DISCARDED

D1597104

DISCARDED

SWITZERLAND
AND THE
SECOND WORLD WAR

SWITZERLAND
AND THE
SECOND WORLD WAR

Edited by
GEORG KREIS
University of Basle

With a Foreword by
DAVID CESARANI

FRANK CASS
LONDON • PORTLAND, OR

First published in 2000 in Great Britain by
FRANK CASS PUBLISHERS
Newbury House, 900 Eastern Avenue
London, IG2 7HH

and in the United States of America by
FRANK CASS PUBLISHERS
c/o ISBS, 5804 N.E. Hassalo Street
Portland, Oregon, 97213-3644

Website: www.frankcass.com

Copyright collection © 2000 Frank Cass & Co. Ltd
Copyright chapters © 2000 contributors

British Library Cataloguing in Publication Data

Switzerland and the Second World War
1. World War, 1939–1945 – Switzerland
I. Kreis, Georg
940.5'3494

ISBN 0-7146-5029-3 (cloth)

Library of Congress Cataloging-in-Publication Data

Schweiz und der Zweite Weltkrieg. English.
    Switzerland and the Second World War / edited by Georg Kreis.
        p.   cm.
    Includes bibliographical references and index.
    ISBN 0-7146-5029-3 (cloth)
    1. World War, 1939–1945 – Switzerland.   2. Neutrality. I. Kreis, Georg. II. Title.

D754.S9 S38 2000
940.53'494–dc21   99-059213

*All rights reserved. No part of this publication may be reproduced, stored in or introduced
into a retrieval system or transmitted in any form or by any means, electronic,
mechanical, photocopying, recording or otherwise, without the prior written permission
of the publisher of this book.*

Typeset by Vitaset, Paddock Wood, Kent
Printed in Great Britain by
MPG Books Ltd, Bodmin, Cornwall

Contents

Foreword

For a few years at the end of the twentieth century Switzerland was the focal point of a frenzy of activity, as diplomats, politicians, and lobbyists battled over one of the last pieces of 'unfinished business' from the Second World War. It began with questions into what had become of the unclaimed assets of Jews who had perished as a consequence of Nazi persecution and mass murder, assets that had been entrusted to banks and financial institutions in Switzerland before 1939. It quickly snowballed into an inquisition into Switzerland's trade in gold with Nazi Germany, whether this included trade in gold looted from Jews, the treatment of Jewish refugees at the country's borders and those who managed to cross them, the trade in works of art plundered by the Nazis, and the behaviour of insurance companies holding the policies of Jews murdered in the death camps. The inquest turned into a spectacle mediated by the global news media to a fascinated public around the world. Within a short time, the way the story was being handled had become a story in itself.

Better-informed Swiss could not understand why facts that were well known inside Switzerland had suddenly assumed such significance abroad and why they were being treated as 'revelations'. Did the world's press have ulterior motives in raising the question of Switzerland's trade in gold with the Third Reich and the treatment of Jewish refugees seeking asylum within its borders? Why was Switzerland suddenly the whipping boy for almost every conceivable sin of commission and omission that could be laid at the door of every neutral and non-belligerent country during the Second World War and, in some cases, the Allies themselves?

It would take several years to disentangle myth from reality and achieve a more dispassionate evaluation of the historical evidence, in the process exposing much of the shoddy 'history' ground out by journalists as 'background' to the breaking news. One welcome effect of the unrelenting political and media pressure was the decision of the Federal Council in late 1996 to set up an Independent Commission of Experts on Switzerland in the Second World War to achieve such 'clarity'. This volume of essays bears testimony to the success of that enterprise and the cathartic effect of Switzerland's experience between

1996 and 1999. That frenzied period ended as suddenly as it had begun, but the essays collected here testify to a legacy that will be of value for a much greater duration.

Georg Kreis, the editor, is one of the distinguished historians who during the 1970s had already contributed to the continuous re-evaluation of Switzerland's wartime record. Much of it was stimulated by officially commissioned work, such as Carl Ludwig's report on refugee policy and Edgar Bonjour's history of Swiss neutrality in 1933–45, as well as the popularisation of this research by authors such as Alfred Haesler and Werner Rings. This volume shows that by end of the 1980s Kreis, Marc Perrenoud, Peter Hug, and Jacques Picard had considerably undermined the self-congratulatory myths about Switzerland's conduct towards Nazi Germany.

However, Josef Mooser, Luc van Dongen, and Sacha Zala explain how a Swiss national myth of resistance to the Nazis and a belief in the existence of a humanitarian policy towards Hitler's victims (within what were considered to be practicable limits) had crystallised and hardened to such an extent that it was nearly impervious to such assaults. Their essays show that this intransigence was neither natural nor accidental. In the 1930s, intellectual and political circles had worked to create a Swiss national spirit, partly to fortify resistance to German demands for compliance with the Nazis' outlook and policies. In the post-war years the convenient elements of this 'spiritual national defence' were accentuated and celebrated, giving it the status of an authentic Swiss tradition. Zala reveals how dissident historians were actually thwarted by the state in their attempts to expose such conceit.

Yet the emergence of myths about Switzerland's wartime record cannot be appreciated without an understanding of the rapidly shifting context: the country's isolation in 1944–45; the period of tense realignment between 1945 and 1948; and the onset of the Cold War. Niklaus Stettler demonstrates that the fear of internal unrest and international ostracism which animated the Swiss elite after the war evaporated after 1948, when the Prague coup cemented Switzerland's place amongst the anti-communist nations and simultaneously ruined the popularity of the far left. Ironically, the bourgeois Swiss leadership, so recently afraid of the masses, was now able to take advantage of the anniversary of Switzerland's democratic constitution, promulgated in 1848, to memorialise the mythic defence of the 'island of democracy' against encroaching fascism. Every national saga needs its heroes and villains, and Neville Wylie and Rudolf Jaun take the examples of, respectively, Foreign Minister Pilet-Golaz and General Guisan to show how they came to personify aspects of the debate on foreign policy and national defence. Even when debate occasionally rocked the pedestal on which national heroes stood, it had the effect of confirming other elements of the story.

For decades, this carefully fabricated (and assiduously defended) narrative guided Swiss self-perception and informed the esteem in which the country was held by foreigners. Its monolithic quality helps to account for the sudden fury that was unleashed when the truth was 'revealed' in the late 1990s. But historical truth is never simple and it is often uncomfortable. Jakob Tanner, Philippe Marguerat, and Madeleine Herren explain that Switzerland's foreign relations, trade in gold, and role in international agencies during the Nazi era are not susceptible to the facile interpretations that enable moral judgements of the sort favoured by sound-bite politicians and journalists. Even so, we would not have the luxury of these sophisticated analyses were it not for the sedulous activity of lobbyists and political actors seeking justice for the victims of Nazi persecution.

Ultimately, though, these essays bear witness to the Herculean endeavours of a corps of historians – some members of the Independent Commission and others operating outside it – who have striven to bring order to an unruly and at times ugly controversy. In an absorbing essay, which is as much about the nature of an archive as it is about the contents of a specific one, Andreas Kellerhals-Maeder sheds light on the vast expanse of documentation that has been consulted and that which awaits future historians. Finally, Jean-François Bergier reflects on the origins and remit of the Commission and its wider implications for scholarship, and raises some profound questions which would otherwise remain implicit in these essays.

Switzerland and the Second World War exemplifies the historical research of the future. It draws on work that is multi-disciplinary and collaborative, involving the recruitment, welding, management, and supervision of large teams of researchers with every conceivable expertise. Yet it still leaves much to be done. Although several of the essays dwell on Switzerland's foreign and economic relations, it does not compare Switzerland to other states and economies. How did Swiss conduct resemble or differ from that of other 'neutrals' such as Sweden, or the USA and the USSR during 1939–41, for that matter? How did Switzerland's democratic political culture and distinctive heritage inflect its relations with the Third Reich in comparison with Spain or Portugal? Could it be that Swiss behaviour was normative rather than aberrant, as has been assumed in much recent commentary?

And why did the onslaught fall on Switzerland in the first place? The Editor's Preface offers some reasons and suggests that Switzerland was an 'ideal target' for those seeking redress for the victims of Nazism. However, it does not mention that after the Cold War ended Western countries enjoyed the luxury of indulging in a more penetrating critique of capitalism than had been possible while the system was under threat from an alternative socio-economic regime in the Eastern Bloc. The spectre of unfettered global capitalism gave added passion to this critique. Paradoxically, at the same time, globalisation of the economy, the internationalisation of formerly national corporations, and new legal instruments for the financial regulation of multi-nationals delivered an armoury of weapons into the hands of those wishing to inflict pain on countries and enterprises they considered to be miscreants.

Once the hyperbole and vituperation had passed, it was clear that while Switzerland was not the only, or in certain matters even the worst, offender, its vaunted neutrality would never be the same again and the reputation of its financial institutions would always bear a stigma of dishonour for their activity during and, more especially, after the Second World War. However, in the long term we may come to see Switzerland as the first victim of the backlash against global capitalism, in which the history of the Second World War was as much a source of leverage for some as it was a genuine source of grievance and suffering for others.

DAVID CESARANI
Parkes-Wiener Professor of Modern European Jewish
History and Culture, University of Southampton
May 2000

Preface

Historiographic evaluation of Switzerland's position during the Second World War has always proceeded along two divergent avenues: on the one hand, along the normal route of ongoing academic research, as is common to virtually all historical subjects; and, on the other, in almost feverish waves of disclosure and denunciation. While the present book owes its existence to the dynamics of the latter, it has been prepared according to the methods of the former.

In 1996 the question of Switzerland's role in the Second World War moved – unexpectedly for most people – to the top of the political agenda. The point of departure was the question of how the Swiss banks had dealt with 'dormant accounts' which had not been claimed because the Holocaust had annihilated the account holders, or which had not been handed over to the descendants of Holocaust victims because they were unable to produce adequate identification. The discussion quickly expanded to include questions of fugitive Nazi funds and the Swiss National Bank's gold trade with the German Reichsbank. Further shadowy issues arose concerning the art trade, insurance companies, slave labour in the German affiliates of Swiss companies, Swiss exports of war matériel, Alpine transit between the Axis powers, refugee policies, and so on.

Why did these questions suddenly become a focus of international scrutiny and – in Switzerland – of violent controversy? One answer particularly gratifying to professional historians posits that history always catches up with those who fail to come to terms with the past when they should have done. But there are two reasons why this view does not hold: first, when history is neglected it – sadly – does not stand up for itself; and, second, as the chapters in this book will show, the subject has already received a good deal of critical study, which politicians and the general public have consistently ignored.

The renewed attention being trained on questions that are, in part, far from new, can be explained above all by the insistent call for 'justice', insofar as such a thing can ever be achieved. We are, after all, not dealing with some arbitrary aspect of the Second World War but with the repercussions of a systematic campaign to annihilate the Jews – an issue that many would like to dismiss as thoroughly analysed before the analysis has even begun. Meanwhile, stolen goods must be returned, debts paid and, as a particularly crucial point, no perpetrators or third parties should under any circumstances be allowed to benefit from the persecutions of the past.

This legitimate demand was already being made – in theory – as early as 1945. But at that time Holocaust survivors and their families had other things on their minds; and the countries of the Western world were not giving individual restitution or even collective compensation particular thought. For them, the larger goals of establishing the peace-time order and rebuilding Europe, and soon of defending the free world against the threat of the Soviet Union, were the prime concerns.

The question of material restitution, with regard, for instance, to the vast amount of property that had been expropriated, derived powerful momentum from the collapse of the Soviet-dominated system in eastern Europe in 1989. The ripple effect also caused certain questions to resurface in the West. In tandem with this – and as a perfect example of the dynamics of a historical constellation – the experiences etched into the memories of the victims of Nazi persecution and the stories they had to tell moved into the public arena in the 1990s. The timing was no coincidence: as they saw the end of their lives drawing near, the survivors of the extermination campaign and the direct descendants of Holocaust victims, who had for so long found it intensely difficult to speak of the unutterable horrors they had experienced, felt a growing need to bear witness, partly out of a sense of obligation to their murdered brothers and sisters. Furthermore, their families and other members of the next generation, who were younger and unencumbered by the burden of having personally become victims of history, were increasingly intent on finally securing the success of a just cause, regardless of the consequences.

So, the past did not re-emerge on its own. There may easily have been a strategic purpose in making Switzerland a 'leading case' as a preliminary to confronting other nations with the same problem. Owing to its historical role as an unoccupied enclave bordering on the areas of persecution, Switzerland was surely an ideal choice. Perhaps it was and remains a perfect example because of the immense discrepancy that prevails between ideal image and normality or reality. Nonetheless, one need only glance at the daily papers to realise that the Switzerland file is merely part of a larger reassessment process.

The authors of the following contributions were not disconcerted by the critical attention suddenly being directed at 'their' country: they did not, through some misplaced sense of identification, feel a need to rush to the defence of 'their own' past. If identification came into play at all, then it was chiefly in the conviction that society is best served when it faces up to history with relentless honesty. Their articles render account in two respects: they show where work on the pertinent issues has been done *thus far* and bring out what remains to be done *in the future*.

For a long while, the history of Switzerland in the Second World War was dealt with almost exclusively by the Swiss, for the Swiss. Now the subject has become international and will also have to be understood in its international context. We therefore welcome the opportunity extended to us by the Arts Council of Switzerland, Pro Helvetia, to present an English-language edition of a book that has, in the original German–French edition, already become a central reference work.

Notes on Contributors

Jean-François Bergier was full professor of economic history at the University of Geneva from 1963–69 and then, until his recent retirement, professor of the history of civilisations at the Swiss Federal Institute of Technology in Zurich. He is Honorary President of the International Association of Economic History. Since the end of 1996 he has been President of the Independent Commission of Experts: Switzerland–Second World War. His main areas of research are the economic history of Switzerland and Europe; the Middle Ages and modern times; the history of the Alps and the history of alimentation. He is the editor of Vol. 13 of *Swiss Diplomatic Documents* (1939–40).

Madeleine Herren is assistant professor of modern history at the University of Zurich; currently she is head of a research project investigating 'Internationalisierungsstrategien als Instrument schweizerischer Aussenpolitik' (Internationalisation Strategies as an Instrument of Swiss Foreign Policy). Her main areas of research are international relations in the nineteenth and twentieth centuries, the history of international organisations, Swiss foreign policy and international history.

Peter Hug is head of the research project 'Die Aussenpolitik der Schweiz 1937–1989' (Swiss Foreign Policy 1937–1989) and, on behalf of the Independent Commission of Experts: Switzerland–Second World War, is currently working on the Swiss armaments industry during that war. His main areas of research are Swiss foreign policy, development policy, peace policy and neutrality; trade in war matériel, armaments industry, procurement of atomic, biological and chemical weapons.

Rudolf Jaun private lecturer at the University of Zurich; director of the archives of the Swiss Army. His main areas of research are the social history of industrial labour and military warfare; history of Switzerland in the nineteenth and twentieth centuries.

Andreas Kellerhals-Maeder is deputy director of the Swiss Federal Archives, responsible for communication, research and public relations. In this capacity he is also responsible for archive-related efforts to investigate the history of Switzerland in connection with the Second World War. He is editor of the 'Dossier' series on themes relating to contemporary Swiss history.

Georg Kreis is full professor of history at the University of Basle and since 1992 has been editor of the *Schweizerische Zeitschrift für Geschichte* (*Swiss Journal of History*). He has been director of the interdisciplinary Institute of Europe at the University of Basle since 1993; an expert on the staff of the national research programme 42 'Foundations and Possibilities of Swiss Foreign Policy' since 1995; and a member of the Independent Commission of Experts: Switzerland–Second World War since 1996. Some of his main areas of research worthy of mention here are international relations, interdependencies of national and international processes, nationalism and migration.

André Lasserre was professor at the University of Lausanne from 1968–92, member of the municipal council of Lausanne, then member of the Cantonal Parliament of Vaud. Works and articles on the history of the Canton of Vaud in the nineteenth century, director of research on the Illème International, author of various published articles, lectures and contribution to a referendum democracy in Switzerland entitled 'L'institution de l'assurance-vieillesse 1889–1947' (The Institution of Old Age Insurance, 1889–1947). Currently, he is engaged in research on the Refuge Policy of the Canton of Vaud under the mandate of the state.

Philippe Marguerat is full professor of modern and contemporary history at the University of Neuchâtel and a member of the national commission for the publication of Swiss diplomatic documents. His areas of research include the history of European banking and the history of the Second World War.

Josef Mooser is full professor of general history of the twentieth century at the University of Basle since 1993. His main areas of research are the social, political and cultural history of Germany in the nineteenth and twentieth centuries, in particular, on problems of rural society, the industrial labour force and Catholicism.

Marc Perrenoud is scientific collaborator of the Independent Commission of Experts: Switzerland–Second World War. Main areas of research: publication of four volumes of Swiss diplomatic documents during the years 1939–47, as well as several articles on the international relations of Switzerland and on economic and social history.

Jacques Picard is a member and head of research of the Independent Commission of Experts: Switzerland–Second World War; a lecturer in history and culture at the Technical College of Berne (HTL); member of the board of trustees of the foundation 'Contemporary Jewish History' at the Archives for Contemporary History of the Swiss Federal Institute of Technology in Zurich (ETH). His main areas of research are contemporary history, minorities, anti-Semitism and human rights.

Niklaus Stettler is an archivist in the Swiss economic archives, Basle, and lecturer at the University of Basle. His main areas of research are economic history of the nineteenth and twentieth centuries, history of science in the twentieth century, especially the bio-sciences.

Jakob Tanner has been full professor at the Research Institute for Social and Economic History at the University of Zurich since 1997. In 1986 his dissertation was published: 'Bundeshaushalt, Währung und Kriegswirtschaft. Eine finanzsoziologische Analyse der Schweiz 1938–1953' (Federal Budget, Currency and Wartime Economy: a Financial-Sociological Analysis of Switzerland, 1938–1953). Following research in Paris and London, he was guest professor at Bielefeld University from 1996 to 1997. In 1996 he was appointed a member of the Independent Commission of Experts: Switzerland–Second World War.

Luc van Dongen has, since 1997, been a collaborator on Swiss diplomatic documents. His main areas of research are the history of the Second World War; Switzerland and the French Resistance; the history of the workers movement.

Neville Wylie is a lecturer in international history at University College Dublin. He has written a number of articles on Swiss diplomacy, economic relations and strategy during the Second World War, and is author of *Britain and Switzerland during the Second World War*, forthcoming in 2001 from Oxford University Press.

Sacha Zala is assistant for contemporary general history at the historical institute of the University of Berne, and is currently scientific collaborator in a research project entitled 'Internationalisierungsstrategien als Instrument schweizerischer Aussenpolitik' (Internationalisation Strategies as an Instrument of Swiss Foreign Policy). Her main areas of research are political history and international relations of the nineteenth and twentieth centuries, Swiss foreign policy and historiography.

Introduction: Four Debates and Little Dissent

GEORG KREIS

If we want to bring some order to discussions since 1945 on Switzerland in the Second World War, we can divide them into four basic types of debate – which have often been combined and have, inevitably, over-lapped. These are debates: (1) over collaboration with Nazi Germany; (2) over neutrality; (3) over the army; and (4) over the refugees and anti-Semitism. Basically, they are all debates about national steadfastness, that is, they apply to the central issue of whether the Swiss – as individuals, in groups, or as a society at large – met demands resulting from the historic situation (the self-survival and defence tasks) and self-styled ideals (democracy, neutrality, humanitarianism or solidarity).[1]

We might imagine that these partial debates have a set framework and a given terrain in the form of a prevailing consensus as to the starting point, and that this consensus corresponds largely to the rather homogeneous self-image of the so-called 'active-service generation'. In the meantime, though, not unjustified doubts about this homogeneity could arise. Differences surely existed to a certain degree within the basic position of national solidarity and need still to be identified more clearly through research.[2]

Two short works written by journalists represent the starting point of discussion on the war years. In 1949, ten years after the outbreak of war, the new editor-in-chief of the liberal *Basler Nachrichten*, Peter Dürrenmatt, explicitly presented a general outline from the perspective of a contemporary observer 'for the younger generation which knows some things only from hearsay'. The message to be passed on was naturally positive in content, spoke of testing and – for similar areas in the future – of proving 'that the federalist Alpine dwarf could resist the northern "giant" and the events it had instigated'.[3] The second work was written by Pierre Béguin, editor-in-chief of the liberal *Gazette de Lausanne*. This appeared in 1951 in the context of the Korean War. It sought to show why Switzerland had stood up to the test of German pressure but also to describe the weaknesses that threatened to surface at a time when Switzerland could have been confronted with problems similar to those of the past war. Under the title *Le balcon sur l'Europe* Béguin took up the ambivalent assessment of the special Swiss position. He conceded that Switzerland had been lucky in remaining unscathed but owed this mainly to its will to resist. This, he said, should also remain a source of inspiration for the future.[4]

During the course of the 1950s the resistance debate had shifted in a military and authoritarian direction, owing largely to political intentions but also to the resistance of a strong-willed democratic country. The memories were now firmly in the hands of the Swiss Federal Department of the Military (EMD), as shown in the 1959 work *20 Years Later*, which reflected what the EMD stood for in those days. Federal Councillor Paul Chaudet also spoke of a 'not unjustified fear of a World War III'. He declared 'our national feelings' and 'our will to defend ourselves' as the timeless bases of 'our history'. He invoked 'confederate unity', congratulated the 'wise vision of the national leadership', and recommended total vigilance as the 'only valid position'.[5] With this background, four types of controversy of varying significance developed from the 1960s on.

THE COLLABORATION DEBATE

The collaboration debate took centre stage first. Its main question asked who had been a political collaborator, or who had taken a wishy-washy position over collaboration and had thus placed Switzerland's political and mental independence at risk. During the entire post-war dispute this type of debate had typically concentrated upon people and values. It was not only the first topic discussed but also the most frequent one.

If we exclude discussions immediately after the war, which we can still understand as an integral part of the period itself, the first debate on this issue occurred in 1961/62, owing to Jon Kimche's thesis that General Guisan had been a much better protector of Swiss interests than the Federal Council.[6] In 1965 a second, yet less controversial debate, took place following Alice Meyer's division of the Swiss microcosm into 'adapters' and 'resisters'.[7] In 1971 Gerhard Waeger took up an opposing position with his thesis that adaptation could also have meant resistance and might even have been a more effective means of resistance.[8]

In 1973/74 Niklaus Meienberg confronted the public with his film documentary on the small-time military collaborator 'Ernst S', comparing him with large-scale political traitors of a citizenry willing to collaborate. But only in 1976/77 did a sharp controversy ignite over the film version: should the film receive a quality award from the government, and should Swiss television transmit it?[9] In 1969/70 a small debate had occurred in connection with works appearing on National Frontism/Swiss fascism (Wolf, Glaus, Zöberlein), and on citizens' ties and sympathies with fascism. These were the genuine debates on collaboration. As we will see, however, later discussions on other issues led repeatedly onto the debate over traitors.

THE NEUTRALITY DEBATE

In 1961/62 it looked for a moment as if the question of military neutrality could become important due to publication of secret wartime military contacts with France before its fall. But, remarkably, because of the parallel release of a paper incriminating the corps commander, Ulrich Wille, the debate focused more on collaboration than neutrality.[10] Cooperation with the Western powers was never a controversial public issue in contrast to the attention which the Federal Council gave to suppressing publications about it in the 1950s.

While it may seem a paradox, in a certain sense it is consistent that *The History of Swiss Neutrality* begun by Edgar Bonjour in 1939/43, then supplemented and extended several times (Vol. 3 in 1967, Vols 4–6 in 1970), triggered no debate on neutralilty.[11] Presentation of Swiss foreign relations was directed so much towards the traditional understanding of neutrality that the 'new discoveries' fit harmoniously into the old pattern of knowledge. Whether the Federal Council which commissioned the work strived for this consciously or unconsciously, all in all the report supplied a confirmation of the old through the new. Even here, however, the controversy got caught up in discussion on assessing Minister Hans Frölicher and Federal Councillor Marcel Pilet-Golaz, quickly turning it into a debate on collaboration.

The economic side of the neutrality problem became more important than the military side. In an initial phase, economic relationships were especially regarded from the supply aspect in the works of Klaus Urner (1968, 1985), Edgar Bonjour (1970) and Daniel Bourgeois (1974, 1981/82). Also discussed was the extent to which the neutrality principle of equal treatment had to be abandoned due to coercion from abroad. In this regard Urner in 1985 made a more critical assessment than Bonjour, and also made it explicitly.[12]

Yet the view that part of Switzerland's trade was carried out not only under coercion but also out of the country's own volition and from a profit motive arose only later. And the notion that independence owed at least as much (if not more) to economic and financial ties gained ground only after Werner Rings' 1985 publication on Swiss National

Bank gold purchases.[13] Gold purchases were first covered in daily press accounts by Peter Utz in 1980,[14] but only accepted in the historiography after Hans-Ulrich Jost's 1983 work. Jost evaluated these purchases as 'trump cards to ensure Swiss existence' but also as 'morally questionable acts'. But, from the Allied–Swiss Washington Agreement of May 1946, he said, menaces and 'blackmail pressure' emerged.[15]

The most important impulse to re-evaluate Swiss economic ties with Germany came in 1989 from two publications. Both were directly or indirectly related to the army abolition referendum and opposition to the 50th anniversary of the mobilisation in 1939. In his work *Dreizehn Grunde: Warum die Schweiz im Zweiten Weltkrieg nicht erobert wurde* (Thirteen Reasons Why Switzerland Was Not Conquered), Markus Heiniger stressed the non-military factors of this problem. To the extent that this discussion was not only directed towards viewing army importance in relative terms, it also had the function of denouncing economic collaboration, that is, treason in facing the precept of a democratic, anti-fascist duty to resist.[16] The other publication concerned a radio programme prepared by Rita Schwarzer, Toni Ladner and Peter Metraux which was aired in March 1989. It called attention, for instance, to the takeover of a Jewish enterprise by the Villiger firm. The programme makers showed that at the time Switzerland not only profited by supplying Germany but was also linked directly to the fate of the Nazi regime's victims by having taken over and operated German branches. This tended to play down the image of a Switzerland innocent because of its neutrality.[17]

Ultimately, the most recent debate over 'unclaimed assets', gold purchases, and the availability of Swiss industrial production led swiftly to a debate over neutrality as perceived by foreigners. Above all, foreign critics stressed that Switzerland had understood how to gain economic profit from its political non-engagement. According to *Time* magazine, for example, in sharpening earlier statements of a similar type, neutrality – 'Switzerland's most quintessential institution' – is the central topic in the whole affair, because it shaped the premise for profitable business dealings with the criminal Nazi regime.[18]

The neutrality problem has also recently become a topic of Swiss domestic debate. It is of central importance to the extent that the issue affects how far one can be present and yet uninvolved. While the moral aspects of not engaging in foreign trade have been emphasised previously, now – and with good cause – the double standard by which Switzerland invoked neutrality only when it saw an advantage in this came in for criticism. By abstaining, in part, it covered the selective role it played and saw itself as the unaffected, the eternal innocent. 'Neutrality', Peter Bichsel notes, 'means above all the eternal guarantee of our innocence.'[19] That brings us to the point – albeit with somewhat broader support – where Friedrich Dürrenmatt already stood in 1981 with his words on the shame of the presumed innocent. Yet that was linked to criticism of cowardice, a vote less on the neutrality issue than on the treason problem.[20]

THE ARMY DEBATE

If one disregards the post-war squabble between General Guisan and the Federal Council in 1946/47, the army debate started considerably later; in fact, with Max Frisch's *Dienstbüchlein* (Service Booklet) of 1974. Before, in 1973, set off by Werner Rings' major television series[21] a small dispute took place in *Die Weltwoche* between Marcel Beck and Sigmund Widmer over the issue of a German attack that never occurred. However, it did not set off further debate. Widmer called Beck's reference to the 'useless' army 'amusing' and a 'gag'. But Beck was only opposed to the army being assigned the 'primary role'; he spoke of terrain and of a subversive resistance of the basis, referred to Swiss Alpine transit as dispensable and to the Alpine *réduit* (redoubt) strategy as part of a Gotthard mysticism – the less said about it the better.[22]

That Switzerland had remained unscathed because of its readiness to collaborate economically was taken into consideration by neither Beck nor Frisch in the following year. On the other hand, we find this viewpoint in the young author and conscientious objector Christoph Geiser (Frölicher's grandson), who by 1970 had already assessed the *réduit* strategy 'rather as an escape' and the army as 'the decor of a fictitious neutrality'. He added: 'Hitler didn't have to occupy Switzerland because Swiss industry worked for him anyway.'[23]

In 1974 Max Frisch also cast doubt on the army's combat readiness. But for him the major criticism was of the undemocratic spirit and lack of anti-fascist attitude. In this way he explicitly reactivated criticism from Niklaus Meienberg. It was primarily Meienberg who, in reportage published at about the same time, set out to denounce the army's class consciousness. But he combined criticism of its being an instrument of domestic repression with the finding that the army, if not useless, had at least become fairly unimportant in guarding against outside dangers.[24] In the great contemporary debates Friedrich Dürrenmatt always stood somewhat in the shadows of the other 'great' author. Yet in a speech on 1 August 1979 he too expressed doubts about the possibility of small states in the Second World War being able to defend themselves, prompting a few letters to the editor.[25]

Though it seems unremarkable today, Hans-Ulrich Jost's comment in 1983 that occupation of Switzerland would have been costly but 'feasible without great difficulties' triggered some annoyance, although his interpretation did not go so far as to ascribe Swiss survival to economic and financial ties with Germany.[26] Publication in 1985 of documents which weighed politically on the army supreme command provoked no debate over the army but rather a variation of the collaborators debate. Typically, it was less General Guisan than the 'exposing historians' who became caught up in the crossfire.[27] The same process repeated itself ten years later and led to the motto 'Ne touchez pas au Géneral!' (Don't touch the general!)[28] The book Willi Gautschi presented in 1989 on army leadership in the Second World War indeed grasped a broad spectrum of procedures, but its critical explanations failed to generate genuine discussion on the central issues. All the more remarkable is the fact that this voluminous book reached a broad market.[29]

Only in 1988/89, in connection with the army abolition referendum, was the traditional way of analysing the military's importance in the national defence of Swiss independence subjected to direct, focused and aggressive questioning. However, in his 1986 dissertation, which was immediately discussed by the newspaper *Friedenszeitung*, Jakob Tanner had already downplayed the military's performance and developed the basis for his later comments.[30] In 1989 Max Frisch appeared with 'Ein Palaver', a work which partially recapitulated the 1974 *Dienstbüchlein* in dialogue form.[31] In addition, several lesser historic contributions appeared in the radical press,[32] among them statements by Jakob Tanner and the somewhat broader book by Markus Heiniger already mentioned, on the '13 reasons' why Switzerland had not been invaded in the Second World War. Jakob Tanner is today a full professor and member of the official Independent Commission of Experts on Switzerland and the Second World War. Yet even as an outsider at the time he represented the thesis of the perfect combination of porcupine mentality and *réduit* (military retreat) on the one side, and intensive cooperation in foreign trade on the other. After the war one honoured the army as the 'decisive factor', while the industrial and banking worlds were so reduced that by contrast, 'they vanished in the nostalgic review of the war years'.[33]

The study undertaken by Klaus Urner and published in 1990 on German invasion plans against Switzerland was a reaction to the thesis on the meaninglessness of the army with reference to economic ties. The major danger occurred in the summer of 1940, but economic supplies first became a trump card in 1941.[34] That Hitler seriously considered conquering Switzerland was presented by part of the press as a 'new thesis', although it actually only confirmed the older but now documented pre-1989 version. Another commentary noted that Urner's study shows how the historic image must be more differentiated 'than the Helvetian historians' dispute suggests'.[35] Along with the latest reactivation of discussion on the function and meaning of economic cooperation with the Third Reich, the question of the importance of national defence in general and the *réduit* in particular has also received a new impetus.

THE DEBATE ON REFUGEES AND ANTI-SEMITISM

Discussion on refugee policy naturally comes up again and again – especially regarding the border closure of 1942 and controversy over the 'full boat'. But the view that Switzerland had failed was at the time unanimous in the sense that discussion of individual aspects (especially of the responsibility of individual councillors and when they knew what) hardly assumed the dimension of a real controversy. Making an issue topical, even if it leads to unpleasant findings, does not stir up controversy in itself. Thus the Ludwig report of 1957 and the Häsler book of 1967 – both milestones in the historiography of refugee history – provided no markers among the controversial episodes about Switzerland's role in the Second World War.[36] Nor did the Favez report of 1988 on the role of the International Committee of the Red Cross (ICRC) really provoke debate.[37]

In 1965 a certain amount of debate arose over refugee history after a literary work by Walter Matthias Diggelmann on the Ludwig report appeared. Yet this discussion also very quickly became caught up in the collaboration debate; Diggelmann, who for his part had already instigated this discussion by attributing a Nazi past to the Cold Warriors of the 1950s, was inundated by accusations of being a communist and an East German sympathiser.[38] The most intensive and sustaining discussion concerned the rehabilitation of St Gall police captain Paul Grüninger (sacked for refusing to implement the harsh policy on refugees). This increased in 1968 and lasted until the verdict against him was overturned in 1995. But even this dispute was basically a variation of the collaboration debate, in that its main object was the morally unjustified punishment of one who failed to adapt and the stubborn refusal to rehabilitate him.

The first signs of a controversy surfaced when Jacques Picard directed attention to the issue, asking to what extent the restrictive refugee policy had been primarily a Jewish policy and not simply a policy towards foreigners in general. This approach met with resistance because it is linked to recognition of the unpleasant fact that a considerable amount of anti-Semitism was at work in Swiss society, and possibly still is.[39]

Yet it should be recalled here that there already was a debate – or could have been – over anti-Semitism in Switzerland during 1970. At the time the opportunity for serious discussion of 'normal' anti-Semitism (this is, not that practised by extreme groups) was missed. Owing to anti-Semitic articles which had appeared during the period 1936–42 in the *Obwaldner Volksfreund*, under the sole editorial responsibility of Ludwig von Moos, the non-conformist monthly magazine *Neutralität* demanded von Moos' immediate resignation at the end of December 1969, shortly before the end of his term as Swiss president.[40] In the following debate, anti-Semitism was played down with the argument that comments 'from that period' had to be understood within the context of the time; that they contained 'nothing new'; that reviving the issue only served the wheeling and dealing of party politics; that the young conservatives had needed to be reinforced against the National Frontists (that is, one had to stick up for them); that there were also contrary comments in the publication cited; that therefore one need not have been a Nazi; that it had only concerned reservations about concentrations in certain professions; that the former editor had never exhibited anti-Semitic behaviour as a federal councillor, and so on.[41]

Only in recent times has there been an admittedly somewhat partisan discussion concerning anti-Semitism in the central Swiss heartland and, in particular, concerning historical writing on Roman Catholicism, especially at the University of Fribourg, which was reproached for ignoring the inherent anti-Semitism in its midst and never seeing political Catholicism as an offender but only as a victim of business-oriented radicals and the left. The major exponent of this recently well-known criticism is Josef Lang from Zug. The accusations were directed primarily at Urs Altermatt, professor of history at the University of Fribourg. The reproaches already raised in the 'alternative scene' in autumn of 1996 would have remained fairly obscure if firm reservations against Altermatt's possible presidency of the Independent Commission of Experts had not been linked to them.[42]

A COMPREHENSIVE DEBATE

These days – and this gives the discourse its special meaning – we are experiencing a comprehensive debate with a reactivation of all four aspects of the discourse. In the army debate, by allegedly using the term *Demutsgeste* ('gesture of humility'), Jakob Tanner stimulated discussion on the letter and spirit of the *réduit*. In the neutrality debate the thesis of war profits and war prolongation was put back on the agenda by the US government's Eizenstat report, which was decisively rejected by

Walther Hofer, but rated as at least worthy of consideration by Jakob Tanner and Hans-Ulrich Jost.[43] We face the question of whether Switzerland has intellectually recognised and emotionally seized the dreadful uniqueness of the Nazi loot-and-annihilate policy. These partial debates were encompassed in the collaboration debate. This can no longer simply sort out good from evil but – after the ongoing judgement of the conduct of various individuals – we must come to grips with the issue of how to deal with the responsibility we have for the acts of past generations and also for contemporary events within our society.

To what extent have these debates changed the face of history itself? Or were they rather products of general social change? Change has obviously occurred. The Centre for Security Studies and Conflict Research at the Swiss Federal Institute of Technology in Zurich recently presented poll findings showing that only 40 per cent of those surveyed still ascribe Switzerland's having escaped the Second World War unscathed to military deterrence 'above all'. This contrasts with 61 per cent in 1983. It is obvious in the current poll that the remaining 60 per cent trace the reason for Switzerland being spared to economic co-operation.[44] The change can also be determined at other levels: for instance, in school textbooks, which have been open to the new research since the 1970s.[45]

However, it is highly doubtful whether professional historians could actually claim to have been the agents of this change. Certainly they have played a major role but mainly one of organising and probing deeper. All in all, it has been less the historians who have determined the general change in consciousness, mentality and values than social change that has conditioned the population's thinking.

Ernst Leisi describes the process correctly: 'After a preparatory and start-up period, a multifaceted process began in the middle of the1960s. It brought about scientific change, in the arts, in social behaviour, and generally in the way of viewing values. Its scientific side represented the now increasing use of historically reappraising the war years.'[46] It is another question whether this change leads to confusion, as Leisi believes, or has not already begun to break down old confusion. One still senses the change most clearly in the differing approaches and assessments of the generations. Leisi appears today as the voice, so to speak, of the active-service generation. The sharpest critics – critics less of the actual Swiss conduct during the war than of the heroic, harmless historic image passed on to those born later, and disregarding exceptions such as Marcel Beck – were members of the post-war generation. The varying assessments began to make themselves noticeable in the early 1970s. Peter Gilg, who a little later would present a study on *das jugendliche Drängen* (youthful urging), determined in commenting on reactions to the Bonjour report in 1970 that a new generation had grown up 'which called the passed-down historic image into doubt – and, indeed, in part mercilessly picked it to pieces'.[47]

THE ROLE OF HISTORIANS

Let us now turn to the question of the role historians played in these discussions and how willing they proved to engage in debate. Historians are by no means a homogeneous group. The most important difference is between historians with university positions or ambitions and other historians. It is also important to take into account the contributions provided by non-professional (amateur) historians, mainly writers. Finally, the generation issue and especially the age issue (which is not identical) play an important role.

It makes sense to differentiate between two basic types of historic discussion, and to keep them separate. The results of these discussions arise from academic historiography on the one hand and sociopolitically motivated historiography on the other. This applies even though there are persons, positions and products for whom such division is unfair. In such cases one would rather speak of a debate among the nation's intellectuals. Academic historiography seeks a scientific basis (a methodically reflected analysis), while sociopolitical historiography wants to express and promote writings which deal mainly with principles and commitment.

The greatest effect on historiography and the historic debates which accompanied it started with documents on Swiss contemporary history becoming known abroad. Such impulses initiated the refugee report of 1957 and the neutrality report of 1970, and also triggered the current need for clarification.

Furthermore, the most important revisionist impulses and the potential for innovation inherent in them did not come from academic historiography but from its sociopolitically motivated counterpart – especially from novelists and reporters. In chronological order, they were the Basle-based Rolf Hochhuth (though with a non-Swiss Vatican theme), Walter Matthias Diggelmann, Christoph Geiser, Alfred A. Häsler, Max Frisch, Werner Rings, Lukas Hartmann, and – if one may also add those with university diplomas – Niklaus Meienberg, Markus Heiniger and Gian Trepp.

Only afterwards did the horde of academic historiographers deal with the still ongoing command to tidy up, in terms of relativising, contextualising and documenting. Perhaps the division of labour is appropriate in this way; at least, it seems unavoidable. Incidentally, it should be noted that the first approach to the now much-discussed Swiss National Bank gold purchases was not written by a historian but a German specialist, namely Peter Utz, who would become professor of German studies at the University of Lausanne, even though his work did not have the impact that it deserved.[48]

An explanation is required regarding the literary contributions: one can understand the impulses of the late 1960s and early 1970s as products of their time. One can thus remain somewhat detached in recognising their innovative service, but they should be granted a certain pioneering or precursory character. On the other hand, the second wave which followed them – contributions from Otto F. Walter, Thomas Hürlimann and Urs Widmer – emerged only after the agenda-setting work undertaken by the professional historians.[49]

The first presentation of the new era beginning in 1961/62 was inspired by the fact that the Federal Council had, in 1962, assigned Edgar Bonjour the task of reappraising the historic period. It was published in 1965 by a non-historian, Alice Meyer, who was nonetheless married to a historian.[50] This work ably assumed the inquisitorial approach of the time: who had 'adapted' and who had 'resisted'? Indeed, the counter-thesis launched by Gerhart Waeger in 1971 – in which certain adaptation proposals had been developed with an intent to resist – did not stem from an amateur historian but from a young specialist on medieval history, a Beck student who did not have the position or authority of a recognised contemporary historian.[51]

In neither 1965 nor 1971 did professional historians make a notable appearance, and few registered in 1970 at the first debate on anti-Semitism.[52] The same can be said – if one ignores my 'objection' – for the 1974–77 debate concerning the execution of Ernst S,[53] and later in 1983 concerning the then provocative general presentation *Geschichte der Schweiz und der Schweizer* (History of Switzerland and the Swiss). The chapter written by Hans-Ulrich Jost on the pre-war and war periods was sharply criticised by defenders of traditional history concepts, yet Jost's colleagues spoke out neither for nor against his presentation or his critics.[54] No historians' debate occurred in 1984/85 as the Federal Archive's director, Oscar Gauye, made public some fairly dubious conceptual notes on Guisan's Rütli report.[55]

As today's discussions show, the professional historians did not keep out of such discussion but were pleased to be called in and even spoke out of their own accord. Yet they failed to debate with their colleagues in public. They preferred to turn individually to the public and offer themselves, so to speak, in competition with colleagues when presenting their suggested interpretations.

If one tries to justify the absence of professional historians in the cases noted on grounds that these controversies seemed unimportant, such a justification would have been out of the question in the public debate on the 1970 Bonjour report. That the handling of the neutrality topic did not stimulate reactions has already been mentioned. On the other hand, there would still have been something to say about the assessment of some contemporary witnesses and the methods used.

Discreet reservations about the Bonjour report were announced by the holder of the history chair at the Federal Institute of Technology, journalist and editor, Jean Rodolphe von Salis, in his *Sonntags Journal*. Salis acknowledged that the 'description was worked out with great care, with critical but also correct meaning and low-key language' yet he also expressed his uneasiness that Federal Councillor Pilet-Golaz could become history's scapegoat; moreover, he made a minor chronological correction based on his own recollection and found fault with the fact that Bonjour had not evaluated the unpublished works of Federal Councillor Karl Kobelt, of which Salis was aware. The summary judgement noted: 'Edgar Bonjour has approached his topic with great honesty and care, even if the cutting edge of critical formulation is lacking. He has weighed all these things against each other like a wise but somewhat sceptical old judge.'[56]

The Zurich medievalist Marcel Beck remained true to himself and expressed his reservations about Bonjour's presentation loudly and clearly. Peter Gilg described Beck's opinions at the time as perhaps the 'most ruthless criticism'.[57] If one overlooks the criticism of missing figures in the business chapters, one can reduce the not very systematically presented complaints in several articles to two points: Bonjour laid too much importance on individual decision-makers and overestimated Switzerland's ability to shape its destiny. 'How much we were rocked about by the deepest effects of the waves around us is not really visible in his thick volume. Yet those Swiss are singled out whose actions or omissions were said to have been decisive for our country during the Second World War.'[58] The criticism running in the same direction within a later work addressed itself less to Bonjour than to an unspecified self-conception of Switzerland: that the Swiss could have been arrogant in assessing what their industry had meant for the German economy. Beck was so fixated on criticising the Swiss penchant for overestimating themselves that he also doubted if the alleged indispensability of Swiss shipments had saved the country from annexation.[59] The second point of Beck's criticism related to creating myths. He said bluntly that Bonjour rather belonged 'to the myth perpetuators of our national history'. Above all, myths were created regarding neutrality, the purpose of the report being 'to make a piece of the Swiss past so harmless that doubts could not be ignited about our neutrality policy in the future'. Furthermore, military heroes became part of the myth. Bonjour wanted to present Guisan as favourably as possible.[60] Destroying the myth through retouching would also have been necessary regarding the history of the officers' conspiracy.[61] Marcel Beck's final judgement was that 'We dismiss this volume too with the conviction that only a very modest first step has been taken toward coming to terms with our past – neutral in name only – during World War II; also under certain conditions it could be an errant first step because Bonjour transforms himself into a verbose advocate, propagating the idyllic neutral path.'[62]

Other historians satisfied themselves by making critical comments within their closed circle. Seen from the professional historians' vantage point, the most hefty objection came from a youthful historian at the time, Klaus Urner. Urner does not have an especially polemical nature. Yet in the *Monatsheften* he criticised the lack of clarity in the basic sources, insufficient emancipation from contemporary 'adaptation or resistance' alternatives, and the danger of cultivating positive and negative myths.[63]

The reservations of University of Zurich history student Elisabeth Alder tended more toward the political realm. In a Socialist Party paper, she criticised the pleasant oversimplifications, the avoidance of profound discussion, especially on the Swiss self-image, the 'shadow boxing' on a purely personal basis, and the overestimation of Switzerland's potential and performance, particularly that of military resistance and the *réduit*; Germany would not have been interested in a 'Swiss change in status' because this would have caused more harm than good.[64]

Criticism also came from Niklaus Meienberg, a former history student at the University of Fribourg who had developed a direct, polemical style of writing in his professional work. Meienberg ranged far afield as a total critic, in the *Zürcher AZ* in 1971 and 1972, and then in the *National Jahrbuch der Neue Helvetische Gesellschaft*. One cannot fail to notice that he was a fairly hard critic. His approach concerned understanding the problem, methods and vocabulary. Military deterrence was exaggerated; the importance of economic cooperation underestimated; the resistance convictions generalised; class relationships were not examined. Finally, in 1973/74, he caught up with the story of Ernst S. Moreover, he criticised the fact that 'there can be no talk of scientific methods. It concerns a justification report which arbitrarily singles out individual episodes and interprets them arbitrarily, veiling rather than enlightening, vagueness instead of precision'. But Meienberg also took exception to his colleagues' failure to react with a basic and methodical system of criticising Bonjour's work. In particular, he explained their reluctance as a matter of not wanting to lay themselves open to accusations of envy and resentment. He also found fault with the fact that an individual and not a team had been commissioned for the job.

While Bonjour overestimated the generosity of the Federal Council's assignment, Meienberg wanted to represent the same mandate as especially restrictive. Bonjour wrote in the foreword to Volume 4: 'It is indeed unique that a nation can afford to explain openly what it has done.' Meienberg, on the other hand, believed incorrectly that France's contemporary historiography could be demonstrated as a liberal model. Regarding the Swiss relationship he noted, 'Bonjour's work would not have been written in a climate of unmerciful intellectual debate.'[65] Yet it should be added that at the time other countries also practised similar procedures: for example, Louis de Jong in the Netherlands[66] or Francis Harry Hinsley in Britain,[67] and in France, where nothing at all was done at the time, the matter was left to the film world.[68]

In particular, Peter Gilg, a private lecturer at the University of Berne, showed in his work the varying reactions to the Bonjour report. But he also expressed his own reservations with the observation, for instance, that Bonjour's interpretations were not likely to tempt you away from the traditional view of the recent past. The central point is Gilg's comment that Bonjour's approach to the writing of history, as with their University of Berne teacher Richard Feller, had more to do with 'shaping and judging than with problems'. He assumes responsibility for the judgements made without revealing all his mental steps in the process. And he speaks here of the courage of leaving gaps where others might have been driven by a passion for asking questions.[69]

Much later, Karl Schib appeared in the *Schweizerische Zeitschrift für Geschichte (SZG)*. Yet he was no university historian but rather a history teacher in Schaffhausen. Referring to Urner, he also criticised Bonjour's dearth of source documentation and objected to the harsh judgement of Switzerland's representative in Berlin, Hans Frölicher, the epic breadth of explanations, and the weighting of material.[70]

Criticism from a like-minded position, if one excludes Beck and Salis, largely failed to materialise. Within the 'inner circle' of scholars, critical words came from junior scholars such as Urner and Gilg. Outside the universities they originated from the history teacher, Schib. The greatest reservations were held by Meienberg, who operated as a professional social critic from a cultivated outsider situation, and finally from contemporaries such as businessman Heinrich Homberger, who quarrelled with Bonjour's tough judgement on Pilet-Golaz and Frölicher.[71]

Further starting points for controversy particularly affected the disputed view of Federal Councillor Pilet-Golaz. Yet the question of whether Pilet had been a strong or weak foreign minister lacked the format of a central theme for argument. At the end of Erwin Bucher's lecturing stint in 1991 at the University of Zurich, he had tried to rehabilitate Pilet-Golaz. But only a few were even slightly moved by the effort. Though he found Bonjour's assessment basically incorrect and compiled an entire book to refute it, even Bucher himself largely avoided exposing his university colleague to overt criticism.[72] He satisfied himself in part simply by saying the opposite without correcting; in part he let it be understood that Bonjour had not seen important files or had interpreted others mistakenly. Only very rarely did he make remarks such as that Bonjour had only cited negative voices and ignored positive ones among press commentary on Pilet-Golaz's radio address of June 1940. Why Bonjour came to the viewpoint he did and what we should think of his attitude was never a theme in itself for Bucher.

Georges-André Chevallaz, who mounted a second rehabilitation effort four years later in strong support of Bucher, clearly took Bonjour to task in much tougher fashion. This occurred after he had become greatly upset by Hans-Ulrich Jost's chapter in the *Geschichte der Schweiz und der Schweizer*. The reaction in focusing on Pilet-Golaz could be explained by Vaudois' personal temperament and his identification with his 'poorly' judged Federal Council predecessor. Tangentially, it could be said that although Chevallez was trained as a historian, he did not belong to the inner circle of professional historians.[73]

THE LACK OF HISTORICAL DEBATE IN SWITZERLAND

Switzerland only knows the phenomenon of 'historical debate' from foreign debates, especially those in Germany on guilt for triggering the First World War, the continuity links from Bismarck to Hitler, the uniqueness of the National Socialist crime,[74] the role of the *Wehrmacht* and the Goldhagen thesis (*Hitler's Willing Executioners*), but also the Italian and Austrian debates over their respective brands of fascism. In this context the term used in both French and English academic circles remained *Historikerstreit* (historical controversy). However, France too has had its debates, though these turned more on the origins and consequences of the French Revolution than the Popular Front or Vichy France. Even Britain had its debates, especially on assessing the appeasement policy and on Churchill. And the USA, which the writer incorrectly made responsible for calling Switzerland's prevailing self-image into question, had its debates on its role in giving rise to the Cold War and on the engagement in Vietnam.

Wider debate among the population at large can be provoked by public discussions among academic historians. But why did no such debate occur in Switzerland? And has the shyness about public debates between colleagues not also contributed to the lack of historic consciousness in Switzerland? Editor Jürg Schoch, who wrote his thesis in 1972 on the Obersten affair of 1916, and who relatively early on (in September 1996) questioned the lack of debate among Swiss historians, saw three main reasons for this omission in Switzerland, as compared with Germany: first, the lesser potential for debating in a quantitative sense; second, the lighter burden of the past; and finally, the strong tendency to check off unpleasant aspects promptly 'in this country'.[75]

The undisputed small size of Switzerland cannot be seen only in a quantitative sense but can also work as a qualitative determinant: it means a handicapping proximity between members of the small community of specialists, and leads, among other things, to false courtesy. Since this also applies to other areas, a general mentality could have been present in the great reluctance to thrash out differences of opinion. The historic debate is marked by feeding the general pattern of this need once more.

Another explanation – and the phrase 'the lighter burden from the past' has already suggested it – could lie in the fact that stable and lethargic Switzerland has no real 'history' (not in the sense of written history, but rather of historical processes) that could stimulate any discussion at all. If nothing happens, there is also nothing to discuss. Yet it could also be said that when nothing is discussed, nothing happens. Until 1996 it could be said that after controversy over the background to the 1918 national strike and the marginal problem of the Jura issue, only Swiss European policy has the format worthy of a major discussion topic.

In the meantime Switzerland has been served with a subject from abroad, focusing on Swiss conduct in the Second World War, and its format is anything but insignificant. Nonetheless, no public debates took place among influential historians. Within the major-theme complex, only Jörg Fisch tried to launch discussion with a pronounced move into the issues of archive access and extending the war. Yet historians still failed to climb aboard.[76]

Are the historians in agreement on all the vital issues and even on what these issues are? Could a further explanation therefore be that the historians pull their punches because a minimum of dissent is lacking or too much consensus exists – even a professional consensus which covers the sensibilities of the various generations regarding questions, methods and assessments? And has this professionalisation reached a degree which is no longer comprehensible to everyday consumers of historical significance?

In this regard, for example, a 1995 debate on General Guisan offers important insights. The six historians who spoke all offered fairly critical assessments of the Swiss army's supreme commander, even if with nuances. They were presented as a united front by the media – 'the historians attack Guisan'. Even in the eyes of the readership they formed a collective – 'a handful of highly qualified people' – whose conclusions cannot have been correct, if we are to believe history's subsequent judgement. Finally, the historians themselves promoted the unified group portrait. André Lasserre, the most moderate of those questioned, explained how the historians understood their task: 'Naturally, by the nature of our profession as historians, we are revisionists.'[77]

Despite the basic homogeneity of thought among the professional historians, there was, and is, a certain degree of difference in individual assessments. However, one obviously prefers to abide by the nation's political culture and stress consensus over division. Marked disagreement confines itself to minor barbs, as shown by Walther Hofer's recent comments in the *Neue Zürcher Zeitung* addressing remarks by Jakob Tanner.[78] Tanner only received a qualified response – naturally in the form of a contradiction – from Hans Senn, former chief of the general staff and a knowledgeable source on military history.[79]

The University of Neuchatel historian Philippe Marguerat is somewhat more combative, but he too avoided naming colleagues in cases of dissent, preferring to adopt the middle ground between 'hard certainties', as one could so refer to the Bonjour report, and the 'corrosive suspicion instilled by the oppositional current', as prompted by Meienberg (mentioned by name) and Jost (whose name was not mentioned).[80]

The successful attack on Urs Altermatt prompted no noteworthy public reaction and certainly no historians' dispute among academic professionals. Almost at the same time, yet with no direct connection, a minor dispute between historians – at least among junior members – was carried out in the magazine *Traverse* about reasons for a lack of Swiss research on anti-Semitism. While Robert Uri Kaufmann presumed a possible cause in the popular mentality of Switzerland for avoiding discussion on Jewish living conditions in Switzerland, Aram Mattioli saw the strong need for consensus as the reason for conflicts with minorities such as the Jews being omitted.[81]

While the professional historians remain rather restrained, from time to time dispute occurs between non-historians in the political arena. Whether debating skilfully or simply powerfully eloquent phrases, lawyer Paul Rechsteiner and entrepreneur Christoph Blocher, for instance, have actually argued in public. On a journalistic level, debate is engaged in by University of Geneva sociologist Jean Ziegler[82] and carried out by retired University of Zurich English studies specialist Ernst Leisi,[83] as well as more recently by University of Basle economist Felix Auer.[84] During the controversy over the Meienberg–Dindo production of 1976/77, the protest of 18 University of Berne professors was at least led by someone better acquainted with history. However, the pre-historian Hans-Georg Bandi used a fairly unprofessional argument and, in the case of his speciality, a problematical one: that is, that Meienberg, born in 1944, had not seen active military service.[85] It rarely happens that specialists debate historical interpretations publicly with non-historians. Neither Bonjour nor Hofer had talked publicly about Max Frisch's *Dienstbüchlein*.[86] Nonetheless, Hofer argued recently with Ziegler on television.

Dispute is hard to create; it either occurs or it does not. If no dispute takes place, one can at least consider why it did not, and what escaped us as a result. Missing a point can obviously only occur with regard to a valuable insight. And this is avowed to be the assumption here: argument, when it concerns intellectual dispute, is something positive. It makes it easier for us to develop necessary positions and to measure our own interpretations in public discussion with other competing interpretations. This sort of argument helps us to orientate ourselves. Intellectual arguments are obviously not arguments between intellectuals. Argument and facts take the foreground in intellectual arguments, as opposed to disputes between intellectuals, in which the main focus is on the disputants and on personal image. In truth, the two cannot be separated from each other so neatly. Indeed, debates over facts still exist out of the need of debaters to gain visibility or – put quite differently – to expose themselves personally to a certain degree. To what extent this willingness is present also depends in part on collective mentalities, on professional interpretation, and on individual personalities. Argument must apply to an issue which is considered crucial for collective self-interpretation. It presumes opposing positions or creates them during the course of debate – usually according to the principle of bipolarity. Argument also has a temporal dimension, with a beginning and an end. It is a temporary compression of an ongoing discourse.

What remains to be said about the function of such debates? We have already noted that carrying out such conflicts is important because they help regenerate the contentious spirit of all involved. But one must also desire debate in the interest of the object debated. Yet, as experience shows, the best chance of determining truth – if it exists at all – is by wrestling within the discursive ring over truths. The question of 'combat readiness' could occupy us as a topic in its own right. However, the issue interests us above all in regard to what part it plays in the altering of historic interpretations. This issue is based on the dual expectation that historic interpretation must change and that readiness to argue promotes such change.

Thus, the issue is not about sustaining the general momentum of permanent change in order to maintain it. There are also positivist expectations of progress at play: 'false' history images must be disposed of; 'correct' ones must be installed. Even if we also understand the insights of today and tomorrow to be in need of further improvement, we still proceed on the unspoken assumption that change from yesterday to today represents progress. Hence, this leads to our assumption that things we failed to see or saw incorrectly at the time will be viewed with hindsight at least more clearly and more correctly. The notion of developing the historical image (to the extent that the word may be used in the singular at all) as one perhaps being carried out in thrusts, yet with successive removal of 'false' images, is touched upon in the literature report on the historiography volume of 1991. It also provides the basis of the *Manifesto* demand of 21 January to further liberate contemporary Swiss history from 'distortions and euphemisms' and to rewrite it more truthfully.[87]

To the extent that public historical debates to satisfy conceited self-image needs are carried out with a great clamour, our regret about the lack of enthusiasm for such debate among Swiss historians ought to be kept within bounds. The question of how much historians should argue publicly with each other is only a side issue which should not let us lose sight of the main issues. The main issues? One of the first of these concerns weighing the various areas of concern within an overall viewpoint. What was actually important? What is important today? How do things relate to each other? Which things were mutually exclusive? Which things could have been better combined with each other? A second main issue applies to the problem of if, and to what extent, 'failure zones' can be balanced against 'relative accomplishments'. The third issue concerns responsibility for earlier events but also current events which result from contemporary roles as well as that of posterity. Finally, the vital question remains of how we stand as a society vis-à-vis the world: whether we turn away from it out of indifference, or turn toward it out of sympathy. Who has what kind of discussions in its culture is a secondary problem in view of these issues, even if there are certain links between one and the other.

NOTES

1 Earlier presentations about these developments with somewhat different approaches are found in Georg Kreis, 'Die Schweiz der Jahre 1918–1948', in *Geschichtsforschung in der Schweiz: Bilanz und Perspektiven – 1991*, Basle, 1992, pp. 378–96; idem, 'Die schweizerische Neutralität während des Zweiten Weltkrieges in der historischen Forschung', in *Les Etats neutres européens et la Seconde Guerre mondiale. Actes du colloque international des Universités Neuchâtel et Berne, 1983*, Neuchâtel, 1985, pp. 29–53; idem, 'Neue Forschungen zum Zweiten Weltkrieg in der Schweiz', in *Neue Forschungen zum Zweiten Weltkrieg, Schriften der Bibliothek für Zeitgeschichte*, Vol. 28 (Koblenz, 1990), pp. 418–26.

2 There was, for instance, a dispute in 1946/47 between the Federal Council and General Guisan concerning in particular the shortcomings of the national defence. This was, however, not an in-depth discussion. See also Chapter 12 by Luc van Dongen in this volume.

3 Peter Dürrenmatt, *Kleine Geschichte der Schweiz während des Zweiten Weltkrieges*, Zurich, 1949. The encouragement for this publication came from his publisher, the Swiss Spiegel Verlag, who in the previous years had dedicated itself to ideological national defence. By the same author the memorial essay, *Ajoie 1944. Eine Landwehrkompanie im aktiven Dienst*, Berne, 1975.

4 Pierre Béguin, *Le balcon sur l'Europe. Petite histoire de la Suisse pendant la guerre 1939–1945*, Neuchâtel, 1951. An article which had already appeared on 9 January 1946 in the newspaper *Gazette de Lausanne* shows that Béguin viewed the years 1939–45 as an exemplary test. See note 27 in the contribution by Luc van Dongen.

5 Hans-Rudolf Kurz (ed.), *Die Schweiz im Zweiten Weltkrieg. Das grosse Erinnerungswerk an die Aktivdienstzeit*, Thun, 1959.

6 Jon Kimche, *Spying for Peace*, London, 1961. German edition: *General Guisans Zweifrontenkrieg. Die Schweiz zwischen 1939 und 1945*, Frankfurt-am-Main, 1961.

7 Alice Meyer, *Anpassung oder Widerstand. Die Schweiz zur Zeit des deutschen Nationalsozialismus*, Frauenfeld, 1965.

8 Gerhart Waeger, *Die Sündenböcke der Schweiz. Die Zweihundert im Urteil der geschichtlichen Dokumente 1940–1946*, Olten, 1971.

9 See note 24.

10 See Chapter 14 by Sacha Zala in this volume.

11 Edgar Bonjour, *Geschichte der schweizerischen Neutralität. Vier Jahrhunderte eidgenössischer Aussenpolitik*, vols 4–6, 1939–45, Basle, 1970. (French edn: *Histoire de la Neutralité Suisse pendant la seconde guerre mondiale*, vols 4–6, Neuchâtel, 1970.) For the antecedents to Bonjour's report, see Georg Kreis, 'Die Geschichte des Bonjour-Berichts', *National-Zeitung*, 5 June 1976; idem, 'Die schweizerische Neutralität während des Zweiten Weltkrieges in der historischen Forschung', in Louis-Edouard Roulet (ed.), *Les Etats neutres européens et la Seconde Guerre mondiale*, Neuchâtel, 1985, pp. 29–53.

12 Bonjour, *Geschichte der schweizerischen Neutralität*; Daniel Bourgeois, *Le Troisième Reich et la Suisse, 1933–1941*, Neuchâtel, 1974; idem, 'Milieux d'affaires et politique étrangère suisse à l'époque des fascismes', *Relations internationales*, 1, 1974; idem, 'Les relations économiques germano-suisse 1939–1945', *Revue d'histoire de la Deuxième Guerre Mondiale*, 121, 1981; Klaus Urner, 'Die schweizerisch-deutschen Wirtschaftsbeziehungen während des Zweiten Weltkrieges', *Neue Zürcher Zeitung*, 27 November, 2 and 6 December 1968; Klaus Urner, 'Neutralität und Wirtschaftskrieg: Zur schweizerischen Aussenhandelspolitik', in *Schwedische*

und schweizerische Neutralität im Zweiten Weltkrieg, Basle, 1985, pp. 250–92.

13 Werner Rings, *Raubgold aus Deutschland. Die 'Golddrehscheibe' Schweiz im Zweiten Weltkrieg*, Zurich, 1985. The report by Robert Vogler which had been written by order of the National Bank of Switzerland appeared in the same year. The economic entanglements are discussed further by Res Strehle, *Die Bührle Saga. Festschrift zum 65. Geburtstag des letzten aktiven Familiensprosses in einer weltberühmten Waffenschmeide*, Zurich, 1981 (2nd edn, 1986).

14 Peter Utz, 'Goldfingers merkwürdige Machenschaften' (publisher's title), *Tages-Anzeiger-Magazin*, 19 April 1980.

15 Hans-Ulrich Jost, 'Bedrohung und Enge', in *Geschichte der Schweiz und der Schweizer*, Vol. 3, Basle, 1983, pp. 172, 173 and 178. Jost on his contribution and the historiography of that time, 'L'historiographie contemporaine suisse sous l'emprise de la "defense spirituelle"', *Archivo storico ticinese*, Vol. 100, December 1984, pp. 299–306; idem, 'Schwierigkeiten beim Aufarbeiten der Geschichte des Zweiten Weltkrieges', in *Die Schweiz im Zweiten Weltkrieg. Forschungsstand, Kontroversen, offene Fragen*, Zurich, 1997, pp. 31–40. Kleine ETH-Schriften No. 32.

16 Markus Heiniger, *Dreizehn Gründe. Warum die Schweiz im Zweiten Weltkrieg nicht erobert wurde*, Zurich, 1989.

17 'Die Villiger-Firmengeschichte. Gratwanderung zwischen Wirklichkeit und Wunsch', Radio broadcast of 23 and 28 March 1989. Federal Councillor Kaspar Villiger, a son of the company's owner at the time, was chief of the Swiss Defence Department in 1989. Expert advice given by Georg Kreis on appeal at Independent Complaint Office. Interview by Roger Blum with Georg Kreis, 'War die Schweizer Wirtschaft Hitlers Komplizin?', *Tages-Anzeiger*, 8 April 1989.

18 *Time Magazine*, 24 February 1997. See Georg Kreis, 'Der Stellenwert der Neutralität in der aktuellen Debatte um die Rolle der Schweiz während des Zweiten Weltkrieges', in *Fluchtgelder, Raubgut und nachrichtenlose Vermögen*, Dossier 6, Federal Archive, Berne, 1997, pp. 59–64.

19 Peter Bichsel, 'Ein Land der Unschuld', most recently in the newspaper *Neue Zürcher Zeitung*, 6/7 September 1997.

20 Friedrich Dürrenmatt on Switzerland during the Second World War, *Weltwoche*, 26 August 1981 (from Stoffe I-II-III).

21 Werner Rings, 'Schweiz im Krieg 1933–1945. Ein Bericht', Zurich, 1974.

22 'Umstrittene Rolle der Armee', *Weltwoche*, 13 June 1973 (interview by Rudolf Bächtold and Ulrich Kägi, pp. 5 and 7). The booklet, *Neutrale Kleinstaaten im zweiten Weltkrieg* (Münsingen, 1973) which appeared at the same time served to emphasise the possibilities of defence.

23 Christoph Geiser, 'Der Anschluss fand statt', *Neutralität*, January 1970, pp. 19–29. Frölicher was the Swiss minister in Berlin, and a leading figure in Swiss efforts to appease Germany.

24 Meienberg wrote in the first edition of his history of Ernst S: 'This army has fired no single bullet during the whole war at the external enemy, but twenty bullets each at seventeen traitors …'. Niklaus Meienberg, *Reportagen aus der Schweiz*, Darmstadt, 1974, p. 162. While Meienberg indicates with his other essays that they had appeared in the *Tages-Anzeiger-Magazin* before, he does not follow this practice in this case. In his revised edition of 1977 – which appeared in association with the film by Richard Dindo – Meienberg corrected the above quoted text with respect to a comment of mine concerning the sorties of the Swiss airforce. The revised text now reads: 'The infantry had during the whole war … (p. 12)'. See also Georg Kreis, 'Geschichtsschreibung mit Film und Klassenkampf. Zur Kontroverse um den Landesverräter Ernst S.', *Neue Zürcher Zeitung*

(*NZZ*), 7 July 1977. Certain media recapitulated the film event '20 years later' in 1996 (newspaper *WoZ*, 13 September 1996, with a contribution by Jakob Tanner, 'Was Ernst S. für die Geschichtsschreibung der Schweiz bedeutet. Oben wurde pensioniert, unten wurde füsiliert'. Also *Tages-Anzeiger*, 20 September 1996).

25 *Neue Zürcher Zeitung*, 10 and 24 August 1979.

26 Jost, op. cit. note 15, p. 168.

27 Oscar Gauye, '"Au Rütli, 25 juillet 1940". Le discours du général Guisan: nouveaux aspects', in *Studien und Quellen*, Vol. 10, Berne, 1984, pp. 5–56. See also Georg Kreis, 'Henri Guisan – Bild eines Generals. Glanz und Elend einer Symbolfigur', *Schweizer Monatshefte*, May 1990, pp. 413–31.

28 *Journal de Genève*, 12 July 1995, as a reaction to two editions of the *Construire*.

29 Willi Gautschi, *General Henri Guisan. Die schweizerische Armeeführung im Zweiten Weltkrieg*, Zurich, 1989, p. 912. The decisive impulse for this work came from the editor Peter Keckeis, who had been looking for an author to undertake a political biography of the general for 15 years.

30 Jakob Tanner, *Bundeshaushalt, Währung und Kriegswirtschaft. Eine finanz-soziologische Analyse der Schweiz zwischen 1938 und 1953*, Zurich, 1986, pp. 268ff. Markus Heiniger, 'Igel im Krieg – ein Trugbild', *Friedenszeitung*, 61, September 1986.

31 Max Frisch, 'Schweiz ohne Armee? Ein Palaver', Zurich, 1989 (written in February/March 1989). Stage version, *Jonas und sein Veteran*, first performance in October 1989 in Zurich. Partly screened by Alexander J. Seiler, 'Palaver, Palaver. Eine Herbstchronik', 1990.

32 Especially the following publications: *Einspruch*, 14, April 1989 (after an event at the culture workshop in Basle produced by Christoph Stratenwerth in January 1989); *Widerspruch*, 17, July 1989, 'Schweizer Armee, Macht, Krieg'; *Friedenszeitung*, 97, September 1989, '1939: Rettete uns die Armee?' with a contribution by Jakob Tanner 'Granit und Guisan' and an article written by Markus Heiniger; *Klunker* (*Anti-Diamant-Zeitung*), also with contributions by Tanner and Heiniger, but also by Josef Lang. The publication by Walter Schaufelberger was, so to speak, from the opposing group: 'Sollen wir die Armee abschaffen? Blick auf eine bedrohliche Zeit', Frauenfeld, 1988. With a contribution by Georg Kreis on the political significance of the army.

33 *Klunker*, 1989.

34 Klaus Urner, *Die Schweiz muss noch geschluckt werden! Hitlers Aktionspläne gegen die Schweiz*, Zurich, 1990.

35 Emanuel La Roche, 'Klaus Urner differenziert Schweizer Historikerstreit', *Tages-Anzeiger*, 11 January 1991.

36 Georg Kreis, 'Wieviel Flüchtlingsgeschichte?', *NZZ*, 14 October 1997, pp. 49 and 50.

37 Jean-Claude Favez, *Une mission impossible? Le CICR, les déportations et les camps de concentration nazis*, Lausanne, 1988. German edn, *Das Internationale Rote Kreuz und das Dritte Reich. War der Holocaust aufzuhalten?* Zurich, 1989. Mandate with unrestricted access 1983.

38 Walter Matthias Diggelmann, *Die Hinterlassenschaft*, Piper, 1965. (Zurich, 1982 edn with an epilogue by Bernhard Wenger on the reactions to the book.)

39 See Chapters 5 and 6, by Kreis and Picard respectively, in this volume.

40 *Neutralität* 8th year, January 1970 (1st and 2nd edns).

41 For instance, articles in the *National-Zeitung* of Basle, 30/31 December 1969 and 2–14 January 1970.

42 Documentation of a meeting of the Socialist-Green Alternative party

(Sozialistische-Grüne Alternative, SGA), *Zug*, 17 September 1996; Josef Lang, '"Ein neuer Artikel: Die Juden". Wie und warum der konservative Katholizismus die Judenemanzpation bekämpfte', in *MoMa*, September 1997, pp. 7–12. idem, 'Katholisch-konservativer Antisemitismus in der Schweizer Geschichte. Professor Altermatts "Freiburger Schule" – zwischen Verdrängung und Verharmlosung', *Widerspruch*, 32, December 1996, pp. 89–98. Urs Altermatt on the question of research on anti-Semitism in *forum*, 9, 1997. Altermatt refuted the reproaches addressed specifically to him and the Catholic milieu and documented in a convincing way that he dealt with Swiss anti-Semitism in his work before 1996 (see interview in *Spectrum. Die Zeitung der Studierenden der Uni Freiburg*, 7, May 1997).

43 Walter Hofer, 'Wer hat den Zweiten Weltkrieg verlängert?', *NZZ*, 7/8 June 1997. Interview with Jakob Tanner. 'Der Frage der Kriegsverlängerung nachgehen', *Basler Zeitung*, 21 May 1997. Hans-Ulrich Jost, 'Die Schweiz im Zielkonflikt zwischen Neutralität, Solidarität und "legitimem Egoismus"', *Tages-Anzeiger*, 15 May 1997.

44 Karl W. Haltiner, Luca Bertossa and Kurt R. Spillmann, *Sicherheit '97*, Zurich, 1996, pp. 37–41 (Zürcher Beiträge zur Sicherheitspolitik und Konfliktforschung No. 42).

45 Excellent article by Peter Haerle, 'Die Mythen sind am Verblassen. Aktuelle Geschichtsbücher für die Volksschule sind besser als ihr Ruf – doch die Verfehlungen in der Vergangenheit wirken noch bis heute nach', *Tages-Anzeiger*, 16 January 1997.

46 Ernst Leisi, *Freispruch für die Schweiz. Erinnerungen und Dokumente entlasten die Kriegsgeneration*, Frauenfeld, 1997, p. 164.

47 Peter Gilg, 'Diskussion um den Bonjour-Bericht. Ein zeitgeschichtliches Werk im Kreuzfeuer der Kritik', *Reformatio*, January 1971, pp. 35–43. Idem, *Jugendliches Drängen in der schweizerischen Politik*, Berne, 1974.

48 Utz, see note 14 above.

49 Themes of the second wave: Roman Bucheli, 'Blinder Spiegel. Die Weltkriegszeit in der Schweizer Literatur?', *NZZ*, 21 March 1997.

50 Karl Meyer, her deceased husband, was professor of medieval history in Zurich and active in the ideological national defence. See, for instance, his paper 'Der Freiheitskampf der Eidgenössischen Bundesgründer', Frauenfeld, 1941.

51 Waeger had received his doctorate shortly before from Marcel Beck after researching the theme of Gottfried von Bouillon in the historiography. The initiative for the book had come from the publisher Walter, who owned the materials of one of the initiators of the project. Waeger says he had been about the third to be asked by Beck. Waeger had then been editor of the journal *Domino* and later chief editor of the television and radio programme guide *TR 7*.

52 *Basler National-Zeitung*, No. 598, 30 December 1969: statements by the politicians Walter Renschler, Heinrich Buchbinder, Andreas Gerwig and Karl Gmünder and the writers Peter Bichsel, Kurt Marti and Walter Vogt.

53 See note 24 above.

54 Curiously, the critique concentrated on this chapter although the following chapter contained, judged from a traditional understanding, more controversial material on the time after the war.

55 Gauye, see note 27 above.

56 In the review of Vol. 3 (1930–39) J. R. von Salis noted that the judgements agreed and recommended the 'excellent report' for reading (*Weltwoche*, 25 August 1967). Vol. 4 (the first of the actual Bonjour report) was reviewed by Bonjour's student

24   *Switzerland and the Second World War*

Hans Fleig who often had non-conformist attitudes but who in this case remained conspiciously soft in his judgement. He praised the language for being almost 'as simple as the language of Tacitus' and the method that 'doesn't foreground the scientist but rather hides him'. Furthermore he noted positively that Bonjour spoke out frankly. The only thing that Fleig criticised was that Bonjour did not show sufficiently the patriotic conformity of those days, 'the atmosphere of fanatical hate found also among the Swiss of diverse political beliefs' (*Sonntags Journal*, 7/8 February 1970). J. R. von Salis' review of Vol. 5 appeared in the *Sonntags Journal*, 20/21 June and 27/28 June 1970. The 'supplement to the Bonjour report' (*Sonntags Journal*, 26/27 September 1970) however is only the additionally published introduction to the dissertation of Peter Stahlberger on Emil Oprecht.

57 Gilg, see note 17 above.
58 *Badener Tagblatt*, 4 April 1970.
59 *Badener Tagblatt*, 4 July 1970.
60 *Badener Tagblatt*, 4 April and 3 July.
61 *Badener Tagblatt*, 18 April 1970.
62 *Badener Tagblatt*, 4 July 1970. Later followed the review of the first volume of documents (Vol. 7) in which Beck took the side of Pilet's defenders: *Badener Tagblatt*, 28 May and 4 June 1977.
63 Klaus Urner, 'Der Bonjour-Bericht in der zeitgeschichtlichen Kontroverse', *Schweizer Monatshefte*, April 1970, pp. 74–82.
64 Elisabeth Alder, 'Mit Edgar Bonjour die Vergangenheit bewältigen?', *Profil*, 1970, pp. 280–6.
65 Niklaus Meienberg, 'Bonsoir, Herr Bonjour', *Zürcher AZ*, 30 April 1971; idem, 'Aufforderung zur seriösen Erforschung der jüngsten schweizerischen Vergangenheit (1939–45). Lesehilfe zum Bonjour-Bericht', in *Die Schweiz. Nationales Jahrbuch der NHG*, 1972, pp. 168–78.
66 Louis de Jong, *Het Koninkrijk der Nederlanden in de Tweede Wereldoorlog*, 27 Volumes, Den Haag, 1969–88.
67 F. H. Hinsley *et al.*, *British Intelligence in the Second World War*, London, 1979–88.
68 Film series, 'Français, si vous saviez!'.
69 Gilg, see note 47 above.
70 Karl Schib in *Schweizerischen Zeitschrift für Geschichte*, 1975, pp. 368–77, and 1976, pp. 375–7.
71 Heinrich *Homberger, Schweizerische Handelspolitik im Zweiten Weltkrieg*, Zurich, 1970, explicitly opposing position on pp. 64ff.
72 Erwin Bucher, *Zwischen Bundesrat und General. Schweizerische Politik und Armee im Zweiten Weltkrieg*, St Gallen, 1991, pp. 550 and 552.
73 Georges-André Chevallaz, *Le défi de la neutralité: Diplomatie et défense de la Suisse 1939–45*, Vevey, 1995.
74 'Historiker-Streit', *Die Dokumentation der Kontroverse um die Einzigartigkeit der nationalsozialistischen Judenvernichtung*, Munich, 1987.
75 Jürg Schoch, 'Bildstörungen', *Tages-Anzeiger*, 21/22 September 1996.
76 Jörg Fisch, 'Die Illusion der abschliessenden historischen Wahrheit. Ein problematischer Bundesbeschluss', *NZZ*, 8 November 1996; with a critical answer by Eric Dreifuss of 20 November 1996. Jörg Fisch, '"Die Kriegsverlängerer". Ein Porträt der neuesten helvetischen Erfindung', *NZZ*, 8 July 1997.
77 *Journal de Genève*, 12 July 1995 on two issues of the *Construire* (Migros-journal).
78 Walther Hofer, 'Wer hat den Zweiten Weltkrieg verlängert?', *NZZ*, 7/8 June 1997.
79 Hans Senn, 'Die Rolle der Schweizer Armee im Zweiten Weltkrieg. Wider-

standswille und Opferbereitschaft der Aktivdienstgeneration', *NZZ*, 25 April 1997. Idem, 'Der Reduit-Vorschlag eine Demutsgeste?', *NZZ*, 22 April 1997.

80 Philippe Marguerat, *La Suisse face au IIIe Reich*, Lausanne, 1991, p. 10. First opposing position already in the colloquium of 1983. See Marguerat, 'La Suisse et la neutralité dans le domaine économique pendant la Seconde Guerre mondiale 1940–fin 1944', in Louis-Edouard Roulet, (ed.), *Les Etats neutres européens et la Seconde Guerre mondiale*, Neuchâtel, 1985, pp. 55–67.

81 *traverse*, 3, 1996 and 1, 1997. See also the article by Karl-Iversen Lapp in *Tages-Anzeiger*, 27 June 1997.

82 Jean Ziegler, *Die Schweiz, das Gold und die Toten*, Munich, 1997. The author claimed to have himself discovered the central document for his thesis, the Memorandum Clodius of 3 June 1943. In reality this document had for the first time already been made public by Jean-Claude Favez in 1970 in the *Cahiers Vilfredo Pareto*, 22/23. And after Favez, Daniel Bourgeois (*Le Troisième Reich et la Suisse*) had analysed it again in 1974.

83 Leisi, see note 46 above.

84 Felix Auer, *Das Schlachtfeld von Thun, oder: Dichtung und Wahrheit bei Jean Ziegler*, Stäfa, 1997.

85 *Tages-Anzeiger*, 20 September 1996.

86 Review by Georg Kreis, 'Der Reiter auf dem Bodensee. Zum Quellenwert von Max Frischs *Dienstbüchlein*', *Basler Nachrichten*, 21 September 1974.

87 *Manifesto*, 21 January 1997. 'Geschichtsbilder und Antisemitismus in der Schweiz', Zurich (*WoZ*), 1997, p. 21.

1

Foreign Trade and Swiss Politics, 1939–45

MARC PERRENOUD

INTRODUCTION: 'THE SWISS MALAISE'

In the March 1946 issue of the *Schweizerische Monatshefte* Ernst Speiser published an article entitled 'Swiss–German Trade Relations during the War'. From the first sentence he conjures up the atmosphere that prevailed in Switzerland at that time: ' "the Swiss malaise" has recently entered the language, though it is much more often encountered in public debates and in the press than in private conversation or discussions around the table in the pub'. As a director of Brown Boveri & Cie, Baden, Speiser held high office: from 1941 he was head of the War Office for Industry and Labour, and was an influential member of the Radical Party and of the Swiss Parliament from 1943. He noted what he called the 'Swiss malaise', mentioning among other aspects a sense of isolation from the rest of the world and doubts about the trade relations with the Axis during the war. To justify the Confederation's attitude, he recalled the legal, political and diplomatic conditions governing foreign relations during the hostilities. He used statistics to paint a reassuring picture of Switzerland, minimising the country's contribution to the German war effort. Calculating that those involved in exports to Germany represented only 2 or 3 per cent of the active population, he concluded that Switzerland had put up a successful military and economic resistance to Nazi and fascist aggression: far from admitting a sense of guilt, Switzerland should be proud of the part it had played during the war.

The statistics provided by Speiser are open to question.[1] However, this oft-quoted article says much about the climate that prevailed in Switzerland at the end of the war: having been spared the destruction and atrocities endured by other nations, Switzerland had to justify the activities and attitudes of which it was accused, both internally and, more especially, beyond its borders. As we know, the controversies prompted by these criticisms would rapidly give way to the tensions caused by the Cold War. However, the malaise described by Speiser did exist, and was probably responsible for a number of studies of foreign relations compiled by lawyers or economists.[2] These works, with a wealth of significant statistical and administrative information, provide us with a better understanding of the legal and institutional traditions existing in Switzerland during the Second World War. In many cases, the authors of these works were, like Speiser, witnesses to or participants in the events.[3] They describe and justify the measures prompted by the war economy, the effects of the Allied blockade and the Axis counter-blockade, and the rights and obligations of a neutral state in wartime economic relations.

SUMMARY OF EXISTING KNOWLEDGE

We know that the publication of documents taken from the German archives provoked reaction in Switzerland. At first, during the 1950s, it was the country's attitude to refugees, and later the policy of neutrality, that prompted the writing of the historical studies now referred to as the Ludwig and Bonjour reports.[4]

During the 1970s, additional research and debate was prompted by foreign trade relations. In 1970 the former director of the Swiss Union of Trade and Industry (SUTI, *Vorort*), Heinrich Homberger, published a very interesting work containing explanations of the agreements negotiated and 'summaries of the events that took place'.[5]

Swiss publications of the post-war period generally tend to offer explanations of the 'Swiss miracle', or to paint a picture of a small country at the mercy of the great powers, which nevertheless succeeds in resisting and defending its independence. These arguments can be understood insofar as these works were written by Swiss participants in the events of a dramatic period which left a deep mark on those who lived through it. However, after the 1970s, historical research both in Switzerland and abroad has tended to retouch this Swiss self-portrait. A degree of distance and a 'longer-term' perspective have tended to modify the image previously created, which shaped the national identity.

In 1970, in an article based on the German archives,[6] Jean-Claude Favez wrote that in the 'spring of 1943 Switzerland thus occupied a relatively important place in the concerns of the Nazi leaders, for strategic and, above all, economic reasons'. On two occasions Hitler himself intervened as a spokesman for moderation, damping the enthusiasm of those who advocated a trade war against Switzerland. The Führer took the side of those who recommended avoiding confrontation with a country that supplied specialised products essential to the war effort, financed its own exports and allowed goods exchanged between the Axis partners to pass through its territory.

From that time a different image of Switzerland began to become apparent, as something more than just a negligible factor at the mercy of an omnipotent dictatorship. Additional information was published in the thesis of Daniel Bourgeois, which was also based on German sources.[7] Without claiming that economic factors alone determined the bilateral relationship, Bourgeois' work is particularly notable for providing unpublished statistics and analyses; he shows that, in some cases, Switzerland was deliberately humoured by the Nazi leaders.[8] Rather than resting on his laurels, Bourgeois continued as he had begun and followed up his thesis with a number of landmark articles.[9] In 1974 he devoted a major article to the activities of business circles in the foreign policy arena, especially at the audience granted by Hitler to Schulthess in 1937, and at the time of the debates regarding recognition of Italian sovereignty over Abyssinia, the 'Manifesto of the 200', the meetings with Nazis with a view to moderating the tone of the Swiss press, and also at the time of the organisation of the mission to the eastern front in 1941. In all these cases, there were close links between political considerations and economic motivations.[10] The debates triggered by these publications demonstrated the need for deeper research into the industrial and banking trump cards available to Switzerland.

Vogler's thesis describes the development of negotiations between Germany and Switzerland in 1940 and 1941:

> Admittedly, the shipments of raw materials to Germany were of central importance. They persuaded Germany to fall in with what the Swiss wanted. But it was only the large credits – a high proportion of which, in turn, was used to finance those very raw materials – that ultimately enabled Switzerland to supply the armaments required, keep Germany at arm's length and assuage its hunger for goods and foreign currency.[11]

We know that at the end of the war Germany's credit line exceeded 1 billion Swiss francs. This was a substantial sum for the Swiss economy (the domestic product at that time being estimated at about 10 billion) and for Nazi Germany.

> Among the neutral trading partners, the completely uncompromising Switzerland always figured as Germany's most important source of credit … At 31 December 1944, the clearing deficit to the neutral states of Europe amounted to RM 762.645 million. Of this sum, Switzerland accounted for RM 685.0 million, Spain RM 108.2 million, Sweden RM 38.1 million and Portugal RM 8.1 million.[12]

Research carried out in Germany shows the changes in various industrial and financial factors that prompted the Nazi leaders to handle Switzerland gently at various periods during the war.[13] Thus, having studied German–Swiss economic relations from 1914 to 1945, Feldenkirchen reaches the following conclusion: 'Germany, therefore, frequently endeavoured to use Switzerland as an instrument of its economic policy, a move against which Switzerland was able to defend itself only occasionally and with varying success. However, its industrial capacities and German dependence on Swiss capital enabled Switzerland – small as its share of German foreign trade was in statistical terms – to become a central focus of German foreign trade policy at critical periods.'[14]

FOUR PROBLEMATIC QUESTIONS

Economic neutrality

Research by historians such as Bourgeois and Urner[15] has shown that Switzerland's economic activities caused greater problems than contemporary publications might suggest: the decisions to prohibit exports of war material, then to allow them in September 1939 and then to prohibit them again in the autumn of 1944 can be understood in the light of arguments of national defence, experience of the previous war and diplomatic pressure or intervention. It must be conceded that the authorities acted more pragmatically than heroically. Despite the repeated assertion of the principle of *do ut des* (give and take), the hard facts of the relative strengths meant unequal concessions, to the detriment of the Confederation.[16]

Similarly, Urner soft-pedals the assertions of respect for economic neutrality. After all, the concept itself is a problematical one and not clearly characteristic of the activities of the various Swiss protagonists. As Georg Kreis noted in 1977, 'Switzerland's trade relations have hitherto been considered from the specifically Swiss standpoint of whether Switzerland could defend her sovereignty and her policy of neutrality. Consequently, the question of the effects of Swiss trade policy has been neglected.'[17]

Escape from invasion

Debate has also focused on the conditions that enabled Switzerland to escape invasion. J. Tanner stresses the close conjunction between foreign trade relations and national defence:

The relatively high density of foreign trade networks in wartime and the military and economic defence of the country were related in two ways: first, exports to belligerent states, especially the Axis powers whose share of Swiss exports rose after 1939, were a factor liable to increase Germany's interest in maintaining the status quo in its relations with Switzerland ... Secondly, the implementation both of the Réduit concept and of the Wahlen plan was to a large extent dependent on the Swiss economy's position in the foreign trade network. This situation was never analysed as a problem by the country's political and military leaders. By contrast, authorities responsible for the war economy, who had to deal with the specific operational problems, made repeated references to it.[18]

Federal government intervention in business

As Jean-François Bergier wrote, 'The war compelled the Confederation to intervene in business life.'[19] The organisation of the war economy tightened the close collaboration between senior officials and the employers. The management and day-to-day surveillance of foreign trade called for a number of administrative structures. For important negotiations, delegations representing the circles concerned were appointed by the Federal Council. As the months went by, the 'permanent economic delegation' became the critical nucleus: a triumvirate comprising the director of the Commercial Division of the Department of Public Economy, Jean Hotz; the director of the SUTI, Homberger; and the Political Department's specialist in financial matters, Robert Kohli, supervised international negotiations. Exceptionally important decisions were discussed by them with the competent federal councillors. Within the government, a 'delegation for economic and financial affairs' brought together the three heads of the Political (Foreign Ministry), Public Economy, Finance and Customs Departments to study the problems.[20]

When the most far-reaching decisions had to be taken, these individuals met at crucial meetings, for which minutes rarely exist. It is all the more interesting, therefore, to study the minutes of the meeting of 21 June 1940, which adopted measures whose impact on industrial activities and federal finances would be considerable.[21]

Although the level of federal government intervention in business remained moderate, it did involve an overlap of activities. For historical researchers, therefore, inspection of the public archives makes it possible to acquire information on trade and on the discussions and activities that took place on both sides.

The post-war economy

From 1943 onwards the prospect of the post-war period gave rise to new ideas among the employers, who were preparing for crises of reconversion, whereas in fact they were on the verge of a long period of expansion.[22] Internal and external factors prompted a substantial increase in public credits during the immediate post-war period. International economic relations would, indeed, initially be strained by Switzerland's international isolation.[23] The Allies dictated their terms to the Confederation, which was to benefit from divisions between the Allies and the effects of the Cold War.[24]

RESEARCH PERSPECTIVES

In a recent article,[25] Linus von Castelmur recalls first that export and import figures are available from customs statistics published over many years, and secondly that diplomatic relations and negotiations have been fairly thoroughly studied. The answers still needed concern questions more associated with 'microhistory'.

- Which companies supplied goods?
- What was the strategic utility and actual use made of the exported products?
- What part did deliveries from Switzerland play in the German war economy?
- What happened to the Swiss companies in Germany and in the occupied countries?
- Did they collaborate with the Nazis? Did they exploit forced labour?

The following research perspectives can thus be identified:

Activities of companies

Company archives would allow a closer analysis of the flows of goods, technical developments and changes in personnel status. Publications on companies nowadays are too frequently more hagiographical than historical. Yet companies' reactions to the upheavals that transformed Europe between 1939 and 1942 would merit a more detailed analysis. What capital expenditures were planned? What industrial reconversions enabled companies to adapt to the new conditions? What social and political activities were contemplated? What was the political and economic impact of the 'New Europe' on companies and their management?[26]

Leading protagonists

More needs to be known about the leading protagonists. However, few of them have published their memoirs.[27] A few have already been the subject of biographies: the head of the Department of Public Economy, Walther Stampfli, is one, and William Rappard another.[28] As long quotations from the latter have been published, we can see the reactions and motivations of a significant personality at the interface between university circles and the political authorities. Rappard questions himself and reveals his reluctance to talk about Swiss impartiality. He recommends greater transparency than has been generated by official pronouncements.

> If we were to admit frankly to ourselves, as was done in Berlin and London, that we had to cut our losses but that there were concessions we could not make in the very interests of our survival, that, in my view, would be both more sincere and more adroit. But, as I have said before, talking like that in Berne meant laying oneself open to a lack of national spirit … The only constructive conclusion that emerges, as I see it, is that it was important to make Berne understand that our attitude fooled no one and that true political realism required that we should save some of the intransigence we showed towards London to display it in relations with Berlin.[29]

One would be glad to find material of this kind in the biographies of other individuals who played more important parts than Rappard. It is a historiographical lacuna that we have no biographies of people like Heinrich Homberger, who was then in charge of the SUTI and frequently played a crucial part in international negotiations. Another example is Hans Sulzer: a leading industrialist in Winterthur, who had served as Switzerland's Minister in Washington at the end of the First World War and then played a central role in employers' organisations in Switzerland,[30] he headed the delegation appointed by the Federal Council for some protracted negotiations in 1942. Similarly, the personality of Walter Stucki is undoubtedly intriguing. His professional career took him to a series of particularly important posts: director of the Commercial Division of the Department of Public Economy, then Federal Council delegate on foreign trade, then, from 1937, Swiss Minister in France (first in Paris, then in Vichy), he returned to Berne after the fall of the Vichy government to become head of the Foreign Affairs Division of the Political Department from January 1945. He led the negotiations with the Allies in 1945 and 1946 before being sidelined to the post of 'Federal Council delegate for special missions'. In this capacity, from the summer of 1946 onwards, he negotiated the application of the Washington Agreement. His political career would thus justify an in-depth study: a member of the Radical Party and of the Parliament from 1935 to 1937, he recommended a way of transcending political divisions.[31] On the eve of war, some accused Stucki of being too far to the left, whereas in Vichy he gained the personal confidence of Pétain, which would be held against him after his return to Switzerland. His personality and his activities make Walther Stucki one of the key personalities of this period.

In addition, it would be useful to analyse the networks of relation-ships which these leading individuals maintained both in Switzerland and abroad, both before and after the war.

Professional organisations

As we know, professional organisations play a vital role in Swiss society. In an analysis of the 1933 Austro-Swiss agreement on the embroidery trade in Vorarlberg, Jean-Claude Favez noted that the effectiveness of Swiss diplomacy was 'largely dependent on the collaboration of the professional associations with the authorities and the convergence of private interests'.[32] In this case, considerations of foreign policy, capital exports and the fight against foreign competition became intermingled to bring about top-level economic and political decisions by Switzerland. However, no historical study exists of the part played by the professional organisations in foreign trade. There is, admittedly, a first study, published in 1997, which provides information on the employers' organisations in the mechanical engineering industry, dealing especially with political interventions.[33] However, it is too incomplete to be regarded as more than a preliminary to an in-depth analysis. As for other organisations, only commemorative publications are currently available. The activities of the SUTI, the Swiss Compen-sation Office and the Swiss Office for the Development of Trade call for historical analysis, taking due account of all the archives and studies available.

One avenue of research may be fruitful: the Industrial Holding Companies Group was founded in November 1942 by eight companies – Alusuisse, Bally, Elektrobank, Suchard, Holderbank, Glaro, Nestlé and Oursina S.A. These companies planned, in this way, to centralise their efforts in order to solve their problems and safeguard their interests, which had been compromised by the rules applied under the clearing conventions. They deplored the fact that an incomplete and caricatured portrayal represented them as companies solely concerned with collecting dividends and interest, whereas their actual activities con-tributed to Swiss exports. 'The efforts made in this direction have greatly benefited the Swiss economy, making it possible, among other things, not only to appoint numerous Swiss citizens to important positions in our companies abroad but also to encourage, very substantially, certain exports such as mechanical engineering exports.'[34] This group, then, was trying to occupy positions similar to that of the Executive of the SUTI or the Swiss Association of Bankers. However, despite numerous campaigns and studies demonstrating the economic importance of its members, this group would never succeed in obtaining as much representation as the other two associations in the delegations appointed by the Federal Council. There is a clear hierarchy: in the person of its director, Homberger, the SUTI occupied a leading position which the Swiss Bankers Association was never able to match. The Industrial Holdings Companies Group therefore occupied third place.

The problem concerning the interaction between commerce and finance in external economic relations can be summarised in the slogan 'Labour takes precedence over capital'. For example, the granting of public loans caused problems: the 850 million francs' credit granted to Germany caused alarm to the Swiss National Bank, wary of inflationist factors, while the SUTI justified the need for it.[35] In the case of the credit for Italy, a dual pressure was brought to bear on the federal authorities: a proliferation of approaches both by the leaders of the fascist regime and by certain Swiss industrialists.[36]

International relations

Relations with countries other than Germany also merit research. The Franco-Swiss relationships have been the subject of two books[37] and several articles. Gérard Levêque stresses the importance of relations with France:

> Trade between Germany and Switzerland, which increased after the total victory of the *Wehrmacht* on the Western front, admittedly sustained a reasonable level of activity, though it was constantly subject to review at the whim of the masters of the *Reich*; in the view of those responsible for Swiss foreign trade, therefore, it would have been a serious error to make the survival of Swiss industry conditional on the goodwill of Switzerland's northern neighbour. It was necessary to ensure at any price that a flow of exports, however reduced its volume, be maintained with neutrals such as Spain or with the enemies of the *Reich*. It would be an even more serious error for this flow of trade not to be negligible by comparison with trade with Germany. Despite all the obstacles set up by the two groups of belligerents (Pilet-Golaz would refer to the 'rings of blockade and counter-blockade' which gradually tightened around Switzerland), it

would be maintained until the end of hostilities, since it was not
in the interest of either camp to strangle Switzerland completely,
enclosed as it was within Hitler's dominions but valuable in more
than one way.[38]

Even so, there are still gaps in the analyses of these relations. Easier
access to the French archives, announced by the French government in
October 1997, may encourage research.

Relations with the United Kingdom also posed the problem of
unlawful exports, which have long been an object of discussion.[39]
Recent studies give a better understanding of the trade, and tensions,
between the two countries.[40] Analysing the economic pressures exerted
by the Allies on Switzerland, and particularly the effects of the
'blacklists', Inglin supplies information on the activities of companies
and businessmen. Alongside other original views on British policy
towards Switzerland, Neville Wylie's argument sheds new light on the
importance of British strategic imports from Switzerland. He was the
first to provide accurate data on the secret operations of the Ministry of
Economic Warfare (MEW), and estimates the total value of the matériel
that the MEW succeeded in procuring secretly on the Swiss market at
72 million Swiss francs. Admittedly, in his view, this figure is only 12 per
cent of what Germany received from Switzerland. In essence, this
unlawful trade related to industrial jewels, watchmaking products and
measuring instruments.

A third country is obviously deserving of attention: the United States
exerted ever-increasing pressure on the countries of Europe and
endeavoured to control Switzerland's economic relations. In the
newspapers, over the radio, in parliamentary debates and diplomatic
negotiations, American criticism mounted. According to Fleury, 'the
importance attached to trade between Germany and Switzerland as
one of the factors prolonging the war may be a cause of surprise'.[41] In
1945, this was a manifestation of America's designs on world leadership.

In Switzerland, as elsewhere, the opening of archives and the
emergence of new problems suggest that major studies may be
published shortly.[42]

Trade and humanitarian activities

The relations between foreign trade and humanitarian activities would
be worth analysing.[43] A tendency still exists to distinguish between
disinterested efforts and mercenary considerations. However, this
divide is not apparent from the study of activities such as the 'medical
missions' to the eastern front or the aid programmes for the reconstruction of a devastated Europe. In 1944 Pilet-Golaz noted that 'the

immediate future of our export industry may be very largely conditional on the future of humanitarian activities'.[44]

Technological stagnation

Another question worth further historical research concerns the relationship between the relative economic prosperity of Swiss industry during the war and its technical advances over a longer period. It may be felt that adapting to the demands imposed by hostilities improved the flexibility of the industrial sector. In his book on a company that was particularly active in foreign trade François Jequier, in a chapter entitled 'Une neutralité prospère: le retour de l'âge d'or (1941–1945)' (Prosperous neutrality: the return of the Golden Age (1941–1945)), mentions the processes of diversification and modernisation.[45] However, other authors consider that industry, with guaranteed markets, introduced virtually no innovations in production technology. In a study of the Paillard company, Laurent Tissot emphasises

> the technical stagnation that typified the various sectors of production between 1938 and 1945. Business increased, but that increase was unaccompanied by any major technological innovation. Whereas new products had been launched at regular intervals in the pre-war years, the global conflict saw no new production at all. By and large, the equipment was no different from that which had been designed and produced during the 1930s.[46]

According to Jean-François Bergier, 'as soon as the war ended industry set off again at full throttle, using the equipment it had retained but done little to renovate'.[47] The unexpected prosperity that boosted the Swiss economy would conceal this weakness on the part of industry. The effects of the technological stagnation during the 1940s would not be felt until the 1960s or later. From that time on, various sectors of industry would pass through periods of crisis – sometimes very severe. In seeking explanations for these, reference was frequently made to the Second World War. It would be interesting to know whether historical studies could confirm these retrospective explanations.

Invisible exports

The structures taken on by the Swiss economy mean that the country's world trade figures cannot be reduced to the figures for products recorded by the Swiss customs. The activities of those who controlled Swiss foreign trade were not confined to bilateral relations or the European continent.[48] Too little is known about the part played by 'invisible exports' and the international connections of companies.

Analysing the Swiss economy 'in the European context from 1913 to 1939', Paul Bairoch recalls the scale and speed of the creation of production units outside the borders, from which he estimates that 'the Swiss capital invested in industrial production sectors abroad was capable of generating a production volume greater than that of all Swiss exports combined'.[49]

The innovative studies of recent years have been conducted both in Switzerland and abroad. This applies particularly to the study of the subsidiaries of Swiss companies in southern Germany. The estimates published by Sophie Pavillon mention a figure of over 150 companies employing about 14,000 people. After the German invasion of eastern Europe, Swiss subsidiaries employed hundreds of people who had been deported from eastern Europe.[50] In short, there is no lack of opportunity for historical research.

NOTES

1 See Klaus Urner, 'Neutralité et politique commerciale pendant la Seconde Guerre mondiale', *Revue d'histoire de la Deuxième Guerre mondiale*, 121, 1981, p. 36.
2 The following list is not comprehensive:
   * Hans Aepli, 'Die schweizerische Aussenhandelspolitik von der Abwertung des Schweizerfrankens bis zum Kriegsbeginn, September 1936 bis September 1939', dissertation, Berne, 1944.
   * Emil Michael Bammatter, 'Der schweizerische Transithandel. Eine Darstellung seiner Struktur und ein Überblick seiner Entwicklung in den Jahren 1934–1954', dissertation, Basle, 1958.
   * Otto Baumgartner, *Die schweizerische Aussenhandelspolitik von 1930 bis 1936*, Zurich, 1943.
   * Hanspeter Brunner, *10 Jahre schweizerisch–amerikanische Handelsbeziehungen 1936–1945*, Zurich, 1946.
   * Max Heuberger, 'Die Strukturwandlungen des schweizerischen Aussenhandels in den Jahren 1938–1949', dissertation, Basle, 1957.
   * Jean Humbert, *Les institutions suisses d'expansion commerciale*, Geneva, 1946.
   * Doris Karmin, *La politique commerciale de la Suisse, 1932 à 1939. Contingents et accords de clearing*, Geneva, 1944.
   * Jean-Flavien Lalive, 'Le droit de la neutralité et le problème des crédits consentis par les neutres aux belligérants', law thesis, Zurich 1941.
   * Walter Peter, 'Die schweizerische Aussenhandelspolitik von der Abwertung des Schweizer-Frankens bis zum Ende des 2. Weltkrieges, 1936–1945. Versuch einer systematischen Darstellung der Lenkungsmassnahmen auf empirischer Grundlage', dissertation, Zurich, 1958.
   * Kurt Rohner, 'Die schweizerischen Wirtschaftsvertretungen im Ausland', dissertation, Berne, 1944.

- Erwin Saner, 'Der schweizerische Maschinen-Export von 1930–1945', dissertation, Fribourg, 1949.
- Schweizerisches Institut für Aussenwirtschafts- und Marktforschungen an der Hochschule St Gallen (ed.), *Die Schweiz als Kleinstaat in der Weltwirtschaft*, St Gallen, 1945 (see in particular the article by William Rappard).
- Max Steiner, *Die Verschiebung in der schweizerischen Aussenhandelsstruktur während des Zweiten Weltkrieges*, Zurich, 1950.
- Adolphe Vaudaux, *Blockade und Gegenblockade. Handelspolitische Sicherung der schweizerischen Ein- und Ausfuhr im Zweiten Weltkrieg*, Zurich, 1948.
- René Vogel, *Politique commerciale suisse*, Montreux, 1966.
- Alfred Zehnder, *Politique extérieure et politique du commerce extérieur*, Geneva, 1957.

3   Particular mention should be made of an article in the book dedicated to the union leader largely responsible for the industrial relations truce signed in 1937, by the former head of the War Economy Board and future Federal Councillor Hans Schaffner, who published 'Gedanken zur Aussenhandelspolitik der Schweiz im Zweiten Weltkrieg', in *Festgabe für Konrad Ilg zum siebzigsten Geburtstag*, Berne, 1947. In 1950 and 1951, the Federal Department of Public Economy published a thick volume devoted to *L'économie de guerre en Suisse, 1939–1948*. The director of the Commercial Division, Jean Hotz, put his name to an important chapter on trade policy.

4   It may be noted that Professor Edgar Bonjour concluded his chapters on economic relations with quotations taken from the SUTI's reports, the arguments of which are frequently reproduced, especially in Vol. 6, Chs 10, 11, 12, 13, 14 and 15.

5   Heinrich Homberger, *Schweizerische Handelspolitik im Zweiten Weltkrieg*, Zurich, 1970, subsequently Neuchatel, 1972 (French translation). See also the pages on 'Aussenhandel' published by Homberger in the *Handbuch der Schweizerischen Volkswirtschaft*, Berne, 1939 and 1955.

6   Jean-Claude Favez, 'La Suisse au tournant de la Seconde Guerre mondiale. Quelques remarques sur les relations germano-suisses au printemps 1943', *Cahiers Vilfredo Pareto – Revue européenne des sciences sociales*, 22/23, 1970, pp. 163–74.

7   Daniel Bourgeois, *Le Troisième Reich et la Suisse 1933–1941*, Neuchatel, 1974, see in particular pp. 158–82.

8   See Marc Perrenoud, 'Aspects des relations économiques et financières de la Suisse avec l'Axe', in *Capitaux en fuite, biens pillés et fonds en déshérence*, Swiss Federal Archive, Berne, 1997, pp. 25–30.

9   Daniel Bourgeois, 'Publications récentes sur la politique commerciale de la Suisse pendant la Deuxième Guerre mondiale', *Relations internationales*, 1, 1974; Daniel Bourgeois, 'Les relations économiques germano-suisses 1939–1945', *Revue d'histoire de la Deuxième Guerre mondiale*, 121, 1981, pp. 49–61.

10   Daniel Bourgeois, 'Milieux d'affaires et politique étrangère suisse à l'époque des fascismes', *Relations internationales*, 1, 1974 (republished in *Page Deux*, March 1997, pp. 7–12).

11   Robert Urs Vogler, *Die Wirtschaftsverhandlungen zwischen der Schweiz und Deutschland 1940 und 1941*, Zurich, 1983, pp. 218–129 (sic).

12   See Willi A. Boelcke, *Die Kosten von Hitlers Krieg, Kriegsfinanzierung und finanzielles Kriegserbe in Deutschland 1933–1948*, Paderborn, 1985, pp. 113 and 153.

13 See Eichholtz, Dietrich, *Geschichte der deutschen Kriegswirtschaft*, Berlin, 1996, in particular pp. 425–8, 453–6, 481–4, 503–7, 567–73.

14 Wilfried Feldenkirchen, 'Die Handelsbeziehungen zwischen dem Deutschen Reich und der Schweiz 1914–1945', *Vierteljahresschrift für Sozial- und Wirtschaftsgeschichte*, 74, 1987, p. 350.

15 Klaus Urner, 'Economie et Neutralité', *Revue d'histoire de la Deuxième Guerre mondiale*, 121, 1981, pp. 35–9; and 'Neutralität und Wirtschaftskrieg: Zur schweizerischen Aussenhandelspolitik', in Rudolf L. Bindschedler *et al.* (eds), *Schwedische und schweizerische Neutralität im Zweiten Weltkrieg*, Basle/Frankfurt-am-Main, 1985, pp. 250–92.

16 Daniel Bourgeois, 'Les relations économiques germano-suisses pendant la Seconde Guerre mondiale: un bilan allemand de 1944', *Revue suisse d'histoire*, 32, 1982, p. 566.

17 Georg Kreis, 'Die Schweiz und der Zweite Weltkrieg. Bilanz und bibliographischer Überblick nach dreissig Jahren', in *La seconda guerra mondiale nella prospettiva storica a trent'anni dall'epilogo*, Como, 1977, p. 231.

18 Jakob Tanner, *Bundeshaushalt, Währung und Kriegswirtschaft. Eine finanzsoziologische Analyse der Schweiz zwischen 1938 und 1953*, Zurich, 1986, pp. 283–4.

19 Jean-François Bergier, *Histoire économique de la Suisse*, Lausanne, 1984, p. 254.

20 Marc Perrenoud, 'L'intervention de la Confédération dans les relations financières internationales de la Suisse (1936–1946)', in Paul Bairoch and Martin Körner (eds), *Die Schweiz in der Weltwirtschaft*, Zurich, 1990, p. 378.

21 Swiss Diplomatic Documents, Vol. 13, Berne, 1991, pp. 739–44.

22 Studies of the commercial policy of Switzerland from 1945 to 1966, financed by the FNRS and directed by H. U. Jost, Hanspeter Kriesi and Sébastien Guex, have recently begun.

23 Antoine Fleury, 'La Suisse et le retour au multilatéralisme dans les échanges internationaux après 1945', in *Die Schweiz in der Weltwirtschaft*, op. cit., note 20, pp. 353–70. Walter Spahni, *Der Ausbruch der Schweiz aus der Isolation nach dem Zweiten Weltkrieg (untersucht anhand ihrer Aussenhandelspolitik 1944–1947)*, Frauenfeld, 1977.

24 See Marc Perrenoud, 'La diplomatie et l'insertion de la Suisse dans les nouvelles relations économiques internationales (1943–1950)', in Georg Kreis (ed.), *Die Schweiz im internationalen System der Nachkriegszeit 1943–1950*, Itinera, 1996, fasc. 18, pp. 130–45.

25 Linus von Castelmur, 'Aspekte der Wirtschafts- und Finanzbeziehungen der Schweiz im Zweiten Weltkrieg', in *Die Schweiz im Zweiten Weltkrieg. Forschungsstand. Kontroversen, offene Fragen*, Zurich, 1997, p. 29.

26 See J. Tanner, op. cit., note 18, p. 366.

27 In particular, Ernst Schneeberger, *Wirtschaftkrieg auch im Frieden*, Berne, 1984.

28 Georg Hafner, 'Bundesrat Walther Stampfli, alt Bundesrat, 1884–1965. Leiter der Kriegswirtschaft im Zweiten Weltkrieg, Bundesrätlicher Vater der AHV', dissertation, Zurich, 1986.

29 Letter dated 22 October 1942 from Rappard to Hans Sulzer, quoted by Victor Monnier, *William E. Rappard. Défenseur des libertés, serviteur de son pays et de la communauté internationale*, Geneva/Basle, 1995, p. 561. See also his analysis of 25 June 1949: 'De tous les pays d'Europe, la Suisse est celui dont le commerce extérieur s'est le plus développé depuis 1938. Et de tous les pays du monde entier, elle est celui qui, relativement au chiffre de sa population, est le plus engagé dans l'économie mondiale.' Federal Archive, Berne, E 2800/1990/106/17.

30 For a list of his numerous positions, see Geneviève Billeter, *Le pouvoir patronal.*

Les patrons des grandes entreprises suisses des métaux et des machines (1919–1939), Geneva, 1985, p. 199.

31 Pietro Morandi, *Krise und Verständigung. Die Richtlinienbewegung und die Entstehung der Konkordanzdemokratie 1933–1939*, Zurich, 1995, in particular pp. 256–72.

32 Jean-Claude Favez, 'Mozart, la broderie et les finances fédérales', in Judit Garamvölgyi and Urs Altermatt (eds), *Innen- und Aussenpolitik. Primat oder Interdependenz? Festschrift zum 60. Geburtstag von Walther Hofer*, Berne/Stuttgart, 1980, p. 349. For details of these negotiations, see Swiss Diplomatic Documents, Vol. 10, Berne, 228, 1982; and Vol. 11, Berne, 1983, 69, 91 and 82.

33 Jan Vonder Mühll, *Die Aktivitäten der schweizerischen Maschinenindustrie und ihrer Verbände ASM und VSM während des Zweiten Weltkrieges (1933–1945)*, Zurich, 1997.

34 Letter from the Industrial Holding Companies Group to the Political Department dated 16 December 1942, Federal Archive, Berne, E 2001(E)1968/78/388.

35 See the correspondence exchanged between the SUTI and the BNS on this matter in 1942, Swiss Diplomatic Documents, Berne, 1997, Vol. 14, 203.

36 See the letter from the Oerlikon-Bührle company, Swiss Diplomatic Documents, Berne, 1992, Vol. 13, p. 915.

37 René Jerusalmi, *Les relations économiques franco-suisses (1939–1945). Un aspect insoupçonné de la Seconde Guerre mondiale*, Berne, 1995.

38 Gérard Levêque, *La Suisse et la France gaulliste 1943–1945. Problèmes économiques et diplomatiques*, Geneva, 1979, p. 10.

39 John Lomax, *The Diplomatic Smuggler*, London, 1965.

40 Oswald Inglin, *Der stille Krieg. Der Wirtschaftskrieg zwischen Grossbritannien und der Schweiz im Zweiten Weltkrieg*, Zurich, 1991; Neville R. Wylie, '"The Riddle of the Swiss": British Policy towards Switzerland 1940–43', dissertation, Cambridge, 1994.

41 Antoine Fleury, 'Les Etats-Unis et la Suisse à l'issue des deux guerres mondiales. Etude comparée de diplomatie économique', *Relations internationales*, 10, 1977, p. 140.

42 As, for example, the proceedings of the colloquium on 'Les relations commerciales et financières de la Suisse avec les Grandes Puissances (1914–1945)', organised at the University of Lausanne in June 1996 by Sébastien Guex.

43 Some interesting information may be gathered from the unpublished thesis by Jörg Kistler, 'Das politische Konzept der schweizerischen Nachkriegshilfe in den Jahren 1943–1948', Berne, 1980.

44 Antoine Fleury, 'La Suisse et la préparation à l'après-guerre', in Michel Dumoulin (ed.), *Plans des temps de guerre pour l'Europe d'après-guerre 1940–1947*, Brussels/Milan/Paris/Baden-Baden, 1995, p. 189.

45 François Jequier (with the assistance of Chantal Schindler-Pittet), *De la forge à la manufacture horlogère, XVIIIe-XXe siècles. Cinq générations d'entrepreneurs de la Vallée de Joux au coeur d'une mutation industrielle*, Lausanne, 1983, pp. 522–38.

46 Laurent Tissot, *E. Paillard & Cie, SA. Une entreprise vaudoise de petite mécanique 1920–1945*, Cousset, 1987, p. 339. See also pp. 320–1.

47 J.-F. Bergier, op. cit., note 19, p. 254.

48 J. Tanner, op. cit., note 18, p. 294, 'Der Leitgedanke der Kriegswirtschaftsbehörden hinsichtlich der Industrie war die Erhaltung der Weltmarktposition der schweizerischen Unternehmungen'. For an example of promising research into the Swiss economic presence in the world market, see Bouda Etemad, 'Le commerce extérieur de la Suisse avec le Tiers Monde aux XIXe et XXe siècles.

Une perspective comparative internationale', *Les Annuelles*, 5, 1994, pp. 7–41. In the same issue of that periodical, see also Lyonel Kaufmann, 'Guillaume Tell au Congo. L'expansion suisse au Congo belge (1930–1960)'.

49 Paul Bairoch, 'L'économie suisse dans le contexte européen: 1913–1939', *Revue suisse d'histoire*, 4, 1984, p. 481. Two other features identified by Bairoch were of particular significance during the Second World War: the relative importance of foreign trade (a statistical comparison based on annual exports and size of population shows that Switzerland is one of the largest exporting countries) and structural changes in terms of products exported (during the inter-war period, exports of metal and chemical products increased considerably at the expense of agricultural produce and textiles).

50 Sophie Pavillon, 'Trois filiales d'entreprises suisses en Allemagne du Sud et leur développement durant la période nazie', *Etudes et Sources*, 1997, pp. 150–94.

2

Switzerland's International Financial Relations, 1931–50

JAKOB TANNER

INTRODUCTION

When the question is raised about the financial relations maintained by Switzerland's banking community and financial market with the Axis powers, the Allies and the neutral countries during the Second World War used a concept that became established as a subject for Swiss historical research only in the mid-1980s. Earlier surveys and studies tended to speak of capital exports, export financing, lending operations, capital flight and capital protection, 'hot money', capital imports, trade in bank notes, clearing and financial agreements and so on. These terms designate different but interdependent phenomena, which were nevertheless rarely analysed *in toto*. The studies that appeared in the wake of the Bonjour report were the first to attempt a coherent inter-pretation of Switzerland's financial sector, with its strong dependence on foreign economies. Particular attention was paid to economic cooperation between the Swiss banking system and the Nazi regime. The examination of the close-knit relationships involving manufac-turing, trade and finance indicated that these business activities created potential complications with regard to neutrality law, and had security-policy ramifications as well. A dilemma, if not a chasm, was identified between reasons of state and state morality. With all their differences in approach and emphasis, the publications by Daniel Bourgeois (1974), Werner Rings (1985), Jakob Tanner (1986) and, in a summing-up, Markus Heiniger (1989) can be placed in this category.[1] More recent studies by journalists also point in the same direction.[2] Because these studies clash with the myth of the *réduit* (Alpine fortress) and with memories of staunch resistance harboured by the 'active service gener-ation' (the mobilisation generation), they were perceived as a critical revision of the established Swiss view of history and were officially received with much reserve in many instances.

The term 'financial relations', with its many connotations and general applications, first became prevalent in the studies of the mid-1980s on Switzerland's relations with the Western Allies.[3] Marco Durrer (1984), Philippe Marguerat (1985), Marc Perrenoud (1987) and Linus von Castelmur (1994) referred to 'financial relations' in their titles or subheadings.[4] For all these authors, the meaning of the term appeared to be self-evident. In any case it was generally used in a descriptive sense. No theoretical treatment of the term as an analytical concept is found. The descriptive approach, however, does permit a certain amount of source-based 'problem monitoring'. Durrer, Perrenoud and von Castelmur adopted a contentious tone, approaching the disputed questions as problems, while Marguerat was more occupied with demonstrating the correctness of the gold purchases from the standpoint of neutrality law and neutrality policy.

Roughly speaking, the following dimensions of the problems at issue were addressed: the geographical distribution of Swiss assets abroad and the provenance of foreign assets held in Switzerland; war economy measures, foreign policy measures and legal measures affecting this transnational asset structure; credit extended in connection with clearing agreements, negotiations and treaties with which disputed questions were resolved and conflicts set aside; and the complex network of protagonists and interests that blurred the lines between political and private-sector institutions. Volumes 13–15 of the *Documents diplomatiques Suisses* (Swiss Diplomatic Documents), appearing between 1991 and 1997, were also devoted to the subject, defined in similarly broad terms. Without mentioning 'financial relations' in the breakdown of topics, these volumes tried to employ questions such as those enumerated above as selection criteria for the sources to be included.[5] The concept of 'financial relations' implies other central questions going beyond these core themes. What sort of tensions existed between the interlocking capital relationships and Switzerland's neutrality policy? In a broader sense, how to define the relationship between the 'small, neutral country' and its internationally oriented financial marketplace, which was so heavily dependent on foreign business? What role did the financial relationships play in warding off military attacks on Swiss territory during the war years? Or, turning the question around, what was the significance of the financial sphere for the Axis powers' weapons industry and military campaigns? How do the financial ties relate to the transactions in (looted) gold, the foreign direct investment, the flows of flight capital, the refugee policy and the trade in plundered goods? And, last but not least, what repercussions did the Second World War have on the long-term growth potential of Switzerland's financial and banking markets in the European and international context? On the whole, it becomes clear that 'financial relations' embrace private-sector activities as well as international law. Markets driven by competition and the profit motive are embedded in a network of interpersonal, legal and political relationships, and are changed by shifting patterns of political and military power.

The next section outlines developments from 1931, the European *annus terribilis* (Gilbert Ziebura[6]) of the Great Depression, to the beginning of the 1950s (European Payments Agreement and founding of the European Payments Union in 1950;[7] Switzerland's compensation agreement with the Allies, 1952).[8] I try to show that, even before the surge of research into economic and social history as the 1960s were about to close, some of the insights which were hardly recognised in Switzerland's ideological view of its own history were already taking shape. This is followed by references to important studies outside the circle of academic historians, which were instrumental in opening up new areas to research. I then deal with the most important publications on the themes that have arisen since the 1970s, and describe where the emphasis lay. The research results available today are then grouped according to two main aspects, which I believe are both particularly relevant and at the same time controversial. The concluding section indicates the most important points that still require further research and makes some suggestions for future historical studies.

GENERAL ACCOUNTS BY INSIDERS AND SPECIAL STUDIES,
INTO THE 1960s

In the first two decades of the post-war era, enough material was available for somebody interested in Switzerland's 'financial relations' to form an idea of the main features and structural characteristics. The *Handbuch des Geld-, Bank- und Börsenwesens der Schweiz* (Handbook on the Swiss monetary system, banking industry and securities trade), published in 1947, together with the *Handbuch der schweizerischen Volkswirtschaft* (Handbook of the Swiss Economy) and the publication *50 Jahre Schweizerische Nationalbank* (50 years of the Swiss National Bank), published in 1955 and 1957, respectively, summarised the state of knowledge at the time.[9] The authors of these works tended to be political and economic decision-makers, who presented very sketchy overviews of events from their own domestic perspective. In addition, a host of economic and legal dissertations have appeared since the beginning of the 1950s, dealing with specific aspects of the subject.[10]

Four structural characteristics or themes were brought out in these studies.

The oldest capital-exporting country north of the Alps

First of all, Switzerland was described as the oldest capital-exporting country north of the Alps. The 'financial centres' initially integrated into various urban societies (Basle, Geneva, Zurich) originated not so much in flight capital but in the course of foreign investment, which was funded by a number of quite diverse sources. Long before the twentieth century began, Switzerland was able to offset its negative trade balance thanks in part to investment income from abroad; statistical time series and data on the regional distribution of these assets, however, can hardly be found in the relevant reference works, and the statements remain largely qualitative.[11]

The link between export financing and capital exports

Second, the close link between export financing and capital exports was emphasised. The commercial banks' loans to the export industry supported Switzerland's external economic relations.[12] Switzerland had been feeling the full impact of exchange controls and bilateral trade problems since the beginning of the 1930s, and the complexities confronting the 'tried and true export credit vehicles' were further compounded by the outbreak of war, while the existing uncertainties were exacerbated by a spate of transfer restrictions. Driven in particular by the need to insure unprecedented transport risks and risks associated with war, in the words of the handbook on the Swiss economy, 'a modern form [of export financing] was developed, adapted to the altered conditions: advances on claims for exports of goods abroad,' that is the 'clearing and transfer receivables'.[13] During the war years, the state stepped forward as the motor driving capital exports, a role it retained in the post-war period. In the years after 1945, the federal authorities were substantially involved in the advance funding of Swiss exports. These advances amounted to CHF 1.3 billion in 1945, with close to another CHF 1.4 billion added by 1954.[14] Because of the shortage of foreign exchange in neighbouring countries, which lay in ruins, the reconstruction of a Europe ravaged by war required the state to assume the function of a bank. While this was interpreted as 'exceptional' and 'contrary to the sound principles of export promotion', there was no recognisable alternative. Also, the official promotion of exports was tantamount to an economic imperative, because 'the leading Swiss banks had turned hesitant' and it was again up to the state to revive the country's languishing capital exports – at considerable risk. The rationale was that if Switzerland proved unable to put up the capital to support the export industry once more, 'not only would a reasonably sustained expansion of exports fail to materialise, but some of the normal foreign sales might even be lost'. The big Swiss banks, in particular, only resumed their traditional role as exporters of capital when the European capital markets were consolidated (formation of the European Payments Union in 1950) and the convertibility of currencies was restored (in the course of the 1950s).[15] The political stability achieved by the chief western European countries at the end of the 1940s and the eminent significance of a hard Swiss franc to Switzerland's function as a hub for international capital flows were emphasised.

Significance of short-term, speculative movements of capital

Third, these general accounts identified the growing significance of short-term, speculative movements of capital.[16] 'Hot money', as the *Handbuch des Geld-, Bank- und Börsenwesen* put it, was a 'new expression for money of a restless, unstable nature, which pops up first here and then there in search of investment' with no intention of finding a permanent abode, and which 'contributes to the inflation of the banks' balance sheets' and made the first Gentlemen's Agreement of 1937 necessary.[17] Financial speculation was fuelled above all by the cascade of devaluations that followed the 1931 devaluation of sterling. While Swiss capital exports stagnated during the loss-ridden years of the Great Depression, 'the flows in the other direction ... of short-term flight capital seeking safe investments took on a growing significance'. The years 1931 and 1932 saw a strong net inflow of capital into Switzerland. Expectations that the Swiss franc would 'capitulate' under all this pressure reversed the direction again. But after September 1936 (30 per cent devaluation of the Swiss franc), the Swiss capital market once again became highly liquid with massive inflows of money from abroad. This enabled it to function efficiently as an *entrepôt* for capital, translating capital imports and savings into capital exports. The expansion of the big banks' networks to include branches in the new international financial centre of New York with the outbreak of war was now seen as directly related to the capital movements triggered by the momentous political events of the day.[18] High volatility was a characteristic of the capital markets of the 1930s: the investors' cumulative expectations and anxieties were mutually reinforcing in the game of short-term maximisation of profit, resulting in completely unpredictable patterns of transactions on the capital markets not only of Switzerland but also of other attractive countries for investors (such as the USA, Canada, Sweden and Argentina). This trend was then brought up short by the panoply of restrictions introduced during the war years (exchange controls, bilateral clearing arrangements, frozen assets and such like).[19]

After 1945 'longer-term loans' took on greater significance again because of the investment in reconstruction.[20] This development favoured Switzerland's financial sector, which was characterised by a strong capital market and a virtually non-existent financial market.

Impact of war

Fourth, the changing nature of the economic cycles and the impact of war on international capital movements were singled out as themes. The assessment of wars is negative; they 'destroy capital, and therefore have always constituted the turning point in international capital movements'.[21] The interpretations mainly cited the experience of the First World War, when 'international solidarity at the economic level broke down'. The subsequent attempt to re-establish the robust gold standard that existed before the war finally came to grief in the depths of the Great Depression. Individual countries, those in debt, felt compelled to 'declare moratoriums on transfers and take foreign exchange measures to prohibit the free export of gold, foreign exchange and their own currencies and to control this traffic'.[22] On the other hand, the creditor nations, and especially Switzerland, with their strong non-interventionist leanings, had to 'take defensive measures in order to limit the adverse impact of exchange controls on their own economies', no matter how much they opposed state intervention in principle, and '15 years of such intervention resulted in a situation where the international payments traffic fell apart, fragmented into a series of separate blocs left to their own fates'.[23] The regimentation of their currencies by many European countries to facilitate armament and serve the war economy then led in 1930 to a 'nearly total crippling of normal international capital flows', to 'capital losses on Swiss foreign assets' that were not quantified further, and to 'an erosion of capital of unimaginable proportions'.[24] But in both world wars, Switzerland found ways to reap a comparative advantage, despite all the negative factors, against the much more straitened currencies of the outside world; 'already during the Second World War', as the *Handbuch der schweizerischen Volkswirtschaft* put it, 'the balance shifted yet again, and Switzerland found itself once more exporting larger amounts of capital for a period of time' in volumes that were to exceed 'even the magnitude of the earlier decades of economic boom'.[25]

This four-point *tour d'horizon* of the various relevant facets of Swiss financial relations shows that these expert insiders also used their knowledge of the material at that time to divert attention from the more delicate issues and disputed questions by a kind of sleight of hand. This is evident in the way the so-called 'clearing billion' was excluded; in the eloquent silence concerning the transactions in looted gold with the Third Reich and Nazi flight capital;[26] and in the absence of anything about how the 'dormant accounts' came to be.

The body of research reviewed here contains a mixture of insider accounts which continued to endorse the received wisdom of traditional Swiss history and specialised studies of individual aspects couched in characteristic scholarly prose. Georg Kreis observed in 1975, correctly, that research into financial relations, based on historical sources, was lacking.[27] In the meantime, however, a process of intellectual fermentation had begun that was also taking issue with the traditional image of Swiss history. In addition, in 1975 the embargo on documents in the Swiss Federal Archive was shortened to 35 years, which made important sources immediately accessible for research purposes for the period up to 1949. More than 20 years after Kreis' statement, Linus von Castelmur came to the conclusion in 1997 that 'the history of Swiss economic and financial relations in the Second World War' was 'well researched'; he did however add the qualifier that 'a comprehensive synthesis' was not yet available.[28]

CRITICAL QUESTIONING OF THE MYTH OF SWITZERLAND SINCE THE 1960s

Consistent with a familiar pattern for innovations in Swiss historiography, a few key initial studies were produced outside the ranks of the academic historians. In 1968, for instance, *Das heimliche Imperium* (The secret empire) by Lorenz Stucki (son of Minister Walter O. Stucki) had a lasting impact on the discussion of Switzerland as a financial centre. Stucki explored the question of 'how Switzerland got rich' and rightly claimed to be the first to investigate this aspect of Switzerland's history.

> While the maritime powers of Europe were establishing their colonial domains, the Swiss pioneers were quietly and secretly building up a world economic empire, as successful businessmen and founders of initially small industrial corporations. No Swiss flags were hoisted above this empire, no Swiss gunboats were used to safeguard export markets and trade relations – and precisely for that reason this empire was only slightly affected by the decolonisation of recent decades.[29]

Stucki went on to explain: 'we of today' could 'never afford our noble intellectual idealism, if our forefathers hadn't rolled up their sleeves and dirtied their hands to amass the money and also to lay the foundations for the modern world'.[30] The author tried to show with his research that 'the history of Swiss "imperialism"' cannot be explained 'by the banking secrecy which attracted flight capital from tax dodgers and profiteers around the world, but goes back to the enormous sums of Swiss capital invested beyond the country's borders'.[31] He presented the history of the capital exports and particularly Swiss direct investments abroad and pointed out the First World War's role as a catalyst for the 'relocation of production abroad'. In the aftermath of the First World War, the Swiss upper class had to suffer further setbacks in a Europe shaken by revolution, as the corresponding capital assets contracted 'from the former eight billion to two and a half billion Swiss francs'.[32] This painful experience of economic losses fused with the trauma of the general strike to solidify an attitude that was (in Stucki's interpretation) to have a lasting influence on Switzerland's domestic politics for the next two decades.

Stucki went on to describe the difficulties of the period between the wars. The 'obstruction, and sometimes near nationalisation of international trade and payments' hit Switzerland, with its dependence on exports, particularly hard. The Second World War, then, intensified the private sector's economic 'dependence on the state'; at the same time, Switzerland, as an 'island of peace', again emerged from the catastrophe as a 'war profiteer', as it had earlier from the 1914–18 conflict. The 'great advantage enjoyed by an unscathed Switzerland over nearly all other European countries' could have been quickly dissipated after 1945, when another wave of internationalisation commenced. But the Swiss, 'instead of rejoicing, were more prone to feel guilty about their prosperity in the midst of an impoverished continent, and so redoubled their efforts and increased their savings as the proven remedy for a bad conscience'. In the slipstream of the liberalisation of international trade, the Swiss managed to take the offensive again after a decade of crisis and, with the help of the state, to wage a 'more or less successful' defence of 'their empire'.[33] In the following decades, the rate of growth of 'Swiss factories' was 'disproportionately slower than the growth of the companies, which were soon employing more workers at their [foreign] subsidiaries than they did at home'.[34] By international standards, Swiss companies were 'medium-sized at best', but 'compared to their European competitors, which had to start lining up credit practically from zero again, they had the advantage of larger capital reserves and a relatively high level of self-financing, supported by a world presence built up over half a century'.[35]

It is indicative that this theme was hardly taken up at all by historians when the work first appeared. Rather, the analysis was continued by the Zurich sociologist François Höpflinger, who published an empirical study in 1977 under the title – echoing Stucki – of *Das unheimliche Imperium* (The Sinister Empire) and who emphasised above all the primacy of external economic affairs.[36] The 'success of the Swiss economy' rested 'to a considerable degree on the ability of its middle class to assume an important position of trust in the structure of international capitalism, whether as reliable suppliers of capital good to companies or as the discreet administrators of financial operations for the world at large', because the country's 'big, financially powerful private organisations ... were beyond the reach of democratic controls'.[37] Without going into the possible long-term effects of the Second World War, Höpflinger stressed that 'the actual era of multinational expansion by the big [Swiss] corporations' only set in 'after the Second World War'.[38]

Professional historians hardly engaged in any critical discussion of such studies. Well into the 1970s, academic historians were still primarily interested in other questions. Nor did the Bonjour report[39] produce any significant change in this regard. The impressive breadth of Edgar Bonjour's study, which nevertheless was largely a tapestry of paraphrasing, did venture a marked (re)appraisal of some of the important figures in Switzerland's domestic politics. By contrast, external economic relations were put on the back-burner. The so-called 'clearing billion', approved in stages after the summer of 1940 in response to the Nazi regime's hunger for credit, was treated in somewhat more detail. This consisted of loans extended by the Swiss Confederation to the Third Reich under the clearing agreement of 1934, which were massively increased to CHF 850 million immediately preceding the German invasion of the Soviet Union in the summer of 1941. At the end of the war, the advances came to CHF 1,119 million, making up something over one-third of the overall volume of the German–Swiss clearing traffic of around CHF 4.3 billion. Bonjour, however, was reluctant to pronounce on this extension of credit, which did not jibe with the principles of neutrality. Certainly, the need to obtain vital supplies played a role – but the fact that the German military was thus enabled to purchase coveted weapons, armaments and war material from Switzerland was only mentioned indirectly.[40] He dealt with the Allies' conduct of economic warfare in the sixth volume but gave the financial relationships only peripheral mention.

Bonjour's study was still oriented strongly towards questions of neutrality, a typically Swiss topic. After it appeared, however, concern with the neutrality issues became internationalised. One landmark contribution was the work by Daniel Bourgeois on *Le Troisième Reich et la Suisse* (The Third Reich and Switzerland), which documented the close synchronisation of the relations of both Switzerland's real economy and its financial sector with the Nazi regime between 1933 and 1941.[41] Research in this area continued to advance gradually in the ensuing decade. Starting in the 1990s, light was shed on a number of empirically shadowy areas, initially by Volume 3 of the *Geschichte der Schweiz – und der Schweizer*, appearing in 1983, and a series of research publications. In an extension of the arguments put forward by Roland Ruffieux, who posited an 'imperialism of banks and bourses' for the turn of the century and a 'covert colonialism' conducted through corporate equity stakes, and who highlighted 'Switzerland's function as a transhipment centre for flows of funds in its capacity as tax haven and financial centre',[42] Hans Ulrich Jost described the 'stable [Swiss] franc' as something 'holy to the state', to which other national economic interests were sacrificed:

> The finance and banking system played a substantial role in the course taken by the crisis. On the one hand, as an international financial centre Switzerland was affected by the collapse of foreign banks; and on the other, the handling of the crisis and monetary policy were largely dictated by the interests of the financial centre and its financial resources.[43]

Jost's findings were consistent with the central statement by Gérard Arlettaz in his essay, 'Crise et déflation. Le primat des intérêts financiers en Suisse au début des années 1930'[44] (Depression and Deflation: The Primacy of Financial Interests in Switzerland at the Beginning of the 1930s). Writers on the economics of the banking industry also stressed the importance of the hard Swiss franc for the banking system's expansion path; 'because of the political, economic and legal stability of our country and the high status of the Swiss banking system in the course of the 20th century', the franc 'became increasingly popular as an investment currency'.[45]

Jost placed the centre of gravity in his discussion on the Swiss financial centre's cooperation with Germany and gave a comprehensive analysis of the role of 'Switzerland as a central entrepôt for movements of gold and foreign exchange', singling out the 'morally disquieting' acceptance of looted gold and the granting of a clearing loan to Germany.[46] In conclusion, he observed in 1983, with good reason, 'The fact that precisely this trade in gold and foreign exchange has hardly been taken up in Switzerland's historiography indicates the uncritical attitude of this discipline in Switzerland as well as a certain tendency to cast a veil over the past.' The gist of this analysis was also endorsed by Werner Rings, Jakob Tanner and Markus Heiniger. Werner Rings, in his 1985 publication *Raubgold aus Deutschland*, provided a whole series of important insights into connections between the financial centre, the 'revolving door for gold', and the 'invisible empire', incorporating as well the flight capital from Germany, which was also partly channelled through Switzerland 'along a complicated, obscure

web of interlocking capital relationships'.[47] The present author, in a study
published in 1986, analysed the 'parallel circuitry controlling financial
and monetary policy under the traditional orientation of Switzerland's
currency policy towards the hardness of the Swiss franc and the
safeguarding of Switzerland's financial centre' and showed how
Switzerland became the 'destination of choice for capital repatriations,
movements of flight capital, the shifting of gold and other financial
transactions'.[48] Markus Heiniger pursued this thesis further in his
general study of relations between Switzerland and the Axis powers
entitled *Dreizehn Gründe. Warum die Schweiz im Zweiten Weltkrieg nicht
erobert wurde*[49] (Thirteen Reasons Why Switzerland Wasn't Conquered
in the Second World War). In the chapter called 'Wechselstube' (Exchange
bureau), the author delved into the factors that assured the flourishing
of Switzerland's financial marketplace precisely under conditions of
war, and showed that only a 'systematic financial blockade and massive
pressure by the Allies' compelled the Swiss authorities, at the war's end,
'to curb the hitherto almost boundless freedom enjoyed by the banks'.[50]

LATER STUDIES ON SWISS FINANCIAL RELATIONS WITH THE ALLIES

With the 1984 publication of Marco Durrer's dissertation on 'Swiss–
American Financial Relations', the perspective shifted from the Axis
powers to the Allies, a shift which was accentuated by the studies
appearing in 1991 and 1992 by Oswald Inglin and Linus von Castelmur,
respectively.[51]

For Durrer, the financial relations maintained by Switzerland with
the USA ranked among 'the most important Swiss problems of the
Second World War', because for this small, neutral country, 'the policies
on the banking industry, capital protection and the currency, as well as
its international economic independence, were at stake'.[52] The author
showed what effects the American blocking of accounts on 14 June 1941
had on Switzerland and how the conditions framing economic and
monetary policy changed, and he identified a correlation between the
course of military events on the front and the conduct of war blockades:
'To the extent that the Allies were more successful on the battlefield
and the Axis powers had correspondingly less means to exert pressure
on the neutrals, the Allied position towards the neutral states hardened.'[53] The US government, however, 'repeatedly held trump cards
it could use against Switzerland', which it nonetheless 'did not play'.
For instance, the 'threats or reprisals against Switzerland – such as
withdrawal of general licence No. 50, the export permits for raw
materials and foodstuffs, and the inclusion of the Swiss banks on the
blacklist – failed to materialize'.[54]

Durrer went on to describe the Swiss bankers' Washington mission, which was intended to 'capitalise on what were often very effective personal contacts in the commercial banking business and the Swiss bankers' good relations with the American private sector and the government', and 'could count on the support of the Swiss foreign ministry'.[55] Because of the considerable divergence of interests, however, the planned joint approach by the Swiss Bankers' Association (Schweizerische Bankiervereinigung, SBVg), the Swiss National Bank (SNB) and Swiss government officials did not come about. Then, when the SBVg's quasi-diplomatic delegation, after half a year of preparations, took up talks with the Treasury Department in October of 1944, the war had entered a phase in which the Allies' economic-warfare measures against neutral Switzerland were tightening further. The economic (or 'Currie') negotiations in Berne from 12 February to 8 March 1945, between Switzerland and an Allied delegation, were also dominated by this tougher approach. Four days after the negotiations started, the Swiss Federal Chancellery announced the immediate blocking of German assets on Swiss territory. Only at the beginning of March (as Klaus Urner observed in his essay on neutrality and economic warfare) could Switzerland bring itself to rein in the brisk trade in bank notes with Nazi Germany as well.[56] Durrer showed how Minister Walter O. Stucki stood 'in the foreground' at this decisive stage of the negotiations: 'The job of coordination within the Swiss camp fell to Stucki. He held all the threads running to and from the Federal Council, the expanded negotiating committee and the Swiss negotiating delegation that was in direct contact with the Allies, in his own hands.' And he prevailed 'against the opposition which had spread to substantial segments of the Swiss economy'.[57] Durrer observed that 'the measures in the financial or "Safehaven" sector, i.e. the exclusion of Swiss property in the USA, the blocking of German assets in Switzerland and the restriction or termination of trade in gold and foreign bank notes, would hardly have been conceivable without the Currie negotiations'.[58] Currie's terse statement on 5 March to the effect that Switzerland had 'capitulated' missed the significance of the substantial room for manoeuvre that still remained and of the cunning tactics employed by the neutral state. The agreement to stop buying German gold was applied so flexibly by Switzerland (for instance, gold was still being carried over the border in April 1945)[59] that a dispute over infringement or compliance with the Currie agreement flared up at once.[60] In the certification of Swiss assets in the USA and the inventory of foreign assets in Switzerland, the Swiss side also exploited the difficulties in implementation and the lack of deadlines. After Stucki had provisionally estimated the German assets at around CHF 1 billion, the interim report by the Clearing Office of 14 November 1945 put the total volume of assets inventoried at CHF 767 million, of which CHF 371 million represented German assets.[61]

The four-power negotiations that began on 18 March 1946 and culminated in the Washington Agreement of 15 May 1946, marked the end of the Allied, and particularly American, economic warfare against Switzerland; Switzerland thus entered the post-war era.[62] This transitional phase, analysed at the conclusion of Durrer's study, also forms the starting point for the study by Linus von Castelmur on Swiss–Allied financial relations between 1945 and 1952. The Swiss National Bank's transactions in looted gold with the German Reichsbank and the German assets and property in Switzerland stood at the centre of the Washington negotiations. The sense of the dramatic choreography of the negotiations, so 'rich in sudden turns', comes across even more fully in von Castelmur's account than in Durrer's. The negotiations were marked by tactical tricks, 'unexpected obstacles', 'the laying of blame' and 'escalating tests of strength'; 'trump cards were played'.[63] Switzerland finally declared its willingness to pay CHF 250 million into the Western Allies' Tripartite Gold Fund for the concerted reconstruction of Europe in order to 'settle' the 'gold question', but without acknowledging any responsibility. As far as the liquidation of German assets in Switzerland was concerned, agreement was reached on an equal split: 50 per cent to be remitted to the Allied governments to help finance reconstruction and 50 per cent to be left at the disposal of the Federal Council, which could be used to pay compensation to German owners.[64] In return, Switzerland obtained the lifting of the freeze on Swiss assets in the USA and the end of the blacklisting of Swiss companies.[65] Not yet mentioned by von Castelmur was Switzerland's secret commitment (which in the event was not observed), in the course of compiling the inventory to also identify assets in Switzerland of Nazi victims who died without issue.[66] The resistance to this restitution measure, primarily emanating from the banks, was the prelude to the 'dormant accounts' story which has now grown into an international scandal.[67]

Following that, von Castelmur concentrated the rest of his investigation on the strategy of 'letting time do its work', which Switzerland, the federal government included, pursued 'along the way to superseding the Washington Agreement' as the Cold War began to take hold.[68] The situation had changed in Switzerland's favour to the extent that a paradigm shift occurred in US politics and the 'safehaven doctrine' aimed at the Nazi regime was replaced by a new approach which can be subsumed under the headings of Marshall Plan, containment and West German currency reform; the prominent exponents of the old confiscation and restitution policy had themselves fallen victim (to 'McCarthyism' in the USA). At Bonn's suggestion, the 'question of German foreign assets was coupled with German foreign debts', which von Castelmur describes as 'a rare stroke of luck' for the Swiss authorities.[69] All in all the existence of this accord can be viewed as a success story. Against payment of CHF 121.5 million, the Allied contracting partners waived the rights they had negotiated in the Washington Agreement on the subject of 'German assets'. Switzerland enhanced its aura as a reliable and impregnable stronghold for flight capital, and could thus boast 'that it hadn't touched the assets of German owners' – and in fact more than 80 per cent of all the owners were released from the terms of the agreement with no financial penalties.[70] In return, the Swiss deputy negotiators achieved a CHF 650 million partial repayment of the so-called 'clearing billion', which was 'all the more respectable since this ill-starred advance had already been widely written off in Switzerland following the war'.[71] Von Castelmur places this story, in which poker-faced negotiations came to a paradoxical arrangement with governmental ethics, against the background of a 'painful normalization process' in the wake of which Switzerland managed to overcome its 'isolation in the community of nations', on the one hand, while continuing to present itself as a 'special case' on the other, in an era of stepped-up geopolitical confrontation between rival blocs.

Marc Perrenoud's study on 'Swiss banks and diplomacy' appeared in 1988 and provided fundamental data, along with approaches to clarification, for the analysis of international financial relations. The author presented statistics on Swiss investments abroad and foreign assets in Switzerland, according to which 'the Anglo-Saxons had greater means at their disposal to exert financial pressure than did the Axis powers'. From the estimated total volume of CHF 12.5–17.7 billion, CHF 5–6 billion alone was in the USA or Canada and just CHF 2.4–4 billion in Germany.[72] Because of the politicisation of cross-border financial relations and the need for (countervailing) regulation, a close alliance formed 'between the authorities and the financial institutions in the 1940s'. The 'defence of private interests abroad' was elevated to an important task of Swiss foreign policy.[73] Like Durrer and von Castelmur after him, Perrenoud then proceeded to the interrelationship between the diplomatic performance delivered by 'financial relations' and the strategic balance of forces in the world conflict, and set the political–commercial alliance in Switzerland in relation to the growing effectiveness of the Allied blockade policy against the Axis powers.[74] In 1943, as again after the war, a policy of playing for time was pursued, whose end result also amounted to a strategy of damage containment. Or, in the words of Robert Kohli on 13 October 1943, as a banking delegation prepared to leave for London, 'The delegation's entire strategy consists of gaining time.'[75]

CONTROVERSIES AND PROBLEMS OF INTERPRETATION

Having reviewed some of the important historical investigations into financial relations, we can now recapitulate the arguments with the focus on two major controversies.

Switzerland's policy of neutrality

First of all, the examination of the issues revolves around the suitability of Swiss-style neutrality in moral terms and in terms of security policy. A number of authors have shown that Switzerland was manoeuvred into a delicate position with regard to neutrality policy after 1940; financial relations were just one aspect of this 'tight predicament' (as Linus von Castelmur put it).[76] That 'the model of maintaining an equidistant position between the two camps in economic and financial policy could not hold up under conditions of total war' was noted by the same author, who went on to show how Switzerland fell willy-nilly into 'Germany's gravitational field' between the summer of 1940 and the beginning of 1944. Gian Trepp gave this statement more bite and formulated the thesis, with a high degree of plausibility, that the economic liberalism maintained by Switzerland for foreign exchange and gold transactions was 'compatible in principle with the doctrine of armed neutrality', but for all 'practical political purposes' it was the Axis powers that benefited from unimpeded access to a convertible hard currency. 'Against this background, the Federal Council's decision to refrain from imposing exchange controls can be interpreted as favouring economic collaboration with Nazi Germany in violation of neutrality.'[77] By contrast, Werner Rings, whose survey covered a longer time frame and thereby also considered compensatory moves in the direction of the Allied side, emphasised the rational motives for adhering to strict neutrality on Switzerland's part. According to Rings, pragmatic analysis of the conditions confronting Switzerland's foreign policy reveals no grounds for 'favouring one or the other belligerent'. Instead, the safeguarding of Switzerland's own interests, as a 'reason of state', would best have been served by a 'policy of absolute neutrality'. Rings' formulation of his 'moral uneasiness' is thus even more pointed with regard to those cases where a 'dubious partnership', a 'reprehensible camaraderie with an inhuman dictator', or the 'sometimes downright conspiratorial collaboration with a regime that was hostile to the Swiss Confederation and its concept of the state'[78] came to light.

This also raises the question of how much leeway was available to the neutrality policy and what criteria should be used to diagnose violations of neutrality in the sphere of financial relations. Linus von Castelmur withdrew from this aspect of the debate with the observation that neutrality, as a concept, is 'weak in explanation, the subject of much fanfare and hype in Switzerland's internal dialogue but not commonly encountered in international research, if at all'. Moreover, 'testing for conformity to neutrality' could be a veiled 'attempt at justification', precisely because the vague definition of economic neutrality allows practically anything to 'slip through the broad mesh of the "neutrality net" thrown out to catch violations'.[79] Peter Hug represents another position, focusing on the dynamics of a normative system of rules whose evolution can be tracked through the war years.[80] From this vantage point, the question of whether Switzerland was legally in compliance with or in breach of neutrality appears too static. The interest here centres on the shifting of standards by which neutral countries can be judged. The question then arises of whether a normative foundation for Switzerland's foreign policy can be derived from the pertinent article of the federal constitution or should be based on the United Nations Charter of 1945 and the human rights declarations of 1948. These last-named codifications, aimed at a condemnation of war and the universal inviolability of individual basic rights, grew out of the disaster of the war itself and represent an answer to the Nazi regime's unparalleled crime, the Holocaust. Tied in with the decision about which values to apply is the question of whether Switzerland is able to see itself as a victim of world history or, conversely, is forced to concede that because of its intensive financial relations it also had a hand in the catastrophe.

Financial policy in an international context

Second (but closely related to the first point), the analysis of Switzerland's financial relations and foreign policy necessarily concerns the European and international context. Initially, this involves judging the Allies' war objectives and thus asking whether Switzerland should not at least have supported the efforts of the anti-Hitler coalition after 1942/43 by refusing to cooperate with the Axis powers.[81] After all, not only were billions of Swiss francs in assets under Allied control, but the Swiss Confederation's prospects for survival depended, for better or worse, on the defeat of Nazi Germany. For the period after 1945 the discussion concentrates on the question of whether Switzerland did not have every reason to actively participate in building the new world order rather than resisting the 'overbearing comportment of the victors'. This point, however, can also be viewed from the opposite perspective. That Switzerland was able to restore its damaged reputation and reduce the external pressure to a minimum as the Cold War proceeded was not primarily a matter of concessions but must be ascribed to the fact that the main thrust of the currency and economic-policy developments under the 'Pax Americana' was equally accommodating to Switzerland.

In the absence of comparative international studies, and given the continued dominance of the 'helvetocentric' point of view, these processes have hardly been analysed. In his review of the history of the world economy after 1945, for instance, Herman van der Wee observed that Switzerland, with its stabilisation policy, 'quickly achieved the pre-war dollar parity, from which the financial sector profited in particular'.[82] What form this 'profit' took remains unclear in the Swiss historical studies reviewed here. In addition, there was a significant shift in the preferred model for recovery from the consequences of the war as the 1940s closed. The London Debts Agreement of 1953 ranked the question of reparations and compensation for victims of Nazi terror below the satisfaction of Germany's pre-war creditors. The upshot, as Jörg Fisch observed in his study on 'reparations after the Second World War', was 'flagrant discrimination against the victims compared to the moneylenders'. The moneylenders, of course, included Swiss creditors (and Swiss creditors, after all, held 15 per cent of Germany's total foreign debt in 1938).[83] The priority given to 'commercial debts' as opposed to money owed for looted assets and other 'ill-gotten gains' was also financially advantageous to Switzerland's financial centre. Obviously, Switzerland had achieved entry into the new Bretton Woods monetary system and launched itself into the expanding post-war capital markets without serious difficulty. The controversy concerning the discrepancy, or perhaps complementarity, between a discredited neutrality and thriving financial relations had not grown intense enough in 1996 to inspire new research projects on this score.

EVALUATION OF PRESENT KNOWLEDGE AND DESIRABLE RESEARCH OBJECTIVES

The studies included in this review, in their development of sources, unearthed a large amount of new knowledge. Nevertheless, the research situation as it stands now is far from satisfactory, primarily due to the almost complete absence of any theoretical framework to guide the approach. Instead of concentrating scientific resources on the dark areas, it would be important at this juncture to map the empty areas in a history of Switzerland's financial relations. The five questions which follow seem to me to be particularly promising avenues for further historical research.

Banking organisations and the balance of payments: stitching together the micro- and macro-perspectives

Because of the desolate state of the archives in the banking sector there is an acute shortage of studies of corporate histories. The material available consists of upbeat, glossy self-portrayals, on the one hand, and occasional critical reporting, on the other.[84] By contrast, hardly any substantiated knowledge is available on the core businesses and the sources of earnings, or the risk structure of the banks and other financial institutions. About all that can be said on the relevance of financial relations to corporate growth, therefore, is that it must have been considerable. A breakdown of capital movements into 'autonomous' flows (portfolio and direct investment) and 'induced' flows (import financing, export credit) would be very useful. There is also a need for empirical research to illuminate the belief that Swiss banking institutions repeatedly seem able to write off massive losses thanks to their 'inner' (or hidden) reserves. Another area calling for study is the effect of the legal codification of banking secrecy in Switzerland's first Bank Act in 1934.[85]

The situation is just as unsatisfactory at the other end of the analytical spectrum. A reconstruction of Switzerland's balance of payments still remains to be done. Some macroeconomic data can be found in Max Iklé's work.[86] As far as long-term and short-term capital movements are concerned, it will hardly be possible today to compile more than a few elements of such a 'balance' (which consists of flow figures rather than stock figures and thus corresponds more to a profit and loss account). But even the record of attempts to put together balance of payments statistics from the scattered and fragmented data in Switzerland and abroad can convey valuable information in itself. The sources show how the projects launched by the Swiss National Bank to gain an overview of the complex range of transactions between the wars and in the post-war period, in its capacity as 'guardian of the currency', were repeatedly frustrated by the banks and the Federal Council.

Communicative learning processes and personal relationship networks

Considering the human factors, interpersonal aspects and communications theory, it is evident that the analysis of financial relations has to be extended to communicative learning processes and personal networks of relationships. 'Credit' stems from 'trust', and this does not happen without verbal communication. The interpretation models that the participants have evolved and solidified in a two-way process of communication are also always embedded in a cross-border capital structure. In the 1930s, communications followed a pattern that Hansjörg Siegenthaler describes as 'typical of a crisis': like all the interactions shaping and shaped by the crisis, communications also suffered 'for the time being ... from a loss of faith in the rules'.[87] Financial relations were particularly vulnerable to this loss of confidence, and the entire credit system proved to be commensurately unstable. The war-shaken transition from the depression era of the 1930s to the boom years of the 1950s can be understood in this theoretical context as a communicative learning process, which also regenerated the 'credit' of the banks; this in turn simply means that the participants were once again able to reach longer-term agreement, which is in fact the case.

Inherent in the observation that Switzerland is a capital-exporting country is the message that the 'Swiss nation', through intensive trans-national communications, has managed to establish itself and repro-duce its presence. The collective representation of the country that surfaces in the image of the stalwart, defence-minded populace had a counterbalance in the involvement of the nation's functional elite in a border-crossing, international division of labour. The latter was propa-gated through a close-knit interpersonal network in which affinities and animosities, loyalties and sensitive areas could all be found. The forced resignation of Federal Councillor Marcel Pilet-Golaz, for instance, and his replacement by the politically inexperienced (but close to the banks and industry) Max Petitpierre in December 1944 made it possible for the banking community and the government to mobilise new reserves of confidence. After reading the existing standard works on 'Switzerland's financial relations', it remains unclear how the (probably specifically Swiss) phenomenon of multiple roles for indi-vidual officials and the hybrid, public–private war economy (mirroring the militia system or reservist army) could be combined with the ability to communicate beyond the national boundaries. It would also have to be worked out, more clearly than in the past, how the interlocking actions of companies, parastatal associations and governmental insti-tutions were related to the low profile of Swiss foreign policy and the strong Swiss presence on world markets.

National identity and collective mentalities

Generally speaking, a strong identification not only with the national symbols but also with the 'stable franc' and 'our own companies' can be observed in Switzerland. Money, capital and savings obviously play a prominent role in the Swiss mentality. The 'metallic foundation of the

Swiss currency'[88] and the firm, crisis-resistant confidence in the Swiss franc formed a symbiosis that contributed to the prosperous Swiss economy. This also helps explain the great plausibility and high degree of acceptance enjoyed by the conservative fiscal policy, which exerted a pro-cyclical influence in the 1930s and exacerbated the crisis. At the same time the savings mentality, the financial entrepôt function and the capital exports mechanism complemented each other well. Without the unshakeable confidence of the Swiss people in 'their' franc, it could not have grown into its disproportionately large role as an international reserve and transaction currency. The 'franc beneath the skin' is a subject worth investigating simply for how it bears on the analysis of financial relations. Perhaps it also helps interpret a statement by Karl Bruggmann (Swiss minister in Washington), cited virtually in passing by Durrer. As the US decision to block Swiss assets was looming, Bruggmann declared that the effect of this measure 'on the morale of the people would be terrific – far worse than a German invasion ... the whole economic structure of Switzerland would collapse and probably anti-Semitism would be the first horrible aftermath'.[89] Even today the public shows a surprisingly strong tendency to equate legitimate demands directed against the banking system with attacks on Switzerland as a whole. How this attitude took root, and whether it represents a typical, small-country reflex, has hardly been the subject of any historical research up to now.[90]

Risk assessment and random walks

The people at the top in the banks of the 1930s and 1940s had their own ideological preferences and positioned themselves mentally somewhere on an imaginary map of the countries of the day. To give the two most important attitudes, some decision-makers in 1940 were convinced of Hitler's 'ultimate victory' and were positive towards it, while others assessed the flow of the war and the geopolitical balance of power more realistically. The Second World War made one thing strikingly clear yet again: how quickly assumptions about 'the way things are going' can be overtaken by events. Under wartime conditions, a company's growth path has to contend with non-economic forces that are almost impossible to predict.[91] It would thus be important to have in-depth analyses of risk assessment and risk diversification strategies for the banking system during a phase when political and military factors severely affected the possibilities of economic expansion and earnings.[92] The starting point could be the proposition that the banks trade in 'promises to pay' (that is a combination of time and money) and substitute 'technology for contingency' as a way of processing the risk.[93] This became much more difficult to the extent that, as the course of the war changed, the uncertainties about the corresponding markets increased and transformation of assets as a specific risk management tool no longer functioned because of the unpredictability of political and military events. When it subsequently began to seem likely that the banks which had pinned their hopes on German victory and a bright future for the Third Reich would instead see their dreams turn to nightmares of smoking ruins and destroyed or confiscated investments, it was too late for institutions such as the Eidgenössische Bank and the Basler Handelsbank. They were forced to take huge write-offs and ended up bankrupt. In the new force fields generated by the strategic geopolitical situation, new (albeit transitory) forms of risk arbitrage also emerged. 'Universal' banks, which had assessed the balance of forces more realistically – in this case Union Bank of Switzerland and Swiss Bank Corporation – were among the winners and were able to translate the failure of their competitors into fresh new momentum for sustained corporate growth.[94] The concentration process that got underway in the Swiss banking sector at the end of the war, and eventually reduced the number of the big banks to four, thus signalled a new allocation of the risks and a reshuffling of the expansion opportunities in the European and intercontinental context. The division of Europe into the Cold War's spheres of influence and the nationalisation measures in the Soviet Union's repressively enclosed satellite states produced even more distortions in the structure of Swiss banking assets and liabilities. This is a field which has hardly been explored.

Playing with asymmetric information

One interesting analytical standpoint for the research into bank transactions is derived from the theory of asymmetric information. It can easily be demonstrated that both domestic and border-crossing financial relations between lenders and borrowers are distorted by systematic information imbalances, because the borrowers, no matter how great an effort the lenders make to gather information, will always be better informed about their own 'inner net worth' and their prospects for success.[95] Especially during the war years, it was hard for the Swiss banks to form a realistic idea of the development potential for investments in the Third Reich (and elsewhere) that would be tenable in the long run. Conversely, the Swiss negotiating delegation brought good bargaining chips to Washington after the end of the war in March of 1946. After all, despite the available intelligence, the Swiss deputy negotiators obviously knew more about the incriminating transactions (looted gold and Nazi accounts, as well as Nazi flight capital) than the Americans did, and they were able to use this information advantage to achieve excellent results in those high-calibre negotiations after a difficult start. The hypothesis that the Swiss elite, owing to their close personal associations, had a competitive advantage in the information game, ought to be investigated in this context.

To sum up, future analysis of financial relations will have to satisfy two requirements that the more recent studies have only partially confronted. On the one hand, the Swiss-centred view of history has to be abandoned, and, on the other, innovations must be made in both methodology and theory. If we start with the assumption that a hiatus exists between the nation erecting its military defences and the 'national economy' intimately involved with surrounding countries and world markets, the environment which generated these contradictions – in which Swiss foreign (economic) policy had to operate – will also become visible. And it will be possible to analyse the interplay between the imaginary autarky of Switzerland as a *réduit* and its tangible external dependence – in so many different areas – as a job market and a financial market, thus juxtaposing the inward-looking and outward-looking perspectives in a new way.

NOTES

1 Daniel Bourgeois, *Le Troisième Reich et la Suisse, 1933–1941*, Neuchatel, 1974; idem, 'Les relations économiques germano-suisses 1938–1945', *Revue d'histoire de la deuxième guerre mondiale*, 121, 1981, pp. 49–61; Werner Rings, *Raubgold aus Deutschland. Die 'Golddrehscheibe' Schweiz im Zweiten Weltkrieg*, Zurich/Munich, 1985; Jakob Tanner, *Bundeshaushalt, Währung und Kriegswirtschaft. Eine finanz-sozologische Analyse der Schweiz zwischen 1938–1953*, Zurich, 1986; Markus Heiniger, *Dreizehn Gründe. Warum die Schweiz im Zweiten Weltkrieg nicht erobert wurde*, Zurich, 1989.
2 Gian Trepp, *Bankgeschäfte mit dem Feind. Die Bank für Internationalen Zahlungs-ausgleich im Zweiten Weltkrieg. Von Hitlers Europabank zum Instrument des Marshall-plans*, Zurich, 1993; Beat Balzli, *Treuhänder des Reiches. Die Schweiz und die Vermögen der Naziopfer. Eine Spurensuche*, Zurich, 1997.
3 Previously, there were references to 'economic relations'. See, for instance, Walter Spahni, *Der Ausbruch der Schweiz aus der Isolation nach dem Zweiten Weltkrieg*, Frauenfeld, 1977.
4 Marco Durrer, *Die schweizerisch-amerikanischen Finanzbeziehungen im Zweiten Weltkrieg. Von der Blockierung der schweizerischen Guthaben in den USA über die 'Safehaven'-Politik zum Washingtoner Abkommen (1941–1946)*, Berne/Stuttgart, 1984; Marc Perrenoud, 'Banques et diplomatie suisses à la fin de la Deuxième Guerre mondiale. Politique de neutralité et relations financières inter-nationales', *Studien und Quellen*, publ. Swiss Federal Archive, 13/14, 1987/88, pp. 7–128; Linus von Castelmur, *Schweizerisch-alliierte Finanzbeziehungen im*

64   *Switzerland and the Second World War*

Übergang vom Zweiten Weltkrieg zum Kalten Krieg. Die deutschen Guthaben in der Schweiz zwischen Zwangsliquidierung und Freigabe (1945–1952), Zurich, 1992; Philippe Marguerat, 'La Suisse et la Neutralité dans le domaine économique pendant la seconde guerre mondiale 1940–fin 1944', in Louis-Edouard Roulet and Roland Blättler (eds), *Les Etats neutres européens et la seconde guerre mondiale*, Neuchatel, 1985, pp. 55–67.

5 Swiss Diplomatic Documents 1848–1945, Vols 13–15 (1939–1945), Berne, 1991–97.

6 Gilbert Ziebura, *Weltwirtschaft und Weltpolitik 1922/24–1931. Zwischen Rekonstruktion und Zusammenbruch*, Frankfurt, 1984; for Switzerland, see Gottlieb Bachmann, 'Die Schweiz als internationales Finanzzentrum', *Die Schweiz. Ein nationales Jahrbuch 1931*, New Helvetic Society, Erlenbach/Zurich, 1931.

7 The European Payments Union was intended to restore the multilateral nature of foreign trade and the full convertibility of the OEEC currencies. It was superseded by the European Monetary Agreement in 1958.

8 See, for instance, Herman van der Wee, *Der gebremste Wohlstand. Wiederaufbau, Wachstum, Strukturwandel 1945–1980 (Geschichte der Weltwirtschaft im 20. Jahrhundert*, Vol. 6), Munich, 1984, pp. 501ff.; Michael R. Darby, *The internationalization of American banking and finance: structure, risk, and world interest rates*, Cambridge, MA, 1986; for the war period, see, for instance, Allen S. Milward, *Der Zweite Weltkrieg (Geschichte der Weltwirtschaft im 20. Jahrhundert*, Vol. 5), Munich, 1977; Will A. Boelcke, 'Zur internationalen Goldpolitik des NS-Staates. Ein Beitrag zur deutschen Währungs- und Aussenwirtschaftspolitik 1933–1945', in Manfred Funke (ed.), *Hitler, Deutschland und die Mächte. Materialien zur Aussenpolitik des Dritten Reiches*, Düsseldorf, 1977.

9 Rudolph J. Kaderli and Edwin Zimmermann (eds), *Handbuch des Geld-, Bank- und Börsenwesens, Thun, 1947; Schweizerische Nationalbank 1907–1957*, Zurich, 1957.

10 See, for example, M. W. Hess, *Die Strukturwandlungen im schweizerischen Bankenwesen von der Schaffung des Bundesgesetzes bis 1958*, Winterthur, 1963; E. Schneider, *Die schweizerischen Grossbanken im Zweiten Weltkrieg 1939–1945*, Zurich, 1959; Max Iklé, *Die Schweiz als internationaler Bank- und Finanzplatz*, Zurich, 1970.

11 Eduard Kellenberger, *Kapitalexport und Zahlungsbilanz*, Vol. 2, Berne, 1942.

12 Kaderli and Zimmermann, *Handbuch des Geld- Bank- und Börsenwesens*, op. cit., p. 210.

13 Ibid., p. 211.

14 W. Hurni, *Entwicklung, Gestaltung und Auswirkungen des gebunden Zahlungsverkehrs in der schweizerischen Volkswirtschaft in den Jahren 1945–1955*, Fribourg, 1960; Emil Küng, 'Probleme des Kapitalexports', in *Schweizerische Zeitschrift für Volkswirtschaft und Statistik*, 1946, pp. 289–301; R. Beriger, *Die internationalen Zahlungsabkommen der Schweiz aufgrund der Zahlungsabkommen von 1945–1949*, Zurich, 1949; E. Hochuli, *Die schweizerische Gold- und Dollarpolitik vom Beginn des Zweiten Weltkrieges im Herbst 1939 bis zur Pfundabwertung im Herbst 1946*, Basle/Stuttgart, 1967.

15 Kaderli and Zimmermann, *Handbuch des Geld-, Bank und Börsenwesens*, op. cit., pp. 213ff.; an important step along the way to the re-establishment of general convertibility was the European Monetary Agreement of 5 August 1955. See Van der Wee, *Der gebremste Wohlstand*, op. cit., pp. 505ff.

16 See the referenced term in Kaderli and Zimmermann, *Handbuch des Geld-, Bank- und Börsenwesens*, op. cit., p. 272. Also, see Henri Blumenfeld, 'Les Capitaux

Migrateurs (Hot Money)', thesis, Neuchatel, 1941.

17 Kaderli and Zimmermann, *Handbuch des Geld-, Bank- und Börsenwesens*, op. cit.

18 Schneider, *Die schweizerischen Grossbanken*, op. cit., pp. 51ff.

19 See Kurt Mueller, *Der Kapitalimport. Studie zur Theorie der internationalen Kapital-bewegungen*, St Gall, 1947.

20 *Handbuch der schweizerischen Volkswirtschaft*, publ. by Schweizerische Gesell-schaft für Statistik und Volkswirtschaft, Berne, 1955, Vol. 2, section on inter-national capital movements, p. 4.

21 Ibid., pp. 3ff.

22 Kaderli and Zimmermann, *Handbuch des Geld-, Bank- und Börsenwesens*, op. cit., p. 560.

23 Ibid. In addition, see Curt Vannini, 'Der zwischenstaatliche Clearingverkehr der Schweiz in den Jahren 1931–1934', thesis, Berne, 1943; Doris Karmin, *La politique commerciale suisse de 1932 à 1939, contingents et accords de clearing*, Geneva, 1943; Eugen Roesle, *Die Finanzforderungen im schweizerisch-deutschen Verrechnungs-verkehr*, Basle, 1944.

24 *Handbuch der schweizerischen Volkswirtschaft*, see note 20 above, subject: capital formation, pp. 4 and 10ff.

25 Kaderli and Zimmermann, *Handbuch des Geld-, Bank- und Börsenwesens*, op. cit., p. 301.

26 An early study does exist on this subject by Hans W. Leuzinger, *Die deutschen Vermögenswerte in der Schweiz und ihre statistische Erfassung auf Grund des Abkommens von Washington vom 25.5.1946 und des Ablösungsabkommens vom 26.8.1952*, Winterthur, 1960.

27 Georg Kreis, 'Die Schweiz und der Zweite Weltkrieg. Bilanz und historischer Überblick nach dreissig Jahren', in *La seconda guerra mondiale nella prospettiva storica a trent'anni dall'epilogo*, Como, 1975, pp. 219–40.

28 Linus von Castelmur, 'Aspekte der Wirtschafts- und Finanzbeziehungen der Schweiz im Zweiten Weltkrieg', in Hans Werner Tobler (ed.), *Die Schweiz im Zweiten Weltkrieg, Forschungsstand, Kontroversen, offene Fragen*, Zurich, 1997, pp. 23ff.; in his thesis, 'Schweizerisch-alliierte Finanzbeziehungen im Übergang vom Zweiten Weltkrieg zum Kalten Krieg', Zurich, 1992, von Castelmur observed that the relevant work had still 'achieved great progress' (p. 11).

29 Lorenz Stucki, *Das heimliche Imperium. Wie die Schweiz reich wurde. Ein erstmals beschriebener Aspekt der Schweizer Geschichte*, Zurich, 1968, pp. 9ff.

30 Ibid., p. 11.

31 Ibid., pp. 9ff.

32 Ibid., p. 318.

33 Ibid., pp. 328ff.

34 Ibid., p. 257.

35 Ibid., p. 333.

36 François Höpflinger, *Das unheimliche Imperium*, Zurich, 1977, p. 12.

37 Ibid., p. 12.

38 Ibid., p. 14.

39 As a rule, the Bonjour report refers to Vols 3–5 of the *Geschichte der schweizerischen Neutralität* (History of Swiss neutrality), published in 1970, covering the period 1933–1945. Three more volumes containing sources had appeared by 1975.

40 Edgar Bonjour, *Geschichte der schweizerischen Neutralität*, Vol. 6, Basle/Stuttgart, 1970, pp. 224 and 232ff.

41 Bourgeois, *Le Troisième Reich et la Suisse*, op. cit.

42 Roland Ruffieux, 'Die Schweiz des Freisinns (1848–1914)', in *Geschichte der*

Schweiz – und der Schweizer, Vol. 3, Basle, 1983, pp. 82ff.
43 Hans-Ulrich Jost, 'Bedrohung und Enge (1914–1945)', in op. cit., p. 149.
44 Gérard Arlettaz, 'Crise et déflation. Le primat des intérêts financiers en Suisse au début des années 1930', *Relations internationales*, 30, 1982.
45 Jean-Paul Chapuis, 'Die Schweizer Banken im internationalen Vergleich', in Hans J. Halbheer and Ernst Kilgus (eds), *Der Finanzplatz Schweiz und seine Bedeutung aus nationaler und internationaler Sicht*, Berne, 1985, p. 77.
46 Jost, 'Bedrohung und Enge', op. cit. note 43, p. 173.
47 Rings, *Raubgold aus Deutschland*, op. cit., p. 189.
48 Tanner, *Bundeshaushalt, Währung und Kriegswirtschaft*, op. cit., pp. 298ff.
49 Heiniger, *Dreizehn Gründe*, op. cit.
50 Ibid., p. 126.
51 Durrer, *Die schweizerisch-amerikanischen Finanzbeziehungen*, op. cit.; Oswald Inglin, *Der stille Krieg. Der Wirtschaftskrieg zwischen Grossbritannien und der Schweiz im Zweiten Weltkrieg*, Zurich, 1991; von Castelmur, *Schweizerisch-alliierte Finanzbeziehungen*, op. cit.
52 Durrer, *Die schweizerisch-amerikanischen Finanzbeziehungen*, op. cit., p. 12.
53 Ibid., p. 311. See Inglin, *Der stille Krieg*, op. cit.
54 Durrer, *Die schweizerisch-amerikanischen Finanzbeziehungen*, op. cit., p. 116.
55 Ibid., pp. 167 and 169.
56 Klaus Urner, 'Neutralität und Wirtschaftskrieg: zur schweizerischen Aussenhandelspolitik 1939–1945', in Rudolf Bindschedler *et al.* (eds), *Schwedische und schweizerische Neutralität im Zweiten Weltkrieg*, Basle, 1985, pp. 250–92.
57 Durrer, *Die schweizerisch-amerikanischen Finanzbeziehungen*, op. cit., p. 194.
58 Ibid., p. 212.
59 Ibid., pp. 224ff.
60 Ibid., pp. 224ff.
61 Ibid., p. 245.
62 A first study on this point was compiled by Daniel Frei as early as the end of the 1960s. Daniel Frei, 'Das Washingtoner Abkommen von 1946. Ein Beitrag zur Geschichte der schweizerischen Aussenpolitik zwischen dem Zweiten Weltkrieg und dem Kalten Krieg', in *Schweizerische Zeitschrift für Geschichte*, 1969, pp. 567–619.
63 Von Castelmur, *Schweizerisch-alliierte Finanzbeziehungen*, op. cit., pp. 49ff.
64 Ibid., pp. 90ff.
65 See Inglin, *Der stille Krieg*, op. cit.
66 Sebastian Speich provided an initial overview in 'Arroganz, Geheimniskrämerei und Antikommunismus', in *Die Schweiz am Pranger. Banken, Bosse und die Nazis* (which he edited), Vienna/Frankfurt, 1997, p. 238.
67 Peter Hug and Marc Perrenoud, *In der Schweiz liegende Vermögenswerte von Nazi-Opfern und Entschädigungsabkommen mit Oststaaten*, a report on historical investigations (prepared on behalf of the Federal Department for Foreign Affairs), Berne, 1996.
68 Von Castelmur, *Schweizerisch-alliierte Finanzbeziehungen*, op. cit., pp. 305ff. and 410.
69 Ibid.
70 Ibid., p. 407.
71 Ibid.
72 Perrenoud, 'Banques et diplomatie suisse', p. 41, see note 4 above.
73 Ibid., p. 125.
74 Ibid., pp. 75ff.

75 Ibid., p. 79.
76 Von Castelmur, *Aspekte der Wirtschafts- und Finanzbeziehungen*, op. cit., p. 23.
77 Gian Trepp, *Der Finanzplatz Schweiz im 2. Weltkrieg. Was wussten und tolerierten die Alliierten?*, Zurich, 1997, pp. 9ff.
78 Rings, *Raubgold*, op. cit., pp. 189 and 191; Heiniger, *Dreizehn Gründe*, op. cit., pp. 118ff.
79 Von Castelmur, *Aspekte der Wirtschafts- und Finanzbeziehungen*, op. cit., p. 409.
80 Peter Hug, address to the conference on *Schatten des Weltkrieges – eine Standortbestimmung* (Shadows of the World War – an assessment), published by Schweizerische Gesellschaft für Aussenpolitik, Lenzburg, 1997, pp. 36ff.
81 This question came up for discussion again in connection with the Eizenstat report: Stuart E. Eizenstat (ed.), *US and Allied Efforts to Recover and Restore Gold and other Assets Stolen or Hidden by Germany During World War II*, Washington, 1997.
82 Van der Wee, *Der gebremste Wohlstand*, op. cit., p. 33.
83 Jörg Fisch, *Reparationen nach dem Zweiten Weltkrieg*, Munich, 1992, p. 120.
84 More demanding than the first-mentioned category, for instance, is Walter Adolf Jöhr, *Schweizerische Kreditanstalt, 1856–1956, Hundert Jahre im Dienste der schweizerischen Volkswirtschaft*, Zurich, 1956; in the second category, *Ganz oben – 125 Jahre Schweizerische Bankgesellschaft*, Zurich, 1987, by Res Strehle, Gian Trepp and Barbara Weyermann; a good place to start is the sound study by Franz Ritzmann, *Die Schweizer Banken*, Berne/Stuttgart, 1973.
85 See, for example, Maurice Aubert, Jean-Philippe Kernen and Herbert Schönle, *Le secret bancaire suisse*, Berne, 1976; Maurice Aubert, *Le secret bancaire Suisse* (no location given), 1979; Hugo Baenziger, *Vom Sparerschutz zum Gläubigerschutz: die Entstehung des Bankengesetzes unter Einschluss seiner wirtschaftspolitischen Bestimmungen*, Berne, 1984; idem, *Die Entwicklung der Bankenaufsicht in der Schweiz seit dem 19. Jahrhundert*, Berne/Stuttgart, 1986; Walter Hadding and Uwe H. Schneider (eds), *Bankgeheimnis und Bankauskunft in der Bundesrepublik Deutschland und in ausländischen Rechtssystemen*, Berlin, 1986; or, written for the more general reader, Christoph Büchenbacher, *Tatsachen über das schweizerische Bankgeheimnis*, Zurich, 1977; Nicolas Faith, *Safety in Numbers: The Mysterious World of Swiss Banking*, London, 1982.
86 Iklé, *Die Schweiz als internationaler Bank- und Finanzplatz*, op. cit., p. 269; see also, Herbert Bachmann, *Der Einfluss der Abwertung auf die Zahlungsbilanz der Schweiz*, Basle, 1950.
87 Hansjörg Siegenthaler, 'Kommunikation und Entwicklung des Bankenwesens', in Youssef Cassis and Jakob Tanner (eds), *Banken und Kredit in der Schweiz (1850–1930)*, Zurich, 1993, p. 101.
88 Eveline Ruoss, 'Die Anfänge der schweizerischen Geldpolitik', in Cassis and Tanner (eds), *Banken und Kredit*, op. cit., pp. 29–52.
89 Durrer, *Die schweizerisch-amerikanischen Finanzbeziehungen*, op. cit., p. 45.
90 See, for instance, *The Swiss Paradox: Rock-solid Social and Economic Fundamentals – Rock-bottom Equity Prices: A Longer-term View*, Geneva, 1988.
91 In such complex situations, however, random walk theory cannot be applied operationally. For a concrete analysis of a concrete phenomenon see, for instance, Erwin Heri's *Random-walk als Erklärungsversuch der kurzfristigen Wechselkursfluktuationen*, Basle, 1980. Nevertheless, the hypothesis remains important as a stimulus to thought.
92 See, for instance, Kenneth B. MacCrimmon and Donald A. Wehrung, *Taking Risks: The Management of Uncertainty*, New York, 1986; Jake Ansell and Frank

Wharton (eds), *Risk: Analysis, Assessment and Management*, Chichester, 1992.

93 Dirk Baecker, *Womit handeln Banken? Eine Untersuchung zur Risikoverarbeitung in der Wirtschaft*, Frankfurt, 1991, pp. 13ff.; Martin Hellwig, *Banking, Financial Intermediation and Corporate Finance*, Basle, 1990.

94 On the system of universal banks, see the comparative study on northern and central Europe edited by Alice Teichova, Terry Gourvish and Agnes Pogany, *Universal Banking in the Twentieth Century: Finance, Industry and the State in North and Central Europe*, Aldershot, 1994.

95 Gerhard Iling, *Geld und asymmetrische Information*, Berlin, 1985; Roland Eisen, *Wettbewerb und Regulierung in der Versicherung: die Rolle asymmetrischer Information*, Berne, 1986; Gerhard Clemenz, *Credit Markets with Asymmetric Information*, Berlin, 1986; Klaus Spremann, *Asymmetrische Information*, St Gall, 1990; Brian Hillier, *The Economics of Asymmetric Information*, New York, 1996.

3

German Gold – Allied Gold, 1940–45

PHILIPPE MARGUERAT

During the Second World War, the Swiss National Bank (SNB) remitted Swiss francs to the Reichsbank in exchange for sales of gold, a large part of which had been seized by German forces from central bank reserves in occupied countries. The overall amounts involved are known: the SNB transferred CHF 1.2 billion to the Reichsbank, to which should be added, as confirmed by the Allies themselves at the end of the conflict, CHF 86 million supplied by Swiss private banks to the Reichsbank, making about CHF 1.3 billion in all. Of this – as far as was known at the time of writing – about CHF 780 million represented looted gold: CHF 400 million in gold from the Netherlands and CHF 378 million in Belgian gold. Paralleling this, the Swiss National Bank also supplied Swiss francs to the Allied governments for gold or foreign exchange (dollars); this was for gold or foreign exchange in blocked accounts to which Switzerland had no access. Figures on these transactions are harder to ascertain. Going by various documents in the Swiss Federal Archive and the archives of the Swiss National Bank, the total is somewhere between CHF 2.2 billion and CHF 2.6 billion, including CHF 1.2–1.6 billion ascribed to the SNB and a little more than CHF 1 billion to the Swiss Confederation.[1]

In short, Swiss currency was sought by both camps. After 1940–41, this was the principal means of international payment, a status based on four qualities: the external stability of the Swiss franc, its genuine convertibility, the ability of foreign holders to use the currency freely within Switzerland (no Swiss exchange controls), and finally its relatively constant purchasing power (low inflation). These qualities reflected actions taken by the Swiss National Bank before and during the war. Under these conditions, the Swiss franc represented the best, and in some cases the only, means of payment for the belligerents on both sides to obtain certain products or services in countries outside the territory they controlled. Gold certainly enjoyed an important role alongside the Swiss franc, but it was still less 'liquid' as money because it might have been obtained illicitly, that is looted, by one belligerent or the other (in reality, by the German Reich). Hence the preference for payments in Swiss francs, even if it meant afterwards converting some of these francs into gold at the SNB; gold which did not appear to be German, even though SNB gold reserves basically came from the Reichsbank ('laundering of German gold').

The Reichsbank sold gold to obtain Swiss francs on a Swiss foreign exchange market that remained totally free until the end of 1942 and partially free thereafter. It may well be asked why the Swiss National Bank and the Swiss Confederation maintained this unique free market with all the related problems that later arose (absorption of looted gold). The answer involves two factors. One was 'existential', the other 'technical'. Both were closely related.

Let us take the 'existential' factor first: the threat of a German invasion. Switzerland had two weapons against this threat: the army massed to defend the *réduit* (Alpine stronghold) from spring 1941, and purchases of German gold for Swiss francs. These francs constituted a privileged currency for Germany, which it needed to procure strategic materials in various countries. The franc could continue to play that role only if Switzerland preserved its territorial integrity and sovereignty.

It is true that the invasion threat is denied by certain historians, who maintain that the 'plans' worked out by the German general staff in the period June–October 1940 were nothing but general staff exercises. This view is incorrect. First of all, and objectively, the threat of an invasion did exist, at least from the summer of 1940, as K. Urner has demonstrated (Urner, 1985). Subsequently, and this is important above all to an understanding of the Swiss authorities' behaviour, the threat was acutely felt subjectively by these authorities. This was definitely the case from summer to autumn of 1940, and also from December of 1942 to autumn of 1943.

In such an environment the sale of Swiss francs for gold was compelling as an invaluable weapon, not during the summer of 1940, when Germany's need for francs remained weak, but from October of that year, when its needs started growing, and above all from autumn of 1941, with the stalemate on the German–Soviet front. The Swiss National Bank and the Swiss government were aware of the relevance and effectiveness of this weapon from autumn 1940. A letter in November 1940 addressed to the Swiss National Bank from the most influential adviser at the Bank for International Settlements, P. Jacobsson (following a meeting with Puhl), underscored the importance to Germany of a free market for gold and foreign exchange in Switzerland. It is fair to assume that Puhl was not just talking out of the blue. The information was taken very seriously at the Swiss National Bank, if its immediate transmission to Federal Councillor E. Wetter and the presence of this letter in various SNB offices and files is anything to go by. Further evidence is provided by various statements by SNB directors (*Swiss Diplomatic Documents*, Vol. 15, 75, p. 210). The government, for its part, gave the information considerable attention. It was the principal argument used by Stampfli against Guisan at a meeting of Pilet, Stampfli, Wetter and Guisan in November 1942, at which the government tried to allay the general's fears about the risk of a German invasion (*Swiss Diplomatic Documents*, Vol. 14, 282, p. 942).

However, invasion was not the only threat. There was also the danger of an economic war, a formidable risk indeed because Germany had the means to exert a stranglehold over the Swiss economy. We know that this hypothesis was taken seriously on the German side from February to June 1943: the purchase of gold by the Swiss National Bank appeared to be the most persuasive argument in the German decision to abandon the idea.

Such was the existential dimension, vital to an understanding of the actions of the SNB and the Confederation. This undoubtedly explains the support given by the government in November 1943 to the acceptance of German gold by the Swiss National Bank, although the dubious origins of this gold and the problems associated with these origins were known to the two protagonists.

Four technical elements must be added to this existential issue. They have been given ample treatment elsewhere and it will suffice here to recall them briefly.

First, the purchase of German gold – as with the purchase of Allied gold – was an instrument of monetary policy. It contributed to maintaining the Swiss franc at the level fixed by law, and thus to the stability of the franc and, in turn, to its convertibility, because without the stability, convertibility would have been impossible. (It helped to maintain the franc in two ways: purchases of gold at parity prevented the franc from appreciating when the Reichsbank wanted to sell the metal; the SNB also acquired the necessary reserves so it could sell gold on the domestic market if the franc showed signs of weakening.) The gold buying did not represent an anomaly by any means. It fitted in with the Swiss National Bank's intervention policy pursued since before the war, with the only difference being that, after 1940–41, gold replaced foreign exchange as the instrument of policy.

Second, buying German gold provided the Swiss National Bank with an important medium of international payment under wartime conditions. A number of countries demanded to be paid in gold for their shipments to Switzerland (Portugal for at least CHF 300 million, Spain,

Romania). And, with Swiss assets blocked by the Allies, the Reichsbank remained the only source of the metal accessible to Switzerland.

Third, from autumn 1943, the purchase of gold represented an instrument of economic policy sought after by the Swiss National Bank. The resale of a fraction of the German gold on the Swiss market helped to moderate the inflationary pressure sparked off by the massive receipts of blocked 'Allied' gold and foreign exchange (around CHF 270–280 million resold between summer 1943 and June 1945).

Fourth, buying German gold was considered necessary by the Swiss National Bank and by the Confederation as an instrument of Switzerland's neutrality policy. As soon as the SNB started buying gold from the Allies in increasingly large amounts (from summer–autumn of 1943), it was more and more difficult to refuse to buy German gold. A neutral state was required to respect the principle of even-handed treatment of the belligerents.

Such were the technical elements that have to be considered. These elements are sometimes seen as simple pretexts used by the Swiss National Bank and the Confederation to justify purchases of German gold, or as simple 'necessities' to assure the functioning of the monetary system consisting of free exchange in the framework of a de facto gold standard which the SNB and the Confederation could have abandoned. The reality, however, is more complex. There was a close connection between the technical and the existential elements. The franc could only protect Switzerland to the extent to which it was sought as payment by suppliers to the German Reich. And it could only serve as this medium of payment under four conditions: it had to be stable, convertible, freely usable in Switzerland from abroad, and unweakened by inflation. These conditions depended, it was felt, on the buying of gold: German gold and Allied gold under the first and third conditions, and German gold for the second and fourth conditions.

The above points raise a number of problems. Gauged against the existential stakes involved, they are secondary in nature, but this does not make them any less important.

A first problem is the origin of the gold 'swallowed' by the Swiss National Bank. A large part of this gold – as was confirmed after the war – had been seized illicitly by the German Reich if not actually looted. This raises three questions. Did the Swiss National Bank know about the origins of the gold or not? Did it have the means to learn the truth? Could it have taken measures to induce the Reichsbank to furnish non-looted gold instead, assuming such reserves were available?

The minutes of various high-level meetings at the SNB leave the impression that the bank began to suspect the possibility that it was taking in looted gold in the summer of 1941, which is earlier than one would have imagined – and earlier than the bank was subsequently willing to admit. Under the circumstances, this poses an important problem from the standpoint of the post-war period: whether the Swiss National Bank was acting 'in good faith' in the legal sense of the term. From the moment the gold was obtained under the taint of doubt and suspicion, the bank had knowingly taken a risk. And, to a lesser degree, the Swiss Confederation had knowingly taken the risk as well (to a lesser degree, because the government was only informed about the problem by the SNB at a later stage, and was only warned that there was a 'theoretical risk' and not of the real suspicions of the bank). They had their reasons for putting the existential issue ahead of any other consideration, but that being the case, they also took on a responsibility which some day they would have to bear. That day came in 1946, in Washington.

A second question has to be raised. Would not the bank have been able, or obliged, to break off the gold purchases at the moment, for instance, when the risk of a German attack ceased to exist? The problem arises from the fact that the threat was perceived as real up to a rather late date, as shown by Volume 15 of the *Swiss Diplomatic Documents*: May–June 1944 by the Swiss army, October 1944 by the Federal Council. So from summer or autumn 1944, the Swiss National Bank would have been able to stop buying German gold. Instead, it continued to take deliveries until April 1945, albeit in smaller and smaller quantities. The rationale was supplied by the considerations given to the neutrality policy from higher up. These considerations may appear specious, but they were not without foundation; they had legal opinions to back them up (*Swiss Diplomatic Documents*, Vol. 15, 181).

The fact that the gold received from the Reich was booty – and that this was suspected in Switzerland – would appear to weaken the neutrality argument. But it should not be forgotten that, from summer 1944, the metal was being received in ever-diminishing quantities (CHF 60 million from July 1944 to May 1945) while shipments of Allied gold were accelerating strongly, making it more difficult to turn down Germany. This would have required a similar gesture to the other side, which was precisely what the Allies did not want. The SNB would certainly have done better to suspend purchases of German gold after summer 1944. But perhaps the Allies could have helped make it easier for Switzerland by renouncing their 'sales' of gold and dollars, or at least really unblocking the gold that they were selling.

A third question has occupied certain historians. Was the SNB policy of accepting German gold not inspired by the profit motive? As has been indicated in the minutes of SNB committee meetings, the resale of German gold on the Swiss market decidedly worked to the advantage of the institution in 1942 and 1944. One cannot deny that there was pressure from certain members of the bank committee, particularly in 1944. It would be a short step to convert this pressure into the driving force behind the bank's purchases of German gold. Proof of this is seen in the reply made by bank president Weber to committee members during a meeting in November 1944: 'The profit aspect should not be allowed to stand in the foreground.' That being said, it should also be seen, as M. Fior (1997) has shown, that the profit motive was too strong when it came to certain purchases of German gold and its re-sale on the Swiss market.

Finally, the main question. Did the SNB not favour the German war effort by accepting its gold? The figures provide an initial answer. The SNB, aided and abetted by the Confederation, accepted nearly twice as much gold from the Allies, and if the source of the German gold was plunder, the Allied gold remained blocked to Switzerland, thus making the Swiss francs paid out a form of real advances (credits). A more general accounting is necessary, however, based on the total amount of Swiss francs remitted to the two sides by the SNB and the Confederation.

Table 3.1 shows the breakdown in billions of francs.

Table 3.1:
Swiss Francs Remitted to the Two Sides (CHF billions)

Axis		Allies[2]	Confederation	SNB
Advance clearing to Germany by Confederation	1.1	Advances on gold or dollars UK and USA	1	1.2–1.6
Purchases of German gold (SNB)	1.2			
Purchases of German gold (banks)	0.09			
Advances to Italy by Confederation	0.18			
Italian gold purchases (SNB)	0.05			
Total	2.6			2.2–2.6
		Plus advances to Belgium, Holland and France		0.35

Altogether, taking into account the late entry of the United States into the war, the services on behalf of the two camps were balanced. There will no doubt be objections that this general balance hides certain discrepancies and in fact what was at work here was an anti-balance of power. This means that Switzerland made concessions to each camp according to the way the wind was blowing: massive services to the German side when the Axis were winning, and massive services to the Allies from 1943. But this objection must be qualified for two reasons:

1. Although by spring of 1943 (mid-April 1943), the actual turning point in the war, the Reich had received around CHF 1.4 billion through sales of gold and clearing advances, the Allies were granted between CHF 830 million and 940 million through the purchase of blocked gold or dollars.
2. This disproportion can also be explained by the late entry of the United States into the war. The American need for Swiss francs did not really become acute until 1943.

So much for the accounts. Let us look now at the 'price' which Switzerland had to pay for making financial concessions to the two camps. The services to the Axis powers consisted of 50 per cent firm purchases of gold and 50 per cent of clearing advances. Only these advances were real credits and as a result represented a financial sacrifice. Moreover, because these credits were covered by public borrowing, they had only a weak inflationary influence. On the other hand, the services to the Allies consisted almost totally (80–90 per cent) of purchases of blocked gold or foreign exchange. These advances were a financial sacrifice to Switzerland and moreover had an inflationary effect. It was equivalent to issuing banknotes in the amount of CHF 1.2–1.6 billion (compared with a money supply of about CHF 2 billion in 1939). To sum up, from the financial or economic point of view, the Allies cost Switzerland more dearly.

One last point, which at the moment is the least understood one. What use did Swiss francs have for the two sides? As far as the Reich is concerned, the clearing advances permitted them to buy strategic material and various other products in Switzerland while guaranteeing the payment of certain expenses (tourism) and debt servicing. The gold sales permitted the purchase of strategic materials in third countries.

In the case of the Allies, our knowledge is less clear. But there is no doubt about the importance of the franc in this Treasury memoire of summer 1944 extracted from a Foreign Office report: 'if the Swiss were to take the line that they must give the same treatment to all belligerents [interrupting gold purchases (Marguerat)], we should be in a complete mess, since we cannot get Swiss francs otherwise than by tendering gold, save in quite small amounts'. As various documents show, the francs remitted to the British had several uses, notably the purchase of weapons in Switzerland (parts for aviation and naval guidance systems) and the financing of a formidable information network in Switzerland. From the end of 1941, this network was responsible for tracking the German economy and acting as scouts for bomber command. It was probably the same with the United States. The francs were used to buy massive amounts of watch movements and to finance the activities of the Office for Strategic Services (OSS) in Switzerland. These activities included the organisation of the French resistance and decisions regarding German industrial targets. It is difficult to determine exactly, in the British and American cases, a breakdown of how the money was used. What can be said is that, of the total Swiss francs that went to the Allies, expenditures not related to the war effort (support, defence of Allied interests, interest on debts owed by the British) represented at the most 25 per cent. The rest went into the war effort in one form or another. The Reich seems to have spent in the same proportion (at least 26 per cent of the amount represented by the clearing advances and the sale of German gold).

In other words, the SNB and the Confederation were contributing to the destruction of what they helped build. That was the kind of neutrality that the war imposed on Switzerland. This neutrality consisted of a free currency market maintained for reasons of survival, in a certain balance between the currency movements and gold in favour of the two camps. This balance was difficult to maintain because, as we have seen, there were two risks: the risk of being a receiver of stolen goods or a money launderer on the one side, and, on the other, the risk of economic distortions and non-recovery of debts (the possible refusal by the Allies to release the blocked gold and foreign exchange). Of course, it can be asked whether, in view of the risks inherent in the purchase of 'German' gold, other less dangerous but equally dissuasive solutions were not possible.

Could the SNB have refused to purchase German gold and left it to the Confederation to supply Swiss francs to Germany within the framework of an expanded clearing credit? The answer is no. The clearing credit essentially supplied Germany with francs useable in Switzerland. What Germany wanted most of all was Swiss currency that could be used anywhere in the world. What is more, an expansion of the clearing credit corresponding to the amount of German gold purchased (CHF 1.3 billion) would have been beyond the capacity of the federal budget and would have overstretched the Swiss financial market. That market was already strained by the existing authorised credit. In fact the

Germans had overshot the credit limit of CHF 850 million to the extent that in March 1943 it was decided no longer to grant a clearing advance to Germany (see *Swiss Diplomatic Documents*, Vol. 14, 328).

In view of this situation, was another solution conceivable: to let the SNB supply the Reich with free Swiss francs without buying German gold? Here again the answer is no. The bank could not have put money into circulation without compensation, without guaranteed security realisable at relatively short notice. Besides this legal obstacle, a blank check would have presented a major risk. Swiss francs spent by Germany in a third country could have come back to Switzerland at any time for conversion into gold at the SNB – a promise the bank could not have kept given the meagre internal reserves at its disposal. The Swiss franc then would not have been convertible, losing one of the basic qualities which made it an instrument of international payments and which in turn held the Reich at bay.

Could the SNB have advanced francs to the Reich against gold 'blocked' in Berlin? This solution would have avoided the situation of having to accept looted gold, provided the necessary security and assured the stability of the franc as well as representing a balanced approach between Allies and Axis. But this option would have undermined two of the pillars which supported the international value of the franc and its power of deterrence: without tangible supplies of gold, the bank would not have had enough reserves to maintain the franc's convertibility or to intervene in the market to reduce inflationary pressures.

Could the SNB have limited its purchases of gold from the German and the Allied sides only to the transactions carried out by the belligerents in Switzerland itself? This is an idea raised by K. Urner in a 1985 article. It would have limited the absorption – at least the actual physical receipt – of German gold, notably looted gold, and it would have avoided the criticism that the franc was being used by the Reich to do business with third countries. But this possibility is hardly more realistic than the previous ones. What interested Germany was money freely useable everywhere in the world. It was the same with the Allies at least in the case where Swiss francs were being used to finance Allied information networks (francs freely available to the American government and from autumn 1943 demanded with more and more insistence; francs freely available to the British government from 1940). Hence there would have been twofold pressure on Switzerland and the potential loss of the Swiss franc's deterrent capacity in the eyes of the Reich. Moreover, there was the obligation of a central bank which wanted to remain linked to the gold standard – the basis of the Swiss franc's strength – to ensure that its currency was convertible into gold and vice versa at least in relations with other central banks.

A final scenario is the introduction of a floating exchange rate. The SNB would then have been able to let the commercial banks buy gold. Such a system would have been less vulnerable politically and legally for the Confederation, but without stability the franc would have lost its convertibility and its status as a deterrent international currency.

Apart from these scenarios, there were no other solutions but those necessitating the refusal of the SNB to buy German gold. Even if one admits that a refusal would not have lessened the dissuasive arguments – a difficult hypothesis to support – it would have met huge obstacles. The weight of the intake of German gold would have fallen on the commercial banks. This would have meant a return to the situation before the end of 1941: then, francs were sold by these institutions to the Reich, which in turn used the francs in third countries from which came requests to the SNB to convert these francs into gold; this arrangement was changed by substituting the central bank for the private institutions, so as to limit losses of gold. Alternatively, it would have been necessary to introduce strict exchange controls, excluding all movement of gold and currency with both Germany and the Allies (balanced treatment). But then Switzerland would have been exposed to double pressure from the belligerents, while its economy would have imploded because of the drastic reduction of exports to the Allies and the likely refusal of one camp or the other to deliver essential supplies. In any case, this last solution would have necessitated a change in the monetary system (the suspension of the gold standard). That would have meant a radical reversal of a monetary policy and of a fragile economic balance that had been in operation since the First World War. It would have reduced the franc to the status of a local, 'non-deterrent' currency.

These counterfactual arguments, as enlightening as they are, should not however create any illusions. They do not seem to have been developed by the SNB but stem from a retrospective view. One would be more reassured to know that the bank had followed such a train of thought and that the strategy it adopted was deliberate. But this does not seem to have been the case. The bank decided almost instinctively what its policy would be because this policy seemed to be in the interests of the country and at the same time to correspond best to the needs of the operations of the bank. It was also perhaps in keeping with the traditional good relations with the Reichsbank, which dated back to the 1920s. Some have spoken of actual collusion with the Reichsbank. But they forget three things: one, that the SNB collaborated just as actively with the Allied central banks even if it was more reluctant to do so because of the freezing of Allied gold and its economic repercussions; two, that the bank took various measures from the summer of 1943 aimed at slowing down the arrival of German gold, notably that gold sold for Swiss francs used in third countries; and three, that the bank seemed to be involved in a policy that supported the purchase of German gold from autumn 1940 and especially from the end of 1941 only at the instigation of the Swiss Confederation and under the pressure of certain economic circumstances.[3]

To sum up, the SNB and the Swiss Confederation were in an inextricable situation. They were torn between the risk of fencing stolen goods or laundering dirty money on the German side and the risk of economic distortion and default on debts on the Allied side. As a result, the SNB and the Confederation tried to strike a 'balance of risks' to assure Switzerland's survival against the Axis and to gain the relative understanding of the Allies. This resulted in what could be described as a policy of financial neutrality, probably the only possible way out. And there was obviously nothing glorious or particularly moral about it at the time. After the war, morality would have consisted in restoring or more generously compensating the gold which had been received as stolen property or laundered – necessarily so, one might add. During the war, morality would have consisted in giving welcome to the refugees crowding at Switzerland's borders – borders made safe because of the protection offered by German gold ingots.

NOTES

1 The sources of the first estimate (CHF 2.2 bn) are as follows: around CHF 1.7–1.8 bn exchanged by the SNB for gold for the period from mid-June 1941 to June 1945 (see minutes of governing board and inventory accounts), to which should be added CHF 263 million remitted to the UK by the SNB against blocked dollars from September 1939 to March 1942 (see Weber's letter to the Federal Political Department, 9 October 1945, Federal Archive), as well as CHF 200 million labelled as 'Confederation guarantees' (see Department of Finance report, 14 February 1946, Federal Archive, E 2001 (E) 1/1968/78/386) and part of the CHF 220 million for *contingents horlogers anticipés* and transfer certificates guaranteed by the Confederation (see Department of Finance, August 1946, Federal Archive, 6100 (A) 26/2479). The sources of the second estimate (CHF 2.6–2.7 bn) are as follows: CHF 200–263 million remitted to the UK by the SNB from September 1939 to March 1942 (see above), CHF 1.2 billion, remitted by the SNB and the Confederation to the USA and CHF 660 million to the UK against blocked gold and dollars from mid-June 1941 to the end of January 1945 (*Swiss Diplomatic Documents*, Vol. 15, 359), CHF 350 million remitted from February to June 1945 (minutes of SNB governing board and SNB inventory accounts); to this are added CHF 200 million in 'guarantees' and part of the CHF 220 million of the *contingents anticipés* and the guaranteed certificates. The reasons for the discrepancy between the two estimates still have to be determined.

2 Perhaps, when comparing the francs remitted to the two warring sides, it would be appropriate to add to the advances made to Britain and the USA, the credits granted at the beginning of 1945 to Belgium, CHF 50 million to the Netherlands and CHF 250 million to France (March 1945). This would bring the total remitted to the Allies to between CHF 2.55 and 2.95 billion.

3 The involvement of the Confederation occurred on two occasions: the first was at the end of October 1940 when the Federal Political Department, during discussions about the gold, expressed the desire that 'business relations with the Reichsbank in this respect [the purchase of gold from the Reichsbank] proceed smoothly' (minutes of bank board, 31 October 1940); the second was at the end of 1941 when the SNB decided for macroeconomic reasons to replace the commercial banks and to monopolise the gold traffic with Germany (*Swiss Diplomatic Documents*, Vol. 15, 446, pp. 1127–8).

REFERENCES

For reasons of space, I have not included archive and bibliographical references.

W. Boelcke, *Deutschland als Welthandelsmacht 1930–1945* (Germany as a world trade power), Stuttgart/Berlin/Cologne, 1944.

D. Bourgeois, 'Les relations economiques germano-suisses' (German–Swiss economic relations), *Revue d'histoire de la 2e guerre mondiale*, 1981, pp. 49–61.

M. Durrer, *Die schweizerisch–amerikanischen Finanzbeziehungen im Zweiten Weltkrieg* (Swiss–American financial relations during the Second World War), Berne/Stuttgart, 1984.

M. Fior, *La Suisse et l'or de la Reichsbank. Que savait la Banque nationale?* (Switzerland and Reichsbank Gold. What Did the National Bank Know?) Neuchâtel, Cahiers de l'Institut d'histoire, 1997.

Philippe Marguerat, *La Suisse face au IIIe Reich* (Switzerland against the Third Reich), Lausanne, 1991.

——, 'La BNS et la position internationale du franc, 1914–1970' (The Swiss National Bank and the International Position of the Franc), in *Les Banques en Europe de l'Ouest* (Banks in Western Europe), Paris, 1995, pp. 243–60.

H. Senn: *Anfänge einer Dissuasionstrategie* (The Beginnings of a Dissuasion Strategy), Basle, 1995.

K. Urner, 'E. Puhl und die SNB' (E. Puhl and the SNB), *Schweizer Monatsheft*, 1985, pp. 623–31.

——, *Die Schweiz muss noch geschluckt werden* (Switzerland Still Has to Be Swallowed Up), Zurich, 1990.

The work of W. Rings may be included: *Raubgold aus Deutschland* (Looted Gold from Germany), Zurich, 1985; praiseworthy but journalistic.

4

Unclaimed Assets of Nazi Victims in Switzerland: What People Knew and What Else They Ought to Know

PETER HUG

The history of Nazi victims' unclaimed assets in Switzerland is a history of neglected responsibilities, accompanied by a recurrent and forceful media debate that comes and goes in cycles, invariably prompting the political authorities or the asset managers to take measures (which later prove inadequate). Public awareness, however, has been shaped by the much longer periods of silence, concealment and fading memories.

Swiss historiography is no exception. Important collections of documents relating to this subject have been accessible in the Federal Archive (FA) since the mid-1980s. Historians of the modern era repeatedly come across the dispute concerning dormant accounts (unclaimed assets, heirless property) in Switzerland emanating from Nazi victims as they work through public collections of press clippings, the annual reports of the Federal Council (Swiss cabinet) and of the professional associations concerned. But the theme was not taken up by Swiss historians, with the exception of two studies undertaken on commission: an initially unpublished report by Jacques Picard for the Jewish Agency (1993)[1] and a second, more comprehensive, study for the Federal Department of Foreign Affairs by Peter Hug and Marc Perrenoud (December 1996).[2] Even the specialised thesis by Linus von Castelmur on post-war Swiss–Allied financial relations devotes just two half-sentences to the problem of unclaimed assets.[3] The reasons for historians' lack of interest in this theme, even after it was subjected to the powerful glare of media attention around the world in 1996 and formed the subject of many books by Swiss and foreign journalists[4] that appeared in 1997, can only be guessed at. Since the end of the 1940s, as this chapter shows, the public has repeatedly been confronted by these issues. An unspoken, latent anti-Semitism was undoubtedly one of the factors in the speed with which events were forgotten. But there is no plausible model to help us find explanations, nor do we

know the extent of the wrongs committed or the individual entitlements still open.

The national and even more the international media played a key
role right from the beginning in helping interested parties such as
the World Jewish Congress (WJC) make their voices heard and in
sensitising the diplomatic community of the Western Allies and Israel
to the issue of Nazi victims during phases when these circles were
receptive.[5] The whole public debate was first precipitated by the WJC's
call – at its war emergency conference of November 1944 in Atlantic City
– for compilation of a record of Nazi victims' assets and use of these
assets to help survivors of Nazi terror to rebuild their lives.[6] A pace-
setting role was played by the *New York Times*. On 29 June 1946, for
example, it reported at length on the resolution of the Paris war
reparations conference to apply US$ 25 million of the German assets
located in neutral countries and another US$ 25 million in 'heirless'
assets in the same countries towards international refugee assistance.[7]
In Switzerland, however, similar proposals by the Swiss Federation of
Jewish Communities initially received no coverage in the press.[8]

The assets of Nazi victims became the subject of public discussion a
few years later when Switzerland concluded an agreement with Poland
which was incompatible with the decisions of the five-power conference in Paris and earlier promises by Swiss diplomats. In an initially
confidential exchange of letters on the Swiss–Polish compensation agreement of 25 June 1949, the Federal Council assured the Polish government that 'heirless' assets held in Switzerland belonging to missing
Polish nationals would be transferred to the Polish central bank's
'nationalization compensation account' at the Swiss National Bank (SNB)
for the benefit of Swiss citizens whose property had been nationalised
by Poland.[9] The Western Allied governments and international Jewish
organisations saw this as an infringement of the promise made by
Minister Walter Stucki as head of the Swiss delegation in an exchange
of letters to the Washington Agreement, stating that the Swiss
government would 'look favourably on the question of introducing the
measures necessary to place at the disposal of the three Allied governments (for the purpose of aid and assistance) the amount of assets in
Switzerland belonging to victims of the acts of violence recently perpetrated by the former German government, who died without heirs'.[10]

That the public would hear about the Swiss–Polish exchange of
letters at all was not a foregone conclusion. The Federal Council, at
the instigation of the Swiss Bankers' Association (SBA) and against
the original intentions of both negotiating delegations, had decided
not to publish the exchange. The head of the Federal Department of
Justice and Police (FDJP), Federal Councillor Eduard von Steiger, also

deliberately refrained from mentioning the Swiss–Polish diplomatic exchange at a reception for representatives of the World Jewish Congress, the Jewish Agency and the Joint Distribution Committee on 8 July 1949, even though the event was dedicated exclusively to the question of how to proceed with regard to Nazi victims' assets held in Switzerland.[11]

So, Max Isenbergh of the American Jewish Committee's European bureau in Paris was all the more astonished when he learned of the Swiss–Polish exchange from none other than the former SBA secretary, UBS (United Bank of Switzerland) senior bank manager and member of the Polish creditors' committee, Adolf Jann. Nevertheless, von Steiger and the head of the Federal Political Department (FPD), Max Petitpierre, were not prepared to receive Isenbergh on this matter.[12] Isenbergh persevered, however, and managed to speak with the legation counsellor, Felix Schnyder, on a pretext on 15 October 1949, when he described the Swiss–Polish exchange of letters as immoral; he urged the Swiss authorities either not to ratify or not to implement the exchange. When Schnyder turned down this demand, Isenbergh said his only alternative was to go public. Schnyder pointed out that this would put pressure on the Federal Council to justify its position publicly.[13] At first, therefore, Isenbergh only informed the Swiss Federation of Jewish Communities, whose president, Georges Brunschvig, lost no time in taking the matter to Petitpierre. Brunschvig and the respected professor of international law in Geneva, Paul Guggenheim, were received by Petitpierre on 4 November 1949. The federal councillor, while not acceding to their demands, permitted them to report the letter exchange in Jewish newspapers.[14] The resultant article in the 2 December 1949 edition of the *Israelitisches Wochenblatt für die Schweiz*, however, went totally unnoticed by the mainstream Swiss press.

With that, Isenbergh and the international Jewish organisations saw no more reason to keep silent. Their public protest against the Swiss deal with Poland appeared in the *New York Times* and its press service. They demanded that Nazi victims' assets in Switzerland should go to international refugee organisations for assistance to the groups that had suffered the most from Nazi terror, as promised by the Swiss government in 1946.[15] Journalists in Washington immediately contacted the Swiss embassy to ask whether the *New York Times* report was accurate,[16] and newspapers in Israel ('Scandal over Jewish assets deposited in Switzerland')[17] and Canada ('Object to Swiss transfer of heirless Jewish funds to Poland') also condemned the agreement.[18] The first diplomatic protests by the International Refugee Organisation, the three Western Allies and Israel were also quick to appear.[19]

The Swiss press remained silent, however, until sensitised members of the Swiss Parliament announced the assignment of the 'heirless' Polish funds, first in parliamentary committees[20] and then in the National Council (National Assembly) during the ratification process on 21/22 December 1949. Swiss diplomacy was supported in the debates by Geneva Radical André Guinand, but was sharply attacked by national councillors Philipp Schmid-Ruedin of the Democratic Party and Paul Meierhans of the Social Democratic Party (SP). In particular, the lack of publication was criticised. Nevertheless, the lower house also refrained from entering the parliamentary debate in the printed version of its stenographic bulletin.[21]

The matter only began to feature in the Swiss press three weeks later, when Swiss politicians on the right started attacking the Swiss–Polish exchange of letters. They were not so much concerned with how to help the Nazi victims' legal heirs as with the 'encroachment of foreign law in our legal sphere for which the gentlemen responsible have every reason to remain silent'.[22] A lead article in *Finanz und Wirtschaft* complained that assets accepted in a fiduciary capacity were now to be used 'for the benefit of Communist circles, of all things', and called on the cantons, 'which alone had the authority to dispose' over the assets, to refuse to go along with the 'ploy'.[23] The series of articles was sparked off by a letter to the editor, which appeared under the title of 'Do we have to take this?' on 10 January 1950 in the independent *National-Zeitung*.[24] Two days later the staunchly conservative *Berner Tagblatt* also criticised the 'disturbing secret clauses'.[25]

For the first time the FPD itself issued a statement to the press on 1 February 1950, because, it said, the exchange of letters 'had already been the subject of many articles in Swiss and foreign papers which deviated in part from the true content'.[26] Checking this statement was difficult, however, because the FPD still refused to release the text. The long-winded 'official justification of the liquidation agreement',[27] as *Der Bund* headlined it, was not well received. The *Anzeiger von Uster* was not at all pleased that the FPD had tried to 'set up the press as a whipping-boy'.[28] 'How will I tell my children?' asked the *Glarner Nachrichten*, and objected that the lengthy explanation did not even reveal who had written it.[29] For the *St Galler Tagblatt*, it was still 'not clear why the Federal Council had not briefed the full session of the two houses about the letters in question "in good and due form"',[30] and, writing in the *National-Zeitung*, attorney Professor Wolfhart Friedrich Bürgi said the 'official version of the matter' should 'not be allowed to go unchallenged' and revealed 'a fresh and grave disregard of elementary Swiss legal principles'.[31] It was, as many papers said in the headlines, 'an attempted justification that failed to convince'.[32]

The 'flowers borne by the secret politics'[33] now attracted the attention of the aggressive populist right. *Die Aktion für freie Meinungs-äusserung* (campaign for free expression of opinion), centred around Robert Eibel, launched a series of polemical advertisements entitled 'We're not putting up with this, you "lords of Berne"!' and spoke of a 'Communist infection' against which 'the people' had to enter their veto: a 'veto to preserve and uphold our Swiss law!'[34] Even the hitherto restrained *Neue Zürcher Zeitung* (NZZ) now wrote: 'The attitude reigning at certain federal offices appears to be that the Confederation does not have to observe any domestic laws at all when negotiating international treaties, not even its own constitution.'[35] The NZZ concluded that 'the commitments undertaken on Switzerland's part are in complete violation of the depositors' property rights or the rights of their private heirs and are in blatant contradiction of our private law'.[36]

A question from Zurich Independent Werner Schmid gave Petitpierre an opportunity to respond to the press attacks in the National Council on 22 March 1950, and at long last to read the text of the Swiss–Polish exchange of letters. However, this answer was also not admitted to the printed minutes of the parliamentary session. Although Petitpierre said nothing materially new, Schmid declared himself satisfied.[37] This settled the matter for the time being as far as the Swiss press was concerned. Professor Paul Guggenheim, however, produced a comprehensive treatise in 1950, which argued that the Federal Council had no right not to publish a treaty that was binding under international law if, as in the case of the Swiss–Polish exchange of letters, Swiss law was transferred to the hands of a foreign state.[38]

That notwithstanding, the Federal Council again decided just a few months later to refrain from publishing the full text of a protocol ('agreed minute') with Hungary in which it undertook to make over to Hungary, as in the agreement with Poland, dormant accounts in Switzerland belonging to Hungarian citizens who had disappeared.[39] But this time the Federal Council mentioned the procedure in a few words of its message on the ratification of the Hungarian–Swiss economic and compensation agreements, in which context the ancillary protocol was drafted.[40] The decision not to publish was all the more remarkable since Petitpierre had described the secrecy concerning the letter exchange a few months earlier as 'mistaken' in his answer to Schmid. Nevertheless, the arrangements with Hungary were hardly placed before the public, any more than in the previous case. Even in the preparatory discussions at the parliamentary commission level, only the Glarus politician, Melchior Hefti (Democratic Party) went into the matter briefly. The compensation arrangements were sharply criticised in the press – along the lines of 'it can't go on like this'[41] – but not the arrangements for 'heirless' Hungarian assets.

Another public debate flared up only a year later, on 26 September 1951, when National Councillor Philipp Schmid-Ruedin called for the problem to be resolved as a matter of principle; he had already been a conspicuous critic of the 'Polish correspondence' and is likely to have had contacts with groups affected. In its answer of 22 January 1952, the Federal Council promised to submit a resolution to the upper and lower house – which would be eligible for referendum – for the introduction of a reporting requirement for 'heirless' assets. This news was carried around the world.[42] The Swiss press, however, only realised what the Federal Council was up to after the decision was heavily criticised by the SDA.[43] Subsequently, the SBA turned to the public, feeling that it was no longer represented by the Federal Council. Henceforth, the SBA also regularly devoted a section of its publicly accessible annual report to this subject, under the heading of 'Information requirements for the banks' from 1951 to 1953, 'Heirless assets' in 1954, 'Information requirements for the banks' (again) in 1957, 'Assets "without heirs"' in 1958, and from 1962 to 1965 under the terse heading of 'Assets of the racially persecuted'.[44] One of the SBA's concerns about a special law on dormant accounts was that it 'would necessarily undermine confidence in Switzerland's asset management services'.[45]

Public interest in the Nazi victims' dormant accounts waned visibly after 1952. For one thing, the Federal Council had announced that a solution was on the way. For another, the Cold War had created a political climate that permitted former Nazis to return to public office under the Adenauer administration and was also not very conducive to a critical assessment of the war years in Switzerland either. Information only started filtering through to the public again in 1954, as the discussions with the FPD and FDJP by the Swiss Federation of Jewish Communities and the Swiss Bankers' Association approached stalemate. The reports on the reception of a delegation from the Federation of Jewish Communities by the head of the FDJP, Markus Feldmann, and a diplomatic note from the Israeli government to the Federal Council a few months later, were only worth a mention in the Jewish press in Switzerland. Coverage at the international level was mainly in Austrian and Israeli newspapers.[46] Additionally, in the same year, Guggenheim published a substantial, basic text on the heirless assets in Switzerland;[47] however, this did not draw much of a response.

The theme was only revived again with the 1957 appearance of a critical report on Swiss refugee policy during the Second World War by Basle professor of law Carl Ludwig, and discussions at the UN about the new outbreaks of anti-Semitism in Germany in 1959/60. On 20 March 1957 a motion by SP National Councillor Harald Huber again demanded special legal provisions to govern the 'heirless' assets.

Replying two years later, on 18 March 1959, the new head of the FDJP, Traugott Wahlen, announced again that a federal law would be drafted with a requirement to report assets of Nazi victims, although at the same time he managed to push through the reclassification of the motion into a non-compulsory *Postulat* or 'proposal'. In the wake of this the subject was taken up by the international press with an enthusiasm hitherto unknown, with heavy attacks on the Swiss banks setting the tone. One of the first was the periodical *Yediyoth Aharonoth* on 22 November 1960: 'The "Bank of Zurich" that pocketed a hefty fee for trafficking in Jewish blood'.[48] The story suddenly spread like wildfire when the chief European correspondent for the *Sunday Telegraph*, Anthony Mann, wrote a very critical article about Nazi victims' assets in Switzerland that was published on 16 June 1961 and picked up by a number of news agencies for worldwide distribution.[49] A Belgian paper on 7 June 1961, drew the dubious but all the more explosive connection between the dormant accounts in Switzerland and the Eichmann trial in Israel which was causing a stir at the time.[50]

The new sensitivity stiffened the Federal Council's resolve to submit a federal decree to the Swiss Parliament (against the opposition of the SBA) on 4 May 1962, concerning assets situated in Switzerland belonging to foreigners or stateless persons persecuted for reasons of race, religion or politics. This was the *Meldebeschluss* Registration Decree. Its passage and implementation were accompanied by another wave of intense media interest around the world. Ten years later, the controversy over the federal decree of 16 September 1974[51] on the allocation of the money paid into the 'heirless accounts' fund (or 'unclaimed assets' fund) under the provisions of the Registration Decree again attracted considerable public interest.

Today, we know that the information given to the public by the Federal Council, in its messages on these two decrees, was incomplete and partially misleading. For instance, not a word was said about the intensive behind-the-scenes diplomacy since 1946 that led up to them. In the case of the message of 1974 this was all the more astonishing because the Federal Council had reaffirmed its willingness – to Poland on 26 June 1964 and to Hungary on 26 March 1973 – to transfer to these two governments the Nazi victims' assets identified as 'heirless' belonging to citizens of the two countries. An initial transfer of CHF 16,347.10 to Poland, or more accurately for the benefit of Swiss citizens whose property had been nationalised by Poland, had already taken place in 1960. This reticence was definitely intentional. Ambassador Emanuel Diez, head of the FPD legal section, bore in mind as the message was being drafted that the Swiss–Polish exchange of letters was originally 'not published out of consideration for the fears expressed by the banks' and only became public under external pressure. Diez observed with satisfaction in 1970 that 'later, on the other hand, the intergovernmental agreement with Poland seems to have been largely forgotten by the public and has also not been adversely cited by other interested states. Thus, we still have a practical interest in allowing the matter to continue to rest quietly by avoiding any publicity.'[52]

The question of whether Parliament should have been informed in the 1974 message on the Polish and Hungarian cases was not a minor issue. Three points must be emphasised. First, the Federal Council decided on 20 August 1965 to credit the Polish 'heirless' assets designated under the 1962 Registration Decree directly to the account of the Polish National Bank. In 1975, however, it withdrew the corresponding sum (CHF 463,954.55) from the 'heirless accounts' fund. Second, in the case of Hungary the Federal Council decided on 27 August 1965 'that Switzerland recognizes Hungary's counter-claim arising from the incorporation of assets of missing Hungarian citizens into the fund, to the extent that Hungary has a proven right to these assets under inheritance law'. Nevertheless, the Federal Council transferred the sum in 1975 with no such proof having been provided. And third, in the very same decision on financing the Hungarian counter-claim, the Federal Council envisaged 'submitting a draft to the two houses on payment of this counter-claim at the appropriate time'.[53] This appropriations bill also did not materialise. Instead, the Finance Administration took the money for the Hungarian government (CHF 325,000) from the 'heirless accounts' fund to be transferred directly to Swiss owners of nationalised property in Hungary via the 'Nationalisation Compensation/Hungary' account. Nonetheless, the Federal Council allowed the Swiss Parliament and public to believe that two-thirds of the money in the 'heirless accounts' fund would go to the Swiss Central Office for Refugee Aid and the other third to the Swiss Federation of Jewish Communities (a total of CHF 3,180,104.73, whereas the government had spoken of CHF 2.2 million) in accordance with the federal decree of 3 March 1975.

Two additional 'information breakdowns' arose because the federal government presented no accountability report explaining the procedure it followed in this matter. Thus, the public remained ignorant of the Federal Council's decision on 28 February 1972 to dispense with the usual procedures for presumption of death and call for heirs in connection with the approximately 125 reported dormant accounts emanating from countries in eastern Europe, amounting to CHF 4.8 million, and to incorporate the assets from Albania, Bulgaria, the German Democratic Republic, Yugoslavia, Poland, Romania, the Soviet Union, Czechoslovakia and Hungary into the 'heirless accounts' fund using administrative procedures.[54] Federal Councillor Ludwig von Moos, who retired in 1971, had argued unsuccessfully that the Swiss Civil Code should be followed with regard to the east European assets, which should 'continue to be administered by the official guardians assigned to those accounts and not integrated into the general fund'.[55] We know today that the Federal Council's decision to the contrary led to the expropriation of assets to which people living in freedom in the West had rightful claims.[56] In addition, the information given to the National Council by Federal Councillor Kurt Furgler, to the effect that 'out of the some CHF 10 million involved in the process in question roughly three quarters of the assets found their way to their owners', was at the very least highly misleading.[57] In fact, the Registration Office, the cantonal authorities acting as custodial guardians and the legal advisers only remitted around one-eighth (or around CHF 1.4 million) of the total funds to their rightful owners. More than CHF 5.4 million remained with the asset managers, because the Registration Office had declared these sums to be beyond its jurisdiction. We now know that the Registration Office, at least in the Lindemann and Dunajewski cases, declined to provide assistance with regard to dormant accounts already registered, based on information received from legal heirs.[58] The claims of Dunajewski's heirs were not satisfied until 1997. These (and other) problems associated with the Registration Decree of 1962, however, were concealed from the public until the end of 1996.

The incomplete information provided by the Federal Council in 1974 had its intended effect. In general, people had the impression that the matter of Nazi victims' assets had been settled. Interestingly enough, this was borne out by the complete lack of references to the issue in 1975 during the increasingly heated debate in Switzerland about the Swiss banks, sparked off by various mishaps in the banking industry. The explosive growth of bank profits in the recession of 1975/76, the acceptance of tax-avoidance flight capital from France and Italy in 1977/78 (the 'Chiasso scandal'), the failure to provide legal assistance in cases of flight capital from the Third World, and the debt crisis of 1981/82 as well as violations of US laws against insider trading in the same years, led to serious foreign policy problems and the launching of the Socialist Party's initiative for tighter controls on the banks in 1978. But not even the harshest critics of the Swiss banks revived the dormant accounts issue. On the contrary, they also incorporated into their own arguments the historical legend that Swiss banking secrecy was introduced in 1934 to shield Jewish accounts from Nazi agents.[59] In the interim it appears to have been proven that attempts by France and Germany to ferret out flight capital lodged in Swiss banks to escape tax and currency problems was behind the move to reinforce banking secrecy with penal sanctions, rather than a desire to protect Jewish property.[60] In the 1970s, during the emotional debate over banking secrecy, it was only the legal experts who retroactively investigated the question of whether or not this secrecy had been impaired by the 1962 Registration Decree.[61]

One of the few who did not give up the search for Nazi victims' funds, even in the 1980s, was Akiva Levinsky, a Swiss emigrant to Israel and former treasurer of the Jewish Agency. He guessed that these funds still had to amount to several dozens of millions of francs at Swiss banks. Neither the international media nor the Swiss Federation of Jewish Communities were interested in Levinsky's hypothesis.[62] In 1989 he contacted the attorney and former National Councillor from Basle, Andreas Gerwig (SP), and gave him and his partner, Stephan Klingenberg, the assignment to research the question of Nazi victims' assets in Swiss banks. The 12 dossiers maintained by Gerwig up to 1994 were closed without showing any results, however. In 1989, Gerwig also turned to the chairman of the Federal Banking Commission, Hermann Bodenmann, and in 1991 the former Federal Councillor, Kurt Furgler. The latter suggested talking to the head of the Federal Department of Justice and Police, Arnold Koller, and convincing him of the need for a new registration decree. On 27 April 1992, Gerwig wrote to Koller that 'for obvious reasons it was impossible for people behind the "Iron Curtain" to submit their claims to Switzerland. In addition, the authorities exercised reserve in locating possible beneficiaries residing behind the "Iron Curtain".' Koller answered on 29 June 1992: 'We have examined your proposal for a federal decree to enable these persons to assert any eventual claims as well, and came to the conclusion that legal measures would not achieve a solution because the assets to satisfy these claims are no longer present.'[63] Furgler and Gerwig then stopped trying.

Levinsky, together with the British newspaper the *Mail on Sunday* and the BBC, therefore commissioned Swiss historian Jacques Picard to produce the study mentioned at the beginning of this chapter. This remained under lock and key until it was discovered in the Archive for Contemporary History at the Institute for History of the Federal Institute of Technology (ETH) in Zurich by economic journalist Beat Balzli, whose summary of its contents appeared in the *SonntagsZeitung* of 5 March 1995. Balzli had already reported an actual case involving 'heirless' funds in the same paper in September 1994, quoting an expert who estimated the probable volume of such funds at roughly CHF 2.6 billion. The SBA's denial ('the heirless assets do not exist') and a parliamentary question concerning the matter by an SP member of the Council of States, Otto Piller, on 6 December 1994, had aroused Balzli's curiosity. There were no worldwide headlines, however, until a grotesque misinterpretation of a 1946 document was published in the Israeli business daily *Globes* by journalist Itamar Levin on 28 April 1995, alleging that the Swiss government had declared its willingness in 1946 to pay the contemporary equivalent of US$ 6.4 billion for the rehabilitation of Jewish victims, drawing the money from heirless funds. In the aftermath, Avraham Burg, chairman of the Jewish Agency, confirmed the central role Levin played in reviving the campaign of the World Jewish Congress to determine the assets in Switzerland emanating from Nazi victims. 'A big fat canard came along here and opened Pandora's box,' commented Shraga Elam, a journalist working in Switzerland who was the first to reveal Levin's misinterpretation.[64]

In contrast to the 1980s, there was considerable readiness around the world to go into the problem of Nazi victims' property. This sensitivity was initially less pronounced in Switzerland. Very little attention was paid to a first report by the SBA dealing with dormant accounts, on 12 September 1995, or to the appointment of the ombudsman for the banking industry, Hanspeter Häni, to act as the central contact point. On 20 December 1995, the Council of States submitted a motion by Piller to make searching easier, but by a remarkably low voting ratio of 6:4 and only in the form of a non-compulsory 'postulate'. Intensive talks were already under way at the time between the WJC and the SBA, which had identified CHF 38.7 million in dormant accounts from the war era on the basis of a new inquiry. In order to keep the search process open, both associations agreed to maintain silence. While WJC president Edgar Bronfmann parried all questions from journalists on this topic at the organisation's annual meeting in Jerusalem in January 1996, the SBA included the figures in a lengthy press release at its regular media conference on 7 February of the same year. The WJC felt that it had been tricked and decided henceforth to go to the public itself more frequently. A particularly effective contact was Senator Alfonse D'Amato of New York, who was chairman of the Senate Banking Committee and knew how to supply the increasingly fascinated media with information that was treated as sensational regardless of how much truth it may have contained.

D'Amato conducted a first hearing before his Senate committee on 23 April 1996, in which Greta Beer appeared as a witness and gave a moving description of the difficulties posed by Swiss banks when she tried to locate the account of her father, who was murdered by the Nazis. D'Amato accused the banks of deliberate concealment and heartlessness. Swiss private banker Julius Bär, a member of the SBA board, informed the hearing of a plan to entrust the clarification of all open questions to a 'committee of eminent persons'. On 2 May 1996, the SBA and the WJC agreed on a memorandum of understanding, named former chairman of the US Federal Reserve Board, Paul Volcker, to preside over the committee, and commissioned three auditing firms to search for further dormant accounts.[65]

D'Amato got even greater play in the media with a second hearing on 16 October 1996, in which he addressed the Swiss government and accused it of having used the money of murdered Polish Jews 'for compensation of Swiss citizens' in 1949 under a 'secret treaty' with Poland. Denials and retractions came thick and fast in Berne, even though the Swiss Federal Archive and the Federal Department of Foreign Affairs would have been able to get the facts internally. These serious information breakdowns led to the deployment of a 'task force' at the Department of Foreign Affairs on 25 October. The task force, under Thomas Borer, was to deal with the matter of Nazi victims' assets and on 29 October commissioned Peter Hug and Marc Perrenoud, as mentioned above, to clarify the historical background. The information breakdowns also had a sequel in the Swiss Parliament.[66]

In January 1997, based on the Hug/Perrenoud report of December 1996, the Federal Council provided the Polish and Hungarian governments with the lists of the original depositors of the funds which had been transferred to them. The Polish government immediately (and successfully) launched a search for rightful beneficiaries, while the Hungarian government initially denied that this was within its remit. For its part, the Federal Council stated on 26 February 1997 that it was prepared (without implying any legal obligation to do so) to render payment to any injured parties and to give the lists of names produced by the Registration Decree to other interested governments and organisations. Moreover, on 25 June 1997, the Federal Council authorised the Department of Foreign Affairs to receive 'further concrete indications of individual claims', to 'investigate all cases drawn to its attention' and to see that 'the persons concerned are apprised of this information in a suitable manner'. At the time of writing (August 1998), the Federal Council had not acted on the recommendation by Hug and Perrenoud to 'examine the dossiers on registered unclaimed assets of east European depositors at the Swiss Federal Archive, which have been preserved in full and are well organised, and to search for any living potential beneficiaries without delay' as far as depositors from Albania, Bulgaria, the former GDR, the former Yugoslavia, Romania, the former Soviet Union and the former Czechoslovakia were concerned, whose assets the Federal Council had expropriated.

In the interim the press has become less aware of the continued great need for clarification and action, especially in the non-bank sphere (governmental authorities, insurance companies, fiduciaries, attorneys, companies and such like), for at least three reasons. First of all, the Swiss Parliament has passed various motions telling the Federal Council to determine what procedures should apply in principle to dormant accounts.[67] Second, the banks' own internal searches for dormant accounts have gained momentum, and by the summer of 1997 had unearthed roughly another CHF 25 million on top of the CHF 38.7 million identified in the original phase of these searches;[68] and on 23 July 1997 the SBA published a first list of 1,872 names for 1,756 dormant accounts belonging to foreign depositors. Third, the Federal Council, on 19 December 1996, had appointed the Independent Commission of Experts under Professor Jean-François Bergier to clarify a long list of questions going far beyond the original problem of dormant accounts. The commission stemmed from a parliamentary initiative for the recording and restitution of 'heirless' assets, introduced by National Councillor Verena Grendelmeier (Zurich, Independents) on 24 March 1995. The proposal led to the passing of the greatly expanded federal decree of 13 December 1996 for the historical and legal investigation of the fate of assets that found their way to Switzerland as a result of the Nazi regime.[69]

The investigation will have to explore 12 'black holes', of which the administration was aware, that swallowed up assets of victims of the Shoah and the war and possibly violated individual entitlements. The questions include:

1. What became of the roughly CHF 5.4 million reported by asset managers to the *Meldestelle* (Registration Office), which was set up for assets of missing foreigners under the Registration Decree of 1962 and was initially located in the Federal Justice Division? These assets remained with the asset managers, but nothing more was done on these cases. In particular, what happened to dormant assets that remained in the non-bank sector (insurance companies, fiduciaries, firms, government agencies and officials) and were not investigated by the Volcker Committee? In general, what is the situation with regard to searches for unclaimed assets in the non-bank sector?

What was the fate of the dormant assets that the federal administration learned of in the context of the freezing, registration and liquidation of German assets between 1945 and 1960 (questions 2–9)?

2. What became of the unclaimed balances included in the assets that were blocked under the federal decree of 16 February 1945, but were later released again successively because they did not belong to 'Germans in Germany' (totalling CHF 521.8 million)?[70]
3. Where did the 114 deposits totalling CHF 1.8 million end up, which were liquidated by the Swiss Central Clearing Office under the so-

called settlement agreements of 26 and 28 August 1952 with the Federal Republic of Germany and the governments of the three Western Allies? The equivalent in deutschmarks was remitted to the German government for compensation of German claimants, but the owners of the accounts concerned were never found.[71]

4. What happened to the CHF 29,848,405 in the 'tax-free' German assets category which were unblocked and which, according to Minister Walter Stucki, included 'thousands' of individual savings 'that had not been claimed by their owners, whose whereabouts were unknown'?[72]

5. What became of the other 'special cases' classified under 'non-contributory released assets' which amounted to more than CHF 53 million and belonged to individuals in Germany, including stateless persons, dual nationals, formerly Swiss women who became German by marriage, 'ethnic Germans', Saarlanders, Busingers and Jestetters as well as victims of racist, political and religious persecution?[73]

6. What happened to the dissolved accounts belonging to citizens of the GDR, to whom compensation could not be paid because, according to Stucki, 'communications with East Germany were not opportune' and who included an undetermined number of cases where 'the creditors no longer existed or their whereabouts were unknown'.[74]

7. Who profited from the CHF 30 million remaining in the FRG government's 'settlement account' at the Swiss National Bank after the Federal Council, on 19 September 1960, revoked the decrees to block the assets, and which had been paid in to cover compensation for German assets but were never claimed?[75]

8. Did the Federal Finance Administration ever pay back the CHF 16,082 owed to six people in Germany, which remained on the 'Blocked Payments/Germany' account of the Swiss Clearing Office at the Swiss National Bank and whose owners at the time could not be found?[76]

9. What did the asset managers do with the 87 cases of unclaimed funds amounting to some CHF 4 million, which were frozen in the accounts of Swiss asset managers following the 1945 blocking decree and which could not be liquidated or otherwise released under the Settlement Decree of 1952 because too little was known of their owners?[77]

10. What became of the thousands of savings passbooks which the banks terminated by notice after the owners had not been heard from in years, in some cases adding the funds to their own reserves, in others transferring the sums to aid organisations (for example,

the Winkelried foundation),[78] and which were not included under the heading of dormant accounts in the banks' first search operation in 1965/66?[79]

11. What are we to make of Walter Stucki's 1957 remark 'that very substantial assets can be found in the coffres-forts (safe deposit boxes) of banks in Western Switzerland – put there by French citizens shortly before the last war' who never contacted the banks again?[80] (Stucki spoke of 'hundreds of millions of francs'.[81])

12. Did the Swiss Confederation ever give back the contents of the refugee custody accounts (amounting to roughly CHF 20,000), which it commingled with the funds 'in the vaults of the Federal Cash Office' to save the custody fees demanded by Swiss Volksbank?[82] These funds resulted from the requirement, introduced in 1943, that refugees had to deposit the funds they held in Switzerland, or received from abroad or from within Switzerland, as security to cover the costs of their own internment.

The following four questions, also still open, are of general historical interest:

1. How should the behaviour of the Swiss authorities, asset managers, Jewish organisations and media be rated by international standards?

2. What motives and decision processes lay behind this behaviour? How should we rate the procedures applied at the 'micro' level, especially by the individual financial institutions? What role was played by latent anti-Semitism?

3. Was the Registration Office's assumption that people living in eastern Europe could be endangered by research activities correct for the entire period the Registration Decree was in force, from 1963 to 1973, for all east European states including Yugoslavia and Albania? In view of the 1973 agreements with Hungary and Poland on free currency convertibility, was the decision justified in 1975 to make money available to both governments out of the 'heirless accounts' fund, but not to provide them with the names of the original Hungarian and Polish depositors?

4. What is the situation with regard to the (dormant and other) assets of the perpetrators?

NOTES

1 Jacques Picard, 'Die Vermögen rassisch, religiös und politisch Verfolgter in der Schweiz und ihre Ablösung von 1946 bis 1973', Berne, 1993 (manuscript initially not intended for publication, also translated into English). Revised and expanded version in Swiss Federal Archive 'Die Schweiz und die Flüchtlinge

1933–1945' (Switzerland and the Refugees, 1933–1945), *Studien und Quellen*, Vol. 22, Berne, 1996, pp. 233–69.

2 Peter Hug and Marc Perrenoud, *In der Schweiz liegende Vermögenswerte von Nazi-Opfern und Entschädigungsabkommen mit Oststaaten* (Assets in Switzerland of Victims of Nazism and the Compensation Agreements with East European Countries), a historical clarification prepared for the Swiss Confederation, Berne, Swiss Federal Archive 1997 (Dossier 4) (available as a manuscript in English translation from the Swiss Department for Foreign Affairs). This was preceded by surveys in the Swiss press, including Georg Kreis, 'Debatte um Holocaust-Gelder in Raten. Fehlende historische Rechenschaftsberichte' (Debate on Holocaust funds in instalments: historical rendering of accounts is lacking), *Neue Zürcher Zeitung* (NZZ), 28 May 1996; Peter Hug, 'Verhandlungs-poker um nachrichtenlose Vermögen. Schweizerisch-polnischer Briefwechsel kein Einzelfall' (Playing poker with dormant accounts at the negotiating table: Swiss–Polish exchange of letters not an isolated case), *NZZ*, 23 October 1996.

3 Linus von Castelmur, *Schweizerisch-alliierte Finanzbeziehungen im Übergang vom Zweiten Weltkrieg zum Kalten Krieg. Die deutschen Guthaben in der Schweiz zwischen Zwangsliquidierung und Freigabe (1945–1952)* (Swiss–Allied Financial Relations in the Transition from the Second World War to the Cold War: The German Assets in Switzerland between Forced Liquidation and Release), Zurich, 1992, pp. 94 and 375.

4 Beat Balzli, *Treuhänder des Reichs. Die Schweiz und die verschwundenen Vermögen der Nazi-Opfer: Eine Spurensuche* (Trustee to the Reich. Switzerland and the Vanished Assets of the Nazi Victims: Looking for Clues), Zurich, 1997, esp. pp. 299–331; Tom Bower, *Das Gold der Juden. Die Schweiz und die verschwundenen Nazi-Milliarden* (The Gold of the Jews: Switzerland and the Vanished Nazi Billions), Munich, 1997; Isabel Vincent, *Das Gold der verfolgten Juden. Wie es in den Schweizer Tresoren verschwand und zur Beute der Banken und Alliierten wurde* (The Gold of the Persecuted Jews: How it Disappeared into the Swiss Vaults and Became the Booty of the Banks and the Allies), Munich/Zurich, 1997; Sebastian Speich, Fred David, Shraga Elam and Anton Ladner, *Die Schweiz am Pranger. Banken, Bosse und die Nazis* (Switzerland in the Pillory: Banks, Bosses and the Nazis), Vienna, 1997, esp. pp. 229–47.

5 For the demands of the Jewish organisations, the diplomatic manoeuvring, the resistance put up by the Swiss Bankers' Association, the Association of Swiss Life Insurers and the Association of Swiss Notaries, as well as the snail's pace of the legislative process in Switzerland and the handling of the so-called Registration Decree of 1962, please refer to the report by Peter Hug and Marc Perrenoud (see note 2 above).

6 Resolution on the question of restitution, point 13, in World Jewish Congress, War Emergency Conference, Atlantic City, NJ, 16–30 November 1944: 'Decisions and Resolutions', Geneva, 1944, p. 23. The WJC was founded in Geneva in 1936. Its second plenary assembly took place in 1948 in Montreux and its third in 1953 in Geneva.

7 Sydney Gruson, 'Germans' Assets to go to victims. $25,000,000 loan on property held by neutrals to aid in resettlement', *New York Times*, 25 June 1946. This resolution is also discussed in two Zurich studies: Karl-Gerhard Seeliger, *Das ausländische Privateigentum in der Schweiz. Rechtsstellung und Rechtsschutz gegenüber dem angelsächsischen und deutschen Kriegsrecht des 2. Weltkrieges* (Foreign Private Property in Switzerland: Legal Position and Protection of Legal Status against Anglo-Saxon and German Martial Law of the Second World War),

Munich, 1949, pp. 203–5; Hans Leuzinger, *Die deutschen Vermögenswerte in der Schweiz und ihre statistische Erfassung auf Grund des Abkommens von Washington vom 25. 5. 1946 und des Ablösungsabkommens vom 26. 8. 1952* (The German Assets in Switzerland and their Statistical Recording Based on the Washington Agreement of 25 May 1946 and the Settlement Agreement of 26 August 1952), Winterthur, 1960, pp. 14ff.

8 On the consequences of the reparations conference for Switzerland, compare the publicly accessible 1946 annual report of the Swiss Federation of Jewish Communities: *SIG-Jahresbericht* 1946, p. 11. All subsequent *SIG-Jahresberichte* give detailed information on efforts to introduce mandatory reporting of Nazi victims' dormant accounts in Switzerland, including those of: 1947, pp. 11ff.; 1948, pp. 21ff.; 1949, pp. 23ff.; 1950, p. 23; 1951, pp. 20ff.; 1952, pp. 12ff. and 22; 1953, p. 22; 1954, p. 22; 1955, p. 18; 1956, p. 19; 1957, p. 19; 1958, p. 17; 1959, p. 21; 1960, p. 8; 1961, p. 3; 1962, pp. 2ff.; 1963, p. 2; 1964, p. 2; 1965, pp. 3ff.; 1966, pp. 4ff.; 1968, p. 5; 1969, p. 5; 1970, p. 5; 1971, p. 6; 1972, p. 7; 1974, p. 7; 1975, p. 7.

9 The leader of the Polish delegation to the leader of the Swiss delegation (Max Troendle), 25 June 1949, Federal Archive, K I. 1506, Vol. 1.

10 Swiss Federal Archive (FA), E 2801/1968/84/32.

11 See Federal Political Department (FPD), Commission for Nationalisation Compensation (Heinz Vischer), memo to Federal Councillor Max Petitpierre, 3 August 1949, FA, E 2001 (E) 1967/113/374 (B.42.13).

12 FPD (Max Petitpierre), telegram to Swiss embassy in Paris, 15 September 1949, FA, E 2001 (E) 1967/113/374 (B.42.13); Tom Bower (cited in note 4), p. 254.

13 FPD, memo for files (D. Robert), 15 October 1949, FA, E 2001 (E) 1967/113/374 (B.42.13).

14 FPD, memo for files (Max Petitpierre), 4 November 1949, FA, E 2001 (E) 1967/113/374 (B.42.13).

15 Michael L. Hoffmann, 'Swiss will turn over to Warsaw property of heirless Polish Jews. Agreement for transfer of funds left by war victims brings strong protests that assets should go to refugee body', *New York Times*, 7 December 1949; also published in Canadian the *Globe and Mail*, 7 December 1949, among other newspapers.

16 Swiss legation in Washington (Karl Bruggmann) to FPD, Politische Angelegenheiten (political matters), 9 December 1949, FA, E 2001 (E) 1967/113/374 (B.42.13).

17 Title of an article in *Haaretz*, the newspaper of Israel's liberal progressive party, 18 December 1949. According to a statement by the FPD press service, the article was written by Arthur Cohn, a student living in Basle.

18 'Object to Swiss transfer of heirless Jewish funds to Poland', *Canadian Jewish Review*, Montreal, 16 December 1949.

19 Protest notes from International Refugee Organisation (Director-General J. Donald Kingsley), 20 December 1949; French embassy in Berne, 20 December 1949; US legation in Berne, 20 December 1949; His Britannic Majesty's legation in Berne, 22 December 1949; Ministry for Foreign Affairs, Tel Aviv, 30 December 1949, FA, E 2001 (E) 1967/113/374 (B.42.13).

20 On 23/24 November 1949 in the National Council committee for customs questions and the Council of States committee for external affairs.

21 An extract of the typewritten version of the stenographic bulletin can be found in FA, E 2001 (E) 1967/113/374 (B.42.13). Until 1971, Swiss Parliamentary debates were only published by special resolution.

22 *Vereinigung für Wirtschaftsgesetzgebung* (Association for economic legislation), 'Eine krasse Rechtsverletzung in einer Geheimklausel zum Polen-Abkommen'

(A crass violation of the law in a secret clause to the Poland agreement), *Badener Tagblatt*, 23, 28 January 1950.

23 'Unhaltbare Rechtslage' ('Untenable legal situation'), *Finanz und Wirtschaft*, 4, 13 January 1950.

24 Letter from P. E., Wil (St Gallen), 'Müssen wir uns das gefallen lassen?', *National-Zeitung*, 14, 10 January 1950.

25 'Bedenkliche Geheimklauseln', *Berner Tagblatt*, 11, 12 January 1950.

26 FPD press release, 1 February 1950, FA, E 2001 (E) 1967/113/374 (B.42.13).

27 *Der Bund*, Berne, 56, 3 February 1950.

28 *Anzeiger von Uster*, 27, 2 February 1950.

29 *Glarner Nachrichten*, 27, 2 February 1950. Some papers seriously thought the Federal Department of Economic Affairs was behind it all.

30 *St Galler Tagblatt*, 56, 2 February 1950.

31 *National-Zeitung*, 67, 9 February 1950.

32 As in the *Tages-Anzeiger*, 29, 3 March 1950; the *Rorschacher Zeitung*, 29, 3 February 1950 carried the headline, 'Eine Erklärung, die nicht überzeugt' (An explanation that doesn't convince); the *Badener Tagblatt* of 4 February 1950 referred to a 'Misslungener Rechtfertigungsversuch' ('Attempted justification misfires').

33 In *Der Landschäftler* of Liestal, 29, 3 February 1950 and *Der Landbote* of Winterthur, 28, 3 February 1950.

34 Appearing in the *Solothurner Zeitung*, 3 March 1950 and the *Schaffhauser Nachrichten*, 53, 4 February 1950, among other newspapers.

35 Professor Wolfhart F. Bürgi, 'Um die Verfassungsmässigkeit des schweizerisch-polnischen Abkommens' (On the constitutionality of the Swiss–Polish agreement), *NZZ*, 460, 6 March 1950, p. 7.

36 'Fragwürdige Geheimabkommen' (Dubious secret treaties), *NZZ*, 469, 7 March 1950, p. 7 ('another missive from the business world'). The Federal Council held the opinion that the Swiss–Polish exchange of letters did not affect the relationship of depositors and asset managers under private law.

37 The manuscript can be found in FA, E 2001 (E) 1967/113/374 (B.42.13). Also see the terse report on the session in the *NZZ*, 606, 23 March 1950, p. 5.

38 Paul Guggenheim, 'Die nicht-veröffentlichungspflichtigen Verträge nach. Völkerrecht und schweizerischem Bundesstaatsrecht', *Staat und Wirtschaft, Beiträge zum Problem der Einwirkung des Staates auf die Wirtschaft, Festgabe zum 70. Geburtstag von Hans Nawiasky*, Einsiedeln/Zurich/Cologne, Benziger, 1950, pp. 91–107; on the arrangements for the Polish heirless funds, pp. 98–100.

39 Meeting of the Federal Council, 28 July 1950, extracts of the minutes, FA, E 7110 1976/16/62.

40 Message of the Federal Council to the Federal Assembly (both houses of Parliament) on the treaty concluded between the Swiss Confederation and the People's Republic of Hungary concerning trade, payments and compensation for Swiss interests in Hungary, 31 October 1960, *Bundesblatt* (*Bbl.*), or 'Federal Gazette', 3, 1950, pp. 263–91, in this case pp. 283ff.

41 Title of a piece by Professor Werner Kägi, *Basler Nachrichten*, 368, 30 August 1950; Professor W. Niederer had a similar tone in 'Ein fragwürdiger Staatsvertrag' (A dubious treaty), *NZZ*, 1883, 10 September 1950. Compare the rebuttal of FPD legal adviser Professor Rudolf Bindschedler, 'Das schweizerisch-ungarische Entschädigungsabkommen und die Rechtsstellung der Ausländer' (The Swiss–Hungarian Compensation Agreement and the Legal Position of Foreigners), *Schweizerische Juristen-Zeitung*, 19, 1950, pp. 285–7.

42 See, for example, the AP report in the *New York Herald Tribune* of 4 February 1952.

43 See, for example, 'Um die erbenlosen Vermögen in der Schweiz. Schweizerische Bankiervereinigung gegen Anmeldepflicht' (Heirless assets in Switzerland: Swiss Bankers Association against reporting requirement), *Volksrecht*, Zurich, 239, 10 October 1952.

44 SBA, *Jahresbericht* 1951/52, pp. 52ff.; 1952/53, p. 55; 1953/54, p. 54; 1954/55, pp. 49ff.; 1957/58, p. 57; 1958/59, pp. 61–3; 1962/63, pp. 66–8; 1963/64, pp. 93ff.; 1964/65, pp. 91ff.; 1965/66, p. 98.

45 Ibid., 1958/59, p. 63.

46 'Um die erbenlosen Vermögen in der Schweiz', *Das Neue Israel*, 11, May 1954; 'Die Bankguthaben jüdischer Naziopfer in der Schweiz' (Bank deposits of Jewish Nazi victims in Switzerland), *Jüdische Rundschau Maccabi*, 44, 5 November 1954, citing a report in *Neue Welt*, Vienna; Siegfried Rosenzweig, 'Ist auch die Schweiz Erbin der Juden?' (Is Switzerland also an heir of the Jews?), *Unser Ziel*, Tel Aviv, 30 November 1954.

47 Paul Guggenheim, 'Die erblosen Vermögen in der Schweiz und das Völkerrecht', in *Festschrift zum 50-jährigen Bestehen des Schweizerischen Israelitischen Gemeindebundes* (The Heirless Assets in Switzerland and International Law, in a Commemorative Volume Marking the 50th Year of the Swiss Federation of Jewish Communities), Zurich, 1954, pp. 108–20.

48 FPD General Secretary (Robert Kohli) to National Councillor Alois Grendelmeier, 14 April 1961, FA, E 2800 1967/59/40.

49 Agency report from London, 6 June 1961, FA, E 2001 (E) 1976/17/97 (B.42.13). See 'Englische Pressestimme zum Problem der jüdischen Bankdepots in der Schweiz' (British press on problem of Jewish bank accounts in Switzerland), *St Galler Tagblatt*, evening edn 262, 7 June 1961, p. 3.

50 Swiss embassy in Belgium (Ludwig Meier) to the FPD, Politische Angelegenheiten (political matters), 7 June 1961, FA, E 2001 (E) 1976/17/97 (B.42.13/1).

51 Message on draft federal decree concerning assets in Switzerland of foreigners or stateless persons persecuted for reasons of race, religion or politics, 4 May 1962, *Bbl.*, 1, 1962, pp. 933–44/49; Message of 16 September 1974 on the application of assets in Switzerland of foreigners or stateless persons persecuted for reasons of race, religion or politics, *Bbl.*, 2, 1974, pp. 801–06/07. I shall refrain from citing the often critical media reactions.

52 FPD Legal Services (Diez) to Justice Division, 28 August 1970, FA, E 2001 (E) 1982/58/84 (B.42.13).

53 Federal Council session of 20 August and 27 August 1965, extracts from the minutes, FA E 2001 (E) 1978/84/144 (B.42.13./3.).

54 Swiss Federal Council, presidential decree (Nello Celio), 8 March 1972, FA, E 4001 (E) 1988/20/373 (64).

55 Federal Department of Justice and Police (Ludwig von Moos) to the director of the Federal Justice Division (J. M. Grossen), 18 January 1971, FA, E 4001 (D) 1976/136/115 (64). Emphasis in the original.

56 On the case of Hilde Sorkin/Walter Loevy, see Jürg Schoch, 'Nachrichtenlose Vermögen: Der Eiserne Vorhang als Vorwand. Die Anspruchsberechtigte lebte gar nicht in Polen, sondern in London' (The Iron Curtain as pretext: the beneficiary lived in London, not Poland), *Tages-Anzeiger*, Zurich, 18 February 1997; on the case of the heirs of Simon Docteur residing in Israel, see Markus Haefliger, 'Jüdische Vermögen. Wer sucht, der findet' (Jewish assets: Seek and ye shall find), facts, Zurich, 26, 26 June 1997, pp. 18–25.

57 *Amtliches Bulletin*, National Council, 1974, p. 1,820.

58 Peter Hug, 'Das Verschwindenmachen der nachrichtenlosen Guthaben in der

Schweiz' (Making dormant balances disappear in Switzerland), in Regina Wecker and Philipp Sarasin (eds), *Raubgold, Réduit, Flüchtlinge*, Zurich, Chronos, 1998, pp. 13–43.

59   There is not a word about Nazi victims' assets in *Die Schweiz über jeden Verdacht erhaben* (Switzerland: The Awful Truth), by Jean Ziegler, 3rd expanded edn, Darmstadt, 1980 (1st edn 1976); 'Die Banken im Blickfeld der Kritik' (The banks targeted for criticism) by Franco Masoni (a lawyer), in *Die Banken im Spannungsfeld wirtschaftlicher Veränderungen* (The Banks in the Force Field of Economic Change) by Adriano Passardi, Berne, 1975, ed. Paul Haupt, pp. 63–80; articles criticising the banks in the socialist *Zeitdienst*, 18, 6 May 1977, pp. 149–51, 20, 20 May 1977, pp. 168ff., 10, 10 March 1978, pp. 76ff., 21, 26 March 1978, pp. 177ff.; 'Materialien zur Bankeninitiative' (Documentation for the bank initiative) by Jakob Tanner, in *Infrarot*, 32, January/February 1978, pp. 4–8 or the contribution by Felix Müller and Andy Gross in 34, June/July 1978, pp. 3–7; 'Banken-Misstände drängen zur Tat. Hintergrundüberlegungen zur Banken-Initiative der SPS' (Banking abuses come to light; points to ponder for the SPS bank initiative) by Rudolf H. Strahm; 'Bankeninitiative – Anstoss zur Überwindung eines wirtschaftspolitischen Notstandes' (Bank initiative – approach to overcoming an economic policy emergency) by Andy Gross; 'Zittern die Gnomen' (Are the gnomes trembling) by Wilhelm Kriescher in *Profil*, 57, 1978, pp. 135–9, 140–44, 145–8; *Bildungsdossier Banken* (Educational Dossier on the Banks) by Rudolf H. Strahm, Berne, 1978; *Zum Streit um das Bankgeheimnis in der Schweiz* (On the dispute over banking secrecy in Switzerland) by Willy Maurer, Basle, 1981; *Schweizer Banken und Sozialethik* (Swiss Banks and Social Ethics) by Hans-Balz Peter, Hans Ruh and Roland Höhn, Berne/Lausanne, 1981 (Studien und Berichte aus dem Institut für Sozialethik, Vol. 31 and Vol. 32); *Les banques suisses en question* (The Swiss Banks in Question) by Claude Torracinta, Lausanne, 1981. Inaccurate interpretation of banking secrecy as being for the benefit of Jews in *Bildungsdossier* by Strahm, op. cit., pp. 8ff., 114; Maurer, op. cit., pp. 10ff.; Torracinta, op. cit., p. 38.

60   Hugo Bänziger, *Die Entwicklung der Bankenaufsicht in der Schweiz seit dem 19. Jahrhundert* (Development of Bank Supervision in Switzerland since the Nineteenth Century), Berne/Stuttgart, 1986, pp. 114–18; Sébastien Guex, 'La Suisse et le secret bancaire', *Le messager suisse. La revue des communautés suisses de langue française*, Paris, January 1996, pp. 14–15, February 1996, pp. 14–15; idem, 'Secret bancaire et développement de la place financière suisse: Suisse secret', *Page 2. Mensuel du différend*, Lausanne, 11, 1997, pp. 33–6. See now Peter Hug, 'Steuerflucht und die Legende vom antinazistischen Ursprung des Bankgeheimnisses. Funktion und Risiko der moralischen Überhöhung des Finanzplatzes Schweiz' (Tax-avoidance flight capital and the legend of antinazism origin of banking secrecy. Function and risk of a moral super-elevation), in Jakob Tanner (ed.), *Gedächtnis, Geld und Gesetz, Vom Umgang mit der Vergangenheit des Zweiten Weltkrieges*, Zurich, 1999.

61   Maurice Aubert criticised the Registration Decree: *Das schweizerische Bankgeheimnis*, Berne, 1978, pp. 180–3 (original edn: *Le secret bancaire suisse*, Berne, 1976).

62   Shraga Elam, 'Am Anfang stand eine Ente. Eine schludrige Medienarbeit löste den Sturm aus, der über die Schweiz braust' (In the beginning was a canard; sloppy journalism set off the storm now buffeting Switzerland), in Sebastian Speich, *et al.* (see note 4 above), pp. 231–7.

63   Johannes Wartenweiler, 'Nachrichtenlose Vermögen. Koller torpedierte Lösung'

(Dormant accounts: Koller torpedoes a solution), *Wochen-Zeitung*, Zurich, 26, 27 June 1997.

64 Shraga Elam (as in note 62), p. 237.

65 See Tom Bower (op. cit. note 4), pp. 353–92, for a description of the interaction between SBA and WJC, although the details are not always exact.

66 See Parlamentarische Verwaltungskontrolle, *Die Informationstätigkeit von Bundesrat und Bundesverwaltung betreffend das Entschädigungsabkommen zwischen der Schweiz und Polen von 1949* (October 1949), report for the attention of the National Council's Control Committee, 3 March 1997. More generally, see 'Schatten des Zweiten Weltkrieges. Nazigold und Shoa-Gelder – Opfer als Ankläger' (Shadows of the Second World War; Nazi gold and Shoah money – victims as plaintiffs), *NZZ-Fokus*, Zurich, 2, February 1997.

67 On the need to devise an arrangement, see Daniel Girsberger, *Das internationale Privatrecht der nachrichtenlosen Vermögen in der Schweiz* (International private law as applied to dormant accounts in Switzerland), Zurich, 26 May 1997 (expanded MS of an inaugural lecture); Nicolas Poncet, 'Swiss Banks' Handling of Dormant Accounts Since the End of World War II', *International Business Lawyer*, 25, 1997, pp. 68–72; Hans Ulrich Walder, 'Rechtliches zur Frage der nachrichtenlosen Vermögenswerte auf Schweizer Banken' (Legal aspects of the question of dormant accounts in Swiss banks), *Schweizerische Juristen-Zeitung*, 93, 1997, pp. 131–5.

68 On the juggling of the figures, see the *SonntagsZeitung* of 27 July 1997, pp. 49ff.

69 See the draft federal decree by the National Council's Commission for Legal Affairs (Kommission für Rechtsfragen), 'Entwurf Bundesbeschluss betreffend die historische und rechtliche Untersuchung des Schicksals der infolge der nationalsozialistischen Herrschaft in die Schweiz gelangten Vermögenswerte', 26 August 1996, *Bbl.*, 4, 1996, p. 1,181. Important impetus for the expansion of the mandate came from a paper, the content of which was inaccurate, by Labour MP and WJC Vice-President Greville Janner on the question of looted gold, which led to a British foreign ministry memorandum and a debate in the lower house on the gold policy of the Swiss National Bank on 10 September 1996.

70 See report of the Federal Council on German assets in Switzerland 1945–58, 22 August 1958, *Bbl.*, 2, 1958, p. 629.

71 Minister Walter Stucki to FPD legal counsellor Rudolf Bindschedler, 17 May 1957, FA, E 2801 1968/84/98 (W. 45).

72 Ibid.

73 Report of the Federal Council (as in note 70), p. 639.

74 Minister Walter Stucki (as in note 71).

75 FPD, Legal Service (Henri Zoelly), memo to Max Petitpierre, head of FPD, 16 November 1960, FA, E 2001 (E) 1972/33/280 (B.42.13/3).

76 Federal Finance Administration (Bernhard Müller) to the Federal Justice Division, 2 March 1964, FA, E 4111 (A) 1980/13/27 (1600).

77 Federal decree on German assets in Switzerland, 19 September 1960, FA, E 2001 (E) 1972/33/280 (B.42.13/3).

78 SBA representative Max Oetterli according to a memo on the talks with the FDJP, the FPD and the SBA, 11 December 1961, FA, E 2001 (E) 1976/17/97 (B.42.13).

79 See the blanket giving of notice on 77 inactive savings passbooks by the Amtsersparniskasse Obersimmental in *Amtsblatt des Kantons Berne*, 33, 30 April 1935, pp. 519ff.; on hundreds of savings books in the *Feuille des avis officiels du canton de Vaud*, Lausanne, 29 January 1960, pp. 164–86; '"Wir haben die Gelder

verschenkt". Die Zürcher Kantonalbank hat nachrichtenlose Vermögen gemeinnützigen Organisationen überwiesen' ('We gave the money away.' The cantonal bank of Zurich transferred funds from dormant accounts to non-profit organisations), interview with Paul Hasenfratz, *Tages-Anzeiger*, Zurich, 28 July 1997; for the publication policy of the Cantonal Bank of Berne, 1938–43 and the Hypothekarkasse von Berne up to 1950, see *Der Bund*, Berne, 10 July 1997.

80 Minister Walter Stucki to FPD legal counsellor Rudolf Bindschedler, 27 May 1957, FA, E 2001 (E) 1972/33/280 (B.42.13).

81 FDJP, memo for files, 22 May 1959, FA, E 4110 (A) 1973/85/2 (XV).

82 Federal Police Division (Tschäppät) to Swiss Volksbank, securities department, Berne, 11 October 1955, FA, E 4260 (C) 1974/34/86 (N.40.5.30).

5

Swiss Refugee Policy, 1933–45

GEORG KREIS

The current debate about the part played by Switzerland in the Second World War focuses on two problem areas: the 'vanished dormant accounts' that had been brought to Switzerland by victims of the National Socialist policy of extermination, and Switzerland's economic cooperation with the Axis powers. At an early stage, however, the controversy also extended to include refugee policy. Why was this? There are two points of contact between the subjects mentioned initially and this additional one. The first is whether the compensation payments should also include the repayment of sums contributed by the Swiss and international Jewish communities to support Jewish refugees in Switzerland during the war. The second is the extent to which Switzerland, on the borders of the dominion of the criminal regime, unilaterally decided its own fate, as it were, to become a welcoming refuge for money and gold but not for human beings. The first part of this chapter will show that the basic facts of Swiss refugee policy in those years have been known to some extent for 30 or 40 years now and can be found in the freely accessible publications. That, however, is not to say that the present controversy is unnecessary, or that all the questions involved have long since been answered, or even known.

THE HISTORY OF THE PROBLEM

By comparison with the attention focused on it today, refugee policy attracted amazingly little interest in the early post-war years. Reports, which were made public and indeed were the subject of public debate, dealt with the organisation of the war economy, the military defence of the country and even press policy and the suppression of anti-democratic activities. Yet, apparently, no such reports were considered necessary on either the executive or legislative aspects of refugee policy. That is not to say that no lessons at all were learned from the experience of refugee policy. The introduction of permanent asylum and the federal contributions to refugee welfare in March 1947 symbolise the country's readiness to make good the shortcomings that had been shown to exist in the basic machinery of its refugee policy. Indeed, over the years some kind of accounting for refugee policy in the war years was actually produced by the Federal Justice and Police Department, while the Federal Council decided in 1951 not to publish it so as not to stir up, once again, an issue 'which can now probably be regarded as largely a closed chapter'.[1]

In general, however, the prevalent opinion after 1945 was that the country had little for which to reproach itself with regard to asylum. In the light of what we know today, the following opinion published in the St Maurice *Nouvelliste Valaisan* in the summer of 1945 is fairly representative: 'in the midst of the war', says the writer complacently, 'when the Jews were being persecuted everywhere and would not even have been given a rock on which to lay their heads, Switzerland's dealings with them demonstrated its respect for mankind'.[2] One exception was probably the *Beobachter*, which published a deeply critical report on refugee policy as early as March 1945 and, in its second 1946 issue, called for a 'White Paper' on the refugee question. Unlike the majority, who wanted to send as many immigrants as possible out of the country as fast as possible, the paper regretted, in an article published in late March 1946, that only some 2 per cent wanted to remain in Switzerland; this, it said, was 'a devastating verdict on our policy for dealing with emigrants'.[3]

The first historiographic work came, with remarkable speed, from the cinema in the shape of the film *The Last Chance*, produced in 1944/45 by Lazar Wechsler and Leopold Lindtberg (both with experience of emigration). The film is still worth watching today.[4] Otherwise, no one in the early post-war period seemed to feel any urgent need to produce an overall account of refugee policy during the preceding years. The first historical accounts were not compiled until 1954, when the documents from German archives, critical of Switzerland, were published.

Once it became known that the suggestion that the passports of Jewish citizens from Germany and Austria should be specially marked with a red 'J' stamp had come from Switzerland in 1938, and following a parliamentary question on the matter, the Federal Council commissioned Carl Ludwig (born 1889), a former government councillor and professor of law at Basle, to produce a comprehensive report on Swiss refugee policy for the Federal Assembly.[5] Ludwig completed his report within a year, although it did not appear until two years later, in the autumn of 1957, so that those primarily responsible for the former refugee policy, Federal Councillor Eduard von Steiger and Head of Federal Police, Heinrich Rothmund, could comment on it. The government wanted to formulate new principles governing its approach to asylum law in periods of heightened international tension or war.

The Ludwig report, largely based on official files, made no claim to provide complete clarification; in the author's own words, residence conditions and the commitment of the relief organisations were touched upon only marginally.[6] What the report did say, however, has stood the test of time very well. Ludwig was determined to expose the restrictive attitude of the authorities unsparingly; he deplored the fact that refugee policy was largely determined by the aliens section of the police or at least from its specific standpoint; and he also referred to the restrictive requirements of the army and the 'not very creditable attitude' of certain cantons. He had no time for the excuse that people had too little knowledge of 'what was going on over there in the Reich'. On the other hand, he did concede that those responsible had acted 'to the best of their knowledge and consciences' and that no one could have known at the time what the future might hold for the country.[7]

An initial survey of press reaction to the report shows that the material released in 1957 did not trigger any self-criticism. References to press censorship were notably frequent, as was the attitude in particular that circumstances at the time had been difficult and should not be judged from the very much simpler present-day situation. Switzerland had done a great deal for the refugees; where it had failed them, the necessary lessons must be drawn for the future. For the liberally inclined *Neue Zürcher Zeitung* (NZZ), however, the lesson lay not in the fact that fear resulted in an overestimate of the danger and hence an excessively restrictive attitude, but more in the fact that the inherently correct principle of 'generous acceptance' had to be kept within limits because of food problems and security requirements.[8] The Zurich socialist paper *Volksrecht* also advised against using the 'significantly more comfortable standpoint of 1957' simply to criticise the authorities, who had borne an enormous responsibility during the war years. After all, they had also to bear in mind the problems of food supply, the danger of epidemics, the risk of undercover activities by the refugees and German threats.[9] The mood of the January 1958 discussion by the National Council was similar. The prevalent opinion was that Switzerland, by and large, had acted correctly.[10] The fact that Switzerland had recently accepted large numbers of Hungarian refugees made it possible to cherish the deceptive illusion that a fundamental change had since taken place in the country's attitude to refugee questions.[11]

As a further consequence of wartime experience, the Federal Council did now make a declaration to the effect that granting asylum was not just a tradition but a principle of governmental policy; its task was to defend not just a territory but principles, too: 'Those principles include the one that states that persecuted people are to be granted asylum in Switzerland.'[12] This commitment, however, important as it was, was not appropriately reflected in legislation.[13] The lessons of the past had at least been sufficiently learnt for the Asylum Act of 1979–81 to extend recognition, formerly confined to political persecution, to include other valid reasons for flight, especially danger arising from one's particular religion or race.[14]

In the 1960s a second major step was taken towards a more open approach to refugee history when interest in the war years underwent a strong revival as a result of the commissioning of Edgar Bonjour's report. It was no coincidence that the Ludwig report, previously published only as an official publication, appeared in book form at this time – in 1966 – and was available from bookshops.[15] It was at this time, too, that the journalist Alfred A. Häsler, at the prompting of the head of the Ex Libris publishing house, Franz Lamprecht, wrote his best-selling book, published in 1967 and subsequently translated into several other languages, *Das Boot ist voll … (The Boat is Full …)*.[16] Häsler was concerned with describing the non-governmental aspects of refugee policy – the refugees themselves, and also the various social forces. He noted with particular sorrow that even the Swiss Society of Authors had supported the restrictive refugee policy at the time.[17] The book, which focused more on those who suffered from the policy than on those who applied it, attracted great attention from the start and subsequently retained the public interest – as did its subject. In the Basle *National-Zeitung* the book was reviewed under the heading 'Swiss refugee policy in the pillory: Those who spoke served their country.'[18]

Two years before Häsler's account appeared, the growing preoccupation with the 'unresolved past' during the 1960s had produced the novel *Die Hinterlassenschaft* by the writer Walter Matthias Diggelmann. He combined criticism of the restrictive refugee policy with a more contemporary indictment of bourgeois Switzerland, which, as a result of the highly emotional reactions to the Hungarian uprising of 1956, had opened the way to a witch-hunt directed against prominent communists. Diggelmann, whose polemical novel anticipated the revisionism of the 1970s and who had been only a child during the war, attracted criticism and rejection not only from the bourgeois he attacked but also from the older left. The socialist protector of refugees, Regina Kägi-Fuchsmann, accused him of one-sidedness, manipulation, spreading a distorted view and giving the impression that Switzerland had offered nothing but weaklings, failures and villains; in fact, she said, there had been others too and even those who bore official responsibility had not simply been unfeeling subhumans and sadists.[19]

Häsler's account said nothing about Paul Grüninger. But the

following year, 1968, saw the start of the long process – lasting nearly 30 years – of rehabilitation of the former St Gallen police captain, who had been dismissed without notice in 1938 for providing illegal assistance to refugees.[20]

The third major milestone in the handling of the refugee story – after Ludwig and Häsler – was André Lasserre's wide-ranging study, published in 1995, of the conditions in which the refugees lived in the camps and hostels.[21] The strength of this work lies in its depiction of the system developed and applied by the host country, thus broadening a perspective that had previously focused entirely on the question of admission. Their living conditions are judged critically but from a general standpoint rather than from the perspective of those concerned, and therefore without anecdotal evidence of the fates of individual refugees.

Between Häsler and Lasserre come the general accounts written by Edgar Bonjour in 1970 and Werner Rings in 1974, both of whom had contemporary experience. Bonjour actually campaigned during the war for an expansive acceptance policy,[22] while Rings came to Switzerland in 1942 as a German emigrant from France. Bonjour's discussion of the subject, within the broader framework of the history of neutrality, deals with the territory marked out by Ludwig and Häsler. He presents and endorses the arguments of reasons of state, and especially the idea that a cautious attitude was essential in order to avoid German intervention. What was achieved despite this is interpreted by Bonjour as a resistance achievement, since after all Switzerland 'under the pressure of the most extreme coercion' – though it must be objected that there is no evidence whatsoever of this – never demeaned itself by abandoning the right of asylum. On the other hand, he observes critically, 'That whole generation failed, and shares the guilt.' That Switzerland was never able to bring itself to derive from its unreserved neutrality a duty of unreserved humanity remains, he says, a 'horrible blot on its escutcheon of neutrality'.[23] The journalist Werner Rings also devotes a chapter of his 12-part television documentary (and the accompanying book) to the refugee question. He draws a rather sharper contrast than Bonjour between the restrictive attitude of the authorities and the tendency of individuals to show willingness to provide 'humane assistance in defiance of regulations'. He describes the refugee episode as a 'dark chapter', though he does conclude by pointing out that some 29,000 Jews were accepted, equivalent to the population of a medium-sized town.[24]

This marked the end of the former image as included, for example, by Fritz Schaffer in his *Abriss der Schweizer Geschichte* (15th edition, 1992) and whose innocent presentation long remained available in reference books: 'In the years before and during the war Switzerland offered asylum to political and military refugees of all nations and races (including Jews, Germans, Poles, Frenchmen and Italians).' The more recent, modified image is probably better represented by Peter Dürrenmatt's account in his 1976 Swiss history, published for the general public. Dürrenmatt provided a fairly balanced view. On the one hand, he stated that the refugee problem had become 'in some respects' a question of guilt, that the country had 'only partly' passed the test, that there had been 'failures' and that it had been a 'fatal error' to define the category of refugees who had to be rejected in similar terms to the National Socialists (meaning that the measures were criticised not in themselves but merely in the wording that justified them). On the other hand, he qualified these concessions by saying that Switzerland had not been prepared for the challenge, had had to consider the 'framework of the external situation', and reasons of state had been determined by the food supply situation and considerations of national defence and so on.[25]

In May 1979, the broadcasting of the television series on the Holocaust resulted in no new publications, but it did lead to a widespread recapitulation of Switzerland's attitude towards refugees in the last world war. Experts gave their opinions in the press and through electronic media,[26] but the general public was also provided with additional material.[27] It was at that time that Max Schmid published his documentation of anti-Semitism in Switzerland.[28] And it was then, too, in all probability that the preparations were made for the film adaptation of *Das Boot ist voll* ... by Markus Imhoof, which appeared in 1981 and won a Golden Bear at the Berlin film festival.

The US televised history of the Holocaust prompted Hansjörg Braunschweig, an SP (Socialist Party) National Councillor from Zurich, to table the question to the Federal Council in June 1979 asking whether the Council felt, in view of the most recent accounts of history and the available files, that it could still maintain the argument of 'lack of information', and whether it was prepared to make arrangements to ensure that the latest historical findings were passed on at all levels of the Swiss educational system. Braunschweig regarded coming to terms with the past as a duty of government policy, though he did emphasise – 'in order to avoid any misunderstanding' – that he was not concerned with the responsibility of individual persons in authority and 'certainly not with any moral verdict or judgement'. The question of what could have been known at the time was left unanswered by the Federal Council, which replied that it had done everything it could to prepare the ground by releasing the files but could not exert any direct influence.[29]

In later years, too, the media made an important contribution to maintaining the collective memory, and not just by paying the necessary attention to books and films on the subject and ensuring that the public knew about them. Lengthy articles also appeared for no particular reason, outside the line of duty, as it were.[30] The media also paid particular attention to major anniversary dates: several articles appeared in 1988 on the Evian conference and the introduction of the 'J' stamp 50 years earlier;[31] in 1990 the press was full of articles about the French and Polish internees accepted in 1940;[32] and 1992 marked the 50th anniversary of the closure of the frontier.[33] These recollective efforts even resulted, in 1992, in the minting of an official commemorative coin bearing an uncompromising image of barbed wire and a portrait of the wartime refugee activist Gertrud Kurz.

Since the 1970s the refugee issue has been a major topic of continuing and high-profile attention.[34] In the *Geschichte der Schweiz und der Schweizer* published in 1983, Hans-Ulrich Jost said of the refugee policy that it had been 'extremely restrictive' in the 1930s, had been 'tightened in an inhumane manner' after the outbreak of war and formed 'the darkest chapter' of the country's history during the Second World War.[35]

Recently, refugee history was certainly among the beneficiaries of the floods of reminiscence that marked the anniversaries of the beginning and end of the war in 1989 and 1995. Various articles appeared in the national press[36] and the same phenomenon was certainly responsible for the volume accompanying the exhibition 'Anne Frank and Us', which appeared in 1995. The same applies to some extent to the collection from the Federal Archive published in 1996, although the research work it contains had been begun much earlier.

In the wake of Ludwig, Häsler and Lasserre, 1994 saw another important broadening of the treatment of the refugee story with the work of Jacques Picard, in which he demonstrated the link between the attitude to refugees and the internal social conditions, particularly anti-Semitism, in Switzerland. The exposure of this problem was in a certain sense a preparation for the 1995 declaration.[37]

The anniversaries of the end of the war brought a new approach to this period of the past in that the national government, in an official apology, distanced itself – as it had often been called upon to do – from the refugee policy of the years 1933–45. In June 1994 the Federal Council, for the first time, distanced itself from the anti-Semitic attitude of its predecessors and, in its answer to a written question by the SP National Councillor Paul Rechsteiner, described the fate of the civilian refugees as a tragedy, and expressed 'its deep regret' that people had died as a result of the policy then pursued by Switzerland.[38] Eventually, in a motion tabled on 1 February 1995 and followed by a statement of grounds on 14 March 1995, heavily based on Ludwig, Häsler and Picard, the SP National Councillor Helmut Hubacher called upon the Federal Council, in the context of the impending commemoration of the end of the war, to offer the apology which it should actually have given back in 1958 on the occasion of the discussion of the Ludwig report.[39] As Federal President Kaspar Villiger stated at the special session of 7 May 1995, 'There is no doubt in my mind that our policy has brought guilt upon us. By introducing the so-called Jewish stamp, Germany was complying with a request made by Switzerland. At that time, in an excessively narrow interpretation of our country's interest, we made a wrong decision. The Federal Council deeply regrets this, and apologizes for it, in the full knowledge that such a failure is ultimately inexcusable.'[40] The apology was both important and necessary, but it was not a progressive act or forward-looking confession, merely a belated ratification of a judgement which, as we have seen, had been arrived at long before. The SP Federal Councillor Ruth Dreifuss, in a separate speech, went somewhat further by associating the 'J' stamp with Swiss anti-Semitism and also drawing attention to the reduced immunity of the bourgeois elite to the incitements of fascism.[41] This, however, laid her open to the charge of indulging in party politics and electoral propaganda ('laid on with a trowel'). A majority might have believed that this official apology drew a line under a melancholy chapter. But, even at that time, Alfred A. Häsler rightly warned that 'Switzerland's penance has only just begun'.[42] In September 1995 a petition launched by the *Jüdische Rundschau* collected some 5,000 signatures in favour of creating a memorial that would commemorate the rejection of refugees after the time of the apology had passed.

A few days previously, Federal Councillor Flavio Cotti had undertaken a kind of official rehabilitation of Carl Lutz. As consul-general in Budapest during 1944/45, Lutz had been responsible for saving thousands of Jews, though after his return home he was repaid not with recognition but with mistrust and suspicion.[43]

In May 1995 the ICRC also found words to express its regret 'for the omissions and errors of the past'.[44] This no doubt included its failure to grant the appropriate recognition to the ICRC delegate Friedrich Born, who had also worked in Budapest, but undoubtedly included the fact that the committee had not had the courage, when it should have done, to draw the attention of the world's population to what was happening in the concentration camps.[45] Admittedly, the ICRC had given notice ten years earlier of its willingness to accept a critical analysis of past problems by allowing Professor Jean-Claude Favez unrestricted access to its archives, thus paving the way for the critical presentation of the ICRC's activities during the war that appeared in 1988.[46]

In the flood of apologies offered in 1995, a fourth instance should be mentioned: Federal President Kaspar Villiger felt it his duty to apologise to Dan Culler, who as a 20-year-old US Air Force internee had been very seriously maltreated by a Swiss camp official after an escape attempt in 1944; the president expressed his 'deepest regrets' and thanked Mr Culler for his efforts in the Second World War.[47]

In that same year an association specifically formed for the purpose, on the basis of a legal opinion by Mark Pieth, a professor of criminal law in Basle, endeavoured to re-open the proceedings which had resulted in the refugee helper Paul Grüninger being sentenced in 1940. The verdict was eventually set aside by the St Gallen district court on 30 November 1995.[48] Among the most recent coverage, mention may be made of one article which admittedly adds nothing new to what has been summarised here but once again sets down what is necessary – a text by Alfred A. Häsler under the title 'Die Schuldfrage ist schon längst geklärt'.[49]

WHAT WE NOW KNOW

Switzerland's refugee policy during the Second World War can be considered to be fairly thoroughly researched.[50] The most important questions have been identified, and valid answers have already been provided to some of them. This applies particularly to the question of what was known, or should have been known, about the extent of the persecution of the Jews, and when it occurred.

Contemporary knowledge of the persecution of the Jews

In 1957 Federal Councillor Eduard von Steiger, who had had primary responsibility for refugee policy, tried to justify his actions on the grounds that not enough information was available and, when reports were received, it was impossible to be sure that they were not war propaganda.[51] Ludwig countered by noting that information could have been obtained through the Swiss foreign service. Since 1994 a work by Gaston Haas has been available, taking Steiger's 1947 words 'If we had known what was going on over in the Reich' as its title, which systematically investigates the question of what was known in Switzerland as early as 1941–43 about the extermination of the Jews.[52] However, there was still no satisfactory explanation of why the majority hardly reacted at all to the horrific reports. In an investigation of press policy no less than 20 years ago, I examined the question of what could have been known or read in the press.[53] There was and still is a tendency to overestimate the restrictive effect of censorship, although demonstrably the supervisory bodies had very little power to influence the journalistic tone of the newspapers.[54] The critical factor, both in press circles and among their readership, was their underlying attitude and the evaluation of the news based upon it. The present day offers a wealth of examples to illustrate that one can 'know' a great deal and yet not perceive it as something that requires a personal commitment. This raises the question of what the emotional attitude was towards the wartime victims.

Anti-Semitism

Even though, as will be shown in due course, Switzerland's humanitarian commitment was and is understood as a fundamental and general duty, it was and remains true that social proximity and mental affinity to the asylum seekers play a major part in determining willingness to accept them. Whereas Ludwig understood the refugee policy at the time as a policy that was applied to refugees in general, Häsler clearly singled out the fact that this policy, because of the nature of the refugees, was ultimately a 'Jewish policy' and that it was fundamentally anti-Semitic. This policy is placed in its overall context in Jacques Picard's comprehensive study. Picard's work demonstrates the ambivalent attitude that existed in certain circles in Switzerland, where Swiss Jews were expected to behave with loyalty but tendencies to marginalise them were encouraged; however, the same book also discloses the tense relationship within which the Jewish community had to exist on Swiss soil, trapped between the threat of Nazi persecution and the vital aid provided privately from the USA. Particularly interesting is the revelation that Federal Councillor Markus Feldmann, in the first treatment of the refugee story, took precautions – successfully – to ensure that the assumption of anti-Semitism underlying Swiss refugee policy was suppressed.[55] We shall only succeed in understanding the refugee policy if we remove it from its fixed association with the National Socialist context, which narrows our viewpoint, and place it in a relationship of continuity with the anti-Semitism that already existed in the 1920s; in fact as early as 1918.[56] We know that Rothmund, the head of the Aliens Branch of the police, said at the beginning of 1939, 'We have not devoted the resources of the Aliens Branch for twenty years to fighting against the increasing domination of Switzerland by foreigners, and especially by Jews, simply to have emigrants forced down our throats today.'[57] Federal Councillor Häberlin, head of the EJPD, felt obliged as early as 1926 to curb Rothmund's frankly anti-Semitic outlook. Details of this, and also of the previous history of refugee policy after 1933 which is highly relevant to our subject, will be found in the recently published dissertation by Uriel Gast about the beginnings of the Swiss Aliens Branch.[58]

Ascribing responsibility

As early as 1958, von Steiger, as the responsible head of department, and his police chief Heinrich Rothmund were declared to be among the main culprits, though at the same time warnings were given that individual persons must not be identified as scapegoats.[59] In 1970 Bonjour felt that he could hold 'that whole generation' responsible because the direct system of democracy would have made it possible to correct government policy if it had been perceived as 'intolerable'.[60] The *NZZ*'s comments on the appearance of the Ludwig report, in October 1957, stated that 'if we are going to talk about responsibility, it affects us all'. The article appealed to Ludwig, who for his part provided an assessment of a 1954 relief programme based on the parable of the good Samaritan, that although we had seen the distress of the refugees we passed by on the other side: 'Not individuals, we have all passed by.'[61] Even if we have no intention of organising 'witch-hunts', we cannot settle for generalisations of this kind, because there is a tendency to use them as a convenient way of disposing of the issue. If all are responsible, ultimately no one is responsible. Even in 1995 there were some who refused to be included in the generalising 'we' of the official apology.

Views that tend to make hard-and-fast distinctions such as contrasting the pro-refugee 'people' with the anti-refugee 'government' or, in an alternative form, the solidarity with the refugees displayed by the left and the hostile attitude of the right. As a third variable, as it were, it would be essential to include the role of the army and/or the army leadership in the assessment. In 1943/44, at least, General Guisan undertook several initiatives demanding (even) greater restraint in the acceptance of refugees.[62]

It can be assumed that the attitude of the authorities corresponded to the attitude of the majority of the population. If the basis for this assertion is the unspoken view that the attitude of the authorities was therefore the right one, it must be pointed out that authorities tend, in their basic attitude, to be more liberal and enlightened than the main lines of popular opinion. In this area, however, to quote Guido Koller, the main activity of the authorities was the conceptual concentration and administrative adoption of prejudices generated in society.[63] The authorities were clearly not afraid to take repressive action if signs of sympathy were shown in some circles of the population. When a school class at Rorschach (partly influenced by press coverage) sent a letter to the Federal Council in September 1942 complaining of the 'heartless refugee policy', the authorities immediately reacted with a police investigation on the instructions of the state security forces.[64]

What attitudes did the political parties adopt? The key debate, which took place in the National Council in September 1942, shows that the large middle-class majority endorsed the Federal Council's policy on refugees, while the Social Democrats and the Landesring, supported by a few representatives of the centre-right, called for a much more liberal policy.[65] That, however, is not to say that the failure of the refugee policy can be blamed solely on the centre right parties. SP National Councillor Walther Bringolf, for example, as a member of the Business Audit Commission in 1939, explicitly approved the tightening of border controls and rejected the allegation that the Aliens Branch was anti-Semitic.[66] Subsequently, in 1943, workers' representatives indicated their concern about the possible competition represented by refugees in the labour market.[67]

There were obvious regional variations, too, in basic attitudes: Basle City, St Gallen and Ticino (and the border cantons in general) proved friendly towards refugees, as did the major cities in comparison with rural areas. Even in Häsler we find information about the wide variations in the cantons' attitudes.[68] And Jean-Claude Wacker's work, pubished in 1992, tells us that Basle had been 'more humane than Berne'.[69]

Within the wide spectrum of the Swiss majority there was a tension, of functional origin, between the administrators of an abstract state policy, who could reasonably regard themselves as the enforcers of the popular will, and the private relief organisations working on the humanitarian front with a close-up view of individual destinies. Within that spectrum, there was perceived to be a reasonable division between necessary hard-heartedness and desirable mercy, between an alleged ethic of responsibility and an ethic of conviction, as if a commitment to a more liberal practice of acceptance could not also claim to be an ethic of responsibility.[70] It was thanks to individual citizens that the official hard-heartedness did not become even more widespread, and that Switzerland was able, at least in part, to accomplish its humanitarian mission.

While individual members of the Christian churches, headed by the clergyman Paul Vogt[71] and Gertrud Kurz,[72] were deeply committed to helping refugees, the churches in their official capacity showed the utmost reluctance. Ursula Käser-Leisibach has used Swiss church publications as a source for studying attitudes to the rise of National Socialism, its struggle against the churches in Germany, the persecution of the Jews, and Swiss refugee policy. It becomes clear that any commitment was confined to members of one's own faith and to

baptised Jews.[73] Pastor Hermann Kocher has now produced a comprehensive study of the attitude of Swiss Protestantism to the refugee issue
and to the Jews in the years 1933–48.[74]

In summary, Switzerland did not adopt a uniform attitude during
the Second World War. Between the extreme judgements, on the one
hand indicting a whole generation and on the other a handful of civil
servants and local officials, it might be possible to arrive at a more
differentiated picture of where responsibility lay.

Identification of motives

In the question of what determined refugee policy, the main interest
understandably has focused, and still focuses, on the restrictive factors.
Their starting point, apart from the permanent effects of anti-Semitism,
was the fear – very widespread even in the inter-war years – of a
political, economic and cultural 'foreign takeover', the vague anxiety
that immigration would leave the Swiss no longer masters in their own
house. To this was added the fear, borne of the experience of mass
unemployment during the world economic crisis, that immigrants
might prove dangerous competitors on the employment market.
Another fear was added by the rationing of food from 1939 onwards –
that the presence of refugees might mean there was no longer enough
to eat.[75] Finally, concerns about security also played a certain part:
acceptance of the 'enemies' of the Third Reich was seen as endangering
relations between Switzerland and Germany, and the presence of
foreigners was regarded as an additional potential hazard in the event
of armed conflict. As far as German pressure was concerned, it took
indirect forms; there has never been any evidence of direct intervention. And, just as in the early years relations with the Axis powers
helped to determine attitudes to refugees, the concern to preserve good
relations with the Allies from 1943 became – in the opposite sense – a
key factor. The cost aspect, although used by the authorities as an
argument to justify a restrictive policy, was not a critical factor in
determining the attitude adopted. All in all, the more materialistic
aspects were less important than the psychological ones.

Along with these various motives, all of which have to be considered
as playing a part in attitudes of rejection, there is another less spectacular but extremely widespread position: indifference. Indifference
both to the fate of the refugees and to the measures taken by the
authorities. In retrospective argument, the justification that people
were afraid plays an important part. However, questions must be asked
about this: to what extent was this fear justified and to what extent was
it a good counsellor, or did it lead to mistaken assessments whose

destructive consequences had for the most part to be borne by others? Apart from this somewhat moralistic analysis, a more structural analysis also has to be taken into account, illustrating the inhumane tendency of the state policy of division of labour. Although Rothmund, during an inspection at the border, evidently could not find it in his heart to send back a group of refugees, once back in Berne he was again able to become a desk-bound activist on the side of restriction.

Ideological criticism and the historical context

The restrictive attitude, whatever its motivation, contrasted with the ideology of humanitarian generosity. On the central avenue of the 1939 National Exhibition appeared the announcement: 'Switzerland as a refuge of the persecuted – that is our noble tradition. It not only expresses our thanks to the world for centuries of peace but also acknowledges the great benefits brought to us over the course of time by homeless refugees.' Even in 1939, a year after the introduction of the 'J' stamp, this impassioned declaration was very far from being the truth; and three years later, with the closure of the borders, it was to appear even more hypocritical. The regulations evolved in the nineteenth century to deal with the problems of immigration by individuals and small groups collapsed under the challenge of modern mass flight from mass extermination. It failed at a time when it most needed to succeed.

Historical elucidations should not confine themselves to ideological criticism, to the identification of discrepancies between theory and practice, but they should first explain how this ideology came about and secondly indicate the relationships between the activities that actually took place and the underlying mental structures and traditions. The notion that Switzerland had a historic mission to be performed as a country of asylum arose from the need, first felt in the second half of the nineteenth century, for a national identity which would enable the country to ascribe to itself a more flattering national characteristic alongside its occasionally unattractive neutrality. This ideology of justification undoubtedly had, up to a point, a self-fulfilling effect as well and is still used today as a reference point for demanding a more liberal refugee policy. This element of the national identity was not pure invention. Because of its linguistic, religious and political diversity, Swiss society also had a corresponding diversity of social formations available as receiving stations for the right categories of refugees: the Reformed Church of French-speaking Switzerland for the Huguenots; the Social Democrats of German-speaking Switzerland for the victims of Bismarck's policy of repression; French Switzerland for the major part of the Communards; Ticino for the republicans of the Risorgimento and so on. Meanwhile, different standards applied even in the nineteenth century. Thus, in the 'progressive' canton of Basle, supporters of the risings in Baden were received much more readily than Jews from Alsace.[76]

These partial commitments, based not on a general humanitarian ideal but on shared convictions which did not draw the dividing line between themselves and others along national borders, gave rise to an ideology which declared humanitarian commitment alongside political non-commitment as being an essential purpose of the nation's existence. These partial commitments were combined by a young nation's determined desire for sovereignty, its acceptance of asylum seekers being at least as much a demonstration of its independence from the outside world as of its desire to help the asylum seekers personally.[77] Similar attitudes were to surface in discussions with the representatives of the mighty Third Reich. Thus Rothmund declared during a visit to Berlin in November 1942 that Switzerland would master the Jewish problem alone, and that the interference of foreign governments was not needed and would not be permitted.[78]

Categories and orders of magnitude

There is no avoiding making distinctions between the various categories of refugees and, in particular, the different treatments received by those categories. It is important to have an idea of the sizes of the various categories, because it is clear that the military internees were by far the largest group among the 295,000 or so people registered as being allowed entry. It is important to compare the 104,000 or so military internees, whose acceptance was, as it were, an obligation under international law, and the 51,129 civilian refugees whose admission could in some sense be regarded as an additional humanitarian service. Another important point is to obtain a more accurate view of the breakdown by religious confession of the approximately 50,000 people in the civilian refugee category.

Table 5.1:
Categories and numbers of refugees

Jewish	19,495
Formerly Jewish	1,809
Catholic	22,303
Protestant	2,638
Orthodox	2,319
Total (September 1939–May 1945)	48,564[79]

It is surprising that the number of Catholics admitted to the country is about the same as the number of Jews. During the war years, in other words, Switzerland admitted only about 21,000 Jewish civilian refugees. It could of course also be said that, after all, 21,000 were admitted, and in the present-day debate it is often emphasised that no other country took as many. Even so, we can say 'only 21,000', because with reference to the total of about 295,000, the opinion is sometimes expressed that the Jews ought to be grateful that so many of them were admitted and, as they say, 'kept fed'. Understandably, the main focus – in research as elsewhere – is on the Jewish civilian refugees. However, it is important not to overlook other refugee groups, especially the gypsies and forced labourers.

Total figures, and especially the total of nearly 300,000, which included the approximately 126,000 very temporary visitors (border crossers, holidaying children caught up in the war), do not tell us how many refugees were living in Switzerland at any particular time. They do suggest, however, that in September 1942, with 9,600 civilian refugees and 12,000 military internees, the boat was far from full, as Federal Councillor von Steiger claimed at the time. But the question of admission was only partly a problem of quantity – to some extent it was a problem of quality, too: the wrong people were trying to board the boat.

To the number of those admitted we should certainly add a 'grey' figure for unofficial refugees, which is mainly referred to in efforts to make the books look slightly better. This contrasts with another 'grey' figure – the number of unrecorded instances where refugees were turned away. Ludwig estimated that about 10,000 had been rejected. Guido Koller showed the figure to be about 24,400. On top of this, 14,500 requests for entry permits were refused by the Swiss foreign service. These figures may yet change slightly as a result of further research. The basic findings, however, are unlikely to change very much.

Living conditions

The main focus of interest has been, and still is in the present debate, the question of admission rather than the question of living conditions for those admitted. Of course, there was and is a close connection between the two aspects of refugee policy. In March 1940 it was decided that civilian refugees who could not be placed with families should be kept in camps.[80] As André Lasserre shows in his 1995 account, camps and hostels not only served practical purposes but also provided a quarantine function: Switzerland had to be protected against political and, even worse, social contusion – 'cultural destabilisation'. On the other hand, the arrangements would also keep foreigners away from the latently xenophobic population. Lasserre's view of this is that greater mingling would have made the refugees (more) unpopular and might possibly even have resulted in tighter closing of the borders. Order and discipline were the key concepts of life in the camps. Refugees – as elements of disorder – inevitably seemed to jeopardise order and hence the mental stability of the natives. The aim of economic self-sufficiency was not achieved, even if the education of the refugees, important for their onward journey, was placed secondary to work service in the 'national interest' and efforts were made to increase efficiency by strict separation based on sex, age and working strength. The refugees, while their acceptance or rejection was based on estimates of their individual situations, were treated as mass groups with no individual responsibility. The extent of this deprival of responsibility, initially taken for granted, became apparent in the final year of the war when greater importance was attached to refugees' personalities. Suddenly, a greater interest was taken in educational requirements and other future plans. And, whereas the initial assumption had been that the rescued victims should simply be grateful, increasing interest was attached towards the end of the war to ensuring that the refugees would later propagate a favourable image of Switzerland in their future journeyings.

   The principle applied to asylum seekers was that they must not be allowed to burden the public budget. Either they brought enough money with them, or their groups in Switzerland had to pay their way for them – for example, Jews for Jews, Catholics for Catholics, socialists for socialists – in accordance with the group-specific partial commitments, which have already been discussed. The umbrella organisation of the Swiss Central Office for Refugee Aid, founded in 1936, made unsuccessful attempts to obtain federal aid in 1939. It was not until the late summer of 1942 that the Protestant community also began to make relief funds available to Jewish refugees.[81] The question of who spent how much on whom is highly complex and can now be reconstructed only with difficulty and incompletely. The fact is that the Jewish community, as the smallest solidarity group, had to fund the largest number of refugees. Implicitly or even explicitly, the authorities were of the opinion that the number of Jews allowed in should depend on the financial contribution made by Swiss Jews. Jacques Picard devotes a special section to the issue of support. It contains additional figures and, in particular, the statement that the special property tax imposed on about 500 prosperous refugees in March 1941 – most of them Jewish – was, at least in part, only made available for Jewish refugee aid when pressure was brought to bear.[82]

   Apart from the key work by André Lassere, already discussed, a few other works are worthy of mention as being specifically concerned with conditions of residence. Chronologically, they were, in 1983, the book compiled by Mathias Knauer and Jürg Frischknecht on the film dealing with living conditions for anti-fascist immigrants in Switzerland;[83] in 1993, Renata Broggini's description of the admission in 1943 of military refugees from Italy;[84] in 1994, the reminiscences of Charlotte Weber, the manager of a refugee home;[85] and in 1995, Fabienne Regard's work on the recollections of Jewish refugees.[86]

Individual fates

Reference to sources always involves a degree of adopting the viewpoint of those responsible for the sources. This is why the Ludwig report, largely based on official files, despite all its efforts to achieve a humane perspective favours an ultimately inhumane standpoint. And it is for this reason that it is important that refugee history also – or even primarily – includes the viewpoint of those directly concerned. Häsler, as stated earlier, achieved this to a certain extent. Stefan Mächler devotes his study in the 1996 anthology to two stories of refugees who were turned away: the Sonabend family, put across the border at Pruntrut, and Mr and Mrs Feingold, turned back at the border in Valais.[87] The search made by Saul Friedländer for traces of his parents, turned back and thus sent to their deaths in the autumn of 1942, also provides the vivid picture that we need in order to understand the full extent of this story.[88] Individual cases are more likely to be familiar if they relate to prominent personalities, such as the fate of the singer Joseph Schmidt, who died in a refugee camp in November 1942 because of lack of medical care;[89] or of the pianist Clara Haskil who was allowed to enter the country in 1942 only after she had twice been vouched for, because the fear had to be overcome that she might remain in Switzerland after the war;[90] or of the Jewish nun Edith Stein, who died in Auschwitz because she had been refused entry into Switzerland in July 1942.

Most of the reports from the refugees' standpoint come from the group of political emigrants: their tone consists of equal parts of anger at the restrictions placed on their efforts by the authorities and triumph at their success in circumventing the restrictive regulations. This is particularly true of the report by Hans Teubner[91] but also applies to the descriptions given by Werner Mittenzwei and Karl Hans Bergmann.[92] In the case of Franz Goldner, a sense of gratitude is uppermost;[93] while Kurt Seliger's view is ultimately conciliatory.[94] The first and only academic attempt to examine the problems of political asylum is the study by Hermann Wichers.[95] Very realistic and non-doctrinaire descriptions can be found in the early book by Max Brusto[96] and the reports by Edith Dietz, who lived in Switzerland as a Jewish refugee in 1942–46.[97] From the standpoint of the host country, the most interesting publications on individual experiences are the recollections of episodes involving refugees in the Basle frontier villages of Riehen and Bettingen.[98] Episodes recounted in Simone Chiquet's collected everyday reminiscences are not numerous, but they are typical.[99]

Assistance abroad

To state the problem in somewhat more general terms, we cannot confine ourselves to considering only what was done for refugees in Switzerland, but must also look into the question of what was done – or, indeed, not done – by Switzerland for the victims of persecution. The part played by the ICRC has already been discussed.[100] So too have the personal efforts made by Carl Lutz and Friedrich Born.[101] Other efforts of the same kind have been documented: Anne-Marie Im Hof-Piguet (born 1916) reports how, as a young Red Cross worker, she looked after Jewish children in occupied France in 1942–44 and smuggled them secretly into Switzerland.[102] Similar reports are provided by the former teacher Sebastian Steiger, who worked for 25 years as a hostel supervisor,[103] and the Red Cross aid worker Friedel Bohny-Reiter on her own work, both of these again being based in France.[104] Alain Dieckhoff documents the efforts made through former Federal Councillor Musy to buy the freedom of a number of Jews in 1944,[105] and Alphons Matt tells the story of the efforts made by Louis Häfliger during the liberation of Mauthausen concentration camp.[106]

A negative counterpoint to assistance abroad is formed by Swiss attitudes which directly or indirectly assisted the persecutions. Mention may be made in this context of the branches of Swiss companies in Germany which employed forced labour, and the trains that carried human freight from Italy to Germany.[107]

RESEARCH QUESTIONS

The fact that refugee policy has been quite well researched does not mean that there are not still many important matters of detail requiring clarification. They include, for example, the individual fates of those turned back (using foreign archives in border areas); the practice of granting visas; the family histories of so-called mixed marriages; and especially the fate of former Swiss women; and what happened to the securities paid for refugees, and the ransom payments for individual

Jews negotiated through Switzerland. More light could and should also be shed on the efforts of the relief organisations and the Swiss Red Cross and their involvement, if any, in the treatment of the various civilian refugee groups, the private efforts made by those who took refugees into their families; and the sometimes striking regional differences in basic attitudes to refugees;[108] the personal reminiscences of those who were allowed in and those who were not (where the latter have survived); the hitherto rudimentary international comparison with other refugee policies; the effects of the 1938 Evian conference; and the repatriation policy after 1945. All these aspects, and many others, should be investigated.

The publication of the 14th volume of the Swiss Diplomatic Documents in June 1997, and of Volume 16 shortly before [sic], means that the most important official documents on refugee policy between 1933 and 1947 are now accessible in printed form.[109] In addition, the Federal Archive produced a specific source documentation on refugee policy in 1997.[110] In 1994/95 the Federal Archive compiled a database from 45,000 files of establishment documents (N) for 67,000 people (most of them refugees). A rejection database is also currently being assembled.[111] The Federal Archive is also working to open up the files of the border cantons and the customs sectors. The situation regarding sources for the activities of the relief organisations is less clear. The Swiss *Archiv für Zeitgeschichte* of the Swiss Federal Institute contains many items that are central to the subject. The main international source material comprises the files of the Swiss Central Office for Refugee Aid, the Swiss Jewish Welfare Association and the JUNA archive; private legacies include, for example, the papers of Otto Zaugg, who worked in the camp system, the 'refugees' clergyman' Paul Vogt, the advocate Veit Wyler, the microfilms of the Saly Mayer archive and such like. The Church Council of the Reformed National Church of Aargau commissioned the young historian Alexandra Binnenkade to investigate the attitudes of its parishes during the war, and the Catholic Synod of the canton of Zurich resolved to commission a similar study in April 1997.

NOTES

1 In April 1947 a first report on military internment was produced by Col. Probst, followed in February 1950 by a report by Otto Zaugg and Heinrich Fischer on the civilian camps and hostels and, finally, in 1950, a report on refugee policy 1933–50 by Oskar Schürch, the publication of which was refused by the Federal Council for the reason stated on 28 December 1951. See Gaston Haas (note 52 below), p. 13.

2 *Nouvelliste Valaisan*, 8 June 1945: 'En pleine guerre nous avons défendu, en eux, le respect de la personne humaine.'

3 Quotation from Alfred A. Häsler, 'Stark für die Schwachen. 55 Jahre gelebte Zeitgeschichte', *Der Schweizerische Beobachter*, Glattbrugg, 1982, p. 196.

4 *Morgarten kann nicht stattfinden*, Lazar Wechsler und der Schweizer Film, Zurich 1966. The Präsens film company had previously made a contribution to the refugee problem with *Marie Louise* (1944), a film devoted to children arriving from France on holiday.

5 Documents on German Foreign Policy 1918–45, Series D, Vol. 5, 642–4. *Schweizer Beobachter*, 6, 31 March 1954 and 8, 30 April 1953. Question tabled by SP National Councillor Hans Oprecht on 8 June 1954, answer dated 16 June 1954, commission to Ludwig dated 23 July 1954. The report: *Die Flüchtlingspolitik der Schweiz seit 1933 bis zur Gegenwart*, Berne, 1957. See also Picard, note 37 below.

6 Ludwig also obtained information from Dr Benjamin Sagalowitz, the head of the press office of the Swiss Israelite Federation JUNA. The documentation provided is today stored as such in the Archive for Contemporary History of Swiss Federal Institute (cf. note 63). Heinrich Rothmund saw fit to accuse Ludwig of having drawn too heavily on Jewish sources. The overall picture resulting, he said, might induce 'certain Jewish circles, filled with ancient semitic lust for vengeance', to see only the adverse aspects of Swiss refugee policy. See note 11, Hubacek, p. 360.

7 Ludwig report, postscript, pp. 372ff.

8 'Asyl Schweiz. Bemerkungen zu einem Bericht', *NZZ*, 20 October 1957 (the author was probably the chief editor Willy Bretscher).

9 'The Steiger Era', *Volksrecht*, 9 October 1957.

10 Hubacek, 'The Ludwig Report (1957) in Retrospect', in *'Zuflucht Schweiz'. Der Umgang mit Asylproblemen im 19. und 20. Jahrhundert*, Carsten Goehrke and Werner G. Zimmermann (eds), Zurich, 1994, pp. 345–67.

11 Hubacek explains the fact that the examination of refugee policy began not in 1946 but only in 1957 by saying that Switzerland did not yet have, in 1946, the internal stability and strength needed to 'confront a few unpleasant facts in its own history' (p. 362). Apart from the fact that the examination of the problem was imposed from outside and resulted in little self-criticism, it could also be said that the predominant self-image in 1946 still contained too much certainty for a report to be considered necessary.

12 Grundsätze für die Handhabung des Asylrechtes in Zeiten erhöhter internationaler Spannungen und eines Krieges vom 1. Februar 1957 (Ludwig report, Berne, 1957, pp. 404ff.).

13 Helga Noe Aeschbach, 'Die Entwicklung der fremden- und asylrechtlichen Grundlagen seit dem Ersten Weltkrieg', *Zuflucht Schweiz*, op. cit., p. 236. The same volume (pp. 257–308) also contains a good survey by Monika Imboden and Brigitte Lustenberger of refugee policy 1933–45.

14 It is known that the police department circular of 13 August 1942 laid down that 'refugees on purely racial grounds, e.g. Jews, are not regarded as political refugees' (Ludwig report, p. 205).

15 Given the external pressure (see note 5 above), the publisher Herbert Lang somewhat inaccurately stated in the foreword to the 1966 edition of the book that the commissioning of Ludwig had been an act of 'courage on the part of a responsible supreme national authority'.

16 Alfred A. Häsler, *Das Boot ist voll ... (The Boat is Full ...)*, Zurich, 1967. Apart from Häsler, the following publications on the refugee problem appeared at that

time: Rudolf Bucher, *Zwischen Verrat und Menschlichkeit*, Frauenfeld, 1967; Regina Kägi-Fuchsmann, *Das gute Herz genügt nicht. Mein Leben und meine Arbeit*, Zurich, 1968; Regina Fuchsmann, subsequently to be involved in refugee aid, had been born in Zurich in 1889 as the child of Jews from the Baltic.

17 Alfred A. Häsler, *Einen Baum pflanzen. Gelebte Zeitgeschichte*, Zurich, 1996, pp. 313–24.

18 Manuel Isler, *National-Zeitung*, 11 June 1967.

19 Regina Kägi-Fuchsmann, 'Wie war es denn damals?', *Volksrecht*, 24 December 1965.

20 The first rehabilitation proposal came in 1968 from FDP Councillor of State Willi Rohner '30 years after' and in the context of the flood of refugees from Czechoslovakia. See Stefan Keller, *Grüningers Fall. Geschichten von Flucht und Hilfen*, Zurich, 1993, p. 219.

21 André Lasserre, *Frontières et camps. Le refuge en Suisse de 1933 à 1945*, Lausanne, 1995. Idem, 'Les réfugiés de Bergen-Belsen et Theresienstadt ou les déboires d'une politique d'asile en 1944–1945', *Schweizerische Zeitschrift für Geschichte 1990*, pp. 307–17.

22 'A sacrifice of the concept of asylum would be a self-inflicted wound to the national sense of honour from which we would find it difficult to recover … Our Christian duty to love our neighbour goes without saying and must not even be the subject of discussion.' Edgar Bonjour, *Die schweizerische Neutralität. Ihre geschichtliche Wurzel und gegenwärtige Funktion*, Berne, 1943. pp. 31ff.

23 Edgar Bonjour, *Geschichte der schweizerischen Neutralität*, Vol. 6, Basle, 1970, pp. 13–44. Quotations pp. 41 and 43.

24 Werner Rings, *Schweiz im Krieg 1933–1945. Ein Bericht*, Zurich, 1974, pp. 315–46.

25 Peter Dürrenmatt, *Schweizergeschichte*, Vol. 2, Zurich, 1976, pp. 938–46. Dürrenmatt was chief editor of the *Basler Nachrichten*, a Liberal Party National Councillor and active in the Evangelical Reformed Church.

26 For example, Alfred A. Häsler, 'Es war noch Platz im Boot', *Brückenbauer*, 4 May 1979. By the same author, 'Auf Vorrat grausam', *Weltwoche*, 9 May 1979. Discussion of a radio programme, 'Holocaust ist über uns gekommen', *NZZ*, 11 May 1979. Discussion of a television debate, 'Schweizerische Asylpolitik im Kreuzfeuer', *NZZ*, 14 May 1979. Numerous readers' letters, for example from Ernst Etter, 'On the origin of the word holocaust', *NZZ*, 15 June 1979. (After the world had spun on several thousand times, the latest debate again gave rise to an instructive reader's letter on the term and – obviously of great importance – the pronounciation of 'Holocaust', this time by Herbert Haag in *NZZ*, 7 February 1997.) At that time, too, an admirably documented series by Jean-Claude Favez and Ladislas Mysyrowicz appeared in the *Journal de Genève* (*Samedi littéraire*) from 21 April to 12 May 1979. In the context of the 1979 debate the central secretariat of the SPS (Swiss Socialist Party) published, under the title 'Mit dem Rücken an der Wand' and with an introduction by Walther Bringolf, an article including the minutes of the National Council refugee debate of September 1942, from which it is apparent that the middle-class majority approved what was then the refugee policy, contrary to the opposition and in particular the Social Democrats. I also expressed an opinion several times in 1979: 'Flüchtlingspolitik und Pressepolitik. Zum Informationsstand der Schweizer im Zweiten Weltkrieg', *NZZ*, 4 May 1979; '"Holocaust" in der Schweiz', *Basler Zeitung*, 17 April 1979; 'Wie war es möglich?', *Weltwoche*, 9 May 1979; 'Das Wirken der "Nation". Nochmals "Holocaust" in der Schweiz', *Basler Zeitung*, 15 May 1979; 'Abschied von "Holocaust"', *Schweizer Monatshefte*, 59,

July 1979, pp. 511–19.

27 The *Schweizer Illustrierte* published a two-page advertisement worded as follows: 'Holocaust file. Are we all guilty? We who already knew in 1942 what was happening in the camps? We who invented the Jewish passport? We who were quite popular with the Nazis? We who said the boat is full? Read all about the Holocaust and the role of Switzerland ... You will find more in the *Schweizer Illustrierten*.'

28 Max Schmid, *Schalom! Wir werden euch töten! Texte und Dokumente zum Antisemitismus in der Schweiz 1930–1980*, Zurich, 1979. See also Schmid's article in the *Tages-Anzeiger*, 8 May 1979.

29 Parliamentary question of 14 June 1979. Answer of 26 September 1979.

30 For example, by Alfred Cattani, 'Die Schweiz und der Judenstempel', *NZZ* of 24–25 April 1982; or Susanne Schorta, 'Arbeitszwang im Land des Asyls', *NZZ*, 26–27 January 1991.

31 Alfred Cattani, 'Flüchtlinge wohin?', *NZZ*, 6 July 1988; Alfred A. Häsler, *Weltwoche*, 13 October 1988; and, with reference to the present day, Markus Knöpfli, *Basler Zeitung*, 4 October 1988.

32 For example, in an article by Jürg Stadelmann in the *Basler Zeitung*, 19 June 1990. For his dissertation, see note 50.

33 As much as ten years earlier, Alfred Cattani, 'Die Grenzschliessung von 1942', *NZZ*, 28 April 1982. From another perspective, by Kurt Staub in *NZZ*, 16 June and readers' letters on 9 July 1982; Alfons Sonderegger, in conversation with Alfred A. Häsler, 'The attitude to foreigners has not changed in the last 50 years', *Tages-Anzeiger*, 28 June 1992; Stefan Mächler, 'Als das Boot für die Juden voll war', *Tages-Anzeiger*, 29 August 1992; reporting of event under the title, 'August 1942 – Tiefpunkt der Flüchtlingspolitik', *NZZ*, 2 September 1992; report on television debate in *NZZ*, 4 December 1992; Rudolf Klein, 'Als das Schweizer Boot voll war', *NZZ*, 10 December 1992.

34 Following on from the same theme and at the same time taking it further, for example Daniel Bourgois, 'La porte se ferme: la Suisse et le problème de l'immigration juive en 1938', *Relations Internationales*, 54, 1988, pp. 181–204.

35 Hans-Ulrich Jost, *Geschichte der Schweiz und der Schweizer*, Vol. 3, Basle, 1983, p. 179.

36 An example for 1989: Renat Künzi, a Bernese student of history and political science, devoted an article to the internment system and showed that the order was issued by official sources to set up 'a large-scale camp on the pattern of the concentration camps on the other side of the frontier' (*Tages-Anzeiger*, 16 September 1989). This article triggered violent protests and a former internee declared that Künzi did not know what he was talking about in making a comparison with the German or Soviet camps (which, in fact, he had not) (*Tages-Anzeiger*, 23 September 1989). An example for 1995: like many other newspapers, the *Winterthurer Landbote* published a special supplement on 6 May 1995. The subject was covered on two pages, each with an evocative title: 'Fleeing Jews sent to certain death' and 'Switzerland soon knew about the holocaust'.

37 Jacques Picard, *Die Schweiz und die Juden 1933–1945. Schweizerischer Antisemitismus, jüdische Abwehr und internationale Migrations- und Flüchtlingspolitik*, Zurich, 1994; idem, 'Die Schweiz und die Vermögen verschwundener Nazi-Opfer. Die Vermögen rassisch, religiös und politisch Verfolgter in der Schweiz und ihre Ablösung von 1946–1973, *Die Schweiz und die Flüchtlinge 1933–1945*, Berne, 1996 (*Studien und Quellen*, 22, pp. 271–324).

38 *NZZ*, 5 June 1994.

39 Oskar Reck, 'Die Schurken von 1938', *Basler Zeitung*, 3 February 1995.

40 Published in full in the *Neue Zürcher Zeitung*, 8 May 1995. Bearing in mind earlier coverage, the statement made in the foreword to the 1996 Federal Archive collection (see note 78) that the official admission of guilt has 'exposed one of the darkest passages in our recent past' is not entirely correct.

41 Extracts from the Thun speech of 8 May 1995 in the *Tages-Anzeiger*, 11 May 1995.

42 *SonntagsZeitung*, 14 May 1995. Häsler also described his personal recollections at the end of the war, 'Erleichterung, Skepsis und Hoffnung', *Tages-Anzeiger*, 3 May 1995.

43 Memorial service of 3 April 1995, marking the 100th anniversary of the birth of Carl Lutz. Lutz had previously been the subject of repeated reports in the media: on 10 March 1994 in a Radio DRS production entitled 'Wenn die Menschlichkeit siegt' by Rita Schwarzer, then in two books by Alexander Grossman, *Nur das Gewissen. Carl Lutz und seine Budapester Aktion, Geschichte und Porträt*, Wald, 1986 and, marking the 100th anniversary of the birth of Theo Tschuy, *Carl Lutz und die Juden von Budapest* (with a foreword by Simon Wiesenthal), Zurich, 1995. Ten years earlier, Johann-M. Werner, 'Konsul Karl Lutz (1895–1975). Im Dienste der Menschlichkeit', licentiateship paper, Berne, 1985 (MS).

44 The ICRC president Cornelio Sommaruga on 30 May 1995 at the annual press conference. Gerhart M. Riegner, who had worked for the Jewish World Congress in Geneva since 1934, considered this declaration to be symbolic of a new basic attitude (*Tages-Anzeiger*, 3 June 1995).

45 On Friedrich Born, see also Drago Arsenijevic, *Otages volontaires des SS*, Paris, 1984.

46 Jean-Claude Favez, *Une mission impossible? Le CICR, les déportations et les camps de concentration nazis*, Lausanne, 1988; German, *Das Internationale Rote Kreuz und das Dritte Reich. War der Holocaust aufzuhalten?*, Zurich, 1989. Idem, 'Le prochain et le lointain. L'accueil et l'asile en Suisse au printemps 1945', *Schweizerische Zeitschrift für Geschichte 1988*, pp. 390–402.

47 See *NZZ*, 31 October 1995. A detailed report also appears in *Tages-Anzeiger*, 31 October 1995. Daniel Culler recorded his traumatic recollections of his time in Switzerland in a book entitled *Black Hole of Wauwilermoos*. Culler came to Switzerland at the invitation of the editor Olivier Grivat (*24 Heures*) and Swiss television. Culler's experiences in Swiss camps were largely described in the book by Peter Kamber, *Schüsse auf die Befreier*, Zurich, 1993, pp. 213ff. and 224ff.

48 *NZZ*, 1 December 1995. Richard Dindo has since made a film of the case.

49 Leading article in *Weltwoche*, 9 January 1997.

50 The Independent Commission of Historians presented a differentiated report on the state of some research in December 1998. Also, Orell Füssli of Zurich published the disseration by Jürg Stadelmann, 'Umgang mit Fremden in bedrängter Zeit. Schweizerische Flüchtlingspolitik 1940–1945 und ihre Rezeption bis heute' (1998, 395 pp.).

51 Appendix to the Ludwig report of 1957, pp. 378–401.

52 Gaston Haas, *Wenn man gewusst hätte, was sich drüben im Reich abspielt ... 1941–1943. Was man in der Schweiz von der Judenvernichtung wusste*, Basle, 1994. See also by Gaston Haas, 'Wer es wissen wollte, der hat es gewusst', *Weltwoche*, 23 February 1995.

53 Georg Kreis, *Zensur und Selbstzensur. Die schweizerische Pressepolitik im Zweiten Weltkrieg*, Frauenfeld, 1973, pp. 189ff.; idem, 'Flüchtlingspolitik und Presse-

politik. Zum Informationsstand der Schweiz im Zweiten Weltkrieg', *NZZ*, 4 May 1979. See also Christoph Graf, *Inventar der Zensurakten des Bundesarchivs*, Berne, 1979.

54 Most recently Stefan Mächler, 1996, p. 197 (see note 87 below).

55 Jacques Picard, note 37 above, pp. 147ff.

56 See Aaron Kamis-Müller, *Antisemitismus in der Schweiz 1900–1930*, Zurich, 1990. On the specific issue of the Aryan certificates issued in Switzerland after 1938, see Georg Kreis, 'Das historische Gegenstück zum berüchtigten Judenstempel', *Weltwoche*, 22 May 1997. On the years 1866–1900 see Friedrich Külling, *Antisemitismus. Bei uns wie überall?* Zurich, 1979.

57 Swiss Diplomatic Documents, Vol. 13, 12, Rothmund to Minister A. de Pury (The Hague), 27 January 1939. The most detailed coverage of Rothmund can be found in Heinz Roschewski, 'Heinrich Rothmund in seinen persönlichen Akten. Zur Frage des Antisemitismus in der schweizerischen Flüchtlingspolitik' in *Die Schweiz und die Flüchtlinge 1933–1945*, op. cit., 1996, pp. 107–36. See also Ladislas Mysyrowicz, 'Le Dr Rothmund et le problème juif (février 1941)' and André Lasserre, 'A propos de la lettre du Dr Rothmund', both in *Schweizerische Zeitschrift für Geschichte*, 1982/83 and 1982/84, pp. 348–55, pp. 561–2.

58 Uriel Gast, *Von der Kontrolle zur Abwehr. Die eidgenössische Fremdenpolizei Im Spannungsfeld von Politik und Wirtschaft 1915–1933*, Zurich, 1997, p. 237.

59 See on the one hand *Volksrecht*, 9 October 1957 and on the other *NZZ*, 20 October 1957.

60 Edgar Bonjour, op. cit., Vol. 6, p. 41.

61 *NZZ*, 20 October 1957.

62 Ludwig report (note 5), pp. 268 and 291. Independent of the refugee problem, there was a debate in 1985 as to the extent to which General Guisan occasionally succumbed to anti-Semitic inclinations. Daniel Bourgeois, an academic employed by the Federal Archive, revealed a letter in which the general asked the adjutant-general on 31 January 1941 how many Jews were employed in the armed forces. See *24 Heures*, 81, 9 April 1985. See also Georg Kreis, 'Henri Guisan – das Bild des Generals. Glanz und Elend einer Symbolfigur', *Schweizer Monatshefte*, May 1990, pp. 413–31. Particularly dubious was Adjutant-General Dollfuss' reply of 6 February 1941, for example, containing the words: 'the film industry in Switzerland is so overrun by international Jewry'. This reflects an attitude which explains why Lazar Wechsler, who originally came from the Russian part of Poland, entered Switzerland in 1914 and was naturalised in 1923, was repeatedly obstructed in 1944 by the army command while producing *The Last Chance* (see note 4 above).

63 Guido Koller, 'Die schweizerische Flüchtlingspolitik zwischen Überfremdungsdiskurs und humanitärer Tradition', 'Die Schweiz im Zweiten Weltkrieg. Forschungsstand, Kontroversen, offene Fragen. Kleine Schriften No. 32', information event at Swiss Federal Institute of Technology, 27 May 1997. Similarly at the Federal Archive's information event of 25 February 1997. See Federal Archive dossier 6, pp. 45–9. Similarly, Stefan Mächlicher, 'Wie der Schreibtischtäter-Staat funktioniert', *Tages-Anzeiger*, 29 August 1992.

64 Dossier 257 of store 4001 (C) 1 of the Swiss Federal Archive. Stapferhaus Lenzburg (ed.), *Anne Frank und wir*, Zurich, 1995, pp. 135–45.

65 Häsler, op. cit. n.16, pp. 160ff. See also 'mit dem Rücken an der Wand ... Flüchtlingsdebatte des Nationalrates vom September 1942', central secretariat of the SPS, Schaffhausen, 1979.

66 As spokesman for the National Council's Business Audit Board, Bringolf declared his agreement not with the introduction of the 'J' stamp for which the Germans would be formally responsible but to the Swiss 'counterpart', meaning a visa requirement for all bearers of that stamp: 'We are in agreement with the suggestion that the frontier controls should be more strictly applied and new entry permits should only be granted if there is certainty that the individual will leave the country again after a temporary stay.' (Ludwig report (note 5), p. 142). Back in the late 1970s, the anarchist and Spanish Civil War veteran Heinrich Koechlin had been careful not to give too positive an assessment of the refugee policy applied by the socialist member of the Basler government responsible for the policeman Fritz Brechbühl. See the debate following a book review by Georg Kreis in the *Basler Zeitung*: 'Zurechttrezensiert', Hp Kehl (9 March 1979); 'SP-Brechbühl und Flüchtling W', Heinrich Koechlin (19 March 1979); 'Der andere Fritz Brechbühl', Ludwig Steffen (28 March 1979); and 'Solidarisch im Versagen', Heinrich Koechlin (12 April 1979).

67 On the parliamentary questions by National Councillor Robert Grimm and State Councillor Max Weber, see Häsler, p. 274.

68 Häsler, pp. 232ff.

69 Jean-Claude Wacker, *Humaner als Bern! Schweizer und Basler Asylpraxis gegenüber den jüdischen Flüchtlingen von 1933 bis 1943 im Vergleich*, Basle, 1992. Similarly, Christiane Ruffieux, 'Les réfugiés dans le canton de Fribourg durant la 2e guerre mondiale', licentiateship paper, Fribourg, 1982, Franco Battel, 'Flüchtlinge in Schaffhausen 1933–1945', licentiateship paper, Zurich, 1992 (MS).

70 One of the so-called 'refugees' mothers', Regina Kägi-Fuchsmann, has passed onto us Rothmund's observation: 'What would you soft-hearted, caring humanitarians say if we gave way to your urging and allowed anyone to enter Switzerland, but allowed entry to Germans at the same time? Then you would be shouting about betrayal of the homeland and its sacrifice to the Nazis. We have to be hard so that you can be soft. Be grateful.' (See note 16 above, p. 168.)

71 See Kocher (note 74 below), pp. 285–308.

72 Gertrud Kurz (1890–1972), already honoured in 1958 with an honorary doctorate in theology by Zurich University for her humanitarian endeavours, was officially honoured posthumously by the federation with the issuing of a commemorative coin. See evaluation by Stefan Mächler in *Tages-Anzeiger*, 19 October 1992. See also the very brief account by Gertrud Kurz, *Unterwegs für den Frieden. Erlebnisse und Erfahrungen*, Basle, 1977.

73 Ursula Käser-Leisibach, *Die begnadeten Sünder. Stimmen aus den Schweizer Kirchen zum Nationalsozialismus 1933–1942*, Winterthur, 1994.

74 Hermann Kocher, *Rationierte Menschlichkeit. Schweizerischer Protestantismus im Spannungsfeld von Flüchtlingsnot und öffentlicher Flüchtlingspolitik der Schweiz 1933–1948*, Zurich, 1986.

75 The introduction of bread rationing on 16 October 1942 was linked to the presence of foreigners. Earlier, on 30 August 1942, Pastor Walter Lüthi had said at the same conference at which Federal Councillor von Steiger referred to the heavily laden lifeboat that it was highly uncharitable to regard a few tens of thousands of refugees as an intolerable burden while at the same time sharing the available food with, perhaps, 100,000 dogs.

76 See Martin Leuenberger, *Frei und gleich ... und fremd. Flüchtlinge im Baselbiet zwischen 1830 und 1880*, Liestal, 1996.

77 Georg Kreis, 'Schweizerische Asylpolitik in Vergangenheit und Gegenwart', in Gernot Heiss and Oliver Rathkolb (eds), *Asylland wider Willen. Flüchtlinge in Österreich im europäischen Kontext seit 1914*, Vienna, 1995, pp. 264–79.

78 Report by Rothmund in late January 1943 on talks held in Berlin in October/November 1942: 'My one exclusive concern was that we should neither depend on assistance from abroad, a method we reject as wrong, nor need or accept hybridization … For us, the main thing is that people should leave us in peace, and I would be very disappointed to think that I was misunderstood on that issue. Otherwise, it seems to me to go without saying that we uphold the right of asylum without any consideration for inconveniences or dangers in dealing with attempts by foreigners to settle here, rather than imitating the shameful example of France.' Document 260 A, in *Swiss Diplomatic Documents*, Vol. 14, ed. Antoine Fleury *et al.*, Berne, 1997, p. 862.

79 Guido Koller, 'Entscheidungen über Leben und Tod. Die behördliche Praxis in der schweizerischen Flüchtlingspolitik während des Zweiten Weltkrieges', *Die Schweiz und die Flüchtlinge 1933–1945*, Berne, 1996, pp. 85ff. (*Studien und Quellen*, 22, Periodical of the Swiss Federal Archive.)

80 The majority of the military internees were in any case accommodated in camps. See also the publication by the journalist Olivier Grivat, *Internés en Suisse 1939–1945*, Chapelle-sur-Moudon, 1995. Also May B. Broda, 'Verbotene Beziehungen. Polnische Militärinternierte und die Schweizer Zivilbevölkerung während des Zweiten Weltkrieges am Beispiel auch des Internierten-Hochschullagers Herisau/St Gallen', *Appenzeller Jahrbücher*, 1991; Bettina Volland, 'Polen, Schweizerinnen und Schweizer, Militärinternierte und Zivilbevölkerung 1940–1945', *Jahrbuch der Historisch-antiquarischen Gesellschaft von Graubünden*, 123, 1993, pp. 197–321.

81 Hermann Kocher, *Rationierte Menschlichkeit. Schweizerischer Protestantismus im Spannungsfeld von Flüchtlingsnot und öffentlicher Flüchtlingspolitik der Schweiz 1933–1948*, Zurich, 1996.

82 Jacques Picard, see note 37 above, pp. 364f.

83 Mathias Knauer and Jürg Frischknecht, *Die unterbrochene Spur. Antifaschistische Emigration in der Schweiz von 1933–1945*, Zurich, 1983.

84 Renata Broggini, *Terra d'asilo. I Rifugiati italiani in Svizzera 1943–1945*, Bologna, 1993. See also Elisa Signori, *La Svizzera ei fuorusciti italiani … Aspetti e problemi dell'emigrazione politica 1943–1945*, Milan, 1983.

85 Charlotte Weber, *Gegen den Strom der Finsternis. Als Betreuerin in Schweizer Flüchtlingsheimen 1942–1945*, Zurich, 1994.

86 Fabienne Regard, *Les réfugiés juifs en Suisse pendant la Seconde Guerre mondiale vu par les prismes de leur(s) mémoires(s)*, Geneva, 1995. See also the contribution by Regard in the 1996 Federal Archive publication.

87 Stefan Mächler, 'Ein Abgrund zwischen zwei Welten. Zwei Rückweisungen jüdischer Flüchtlinge im Jahre 1942', in *Die Schweiz und die Flüchtlinge 1933–1945*, Berne, 1996, pp. 137–232. (*Studien und Quellen*, 22, Periodical of the Swiss Federal Archive.) For the Sonabend case the television journalist Irene Loebell also undertook research and, in particular, made it clear that the rejected family must have had a bank account in Switzerland. Most recently, see *Weltwoche*, 11 July 1996. There was a Rundschau TV programme as early as the summer of 1994, see *NZZ*, 10 June 1994.

88 Saul Friedländer, *Wenn die Erinnerung kommt …*, 1979 first German edn, 1991, Fischer paperback edn. According to the report by border guard Cpl. A., the

Friedländer parents were denounced by two young people. The border guards knew what was at stake: 'These people have entered Switzerland in order to escape deportation in Germany' (Federal Archive, Berne E 4264/1985/86/547, N 6488).

89 Article marking the 50th anniversary of his death in *Tages-Anzeiger*, 4 March and 19 November 1942; then again on the 90th anniversary of his birth in *ZEIT*, 4 March 1994. Géza von Bolvary had already made a feature film of his life in 1958.

90 Jean-Claude Favez and Ladislas Mysyrowicz in *Journal de Genève*, 28 April 1979.

91 Hans Teubner, *Exilland Schweiz 1933–1945*, Berlin, 1975.

92 Werner Mittenzwei, *Exil in der Schweiz*, Leipzig, 1978; Karl Hans Bergmann, *Die Bewegung 'Freies Deutschland' in der Schweiz 1943–1945*, Munich, 1974.

93 Franz Goldner, *Die neutrale Schweiz und die österreichische Emigration 1938–1945*, Vienna, 1983.

94 Kurt Seliger, *Basel – Badischer Bahnhof*, Vienna, 1987. At the same time Paul Müller, *Wir wollten die Welt verändern*, Frankfurt, 1987.

95 Hermann Wichers, *Im Kampf gegen Hitler. Deutsche Sozialisten im Schweizer Exil 1933–1940*, Zurich, 1994.

96 Max Brusto, *Im Schweizer Rettungsboot*, Munich, 1967.

97 Edith Dietz, *Den Nazis entronnen. Die Flucht eines jüdischen Mädchens in die Schweiz. Autobiographischer Bericht 1933–1942*, Frankfurt am Main, 1990; idem, *Meine Internierungszeit in der Schweiz 1942–1946*, Frankfurt am Main, 1993.

98 Lukrezia Seiler and Jean-Claude Wacker, *'Fast täglich kamen Flüchtlinge'. Riehen und Bettingen – zwei Grenzdörfer in der Kriegszeit. Erinnerungen an die Jahre 1933–1948*, Riehen, 1996.

99 *'Es war halt Krieg'. Erinnerungen an den Alltag in der Schweiz 1939–1945*, Zurich, 1992. One scene reports the resentment shown to a female Jewish refugee, who was accused of smoking, having painted fingernails and ironing her pullovers wastefully (p. 56). Another recalls a schoolgirl with a Jewish name (and a baptised father) being taunted with the playground insult: 'Jew brat' (p. 69).

100 See note 46 above.

101 See note 43 above.

102 Anne-Marie Im Hof-Piguet, *La Filière en France occupée 1942–1944*, Yverdon-les-Bains, 1985; German, *Fluchtweg durch die Hintertür*, Frauenfeld, 1987.

103 Sebastian Steiger, *Die Kinder von Schloss La Hille*, Basle, 1992.

104 Friedel Bohny-Reiter, *Vorhof der Vernichtung. Tagebuch einer Schweizer Schwester im französischen Internierungslager Rivesaltes 1941–1942*, Constance, 1995.

105 Alain Dieckhoff, *L'action Musy: une opération de sauvetage de Juifs européens en 1944–1945*, Basle, 1995. See also Yehuda Bauer, *Jews for Sale?*, New Haven, CT, 1994, pp. 222–38.

106 Alphons Matt, *Einer aus dem Dunkel. Die Befreiung des Konzentrationslagers Mauthausen durch den Bankbeamten H*, Zurich, 1988.

107 For details of the transit traffic, see Richard Ochsner, 'Transit von Truppen, Einzelpersonen, Kriegsmaterial und zivilen Gebrauchsgütern zugunsten einer Kriegspartei durch das neutrale Land', in Rudolf L. Bindschedler *et al.* (eds), *Schwedische und schweizerische Neutralität im Zweiten Weltkrieg*, Basle, 1985, pp. 216–35. Quite recently, rumours have again surfaced regarding concentration camp transport through Switzerland. The most detailed account was in *Jüdische Rundschau*, 19 June 1997, and see also *Tages-Anzeiger*, 2 July 1997. The rumours were triggered by a BBC television production. Experts such as Liliana Picciotto-Fargion, Milan, and Brunello Mantelli, Turin, were unable to

confirm this or show it to be false.
108 Recent television documentation by Hansjörg Zumstein on the refugee helpers of Diepoldsau, St Gallen.
109 Vol. 16, produced under the supervision of Antoine Fleury and covering the period from 9 May 1945 to 31 May 1947, is the first volume of the new series coordinated by Chronos-Verlag, Zurich. It refers to the documents concerning our subject-matter under the heading 'migratory movements'.
110 Documentation by Guido Koller, dated 25 February 1997.
111 See also Irene Loebell, 'Über Bern nach Auschwitz', *Weltwoche* 9 November 1995.

FURTHER READING

Broggini, Renata, *La Frontiera della speranza. Gli ebrei dall'Italia verso la Svizzera.* Milan, 1998.
Flüchtlingsakten 1930–50, *Thematische Uebersicht zu den Beständen im Schweizerischen Bundesarchiv.* Bern, 1999.
Hoerschelmann, Claudia, *Exilland Schweiz. Lebensbedingungen und Schicksale österreichischer Flüchtlinge 1938–1945.* Innsbruck, 1997.
Schmidlin, Antonia, *Eine andere Schweiz. Helferinnen, Kriegskinder und humanitäre Politik 1933–1942.* Zürich, 1999.

6

Investigating 'Anti-Semitism'?: On the Concept and Function of 'Anti-Semitism' and Problems Involved in Research

JACQUES PICARD

DEFINING ANTI-SEMITISM

I am often asked: 'If I criticise a Jew, am I being anti-Semitic?' This question is as interesting as it is wrong. It is wrong because this line of reasoning equates the questioning of ideas that may deserve to be critically challenged with a personal aspersion on somebody's origins or background. It is interesting, since the incorrectness of the question reveals that there are rather varied perceptions of what 'anti-Semites' – and by implication 'Jews' – are supposed to be. Unfortunately, there can be no doubt that anti-Semitism has been a continuous phenomenon throughout history and has remained topical up to the present day, even if it appears in different functions and forms. The tasteless quip that anti-Semitism is when you dislike Jews even more than nature intended is also an answer that I cannot let stand.[1] That statement, too, is just as spurious as it is interesting. It is false because a dislike of Jews, as an explanation, misses the point that anti-Semitism is a symptom of conditions and norms that characterise a society. It is interesting, since, with its personalised definition, anti-Semitism is implied to be a natural occurrence for which the presence of actual Jews is no longer needed. In the meantime we know that anti-Semitism without Jews is indeed possible and can thus be directed against imaginary 'Jews'.

At this point it must be added that an 'anti-Semitism without anti-Semites' also exists.[2] This can be seen in the fact that patently anti-Semitic attitudes are credited and disseminated by people who earnestly assure you that they are not anti-Semites – on the contrary, they think that they are friends of the Jews. This shows that even today the debate on anti-Semitism is unfortunately shaped by the idea that Jews, real or imaginary, represent either friends or foes, as an incarnation of the inherently good or the inherently evil. When the imaginary character of anti-Semitism is at work, there is a pattern in which people involved in a debate deny that they themselves hold anti-Semitic views while ascribing such views to their political opponents. This does not mean that there is no real need – in social and political terms – to reveal and label anti-Semitic logic and intrigues for what they are. The danger lies in reproaching somebody else's anti-Semitism only to make yourself appear in a better light, while it remains unclear in individual cases what 'anti-Semitic' really means.

In sum, critical argumentation, where anti-Semitism is concerned, requires clear definition of terms. The need for clarification of both the terms used and the functions of anti-Semitism itself is a hard nut to crack. The phenomenon demarcated by the term 'anti-Semitism' is very narrowly defined and barely capable of capturing all the facets and complexities of the ambivalence towards Jews and Judaism. Over the course of history, anti-Semitism has changed not only its intentions, functions and forms but also the target and rationale of the ostracism it entails. We can genuinely speak of a phenomenon which, by definition, is difficult to define. To illustrate this point, let us refer to a conceptual absurdity: anti-Semitism in Europe, as a form of obsession and animosity with complex roots and as a historical manifestation of a racist–colonialist sense of mission, reaches a level of tragic irony against the backdrop of the Israeli–Palestinian conflict, if one considers the meaning of the highly questionable linguistic constructs 'Semitic' and 'anti-Semitic'. The beginning of my analysis does not deal with these rather far-reaching connections but with summary references to the somewhat doubtful contribution of the academic disciplines in explaining and establishing what is 'anti-Semitism'.

Therefore, in this chapter I intend to address the problems posed by research into the phenomenon of anti-Semitism.[3] Current contributions to the history of anti-Semitism are nowhere near adequately comprehensible without some knowledge of the theoretical frameworks developed by various approaches. These theories have freed themselves of the foundation of anti-Semitism or have been formulated, particularly since 1945, in defence of human values. The narrative is neither systematic nor chronological but attempts to recognise the traces of anti-Semitic thinking as reflected throughout history in deeds of a discriminatory and destructive nature. My comments examine the concept and functions of anti-Semitism itself, and in particular its development in Germany and France. Its manifestations as a function of the wielding of political power are also placed in relation to the history of Switzerland in individual cases but not in a representative or systematic manner.

FIGMENTS OF THE IMAGINATION: 'SCHOLARLY' TERMS WITH A DUBIOUS HISTORY

Anti-Semitic interpretations of historical and social events are well documented in philosophy and in the other arts and sciences. The word 'anti-Semitism' is a fashionable, popular neologism dating from the last 30 years of the nineteenth century.[4] The linguistic and conceptual prerequisite for the term 'anti-Semitism' is the prior creation and dissemination of the word 'Semitism'.[5] This term was taken over from the theological literature of the eighteenth century and introduced somewhat later into linguistics. In anthropology, it stands in contrast to the terms 'Aryan' and 'Indo-European' which were also borrowings from linguistics. The 'Semitic' and 'Aryan/Indo-European' linguistic groups were placed in contradistinction to each other in the wake of Romanticism and its academic traditions. 'Semites' were connoted with oriental studies which, as a branch of the humanities, created an academically construed reality out of an imaginary geographic area: the European world, and with it the interest of archaeologists, extended as far as Greece, while the world beyond Troy appeared alien and even ahistorical in terms of cultural history.[6] This demarcation was used by the opponents of European Jews to present them as a defined group in ethnological, national terms, which would have appeared 'foreign' to the European mind. Thus, a 'scientifically' legitimised definition made it possible to set up 'Jews' and 'Judaism' as the negative images of Western culture.

As a result of this definition of European Judaism, the term 'race' came to be applied in the sense of a group with a common biological origin.[7] Racial theorists in the second half of the nineteenth century soon wrote about the 'Semites' in a pseudo-biological, scientific-sounding, popularised social-Darwinist manner. At the same time, the ethnological or 'biologised' definitions signalled that the character of Judaism had been cut loose from the former religious definition, which would have clearly linked the Jews to their Christian environment and made them part of Western European culture.[8] Anti-Semitism, as a movement of the late nineteenth century, mixed and matched these various constructions – semantically derived from the term 'Semitism' – according to the political or ideological agenda at the time. Interestingly, in 1935 the German Ministry of Propaganda issued instructions – based on considerations of foreign policy – that the phrase 'anti-Semitic' should not be used, in 'consideration of other Semitic groups'.[9]

The term 'anti-Semitism' thus derives from a largely secular hatred of the Jews, which attempted to become socially acceptable both as regards logical and scientific backing. The pretension to legitimacy proved untenable even though several racial theorists devised and disseminated putative scientific systems to this end. The purportedly scientific combination of terms was much more successful in the popularisation of a warped idea and distorted image, although its use in debates was first made acceptable by the statements of various academic luminaries. Once the words 'Semitism' and subsequently 'anti-Semitism' had become slogans in Germany and spread rapidly to other linguistic areas, the label was taken up by anti-Jewish groups which organised themselves in a great variety of societies and associations.

The movements that had considered themselves anti-Semitic since 1871 in Berlin and soon after in Vienna, Paris and London wanted to be clearly distinguished from the Christian church's old hatred of the Jews, with its theological underpinnings. Anti-Semitism aimed at acquiring validity as something new, a 'modern' idea, even while appearing to continue an old theme of the churches. The new anti-Semite did not see his target in the traditional, religious Jew or an isolated class, eking out a living but relatively powerless. Instead, the hatred was now directed at the educated, bourgeois, emancipated or assimilated Jews. It was ultimately a conservative reaction to the politics of emancipation, debated as the modern 'Jewish' question.

AMBIVALENCE AND VAGUENESS – NECESSARY PRECONDITIONS FOR FUNCTIONAL BENEFITS

If we consider the above circumstances, the shift in the objects of hatred becomes clear. Images of symbolic enemies which convey the idea that discrimination is a hypothetical or even a practical option can gradually become assimilated to other targets or, more rarely, become inter-changeable. This change in the form of animosity towards Jews and the popular reception given its arguments reflect the social crisis of those classes and sections of society which found themselves painfully exposed to what they perceived as the aggressive potential of indus-trialisation or modernisation. But this does not adequately explain the anti-Semitic reaction if we assume that anti-Semitism obviously outlives the social conditions which give rise to it. Furthermore, there are also psychological qualities which give a certain continuity to the notorious hostility towards the Jews. It is the social individual who, out of ambivalence and in emotional terms, expresses a preconceived and often personifying image as an explanation for situations producing a collective malaise. In reference to the historian of science Thomas Kuhn, Saul Friedländer remarked: 'As regards what I perceive to be the essential nature of Nazism [and anti-Semitism] – its psychological dimension – historical research appears to suffer from an irreducible anomaly.'[10] We can thus state the following: social and ideological moments of hostility towards the Jews always correspond to the dual psychological–economic nature of anti-Semitism. This convergence indicates a degree of uncertainty as one of the main historical characteristics of anti-Semitism when the question is raised as to what it is.

It is in the open-ended nature of the term 'anti-Semitism' that its appeal and political function lies, as Salo W. Baron has noted.[11] Its vagueness causes it to appear as a type of omnibus, a vehicle on whose running boards a considerable number of different motives, fixations and intentions can travel. The pretence of scientific authority in the choice of the term 'anti-Semitism', which should at least rationally have provided a foundation for anti-Semitic theorising – as nonsensical as this must seem – quickly turned into the opposite. The anti-Semites' patterns of perception proved to be a manipulative mixture of abstruse judgements and poorly thought-out attributions of guilt. Demagogic propaganda thrived on the vagueness of the term and ultimately produced the doublespeak that would later be so useful to the murderers of the National Socialist reign of terror. It continues to be employed in the pseudoscientific arguments of the Auschwitz revisionists who conjure up the old spectres again.

The false linguistic images were excellent material from the very beginning for propaganda purposes. The rise of racist movements in the first decades of the twentieth century made anti-Semitic racism a popular explanation for the complex realities of modern life.[12] Between 1880 and 1930, Europe was characterised by social conflict. A large number of political movements believed they had the answers to these tensions. The anti-Semites used the end of the era of liberal openness to channel nationalist sentiment in their direction by claiming that Judaism was an international conspiracy.[13] The ideology relied mostly on a kind of credibility by association, whether in conjunction with anti-liberalism or anti-Marxism, or even, as the example of the Dreyfus Affair shows, in the mentality of the Catholic–conservative right which reflected an 'unholy trinity' of all three currents.[14]

Individual functional benefits can be ascribed to elements of the 'omnibus': conservative-minded members of economic, academic and military circles used anti-Semitism to maintain their hold on power, farmers' associations and the militant traditionalist groups (*Heimatwehren*) accentuated the increasing contrast between town and country. Christian circles on the political right backed the anti-Semites because they saw the Jews as representing cultural modernity. Populist charismatics integrated anti-Semitic brickbats into their anti-communist doctrines to personify simplistically deplorable social conditions. Those on the extreme left who did not belong to the Social Democratic reformist ranks used the negative stereotype of the 'Jew as exploiter' in their revolutionary anti-capitalism. From place to place, from country to country, these images assumed different functions. Anti-Semitism, in conjunction with ideology or emotion, was used again and again to explain economic situations, to wage a struggle for political or administrative power, to justify social disadvantages or discriminatory measures, to divert attention from the causes of crises or to give a new image and purpose to folk traditions.

The social base for the phenomenon known as 'anti-Semitism', whether in the form of organised movements or 'fellow travellers', was very uneven in terms of the groups represented. The common denominator – which is the object of sociological analysis – was that they saw themselves as the losers in the modernisation process, disadvantaged by the bourgeois constitutional state and the capitalist system. Members of the old ruling and educated classes on the one hand, and socially segmented workers, small tradesmen and farmers, on the other, they saw themselves losing status and being threatened by the dynamics of urbanised industrial society. Conservative forces used anti-Jewish caricatures to project a social and ideological anti-Semitism in their Romantic–pessimistic cultural criticism, which was founded on concern for a Christian lifestyle or spearheaded by the accusation that the educated were particularly out of touch. To compensate for wounded national pride, the anti-Semitic movement was ultimately styled as a battle for political power and national dominance. In the process of creating national order, it was the nationalistically minded who abhorred everything deemed 'foreign' or ambivalent to the 'essence' of the idea of a nation-state. In the midst of these dynamics, modern anti-Semitism saw itself in relation to society as the result of a nationalistically channelled process of modernisation.

In individual European countries, especially Germany and France, the anti-Semitic movement was not able to assert itself politically between 1870 and 1914, even though 'pale imitations' of anti-Semitism, in the form of an anti-Jewish 'social mood' [15] repeatedly succeeded in making inroads in polemics and discriminatory barriers. The actual genesis of the modern 'Jewish question', the integration of Jewish segments of the population in the leading nation-states, was little influenced by this in general, even if zones of discrimination continued to exist despite this acceptance by and in society. In France, the victors of the Dreyfus rehabilitation over the anti-Semitic enemies of democracy continued to act as the guarantors of progress and emancipation. In

Germany, the principle of equality before the law remained uncontested, despite the occasional case of social discrimination or murmurings concerning world views. This changed after the end of the First World War, with Germany's defeat, the creation of new nation-states in eastern Europe and social crises that encouraged unsettled social moods and revolutionary agitation.[16] Virulent anti-Semitism became current and found a political echo in a psychotic search for scapegoats.

BIOLOGISATION, DEMONISATION AND THE ECONOMY OF PLUNDER
IN ANTI-SEMITIC NAZISM

Hitler elevated what he perceived as the older superficial anti-Semitism to an organised 'struggle' against the Jews based on 'scientific' racial theories.[17] The term 'anti-Semitism' as an expression of a previously diffuse, if politically expedient, trend became obsolete in view of the declared 'final solution to the Jewish question' which Hitler broached in a political campaign and then put into practice. Under the Nazis anti-Semitism became part of a comprehensive political concept which sought to destroy people, colonialise eastern Europe and establish a new German order in Europe as elements of a 'view of world history' with its catastrophic conclusion. Birth, genetics and gender as determinants of social and hierarchic status supported the ideological, political and economic thrust of Nazism. The emphasis on the biological aspects of social order, armed with a Manichaean world view, culminated in systematic mass murder, which was preceded by ostracism, deprivation of rights, expulsion and looting by the unlawful state.

The enlisting of 'scientific' proof to legitimise systematic campaigns may have occurred with the intention of promoting anti-Semitism as a product for export which would serve to propagate a new political order. In Switzerland, the National Socialist slogans were heard and heeded by only a small segment of the population. The following example of a type of pornographic anti-Semitism, such as was disseminated eagerly by Julius Streicher, shows how different motives were mixed and matched in radical and propagandist publications, including biological, sexual, religious, ideological and economic 'views', which were allegedly 'confessed' to physicians and welfare workers.

Example: 'Swiss maid, beware!'

> The Jew, who has now hoarded and stored 80 per cent of our national wealth, conjured up this large-scale unemployment not least to use the suffering workers in his devilish, Marxist–Leninist organisations

as a tool for his wicked plans against the Aryan people, and also to force our women to their knees before him. In the department stores and all Jewish companies he attempts, by not paying adequate wages, to force our blonde women to engage in meretricious pursuits. In these needy times he causes the Aryan girl to throw herself into his arms, uses her shamelessly for his lustful urges without of course thinking for a moment that he leaves behind a human being who is broken inside. The Jew's eroticism is abominable, and he uses it, supported by his national Talmudic teachings, as a weapon against the non-Jewish peoples, to ruin them by mixing his blood with theirs. If he wants to win a woman he finds attractive, he knows no barriers, no inhibitions. With gold and connections of all kinds he approaches the Aryan woman who, with her blonde hair, drives him – the mongrel of a Semitic and oriental race – to distraction. The Jew does not feel love for these women, only the desire to satisfy his lust. Physicians and social workers have sometimes heard confessions of what these women have suffered in the hours of their surrender ...[18]

When such texts are read and an attempt is then made to analyse them, the analysis of 'anti-Semitism' as a concept and the social factors which generate it always seems inadequate to the graphic nature of anti-Semitic thought patterns. If it is still possible to understand 'anti-Semitism' in historiographical terms as a lever to advance political interests or as a way to explain social conflicts, an analysis of the subjective factors and links between motives appears particularly difficult. This has already been pointed out when discussing the psychological–economic dual nature of anti-Semitism. Emotional inner spaces and key motifs in anti-Semitic arguments reveal irrational aversions and images beset with emotion, which stand in contrast to the purportedly rational and at least partially 'scientific' justifications for anti-Semitism and likewise to the apparently 'obvious' solutions put forward by its opinion-shapers. The power of Nazism, the fascination it holds for social and political circles, cannot be understood unless the convergence of ideas and emotions, of the 'scientific' and the phantasmagoric – which are usually kept distinct in modern societies – is analysed sufficiently. In Nazi anti-Semitism, the antagonism between practical rationality and suggestive irrationality – merely hinted at in the uncertainties that fostered the ambivalent situation – becomes manifest and, what is more, becomes reality.

The Nazi programme of anti-Semitism and the destruction of the Jews gave obsessions, the irrational and the propagated phantoms a political reality. The resulting problem is that historiography cannot adequately investigate Nazism or the anti-Semitism which preceded it with rational, sometimes theoretical and sometimes phenomenologically presented but always schematically active approaches to research. A certain amount of dissatisfaction and bewilderment always remains if one attempts to understand what constituted the obsessiveness of Nazi anti-Semitism. The historian and biographer of Hitler, Alan Bullock, compared deciphering the virtually occult force of Hitlerism to the understanding and ability of a shaman who knows how to captivate his listeners.[19] The quote from a passage in Goethe's *Dichtung und Wahrheit* (Poetry and Truth), referring to the demonic element in man, by one of the defendants in the Nuremberg trials and its application to the realities created by Hitler, speaks volumes.[20] Harry Mulisch points out that the 'images', the dream of working on human material, were there long before they were implemented by Hitler.[21] What is so terrible in this confusing concoction of thoughts, as Rüdiger Safranski puts it, is the 'unrelenting consistency with which some crazy premises gave rise to an entire system and a strategy for action'.[22]

This marks the outer limits for the rational mind, and not only there where the mind withdraws from analysis into legalistic or positivistic positions. It thus makes sense to investigate the metaphors when dealing critically with anti-Semitism, if this will result in a psychological understanding of the functions of anti-Semitism and especially its seductive side. However, the limits of such a perspective must also be defined: criticism of the 'Aryan' images and formulas and ideological–historical analyses of their origins does not go far enough to comprehend the myth which produces these images. It is not possible to combat the false and dangerous appearance of these myths by again creating a type of negative wonder in the process of penetrating Nazi propaganda. Critical science must thus read formulas and images from a distance – distanced from the 'mythical' as well as from the 'modern', precisely because traditional and Nazi anti-Semitism have used these references to such great effect. This methodological prerequisite means that metaphors are often an enlightening way of uncovering theses and contexts.

ANIMISTIC REGRESSIONS AND HOW THE 'JEWISH QUESTION' BECAME A TABOO IN SWITZERLAND

In Switzerland, too, the characterisation of the relationship with Nazi anti-Semitism cannot escape a touch of metaphorical imagery. The legend in the canton of Uri of the pact with the devil was often cited in the Middle Ages as the explanation for the creation of the passage through the Alps. It was published in the late 1920s as part of Switzerland's folklore. The devil, who magically creates the bridge over the

Reuss in return for the first soul to cross the bridge, has to be satisfied with a billy-goat sent across by the villagers.[23] This deception of evil is now used to portray wantonness and ignorance, to the extent that the country's elite must have known of its advantageous relationship with the miscreant Nazi state, whose most striking attributes were anti-Semitism, totalitarianism and plunder. The controversial use of the image of a deal with the devil in reference to the relationship between the Swiss banks and the Third Reich was not invented for the current debate,[24] but is documented in historical sources as a self-descriptive statement. In the final report, written in 1942, on a study by Bernhard Bernstine, consul-general for the US Treasury Department[25] and later director of the CIA's financial department, the 'devil's bridge' is mentioned in correspondence, censored by the intelligence service, between two Swiss bank representatives as a code which obviously referred to knowledge of the provenance of the gold sold to Switzerland.[26] Admittedly, this can only be interpreted on the basis of the facts, as the source with this quote only mentions the 'memorial underneath the bridge', in other words, the memorial to Russia's Field Marshall Suvorov from the time of the French revolutionary wars.[27]

In my opinion, another legend, also from the canton of Uri, offers a much more appropriate picture of the reactions in Switzerland to anti-Semitic Nazism and Nazi Germany in general, as well as to historically unpleasant truths in Switzerland. The physician and researcher of myths, Karl Renner, writes of cattle being driven down from Alpine pastures and of how the herdsmen were suddenly confronted with 'black holes' which swallowed up possessions and the landscape:

> In broad daylight, somewhere on the broad military road, an entire herd of cattle can disappear before the herdsmen. They hardly wonder at this at all – *they do nothing at all* – as it says in the legends, they crack their whips, point the way and shout with joy, and behold: at the next turn in the road the animals have reappeared![28]

In his writings, Renner described three constitutive 'figures' of animistic–magical experience, the numinous 'it', the magic 'ring' and the 'crime' as 'deafness to warning from the environment'.[29] Renner's book, *Goldener Ring über Uri*, appeared in 1941, and the Swiss Jewish author Kurt Guggenheim, whose novel *Wir waren unserer vier* was published just a few years after the end of the Second World War, allowed the character of the Jewish biologist Glanzmann to report on Renner's observation.[30] 'Doing nothing at all', 'knowing, but not wanting to know': this is how the magic spell of the Alpsman refers to the only hesitantly expressed, ambivalent reactions with which the temptations of Nazism and its numinous nature were inwardly warded off. In the realm of the novel (which is most enlightening), however, this must be interpreted in a political context, since, in historical terms, making the anti-Semitic 'Jewish question' into a taboo also involved warding off the Jews themselves.[31] German foreign policy's use of the 'Jewish question' as an aggressive instrument was an ideal opportunity to fade the Jews out of the picture as foreign neighbours or citizens of Germany. Instead of combating anti-Semitism, the authorities and individual politicians responsible for Swiss policy on aliens and refugees[32] considered the Jewish victims to be undesirable – thus virtually following the logic of an animistic regression.

The same dynamics of selective vision also appear to have slowed the historical confrontation and the legal and moral clarification of the questions associated with this policy for a considerable time, whose shadows extended far beyond refugee policy into other areas. 'Doing nothing at all' as a form of regression in collective memory characterises the missing relation to Auschwitz as a place and a metaphor of the destruction of humanity as a whole. Finally, the regression qualifies neutrality itself as more of a metaphorical neutrality, whose nature is more of a mythical type than a substantial reality or a way of relating to the world. The 'prevented or missed opportunity' to join the UN[33] after the war also finds its ultimate metaphorical reflection in the image evoked by the numinous element of driving cattle down from Alpine pastures.

Critical reflections on possible relations between gold and magic, rationality and shamanism, irrationality and science should thus only be made in order to arrive at the question of how deeply ambivalent feelings, as conjured up in the fascination of anti-Semitism and Nazism, can exist in human awareness across generations and beyond historically determinable moments. Counter-myths, or numinous justifications for the fight against this threat, are also observed.[34] In contrast to this – rationally speaking – the intellectual and social contexts for their justification should have long since disappeared. If this is not the case, however, and there are reasons why this is so, the question must be asked as to how the duration and effectiveness of Nazi phantoms and anti-Semitic prejudices and the stream of stubborn anti-Jewish opinions can be explained both individually and collectively. This is a delicate question which cannot be discussed without critical consideration of scientific and theoretical assumptions. It was on the basis of a deterministic–positivistic understanding in science that those racial theories were formulated according to which long-term patterns of thought and action were attributed to somehow unchangeable hereditary or racial characteristics in both individuals and groups. Psychological and economic structures attributed as an imaginary assumption to a collective group – in this case the Jews – appeared to be paradig-matically and immovably displaced in this type of scientific assumption.

With these questions we find ourselves on a level on which science, that is anti-Semitism research, arrives at a critical theory suitable for the object characterised by its ambivalence and uncertainty. 'Critical' is, at this point, a necessary label for the fact that, on the one hand, research is confronting its own scientific tradition, and, on the other, clearly distancing itself from certain intentions of this science. There were also scientists who, in the late nineteenth century, contributed to the allegedly scientific substantiation of racism; and more than a few Nazi academics – including physicians, chemists and biologists, as well as lawyers, historians and psychologists – played a determining role in Hitler's campaigns of destruction.

Anti-Semitism in the context of eugenics and family policy in Switzerland

Eugenics and 'racial hygiene', being understood as intervention sciences, stood in a direct relation to politics, to the extent that they aimed at changing social conditions. Based on the law for the 'prevention of children with hereditary diseases' (GzVeN) which came into force in 1934, around 300,000 people were forcibly sterilised in Nazi Germany by the outbreak of the war. Ernst Rüdin, with dual German and Swiss nationality, a professor of psychiatry in Basle and head of the genealogical–demographic department of the German research institute for psychiatry in Munich, who was also one of the authors of the commentary on the GzVeN, advocated 'carrying out sterilization … even against the will of the person to be sterilized'.[35] Together with the GzVeN a number of Nazi laws came into force which were of an anti-Semitic nature and rested on eugenic assumptions: for instance, laws concerning the 'protection of German blood and German honour' and the 'protection of hereditary health of the German people'. Marriages, sexual intercourse and reproduction between Jews and 'citizens of German and related blood' were forbidden. Anti-Jewish racism was linked with family policy and birth control.[36]

It is not possible to make a comparison between the conditions in Germany in this period with the demands put forward by scientists in Switzerland for eugenic programmes without distinguishing clearly between the different general conditions. As regards legal regulations concerning 'negative eugenics', after 1933 there were considerable differences between Switzerland and Germany, even if the sterilisation law in the canton of Vaud at the time may have served as a precursor for 'negative eugenics'. However, legalistic differences do not explain the questions relating to the intervention and scientific understanding of scientists interested in eugenic demands. It would thus be incorrect to base our evaluation on a research perspective that was formulated without consideration for the backdrop of Nazism. But it would be equally false to make light of the fact that social questions were turned into a medical issue and eugenics was espoused by professionals as a political option, thus paving the way for racist points of view. This is borne out by the eugenic debates in professional journals, the sterilisations carried out in a 'grey area' of medical and legal practice, and the failure to distance themselves from racial hygiene and racial–psychological practice in Nazi Germany.

So far the topic of eugenics in Switzerland has been examined mainly in the context of policies concerning women and social policy.[37] This was compounded by a strange and ultimately unsuccessful attempt to develop a semi-official Alpine racial typology by combining skull measurements with anatomical–anthropological and geographic–tectonic logic.[38] The sources would have to be very carefully examined in order to determine the extent to which anti-Semitic traditions existed in the context of eugenic discourse and plans. Likewise, links with the persecution of gypsies (travellers, Roma, Sinti) must be considered empirically and factually, as well as on the level of what could possibly be understood of these interventions that could claim to be supported 'scientifically'.

In general, scientific or academic elites must be cited with care, partly to avoid suggesting a direct relationship with Nazi racial ideologies but also to avoid supporting any attempt to play down the interrelations that exist. By way of differentiation: Auguste Forel, a member of the Social Democratic party and of an earlier generation than the Nazi sympathiser Ernst Rüdin or the psychiatrist Eugen Bleuler, was clearly opposed to the 1893 prohibition of ritual slaughter and stood up in opposition to anti-Semitic movements.[39] But this is not to say that it was merely an insignificant exception, because Forel's work contributes to an understanding of later eugenists. Whether and to what extent his scientific successors Rüdin and Bleuler supported or distanced themselves from anti-Semitism and racism as official Nazi policies is an obvious question when dealing with the programmes, the degree of planning and institutionalisation and especially the implicit or explicit understanding of medicine and science in Switzerland at the time held by the practitioners themselves. There has so far been no answer to the question as to how Theo Lang, who worked for a long time in Munich under Rüdin, was able to carry out a 'psychiatric, hereditary–biological study on Jewish refugees' in Switzerland with the support of the Swiss central administration of labour camps for immigrants and refugees.[40]

AN END TO APOLOGETICS? RESEARCH ON ANTI-SEMITISM AND RACIAL IDEOLOGIES AFTER 1945

Anti-Semitic theories which emerged around 1890 were a reaction to the initial attempts at a critical consideration of the older anti-Semitism of a hundred years earlier, when Christian humanists and radical proponents of the Enlightenment, such as G. E. Lessing, C. W. von Dohm, Henri Grégoire, Adolphe Thiéry and Bettina Arnim, attempted to change the 'Jewish question' by making a positive change to social conditions.[41] The theory inspired by the Enlightenment reversed the previously uncontested view that the cause of anti-Semitism lay with the Jews themselves, and went on to advance the demand for emancipation as a logical conclusion. The Enlightenment project used mainly social and economic arguments, ultimately with a social purpose. By contrast, the scholars and scientists who were moving towards a rejection of the emancipatory approach motivated by racial theories, far from taking a critical view of anti-Semitism were using it as their theoretical foundation. Having examined how anti-Semitic policy was turned into a biological issue, culminating in the organised destruction of people on an industrial scale with the help of chemical technology, the next issue to be examined is the historicisation of the sciences – mainly the natural sciences, but also the humanities and social sciences – in an attempt to explain this period.

The first, early political analyses of Marxist or bourgeois origin from the pre-war period, which were mainly in the nature of apologetics aimed at mobilising political forces, were followed by the actual formulation of new theories in the aftermath of the Holocaust and Nazism. The various psychological schools first used the key word 'stereotype' or 'prejudice' to examine the ability or inability of individuals to recognise or not to recognise social realities. The Gordon Allport school used the stereotype of Jews to show the rules according to which such processes occur.[42] Theodor Adorno explored this process using the structure of authoritarian personality.[43] Several anthologies, published in the USA during the Second World War, have become pioneering works in the field of anti-Semitism analysis, including *Studies in Prejudice* published by Horkheimer and Flowerman, which took a systematic, historical approach.[44] This influential area of discussion was revived after the return of the Frankfurt Institute of Social Research from New York to the German-speaking countries, in that the authoritarianism theory first linked psychoanalytical concepts to neo-Marxist social theory. The psychoanalytical teachings pointed to the contradiction between an emotional fixation and rational justification of anti-Semitism in that negative experiences in early childhood would later drive the individual to compulsive, unconscious acts. Individual weakness, low tolerance of frustration and feelings of being threatened result in a need for the security of your own group and the projection of negative feelings on to other groups, compounded by a fixation on feared authorities and a rejection of the weak.[45]

Sociological research used these socio-psychological and depth psychology (psychoanalytical) approaches to understand the Jews as a minority or unprotected group – an obvious target for economically disappointed classes or for rivalries being played out between sub-groups.[46] The theory obviously had to be buttressed by empirical studies. It is interesting to note that there are no comparative studies on anti-Semitism in the various linguistic and cultural areas, with the exception of an internationally conducted, but unpublished, study by Melvin Tumin in 1962, which was a reaction to a wave of anti-Semitism in the context of the Eichmann trial.[47] By contrast, we have synoptic interpretations of various survey data in Western countries, which all show a declining trend in anti-Semitism during the 1980s.[48] The beginnings of empirical research in the Federal Republic of Germany included studies by the Institute for Demoscopy in Allensbach,[49] various surveys conducted by the EMNID institute and others, as well as data collected by the US military administration (OMGUS) in the former Federal Republic of Germany.[50] These empirical studies by American and German researchers after the Holocaust contain individual references to Switzerland. For example, between 1970 and 1989 the Institute for Consumer and Social Analysis (KONSO) conducted surveys on behalf of the Swiss Federation of Jewish Communities (SIG), which should be understood primarily in the context of public criticism of Israeli policy. In 1979, 50 per cent of the population believed that Swiss citizens definitely harboured anti-Semitic feelings. The number of Jews living in Switzerland is regularly overestimated.[51]

An example of contrasts: utilising empirical statistical data

It is well known that empirical data can be used for political or economic purposes. Empirical surveys of anti-Semitic attitudes after 1945 stand in contrast to descriptions dating back to before 1945 which attempted to justify or renounce anti-Semitic attitudes with empirically gathered data. An attempt by the 'defence' to argue against anti-Semitism with statistical data appeared in the Basle newspaper *National Zeitung* on 17 November 1938. The following extract describes the individual occupations in statistical detail:

> The Jewish population is a minority in every country. The Jewish question thus ultimately depends on the intelligence, skill and tact

with which the non-Jewish majority integrates the Jewish minority into the state. This applies at least to democratic countries. According to the latest census there are 17,973 Jews in Switzerland (in 1920 there were 20,979). The Jews thus constitute only a fraction of four thousandths of the total population ... Of the directly employed 1.9 million people in Switzerland, 7,877 are registered as Jews, and the question now arises whether individual occupations can be considered to be 'dominated by the Jews' – to use the vulgar slogan. One consequence of historical developments is that the occupations with the strongest connections to the land, such as agriculture, number almost no Jews, the industries and crafts have only a few, and here these are mainly tailors and photographers. By contrast, the professional groups in trade, banking, insurance and administration number 2,248 self-employed and 2,949 Jewish employees ... Of the 4,358 male shop owners in the textile and clothing industry, 942 – a good fifth – are Jews. In livestock trading we find [etc.]. Neither these overall figures nor the figures in the individual industries permit us to claim that there is any sort of 'Jewish dominance'. Trade is the profession par excellence of the Jewish population in Switzerland. In all other professions the share of the Jewish population is smaller than the proportion of Jews in the population of the country ... . Professions which numbered a strong Jewish presence in Germany are completely devoid of Jews.[52]

The author based his article on a publication by Carl Brüschweiler, director of the Swiss Federal Statistical Office. Brüschweiler himself never had reservations about backing demands relating to population policy which reflected the character of 'positive eugenics'. Brüsch-weiler, who in particular feared that Switzerland would be 'overrun by foreigners' did not see 'any reason for concern on account of 18,000 Jews, as some un-Swiss minds seem to believe' as he wrote on the occasion of the national exhibition in 1939.[53] The refutation of anti-Semitic statements with demographic statistics, as in the *National-Zeitung*, is understandable against the backdrop of the November 1938 pogroms in Germany. This source should thus be understood in the context of Switzerland's foreign policy, defence and appeasement strategy vis-à-vis Nazi Germany. It is particularly interesting that the anti-Semitic movements in Switzerland worked by distorting and mixing 'figures' and 'facts' for propaganda purposes. Precisely because their anti-Semitism could not be supported by hard numbers, it was presented in slogans designed to sound modern that were at bottom just 'theory' ('domination of the professions by the Jews'). The refutation of anti-Semitic propaganda in Switzerland implied or explained a corresponding line of argument which, in contrast to Germany, suggested a Switzerland which would be 'reasonable' in human terms even if 'free of Jews'. This in turn allowed ambivalence towards the country's own Jews to become manifest.

Such examples show that empirical research is of interest not only because of the data gathered but also in the context of the political order and a psychological–social discourse of enlightenment.

This applies in particular to research considered to be of a critical nature: this is where the methodological and scientific understanding of the analysis is reflected, in this case with regard to anti-Semitism research. In the example of the Frankfurt school we see that the significance of empirical study lay not solely in the investigation of specific prejudice patterns but equally of the underlying ideological contexts and structural conditions. Anti-Semitism was seen as one of many forms of racism and ethnocentrism and at the same time was linked to the critical theory of the bourgeois–capitalist society.

But theory itself is subject to political conditions and the historical processes on which these are based, and in no way constitutes an end to the apologetics which are reproduced at a different level. The socially critical beginnings of anti-Semitism research were later taken up by the student movements of the 1960s as part of the process of settling the score with the previous generation. The strength of Marxist dialectic in analysing socio-historic processes breaks down where the impact on the men and women actually affected is concerned. First, anti-Semitism appeared obsolete as an object of analysis to the extent that fascist theories and Marxist interpretations of anti-Semitism declared animosity towards Jews to be solely a manifestation of the social contradictions of bourgeois power. This reductionism bypassed Auschwitz completely; in addition, it contrasted with the repeatedly refuted reproach that anti-Zionism was a form of anti-Semitism. With the end of the Cold War, the admission that the connection between anti-Semitism and anti-Zionism had not been adequately understood plunged the sons and daughters into a process of cultural and emotional soul-searching.[54]

MINORITIES RESEARCH AND THE DILEMMA OF CULTURAL–ANTHROPOLOGICAL APPROACHES

Minorities research constitutes another approach to investigating anti-Semitism. This research challenge arises primarily from attempts to classify and analyse prejudices towards races. The efforts are understandable given that the idea of a harmonious coexistence of the various cultures in the melting pot of the USA does not correspond to reality. In all attempts at overcoming the American 'race problem' the approaches vary even today, as reflections on the relationship between the races end in a paradox, since social integration is inextricably linked with the segregation demanded by the minorities themselves. This is compounded by the fact that the discourse has continued on into broader contexts intended to legitimise minorities research: the criterion of race was supplemented by other, predominantly ethnic affiliations, in addition to specifically cultural identifications, for instance, religious, sexual or intellectual forms of self-definition.

In historical terms this approach can already be seen in the American research on prejudice conducted before the war and in the methodical OMGUS surveys based on this research, which examined the extent of rejection of black American troops in Germany since the 1940s and the continuity of anti-Semitic views in occupied Germany.[55] Finally, anti-Semitism was of course a subject of investigation – either implicit or explicit – in projects sponsored by the UN which dealt with racism precisely in the context of inter-ethnic and group or minority-related relations or which discussed racism as an issue in a multicultural society.[56]

Example: black allies?

A study by the Swiss army HQ of 24 October 1939 of the military basis of cooperation with the Western powers in the event of a German attack systematically explored the security conditions and military prepara-tions which, from the Swiss point of view, would arise if negotiations were imminent or if links were forged with the Allies. The historio-graphic value of this study on the *Fall Nord* (The case of the north, that is a possible German invasion) is certainly not slight, as it discusses in detail what would have had to be considered to prepare for military cooperation with Britain and France. It assumes that Switzerland, on account of its poor level of military preparedness and education, would of necessity have to rely on the presence of Allied troops in force. The questions of chain-of-command, the 'mixing' of units and respect for 'a sense of justice' are discussed in depth. At this point the author raises an unusual concern which he voices to the possible readers of his report:

> Our people very likely also wish that the Allies will not use any troops from the Colonies, i.e. Negroes, in Switzerland. Can this wish, a result of emotional and political motives, be justified in military terms? Does it not conflict with the understandable desire of the French to protect their sparsely numbered young men and to make up the deficiency by using their black African troops? An invasion of foreign armies in Switzerland would make Switzerland the most important battle-ground where the decision would be sought. The Allies thus have an

interest in using their best troops here. The French army considers its black soldiers to be among its bravest and apparently also its most reliable units. The claim can therefore not be justified purely on military considerations. On the other hand, it is doubtful whether the Negroes would tolerate our harsh climate easily.[57]

The subsequent hindsight of minorities research – as part of a preventive fight against racism – was preceded by the fear of the Allied occupying troops in Germany that those among their ranks of African origin could encounter racial prejudice which would make acceptance difficult. There is no need here to interpret the Swiss example testifying to similar fears with a different intention and originally couched in another language.

In Switzerland, minorities research has been taken up in scientific and political circles over the past ten years, reflecting the changed realities and attitudes of younger generations. In the context of the heated debate on whether Switzerland is overrun by foreigners, which centres around the immigration of people from neighbouring, European and non-European countries, and the multicultural nature of the society which, as a tenet of national identity, accepts various lifestyle choices, anti-Semitism has not been a weighty issue for some considerable time.[58] This certainly corresponded to the publicly recognisable realities, in that obviously negative, emotional energies were directed towards minorities other than Jews. Whereas in German research anti-Semitism was always made an issue in the context of National Socialism or neo-Nazi tendencies, in the Swiss perception it has been used – if at all – mainly as a reference point in history for the historically legitimised explanation of prejudice against cultural minorities.

It should not be surprising that sensitisation to minority issues took place and takes place in the context of a loosely articulated concept of culture. The dynamics of the post-war era, the accelerated change in the economy and society and the intermingling of different lifestyles contrast with the intolerance shown to different ways of life and cultures perceived as foreign in one's own country – depending on how one relates to life. What is more, the large proportion of foreigners in Switzerland contrasts to the continued slowness of the naturalisation process. And yet, precisely in Switzerland, with its linguistic, regional, confessional and social variations, which can be understood as 'minorities within minorities', the appeal of the idea of 'cultural diversity' is unexpected, especially since in a political system of democracy by referendum the constant political multiplication of decisions is intended to impart integrating impulses.[59] The simultaneous homogenisation and heterogenisation of culture is perhaps seen only implicitly as a question of fighting racial prejudice and rather understood as an explicit opportunity – based on tradition-induced behaviour – to fix or expand and if necessary also revise personal and collective formulations of identity.

Today, topical events are causing a shift in perspective: in Germany, where anti-Semitism research is institutionalised, the public is increasingly concerned with the ethnologisation of social conflicts and the mutual perceptions of the dominant culture and minorities living in the country; whereas in Switzerland research is turning to the phenomenon of anti-Semitism and racism as a specific subject of studies, since this issue has become a matter of legal, political and historical concern as a result of the anti-racism law and the debate about dormant accounts.[60]

REFERENCES TO HISTORICAL RESEARCH

The cultural–anthropological approach to minorities research, which is now preoccupying both the left and the liberals, especially in connection with asylum and aliens' policy, is definitely problematical. In my view there is a considerable need for clarification of the terms and discussion as regards the categories 'minority' and 'alien'. In the discussion on interculturalism, which continues to be contrasted historically with racism and anti-Semitism, elements such as integration and separation, identity and identification constitute a matrix expressing the difficulty of achieving a conciliatory understanding of the terms 'own' and 'foreign'. In any case these categories are fraught with dilemmas. Georg Simmel once penned the illuminating sentence that the foreigner is not he who came yesterday and goes tomorrow but rather he who came yesterday and stays tomorrow.[61]

At this point I should like to remark that the word 'foreign' is understood to mean different things in the scientific terminology of various disciplines. Historians discuss the concept of 'foreign' primarily as a question of policy towards aliens and thus of refugee or naturalisation policy as well.[62] This may be justifiable as a legal category or as a result of being occupied with administrative history but cannot be upheld so clearly in terms of historiography: for example, if questions are to be raised regarding Switzerland's own domestic policy as a logical adjunct to researching the history of Swiss refugee policy. Certain convergences of anti-foreigner attitudes towards Swiss Jews and other minorities and groups in Switzerland can be observed and are more precisely visible in the aliens' policy (foreigners, naturalisation, gypsies). At the same time we note that today 'foreign' is a category documented primarily by the study of literature in order to distance oneself from Eurocentric prejudices with a view to non-European literatures. The supreme discipline in this question, ethnology as the science of the foreign, has formulated the dilemma of ethnographic endeavour in such a way that an adequate description of that which is foreign is not possible but can only emerge in a narrative dialogue between the scientist and the native of that country. There, the scientist himself has unexpectedly become the 'foreigner' who, as a 'guest' in the history of another person, learns to see his own history.

Let us return to the point of departure, to the question of investigation of anti-Semitism and its derivatives. The shaping of sociological anti-Semitism research, especially the sociological concepts and social and psychiatric models, have had a considerable influence on historians since the Second World War. It can also be said in advance that the term 'anti-Semitism' was now no longer oriented to the post-emancipatory phenomenon which constituted an object since 1870. Instead, the term 'anti-Semitism' as a label of scientific discourse was expanded to embrace research into the dislike of Jews since antiquity, including the Middle Ages. Today the term 'anti-Semitism' has established itself in this comprehensive sense as an object of research. In-depth studies have focused on ancient history, the mediaeval era and the early modern age.[63]

In recent years this has been supported by special literature dedicated to the Christian, theological problem of anti-Judaism; it is an undisputed fact that anti-Semitism in modern times cannot be investigated without a deeper understanding of anti-Semitism in Christianity and in the churches. The historical analysis of the nineteenth and twentieth centuries has nevertheless become important for anti-Semitism research, and is considered retrospectively mainly in connection with genocide and the totalitarian Nazi regime. Much has already been done to describe anti-Semitism in Switzerland,[64] even if considerable gaps still exist. The period from the founding of the federal state up to and including the Second World War[65] and the period after the Holocaust[66] offer sufficient aspects for further work.

The results of anti-Semitism research stand out in the framework of research questions in the humanities and social sciences in the context of ultimately self-destructive eradication of the other. The Holocaust and with it the reconstruction of the Nazi state has occupied researchers over the past ten years in a previously non-existent intensity. In Germany and also in the countries of Europe which were directly or indirectly affected by the Holocaust, this has been accompanied by debates whose intensity makes clear the dialectics of impulse and defence, of that which is one's own and that which is foreign. For anti-

Semitism research, the long-standing lack of studies of the socio-economic contexts of the history of anti-Semitism can be seen today. This is now being addressed for the Nazi period in Germany where special research is analysing the financial and industrial–economic links in the Nazi state.[67] That this can affect other countries in or outside Europe, whether they were neutral, occupied or belligerent, is evident, given the debates on dormant accounts and the question of the transfer of Nazi funds to Switzerland. Under the 'shadows of the Second World War' which are cast over Switzerland or which emanate from it, and the related political pressure, forms and formulas from an anti-Semitic stronghold which had previously remained invisible are grudgingly coming to light.

NOTES

1 Quoted according to Henryk M. Broder, *Der ewige Antisemit. Über Sinn und Funktion eines beständigen Gefühls*, Frankfurt, 1986, pp. 23ff.
2 Bernd Marin, 'Ein historisch neuartiger "Antisemitismus ohne Antisemiten"', *Geschichte und Gesellschaft*, 5, 1979, pp. 545ff.
3 I would like to thank the following for their comments: Jakob Tanner, Saul Friedländer, Daniel Wildmann and Regula Ludi.
4 Paul W. Massing, *Vorgeschichte des politischen Antisemitismus*, Frankfurt, 1959 (1986).
5 Reinhard Rürup and Thomas Nipperdey, 'Antisemitismus', in *Geschichtliche Grundbegriffe. Historisches Lexikon zur politisch-sozialen Sprache*, O. Brunner *et al.*, Vol. 1, Stuttgart, 1972, pp. 129–53, provides an illuminating study of the history of the terms. Reprinted in R. Rürup, *Emanzipation und Antisemitismus. Studien zur 'Judenfrage' der bürgerlichen Gesellschaft*, Göttingen, 1975.
6 Edward W. Said, *Orientalism*, New York, 1979, as a study in literature and scientific criticism, offers an insight into the conceptualisation of the Orient and the Arab world in the minds of French and British intellectuals.
7 See Eleonore Sterling, *Judenhass. Die Anfänge des politischen Antisemitismus in Deutschland (1815–1850)*, Frankfurt, 1969.
8 See also Peter G. J. Pulzer, *Die Entstehung des politischen Antisemitismus in Deutschalnd und Österreich 1867–1914*, Gütersloh, 1966; Jacob Katz, *Zur Assimilation und Emanzipation der Juden*, Darmstadt, 1982.
9 Instruction of the press conference of the government of the Third Reich on 22 August 1935; see C. Berning, *Vom 'Abstammungsnachweis' zum 'Zuchtwort', Vokabular des Nationalsozialismus*, Berlin, 1964, p. 14.
10 Saul Friedländer, *Kitsch und Tod. Der Widerschein des Nazismus*, Munich, 1986, p. 106; with reference to Thomas Kuhn, *Die Struktur wissenschaftlicher Revolutionen*, Frankfurt, 1967.
11 Salo W. Baron, *A History of the Jews*, Vol. 2, New York, 1937, p. 296.
12 For an analysis which is critical of the ideology and political consequences of anti-Semitism, see Léon Poliakov, *Le Mythe arien*, Paris, 1971. Rupert Breitling analyses the transition from 'traditional' to National Socialist anti-Semitism and the resulting ideological–political use, *Die nationalsozialistische Rassenlehre.*

Entstehung, Ausbreitung, Nutzen und Schaden einer politischen Ideologie, Meisenheim am Glan, 1971.

13 Werner Jochmann, 'Struktur und Funktion des deutschen Antisemitismus', in Werner E. Mosse and Arnold Paucker (eds), *Juden im Wilhelminischen Deutschland 1890–1914*, Tübingen, 1976, pp. 389–477; Saul Friedländer, 'Die politischen Veränderungen der Kriegszeit und ihre Auswirkungen auf die Judenfrage', in Werner E. Mosse, *Deutsches Judentum im Krieg und Revolution 1916–1923*, Tübingen, 1971, pp. 65–83. In general, see the study by Eva G. Reichmann, *Flucht in den Hass. Die Ursachen der deutschen Judenkatastrophe*, Frankfurt, 1958.

14 See also, Zeev Sternhell, *La Droite révolutionnaire 1885–1914. Les Origines françaises du fascisme*, Paris, 1978; Michael R. Marrus, *Les Juifs de France à l'époque de l'Affaire Dreyfus*, Paris, 1971.

15 Friedrich Naumann, *Die Leidensgeschichte des deutschen Liberalismus (1908)*, Vol. 4, Cologne/Opladen, 1964, p. 292.

16 Saul Friedländer, *L'antisémitisme Nazi. Histoire d'une psychose collective*, Paris, 1971. See also notes 12 and 13.

17 Quotes from Adolf Hitler, *Mein Kampf*, Munich, 1930 (1939), pp. 628ff.

18 'Schweizermädchen, hüte Dich vor schändenden Juden', *Eidgenoss*, 12, Zurich, 1933. The article was, among other things, the cause and object of the lawsuit for the so-called Bernese trial (1934–37) brought against the 'Protocols of the Elders of Zion'.

19 Allan Bullock, *Hitler. Eine Studie über Tyrannei*, Düsseldorf, 1967, p. 356.

20 Quoted in Bullock, op. cit., p. 357.

21 Harry Mulisch, *Strafsache 40/61. Eine Reportage über den Eichmann-Prozess*, Berlin, 1987, p. 17.

22 Rüdiger Safranski, *Das Böse oder das Drama der Freiheit*, Munich/Vienna, 1997, p. 278.

23 Regarding the Uri legends, see Josef Müller, *Sagen aus Uri*, 2 vols, Basle, 1926/29.

24 The legend which centres around the devil's bridge was quoted by me in the programme 'Sternstunde Philosophie' on the subject of anti-Semitism on Swiss–German television on 2 March 1997. The legend is used by Jane Kramer, 'Manna from Hell: Nazi Gold, Holocaust accounts, and what the Swiss must finally confront', *New Yorker*, 28 April/5 May 1997. I assisted Jane Kramer with her research into this legend.

25 On Bernstine, see Catherine Schiemann, *Neutralität in Krieg und Frieden. Die Aussenpolitik der Vereinigten Staaten gegenüber der Schweiz 1941–1949. Eine diplomatiegeschichtliche Untersuchung*, Chur, 1991, pp. 201ff.

26 National Archive, Washington DC: *Final Report Swiss Bank Investigation (1942)*, by Bernhard Bernstine, general attorney, US Treasury Department, RG 59, E77-52, Box 5.

27 This reference made by the banker to the provenance of the gold accepted from the Soviet Union is likely to be factually correct for 1940/41.

28 Karl Renner, *Goldener Ring über Uri*, with illustrations by Heinrich Danioth, Zurich, 1976 (1941), p. 19. A book about the experiences and mentality of our mountain people, about magic and spirits and about the first and the last things. Renner concentrated less on the legend which arose around the route through the pass in the main valley and more on the magical–animistic experience of the population in the lateral valleys (Schächental, Maderanertal); as a physician he was particularly interested in this.

29 Renner, op. cit., p. 241. The numinous element ('it') and with it the 'ring' and the 'crime' of the shamanist's world are emphasised much more strongly than

the legends or tales as they appear in the mythological approaches of Josef Müller.

30 Kurt Guggenheim, *Wir waren unserer vier*, Zurich, 1949 (see Ch. 10).

31 See statements in Jacques Picard, *Die Schweiz und die Juden 1933–1945. Schweizerischer Antisemitismus, jüdische Abwehr, internationale Migrations- und Flüchtlingspolitik*, Zurich, 1994, pp. 41–50.

32 See Guido Koller, 'Entscheidung über Leben und Tod. Die behördliche Praxis in der schweizerischen Flüchtlingspolitik während des Zweiten Weltkrieges', in *Studien und Quellen, Zeitschrift des Schweizerischen Bundesarchivs*, Vol. 22, Berne, 1996, pp. 17–106.

33 See Peter Hug, 'Verhinderte oder verpasste Chance? Die Schweiz und die Vereinigten Nationen 1943–1947', in Georg Kreis (ed.), *Die Schweiz im internationalen System der Nachkriegszeit 1943–1950*, Itinera Fase 18, 1996, pp. 84–97.

34 A contemporary legend appears to centre around the experience of the war years: the people from Wengen in the Bernese Oberland tell that there is an unknown cave below the Jungfrau glacier which has opened only twice, before the outbreak of both world wars (as related by Bernhard Schaer, bookseller, in Interlaken, to me).

35 Peter Emil Becker, *Zur Geschichte der Rassenhygiene. Wege ins Dritte Reich*, Stuttgart, 1988, p. 128.

36 Gisela Bock, *Zwangssterilisation im Nationalsozialismus. Studien zur Rassenpolitik und Frauenpolitik*, Opladen, 1986, pp. 102ff.

37 Nadja Ramsauer and Thomas Meyer, 'Blinder Fleck im Sozialstaat. Eugenik in der Deutschschweiz 1930–1950', *Traverse*, 2, 1995, pp. 117–21. Anna Gossenreiter, 'Psychopathinnen und Schwachsinnige. Eugenische Diskurs in Psychiatrie und Fürsorge: Die Sterilisation von weiblichen Mündeln in der Vormundschaftsbehörde Zürich 1918–1933', Zurich, 1992 (thesis for university degree).

38 Christoph Keller, *Der Schädelvermesser. Otto Schlaginhaufen – Anthropologe und Rassenhygieniker. Eine biografische Reportage*, Zurich, 1995; Georg Kreis, 'Der "homoalpinus helveticus". Zum schweizerischen Rassendiskurs der 30er Jahre', in Guy P. Marchal and Aram Mattioli (eds), *Erfundene Schweiz. Konstruktion nationaler Identität*, Zurich, 1992, pp. 175–90.

39 Aaron Kamis-Müller, 'Juifs en Pays de Vaud', in *Musée historique de Lausanne, Vie juive en Suisse*, Lausanne, 1992, pp. 147–51.

40 Theo Lang, 'Erste Ergebnisse psychiatrisch-erbbiologischer Untersuchungen an jüdischen Flüchtlingen', *Bulletin der Schweizerischen Akademie der Medizinischen Wissenschaften*, 1, Basle, 1945, pp. 281–95.

41 Arthur Hertzberg, *The French Enlightenment and the Jews*, New York, 1968, pp. 264ff. Jacob Katz, *Aus dem Ghetto in die bürgerliche Gesellschaft. Jüdische Emanzipation 1770–1870*, Frankfurt, 1986, pp. 70ff. Jacques Picard, Recht auf Abweichung. Das Juden- und Frauenbild der deutschen Romantik und Bettine von Arnims Seitensprung', in Erhard R. Wiehn, *Judenfeindschaft*, Konstanz, 1989, pp. 73ff.

42 Gordon W. Allport, *Die Natur des Vorurteils*, Cologne, 1971.

43 Theodor W. Adorno *et al.*, *The Authoritarian Personality*, New York, 1950. For a discussion, see Detlev Claussen, *Die Grenzen der Aufklärung. Die gesellschaftliche Genese des modernen Antisemitismus*, Frankfurt, 1994 (revised edn).

44 Max Horkheimer and S. H. Flowerman (eds), *Studies in Prejudice*, 5 Vols, New York, 1949–50.

45 For a basis, see Max Horkheimer and T. W. Adorno, 'Elemente des Anti-

156   *Switzerland and the Second World War*

semitismus', in *Dialektik der Aufklärung*, Frankfurt, 1947, pp. 199–244.
46 Alphonse Silbermann, *Der ungeliebte Jude. Zur Soziologie des Antisemitismus*, Zurich, 1981. Alphonse Silbermann and J. H. Schoeps (eds), *Antisemitismus nach dem Holocaust. Bestandesaufnahme und Erscheinungsformen in deutschsprachigen Ländern*, Cologne, 1986.
47 Melvin Tumin, 'Intergroup Attitudes of Youth and Adults in England, France and Germany', Princeton University, 1962.
48 Werner Bergmann and Rainer Erb, *Antisemitismus in der Bundesrepublik Deutschland. Ergebnisse der empirischen Forschungen von 1946–1989*, Opladen, 1991.
49 IFD, Institut für Demoskopie Allensbach, *Jahrbuch der öffentlichen Meinung*, Vols 1–8, 1947–83; Renate Köcher, *Ausmass und Formen des heutigen Antisemitismus in der Bundesrepublik Deutschland*, Allensbach, 1987 (Institut für Demoskopie).
50 Overview in Bergman and Erb, see note 48, pp. 11–16 and 318–19. See also Frederick D. Weil, 'The Extent and Structure of Antisemitism in Western Population since the Holocaust', in Helen Fein (ed.), *The Persisting Question. Sociological Perspectives and Social Contexts of Modern Antisemitism*, New York/Berlin, 1987, pp. 164–89.
51 KONSO surveys 1970, 1975, 1979, 1989. See Heinz Roschewski, *Auf dem Weg zu einem jüdischen Selbstbewusstsein? Geschichte der Juden in der Schweiz 1945–1994*, Basle, 1995, pp. 51–69.
52 *National Zeitung*, Basle, 17 November 1938. Carl Brüschweiler, *Beruf und Konfession in der Schweiz*, Olten, 1938.
53 Carl Bärschweiler, *Wir als Viermillionen-Volk*, Olten, 1939 (special edn), p. 20.
54 Dietrich Wetzel (ed.), *Die Verlängerung der Geschichte. Deutsche, Juden und der Palästinakonflikt*, Frankfurt, 1983; Micha Brumlik, 'Die Angst vor dem Vater. Judenfeindliche Tendenzen im Umkreis neuer sozialer Bewegungen', in A. Silbermann and H. J. Schoeps, *Antisemitismus*, 1986, pp. 133–63. For the past ten years a connection between anti-Semitism and anti-Zionism has also been discussed among the members of the left in Germany. In the case of Switzerland a historic analysis will need to be conducted to determine whether and how this type of discourse has developed since the 1970s.
55 Daniel Katz and Kenneth W. Braly, 'Racial Prejudice and Racial Stereotypes', *Journal of Social Psychology*, 30, 1935, pp. 175–93; Anna J. Meritt and Richard L. Meritt (eds), *Public Opinion in Occupied Germany: The OMGUS Surveys 1945–1948*, Urbana, 1970; idem, *Public Opinion in Semi-Sovereign Germany HICOG Survey 1949–1955*, Urbana, 1980.
56 Kripal Singh Sodi and Rudolf Bergius, *Nationale Vorurteile*, Berlin, 1953. A similar approach to prejudice and minority research can be found in Gertrude Selznik and Stephen Steinberg, *The Tenacity of Prejudice. Anti-Semitism in Contemporary America*, New York, 1969.
57 Swiss Federal Archive, E 5795, Vol. 300. Army Command, Germann report, 24 October 1939.
58 Georg Kreis, *Die Schweiz unterwegs*, final report of the National Research Programme (NFP) 21, 'Kulturelle Vielfalt und nationale Identität', Basle, 1993.
59 Ibid., esp. pp. 17–32.
60 The topic was first publicly debated in a manner which was significant for the 1990s by the *Israelitische Cultusgemeinde Zürich* with the *Gesellschaft Minderheiten in der Schweiz*. See Gaby Rosenstein (ed.), *Fremdenfeindlichkeit, Rassismus, Antisemitismus, Konstanz*, 1991 (Zurich symposium of 2 December 1990).
61 Georg Simmel, 'Der Fremde', in *Das individuelle Gesetz*, (Philosophical discourses),

Frankfurt, 1968, p. 63.

62 References to sources and literature in Georg Kreis and Patrik Kury, *Die schweizerischen Einbürgerungsnormen im Wandel der Zeiten*, Berne, 1996 (Swiss UNESCO Commission and Europe Institute/Historical Institute of the University of Basle).

63 Representative of mediaeval studies: Frantisek Graus, *Pest, Geissler, Judenmorder. Das 14. jahrhundert als Krisenzeit*, Göttingen, 1987, with references from the area of modern-day Switzerland; and Norman Cohn, *Das Ringen um das Tausendjährige Reich*, Berne, 1961, as an important study of the history of ideology.

64 See Annie Fraenkel, *Bibliografie zur Geschichte der Juden in der Schweiz*, published and edited by Uri R. Kaufmann, Munich/London/New York/Paris, 1993, pp. 59–89.

65 Friedrich Külling, *Bei uns wie überall?* (*Antisemitismus in der Schweiz 1866–1900*), Zurich, 1977; Aaron Kamis-Müller, *Antisemitismus in der Schweiz 1900–1930*, Zurich, 1991; Jacques Picard, *Die Schweiz und die Juden 1933–1945, Schweizerischer Antisemitismus, jüdische Abwehr und internationale Migrations- und Flüchtlingspolitik*, Zurich, 1994; Aram Mattioli (ed.), *Antisemitismus in der Schweiz*, Zurich, 1998.

66 Willy Guggenheim, 'Antisemitismus in der Schweiz nach dem 2. Weltkrieg', in A. Silbermann and H. J. Schoeps, *Antisemitismus nach dem Holocaust*, 1986, pp. 71–90; 'Öffentliches antisemitismus in der Schweiz, Nach 1945', in Mattioli (ed.), *Antisemitismus in der Schweiz, 1948–1960*, Zurich, 1998, pp. 555–76.

67 See Hans-Erich Volkmann, 'Die NS-Wirtschaft in Vorbereitung des Krieges', in Wilhelm Deist *et al.*, *Ursachen und Voraussetzungen des Zweiten Weltkrieges*, Stuttgart, 1979. Likewise Richard J. Overy, Gerhard Otto and Johannes Houwinkten Cate (eds), *Die 'Neuordnung' Europas: NS-Wirtschaftspolitik in den besetzten Gebieten*, Berlin, 1996.

7

Pilet-Golaz and the Making of Swiss Foreign Policy: Some Remarks

NEVILLE WYLIE

In the recent public controversies surrounding Switzerland's wartime history, Marcel Pilet-Golaz, Swiss foreign minister from 1940 to 1944, has been noticeable by his absence. This is a curious omission, for Pilet has long been an intensely controversial figure for Swiss historians and public alike. His 'defeatist' presidential radio address of 25 June 1940, audience with the Swiss fascist party the following autumn and supposed 'peace brokering' later in the war, have been the subject of much debate. If the current furore is to produce a fundamental reassessment of Switzerland's role in the war, the historical image of Pilet-Golaz is likely to require careful examination. This will be no easy task. Pilet was by nature cautious and left few clues as to his true attitudes or opinions. The strong emotions he aroused in his contemporaries have also meant that the historical record is often strongly flavoured with personal prejudice. Perhaps for these reasons, Pilet has yet to find a biographer, and there is still considerable darkness surrounding many aspects of his life and attitudes. So as to help assist in this reassessment, this essay will outline how Swiss historians have portrayed Pilet in the past, and then sketch out some aspects of Pilet's foreign policy decision making.

PILET AND THE HISTORIANS

The 'traditional' view of Pilet was enunciated in its most unambiguous form in Edgar Bonjour's monumental *Geschichte der schweizerischen Neutralität*.[1] Reflecting the views of Pilet's many political opponents, Bonjour portrayed Switzerland's war as a simple struggle between adaptation or resistance, and cast Pilet in the role of leading appeaser. Pilet was the weak 'Pontius Pilate', easily swayed by the raucous criticisms emanating from Berlin and Rome, and in the end, prepared to mortgage Swiss independence and traditions in order to fit

Switzerland quietly into Hitler's New Order. Bonjour did not go so far as to liken Pilet with Laval, nor did he consider Pilet a genuine 'Quisling'. But Pilet's excessive pessimism and belief in an ultimate German victory were considered important factors in weakening the morale of the federal authorities, at the very moment when a strong lead was required. Amidst the population at large, Bonjour's magisterial report had the effect of cementing the popular view that Switzerland's difficulties in 1940 and beyond were caused, or at least aggravated, by Pilet's pusillanimity.

The opening of the federal archive to researchers quickly stimulated views of Pilet which differed from that offered by Bonjour. Initially, discussion centred around those aspects of the story which were most at odds with the popular perceptions. The proposals of the commander-in-chief of the armed forces, General Guisan, for the dispatch of 'special missions' to Washington, London and most notably Berlin in the autumn of 1940 and spring of 1941 came under close scrutiny. While the motives of Guisan, hitherto considered the personification of Switzerland's will to resist, were open to a range of interpretations, Pilet's refusal to countenance any pilgrimage to Berlin obviously stood in his favour, and contradicted his image as an arch appeaser.[2] But other areas were also considered open for reassessment. Whatever his motives in articulating a pro-German line and giving Berlin the impression that he genuinely considered an accommodation to be in Switzerland's best interests, Pilet almost certainly helped ease Swiss–German relations at a critical time. Given the state of Swiss defences, especially in the air, Pilet had just reason to consider Guisan's heroic public utterances inappropriate and even counter-productive.[3] Commentators in the *Suisse romande* were particularly responsive to the new research, and to the argument that Pilet had been unjustly branded a scapegoat to excuse the more ignominious chapters of Switzerland's wartime history. Though some of the works were blatantly hagiographic, and an apologetic strain exists in much of the literature, they did have the effect of popularising a more sympathetic appraisal of 'their' federal councillor.[4]

The latest retouches to Pilet's historical image have been applied by the Winterthur historian Erwin Bucher. In *Zwischen Bundesrat und General* (1991), Bucher examined Pilet's foreign policy from the perspective of his internal political situation.[5] For all the difficulties associated with this perspective, the belated acknowledgement of a connection between Switzerland's *Innen-* and *Aussenpolitik*, advanced our appreciation of the circumstances within which foreign policy was allowed to develop. The array of domestic forces which Bucher sees pitted against Pilet, from virulent left-wing politicians to a cabal of restive intelligence officers, may not find agreement in all quarters, but by shifting the analysis away from Switzerland's diplomatic relations, Bucher has highlighted the fact that even Switzerland's apparently tranquil domestic polity was not immune from the kind of stresses and strains which impinge on foreign policy considerations. Pilet was clearly more constrained by internal forces than his peers and whether these forces ultimately worked in Switzerland's favour, or whether they merely exacerbated Pilet's already difficult task remain a matter of debate.

PILET AND THE MAKING OF SWISS FOREIGN POLICY

Any assessment of Pilet's role as foreign minister must take into account not only his own political inclinations, but also his handling of foreign policy decision making, particularly the extent to which he permitted a free exchange of ideas before taking action. Pilet had been groomed to succeed Giuseppe Motta as head of the Swiss foreign ministry, the Federal Political Department, when failing health brought Motta's 20-year tenure as foreign minister to an end in early 1940. Pilet's own outlook on foreign affairs typified that held by many Swiss, especially from the *Suisse romande*, being overwhelmingly central European in its orientation, with a healthy regard for Italian patronage, and French cultural and military hegemony. Added to this was a visceral hatred of bolshevism, which had been sharpened by many years of strained relations with socialist politicians in Switzerland.

Historians have rightly noted that Pilet's grip on foreign policy decision making was unusually strong. Much of Pilet's authority stemmed from his commanding position in the seven-man federal council. All councillors enjoyed considerable authority over their own departmental interests. During the 1920s and 1930s, the traditionally collegiate nature of council's decision-making was gradually over-whelmed by the waxing volume and complexity of government business. The council tended increasingly to confirm the recommendations presented by the relevant councillor with little detailed discussion.[6] For Pilet, this process was accentuated by the fact that there was on the council no intellectual counter-weight to challenge his view. After the resignations of Obrecht, Minger and Baumann in 1940, Pilet's peers on the council were united in their mediocrity, barely capable of managing their own departments, far less rising to meet the dangers of a European war. There is ample evidence to show that when Pilet's interests collided with those of other councillors, particularly Kobelt (military) and Celio (Post & Railways, Pilet's former department), he had little difficulty in running rings round them and winning his case.[7] In the council sessions, Pilet's recommendations also rarely appear to have stimulated dissent, nor did he encourage any debate.[8] He was usually coy in discussing foreign policy matters and his infuriatingly evasive answers spawned many of the suspicions which shrouded his political career. Since Pilet's own personal relations with his (predominantly) German-speaking colleagues were not warm, there was seldom an opportunity to discuss matters informally. 'Man sei bei Pilet nie sicher', federal councillor von Steiger complained once, 'was er von sich aus mit fremden Diplomaten abgemacht habe'.[9] The only exception to this rule was Philipp Etter, who deputised as foreign minister for Pilet in his absences.[10] On the whole however, when Pilet's colleagues complained of being kept in the dark, there is more than a hint that they were relieved to be able to plead ignorance, and let Pilet shoulder the burden of steering the country's external relations.

The absence of any challenge to Pilet's hold on foreign policy in the council is of particular note, because of the marked curtailment of parliamentary business and heightened centralisation of executive authority in the hands of the federal council brought about by emergency legislation on the outbreak of war. The only forum for parliamentary oversight of federal policies during the war was the quarterly meetings of the National Council's *Vollmachtenkommissionen*.[11] These were undoubtedly uncomfortable occasions for Pilet, and he invariably encountered a barrage of hostile questioning from opposition socialist or 'independent' politicians. But the *Vollmachtenkommissionen* never developed into an alternative arena for policy making. The national councillors were restricted to commenting on decisions already made and the bourgeois parties quickly closed ranks whenever opposition factions looked like causing their representatives on the federal council serious embarrassment. This was the case in the spring of 1943, when Pilet's Radical party defended him against accusations that he was trying to broker peace between Berlin and Washington.[12]

If councillor and parliamentary leverage over Pilet's foreign policy appear to have been relatively limited, so too were other 'external' influences. Ironically, at a time when Swiss banking and business barons were busily profiting from the war, they were faced with the unaccustomed situation of having an independently minded federal foreign minister who was neither 'in their pocket' nor deeply interested in economic affairs. Two points arising from this are of particular significance. On the one hand, since Pilet had shunned all offers of business or banking sinecures and kept his contacts with the business community to a minimum, he was able to keep this powerful lobby at a distance and operate with a freedom of manoeuvre which few in his position would have enjoyed. According to Clifford Norton, Britain's minister in Berne, Pilet had so little respect for Swiss industrialists that he often had a 'sly laugh' with Norton whenever 'he went through the motions of defending someone whom [the Allies] had blacklisted'.[13] Swiss industrialists were no doubt well aware of Pilet's opinions and, almost unique in private and official paper collections of Swiss politicians, one finds hardly any letters from Swiss businessmen amidst Pilet's voluminous correspondence.

On the other hand, Pilet's disinterest in commercial matters tended to make him undervalue economic considerations in his foreign policy. Trade quotas and financial credits were, for Pilet, concessions which could be dispensed, freely if necessary, to assist Switzerland's passage through the war.[14] He therefore left commercial policy to the economic authorities, and remained only partially informed through reports from Robert Kohli, the Federal Political Department official in charge of economic and financial affairs. Consequently, for most of the war, while Swiss trade and finance policy matched the interests of the central bank, businesses and banking, it lacked a strong political component. After the initial concessions granted to the Axis after the collapse of France, overt political considerations came to the fore rarely, most notably in the autumn of 1943 and during negotiations with the Allied powers in early 1945. On the whole, in the absence of a strong political lead from Pilet's department, the smooth swing-doors between business, banking and politics revolved quietly, enabling commercial interests groups to dominate federal trade and financial policy.[15]

Measuring the influence exercised by other elements in Switzerland's complex social mosaic on Pilet is even harder to assess, especially since so little research on Switzerland's 'hidden wiring' has been carried out since Daniel Bourgeois' seminal article in 1974.[16] Pilet was fully conscious of the arguments of those wishing to appease Germany and Italy. As federal president, he received the famous 'petition' of 15 November 1940 signed by leading figures, calling for the introduction of arbitrary and undemocratic measures to defend Swiss independence. Although Pilet was in contact with former federal councillor Jean-Marie Musy, who was active in courting German personalities during the early war years, Pilet was certainly not Musy's 'parrot', as Musy boasted.[17] Gonzague de Reynold, one of the most articulate Swiss with authoritarian inclinations, also sent Pilet a number of reports during 1940, encouraging him to ignore popular pro-British sentiments.[18] More influential perhaps was Philipp Etter, councillor for the interior department, and the one councillor with unambiguous authoritarian leanings. Again however, Etter's exact influence over Pilet is unclear. If there are doubts over specific relationships, it is nonetheless clear that Pilet was not a natural confederate for these groups, even when France's collapse had so profoundly shaken his confidence and political beliefs. He was not counted amongst Switzerland's patrician society, to whom, like their cousins elsewhere in Europe, the call 'better Hitler than Blum (or Stalin)' found such a strong resonance before and during the fascist ascendancy. For every example of Pilet bowing to German pressure or flirting with authoritarian views, can be found others, demonstrating his determination to maintain his, and Switzerland's freedom of action.

Within the Federal Political Department (FPD), Pilet's intellectual isolation continued. Policy decisions were ruthlessly centralised under his personal control. The only official whose advice Pilet consistently valued and relied upon was the head of the division for political affairs, Pierre Bonna. Born into a Genevan banking family, Bonna had spent almost his entire career in Berne as a functionary of the FPD. Though knowledgeable and intelligent, his lack of foreign experience meant that his world view revolved almost exclusively around the Federal palace. Added to this intensely Swiss-centric outlook, was a naturally cautious, almost unimaginative attitude towards the art of diplomacy which perfectly embodied Talleyrand's dictum, 'above all, no zeal!' In Bonna therefore, Pilet had an official whose innate prudence, political and cultural references mirrored his own, and whose temperament inclined him towards compromise; hardly the person to contest Pilet's handling of foreign policy. Yet it was with Bonna that Pilet would meet to decide foreign policy matters, whether they concerned Bonna's division or not, as in the case of Berne's protecting power duties. Other senior officials invariably had to reach Pilet through Bonna, or submit written memoranda for Pilet's attention. Though undoubtedly exaggerating, the head of the FPD's press section claimed in October 1942 to have met with Pilet only once during the entire year, and with Bonna only twice.[19] Pilet countenanced no independent initiatives from his officials. No press announcements about Berne's protecting power activities could be released without Pilet's prior consent. One of the reasons behind the FPD's reputation for being so uncommunicative to public or press enquiries lay in the fact that, since most of the officials did not have access to Pilet, far less were privy to his ideas, they were almost incapable of answering questions on foreign policy matters.[20]

Curiously, for someone whose experience of foreigners was so restricted, foreign diplomats played a vital part in Pilet's diplomacy. Having considered a problem, requested 'Notizen' from his staff, and perhaps discussed the matter with Bonna or other senior officials, Pilet's next step was to take the matter up with the relevant diplomat in Berne. Here was the crux of Pilet's diplomatic technique – confidential, often secret, but above all personal, negotiations with foreign diplomats. In fact, to some extent, Pilet's desire to play all the cards himself did his country no disservice. Pilet's penchant for 'secret diplomacy' suited the type of work Berne was called upon to fulfil in representing the interests of one belligerent in the territory of another, as their protecting power. Historians have generally been slow in recognising the importance of this aspect of the FPD's wartime work. Pilet's negotiations with foreign diplomats in Berne were generally commendable. While in public Pilet came across as contemptuous, affected and autocratic, in private discussions he was much more appealing.[21] To foreigners, bored by Berne's sombre social circuit, Pilet's sociability and lively mind were a welcome breath of fresh air. Even as late as November 1944, an American official found Pilet 'an admirable and entertaining conversationalist [who] was quite frank in expressing his views on many subjects'.[22] Pilet rightly prided his ability to cultivate friendships with the senior belligerent diplomats. He could speak his mind freely with the German minister, Otto Köcher, who was especially grateful for Pilet's part in hushing up news of a car accident in July 1940 in which Köcher had run over and killed a Swiss citizen.[23] More surprisingly, Pilet also maintained excellent relations with the Anglo-Saxon diplomats, of whose world and cultural background he knew so little. With Leland Harrison, the US minister, Pilet enjoyed good relations.[24] He developed a warm, lasting friendship with the British minister, David Kelly, and Kelly's successor, Clifford Norton, though not uncritical of Pilet, clearly admired him. On Pilet's retirement Norton remarked, 'It is a fitting, if ironic, commentary that the outspoken and general dislike felt for him by his countrymen should find so little echo, at any rate in official circles, among the principal European belligerents, against whose exigencies it was his daily task to defend the material and political interests of his country'.[25]

For all the points Pilet scored with foreign diplomats, there were however significant problems inherent to his private style of diplomacy. Although Pilet's reliance on the diplomatic missions in Berne suited the confidential nature of much of Switzerland's protecting power activities, it gave Pilet precious little insight into the 'minds' of the major belligerent governments. Köcher's ability to talk for Berlin was always problematic given the chaotic nature of Nazi decision-making, and it diminished noticeably as the standing of the Reich's foreign minister Joachim Ribbentrop waned. Pilet's relations with von Bibra, the party official and main power broker in the German legation, were never good. The French ambassador, de la Baume, lacked influence amongst the ruling clique in Vichy, while David Kelly, an 'old-school' diplomat who was starved of information from London, was undoubtedly out of touch with 'Churchillian' Britain after May 1940. Moreover, Kelly's freedom to formulate British policy towards Switzerland before mid-1941 was soon contested by competing government departments in London, and even by maverick commercial officials in his own legation. The same was true with Leland Harrison, who was bewildered by the demise of the State Department's influence over US foreign policy and faced grave difficulties with some of his staff who rejected his excessive neutralism. In short, when Pilet relied on foreign heads of missions as prisms to survey the world beyond Switzerland's frontiers, he received a distorted picture. Pilet completely exaggerated their importance within the diplomatic matrix; the weight he placed on his relations with foreign diplomats was not shared by the governments which they represented.

A further problem with Pilet's preference for personal action was that it ignored the resources provided by Switzerland's own diplomatic service. Admittedly, some sensitive correspondence relating to Switzerland's protecting power work was specifically channelled by the belligerents through Pilet alone. But Pilet's marginalisation of Swiss diplomats went beyond merely a question of tactics. By the end of the war, there were few Swiss diplomats who had not felt themselves slighted by Pilet, either for being kept waiting for days before being granted an audience, or having the impression that their dispatches were left unread.[26] Walter Thurnheer in London was so much left in the dark over official policy that he invariably had to call on the Foreign Office to find out what Pilet had just arranged in Berne. Being a diplomat of a small neutral was a rough job at the best of times; Pilet made it doubly difficult. Personal animosities may well have influenced Pilet's behaviour; particularly so with the prickly Walter Stucki in Vichy, and the banker Vieli, whose backers in Berne, including Etter, may have secured him his position as minister in Rome against Pilet's wishes. There were also diplomats, such as Frölicher in Berlin, who Pilet felt had 'gone native' and whose judgements were therefore considered unreliable.[27]

It was, however, Pilet's jealousy and desire to keep undisputed control of Swiss foreign policy which lies at the heart of his treatment of Swiss diplomats. His relations with Thurnheer bare out this point. Thurnheer's health problems frequently caused him to be absent from his desk for long periods from early 1942. This, and his meek demeanour had encouraged certain sections of the press to call for his replacement. Despite the problems of Thurnheer's position in London, Pilet steadfastly refused to find a substitute until May 1944, by which time the London post had been vacant for six months. Pilet's attitude towards Thurnheer was not due to any lingering sense of duty or affection. For Pilet, Thurnheer possessed one inestimable advantage. As a career diplomat Thurnheer lacked powerful sponsors in Berne, which meant that he could be ignored with impunity.[28] Moreover, given the dearth of qualified candidates, Thurnheer's obvious replacement for most of the war would have been Henri Vallotton. President of the National Council in 1939, president of the *Vollmachtenkommission* for foreign affairs until June 1940, a Vaudois Radical (like Pilet), and one of the leading French-speaking politicians, Vallotton was a potential substitute for Pilet, should his adversaries succeed in ousting him from the council. Pilet may have had good reason to wish Vallotton out of Berne, but he certainly did not want to see him in an important diplomatic post. Rio de Janeiro, the post eventually secured for Vallotton in September 1943 was much more to Pilet's liking![29] In the event, neither Vallotton nor Thurnheer gave Pilet much trouble. Thurnheer suffered his ignominious situation in stoic silence, and Vallotton gradually gave up his ambition to occupy the *Suisse romande* seat on the council, and is best remembered today for providing a 'Zeitungs-Zimmer' (cafeteria!) for the federal palace.[30] But such improvements in Pilet's political position were a heavy price to pay for Switzerland's inadequate representation in one of the major belligerent capitals. Pilet may have been bequeathed a Mini-sized diplomatic service, but under his direction it gave the performance of a Trabant.

Pilet's attitude towards the Anglo-Saxon world both illustrates the problems associated with his style of decision-making, and represents one of the principal areas where these failings were at their most acute. Pilet never understood the Anglo-Saxon world. His view of Britain was typically Gallic: of the 'perfidious Albion' variety, rather than of the magnanimous Britannia, ruling the waves for the common good. As for the 'land of the free', this was populated by uncouth cowboys, as unrefined in their manners as they were in the intricacies of diplomacy. Pilet made some paltry attempts to make up for the gaps in his knowledge by drawing on the advice of Switzerland's pre-war minister in London in early 1940. But once every Francophone's suspicion of the British had been confirmed at Dunkirk, Oran and Dakar, Pilet seems to have given up expecting anything from London. He remained wedded to this mind-set until late 1943, paying little attention to Thurnheer in London (who was, in his opinion, 'völlig anglisiert') and rejecting all suggestions to employ an Anglo-Saxon specialist on his staff.[31] The one FPD official capable of fulfilling this function, former councillor in London, Clemente Rezzonico, was shunted off as head of the press division. Pilet only drew on his talents in the spring of 1944 when, bewildered by the sudden aggressive tone in Allied attitudes towards Switzerland, Pilet belatedly dispatched him on a fact-finding mission to London.

As a result, Pilet remained out of touch with the changing currents of opinion in the Allied capitals and blind to the implications of their irresistible military successes. When confronted with evidence of Switzerland's poor standing, Pilet invariably discounted it, blithely assuming that gratitude for his humanitarian work, and his good relations with the Allied diplomats would be sufficient to defend Switzerland's vital interests. As a last resort, after reading Rezzonico's mission report in early 1944, he grudgingly agreed to augment the London legation's entertainment allowance! Quite how long Pilet believed in a German victory is a matter of conjecture, but the conviction that neither Britain nor America could solve Europe's problems, meant that a compromise peace always appeared to be the war's most likely outcome. Keeping on good relations with Nazi Germany was therefore not simply a requirement of Swiss neutrality, but was based on the assumption that Berne would have to deal with Berlin's criminal regime for some time to come.

Switzerland's relations with the West were also significantly influenced by Pilet's disregard for commercial matters. Since his involvement in Swiss trade policy was as negligible as his interest in it, Berne's commercial relations with the West were allowed to develop in a political vacuum. Consequently, as economic and financial matters began impinging on Allied relations with Switzerland from 1942, the Swiss deluded themselves that all was well, and continued to view Swiss–Allied economic relations in terms of their impact on Switzerland, rather than *vice versa*. Ignorant of the exact nature of Switzerland's commercial commitments with Germany, Pilet was taken by surprise when the Allies embarked on an aggressive campaign against Swiss metallurgical firms in the autumn of 1943, and 'black-listed' the firm of Hans Sulzer, one of Switzerland's pre-eminent business/political figures. Stirred into action, Pilet injected some political sense into the debate, forcing the council to resist the demands of the metallurgical industry, and reach a settlement with the Allies. However, Swiss commercial and financial affairs with the West continued to be largely divorced from Pilet's handling of Switzerland's political relations over the following year, and remained so with the exception of a brief interlude in early 1945 during the so-called 'Currie' negotiations.

The historical jury is still out on Pilet. This remote, aloof figure, continues to intrigue, beguile and baffle historians. What is beyond doubt however, is that the conduct of Swiss foreign policy from 1940 to 1944 was in many critical respects indelibly stamped with Pilet's character. Isolated from his federal colleagues, fellow politicians, interest groups and even departmental officials, Pilet had a remarkably free hand in defining foreign policy. More research is required on Pilet's political attitudes after the shattering experience of the fall of France, especially the allure of authoritarian Pétainist political solutions in the second half of 1940. However, in jealously 'cocooning' himself and his work from outside influences, Pilet allowed Swiss foreign policy to develop in a sterile intellectual environment. Debate was too often reduced to memoranda, with inadequate discussion on policy issues, and insufficient opportunities for officials to present opinions which challenged Pilet's view of Switzerland's place in Europe or the course of the war. Likewise, little was done to question Pilet's definition of Switzerland's political interests, a definition which failed to give sufficient weight to economic and financial considerations. The political implications of Switzerland's commercial policies were therefore overlooked by the very department whose job it was to secure Switzerland's interests abroad. As a result Switzerland's banking and business interests groups enjoyed unfettered influence and were permitted to mortgage federal trade policy and the country's economic independence to the Axis powers. Switzerland may well still be paying the price for Pilet's oversight today.

NOTES

1 Edgar Bonjour: *Geschichte der schweizerischen Neutralität. Vier Jahrhunderte eidgenössischer Aussenpolitik*, Basle, Helbing & Lichtenhahn, vols 4–6, esp. Vol. 5, Ch. 17. See also Alice Meyer, *Anpassung oder Widerstand. Die Schweiz zur Zeit des deutschen Nationalsozialismus*. Frauenfeld, Huber, 1965.

2 See O. Gauye, 'Le général Guisan et la diplomatie suisse, 1940–1941' in *Studien und Quellen*, 4, Berne, Schweizerisches Bundesarchiv, 1978, pp. 5–63.

3 Daniel Bourgeois, 'L'image allemande de Pilet-Golaz, 1940–1944', *Studien und Quellen*, 4, 1978, pp. 68–125, and 'La Suisse et la Deuxième Guerre Mondiale. Guisan, Pilet-Golaz? Le cas des relations Germano–Suisse', *Alliance Culturelle Romande*, 23, 1977, pp. 11–16. For a critical balanced summary of Pilet's career, see J.-C. Favez and M. Fleury, 'Marcel Pilet-Golaz 1889–1958', in Urs Altermatt (ed.), *Die Schweizer Bundesräte. Ein biographisches Lexikon*, Zurich, Artemis & Winkler, 1991 (2nd edn, 1997), pp. 366–71.

4 Alfred Bonnet: *Le grand mérite de Pilet-Golaz*, Lausanne, private publication, 1977. Georges-André Chevallaz: *Le Défi de la Neutralité. Diplomatie et défense de la Suisse 1939–1945*, Vevey, L'Aire, 1995.

5 Erwin Bucher, *Zwischen Bundesrat und General. Schweizer Politik und Armee im Zweiten Weltkrieg*. St Gallen, Verlagsgemeinschaft, 1991, esp. pp. 575–98.

6 See discussion in J. F. Paroz, 'La décision de satisfaire les exigences allemandes relatives aux incidents aériens de l'été 1940', *Relations internationales*, 49, 1987, pp. 33–54.

7 The same was also true with regard to General Guisan. See W. Gautschi, *Le Général Guisan*, Lausanne, Payot, 1991 (from German, 1989), pp. 423–34.

8 But see views of Bucher on the discussions surrounding the presidential address of 25 June 1940, Bucher, *Zwischen Bundesrat und General*, pp. 536–56.

 9 Federal Councillor Eduard von Steiger to National Councillor Markus
   Feldmann, Feldmann Diary entry for 1.3.1943. BA. JI. 3/31. fo. 2199. (With Pilet,
   one can never be sure what he may have discussed with foreign diplomats.)
   Papers consulted with kind permission of Dr Hans Feldmann.
10 In the absence of a full biography see J. Widmer: 'Philipp Etter 1891–1977', in
   Altermatt (ed.), *Die Schweizer Bundesräte*, pp. 389–94. Etter was a member of the
   ICRC, but his discussions with Pilet were not restricted to humanitarian matters.
   Ernst Wetter later claimed to be the closest councillor to Pilet, but there is little
   evidence to support this view. See E. Bonjour: 'Wie lange glaubte Pilet-Golaz an
   den deutschen Endsieg?', in *Die Schweiz und Europa*, Vol. 7, Basle, Helbing &
   Lichtenhahn, 1981, pp. 313–15.
11 Members of the council also occasionally met deputations from political parties,
   in which policy matters would be discussed.
12 For this episode see Bucher, *Zwischen Bundesrat und General*, pp. 79–220.
13 Confidential memo. by Norton in Norton to Howard (FO) 24.2.1945. PRO.
   FO371/49687 Z2585. For the listing of Sulzer see Oswald Inglin, *Der stille Krieg.
   Der Wirtschaftskrieg zwischen Grossbritannien und der Schweiz im Zweiten Weltkrieg*,
   Zurich, Neue Zürcher Zeitung Verlag, 1991, pp. 172–81, and Neville Wylie,
   Britain and the Swiss, 1939–1945, Oxford, Oxford University Press, 2001.
14 See his comments on 21 June 1940 to the federal financial delegation in
   Documents Diplomatiques Suisses, Vol. 13, Berne, Benteli, 1991, No. 314/1.
15 The numerous self-congratulatory histories of Switzerland's leading business
   do little to illuminate their role in Swiss foreign affairs. One of the primary
   challenges facing analysts today is to examine the link between Swiss government, industries and banks in the making of federal trade policy, especially the
   role of business lobby groups and the chamber of commence (Vorort), whose
   chairman, Heinrich Homberger, was one of the primary architects of Swiss trade
   policy during the war.
16 Daniel Bourgeois, 'Milieux d'affaires et politique étrangère suisse à l'époque des
   fascismes', *Relations internationales*, 1, 1974, pp. 181–207.
17 According to information reaching the US legation in Berne, UK embassy,
   Washington, to Foreign Office, 2.12.1941. PRO. FO371/26344 C13022.
18 See correspondence in BA. E2001 (D) 2/29, and, *inter alia*, A. Mattioli, *Zwischen
   Demokratie und Totalitärer Diktatur*, Zurich, Orell Füssli, 1994, pp. 256–91.
19 Diary of Markus Feldmann (then National Councillor), 16.10.1942. 3A. JI. 3 Vol.
   30 folio. 1959.
20 See Pilet's remarks to federal councillor Kobelt about his staff cited in
   P. Braunschweig, *Geheimer Draht nach Berlin*, Zurich, Neue Zürcher Zeitung
   Verlag, 1989, p. 450, n.185.
21 The diary of National Councillor Markus Feldmann provides an excellent
   illustration of how Pilet was able to soften the views of one of his most ardent
   critics after a private meeting between the two men in April 1943. BA. JI. 3 Vol.
   31 fols 2258–65 for April 1943.
22 N. Lankford (ed.), *OSS against the Reich: The World War II Diaries of Col. David K.
   E. Bruce*, Kent OH, Kent State University Press, 1991, p. 193.
23 BA. JI. 17. 1990/98/174. FPD Note 'Streng Vertraulich', 15.7.1940, and Bourgeois,
   'L'image allemande de Pilet-Golaz', p. 110.
24 See forthcoming PhD thesis by Monika Bachmann, 'Leland Harrison and
   Swiss–American relations during the Second World War', London School of
   Economics, University of London.
25 Norton to Eden, 28.12.1944. PRO. FO371/49687 Z519. On Pilet's relations with

Britain's ministers see Neville Wylie: 'Marcel Pilet-Golaz, David Kelly and Anglo-Swiss relations in 1940', *Diplomacy & Statecraft*, 8/1, 1997, pp. 49–79.

26   See remark by William Rappard in the *Vollmachtenkommission* debate, 16.9.1942. BA E2809/1.

27   For Frölicher and Swiss representation abroad see, G. Kreis, 'General Guisan, Minister Frölicher und die Mission Burckhardt 1940', *Zeitschrift für schweizerische Geschichte*, 19, 1977, pp. 99–121.

28   Similar attitudes may in some small part lie behind Pilet's refusal to recall Frölicher from Berlin.

29   Vallotton had been offered the London post in 1939, but had declined it, probably in order to further his political career in Berne. BA. E1004.1 1 Minutes of the Federal Council, 14.7.1939. Bucher, *Zwischen Bundesrat und General*, pp. 128, 529.

30   Thurnheer mentioned his difficulties to William Rappard, and other people during his occasional visits to Berne, but his professionalism prevented him from making his criticisms too vocal.

31   William Rappard to Federal Councillor Walter Stampfli 1.6.1942. BA. JI 149/1977/135 Vol. 118, and Daniel Bourgeois, 'William Rappard et la politique extérieure suisse à l'époque des fascismes, 1933–1945', *Studien und Quellen*, 15, 1989, pp. 7–76.

8

'Neither this Way nor any Other': Swiss Internationalism during the Second World War

MADELEINE HERREN

The remarks that follow are an attempt at a structurally oriented presentation, confined to the Second World War, of that aspect of Swiss foreign policy which found expression in the sending of official representatives to international conferences, and governmental support for international organisations, irrespective of whether the institution concerned was a governmental one or, formally, non-governmental.[1] This governmental internationalism was based on the concepts of multilateral cooperation that stretched back into the nineteenth century and also played a major part, alongside the League of Nations system, in international relations and Swiss foreign policy during the inter-war period. At the outbreak of the Second World War, the Swiss version of internationalism clashed with an expansionist National Socialist version. Trapped in a policy vacuum that was only skimpily camouflaged by protestations of neutrality, Swiss foreign policy unintentionally drifted off course, a position that was confirmed and reinforced by the lack of differentiation from National Socialist internationalism and the country's reluctant attitude – justified by the policy of neutrality – towards the internationalisation strategies launched by the Allied side.

INTERNATIONAL ORGANISATIONS, CONGRESSES AND CONFERENCES AS A MEDIUM OF STATE FOREIGN POLICY

In the second half of the nineteenth century, international gatherings of the most varied origins breached Europe's internal frontiers. Apart from politically motivated alliances, such as the Socialist International, the 'flood tide of internationalism' was borne along by a broad spectrum of apparently non-political processes of internationalisation. What seemed at first sight to be the internationalisation of civilian associations and a strengthening of scientific internationalism had in fact acquired an unmistakably strong governmental component. Foreign ministries issued invitations through their diplomatic representations to congresses which, although they were by no means formally official, were nevertheless eventually attended not only by private participants but also by official government delegates from many countries. Governments supported, and sent delegates to, international institutions which did not necessarily meet the criteria of an intergovernmental organisation, while on the other hand most of the international unions were subject to the political control of the host country. This governmental internationalism made it clear that the trend towards international networking, dictated by modernisation, also and especially included the state. By providing facilities for cross-border communication, creating internationally compatible rules and standards, ensuring the international transfer of information and, consequently, the governmental provision and safeguarding of infrastructures with a cross-border functional capability, the state made it possible to take advantage of the world market, and in so doing had to rely on co-operation with non-governmental experts. Whereas the concept of the sovereign and therefore autonomous and autarchal state had already become unrealistic in the age of the creation of nation-states and exaggerated nationalism, the underlying principle of governmental internationalism – the insight into the need for state participation in multilateral networks – is still not obsolete today.[2]

Only certain aspects of national foreign policy become visible through the filter of governmental internationalism: exclusively multilateral contacts with a primarily technical objective. Yet internationalisation strategies have the methodological advantage of breadth. They make it possible to show the consequences of modernisation in foreign relations and highlight the dialectical tension between traditionally secret diplomacy and multilateral cooperation designed for public consumption. From the Swiss standpoint, probably the most essential advantage of this concept is that there is no need to discuss Switzerland as a *Sonderfall*. Internationalisation strategies were apparent in Europe in the nineteenth century, but even before the First World War they could be seen throughout the world. The structure of these foreign relations encompasses both non-governmental and governmental activities and suits the Swiss militia system, which is by no means unusual in this field. In addition, the lack of a strong foreign ministry proved not obstructive but beneficial for Swiss internationalism. The objective of governmental internationalism – networking dictated by modernisation – enforces a view of Switzerland as a country involved multilaterally in international relations. The technical orientation casts light on the everyday business of foreign policy and not the grand gestures of declarations of principle rooted in the policy of neutrality. Internationalisation strategies also reduce the apparent gap between great powers and small states, because economic potential and the national capability for modernisation raise the status of the smaller state. Furthermore, even after the foundation of the League of Nations, the structure of which was dictated by the great powers, Switzerland was in charge of the international offices of the five largest and most important international unions.[3]

GOVERNMENTAL INTERNATIONALISM ON THE EVE OF THE SECOND WORLD WAR

The growing political tensions and the collapse of the League of Nations system in no way reduced governments' need for official congress invitations. The number of invitations to international gatherings debated by the Swiss Federal Council had declined in 1933 and 1934, but then rose steadily until the outbreak of war; and, as the number of invitations increased, fewer were rejected than in the period before 1933.[4] In 1936, the year of Italy's attack on Abyssinia and the outbreak of the Spanish Civil War, the Swiss Federal Council did not refuse any congress invitations at all. Switzerland's commitment to internationalism cannot be explained solely by the fact that the country's presence at foreign congresses was a necessary part of the preparations for the international events accompanying the Swiss National Exhibition of 1939. When Swiss foreign policy switched to absolute neutrality in 1938, Swiss internationalism took over the function of demonstrating that Switzerland was nevertheless active in foreign policy. 'At a time when we are considering the means of definitively recovering our complete neutrality within the framework of the League of Nations, it would be of some significance for Switzerland to demonstrate its support for international collaboration in areas where there is no danger of our political status becoming an issue.' According to Federal Councillor Motta, the Red Cross created favourable opinion abroad, and the International Bureau of Education 'adds ... to our country's moral stature. ... Neutrality need not mean isolation, and Switzerland, which in any case depends on its foreign trade, has everything to gain by making a direct contribution to the general work of civilization.'[5]

The concept of a Switzerland which could be internationally active even under conditions of absolute neutrality was not confined to the rhetoric of the 'spiritual national defence'. But the Swiss internationalism of the inter-war years suffered from a mistaken lack of universality and expressly excluded any involvement of the Soviet Union. Invitations to events held in Switzerland and attended by emissaries of foreign governments were distributed through diplomatic channels, in accordance with the model of governmental internationalism, invitations being sent on each occasion to those countries with which Switzerland maintained diplomatic relations. The Soviet Union was not one of them. The congress organisers, who had set out in 1938 with the notion that the Swiss could mediate between political opposites, would have preferred official participation by the Soviet Union, as in the case of the organising committee of the eighth International Congress of Historical Science,⁶ held in Zurich in 1938. The organising committee of this history congress – and of the physiology congress held in the same year – tried at least to arrange easier travelling conditions for those coming to Switzerland privately to attend the congresses.⁷

Since the multilateral nature of Swiss internationalism from the end of the First World War had not been universal and global in its intent, it was difficult to achieve any credibility in 1938 by presenting a willingness to cooperate internationally as an expression of total neutrality. Switzerland's decision not to adopt a broadly based internationalism was all the more serious in that, even in the case of the Soviet Union, cross-border contacts certainly did exist. After all, as the successor state of Tsarist Russia, the Soviet Union was a member of various international unions based in Berne, which in itself meant that it was in contact, through political agencies, with the EPD (Federal Political Department), which was responsible for supervision of the international offices. In addition, the Federal Council was willing to finance a fairly long study trip in 1930 for a delegate to a conference on soil sciences in Moscow. In accordance with instructions from the Federal Council the delegate, Professor G. Wiegner, spoke as a 'scientist without government mandate'.⁸ During the Second World War, the officially non-existent relationships were consolidated at least to the point at which the Swiss legation in Ankara obtained weather information from the Soviet representation there to pass on to the International Meteorological Organisation.⁹

While the Swiss authorities refused to issue an official invitation to the Soviet Union to attend the historical science congress in Zurich, the invitations sent out to the German Reich and Italy through diplomatic channels brought large National Socialist and fascist delegations to Zurich.¹⁰ The fact that the Swiss version of internationalism did not include the Soviet Union was to develop into a fundamental problem during the 1930s, as the Federal Council's increasing enthusiasm for participating in international congresses now encountered the increasing presence of the Axis powers in the process of internationalisation.

The Federal Council refused none of the offers received from Italy after 1929, while official congress invitations from Berlin were all accepted from 1936. Although the Federal Council's response to invitations from France was also totally favourable in 1935 and 1936,[11] by 1939 German offers exceeded those from France and reflected a growing interest on the part of the National Socialist state in the instrument of governmental internationalism. German efforts to bring about the official combination and centralisation of multilateral activities resulted in the formation of an institution for that specific purpose. The Deutsche Kongress-Zentrale, an institution which had been under the control of the German Reich Ministry for Popular Enlightenment and Propaganda since 1936, was the ultimate affirmation of the political importance of official congress participation as a powerful tool of foreign policy. In Berne, as elsewhere, the German legation asked the Federal Political Department to support the *Yearbook of Congresses* published by the Kongress-Zentrale by supplying details of those held in Switzerland. The Federal Department of Posts and Railways expressed reservations: 'The request made by the German Legation, or by its principal, makes us wonder what is behind it, and particularly whether it is appropriate to supply detailed information on the Congress organizers (names and addresses).'[13] By this time, however, congress lists had already been sent to Germany.[14] In 1938/39, therefore, a growing Swiss interest in internationalism coincided with an increase in governmental internationalism in National Socialist Germany.

'NEITHER THIS WAY NOR ANY OTHER'

The outbreak of the Second World War saw a dramatic decline in international congress activity, though it did not put an end to efforts at governmental internationalisation. The importance of Switzerland as a centre of internationalist activity grew. Some organisations transferred their headquarters to Switzerland, Swiss citizens were appointed as interim secretaries, government departments in Berne sometimes handled the business of international organisations, and multilateral meetings in Switzerland were concerned with the safeguarding of international agreements. The International Meteorological Committee, implementing a resolution adopted before the outbreak of war, moved its headquarters from the Netherlands to Lausanne in 1939. In the same year, the director of the Swiss Federal Veterinary Office became president of the International Office of Epizootics. Similarly, with German consent and the approval of the Federal Political Department, the interim secretariat of the International Hospital Association had also been based in Switzerland since 1939.[15] In 1940 a *petit comité consultatif*, comprising representatives of the member states of the International Broadcasting Union (IBU) not involved in the war at that time, met in Lausanne. Delegates from Norway, Italy and Switzerland tried – albeit unsuccessfully – to implement an arrangement that had been made shortly before war broke out. In 1942 the International Confederation of Authors' and Composers' Societies moved its headquarters from Berlin to Berne. The increase in the number of international bodies in Switzerland increased the administrative expense of foreign policy, simply because of the visas and residence permits required. Finally, the war also resulted in a thematic expansion of the spectrum of existing internationalisation measures, since the creation of a Swiss navy, owing to the war, compelled the government in Berne to become involved in the complex system of international maritime law.[16]

The increase in Swiss internationalism coincided with an increase in the importance of international organisations that was ultimately independent of Switzerland. Its information service – from weather reports to cereal production statistics – was strategically important, and internationally networked communication facilities were an essential requirement of modern warfare.[17] Even associations of marginal significance in the government's eyes, such as the International Federation for Housing and Town Planning, found their value enhanced by the war.[18] At a time when international communications were difficult, international organisations also offered a politically important opportunity for the multilateral confirmation of territorial changes. Newly created states were exceptionally quick to turn to the Universal Postal Union (UPU),[19] with a view to gaining indirect recognition of their new status within this organisation with its broad multilateral basis. As demonstrated by the issuing of postage stamps by the Polish government in exile, the Universal Postal Union was also a convenient platform on which to mount a show of resistance.[20] These politically explosive activities had in each case to be notified through the diplomatic channels of whichever state was in control of the organisation, since most international offices of the Public International Unions did not communicate directly with the member states. In the case of the offices located in Berne, the Federal Political Department was therefore involved. The fact that the Federal Council was more than just a 'postman' in such cases was confirmed by the UPU congress of 1939. The congress was particularly important politically because of the dispute regarding the deletion of Czechoslovakia from the preamble to the Universal Postal Convention – a deletion that eventually did not take place. The accession of Slovakia to the existing postal conventions was confirmed at the same congress, 'although the British delegation suggested in the course of conversation that the Federal Political Department should first put out diplomatic feelers to the Contracting States'.[21] Although the Federal Council did not take the opportunity for international action, internal activities were unavoidable in this matter, especially since not only the bureau of the Universal Postal Union but also the other international offices based in Berne did not take politically explosive decisions without involving the Federal Political Department. For example, the Director of the United International Bureaux for Industrial, Literary and Artistic Property first obtained the approval of the Federal Council before accepting the registration of the 'Protec- torate of Bohemia and Moravia' as a designation of origin and trying to initiate the accession of Slovakia.[22]

Reactions abroad confirmed that decisions by the international offices in Berne were also interpreted as an expression of Swiss foreign policy. Thus, in 1941, the director of the United International Bureaux of Industrial, Literary and Artistic Property, after consultation with the Federal Council, denied a report in the *Deutsche Volkswirt* asserting that the Federal Council was blocking Slovakia's accession to the existing trademark protection conventions for political reasons.[23] The political consequences of this area of foreign policy extended into the post-war years, when in 1946 the Polish delegation to the postal conference at Lake Success explicitly criticised the rapid recognition of Slovakia.[24] The extent of Switzerland's interests in the policy of the international offices was also confirmed by the case of Abyssinia, when problems were caused in the second half of the war by the hasty deletion from the list of UPU members of this country that had been a member of the union since 1908. What happened was that in 1942 the Abyssinian ministry responsible asked to be sent the documentation on the UPU congress in Buenos Aires. Since Abyssinia was not included among the member states named in the preamble and its postal authority had been run by Italy since 1936, the question arose of whether it was entitled to make this request, particularly since the territory now appeared to be under British administration.[25] When the Abyssinian post office also issued stamps, the question again arose at the end of February 1943 of whether the country could join the Universal Postal Union or could claim the benefit of its pre-1936 membership. The director of the UPU bureau, Reinhold Furrer, was of the opinion that the case of Abyssinia was not comparable with those of Poland, Yugoslavia and Czechoslovakia, because although the last named no longer had any territory, it did nevertheless maintain relations with the Universal Postal Union. In addition, in view of the uncertain political situation, it was desirable 'not to apply for membership at this early stage'.[26] The case resulted in lengthy investigations within the Federal Political Department, which recommended playing for time in the hope that events would arise 'to prevent a situation in which the first official document which internationally establishes the loss of Italy's colonial empire in Abyssinia originates from a Swiss authority'.[27]

Despite the increasing politicisation of the international organisations, the Federal Council was not prepared to provide any clearer definition of its supervisory tasks. The Federal Political Department was stranded in a twilight of uncertainty and dealt with issues of increasing political importance as purely technical problems of content. In an opinion drafted in September 1942 on the issue of the federal director of building's personal membership of the German-dominated International Federation for Housing and Town Planning, the lack of strategic planning had become a maxim of foreign policy. The Federal Political Department felt that the question of membership was a difficult one to answer 'because it is impossible at this stage to predict either the consequences of refusal or the effects of agreement. Either could result in inconvenience, which it is very much in our interest to avoid. It would therefore appear to us to be advisable not to anticipate events and, if possible, to endeavour to rule neither this way nor in any other until the end of the war.'[28] The policy of 'neither this way nor any other' strengthened the reactive component of Swiss foreign policy at a time when the importance of Swiss internationalism was enhanced and when clear limits should have been imposed on the expansion of National Socialist internationalism.

SWISS REACTIONS TO NATIONAL SOCIALIST INTERNATIONALISM

National Socialist strategies of internationalisation were directed towards infiltrating existing international organisations, founding competing organisations and attempting to involve Swiss and international officials in German-dominated associations. The scope of this movement, hitherto neglected by researchers into National Socialism,[29] was considerable. It was aimed at contacts with governments, institutions and individuals, and focused on the politically sensitive areas of communication, information transfer and the harmonisation of law. The multilateral nature of governmental internationalism was confined to the Axis powers, their satellite states and a few neutrals, while occupied territories were specifically not invited. As Sweden, in particular, applied a more restrictive policy than Switzerland when it came to sending delegates, the group of neutrals invited on each occasion increasingly consisted of states whose neutrality was in no way linked to democratic structures. This contextual disavowal of neutrality also needs to be borne in mind in connection with the establishment of the post-war order. In 1944, for example, the Soviet Union blocked the inclusion of neutrals in the United Nations Relief and Rehabilitation Administration (UNRRA), but at the same time, and most notably, tried to prevent the accession of Spain and Argentina (the latter still a neutral at that time).

The authorities were well aware of the attempt to exploit Swiss participation in National Socialist internationalism. As far as the Federal Political Department was concerned, even such apparently secondary issues as sending a delegate to a spa congress in Bratislava had dangerous political overtones, since the circumstances of the time 'require us to be extremely circumspect in the matter of official participation at international meetings where the organisers, under more or less overt pressure from their governments, sometimes tend to involve the "neutral" delegates in decisions outside the framework of such meetings; this often places the delegates concerned in a very invidious situation'.[30] However, there had been no indications hitherto that the Federal Political Department had refused an invitation from Berlin on the grounds that Swiss internationalism, interpreted as a multilateral concept, could not participate in National Socialist belligerent internationalism specifically for reasons of neutrality.

The belligerent internationalism of National Socialism was conceived as a broadly based movement and related in particular to the process of harmonisation of law. The year 1940 saw the creation in Germany of an association on International and Foreign Criminal Law, whose aim was to 'discuss the reconstruction of international scientific associations'.[31] A similarly broad objective was pursued by the International Chamber of Law, founded in 1941: the objective of this corporate organisation, as stated by its president, Reich Minister Hans Frank, was 'the preservation of order in the German sphere of influence by means of a new continental legal system meeting the natural needs of the peoples living there'.[32] The structure of the International Chamber of Law was geared to taking over international functions of existing organisations. Individual technical sections published 'archives', including an archive for the law of international organizations, which appeared to the Swiss envoy Hans Frölicher to be a takeover of the publications documenting international life previously published by the Belgium-based Union of International Associations.[33] Other subject areas appropriated by the International Chamber of Law dealt with the law on bills of exchange, intellectual property, cinema law and the regulation of the postal and telegraphic services – areas, then, which had long been the subject of international discussion and for which international organisations existed that had been set up in the early days of governmental internationalism. While the International Chamber of Law, as a corporate organisation, established international contacts at a personal and professional level and tried – unsuccessfully – to recruit the director of the United International Bureaux for Industrial, Literary and Artistic Property as a member of its copyright section,[34] a whole series of newly established or radically restructured organisations formed the basis of a competing international system. The harmonisation of law found its institutional continuation in the Association of European Copyright Associations (VEU), founded in 1942. This organisation aimed to establish links between the European copyright associations with a view to discussing questions of content, offered support to individual associations, and guaranteed their interests in dealings with non-member associations and with third parties. The organisation, based in Berlin and Rome, even dictated relations with the competing International Confederation of Authors' and Composers' Societies (CISAC), which was integrated into the structure of the new association through the persons of its members.[35]

By dealing with the subject of film rights, the International Chamber of Law was turning to an area of internationalisation that had its own, National Socialist-dominated organisation. The International Film Board had set itself the task 'of advancing understanding between nations within the framework of the international new order'.[36] The film board had been in existence since as early as 1935, but had been restructured at an international convention in Berlin in the summer of 1941, where new statutes were adopted. The deputy chairman of the Reich Film Board, Karl Melzer, in his invitation, asked foreign governments to send plenipotentiaries to the conference, and announced a session 'at which binding resolutions are to be adopted on the transformation of the International Film Board, the adoption of new statutes, the initiation of the working programme and the appointment of members'.[37] The convention was thus vested with an official status hitherto reserved exclusively for diplomatic conferences. The refounding of the International Film Board, which eventually also took place, instituted the internationalisation of the corporate principle. The implementation of this characteristic feature of fascist internationalisation first came about in an area which had been energetically canvassed in the inter-war years by Italy, France and Switzerland, with the participation of the League of Nations, and eventually resulted in the founding of various (educational) film institutes in Rome, Basle and Paris. Back in 1938, when the possible accession of Switzerland to the International Educational Film Institute was under discussion in Berne, the question of the internationalisation of cinema was considered by the Swiss film expert Dr Gottlieb Imhof to be one of crucial importance, because 'apart from the armaments industries, only the film industry has such extensive international links that every possible effort must be made to find an international solution to its present and future problems'.[38]

In 1941 Switzerland participated in the legal establishment of a National Socialist-dominated film centre, sending an official delegate and an expert to the founding conference in Berlin. However, the Federal Council expressly refused to give the delegates any power to make binding declarations, and in fact sent them to Berlin for reporting purposes only.[39] The report delivered to the Federal Council by these delegates was far-sighted but proposed a position which combined the special case of Switzerland with benevolence and willingness to cooperate. A 'legal innovation', according to the delegates, was cross-border corporate cooperation, which was of interest not only to the Reich Propaganda Ministry but also to the Foreign Ministry. Furthermore, there was 'no denying that the refounding of the International Film Board in the context of the reorganisation of European industry, as intended by the Axis powers, is happening'.[40] But, they added, the interests of Switzerland would be better served by joining in, and experience in Berlin showed that Switzerland could 'even today, thanks to its honest desire to participate, make itself useful and successful internationally'.[41] The Federal Political Department (EPD) was not averse to Swiss involvement in the Film Board, and welcomed the founding of a Swiss Film Industry Association, because, as the EPD put it, the association would have made Swiss membership of the International Film Board possible without official involvement.[42] However, Switzerland was still not a member of the International Film Board by 1942, despite a further initiative by Melzer,[43] because a press campaign and many petitions to the Federal Council in the summer of 1941 prevented Swiss membership.[44]

In 1942 the number of conferences and congresses arranged by the Germans proliferated to the point where Franz Kappeler from the Swiss legation identified a '[strong] determination to impose a European order precisely in association circles ... with no intention whatsoever of abandoning the international ... ties'.[45] The internationalisation policy of the Third Reich, based on the professional classes, suited the structural significance of the Swiss associations and caused problems of control and supervision within the EPD. As letters and invitations from Germany went straight to the Swiss associations, their willingness to cooperate with the state determined whether the Federal Political Department would be notified of their presence at all, though ultimately that presence was portrayed as Swiss participation. Thus, it was from a newspaper report that the Federal Political Department learned that Switzerland had attended a VEU conference in Berlin. Enquiries by the Federal Justice and Police Department revealed that the Federal Intellectual Property Office had not been represented, though the *Mechanlizenz*, the Swiss Association for Mechanical Copyrights had been, subject to the reservation of freedom to associate with the VEU member states hostile to the Axis.[46] This failure to inform the Federal Political Department recurred in the summer of 1943, when another VEU conference was held in Madrid and the department asked the Swiss legation in Madrid to enquire into the presence of Swiss delegates.[47] The *Mechanlizenz*, when questioned by the Federal Political Department, had promised in the spring of 1943 not to send representatives to this event, though it did defend itself in a manner that makes it easier to understand the later investigations by the Federal Political Department. The *Mechanlizenz* had argued that its presence in Berlin had been following the example set by the Swiss attendance at the European Postal Union Congress in Vienna.[48] Furthermore, the *Mechanlizenz* pointed out that its commitment abroad was attributable to the unsatisfactory situation in Switzerland. The opinion expressed by the *Mechanlizenz* ended with a request that it be granted a monopoly right of exploitation similar to that of the *Suisa*, the Swiss Association of Authors and Publishers. Otherwise, argued the *Mechanlizenz*, it would have to resort to international cooperation. The *Mechanlizenz* case highlights the difficulty created by National Socialist internationalism when it came to ensuring governmental control over foreign policy. The example also underlines the significance of the neutrality argument as an instrument of discipline in domestic policy.

Berne was also compelled to take action by the National Socialist attempt to undermine international organisations based in Switzerland. In the summer of 1942 Robert Hercod, the secretary-general of the International Bureau against Alcoholism, requested an audience with Minister Pierre Bonna because the president of the World League against Alcoholism, the head of the Reich health administration Dr Leonardo Conti, wanted to arrange an international conference in Berlin. Hercod feared that resistance to the convening of the conference would result in the abandonment of the Swiss headquarters and the re-establishment of a politicised union under German control. He therefore proposed a compromise solution and wanted assurances that the anti-alcohol associations of the occupied countries would participate, that delegates would be nominated without political pressure and that no binding resolutions would be adopted, though he was aware that this approach would annoy the Swiss associations.[49] The agreement finally reached with the EPD was that Hercod should agree to the conference in Berlin, subject to the requirements proposed by him. However, his compromise proposal that the associations in the occupied territories should be included came to nothing, because the associations concerned refused to put in an appearance in Berlin.[50] Fears that an event would now be held in Berlin and would be dominated by the Axis powers eventually proved unfounded: the conference was postponed 'sine die' in November 1943.[51]

Hercod was not the only internationalist to report to the Federal Political Department on National Socialist takeover bids. Marcel Godet, Director of the National Library, travelled to Salzburg – admittedly not as an official delegate, but nevertheless by arrangement with the Federal Department of the Interior (EDI) and the consent of the Federal Political Department – to attend a conference of the enlarged advisory board of the German Association for Documentation. Godet was chairman of the International Association of Librarians and feared that the question of the formation of a European Association of Librarians might be raised, in which case he proposed to adopt delaying tactics.[52]

The instances mentioned above resulted in no official interventions by Switzerland as a matter of foreign policy, though action was taken domestically.[53] However, they do demonstrate that the Federal Political Department was well informed, and they also provide proof that National Socialist internationalism was systematically trying to exploit even minor international movements. The scope of the movement and the evidence of deliberate efforts at internationalisation thus confer additional importance on the most significant of these cases, the creation of a European Postal and Telecommunications Union.

The Swiss legation reported that there was discussion in the *Reichsanzeiger* in September 1942 to the effect that 'all European postal administrations' had been invited to attend a congress in Vienna in October.[54] This congress culminated in the foundation of a European Postal and Telecommunications Union, which the Swiss legation was not alone in viewing as 'a further step towards the concentration of Europe under Axis leadership'.[55] Efforts at postal internationalisation had begun in late 1941, when the German post office began endeavouring to conclude bilateral agreements. The overriding aim of these initiatives, even at that stage, was to create a European organisation.

In the run-up to the Vienna congress, an interview took place between Dr Risch, the head of the German ministerial department concerned, and the director of the Universal Postal Union Bureau, the Swiss Reinhold Furrer. Furrer notified the Federal Political Department of this conversation before it took place. He felt that the matter was nothing to do with the bureau, particularly since numerous regional postal unions – such as the American, Scandinavian and Balkan Postal Unions – already existed.[56] While the Universal Postal Union did not oppose the creation of the European Postal Union, the political decision was viewed with considerable misgivings in the Swiss Parliament. The Federal Department of Posts and Railways considered the pros and cons of a postal convention between Germany and Switzerland, and concluded that the advantage of simplified postal and telegraph traffic between the two countries would be offset by two important disadvantages – financial losses, further increased by the threatened adoption of the mark instead of the gold franc as the basis of payment, and political problems. In the EPD, Daniel Secrétan again adopted the strategy of 'neither this way nor any other', and proposed to undermine the political intentions of the German invitation by making a decision on an exclusively technical basis.[57] The Swiss Federal Council endorsed this strategy and sent two observers representing the postal, telephone and telegraph authority to Vienna, though it expressly refrained from describing them as delegates of the Swiss Federal Council.[58] At the Vienna congress, the Axis powers and their European allies were represented by plenipotentiaries.[59] Observers came from Switzerland, Spain, Turkey and the Vatican. France and Belgium had not been invited, on the grounds that they were territories under military occupation. On the other hand, the 'representatives of the German Reich Post abroad', who worked with various diplomatic missions, were present.[60] In the report by the Swiss observer Ernest Bonjour, which also refers to a Japanese observer, importance is attached to a list of the countries not represented. Apart from Greece and Portugal, the main absentee was Sweden. Sweden's refusal, as Bonjour was able to report, was the result of a foreign policy decision – the Swedish Post Office would actually have liked to attend.[61]

National Socialist activities in 1942 coincided with the greatest territorial extent of the Third Reich, though National Socialist internationalism was not confined to this phase and did not collapse after Stalingrad. Internationalisation strategies were pursued with meticulous bureaucratic enthusiasm. On 12 August 1944 the Reich post minister sent out invitations to attend a conference of the European Postal and Telecommunications Union in Vienna, to discuss 'issues of telecommunications technology for the first time'.[62] The International Forestry Centre, founded in 1939 and a member of the institutional clan of the International Institute of Agriculture, is further confirmation of the persistence of National Socialist internationalism.[63]

In March 1940 one of the numerous sessions of this organisation took place in Berne,[64] and in the summer of 1942 the Swiss Federal Council resolved to increase the Swiss contribution to the Forestry Centre. In reaching this decision, the Swiss government was following a recommendation by Georges Golay, the Swiss member of the International

Forestry Centre. The Swiss legation in Berlin had supported this proposal and emphasised the importance of the contacts made through the Forestry Centre. As Minister Hans Frölicher said, Golay had 'through his position ... in the International Forestry Centre established valuable links with circles close to Reichsmarschall Hermann Göring, who is known to take a particularly close interest in forestry matters because of his enthusiasm for German forests'.[65] When the sixth regular session of the Committee of the International Forestry Centre was due to take place in Vienna in September 1942, Switzerland was represented by federal senior forestry inspector Marius Petitmermet as an official delegate, who combined his trip with a visit to the Slovakian forestry authorities 'with whom Switzerland is currently maintaining active relations in connection with the timber trade'.[66] Nor did Switzerland's relations with the Forestry Centre become any less close in the following year, when the new board of directors was appointed. The new chairman was the former deputy chairman, forestry commissioner General Friedrich Alpers, 'who is known to be Reichsmarschall Göring's man'.[67] When it was proposed that a deputy chairman should be elected from a neutral country, 'to confirm the international character of the Centre',[68] and the Swiss senior forestry inspector was proposed for this reason to take on the deputy chairmanship, Petitmermet excused himself on grounds of health, after consultation with Federal Councillor Etter. Nor was he willing to attend the session in question, in Berlin. In the autumn of 1943, however, the senior forestry inspector did once again attend a conference of the Forestry Centre, together with his deputy delegate, and expense accounts confirm that German specialists also visited the Federal Institute for Snow and Avalanche Research and the avalanche barriers on the Alp Grüm at Poschiavo.[69] Even after the German surrender, Switzerland was prepared to pay contributions to the International Forestry Centre. The general secretariat was now in Swiss hands and was being run by Georges Golay, who had returned to Switzerland in March 1945. Golay was pressing for the Swiss contribution to be paid, because his arrangement with the Forestry Centre specified that his fee was to be paid out of the Swiss subscription.[70]

1943: NO NEW ORIENTATION FOR SWISS INTERNATIONALISM

Whereas the policy of 'neither this way nor any other' suggested to outsiders the absence of a clear standpoint, the Swiss Federal Council did attempt, in domestic policy, to use the neutrality argument to counter the corporative approach of National Socialist internationalism, as a way of regaining control over Swiss foreign policy. It was not only individual associations and persons who were requested not to jeopardise Swiss neutrality by participation in international conventions and organisations. In March 1943 a circular signed by Federal Councillor Etter was sent to the major scientific associations and cantonal directors of education. Their attention was drawn to the fact that Swiss scientists should not participate in international conventions without discussing the matter with the authorities and legations. The intention, said the letter, was not to apply censorship but to advise against attendance in certain cases 'in order to avoid, so far as possible, the disadvantages of all kinds to which the representatives of neutral states are particularly exposed, in the present circumstances, when attending international meetings or events'.[71] These efforts, dictated by neutrality, to restore control of foreign policy to the Federal Council were now encountering the growth of a broadly conceived Allied internationalism.

As the Political Department stated in its annual report for 1945, the foundation of the UN was accompanied by a 'comprehensive programme of international cooperation and peace activities', which had begun to take shape on major diplomatic occasions even before the end of the war.[72]

Since the agricultural conference at Hot Springs in the summer of 1943 it had been clearly apparent that the Allied internationalism was a belligerent internationalism in which the belligerents had an obligation to plan the future peacetime order. A 'depoliticised' internationalism, based on playing for time and postponing realignment until the end of the war, made little sense in the face of these Allied efforts at internationalisation. Switzerland's foreign policy leadership, which had just declared its controlling function, reacted by referring to Swiss neutrality and refrained from action. This was another instance where little thought was given to the international context of these protestations of neutrality, since in view of Switzerland's admittedly reluctant but nevertheless demonstrable involvement in National Socialist internationalism its posture of rejection towards Allied processes of internationalisation looked like support for the other side.

The UNRRA illustrates this dilemma. This most comprehensive and oldest of the major Allied organisations had a clearly military objective, since its purpose was to secure the hinterland conquered by the Allies.[73] In total contrast to Swiss industry, which, in the Swiss Committee for Economic Participation in European Reconstruction, showed a lively interest in Swiss participation in UNRRA, the Federal Political Department adopted an aloof attitude. In a report written in the summer of 1944 it was stated that accession to UNRRA was incompatible with Swiss neutrality, and universality was emphasised as a precondition for

Swiss involvement. When the American government asked for official recognition of the UNRRA and proposed to accredit a former member of the American legation staff as the new organisation's diplomatic representative, Berne refused. This action, which caused annoyance to the USA, eventually resulted in the unofficial recognition of the UNRRA representative, who was granted, de facto although not formally, the rights of a head of mission.[74]

Since Allied internationalism was hallmarked by Anglo-Saxon concepts, which in turn differ from the continental model, specific efforts had to be made to remind London and Washington of Switzerland's contribution to the process of internationalisation. However, such measures were undertaken only in isolation and too late. The International Bureau of Education kept the Federal Council regularly informed of Allied efforts to establish a post-war order in educational policy even before the London conference took place. The Department of the Interior also requested the EPD to intervene in favour of the International Bureau of Education. However, the EPD observed in May 1944 that it was too early as yet for any such approach.[75]

In the summer of 1944 the Allies felt that the Swiss government seemed to be uninterested in continuing any internationalist strategies. As the Swiss correspondent of the *NZZ* in the USA, Walter Bosshard, said in his report on the conference at Bretton Woods, 'the question often arose of whether our country still has any interest at all in international organisations'.[76] The same report made it extremely clear that a re-orientation of Swiss foreign policy was a matter of urgency, not to say well overdue.

In the remote forests of New Hampshire, in the summer of 1944, 'the discussion began with the question: "Does your foreign minister still believe in German victory?"' British delegates advised the Swiss that they needed not only a change of personnel at the top of the Foreign Ministry but also a change of generation at the head of the National Bank, and described the Swiss National Bank's reaction to the post-war order as 'stubborn, small-minded incomprehension'.[77] The conclusions Bosshard formed as a result of his discussions at Bretton Woods are not without a certain prophetic foresight. He observed that 'the facts of the matter regarding the BIS and Switzerland's attitude should be unambiguously clarified'. Switzerland should make up its mind 'promptly to state a clear opinion' regarding the requested assistance with the 'identification and disclosure of concealed assets of all kinds from hostile foreign countries and the occupied territories' and should send a high-calibre study group to the USA to win back American goodwill. However, treatment of the symptoms must also be followed by a fundamental realignment of policy. Bosshard called for a more active and strategically thought-out foreign policy and criticised Switzerland's absence from international conferences particularly as it would have been possible for Switzerland to participate at Bretton Woods, even if not officially. There were no alternatives, because 'our previous mute irresolution, which is being seen in many quarters as helplessness and misinterpretation of our neutrality, a lack of courage and foresight, could quite soon have consequences that would be very serious for our economic position'.[78]

NOTES

1 This chapter presents some of the results of a project investigating 'internationalisation as an instrument of Swiss foreign policy' as part of the National Research Programme of the Swiss National Science Foundation, Capabilities of Swiss Foreign Policy (NFP 42). Thanks are due to Sacha Zala for his stimulating comments.

2 Madeleine Herren, *Hintertüren zur Macht. Internationalismus und modernisierungs-oriente Aussenpolitik. in Belgien, der Schweiz und den USA* (forthcoming).

3 The following administrative unions, founded back in the nineteenth century, were based in Berne during the period under discussion here and were under the supervision of the Swiss Federal Council: the Bureau of the International Telecommunications Union, the International Bureau of the Universal Postal Union, the Central Office for International Railway Transport, and the two United International Bureaux for Industrial, Literary and Artistic Property, which were merged to form a single institution. On the significance of the administrative unions as the first generation of international organisations, see Craig N. Murphy, *International Organization and Industrial Change: Global Governance since 1850*, New York, 1994.

4 Official participation in international conferences and congresses can be established on the basis of the Federal Council decisions. Swiss Federal Archives (hereinafter abbreviated as BAR), Register of the Proceedings of the Federal Council, E 1004.3-/3.

5 Letter from the Federal Political Department (EPD) to the Federal Department of the Interior (FDI), Berne, 13 January 1938, BAR, E 2001 (D), –/4, Vol. 31.

6 The EPD informed the organising committee that, in the absence of any diplomatic relations, the Soviet Union could not be officially invited to attend the congress, EPD to the secretary of the eighth International History Congress, G. Hoffmann, Berne, 10 August 1937, BAR, E 2001 (D), –/1, Vol. 126. For the History Congress in Zurich, see Karl Dietrich Erdmann, *Die Ökumene der Historiker, Geschichte der Internationalen Historikerkongresse und des Comité International des Sciences Historiques*, Göttingen, 1987, pp. 221.

7 Letter from Professor Dr W. R. Hess to the FDI, Zurich, 27 February 1936, BAR, E 3001 (A), –/3, Vol. 18. However, no Soviet historians were represented at the historical congress.

8 Report by Georg Wiegner to the director of the Agriculture Department, Zurich, 2 November 1930, BAR, E 7220 (A), –/1, Vol. 12.

9 The legation had explicitly inquired in Berne whether it should be responsible for such services, and received an affirmative reply. Letter from the EPD to the

Swiss legation in Ankara, Berne, 18 January 1943, BAR, E 2001 (D), –/3, Vol. 494.

10 The Italian delegation alone comprised 14 people, including Giovanni Gentile, Francesco Ercole and former under-secretary of state Silverio Leicht. Swiss legation in Italy to the EPD, Rome, 1 June 1938, BAR, E 2001 (D), –/1, Vol. 126.

11 In 1935 invitations from Germany matched the number of international events held in France. A quantitative evaluation of the Federal Council's policy on sending delegates is currently in preparation.

12 Letter from the German legation in Switzerland to the EPD, Berne, 28 January 1939, BAR, E 2001 (D), –/1, Vol. 126.

13 Letter from the Federal Department of Post and Railways (EPED) to the EPD, Berne, 11 February 1939, ibid.

14 Ibid.

15 Letter from the temporary secretary of the International Hospitals Association, Dr Otto Binswanger, to the director of the Federal Office for Public Health, Charles Fauconnet, Kreuzlingen, 17 December 1943, BAR, E 2001 (D), –/3, Vol. 495.

16 The law of the sea was so complex that the Federal Council resolution creating a Swiss navy confined itself to mentioning the existing international conventions. For a few comments on the draft of a Federal Council resolution on seagoing shipping under the Swiss flag, see memorandum by Reinhard Hohl, EPD (Berne), 6 March 1941, BAR, E 2001 (D), –/2, Vol. 223.

17 For the significance of the communications systems in wartime, see Daniel R. Headrick, *The invisible weapon, Telecommunications and International Politics 1851–1945*, New York/Oxford, 1991.

18 The president of the association, Mayor Strölin of Stuttgart, wanted to use this organisation to achieve the international protection of cities from bombing, negotiated by Switzerland. By 1943, only technical cooperation was under discussion. However, the EPD mistrusted this offer of cooperation and passed the inquiry on, noting 'that at present a degree of caution is appropriate even in matters of purely technical cooperation, since under the present circumstances such organisations generally tend to be set up with certain secondary or underlying political ideas'. Letter from the EPD to the Swiss legation in Germany, Berne, 3 April 1943, BAR, E 2001 (D), –/3, Vol. 494.

19 The Slovak ministry responsible for the mail informed the bureau of the Universal Postal Union that stamps overprinted with the words 'Slovensky stat 1939' had been issued. The timing is interesting, since the international announcement of postal sovereignty occurred even before the country's declaration of independence on 14 March 1939. Letter from the Ministry of Communications and Public Works of the Slovak state to the International Bureau of the Universal Postal Union, Bratislava, 6 March 1939, BAR, E 2001 (D), –/2, Vol. 200. Formal notification of Slovakia's accession to the UPU Convention was given on 4 April 1939 in a letter sent by the Slovak foreign ministry to the EPD, ibid. The EPD referred to the indirect recognition of Slovakia resulting from the Federal Council's acceptance of the declaration of independence, and therefore raised no objection to passing on notification of Slovakia's accession to the contracting states as early as 25 April 1939, with the proviso that the EPED should be consulted. EPD to UPU bureau, Berne, 25 April 1939, ibid. The influence of accessions of new states to the Universal Postal Union and the deletion of states on Swiss recognition practice is currently being investigated. Regarding formal recognition of new states, see Walther Hofer, 'Gestaltung der diplomatischen Beziehungen der Schweiz zu neuen oder untergegangenen

Staaten sowie zu Staaten mit grundlegenden Systemänderungen', in Rudolf L. Bindschedler, Hans Rudolf Kurz, Wilhelm Carlgren and Sten Carlsson (eds), *Schwedische und schweizerische Neutralität im Zweiten Weltkrieg*, Basle, 1985, pp. 176–96.

20 The stamps were used, in the absence of any territory, on Polish vessels in international waters. Verbal note from the Polish legation in Switzerland to the EPD, Berne, 3 December 1941, BAR, E 2001 (D), –/2, Vol. 200.

21 Report by the Swiss delegation on the 11th Congress of the Universal Postal Union in Buenos Aires, 1939, to the secretariat of the directorate-general of the PTT, 13 May 1939, ibid.

22 EPD to the United Bureaux for Industrial, Literary and Artistic Property, Berne, 13 June 1939, BAR, E 2001 (D), –/2, Vol. 202.

23 Letter from the International Bureau for the Protection of Industrial Property to the EPD, Berne, 20 March 1941, ibid.

24 Within the EPD, inconsistencies were subsequently found between the attitude of the EPD and that of the UPU bureau: 'It seems ... that the Bureau of the Universal Postal Union went farther than the Political Department would have wished in adding Slovakia to the preamble of the Cairo Convention, for which we cannot take responsibility.' UB (E. Vallotton), memorandum on Slovakia's accession to the Universal Postal Union Convention, 1 May 1947, BAR, E 2001 (D), –/2, Vol. 200.

25 Wilhelm Triest, deputy director of the bureau of the UPU, to the EPD, Berne, 1 February 1943, BAR, E 2001 (D), –/3, Vol. 496.

26 Reinhold Furrer, director of the bureau of the UPU, to the EPD, Berne, 26 February 1943, ibid.

27 Memorandum to Daniel Secrétan from Pierre Zumbach, Berne, 27 October 1944, ibid.

28 Letter from EPD to the EDI, Berne, 12 September 1942, BAR, E 2001 (D), –/3, Vol. 494.

29 Michael Ruck, *Bibliographie zum Nationalsozialismus*, Cologne, 1995.

30 Memorandum from Pierre Zumbach to Minister Pierre Bonna, Berne, 10 September 1942, BAR, E 2001 (D), –/2, Vol. 205. Eventually no official Swiss delegate attended the congress because the German transit visas were never received. However, the Swiss consul-general in Bratislava did attend the congress. The Swiss consulate-general in Bratislava to the EPD, Bratislava, 15 September 1942, ibid.

31 *Zeitschrift der Akademie für Deutsches Recht*, 15/16, Berlin, 1 August 1940, p. 249, BAR, E 2001 (D), –/2, Vol. 206.

32 Hans Frank, 'Internationale Zusammenarbeit auf dem Gebiete des Rechts', in *Berlin–Rom–Tokio*, March 1942, quoted under 'International Chamber of Law, headquarters Berlin, founded in April 1941 in Berlin'. Report by the Swiss legation in Berlin, late July 1942, Swiss legation in Germany to the EPD, Berlin, 3 August 1942, BAR, E 2001 (D), –/3, Vol. 493. The inaugural meeting was attended by representatives from Bulgaria, Denmark, Finland, Japan, Italy, the Netherlands, Norway, Portugal, Romania, Slovakia, Spain and Hungary.

33 Ibid.

34 Dr Willy Hoffmann to Bénigne Mentha, Leipzig, 6 May 1942, BAR, E 2001 (D), –/3, Vol. 495. Mentha submitted all such enquiries to Federal Councillor Marcel Pilet-Golaz. The EPD recommended Mentha not to get involved personally but, as the director, to stress the obligation to provide information to member states. EPD to Mentha, Berne, 28 July 1942, BAR, E 2001 (D), –/3, Vol. 495.

35 The secretary-general of the CISAC had the right of 'advisory opinion'. The members of the legal committee of the CISAC formed the Legal Committee of the European Union. Statutes of the Union of European Copyright Associations, Berlin, 26 October 1942, ibid.

36 Draft statutes of the International Film Board, Berlin, 12 May 1941, BAR, E 3001 (A), –/5, Vol. 28.

37 Circular from the deputy chairman of the Reich Film Board, Karl Melzer, Berlin, 21 June 1941, ibid.

38 Soll sich die Schweiz um das Internationale Lehrfilminstitut bemühen? Report by Dr Gottlieb Imhof to the Federal Film Commission, Basle, 9 February 1938, ibid.

39 Extract from the minutes of the meeting of the Swiss Federal Council, 11 July 1941, ibid.

40 Report by the Swiss delegation on the conference in Berlin (15–21 July 1941) on the conversion of the International Film Board, to the Swiss Federal Council, Lausanne, 30 July 1941, ibid.

41 Ibid.

42 Letter from the EPD to the FDI, Berne, 16 August 1941, ibid.

43 Letter from the secretary-general of the International Film Board, Karl Melzer, to Albert Masnata, Berlin, 14 February 1942, BAR, E 3001 (B), –/1, Vol. 52.

44 The Swiss Workers' Education Centre protested against Switzerland's membership of the International Film Board in a letter dated 22 August 1941, as did the Cinematographic Association of French-Speaking Switzerland on 21 August 1941 and the Working Group on Women and Democracy on 28 August 1941. BAR, E 3001 (A), –/5, Vol. 28.

45 Letter from the Swiss legation in Germany to the EPD, Berlin, 9 September 1942, BAR, E 2001 (D), –/3, Vol. 495.

46 Letter from the EJPD to the EPD, Berne, 18 November 1942, ibid.

47 Letter from the EPD to the Swiss legation in Spain, Berne, Wednesday, 7 July 1943, BAR, E 2001 (D), –/3, Vol. 495.

48 *Mechanlizenz* to the Swiss Federal Intellectual Property Office, Berne, 27 May 1943, ibid.

49 Letter from Robert Hercod, secretary-general of the International Bureau against Alcoholism, to the chairman of the EPD, Lausanne, 20 June 1942, BAR, E 2001 (D), –/3, Vol. 493.

50 Letter from Robert Hercod, secretary-general of the International Bureau against Alcoholism, to Minister Pierre Bonna, Lausanne, 3 December 1942, ibid.

51 Letter from Robert Hercod, secretary-general of the International Bureau against Alcoholism, to Minister Pierre Bonna, Lausanne, 11 January 1943, ibid.

52 EPD memorandum, Berne, 12 September 1942, BAR, E 2001 (D), –/2, Vol. 206.

53 For example, the lawyer, Wilhelm Frick, after an interview with Federal Councillor von Steiger, refrained from accepting a position as Switzerland's unofficial representative at the International Chamber of Law. Letter from Wilhelm Frick to the EPD, Zurich, 6 July 1943, BAR, E 2001 (D), –/2, Vol. 493.

54 Letter from the Swiss legation in Germany to the EPD, Berlin, 9 September 1942, BAR, E 2001 (D), –/3, Vol. 495.

55 Letter from the Swiss legation in Germany to the EPD, Berlin, 24 October 1942, ibid.

56 Letter from Reinhold Furrer, director of the Bureau of the UPU, to the EPD, Berne, 20 August 1942, ibid.

57 Memorandum from Daniel Secrétan to Minister Pierre Bonna, Berne, 16

September 1942, ibid. Secrétan's proposals were to the effect 'that our stand-point should be the same as that which we follow with regard to the inter-national bureaux: depoliticisation. For my part, therefore, I would be tempted to reply that political arguments must be taken into account and that only the postal, telegraphic and financial aspects should be decisive.'

58 Extract from the minutes of the meeting of the Swiss Federal Council, 28 September 1942, ibid.

59 Those represented were Albania, Bulgaria, Denmark, Germany, Finland, Italy, Croatia, the Netherlands, Norway, Romania, San Marino, Slovakia and Hungary. Confidential letter from the Swiss consulate-general in Vienna to the EPD, Vienna, 28 October 1942, ibid.

60 Confidential letter from the Swiss consulate-general in Vienna to the EPD, Vienna, 28 October 1942, ibid.

61 E. Bonjour, inspector-general of post, memorandum on the Vienna Postal Congress to the head of the Political Department, Berne, 6 November 1942, ibid.

62 The Reich post minister to the directorate-general of the Post, Telegraph and Telephone Authority, Berlin, 12 August 1944, ibid.

63 Members of the organisation included, in addition to the German Reich, Bulgaria, Croatia, Denmark, Spain, Finland, France, Hungary, Italy, Norway, the Netherlands, Romania, Slovakia, Sweden, Switzerland and Turkey. Regarding the International Forestry Centre, see Heinrich Rubner, *Deutsche Forstgeschichte 1933–1945. Forstwirtschaft, Jagd und Umwelt im NS-Staat*, St Katharinen, 1985, pp. 141–58.

64 Letter from the Federal Inspectorate of Forestry, Hunting and Fisheries to the EPD, Berne, 8 March 1940, BAR, E 2001 (D), –/3, Vol. 492.

65 Letter from the Swiss legation in Germany to the EPD, Berlin, 15 April 1942, ibid.

66 Letter from the EDI to the EPD, Berne, 2 October 1942, ibid.

67 Letter from the Swiss legation in Germany to the EPD, Berlin, 5 May 1943, ibid.

68 Ibid.

69 Letter from the EDI to the EPD, Berne, 18 September 1943, ibid.

70 The accounts department decided to side with the accountancy section of the Federal Political Department, which argued that, after all, the payment should be made to a Swiss national. Letter from the EPD, Section for Accountancy and Private Assets Abroad to the Swiss accounts department, Berne, 17 May 1945, ibid.

71 Circular from the EPD, signed by Federal Councillor Philipp Etter, to the Swiss Sciences Association, the Swiss General History Association, the Society of Swiss Writers and the Society of Swiss Musicians, Berne, 30 March 1943, BAR, E 3001 (B), –/1, Vol. 61. An identical circular was sent to the cantonal directors of education.

72 Report by the Swiss Federal Council to the Federal Assembly on its conduct of its business in 1945, p. 108. No official Swiss delegates attended the conferences at Hot Springs, Atlantic City, Bretton Woods and London, which were concerned with agricultural internationalism, reconstruction, cross-border economic aid and scientific internationalism.

73 The UNRRA saw itself as 'the first great international agency to go out into the world and wrestle with the problems that arrived with the peace. It was a global approach to a global problem.' Office of Public Information, United Nations Relief and Rehabilitation Administration, *The Story of UNRRA*, Washington, 1948. The breadth of the objective pursued by the UNRRA was apparent when it was dissolved and its resources passed to the FAO, ILO, WHO and UNICEF.

R. F. Gorman, *Historical Dictionary of Refugee and Disaster Relief Organizations*, Metuchen, NJ, 1994, p. 82.

74 Report on the UNRRA by Carl Albert Egger, Berne, 5 July 1944, BAR, E 2001 (D), –/3, Vol. 490.

75 Letter from the EPD to the FDI, Berne, 24.5.1944, BAR, E 2001 (D), –/3, Vol. 493. It also proved impossible to enable the Geneva bureau to share the same institutional basis as UNESCO.

76 B. (Walter Bosshard), 'Bericht über die Finanz- und Währungs-Konferenz von Bretton Woods, N.H. 1–23 July 1944', confidential and not intended for publication, New York, 3 August 1944 in Swiss legation in the USA to the EPD, Washington, 7 August 1944, BAR, E 2001 (D), –/3, Vol. 499.

77 Ibid.

78 Ibid.

9

The Military National Defence, 1939–45

RUDOLF JAUN

In the controversy about 'Switzerland in the Second World War', the subject of national defence is of secondary, not to say tertiary, importance when compared with the issues of refugee policy, foreign trade, and Switzerland's dealings in financial services and gold with the belligerent powers. Nevertheless, the question of the importance of the deterrent effect of the Swiss army against the military potential of the belligerent powers is one of the topical issues of debate concerning Switzerland in the Second World War. It was in the specific context of that debate that a disagreement flared up regarding the military, political and identifying significance of the Swiss army's redoubt (réduit) concept.

When we consider the subject of 'national defence in the Second World War', there are two aspects that must be borne in mind. It is not just since 1996 that the debate about the Swiss army in the Second World War has been conducted on the assumption that historians have exaggerated the deterrent effect of the Swiss armed forces and that the description of the part played by the army in the Second World War has been in need of revision. Ever since the early 1970s there has been evidence of disagreement regarding the importance of the Swiss army in the Second World War, a disagreement motivated by military policy and characterised by increasingly fierce attacks and increasingly stubborn defences.

In my view, however, this battle regarding the value and capabilities of the Swiss armed forces also has to be considered from a long-term perspective. The national defence of the Swiss Confederation had been controversial since the early nineteenth century, in terms of the military concept, and since the early twentieth century in terms of politics too.[1] It was not until shortly before the outbreak of the Second World War that it received support from all parts of the political spectrum, while the further development of the military concept and the question of the relationship between the military and society were left unresolved. In 1945 the consensus, both in terms of military concept and in terms of politics, about the Swiss army was called into question. As far as the military concept was concerned, the consensus collapsed immediately after the end of the war, resulting in the 'concept dispute' about the combat principles of the Swiss army, which lasted into the 1960s. The political consensus about the Swiss military was first called into doubt by the effects of the 1968 movement and the barracks unrest of the 1970s, resulting in the Swiss electorate being asked in 1989, under the influence of the peace movement of the 1980s, the question: Abolish the army – yes or no? The sovereign Swiss people answered this question in the negative. After 1989, against a background of the problems of Switzerland's political positioning in Europe, the revolutionary changes in European strategic and security policy, and the problems of a 'joint' suppression of outbreaks of political violence inside and outside Europe, the armed forces debate flared up again, and with it the debate about the Swiss army in the Second World War.

Against that background, the first part of this chapter deals with the changing way in which historians and publicists have portrayed the military defence of Switzerland in the Second World War. The chapter then goes on to consider the achievements and failures of research. Although in Switzerland, as elsewhere, the Second World War marked the first occasion on which the various elements had come together to form a comprehensive defence or 'total war', this chapter focuses primarily on the military defence of the country, leaving aside the political, economic and spiritual aspects of that defence.

HISTORIANS' CHANGING VIEW OF THE MILITARY DEFENCE OF SWITZERLAND IN THE SECOND WORLD WAR

In contrast to events in (private) financial and industrial circles, and in contrast to foreign and refugee policy, it was a matter of course that, immediately after the conclusion of active service, the supreme commander of the army would present a report to the political authorities on the period of mobilisation. The tradition of generals' reports in Switzerland dated back to the *Sonderbund* civil war of 1847. The 'Report to the Federal Assembly on the 1939–45 Period of Active Service' by General Henri Guisan was the first of many descriptions of Switzerland's military activities in the Second World War.[2] General Guisan wrote his report on the period of active service with the confidence of a great military leader and was unsparing in his criticism of events and the military leaders responsible for them. The appearance of the report in 1946 was the starting signal for what became nothing less than a war of reports: the Federal Council and the much-criticised head of the air corps and anti-aircraft troops, General Bandi, published counter-reports.[3]

Once censorship was lifted, the public received its first detailed information, from the standpoint of the supreme commander, on the military threat that had existed during the war and the operational and strategic activities of the army command. However, the report undertook no actual discussion of operational ideas and how they had arisen in the context of external political and economic relations. General Guisan, whose operational and strategic abilities had been questioned, not without reason, succeeded through his report in focusing attention on himself. His surprising frankness – he was repeatedly accused of betraying military secrets – and his provocative ideas for modernising the army, such as his support for recruiting officers from working backgrounds, set him apart from the majority of the army leadership but made him more popular with the majority of the press. The general's report and the debates that followed would subsequently exert a strong influence on the presentation of the military aspects of 'Switzerland in the Second World War' and would themselves become the subject of historical studies.[4]

Less prominently, if not entirely remote from the public, two groups of officer-instructors and militia officers had already formed within the army before the end of the war, and after it revealed to the public their differing views of the future structure of the Swiss army. This argument about future directions, which has become known to historians as the 'concept debate', explicitly referred to the military structures, discretionary powers and shifts in orientation during the period of active service.[5] The group identified as reformers tried to retain the leadership style exemplified by the younger generation of officers and supported by General Guisan, based on republican-style citizen officers and geared to skirmishing tactics. By contrast, the 'Willeans', who still took their cue as well as their name from General Ulrich Wille, attempted to continue developing the Prussian/German style of leadership, based on conventional forms of warfare as previously practised by the German army. The periodical *Volk und Armee*, published by the reformers from 1943 to 1950, gives a good example of the contentious treatment of the military experience of the Second World War.

Since the start of the active service period, there has also been a high output of reminiscences – both collective works dealing with military units and the recollections of individuals serving in the forces – and these continue to appear today. Individual works of reminiscence include Max Frisch's *Blätter aus dem Brotsack* and Josef Konrad Scheuber's *Gewehr von der Wand*. The armed forces newspapers and service records of dozens of military units, carefully preserved in the Federal Military Library, are a genuine treasure trove in their portrayal of states of mind, everyday activities and the roles of the sexes. In the post-war years, the production of memoirs as such also began: the general's chief of staff, Major Barbey, published his diary, and the general himself gave a whole series of interviews to Radio Lausanne, subsequently published as *Entretiens*.[6]

The first discussions of aspects of Swiss national defence in the Second World War were based on reminiscences, memoirs published in Switzerland and abroad, and privileged access to printed source material – the documents in the Federal Archive were, until 1974, sealed for 50 years.[7] The first debate about the deterrent value of the Swiss army in the First and Second World Wars seems to have been triggered by the 'Chevallier initiatives', named after their instigator, of 1954 and 1956, which aimed to 'restrict military spending'.[8] In the course of the 1950s, a civil servant with a legal background employed at the Directorate of Military Administration emerged as the official historian of the EMD (the Federal Department of the Military). Hans Rudolf Kurz had previously worked in the late 1940s and early 1950s on the 'history of the Swiss redoubt concept' and the 'military threat to Switzerland in the Second World War'.[9] Since 1957 he had produced, at short intervals, works on the status of military strategy in Switzerland and an anthology on 'Switzerland in the Second World War'.[10] This 'extensive collection of reminiscences of the active service period, 1939–45' from the 'most authoritative sources', compiled under his editorship, is very typical of much Swiss military historiography, strongly influenced by personal reminiscence, explanations and excuses. Hans Rudolf Kurz, who preferred his work to appear in publications for non-commissioned officers, also published a popular work on General Guisan in the 1960s and a popular collection of documents on the Second World War, *Dokumente des Aktivdienstes*.[11] When the importance of the Swiss army's role in the Second World War was again called into question during the 1970s, Kurz updated his works from the 1950s.[12]

Kurz was not alone in publishing his views on General Guisan in the 1960s. In 1961 Jon Kimche, a British journalist of Swiss descent, made General Guisan the subject of an updated heroic saga for the international book market, *Spying for Peace*. This book focused primarily on Guisan's risky contacts with the intelligence services and also caused a stir in Switzerland, where it was published in German as *General Guisans Zweifrontenkrieg* and in French as *Un général suisse contre Hitler. L'espionnage au service de la paix*.[13] This 'report' was followed by a whole series of books dealing, in one way or another, with the interlocking themes of Switzerland's intelligence and foreign policy dialogue with

Nazi Germany and internal policy developments in Switzerland, under the general heading 'accommodation or resistance'.[14] Not only that, but the Federal Council saw fit to commission from the distinguished Basle history professor Edgar Bonjour 'a comprehensive report on Swiss foreign policy during the last world war' which was also to deal with 'the activities of the army command and events in domestic policy which affected foreign policy'.[15] Bonjour's history of Swiss neutrality in the Second World War has thus also become the standard work on the military defence of the country. However, in accordance with his remit, Bonjour confined himself to the effects of military decisions and events on foreign policy and to military intelligence contacts relevant to foreign policy. Although the report did describe the major consecutive stages in military strategy and the sequence of military events (central position – Rütli briefing – redoubt), it did not examine the structure and problems of the available military human, planning and armament resources, or the attitudes and politico–military orientations of the various hierarchical groups and age-groups among the officers, NCOs and other ranks. In terms of military concepts, however, the standard work *Die Konzeption der schweizerischen Landesverteidigung 1815–1966* by corps commander Colonel Alfred Ernst supplemented Professor Bonjour's report.[16]

Bonjour's wide-ranging studies had a twofold effect. First, they made it possible for 'Switzerland during the war' to receive the mass media treatment for television presentation;[17] secondly, the official account of Swiss foreign policy during the Second World War gave rise to a great many academic studies dealing with, among other things, individual aspects of the military national defence.[18] Adolf Jöhr tried to use the Bonjour report as a basis for a game-theory analysis of Swiss strategy.[19] A first general overview of the development of relations between Nazi Germany and Switzerland, including the evolution of the military situation, was produced by Daniel Bourgeois in his study, *Le Troisième Reich et la Suisse*.[20] The compromising cache of documents found at La Charité-sur-Loire was analysed by Georg Kreis in the context of French and German influence on the Swiss armed forces.[21]

While Professor Bonjour's mass-media coverage by press, radio and television and Werner Rings' television documentary were familiarising the general public with the achievements and perils of the Swiss army command in its successful confrontation with the Axis powers, non-conformists old and new, the latter under the influence of the 1968 movement, were radically questioning the importance of the role of the Swiss armed forces in the Second World War.[22] The existence of an acute military threat from Nazi Germany was disputed, and the Swiss armed forces were (re)discovered as an instrument of class domination. Max

Frisch in his *Dienstbüchlein* and Niklaus Meienberg in his reports on 'Die Erschiessung des Landesverräters Ernst S.', filmed by Richard Dindo, drew vivid pictures that helped to popularise the theory of a class-dominated army.[23]

By the mid-1970s the old historiographic approach, based on conventional political history, was on the way out, though the new style of historical research, focusing on social, economic and intellectual history, was still in its early stages. Zurich University provides one example: while Professor Erwin Bucher still focused on the performance of the 'leaders',[24] the Seminar at History Faculty in May 1975 saw the formation of a student working group which proposed to examine the history of Switzerland in the Second World War along the lines of the study *Klassengesellschaft im Krieg, Deutsche Sozialgeschichte 1914–1918* by Jürgen Kocka.[25] The fundamental questioning of the effectiveness of the military defence of Switzerland during the Second World War brought traditional military history into the arena during the 1970s. As early as 1972 the Swiss Military History and Military Science Association was addressing the 'politically rather than historically motivated tendency to claim that the Swiss armed forces were not a factor at all in 1939–45', and was hoping that a new version of Hans Rudolf Kurz's studies of the threat faced by Switzerland would 'refute these tendentious claims by the opponents of the army'.[26] As far as refuting 'tendentious claims' was concerned, however, Kurz's studies suffered from the drawback that they had originally interpreted the operational plans for the conquest of Switzerland as purely theoretical works designed to provide intellectual stimulation for under-employed German army staff personnel.[27] Now Walter Schaufelberger, professor of military history at Zurich University, and his students Werner Roesch and Hans Rudolf Fuhrer joined the fray. Werner Roesch undertook a re-examination of the operational plans to attack Switzerland and compared them with the Swiss army's defensive preparedness,[28] while Schaufelberger and Fuhrer made no further search for studies and tactics of an attack on Switzerland but, referring to German intelligence sources, demonstrated the Germans' considerable respect for the fighting qualities of the Swiss army and the serious espionage activities undertaken by the *Wehrmacht* against the Swiss defences.

After the founding of the Unarmed Switzerland Association (GSoA) in 1981, the tabling of a motion for the disbandment of the armed forces in 1986 and the November 1989 referendum, the debate on the value of the Swiss army in the Second World War came well and truly into the sphere of current controversy on military policy. This lesson was brought home to, among others, Oscar Gauye, director of the Federal Archive and, as an officer in the militia, head of the Armed Forces

Archive. He obtained the documents relating to General Guisan's address on the occasion of the Rütli briefing and – though he was not a particular GSoA sympathiser – decided to publish these source documents, which appeared to confirm Guisan's affinity for the corporate state and antipathy to communism.[29] The press dramatised Gauye's analyses as 'shocking revelations': the symbolic figure of Guisan was drawn into the crossfire between abolitionists and supporters, but eventually survived – as he had previously after the appearance of the Bonjour report – still on his pedestal though, once again, somewhat tarnished. A very major contribution to this was made by Willi Gautschi's academic study of the army leadership under General Guisan's command, which resulted in 'no fundamental corrections' to the general's image but merely a few 'retouches'.[30]

In 1989, the year of the political and strategic upheaval in Europe, the debate on the deterrent effect of the Swiss army in the Second World War came to a head: the motion to abolish the Swiss army was put to the vote. Since the mass media were successful in their campaign to minimise the deterrent effect of the Swiss army and play off the younger, revolutionary generations against the incorrigible active service generation, the 'Switzerland of old comrades', a central cog in the argument for retaining national armed forces was disabled and the younger generations were given an opportunity to put one over on the custodians of the myth of Guisan and the redoubt.[31] One contribution to the debate, Markus Heiniger's book, *Dreizehn Gründe. Warum die Schweiz im Zweiten Weltkrieg nicht erobert wurde*,[32] written in informal style, proved a treasure trove for the abolitionists' efforts in the mass media. Heiniger summarised the literature that had appeared before 1989 and emerged with one major argument: that the Swiss army had not been a serious factor as an instrument of national defence but had, in fact, been an internal administrative force under the command of its 'Führer' Guisan, satisfying the 'home front' and, with its redoubt concept (seen as a defensive propaganda bluff), enabling Swiss industry to produce goods for Nazi Germany. In addition to older approaches inspired by class theory, Heiniger based his ideas regarding pacification and the redoubt on Jakob Tanner's dissertation, published in 1986.[33] Basing his arguments on financial sociology and the politico–economic theory of the 'strategic synthesis' of internal and external 'fronts', Tanner was able to show that the allocation of resources to the army in the form of weapons and raw materials, especially for the building of the fortifications, would have been impossible without trade relations with Germany, just as the emergency farming campaign could not have succeeded without imports of seed and artificial fertilisers from Germany.[34] If the redoubt was ultimately seen as a resource-devouring system of fortifications rather than an operational military option, the central districts strategy could be shown to be 'totally dependent on and overshadowed by cooperative economic efforts'.[35]

Just how important the depiction of Switzerland in the Second World War was in the context of the army abolition referendum is shown by, for example, the fact that the leftist *Wochen Zeitung* published a whole series of articles on Switzerland in the Second World War under the title 'Collapse of a myth', while old Max Frisch roused himself to write one more play, *Schweiz ohne Armee? Ein Palaver*.[36] Another example was the publicity put out by supporters of the army, giving a negative answer to the question 'Should we abolish the army?' based on, among other things, a 'look back at a dangerous period'.[37] The diamond jubilee celebrations held throughout Switzerland in 1989, to commemorate the 1939 mobilisation of the army and honour those who had served, proved a perfect medium for stressing the role of the military national defence. Anxious technical college teachers from the canton of St Gallen, assisted by the New Helvetic Society, marked the diamond jubilee for the active service veterans by producing a complete federal dossier containing pupils' and teachers' books, transparencies, facsimile newspapers and reproductions of army documents from the Second World War period.[38] The Federal Institute of Technology (ETH) Department of Military Sciences organised a conference and publication, *Kriegsmobilmachung 1939*, which was intended to be seen as an 'academic and critical analysis marking the 50th anniversary of mobilisation day in 1939' and not as a memorial.[39] The Swiss Military History and Military Science Association published a bibliography on the history of the armed forces in the Second World War.[40]

A year after the battle of the referendum, Klaus Urner's studies of the Wehrmacht's preparations for attack in the summer of 1940 brought the subject of the Swiss army in the Second World War back into the spotlight.[41] Urner was the first to prove by means of source material that, after the defeat of France, the German army was not merely indulging in 'theoretical studies' but was preparing troops for the assault on Switzerland, conducting propaganda and instructing staff officers in the requirements of this 'special task' – all this allegedly being ordered by the unpredictable Hitler.[42] This largely demolished the theory advanced by Hans Rudolf Kurz in the 1950s that the planned attack was merely a project to be held in reserve. Although the publication of long-term research projects continued in the first half of the 1990s (Bucher on the relationship between Pilet-Golaz and Guisan; Senn on the history of the Swiss general staff in the Second World War), the Second World War became a secondary interest in the media; nor was there any longer a link to current controversies.[43] In addition, the production of unit histories, enormously increased since the 1970s, continued to produce more or less academic analysis of the deployment of individual units during the Second World War.[44] Although Philippe Marguerat undertook, as early as 1991, a critical analysis of the theme, developed in the course of the debate on the abolition of the army, that the redoubt strategy had been primarily a politico–economic accommodation, it was not until the present debate on Switzerland in the Second World War that the dispute about the military, political, economic and identity-creating significance of the Swiss army's redoubt concept in the Second World War received a fresh airing.[45]

RESEARCH: STATUS AND SHORTCOMINGS

Although many works have been published on the defence of Switzerland in the Second World War, it is becoming apparent that – because of the strong political influence on researchers' interests – some areas have been very thoroughly investigated, or at least cultivated for their publicity value, while many others have been the subject of no systematic investigation at all. In essence, there have been four main lines of inquiry, depending upon the knowledge which researchers hope to find, but these have pointed to conflicting results, depending on the military and political interests of the researcher concerned. First, the foreign policy aspect of the military national defence and its adventurous intelligence activities (Kimche, Bonjour, Gautschi, Braunschweig and Bucher). Second, the question of the military threat posed by the belligerent powers and their assessment of Switzerland's defence capability (Kurz, Schaufelberger, Roesch, Fuhrer and Urner). Third, the offsetting of economic, financial and intelligence accommodations against the military defence of the country (Tanner, Heiniger and Marguerat). And, fourth, the depiction of the military measures adopted, and especially the redoubt strategy as a successful emergency solution to the problems of a politically and militarily encircled Switzerland (Senn and Odermatt). The great majority of studies are based on a traditional approach to the history of events and individuals. Modern methods and theories, guided by social sciences and the humanities, have played little part, Jakob Tanner's study being a major exception.

No aspect of the national defence in the Second World War has been so thoroughly illuminated as the Swiss army's walking of its foreign policy and intelligence tightrope; the only thing missing is a biography of Hausamann, a background figure but an influential lobbyist and intelligence figure. The question of the military threat and the assessment of the fighting qualities of the Swiss army are also likely to be widely known, although Klaus Urner promises more detailed information in his study of the acute threat that existed in the summer of 1940.[46] However, the relationship between economic and financial accommodations and military national defence calls for further study. It is precisely in the area of military national defence, with which we are exclusively concerned here, that what Tanner calls the 'petrified myth of the redoubt' requires 'softening' by way of a range of social and military historical studies.

As a military problem, the redoubt could be 'attacked' from three sides. First, the aspect of recollection and tradition would have to be a central theme. An initial approach to this, inspired by oral history and popular accounts, is to be found in the collection of reminiscences, *Es war halt Krieg* by Simone Chiquet, and the catalogue of the 'Basle redoubt' exhibition edited by Nadia Guth and Bettina Hunger.[47] The experiences and achievements of women have been touched upon, but still require more in-depth study.[48] The massive literature of military reminiscences, mentioned earlier, is a mine of information on the 'consciousness' of the (male) generation that saw active service. It would be important to remember here both the 'invention of tradition' and the 'tradition of invention' in connection with Swiss fighting prowess: few events have matched the Second World War in its power to reconstruct such national stereotypes.[49] And there was a rich store of stereotypes from which to draw, tracing the development of Swiss military ability in the context of the country (mountain terrain), the people (the combativeness of free men) and the passage of time (the history of their rise and fall).

Second, did so-called 'pro-German' officers try to portray the army's redoubt positions as a gesture of deference to National Socialist Germany? The dispute between Hans Senn and Jakob Tanner has exposed the dubious nature of the terms 'pro-German' and 'pro-French'. Is the implied equation, pro-German equals pro-fascist, not too much of a simplification? Were there not pro-French officers who were strongly influenced by the French right and whose stance was much farther to the right than that of many so-called pro-German officers? The distinction between pro-German and pro-French officers, and the question of factions in the officer corps, should be re-examined in the light of studies based on social and ideological history. In this context, too, the issue of Guisan's political ideas should be given more careful consideration. Very little is known about the development of the supreme commander's philosophy, as is clear from the attempts – some of them quite futile – to interpret his thinking in the context of his Rütli address.[50] Even Gautschi is notably monosyllabic here. In the case of Guisan, who was no intellectual and published little (on his own account), this is no simple matter.[51] But it can be done with many other officers, who were enthusiastic and copious authors of published material. For example, Gustav Däniker and Hans Frick produced many writings which could be the subject of analysis.[52] Their affinities with bellicose German militarism, which played a constituent part in National Socialism, could be demonstrated in the context of their activities. The divisions within the Swiss officers corps cannot be understood without a knowledge of the clashes of tendency and orientation within the Swiss army's corps of training and militia officers, which had persisted since the late nineteenth century.[53] The question also arises of the attitudes of the *Offiziersbund* (League of Officers), which also hankered after a 'new Switzerland' based on 'soldierly comradeship and discipline', or what the attitudes of the so-called 'pro-French' officers were. This calls for modern approaches to research, which have mastered the linguistic turn and can launch a modern ideological history of the Swiss relationship between military, state and society. The period of the Second World War must not be considered in isolation but should be seen in the context of the 'long development' that began in the nineteenth century, as Switzerland set out on the road towards acquiring a sovereign, militarily equipped national identity in accordance with its idealistic national philosophy. Against this background, statements such as Germann's 'the purpose of the redoubt position was to demonstrate the right to existence of a free Swiss people through the defensive capability of its army' can be interpreted and assigned to the correct place in the thinking of those responsible for making decisions.

Also lacking is any long-term political history of the Swiss armed forces which, by giving an account of the structural, ideological and factual history of the country, could provide an analysis of the relationship between politics and the military from 1918 to 1945. Arguments which reproachfully rub the noses of the left in their anti-militarism and their half-hearted support for the national defence are unhelpful here. So too are studies inspired by class theory, which assume the social and political formation in Switzerland of a working class equipped for the class war which had nothing to do with the (bourgeois) military and had now achieved social, political and military integration as a result of the Second World War.[54]

Even less researched than the relationship between politics and the military is the relationship in Switzerland between the military and society in the first half of the twentieth century, thus including the period of the Second World War. The social composition of the various ranks in the army – officers, NCOs and other – is not a completely closed book, but it has been the subject of no empirical, detailed study.[55] What were the socially and locally structured backgrounds from which soldiers were recruited into the individual battalions and regiments that form the active service generation against which hostility is directed today? Who were the NCOs? Who were the officers? Who were the officers who attended the Rütli briefing, and what were their social, political and intellectual backgrounds and their attitudes towards the threat posed by National Socialism and fascism? What was the background of the officers who helped bring about the change in style of military leadership supported by Guisan and worked towards a radical reform of the army? [56]

Third, there are a great many questions concerning military history in the narrower sense during the period 1918–45 which require clarification in the light of a study of military national defence based on political, social and ideological history. Apart from the general overview of the development of the Swiss general staff by Hans Senn, there are only isolated detailed studies.[57] How did operational and tactical ideas change when confronted with the rapid advance in mechanisation and technology that had revolutionised warfare since the First World War? How important were concepts of total war and the people's war?[58] Along what lines did Swiss armaments develop in the light of the political, financial, production engineering and operational para-meters? What were the underlying principles behind the technical and psychological military training of the Swiss reservists? Equally unclear are the interactions between military and economic national defence, especially the issue of the food supply, which also affected refugee policy.

The military defence of Switzerland in the Second World War cannot be fully understood unless due account is taken of the specific tensions and problems of the Swiss militia army, which is not a reserve to supplement a regular, standing army but a militia which applies the organisational and fighting principles of regular armies. These tensions and problems, which surfaced constantly as the Swiss militia army optimised its equipment, strategic and human resources in the course of the nineteenth and twentieth centuries, became particularly appar-ent during the Second World War. Further studies of the measures taken for the military defence of the country in the Second World War – not excluding the redoubt strategy – will have to take due account of these problems confronting the Swiss armed forces.

NOTES

1 It was only under the pressure of the threat posed by National Socialism and fascism that the social democratic and communist left supported the military

defensive efforts. Until 1917 the left supported the army as a means for defending republicanism, and also appointed many officers; subsequently, the army was rejected as a tool of the class enemy.

2 Henri Guisan, *Bericht an die Bundesversammlung über den Aktivdienst 1939–1945*, Lausanne, 1946; *Bericht des Chefs des Generalstabes der Armee an den Oberbefehlshaber der Armee über den Aktivdienst 1939–1945* (supplement to the general's report); *Bericht des Kommandanten der Flieger- und Fliegerabwehrtruppen, des Generaladjutanten der Armee, des Chefs der Ausbildung der Armee, des Chefs des Personellen der Armee an den Oberbefehlshaber der Armee über den Aktivdienst 1939–1945* (supplement to the general's report).

3 *Bericht des Bundesrates an die Bundesversammlung zum Bericht des Generals über den Aktivdienst 1939–1945*, Berne, 1947; *Eingabe zum Bericht von General Henri Guisan und zum Bericht des Kommandanten der Flieger- und Fliegerabwehrtruppen von Oberstdivisionär Bandi*, Berne, 1947.

4 Viktor Hofer, *Die Bedeutung des Berichtes General Guisans über den Aktivdienst 1939–1945 für die Gestaltung des Schweizerischen Wehrwesens*, Basle, 1970; Hermann Anthmatten, 'Der Fall Bandi', Berne University licentiateship thesis, 1986 MS; Hans-Georg Bandi, *Oberstdivisionär Hans Bandi 1882–1955: Späte Rehabilitierung des ersten Kommandanten der Flieger- und Fliegerabwehrtruppen*, Berne, 1989.

5 Alfred Ernst, 'Geschichte der Landesverteidigung', in Erich Gruner (ed.), *Die Schweiz seit 1945*, Berne, 1971; idem, *Die Konzeption der schweizerischen Landesverteidigung 1815–1966*, Frauenfeld, 1971; Chantal de Riedmatten, *Général Henri Guisan. Autorité et Démocratie ou la question de l'inspecteur et celle de la démocratisation dans l'armée 1939–1947*, Fribourg, 1983.

6 Bernard Barbey, *P.C. du Général. Journal du Chef de l'Etat-Major particulier du Général Guisan 1940–1945*, Neuchatel 1948; Henri Guisan, *Entretiens accordés à Raymond Gafner à l'intention des auditeurs de Radio-Lausanne*, Lausanne, 1953.

7 Peter Dürrenmatt, *Kleine Geschichte der Schweiz im Zweiten Weltkrieg*, Zurich, 1949; Pierre Béguin, *Le Balcon sur l'Europe: Petite Histoire de la Suisse pendant la Guerre 1939–1945*, Neuenburg, 1951; Edgar Schumacher, 'Die schweizerische Armee in ersten und zweiten Weltkriege', in Hans Hemmeler (ed.), *Festschrift for Eugen Bircher*, Aarau 1952, p. 25.

8 Raymond Gafner again invited General Guisan to speak on Radio Lausanne and to defend the army against the 'attacks' of the anti-militarist left by explaining the 'lesson of two general mobilisations': Henri Guisan, 'Les Leçons de deux Mobilisations', interview with Major R. Gafner broadcast on 30 August 1954, Lausanne 1954.

9 Hans Rudolf Kurz: 'Zur Geschichte des schweizerischen Reduit-Gedankens', *Schweizerische Monatsschrift für Offiziere aller Waffen*, 1, 1947, pp. 1–10 and 2, 1947, pp. 45–58; idem, 'Die militärischen Bedrohungen der Schweiz im zweiten Weltkrieg', *Allgemeine Schweizerische Militärzeitschrift (ASMZ)*, 11, 1951, pp. 757–92.

10 Hans Rudolf Kurz, *Die Schweiz in der Planung der kriegführenden Mächte während des Zweiten Weltkrieges*, Biel, 1957; idem, *Die Schweiz in der europäischen Strategie vom Dreissigjährigen Krieg bis zum Atomzeitalter*, Zurich, 1958, idem (ed.), *Die Schweiz im Zweiten Weltkrieg. Das grosse Erinnerungswerk an die Aktivdienstzeit 1939–1945*, Thun, 1959; idem, 'Nochmals: die militärische Bedrohung der Schweiz im Zweiten Weltkrieg', *ASMZ*, 7, 1961, p. 296. In the latter article Kurz refers to the 'Zimmerman study' of Army Group C of 4 October 1940, which was shown to Kurz by Hans-Adolf Jacobson.

11 Hans Rudolf Kurz, *General Henri Guisan*, Zurich, 1965; idem, *Dokumente des Aktivdienstes*, Frauenfeld, 1965.

12 Hans Rudolf Kurz, *Operationsplanung Schweiz. Die Rolle der Schweizer Armee in zwei Weltkriegen*, Thun, 1974.

13 Jon Kimche, *General Guisans Zweifrontenkrieg. Die Schweiz zwischen 1939 und 1945*, Zurich, 1962. In 1964, while at secondary school, I bought this book with money earned during the summer holidays, thus laying the foundation for my library.

14 Alice Meyer, *Anpassung oder Widerstand. Die Schweiz zur Zeit des deutschen Nationalsozialismus*, Frauenfeld, 1965; Pierre Accoce and Pierre Quet, *La guerre a été gagnée en Suisse, 1939–1945*, Paris, 1966; Otto Püntener, *Der Anschluss fand nicht statt. Geheimagent Pakbo erzählt*, Zurich, 1967; Alphons Matt, *Zwischen allen Fronten. Der Zweite Weltkrieg aus der Sicht des Büros 'Ha'*, Frauenfeld, 1969.

15 Edgar Bonjour, *Geschichte der schweizerischen Neutralität. Vier Jahrhunderte eidgenössischer Aussenpolitik*, Vols 3–6, Basle, 1967–70.

16 Alfred Ernst, *Die Konzeption der schweizerischen Landesverteidigung 1815–1966*, Frauenfeld, 1971.

17 As an accompaniment to the television series 'Schweiz im Krieg 1933–1945', broadcast in 1973, there appeared a report by Werner Rings, *Schweiz im Krieg 1933–1945. Ein Bericht*, Zurich, 1974.

18 Hofer (as note 4 above); Oskar Felix Fritschi, *Geistige Landesverteidigung während des zweiten Weltkrieges. Der Beitrag der Schweizer Armee zur Aufrechterhaltung des Durchhaltewillens*, Dietikon/Zurich, 1972; Christian Vetsch, *Aufmarsch gegen die Schweiz. Der deutsche 'Fall Gelb'. Irreführung des Schweizer Armee*, Olten, 1973; Philipp Wanner, *Oscar Frey und der schweizerische Widerstandswille*, Münsingen, 1974.

19 Walter Adolf Jöhr, 'Zur Strategie der Schweiz im Zweiten Weltkrieg. Versuch einer spieltheoretischen Auswertung des Bonjour-Berichtes', *Wirtschaft und Recht*, 1, 1971, p. 14.

20 Daniel Bourgeois, *Le Troisième Reich et la Suisse 1933–1941*, Neuenburg, 1974.

21 Georg Kreis, *Auf den Spuren von 'La Charité'. Die schweizerische Armeeführung im Spannungsfeld des deutsch-französischen Gegensatzes*, Basle, 1976. See also Laurent Wehrli, 'L'hypothèse H. L'image de l'Armée suisse au sein du haut-commandement français 1935–1940', Lausanne University licentiateship thesis, 1987 MS.

22 'Nur eine nationalistische Nabelschau kann deshalb die territoriale Unversehrt-heit der Schweiz den eigenen Anstrengungen zugutehalten, anstatt sie aus deutschem Desinteresse zu erklären', according to Niklaus Meienberg, in *AZ* (SP-Presse), 1 May 1971, quoted by Hans Senn, 'Schweizerische Dissuasions-strategie im Zweiten Weltkrieg', in Rudolf L. Bindschedler *et al.*, *Schwedische und Schweizerische Neutralität im Zweiten Weltkrieg*, Basle, 1985, p. 207. 'Umstrittene Rolle der Armee. Interview mit Marcel Beck und Sigmund Widmer', in *Die Weltwoche*, 13 June 1973. See also the left-wing periodicals *Focus* and *Konzept*.

23 Max Frisch, *Dienstbüchlein*, Frankfurt-am-Main, 1974; Niklaus Meienberg, *Reportagen aus der Schweiz*, Darmstadt, 1974. For a critical view of Meienberg and Dindo, Georg Kreis, 'Geschichtsschreibung mit Film und Klassenkampf. Zur Kontroverse um den "Landesverräter Ernst S."', *NZZ*, 157, 7 July 1977. See also Peter Noll, *Landesverräter. 17 Lebensläufe und Todesurteile 1942–1944*, Frauenfeld, 1980. Jost auf der Maur, 'Warum der Bundesrat Oblt. Reimann erschiessen liess', *Die Weltwoche*, 28, 9 July 1992.

24 Erwin Bucher, 'Die Schweiz im Sommer 1940', *Schweizerische Zeitschrift für Geschichte*, 2, 1979, p. 355.

25 Paper entitled 'Diskussion über die Methode, nach der die historische Wirklichkeit in der Schweiz zwischen 1930 und 1950 erschlossen werden soll', 12 May 1975 and 'Bericht der Arbeitsgruppe "Die Schweiz im 2. Weltkrieg"', June 1976 by Andy Gross. Both papers are in my archives.

26 Corps commander Colonel Alfred Ernst, in foreword to Kurz (as note 12 above). See also Alfred Ernst, *Neutrale Kleinstaaten im Zweiten Weltkrieg*, Münsingen, 1973.

27 As far as he could, Kurz tried to retract the theory of 'occupational therapy for the staff'. See in particular the series of articles entitled '"Operation Tannenbaum": Die deutschen Angriffspläne gegen die Schweiz', *Die Weltwoche*, 9–11, 1973. In my view, Kurz copied his interpretation of the operational planning against Switzerland as a 'draft to be kept in reserve' from Bernhard von Lossberg, *Im Wehrmachtsführungsstab*, Hamburg, 1949.

28 Werner Roesch, *Bedrohte Schweiz. Die deutschen Operationsplanungen gegen die Schweiz im Sommer/Herbst 1940 und die Abwehrbereitschaft der Armee im Oktober 1940*, Frauenfeld, 1986.

29 Oscar Gauye: '"Au Rütli, 25 juillet 1940". Le discours du général Guisan: nouveaux aspects', *Studien und Quellen*, 10 (periodical of Swiss Federal Archive), Berne, 1984, pp. 5–55. Gauye had already published, back in 1978, comments on another Guisan 'story', though this was only attributed to the general at a later date: his proposal, after the defeat of France in summer 1940, to send a Swiss delegation to Berlin under the leadership of Carl-Jacob Burckhardt. Oscar Gauye, 'Le général et la diplomatie suisse, 1940–1941', *Studien und Quellen*, 4, Berne, 1978.

30 Willi Gautschi, *General Henri Guisan. Die schweizerische Armeeführung im Zweiten Weltkrieg*, Zurich, 1989. On the development of popular and academic historiographical recollections of General Guisan, see Georg Kreis, 'Henri Guisan – Bild eines Generals. Glanz und Elend einer Symbolfigur', *Schweizer Monatshefte*, 5, 1990, pp. 413–31.

31 'Die wichtigste Errungenschaft der GSoA: Das Zusammenbringen der junggebliebenen 68er, der rebellisch gebliebenen 80er und der frisch politisierten GSoA-Generation.' Jo Lang, 'Über die Bedeutung von GSoA-Bewegung, GSoA-Kampagne und GSoA-Resultat. Vom kleinen zum grossen Polit-Wunder', *GSoA-Zitig*, 36, March 1990, p. 6. '1939: Rettete uns die Armee? Sonderbeilage: Schweiz im Zweiten Weltkrieg', *Friedenszeitung*, 97, September 1989.

32 Markus Heiniger, *Dreizehn Gründe. Warum die Schweiz im Zweiten Weltkrieg nicht erobert wurde*, Zurich, 1989.

33 Jakob Tanner, *Bundeshaushalt, Währung und Kriegswirtschaft. Eine finanzsoziologische Analyse der Schweiz zwischen 1938 und 1953*, Zurich, 1986.

34 Peter Maurer, *Anbauschlacht. Landwirtschaftspolitik, Plan Wahlen, Anbauwerk 1937–1945*, Zurich, 1985.

35 See my discussion of Tanner in 'Widerspruch', *Sonderband Arbeitsfrieden*, 1987, pp. 203–5.

36 Jakob Tanner, 'Schweizer Armee 1939–1945: Réduit-Mythos und Igel-Syndrom. Der Gotthardgranit und der General', *Wochen Zeitung*, 35, 1 September 1989.

37 Walter Schaufelberger (ed.), *Sollen wir die Armee abschaffen? Blick auf eine bedrohliche Zeit*, Frauenfeld, 1988 (No. 8 der Schriftenreihe der Schweizerischen Gesellschaft für militärhistorische Studienreisen GMS). Schaufelberger used the argument of the military threat to reply to Heiniger, 'Die militärische Bedrohung der Schweiz im Zweiten Weltkrieg', *NZZ*, 265, 14 November 1989; idem, 'Die "dreizehn Gründe" des Markus Heiniger. Eine kritische Entgegnung', *ASMZ*,

11, 1989, p. 723. As early as 1985, Edmund Wehrli had published, as part of the GMS series, a slim volume entitled 'Schweiz ohne Armee – eine Friedensinsel?'.

38 *Die Schweiz und der Zweite Weltkrieg*, edited by a working group headed by Josef Weiss and Silvio Bucher, Winterthur, 1989.

39 Roland Beck (ed.), *Kriegsmobilmachung 1939. Eine wissenschaftlich-kritische Analyse aus Anlass der 50. Wiederkehr des Mobilmachungstages von 1939*, Zurich, 1989.

40 Louis-Edouard Roulet (ed.), *La mobilisation de guerre de l'armée suisse et le service actif 1939–1945*, Berne, 1990.

41 Klaus Urner, *'Die Schweiz muss noch geschluckt werden!' Hitlers Aktionspläne gegen die Schweiz*, Zurich, 1990.

42 See the somewhat acidic discussion by Jakob Tanner, *Wochen Zeitung*, 28–30, 13 July 1990, and by Alfred Cattani, *NZZ*, 280, 1–2 December 1990.

43 Erwin Bucher, *Zwischen Bundesrat und General. Schweizer Politik und Armee im Zweiten Weltkrieg*, St Gallen 1991 and Zurich 1993; Hans Senn, *Erhaltung und Verstärkung der Verteidigungsbereitschaft zwischen den beiden Weltkriegen. Der Schweizerische Generalstab*, Vol. 6, Basle, 1991; idem, *Anfänge einer Dissuasionsstrategie während des Zweiten Weltkrieges. Der Schweizerische Generalstab*, Vol. 7, Basle, 1995. The dissertation by Pierre-Th. Braunschweig, *Geheimer Draht nach Berlin. Die Nachrichtenlinie Masson–Schellenberg und der schweizerische Nachrichtendienst im Zweiten Weltkrieg*, Zurich, also produced as part of the general staff history project, had appeared back in 1989.

44 The following are just a few examples dating from the 1990s: Robert Gubler, *Felddivision 6. Von der Zürcher Miliz zur Felddivision 1815–1991*, Zurich, 1991, and *Die Gotthard-Division. La Divisione del Gottardo 1938–1993*, Locarno, 1993. For an overview of divisional and corps histories published earlier, see, Walter Schaufelberger, 'Von der Kriegsgeschichte zur Militärgeschichte', in *Geschichtsforschung in der Schweiz. Bilanz und Perspektiven – 1991*, edited by the Allgemeine Geschichtsforschende Gesellschaft der Schweiz, Basle, 1992.

45 Philippe Marguerat, *La Suisse face au IIIe Reich. Réduit national et dissuasion économique*, 1940–1945, Lausanne, 1991. Hans Senn, 'Die Rolle der Schweizer Armee im Zweiten Weltkrieg. Widerstandswille und Opferbereitschaft der Aktivdienstgeneration', *NZZ*, 95, 25 April 1997; idem, 'Nützling oder Nichtsnutz? Unsere Armee im Zweiten Weltkrieg', *ASMZ*, 6, 1997, pp. 12–13; idem, 'Der Reduit-Vorschlag eine Demutsgeste? Nachlese zu einer Debatte über die Rolle der Armee', *NZZ*, 193, 22 August 1997. Gotthard Frick, 'Die Schweizer Armee im Kalkül der Wehrmacht. Positive Beurteilung der Verteidigungsbereitschaft', *NZZ*, 132, 11 June 1997. Frick had commented on the redoubt strategy ten years earlier. Idem, 'Die Reduitstrategie – aus der Sicht des möglichen Aggressors', *ASMZ*, 11, 1987, p. 746. On the problems of the redoubt, see also Franz Odermatt, 'Zur Genese der Reduitstrategie. Die Reaktion der schweizerischen Armeeführung auf einen strategischen Sonderfall im Sommer 1940, Berne University seminar paper, 1983, MS; idem, 'Zwischen Realität und militärischem Mythos: Zur Entstehung der Reduitstrategie im Jahre 1940', *ASMZ*, 7, 8 and 9, 1987, p. 447; Edmund Wehrli, 'Vom zaghaften zum wehrhaften Reduit. Anmerkungen zu General Guisans operativen Überlegungen', *NZZ*, 29, 5 February 1987, and 34, 11 February 1987; Hans Senn, 'Schweizerische Dissuasionsstrategie im Zweiten Weltkrieg', in Rudolf Bindschedler and Hans Rudolf Kurz (eds), *Schweizerische und schwedische Neutralität im Zweiten Weltkrieg*, Basle, 1985; Walter Schaufelberger, '"Das Réduit national", 1940, ein militärhistorischer Sonderfall', in Guy P. Marchal and Aram Mattioli, *Erfundene Schweiz*

210   *Switzerland and the Second World War*

- *Konstruktionen nationaler Identität*, Zurich, 1992, p. 207; Jakob Tanner, 'Réduit National, Exportindustrie und Finanzplatz: Wechselwirkungen zwischen Dissuasion und Kooperation mit den Achsenmächten', in Philipp Sarasin and Regina Wecker (eds), *Raubgold, Réduit, Flüchtlinge. Zur Geschichte der Schweiz im Zweiten Weltkrieg*, Zurich, 1998.

46 Urner refers to as yet incomplete studies by Michael Müller, NZZ, 149, 30 June/1 July 1990, p. 95.

47 Simone Chiquet (ed.), *'Es war halt Krieg'. Erinnerungen an den Alltag in der Schweiz 1939–1945*, Zurich, 1992. Nadia Guth and Bettina Hunger (eds), *Reduit Basle 39/45*, exhibition catalogue, Basle, 1989.

48 Mary Anna Barbey, *et al.*, *39–45: Les femmes et la mob*, Carouge, 1989; Monique Pavillon, *Les Immobilisées. Les femmes suisses durant la seconde guerre mondiale, Essai historique*, Lausanne, 1989; Jürg Stüssi-Lauterburg and Rosy Gysler-Schöni, *Helvetias Töchter. Frauen in der Schweizer Militärgeschichte von 1291–1939*, Frauenfeld, 1989; Simone Chiquet, 'Viel Bewusstsein – wenig Erfolg. Der Schweizerische FHD-Verband, 1944–1948', in Rudolf Jaun and Brigitte Studer (eds): *weiblich – männlich. Geschlechterverhältnisse in der Schweiz: Rechtsprechung, Diskurs, Praktiken*, Zurich, 1995.

49 On the army's part in shaping national conceptions, see Yves-Alain Morel, *Aufklärung oder Indoktrination? Truppeninformation in der Schweizer Armee 1914–1945*, Zurich, 1996.

50 'Es ist denkbar, dass Guisan, der ja im Kanton Freiburg aufgewachsen ist, dem Gedankengut Gonzague de Reynolds nicht fernstand.' ('It is conceivable that Guisan, who actually grew up in the Canton of Freiburg, failed to understand Gonzague de Reynold's thinking.') Katharina Bretscher-Spindler, 'Konservativismus, Korporativismus und Faschismus', NZZ, 90 19 April 1985.

51 Antoine Schuelé, 'La pensée militaire d'Henri Guisan', in *La Suisse et la Seconde Guerre mondiale*, Actes du Symposium 1995, Pully, 1997, p. 293.

52 Neither the extremely clear and precise biography of Gustav Däniker by Franziska Keller nor the somewhat superficial licentiateship thesis by Philibert Frick on his grandfather Hans Frick uses semantics to evaluate the texts of these two exponents of bellicose militarism. Franziska Keller, *Oberst Gustav Däniker. Aufstieg und Fall eines Schweizer Berufsoffiziers*, Zurich, 1997; Philibert Frick, 'Hans Frick: Années de Formation et Début de Carrière d'un Chef militaire (1888–1940)', licentiateship paper, Geneva University, Bougy-Villars, 1992, MS.

53 For the rise of the Prussian/German military ethic in Switzerland, see Rudolf Jaun, 'Vom Bürger-Militär zum Soldaten-Militär', in Ute Frevert, *Militär und Gesellschaft im 19. und 20. Jahrhundert*, Stuttgart, 1997; idem, *Preussen vor Augen. Das Schweizerische Offizierskorps im militärischen und gesellschaftlichen Wandel des Fin de Siècle*, Zurich, 1999.

54 Jann Etter, *Armee und öffentliche Meinung in der Zwischenkriegszeit 1918–1939*, Berne, 1972; Rudolf Jaun, 'Vom "Luftkrieghorror" zur Aktion "1000 Flugzeuge"', *Tages-Anzeiger*, 21 May 1993; Otto Lezzi, *Sozialdemokratie und Militärfragen in der Schweiz*, Frauenfeld, 1996.

55 Rudolf Jaun, *Der Schweizerische Generalstab, Vol. 8: Das Schweizerische Generalstabskorps 1875–1945. Eine kollektiv-biographische Studie*, Basle, 1991.

56 Chantal de Riedmatten, *Général Henri Guisan. Autorité et démocratie ou la question de l'inspecteur et celle de la démocratisation dans l'armée 1939–1947*, Fribourg, 1983.

57 Hans Rudolf Fuhrer, 'Les conceptions opératives de l'armée suisse 1921–1939', *Revue militaire suisse*, 3, 1994, p. 34; idem, 'Zum Vorwurf fehlender Aufmarschpläne bei Kriegsbeginn', in *La Suisse et la Seconde Guerre mondiale*, Actes du

Symposium 1995, 1997, p. 60; Hans Rudolf Kurz, 'Problèmes militaires: l'entre-deux-guerres', *Revue d'Histoire de la deuxième Guerre mondiale*, 121, January 1981; Antoine Fleury, 'La Suisse et la question du Désarmement dans l'Entre-deux-Guerres', in Alessandro Migliazza and Enrico Decleva (eds), *Diplomazia e Storia delle Relazioni internazionali*, Milan, 1991, p. 303; idem, 'Enseignements de la guerre civile espagnole selon les observations militaires suisses', in Actes du Symposium 1983, p. 61; Gerhard Wyss, 'Das Dienstreglement von 1933 und sein Einfluss auf die Kriegsbereitschaft der Armee 1939', licentiateship paper, Berne University, 1986, MS; Hans Senn, 'Kriegsmobilmachung und Verteidigungs-bereitschaft 1939', *NZZ*, 197, 26/27 August 1989.

58 Hans Georg Wirz, *Totale Landesverteidigung? Volkskrieg?*, Zofingen, 1939.

10

Political and Humanitarian Resistance in Switzerland, 1939–45

ANDRÉ LASSERRE

The word 'resistance' will be used here in a restrictive sense, excluding the defence conducted by the authorities through foreign policy, and excluding the military defence. Its purpose is to preserve national independence, or to recover it if it is lost. The enemy is the invader, naturally, but may also include a national government which is timid in the face of threats or servile under occupation. On the other hand, in order to prepare its defence against possible invasion, the government of a neutral state has to adopt military measures and, at the same time, sustain the spirit of resistance within the population while also maintaining correct relations with tomorrow's potential enemy. This ambiguity is reflected in the uncomfortable relations that exist between the public authorities and the advocates of unbridled resistance. The ideal soil for conflict is censorship. The simplistic antithesis 'accommodation or resistance' really obscures the fluctuating relations between the state and those resistance idealists who refuse any compromise with the enemy. With the benefit of hindsight, the reactions and arguments of the resistance may be seen as unrealistic or exaggerated. They are a given, which the historian has to accept as an authentic ingredient of public opinion.

In recent times Swiss economic and financial relations with Germany have been the subject of many heated debates, extending well beyond the circle of historians. These debates supply historians with little original data but compel them to re-examine the reality of Swiss sovereignty and its limitations, looking beyond the long-standing and exaggerated admiration for the part played by the military defence. A wide avenue of exploration has thus opened up to the historians involved, and to all those who consider it their duty to pass moral judgements on the past.

As for the means to be employed by the resisters, some prefer to act through civilian groups, some of them secret, while others join the political parties and authorities in proclaiming the sacred union, the *Burgfrieden*, enshrining the desires of patriots of all shades of opinion. Within this framework, each individual has to forget outdated differences to protect what is essential. First instituted between the major parties in 1937, and wavering somewhat until war broke out, this inter-party consensus took on new life in 1939, and especially in 1940. Yet even when danger was most pressing, cracks appeared, and the passing of time deepened them. For the Swiss, the new problems posed by the course of the worldwide conflict and the variations in the threat inevitably reawakened ancient conflicts, but in a different atmosphere. Is not the sacred union necessarily conservative but compelled to compromise with minority ideologies and interests? After all, even if it splits along the line between innovators and reactionaries, it will not necessarily lose all its unifying virtues.

These initial propositions are deliberately simplified: the only true resistance workers, it might be said by way of example, were the communists, since the banning of their movement compelled them to go (partly) underground and brought them into direct confrontation with the state. If one adopts the customary interpretation of resistance, it is hard to bring the communists into the picture before 1941. As for the opportunists and the convinced supporters of appeasement, they certainly resisted – against the government but not against the potential invader! In any case, their absence from these pages should not be taken as meaning that they did not exist.

THE MYTH OF THE ALPS

Until the spring of 1940 resistance remained a fairly abstract or remote concept: the dangers that the war had brought did not greatly affect the population, whose determination to fight for their independence was being exercised by others on their behalf. The best example was the campaign conducted by the Finns against the USSR. This far-away conflict showed that David could defeat Goliath and a communist Goliath at that! At any rate, when combined with the passive attitude of the Allies, who feared confrontation with the Reich, the war in Finland did no harm to the spirit of resistance as defined, in the spirit of the age, by the famous Federal Council message of 1938, drafted by Etter. This determination had been reinforced by the National Exhibition of 1939 with its *Dörfli* (archetypal Swiss village) and its 'Swiss way' leading to the mighty statue of the citizen pulling on his military uniform. The government document drew heavily on the theories of

Gonzague de Reynold, who held that the heart of Switzerland was the Gotthard massif and the unchanging virtues of a primitive, Alpine and peasant Switzerland; the *Landi* (*Landesaustellung* – national exhibition) – of which this was not the only message – had left in people's minds the image of a people united in its roots in the soil, a nation born in 1291. In Switzerland, 1848 and the rise of democracy yielded pride of place to a remote, mythic past. With some perspicacity, Max Frisch would later recall his visit to the Great Exhibition: 'With no Utopia, immunised against everything that is not truly Swiss. Self-confidence through folklore. And something that didn't strike me at the time: the subtle odour of Swiss blood and soil.'[1]

Leaving aside the issue of blood, more likely to be divisive in a multi-ethnic country, let us confine ourselves – alongside history – to the exaltation or cult of the soil on which the 'constants' of the national essence are founded. Other examples could also be found in the Europe of that deeply crisis-riven era: the Great War, the Bolshevik, Fascist and National Socialist revolutions enervating the reflexes of the democratic states and even undermining the foundations of their systems, the economic disaster of 1929 which eroded confidence in the state and in traditional society, encouraging in many people a refusal to look forward and a desire to return to the safety of their origins. How could an identity that was fraying be rediscovered elsewhere? 'To integrate a Helvetic myth into the general mentality' – that was the mission which the historian of the *Neue Zürcher Zeitung* retrospectively attributed to his newspaper.[2] This is the territory of full-scale historical myth, but 'the exaltation of the national power or conscience is still one of the great reasons for the existence of narrative history, just as it was no doubt its original stimulus: all nations need to know the story of their origins, a memory of greatness, which are at the same time the guarantees of their future'.[3] Prepared since before the war by a whole school of historians, the success of the spiritual resistance is largely attributable, as we know, to the thirst for a greater national cohesion. It was thanks to the war, one might say, that this need could be satisfied. With the stunning successes of the *Wehrmacht* in the spring of 1940, German threats and virtually complete encirclement of the country by the victors of the hour, the military defence acquired a solid backing of patriotic con-science. By means of the war of nerves, as Hitler had said, 'the enemy nation must be demoralised and ready to capitulate before one is entitled to consider military action'. We may deny to our hearts' content the objective reality of the military threat to Switzerland. Without even considering the revival of the right-wing groups generated by the *Wehrmacht*'s victories, it is impossible to disregard this type of offensive and the enormous, skilfully modulated economic and psychological pressures that went along with it. The recent publication of the report submitted to the government by Oprecht on the German plan for the subjugation of Switzerland is a useful reminder of Daniel Bourgeois' analysis of this type of National Socialist strategy.[4] Confronted by this type of attack, it was important to exalt the defence of values that justified the protection of independence. It was on this ideological battlefield that it was first important to find some answers. *Armée et Foyer* was the agent of psychological warfare, as a quartermaster-general's department, among troops and civilians alike. A propaganda tool in the service of an imposed ideology? The point is arguable, but its working methods, its structure, its receptiveness to argument and its ignorance of the principles of manipulation left it far behind Goebbels' headquarters.

Until 1942, or even the winter of 1943, these priorities would generally be established in people's minds, even if there was no shortage of accidents and false notes. Their effectiveness could only be temporary, associated with the duration of this type of offensive. To reduce, as a matter of a particular mental tradition, the spiritual resistance to the expression of a reaction to the crumbling of the bourgeois conscience or to a 'revenge of the defeated Sonderbund' is not without interest and may help to explain the origin of the movement, though not its effectiveness and widespread nature – or its brevity. It would be an exaggeration to say that 'throughout the war, the collective expression would be deeply marked by this ideology, this political culture of resistance':[5] once the danger was over, the spiritual resistance died away and many processes of renewal began. An analysis of political speeches would provide a clearer insight into this multifarious concept of spiritual resistance.

The Federal Council message of 1938 was a preparation for the isolation of an encircled Switzerland, though without predicting it: after all, how could Switzerland deal openly after 1940 with a Europe under construction when its architects were the victorious Nazis? Even if the message asserted a desire for a policy of outward openness, it would be easy enough to remember, first and foremost, its invitation to fall back on the Alpine virtues and the Alpine heights. At all events, its ideology was incarnated in the new strategy based on the national redoubt. It is impossible to be unaware of this when analysing the constituents of the spirit of resistance. The popularity of the Wahlen plan follows the same line: its economic successes cannot be compared with its psychological impact.[6]

Our political system was born in the Alpine centre of the country. 'Ex Alpibus salus patriae' – the health of the country comes from the Alps.[7] Those ringing words from a genuine poet of the independence

216 Switzerland and the Second World War

and greatness of the country do not summarise the spirit of the entire resistance. They characterise one of its trends – no doubt the most popular – the trend most closely associated with the ideology that underpinned the strategy of the national redoubt, and the most suited, too, to the siege mentality so characteristic of the times. It is notable how few references to democracy there are in the 1938 message and the literature that drew upon it to galvanise the spirit of resistance – at least until the point at which the Allied victory was becoming more and more obvious. Going beyond this trend, it would be quite interesting to analyse the various perceptions of democracy between the German-speakers on the one hand, associating democracy with ancient Switzerland,[8] and the French- and Italian-speaking Swiss on the other, who historically were more the victims than the beneficiaries of the German-speaking cantons. The latter drew their inspiration from the philosophy of the Enlightenment and the 'immortal principles' of 1789, so roughly treated between the wars and during the early years of the new global conflict. What hope remained for their disappointed disciples? Their silences, their hesitations, their quest for a new political creed, their reversals of attitude during the war whose ideological nature was in any case obvious – all these would be deserving of attention. And one might add the enthusiastic expectation of communist democracy on the far left of the resistance.

The vagaries of changing attitudes among the resistance could usefully be studied by reference to the content of the press, especially that of satirical papers such as the *Nebelspalter* in particular, to which might be added the productions of cabarets such as the *Cornichon* in Zurich or the *Coup de Soleil* in Lausanne.[9] To be successful, humour and caricature must constantly adapt to the events and feelings of the moment and prise out the unspoken ideas of the time. Powerful as it was in the period of confusion that followed the French defeat, the *Nebelspalter's* image on 21 June 1940 of Tell's boat under the caption 'We've got a good pilot on board' would have been a ridiculous anachronism three years later.

RESISTANCE MOVEMENTS

A period of vacillation followed the French defeat, until the defensive spirit was rallied by the efforts of the general in late July. A feature of this interval was the officers' conspiracy, headed by Alfred Ernst and a number of other captains, with a view to preventing the federal authorities from sliding into defeatism in the face of German aggressiveness.

The story is well known. We will confine ourselves here to noting the behaviour of the general, who had no choice but to impose (light) punishment for this serious insubordination but assured the conspirators that he still had full confidence in them: this is one instance, and not the last, of the ambiguity of resistance activity, simultaneously aligned with and opposed to the state institutions and authority. Humanitarian resistance supplies other, more damaging examples of the same thing. Moreover, the somewhat rudimentary political agenda of the conspirators has attracted little attention, as has their sense of being a caste on which the national destiny depended, contrary to Swiss tradition. There were other examples of this at the same time. And the part subsequently played by these officers, who continued to meet regularly and remain active in various civilian organisations, proved more important than their burst of patriotic energy in the summer of 1940, as Bonjour has already pointed out.[10]

One example of this kind of involvement was the *Aktion Nationaler Widerstand*, more deserving than some of its self-styled label of resistance: secretive, with no horizontal links between members, it had infiltrated the public service and remained mistrustful or even hostile towards the Federal Council, which it felt was too docile towards Germany, but close to *Armée et Foyer* (August R. Lindt, for example, belonged to both organisations). Its recruitment policy targeted leading figures in political, economic and other circles and – a notable innovation – transcended party politics: its ranks included not only the Liberal National Councillor Albert Oeri from Basle but also his Socialist colleague Hans Oprecht from Zurich, who was chairman of the movement. The socialist involvement is an important testimony to the way in which the major party of the left was brought by the war into the patriotic establishment. This may be one of the reasons why, unlike other resistance movements, it proposed no agenda of political or social reforms, confining itself to watching over the independence of Switzerland and preparing to fight against any occupying power. Its fragmented and disparate activities are, naturally, not well known.[11] From November 1940 until early 1944 it published a mimeographed periodical for its members, *Die Information der Woche*. Its main thrust was opposition to Nazi Germany, and it had basically achieved its purpose well before it ceased publication.

The Gotthard League brings us to a different type of resistance – although Alfred Ernst was at one time among its supporters. Created by the joint initiative of Denis de Rougemont and Theophil Spoerri, its membership climbed rapidly to about 8,000. Its aim – as its symbolic name clearly suggests – was to strengthen the spirit of independence among the people and the authorities and ensure that it prevailed. Another, stronger determination was the renewal of Switzerland. Its 'charter' of 1942 thus postulated activities based on professional organisation, pension schemes based on compensation funds, protection of the family among others. It is difficult to quantify the league's real achievement, the more so since from the time of its first general meeting in September 1940, and then later when political and social reforms were proposed, it had ever-increasing difficulty in keeping the movement together; one reason being that it brought together people of all shades of opinion, even including supporters of the far right or believers in Switzerland's alignment with the new Europe.[12] Other, more homogeneous groups, such as the political parties, proved more effective in influencing the institutions. Did the league and its civilian associations ultimately have a greater impact on people's thinking than on practical reforms, as if there had been a kind of de facto division of the areas of influence? According to de Rougemont, at all events, the league had achieved its true objective by the summer of 1940, when the government's determination to resist was irrevocably asserted[13] (this was also the point at which de Rougemont left Switzerland!).

The New Helvetic Society, older and more deeply rooted in the country, offered an organisational model based on diversity and even conflict of opinion. Its undeniable dedication to national independence and pluralism did not prevent it from addressing the major problems of the day. However, it was less interested in political activity than in providing information and maintaining a constructive spirit based on mutual respect. This tradition denied it any direct influence on events, all the more so since its lack of numbers prevented any thought of large-scale campaigns. Its role during the war is thus difficult to measure, especially since its structure, based on large numbers of highly independent sections, makes things difficult for researchers, but it never disarmed throughout the period of conflict.[14]

Among the civilian movements that were active from time to time, mention could also be made of *Forum Helveticum*, an umbrella association bringing together several groups such as the New Helvetic Society, the Young Liberals and such like, and the *Eidgenössische Gemeinschaft*, initially secret and never very numerous, which was ultimately to be converted to a political party in 1943/44, or *Res Publica*, launched in 1939.

With their public conferences, their seminars, their publications, their points of contact and their more or less systematically organised networks, all these movements sustained the spirit of independence and backed up the efforts of *Armée et Foyer*. No general overview of their activities has yet been produced.

THE MEDIA

The newspapers played a leading part: 'one of the pillars of the resistance', in the words of Edgar Bonjour.[15] Except for those committed to a party line, they fought the same fight as the state, to varying degrees, but – even more tightly squeezed than the state between the need for a degree of fear in order to fight defeatism and the need for reassurance in order to prevent panic or diplomatic intervention – they suffered from the close constraints brought about by the encirclement of the country and a vigilant censorship. Entrusted to the army's Press and Radio Division, media surveillance had been organised during the phoney war. Even so, a system had grown up whereby the press was largely dependent on the government. Without being under any formal obligation to set forth arguments dictated by propaganda, there were certain limits beyond which the editors could not go – limits laid down by instructions that were often vague and, above all, varied as events progressed and Switzerland's foreign relations changed. The personalities of the military district censors also influenced the behaviour of journalists, who in fact had varying degrees of freedom of expression: very narrow in some cases, as shown by the example of Lausanne, more relaxed elsewhere. Not without some second thoughts and U-turns, the censorship tended to relax its grip as the German threat became less urgent. According to a report by the Press and Radio Division, 'The result is a certain tension between the two sides; they have difficulty in agreeing on exactly where the fine line lies between discipline and neutralisation, meaning the standardisation of public opinion.'[16] The newspapers were thus both a powerful boost to the spirit of resistance and a menace to foreign policy and neutrality, especially towards a very watchful and highly sensitive Germany. Finally, the press served as a convenient scapegoat for the federal authorities caught in the diplomatic crossfire. Paradoxically, journalists had less independence in what they could say than *Armée et Foyer*, an adjunct of the army which had the self-appointed task of saying at seminars and conferences what the press could not say.

Within the kaleidoscope of a geographically fragmented press, certain organs emerged as representatives of the spirit of resistance: the *Neue Zürcher Zeitung*, the *Bund*, the *Nation*, the *Basler Nachrichten*, the *National-Zeitung* above all, the *Sentinelle* (and the other socialist papers) and so on. And the local press, under less strict surveillance and therefore probably enjoying more room for manoeuvre, should not be forgotten either.

Though there were exceptions and instances of backtracking, the press as a whole played a positive role in maintaining national morale, which was conceived of as meaning spiritual resistance, especially between the spring of 1940 and 1942/43, when German pressure was unrelenting. We need only mention the famous Trump campaign of June 1940, designed to remove certain editors, primarily Schürch at the *Bund* but also Bretscher at the *NZZ*, Oeri at the *Basler Nachrichten* and Lüdi at the Swiss Telegraphic Agency. The scheme failed, thanks more to the journalists than to a timid administration. Then again, there were the reactions to the *Blutschuldthese* (blood-guilt theory), which held that anti-German outbreaks in the press would lead to retribution in the form of an invasion of Switzerland. Giving in to blackmail would obviously have had grave consequences for the country. In the words of Theodor Gut, summarising the principle of press resistance: 'The intellectual neutralisation of the press has done nothing to save other countries which have since been liquidated; if the press were to hold its peace, our democracy would very soon be seriously disrupted.'[17]

Resistance to pressure, and sometimes to the temptations advanced by the victorious Germans, went hand in hand with the rejection of European unity associated with a Nazi victory. There was no shortage of vilification and mockery of the Swiss for refusing to climb aboard this bandwagon or, after 1941, to participate in the 'Swastika crusade' as Oeri derisively called the anti-Bolshevik crusade which was to save Europe from the red peril. These reactions by the Swiss were perfectly consistent with their strategy of protective and isolationist spiritual defence.

In the final stages of the war, from 1943 to 1945, these reflexes no longer had a part to play in the new map of Europe and the world that was beginning to take shape and in which Switzerland had to prepare a place for itself. The problems were less of a direct threat to survival, but they still existed: the Allies and their press now took their turn in criticising a neutrality that was no longer any use to them. In turn, too, they brought greater pressure to bear on Switzerland, not to mention the USSR in its dual role of salvation and threat. The Atlantic Charter and the leftward trend towards the welfare state, which was very marked in the Allied states (and in the national resistance movement), also displeased the right wing of the press and threatened the solidarity and cohesion of the resistance supporters of the earlier period. In addition, conservatism was no longer a force. The Swiss easily become depressed when confronted by the imminent victory of their saviours and the prospect of new, ambitious great powers.

The press has already been studied on several occasions and from various aspects. Journalists have published their memoirs or reprinted collections of their main articles.[18] To quote just one example, there was Ernst Schürch, who apparently harboured few illusions about the prospects of armed resistance but harped incessantly on about the need for self-determination and its inevitable victory in the long run, on national solidarity, on the fundamental illegitimacy of a government imposed from outside and so on: in short, a theme which has much to say about the atmosphere of psychological warfare and the weapons available at a time when the only guarantee of safety was the graveyard, as Schürch wrote on 3 October 1940.

What has hitherto been lacking, however, is any analysis of content which would enable us to follow more closely the changing trends in journalistic opinion and messages.[19] We still know too little about attitudes to particular events, countries and problems (anti-communism, for example, which was twice as virulent in the aftermath of the Russo-Finnish war), just as we know too little about the disagreements between the various parts of the country. For example, the temptations of Pétainism imparted a specific hue to the resistance in French-speaking Switzerland. There still remains the nebula of the professional press, the political parties and the churches, where the interests and convictions expressed sometimes defy the censor's prohibitions, even at the expense of their authors.

Book publishing, also subject to state supervision, faced different problems from the press: in German-speaking Switzerland it traditionally depends on German customers. The cultural nationalism which it was now expected to support was broadly equivalent to the loss of an important market, monitored by a censorship of exceptional strictness, or abandoning publication of emigré German authors. On the other hand, competition from Germany fell away sharply. Ultimately, the war was a golden age for those Swiss book publishers who were able to organise their markets in time. The history of Swiss book publishing, too, is as yet largely unwritten.[20]

Radio broadcasting was much easier to control than the press or the book trade because attention could be focused solely on the Swiss Broadcasting Association. Its licence was suspended on 29 August 1939, and broadcasting from then on was under the direct control of the Federal Department of Posts and Railways. As the agent of spiritual defence, the department's mission was to strengthen national cohesion through its cultural activities, while remembering to make them comprehensible to listeners abroad. The various types of link between each of the three linguistic regions and their foreign counterparts made it difficult to carry out this task in a uniform manner – and makes it equally difficult to analyse today. The handful of areas of jurisdiction reserved to the army did nothing to simplify matters but, at the instigation of Schenker, enabled broadcasts to be geared towards cultivating a spirit of resistance. The best known agents of this policy were to be

René Payot at Sottens and Jean Rodolphe de Salis at Beromünster. Although a few studies have been produced, the content and evolution of the messages put out in news bulletins, and historical, political, social and other types of comment, still lie dormant in sound archives, some of which have been better preserved and indexed than others.[21] This, however, is an essential field of investigation: for a period when radio was one of the propaganda weapons of choice and Switzerland was a sealed arena for conflicts between those who wanted to use broadcasting for psychological warfare and those who kept a jealous eye on neutrality. This was probably one of the most intense sectors of the struggle between institutionalised state resistance and the active resistance born of conviction.

Cinema, too, held a privileged place in the arsenal of psychological warfare. The 1938 Federal Council message established a place for the cinema among the key instruments of spiritual defence. Indeed, a whole series of productions would come about, placing appropriate emphasis on national values and sacred traditions. At the same time, every cinema would compulsorily screen a weekly review of Swiss news, heavily slanted towards folklore and festivals, under the aegis of the Swiss Cinema Board with its tortured history.[22]

When we come to the modern media we enter an even more unfamiliar cultural maze. For example, a study of broadcast jazz and the spiritual resistance has been written, and shows what unexpected implications this concept had. Until the National Council of 1943, in particular, this was an area of conflict between the opponents of this kind of music and its partisans. One side was critical of its foreign, degenerate, not to say negro origins, and expected musical works of genuinely Swiss origin. Others, conversely, applauded a form of music aimed at the young, at ordinary people, a new popular music formula. French- and Italian-speaking Switzerland were more inclined that the German-speaking areas to adopt this socially favourable interpretation of the new music.[23]

POLITICAL PARTIES

Regarded as nationally divisive factors, capable of paralysing democracy, the political parties were unpopular for many years while the dictatorships flaunted their successes. However, apart from those who would have had everything to gain from being placed under the tutelage of larger neighbouring states, they knew that they would be among the first victims of an imported *Gleichschaltung* (totalitarian homogenisation). No question, then, of giving in to threats or blackmail, and no question either of abandoning the means of ensuring the national defence. We know how the Socialist Party was converted to this point of view. But there is no shortage of finer points: one of the most revealing, perhaps, says much about what the myth of rural patriotism meant in reality – the refusal of the *Bauernheimatbewegung* (Farmers' Homeland Movement) to participate unconditionally in the strengthening of the national defence: 'Either the State can help me escape from my grinding poverty or I shall take no interest in defending it.'[24] Those words, admittedly, date from 1936, and the party would increasingly be tempted by the bait that the Nazis had carefully laid for the farmers of the *Nährstand* (peasantry), but what a weakening of one of the central pillars of Swiss patriotism! On the positive side, we should recall the effort towards convergence undertaken with the Socialists through joint meetings and projects. It enjoyed little direct success outside the Canton of Berne, but maintained a general state of mind that made it possible for the Radicals to give up a seat in the government in December 1943 to the first Socialist Federal Councillor, Ernst Nobs.

As participants in the political resistance, the parties' main interest for us here is their agendas: on the one hand, they had to adapt these to the needs of the moment, and above all to the requirements of national unity, which demanded sacrifices from all in the interests of solidarity; on the other hand, it was essential for them to be able to offer people hope for the future, social projects in tune with traditional ideologies and with the expectations of the voters, who also wanted to benefit from the concessions granted by the other political partners. This active and passive solidarity was appropriate to a system of consensus that became established within the 'sacred union' – a union that constituted an integral part of the concept of resistance.

Pride of place must go to the Radical Party, which prided itself on incarnating the great principles of the federal state: 'its duty is to be in the forefront of the fight to defend spiritual Switzerland and repel any attack from an ideological aggressor', whether from left or right.[25] The official spirit of defence thus went without saying, but by taking its stand on ideological grounds it also formed an important part of the psychological resistance. At the same time, good relations had to be maintained with foreign states. In such a large party, tensions were in any case inevitable and individual reactions took many forms.

Resolutely opposed to Nazism, though more sympathetic to Italian fascism, the Catholic Conservative Party shared the same ideas about national defence in a different spirit, shaped by religion and by its deeply ingrained anti-socialism. While the Radicals moved forward cautiously into the territory of political and economic innovation, the Catholic Conservative Party barely set foot in it: equally dedicated to independence and social harmony within the country, it based its policies on the defence of federalism and the family and was more inclined to seek its advances in the permanent values of society, if not actually in past formulas.

The Socialist Party was the most original and innovative of the major parties. Gradually brought round to the concept of national defence from 1936 onwards, its fundamental anti-fascism led it to emphasise military defence at the outbreak of war, with a view to safeguarding territorial independence; the interests of the working class took second place. This change of heart involved participation in the spiritual defence and collaboration with the other political groups. However, at the May 1941 congress, the imperatives of social reforms were voiced, and the move to achieve them triumphed in the 'New Switzerland' Programme in late 1942, envisaging radical social and economic change but without revolution. The programme stated the need to put an end to capitalism, and set out how it should be done. This was a serious blow to the 'sacred union', a sign of the times; a German victory was becoming more and more improbable and the war was entering a new phase, where the international situation was losing its priority status and moving back to an equal footing with domestic problems. Bringolf, from Schaffhausen, would make the point clearly at the 1943 congress. The concern with preparing Switzerland's future and its place in a new world order, already established in certain circles, would now become increasingly important. The Socialists enjoyed a strong position in this new turn of events: receptive in principle to changes in society, they attracted increasing support at a time when, in Switzerland and everywhere else in the world, people were agreeing on the need to seek improved social security, guaranteed employment, state control or the end of liberal capitalism and such like. The middle-class parties themselves went along with the movement, though naturally without the same revivalist enthusiasm as the left. This, however, did not mean that the Socialists disregarded the internal crises; their relations with the Communists and with their own youth movement, which had rallied to the Communists, remained chaotic. To confirm their position on class, they naturally repudiated the 'sacred union', but not participation in the Federal Council.[26]

The wartime history of the far left, under its various labels, is even less well known.[27] It naturally followed the twists and turns of Soviet policy, from the Ribbentrop–Molotov Pact of 1939 to Operation Barbarossa in 1941. Always opposed to official Swiss policy, operating underground from the banning of the Communist Party on 26 November 1940 until its official resurrection under the name of the Swiss Labour Party in October 1944, and vigilantly monitored by the police and the army, it would take the view that the USSR alone had won the victory over fascism. It did, therefore, conduct a resistance campaign, but in a very different sense from the other parties.

The priority which the political parties, and the population as a whole, accorded to economic and social problems was almost suggestive of resistance on their part to liberal capitalism. The economic crisis with its saga of unemployment and poverty, fears of a repetition of the well remembered general strike of 1918 and a price escalation comparable to what had occurred during the First World War – a recurrence of these scourges had to be prevented at all costs. The objective of the 'sacred union' and national resistance also made it essential to find new ideas that would prevent workers and peasants drifting towards Nazism or communism. These circumstances favoured the left, which had every interest in profiting from this climate, but were difficult for the other parties, which were probably more inclined to argue in terms of concessions than of sacrifices! Under the fashionable slogans of community spirit and solidarity, and following the line of spiritual defence, the years 1940–43 saw numerous projects for reform which ran counter to traditional socialist or trade union demands. One of the most interesting and elaborate was that of Ducommun and the Gotthard League, calling upon the professional community to bring employers' associations and workers together for the joint management of businesses and economic sectors. This would be a way of avoiding government interventionism without jeopardising the interests of the workers. Quite the reverse – the workers would in fact be re-integrated into the national community on equal terms. A new humanism would arise from this process of renewal: over and above material or political concerns, the spiritual references and echoes of authentically Swiss cooperative traditions bear the stamp of the time.[28] Adopted by a conference of the French-speaking unions in October 1940, the project had little success in German-speaking areas despite its ratification by the Swiss Union Commission in May of the following year.

THE CHURCHES

The federal authority officially advocated spiritual defence, but did not welcome interference by the churches in this form of spirituality. Among the Protestants, men like Karl Barth, Leonhard Ragaz and Arthur Frey, director of the Press Service, rejected any form of alignment with the new Europe and criticised the government for its defeatism. In particular, they rejected the idea that the church should confine its activities to the private sphere, as it was exhorted to do by the Press and Radio Division. In an echo of the *Kirchenkampf* (the struggle between the German churches and the Nazi government), the dispute related primarily to the relations between church and state. The first subject of controversy was censorship: was not this the first step towards the extinction of liberty and destruction of democracy? The leading lights of the resistance[29] made no attempt to conceal their opinions on this. Hence their clashes with the official watchdogs, aware of the threat to authority represented by an influential press agency and strong-minded, respected advocates of freedom of expression. Not all their co-religionists followed suit, in particular the Federation of Protestant Churches, which kept a very low profile. There was no shortage of reflection and criticism, and these again have not been studied hitherto. For once, however, the problem of the conditions of the Christian profession of faith and the social responsibilities of the church arose, during those years, not as an academic issue but as a direct and tangible one.[30]

The Protestant rebels were advised by the Press and Radio Division to take their cue more from the Catholic Church, whose policies were indeed very cautious. The fact that Catholics were in a minority among reservists and that the Catholic Church lacked any figures as outstanding as Karl Barth, together with reservations on the part of Rome, may explain this Catholic docility. However, there were exceptions in French-speaking Switzerland, where Charles Journet and Albert Béguin also committed themselves to the fight against totalitarianism.[31]

LEADERS OF OPINION

'Enough action, time for a word,' suggested the journalist Edmond Gilliard in the October 1940 edition of the Vaudois periodical *Traits*. This paradoxical yet suggestive demand could suggest the general expectation that the authorities would be truthful and at the same time offer hope for the future. This need, arising out of the collapse of France and the seizure of Europe by the dictators, would thus explain the many public utterances by individuals who enjoyed high moral or intellectual standing in the media, the political parties or the civilian, religious or humanitarian groups. It was they who, through the spoken and written word, wove the networks that passed on and propagated the spirit of resistance. Their influence is difficult to quantify, but must not be underestimated in any attempt to analyse public opinion. Some idea of it can be formed from the suggested lists of works and brochures regularly published by the Livre Suisse (not to mention newspaper articles). Oral propaganda is more difficult to track down. Such research could be most fruitfully conducted at canton level, where the influence of the persons involved is easier to measure.

If it is assumed that a propaganda offensive existed, orchestrated from above, these writings and conferences could be seen as organised relay stations. Apart from the members of *Armée et Foyer* or the army officers, there is no evidence so far to uphold this assertion.

In conclusion, we come to the most active phase of political resistance, up to the time of Stalingrad: its dominant features were psychological offensives and the threats of suppression or even invasion. This exceptional time of destabilisation created, by way of reaction, a no less exceptional spiritual resistance. Subsequently, a more or less guaranteed relaxing of the pressure calmed people's minds and weakened the springs of resistance as the threat became less distinct – or was felt to be increasingly remote. *Armée et Foyer* rebelled against this happy-go-lucky holiday spirit, together with all those who felt the situation was still serious and the exhortation of patriotic solidarity still essential.

This resistance in the early years was very largely based on the Alpine myth. Would it be an exaggeration to say that once that myth had become worn out, it was replaced by another – the myth of General Guisan, which had been forged bit by bit during the period of acute danger when he increasingly emerged as the saviour of his country? Historians have still not tired of making fun of him. Yet the objective reality was less important at the time than the perceived image of that reality. Public opinion is the object of the history of mentalities, and not the subject which provides testimony that is subject to the criticism of truth of testimony.

The battle of Stalingrad makes a convenient landmark to identify the turning point in the war: it lasted several months, until the surrender on 2 February 1943, allowing time for attitudes to develop slowly. While its allies were hesitant or slow to land on the European mainland, the USSR was giving repeated demonstrations of its military might. The contagious power of its ideology benefited from this and undermined convictions or created doubts among the Swiss. Some glorified the Soviet liberators of the peoples of Europe; others execrated the oppressors of the proletarian dictatorship and were reluctant to abandon the comfortable cushion of reliance on national values. At the same time, rising prices, material difficulties and privations sometimes paved the way to latent social conflicts.

Despite the conservative or even reactionary ethos of the spiritual defence, political thought proved to be both lively and imaginative in some quarters, mainly in the social field. This was one way of consolidating national cohesion, a form of resistance which made no concessions to external pressures.

A number of indications supplied by the titles of political essays suggest that between 1940 and 1942 a copious – though decreasing – amount of literature dealt with the essence of Switzerland and its constants; from 1943, however, preparation for the post-war period and the country's position in a new and alarming world became the dominant issues.[32] That year marked a genuine change in atmosphere, an important advance in attitudes. Since an increasing proportion of public opinion felt there was no longer any justification for the 'sacred union' to confront the Nazi peril, concerns about the future became more important, with all the confrontations that the various visions of society produced. However, one important element of national solidarity remained, social anxieties and the search for peaceful solutions to domestic conflicts: there was very widespread acceptance of the fact that the laws must impose a more equitable society. The creation of the pension scheme for retired people and surviving dependants would be its clearest symbol, though not the only one.

HUMANITARIAN RESISTANCE

The moral justification for neutrality lay in humanitarian activity, which, incidentally, no diplomatic formality required the country to undertake. Although this requirement was never forgotten, it was necessary to await the creation of the Swiss Gift to war victims in October 1944 and the election of Max Petitpierre to the Federal Council in January 1945 before it became a major principle of foreign policy. Proposed to the Federal Council in December 1943, this aid programme only got off the ground in the autumn of 1944, at the instigation of Pilet-Golaz. At the same time – and not by chance – it would take on the colouring of a 'humanitarian catching-up exercise', designed to bring the country out of its growing isolation.[33] The importance of the private contributions justifies the mention of the Swiss Gift in this account, even if its political and official ramifications have nothing to do with the resistance.

Nor was it a matter of chance that it was in the last stages of the war, from 1942/43 onwards, that efforts at solidarity greatly increased: the burden of the German occupation of Europe was becoming inexorable. The Jews were now destined for the 'final solution', other victims were accompanying them to their fate, and privations were affecting every-one. Switzerland could no longer ignore this situation.

Aid to war victims was primarily a private initiative. It is difficult to trace, in view of its scattered nature and the lack of readily accessible data. The International Committee of the Red Cross constitutes a dual exception: it is a subject of international law and it has had its own historian. The domestic and international activities of the Swiss Red Cross, which both suffered and profited from its semi-official status, are less well known.[34]

As my concern is with the resistance, I shall confine myself here to the activities on behalf of refugees, which can effectively be subdivided between joint efforts with the authorities, simple legality and illegality. It had of course to operate within the context of the federal policy on asylum, since it was this that laid down the rules of refugee status: hard-line resistance would have deprived those involved of any influence over the way in which those rules were formulated and applied, to the detriment of the asylum seekers themselves. A good example is Gertrud Kurz, the head of the *Chevaliers de la Paix*, who was undeniably stubborn in her dealings with Rothmund or von Steiger but did not burn her bridges with the authorities, and was thus able to make her famous direct intervention with the Federal Council in 1942.[35] The essential facts of the situation are known here, except as they apply to the re-emigration of the refugees, which in most cases took place after the end of the war.[36]

Among the humanitarian activities, pride of place must of course go to the Swiss Jews, who demonstrated a remarkable solidarity.[37] For a numerically small and politically moderate community, this was also the only possible form of resistance. That is not to say that there were no internal crises: some felt the necessary financial sacrifices were excessive while others, more radically inclined, thought it a scandal that the law-abiding approach necessary for collaboration with the federal police made it impossible to save victims from the Holocaust.

Recent events have also shown that we know little about the public's awareness of the 'final solution' or the time at which that awareness genuinely dawned. The contribution made to this ignorance by censorship was greater than is generally thought: the censors did nothing to allow the facts to become known – quite the reverse.

To facilitate relations with the authorities and coordinate their activities, the leading charitable bodies formed the Swiss Central Refugee Aid Office (OSAR), which was compelled by its statutes to abide by Berne's decisions but could influence them. There is still some doubt about the exact part it played. Its clashes with the federal police related mainly to the criteria for admission to Switzerland, the financing of asylum, admission to the camps after 1940 and re-emigration. Also, the chief of the federal police deliberately short-circuited the OSAR; for example, he often negotiated directly with the Federation of Israelite

Communities. On the most contentious issue, the admission of refugees, he was able to play his biggest trump card of the first trick: no association would be recognised unless it declared every refugee it helped. The risks of a break with the authorities were too fraught with consequences to be taken light-heartedly. With a few exceptions, then, it is not here that we should be looking for humanitarian resistance. On the other hand, Rothmund agreed to negotiate on special cases or rules: the independence of his contacts and their influence were greater than might be thought. This was probably especially true until 1940 or 1942, at a time when the Confederation was not taking responsibility for the cost of supporting the refugees, the burdens accepted by the private groups increased their independence, even if only slightly.

To find determined resistance to the official policy on admission to the country or the camps, we need to look at lower levels: first, the cantons, which still had a certain freedom of decision and were involved in the guarding of the borders and in the federal police conferences. Although the independence of the high officials, as demonstrated at those conferences, was less than dazzling, the same did not necessarily apply in day-to-day practice. Some authors have already studied the cantonal policies or the activities of individual officials, in Basle and especially in Ticino, but more detailed inquiries would identify many cases where the law as laid down in Berne was mitigated, either in favour of certain categories of refugee (such as fugitive members of the French resistance) or more generally.[38]

Illegal humanitarian activities took place primarily at an individual level, in connection with border crossings. There was no shortage of volunteers, paid or otherwise, to smuggle refugees across the mountain borders of the Jura or Alps, adding to the obsessive fears of an administration that hated the smugglers even more than the refugees they were helping. The ranks of the administration itself included a number of independent operators: among the frontier guards and police, like Grüninger before the war; in the diplomatic or consular service, such as Carl Lutz in Budapest; and in humanitarian missions abroad. Secretive by necessity, they rarely revealed themselves; their motives and the extent of their activities are thus largely unknown, despite occasional memoirs and oral testimony, but they undoubtedly left their mark on the police archives or court files.[39] The political parties, too, even leaving aside the communists, sometimes played a not insignificant part – probably more so in the finding of accommodation than in border crossings. Finally, there were some more or less dubious characters who naturally gravitated to activities in which ambiguous behaviour benefited from illegality: the most famous member of this underworld was the former Federal Councillor Musy.[40]

A distinction has to be made between these two phases of refugee activity before we address the most essential yet least known aspect of the subject: public opinion. Easier to illustrate by examples than to quantify, it determines the very existence of private aid and, to some extent, actual official policy. The permanent fear of excess foreign immigration that steered official policy was largely irrational; the authorities nurtured it carefully as part of a public opinion that was thoroughly conditioned by the spiritual defence but had already been naturally receptive to it in the first place. Latent anti-Semitism played its part. As an assumption, it may be said that the asylum policy generated no strong resistance within the country, that it was rejected or even ridiculed in the border regions where the hard-pressed fugitives were to be seen, and often criticised for what was considered its over-generous application in the refugee camps inside the country.

Finally, there were the refugees themselves, the central focus of humanitarian policy. They were often treated as inanimate objects on arrival, but increasingly as individuals as they progressed towards the camps. Their testimony is often unbiased, whether critical or laudatory. That testimony is irreplaceable, but difficult for the historian to use.[41]

NOTES

1 Max Frisch, *Livret de service*, Geneva/Zurich, 1977, p. 55. See Georg Kreis, 'Der homo alpinus helveticus, Zur Darstellung des schweizerischen Rassendiskurs der 30er Jahre'; André Lasserre, 'Le peuple des bergers dans son "Réduit national"', in Guy P. Marchal and Aram Mattioli, *Erfundene Schweiz – La Suisse imaginée*, Zurich, 1992; Werner Möckli, *Das schweizerische Selbstverständnis beim Ausbruch des Zweiten Weltkrieges*, Zurich, 1973, analyses the image of Switzerland as the inheritor of its glorious past by reference to the National Exhibition.
2 Fred Luchsinger, *Die NZZ im Zeitalter des 2 Weltkrieges, 1930–1955*, Zurich, 1955, p. 244.
3 François Furet, *L'atelier de l'histoire*, Paris, 1982, p. 75.
4 Swiss Diplomatic Documents, Vol. 14, Berne, 1997, pp. 166ff., secret German report passed on 12 June 1941; Daniel Bourgeois, *Le 3e Reich et la Suisse, 1933–1941*, Neuchatel, 1974, Ch. 10.
5 Jean-Claude Favez, 'Tu m'as dit d'aimer', in *Union et division des Suisses*, Lausanne, 1983, pp. 106 and 95; see also Georg Kreis, 'Die Schweiz der Jahre 1918–1948', pp. 378ff., in *Geschichtsforschung in der Schweiz*, Basle, 1992. It is characteristic that the Socialist Party published Hugo Kramer's *Die Quellen der schweizerischen Demokratie*, Zurich, 1941, which traces a continuous tradition of egalitarianism down the centuries, from the medieval *Markgenossenschaften* to the impending dawn of socialist democracy.
6 Peter Maurer, *Anbauschlacht, Landwirtschaftspolitik, Plan Wahlen, Anbauwerk 1937–1945*, Zurich, 1985.
7 Georg Thürer, 'Der Sankt Gothard als Wegweiser', *Neue Zürcher Zeitung*, 23–24 August 1943.

8 A good example of the rejection of French-style democracy in the name of primitive Swiss democracy is to be found in Arnold Jaggi, *Eidgenössische Besinnung*, Berne, 1941.

9 Peter Métraux, *Die Karikatur als publizistische Ausdrucksform untersucht am Kampf des 'Nebelspalters' gegen den Nationalsozialismus 1933–1945*, Berlin, 1966; Elsie Attenhofer, *Cabaret Cornichon*, Berne, 1975.

10 Edgar Bonjour, *Histoire de la neutralité suisse*, Vol. 4, Neuchatel, 1970, p. 185. I have already addressed a number of the subjects discussed: André Lasserre, *La Suisse des années sombres, courants d'opinion pendant la seconde guerre mondiale*, Lausanne, 1989, pp. 105ff.; Philipp Wanner, *Oberst Oskar Frei und der schweizerische Widerstandswille*, Münsingen, 1974, pp. 118–23; Alfred Ernst also expressed his opinion in the anthology dedicated to Hans Oprecht, *Unterwegs zur sozialen Demokratie*, Zurich, 1969, August Lindt, *Le temps du hérisson, souvenirs 1939–1945*, Carouge/Geneva, 1995.

11 Bonjour, *Histoire de la neutralité*, op. cit., Vol. 4, pp. 212ff.; Ernst v. Schenk, 'Aktion Nationaler Widerstand', in *Unterwegs zur sozialen, Demokratie*, see note 10, pp. 107ff.; A. Lindt, *Le temps du hérisson*, op. cit., pp. 59ff.

12 Lindt, *Le temps du hérisson*, op. cit., p. 43; Christian Gruber, *Die politischen Parteien der Schweiz im Zweiten Weltkrieg*, Zurich, 1966, p. 102.

13 Denis de Rougemont, *Journal d'une époque, 1926–1946*, Paris 1968, p. 422 and *passim*; Christian Gasser, *Der Gotthard-Bund, eine schweizerische Widerstands-bewegung ...*, Berne, 1984 (the part which de Rougemont attributes to himself is reduced by the author to more modest proportions. His testimony is too closely linked to the movement he helped to found to be a sufficient basis for understanding of the internal history and true role of the league); Alice Meyer, *Anpassung oder Widerstand*, Frauenfeld, 1965, pp. 188ff.; Théo Bovet, *Credo helvétique*, Neuchatel, 1942; idem, *Schweizer heute ...*, Berne, 1942, see also the movement's publication *Lettre du Gothard* (Gotthard-Brief) which appeared under various titles from 29 August 1940.

14 Neue Helvetische Gesellschaft (ed.), *Die Schweiz und der 2. Weltkrieg, 1990. Die Schweiz, la Suisse, la Svizzera*, published annually, 1930ff. (under various titles). Gives a good overview of the trends affecting major political and social problems and changing public opinion.

15 Bonjour, *Histoire de la neutralité*, op. cit., Vol. 4, p. 203; Alice Meyer, *Anpassung*, op. cit., pp. 185ff.; Peter Gilg, 'Die eidgenössische Gemeinschaft', in *Festschrift zum 65. Geburtstag von Professor Dr Ulrich Im Hof*, Berne, 1982.

16 Quoted in Lasserre, *Courants*, op. cit., p. 26.

17 Quoted in Karl Weber, *Die Schweiz im Nervenkrieg. Aufgabe und Haltung der Schweizer Presse, 1933–1945*, Berne, 1948, p. 129; Daniel Bourgeois, *La presse suisse pendant la 2^e guerre mondiale*, Lausanne, 1983, provides a useful reminder of the organisation of the press, German pressure, censorship and so on.

18 Jost Adam, *Die Haltung der Schweiz gegen das Nationalsozialistische Deutschland im Jahre 1940*, Mainz, 1972; Georg Kreis, *Juli 1940, die Aktion Trump*, Basle, 1973; idem, *Zensur und Selbstzensur. Die schweizerische Pressepolitik im 2. Weltkrieg*, Frauenfeld, 1973; Marc Perrenoud, 'La Sentinelle sous surveillance. Un quotidien socialiste et la censure de la presse (1939–1945)', *Revue suisse d'histoire*, 1987, pp. 137ff.; Forbes-Jaeger, *La presse lausannoise et la censure ...*, *Mémoire de Lettres*, Lausanne, 1990; Ernst Otto Maetzke, *Die deutsch-schweizerische Presse zu einigen Problemen des 2. Weltkrieges*, Tübingen, 1955; Jean-Charles Biaudet, 'Edmond Rossier et la censure pendant la 2e guerre mondiale', *Etudes de Lettres*, 2, 1968; Jacques Meurant, *La presse et l'opinion publique de la Suisse romande face à*

l'Europe en guerre, 1939–1941, Neuchatel, 1976; *Die Schweizer Presse, bulletin de l'association de la presse suisse*, 1918ff. Works by journalists: Willy Bretscher, *Neue Zürcher Zeitung 1933–1944. 70 Leitartikel*, Zurich, 1945; Adolf Gasser (*National-Zeitung*), *Für Freiheit und Recht, 1940–1945*, Berne, 1948; Albert Oeri, *Oeri's Tagesberichte* (*Basler Nachrichten*), Berne, 1946; Paul Schmid-Ammann, *Mahnrufe in die Zeit, vier bewegte Jahrzehnte schweizerischer Politik, 1930–1970*, Zurich, 1971; Ernst Schürch, *Bemerkungen zum Tage*, Berne, 1942 among others.

19 But see Jacques Meurant, *La presse*, op. cit.

20 Primarily focused on the pre-war period and corporate problems, Martin Dahinden, *Das Schweizerbuch im Zeitalter von Nationalsozialismus und geistiger Landesverteidigung*, Berne, 1987. Dedicated to the main anti-Nazi publisher, Peter Stahlberger, *Der Zürcher Verleger Hans Oprecht und die deutsche politische Emigration, 1933–1945*, Zurich, 1970. See also Jürg Zbinden, *Sternstunden oder verpasste Chancen. Zur Geschichte des Schweizer Buchhandels 1943–1952*, Zurich, 1995.

21 J. R. von Salis, *Weltchronik 1939–1945*, Berne, 1966; Ruth Halter-Schmid, *Schweizer Radio 1939–1945. Die Organisation des Radiokommunikators durch Bundesrat und Armee*, Berne/Stuttgart, 1980 (see, in particular, pp. 158ff.); Philippe Gex, *Radio et cinéma en Suisse, 1936–1942. Le cas de la Suisse romande en période de repli culturel, Mémoire de Lettres*, Fribourg, 1982; Jean-Claude Favez, *Tu m'as dit*, op. cit., pp. 96ff.

22 For further details, I refer the reader to Rémy Pithon, 'Essai d'historiographie du cinéma suisse (1945–1991)', in *L'histoire en Suisse, Bilan et perspectives – 1991*, Basle, 1992, pp. 228–37. For more direct relevance to our subject, see idem, 'Cinéma suisse de fiction et défense nationale spirituelle de la Confédération helvétique (1933–1945)', *Revue d'histoire moderne et contemporaine*, 1986, pp. 254ff.; idem, 'Le cinéma suisse et les mythes nationaux (1938–1945)', in Bernard Crettaz et al., *Peuples inanimés avez-vous donc une âme? Etudes et mémoires de la section d'histoire de l'Université de Lausanne*, 1987, pp. 39ff.

23 Theo Mäusli, *Jazz und geistige Landesverteidigung*, Zurich, 1995.

24 Quoted in René Riesen, *Die schweizerische Bauernheimatbewegung*, Berne, 1972. Christian Gruber, *Die politischen Parteien*, op. cit. gives the only general picture of the subject. He conscientiously and usefully traces the official positions of the political parties, but does not go much further than that.

25 Quotation from W. Bretscher at the 1943 congress, in Gruber, *Die politischen Parteien*, op. cit., p. 16.

26 Gruber, *Die politischen Parteien*, op. cit., p. 98ff.; Erich Gruner, *Die Parteien in der Schweiz*, Berne, 1969, pp. 13ff.; Lukas Rölli-Alkemper, *Die schweizerische konservative Volkspartei, 1935–1943*, Fribourg, 1993; Beno Hardmeier, *Geschichte der sozialdemokratischen Ideen in der Schweiz*, Winterthur, 1957; Hans Oprecht, *Die Arbeiterschaft der Schweiz im 2. Weltkrieg*, Zurich, 1943; Walther Bringolf, *Mein Leben. Weg und Umweg eines Schweizer Sozialdemokraten*, Berne, 1965; Walter Wolf, *Walther Bringolf. Eine Biographie. Sozialist, Patriot, Patriarch*, Schaffhausen, 1995.

27 Apart from the memoirs of leaders such as Humbert-Droz, Hofmeier and Wullschleger, we have an official history by the Labour Party Historical Commission, *Zur Geschichte der kommunistischen Bewegung*, Zurich, 1981. See also Brigitte Studer, *Un parti sous influence, le parti communiste suisse, une section du Komintern, 1931 à 1939*, Lausanne, 1994, and especially André Rauber, *Histoire du mouvement communiste suisse*, Geneva, 1997, the fullest analysis, particularly interesting from Stalingrad onwards, but suffering from the fact that the archives are too slender and scattered.

28 Charles-Frédéric Ducommun, *Destin national et organisation professionnelle*, Zurich, 1941; idem, 'Les données du problème ouvrier', in *La Suisse forge son destin*, Lausanne, 1942, pp. 41ff.

29 Karl Barth, *Im Namen des Allmächtigen, eine Schweizer Stimme, 1938–1945*, Zollikon, 1945; Daniel Cornu, *Karl Barth et la politique*, Geneva, 1968. His overt support for the German communist refugees who were preparing their new Germany in Switzerland highlights the destabilising impact of Soviet propaganda and victories on the united front of spiritual resistance. See Hans Teubner, *Exilland Schweiz, Dokumentarischer Bericht über den Kampf emigrierter deutscher Kommunisten 1933–1945*, Frankfurt-am-Main, 1975, pp. 262, 268ff.

30 Meyer, *Anpassung*, op. cit., pp. 178ff.; Erland Erkenrath, *Die Freiheit des Wortes, Auseinandersetzungen zwischen Vertretern des schweizerischen Protestantismus und den Zensurbehörden während des zweiten Weltkrieges*, Zurich, 1972; Beat Raaflaub, *Kirchlicher Mahnruf in kritischer Zeit. Der schweizerische Evangelische Pressedienst 1928–1955*, Berne, 1977; Rudolf Pfister, *Kirchengeschichte der Schweiz*, Vol. 3, 1720–1950, Zurich, 1985, pp. 393ff.

31 Victor Conzemius, 'Christliches Exil und christlicher Widerstand', in *Ein Symposium an der katholischen Universität Eichstätt 1985*, Regensburg, 1987, pp. 225ff.

32 Roland Ruffieux, 'De l'"Ordre Nouveau" à de nouvelles préoccupations: le débat idéologique en Suisse romande', *Revue d'histoire de la deuxième guerre mondiale*, January 1981, pp. 97ff. For the debate from 1943 onwards, see also Georg Kreis (ed.), 'La Suisse dans le système international de l'après-guerre 1943–1950', Basle, 1996.

33 Swiss Diplomatic Documents, Vol. 15, pp. 139ff., Jean-Claude Favez, 'Le Don suisse et la politique étrangère. Quelques réflexions', *Des archives à la mémoire, mélanges d'histoire politique, religieuse et sociale offerts à Louis Binz*, Geneva, 1995, p. 337.

34 Jean-Claude Favez, *Une mission impossible? Le CICR, les déportations et les camps de concentration nazis*, Lausanne, 1988. See also report by the Swiss Red Cross on its activities from 1938 to 1948, Berne, 1948.

35 Even a hostile and straightforward analysis of asylum policy acknowledges the value of this kind of attitude: see Catherine Boss, 'Asylpolitik und Flüchtlingshilfe 1938–55', in *Streitfall Friede*, Berne, 1988, pp. 23ff.

36 Carl Ludwig, *La politique pratiquée par la Suisse à l'égard des réfugiés au cours des années 1933 à 1955*, Berne, 1957; Alfred-A. Häsler, *La Suisse terre d'asile? La politique de la Confédération envers les réfugiés de 1933 à 1945*, Lausanne, 1971, André Lasserre, *Frontières et camps, le refuge en Suisse de 1933 à 1945*, Lausanne, 1995; Jacques Picard, *Die Schweiz und die Juden 1933–1945*, Zurich, 1994; Swiss Federal Archive Review, various authors, 'La Suisse et les réfugiés', Berne, 1996; Fünfzehn Jahre Arbeiterhilfswerk (Commemoration of 15 years' aidwork). Personal recollections or biographies illustrate the part played by various individuals who devoted themselves to the refugee cause: Regina Kägi-Fuchsmann, *Das gute Herz genügt nicht. Mein Leben und meine Arbeit*, Zurich, 1968; Nettie Sutro, *Jugend auf der Flucht 1933–1948*, Zurich, 1952; Gertrud Kurz, *Unterwegs für den Frieden, Erlebnisse und Erfahrungen*, Basle, 1977.

37 Otto Heim, 'Jüdische soziale Arbeit und Flüchtlingshilfe in der Schweiz', in *Schweizerischer israelitischer Gemeindebund 1904–1954*, 1954, n.p.

38 Jean-Claude Wacker, *Humaner als Bern. Schweizer u. Basler Asylpraxis gegenüber den jüdischen Flüchtlingen v. 1933 bis 1943 im Vergleich*, Basle, 1992; Elisa Signori, *La Svizzera e i fuorusciti italiani … Aspetti e problemi dell'emigrazione politica, 1943–1945*, Milan, 1983; Renata Broggini, *I rifugiati italiani in Svizzera e il foglio*

Liberta, Antologi di scritti 1944–1945, Rome, 1979; idem, *Terra d'asilo. I rifugiati italiani in Svizzera 1943–1945*, Bologna, 1993; Christiane Ruffieux, 'Les réfugiés dans le canton de Fribourg durant la 2ᵉ guerre mondiale', licentiateship paper, Fribourg, 1982.

39 Anne-Marie Im Hof-Piguet, *La filière, en France occupée 1943–1944*, Yverdon, 1985.
40 Johann-M.Werner, 'Konsul Karl Lutz (1895–1975) Im Dienste der Menschlich-keit', licentiateship paper, Berne, 1985. Alain Dieckhoff, *Rescapés du génocide. L'action Musy, une opération de sauvetage de Juifs européens en 1944–1945*, Basle, 1995.
41 Mention should be made here of the pioneering work undertaken by Fabienne Regard in an article in the *Federal Archive Review*, op. cit., and in her forthcoming thesis.

11

'Spiritual National Defence' in the 1930s: Swiss Political Culture between the Wars

JOSEF MOOSER

It is not easy for an outside observer to penetrate the tangled thicket of clichés that is Swiss history and politics. He therefore turns gratefully to apparently unusual aspects which offer the hope of clearing paths through the maze. 'But what is all too rarely borne in mind' – as a commentator wrote in a German newspaper in 1993 – 'is that Switzerland is the only European country in which the 1848 revolution succeeded and … a successful example of a functioning, non-ethnic citizen's state'.[1] Is that just another 'Swiss' cliché? Whether or not, it is at least a possible and by no means new interpretation of Swiss history. If, on a second glance, one changes location and perspective and investigates the way the Swiss see themselves, one immediately encounters further obstacles. In the intensive self-preoccupation with what is 'Swiss' in history, culture and politics that characterises the 'spiritual national defence' in the inter-war period, federalism – the national 'unity in diversity' of the nationalities and linguistic regions – forms a basic assumption which, again, is almost a cliché in itself. Yet powerful forces in the interpretation of this self-image have at the same time turned massively against seeing this feature of 'Switzerland' as being grounded in the successful liberal and democratic revolutions of the nineteenth century and in the federal state after 1848.

In the case of the 'spiritual national defence' this contradictory nature refers to something much more than the fact of competing interpretations of history – or the limited abilities of an outside observer. (And, perhaps, to the impossibility of reducing the hypercomplexity of Swiss history to a simple denominator?) The significance of the 'spiritual national defence' extends further. This key phrase is associated with the experience and memory of the country's critical situation in the period between the two world wars and, in particular, the collective experience of standing up to National Socialist Germany, which since 1933 had been perceived by a great majority of the population as a threat to their very existence. Thus the values, attitudes and objectives of the Swiss self-image in the context of the 'spiritual national defence' took on, as it were, an epoch-making dimension, were in many ways linked to other, extra-political aspects, and exerted an influence that lasted until well after the Second World War. This made them a sensitive factor in the political culture, imposing conformity and yet also necessarily issuing a challenge to contradiction and criticism when, with the passing of time, the marginalised or suppressed dark sides of the heroic collective experience of the Second World War became more apparent after the 1960s. In particular, the restrictive and selfish refugee policy after 1933 brought shame to another strand in the national self-image – the humanitarian tradition of Switzerland. The political culture of the 'spiritual national defence' took on a sinister aspect.[2] It seemed less a factor of self-assertion and 'resistance' and more one of 'accommodation',[3] responsible for the turning-back of refugees and, in the post-war period, for a self-righteous political inertia. Hans Ulrich Jost's polemical thesis on 'Swiss totalitarianism' struck, as it were, at the very heart of Switzerland's historical tradition: it suggested there had been an 'adjustment by large groups within the population', including some of the country's leaders and its political system, to the National Socialist enemy, even in the endeavour to preserve national independence, because this defence involved absorbing certain elements of Germany's political culture.[4] This accusation of conjuring Beelzebub to cast out the Devil devalued the self-image of a political generation. With the same idea in mind, the literary historian Charles Linsmayer referred to 'democratic totalitarianism' and concluded from the anti-Semitic overtones of Switzerland's asylum policy 'that the emotional commitment to the spiritual national defence was hollow and mendacious'.[5] It is worth noting that this verdict in 1983 was based on the unequivocal words of Edgar Bonjour in 1970 about the 'failure of that entire generation', rather than just of a few senior officials, to help the refugees.[6] In the opposite camp, André Lasserre has defended the anti-totalitarian values of the 'spiritual national defence' and their decisive effect in the 'war of nerves' into which Switzerland had been forced.[7]

These highly contrasting views of the 'spiritual national defence' should be borne in mind in order to emphasise, for those undertaking the academic task of a critical and historical analysis of it, that any such undertaking would be highly complex. This central phenomenon of Swiss political culture in the twentieth century needs to be seen in all its multilayered aspects: the differing ideological, cultural and political currents that contributed to it; the various groups and institutions that propagated it; the influence exerted by its ideas and values on everyday and collective life, including, for example, education, art, literature and the mass media; the expectations placed in it; and its significance in each of the various political contexts of the pre-war, wartime and post-war periods. In other words, what is necessary is a study of the political ideology and mentality of the 'Swiss nation' in the context of the 'spiritual national defence' in a precise and differentiated fashion, taking into consideration ideological and cultural history, political and social history, and not least the history of everyday life and the gender of those studied. Under these conditions, it would also be possible to form a more accurate assessment of its effect, which hitherto has perhaps been too quickly and generalisingly accepted or assumed as being overpowering.

This plea follows the development of research.[8] In the wake of important studies undertaken by Gonzague de Reynold[9] and of trends in cultural criticism since the turn of the century,[10] fundamental analyses of party-political and mass-media communication[11] and the reconstruction of the phenomenon – obviously long underestimated – of the 'crisis initiative' and 'guideline movement' of the 1930s,[12] it is becoming apparent that the landscape is much more varied than the argument of 'Swiss totalitarianism' had previously assumed. This label was not only theoretically inconsistent and polemically exaggerated as compared with the way the term is normally understood; it is also empirically obsolete, because the multilayered political nature of the 'spiritual national defence' has become apparent. As well as conservative trends (such as those on which Jost based his verdict), social liberal and leftist references to and expectations of this code phrase of the 1930s are becoming apparent which, despite all the tendency to integration, have failed to overcome or circumvent old and new differences. In addition, the long-term 'internal' origins and relationships are now much clearer than before by comparison with the 'external' impulses inherent in the very meaning of the words 'spiritual national defence'. Thus the question of timing and origin has shifted, while the question of the interrelationship between internal and external factors requires reformulating in view of the multilayered nature of the phenomenon in the 1930s. In all these aspects and contexts, too, the argument about its totalitarian nature can be taken up productively and changed to suit the question of whether, and in what form, certain layers of the 'spiritual national defence' contributed to the ideological and cultural manifestations of criticism of bourgeois society as expressed in many European countries since the turn of the century. The chapter which follows endeavours to explain this multilayered nature and its context, and to place the issue of the history of effects in the precise context of this multilayered nature; unresolved problems, too, will be referred to. For reasons that will be discussed briefly at the end, I confine my remarks here to the pre-war period.

HISTORY OF THE PHRASE 'SPIRITUAL NATIONAL DEFENCE'

The mere history of the phrase 'spiritual national defence' gives an indication of its multilayered nature, its content by no means being defined by the phrase itself. Although the term first became fashionable in 1933, similar phrases can be found earlier. In 1929 National Councillor Jakob Zimmerli appealed to the 'cultural national defence' to safeguard the literary market, and especially theatre, against 'a foreign takeover' and to promote Swiss literature.[13] In the autumn of 1933 the phrase had already taken on different connotations. A Frontist paper proclaimed the 'spiritual national defence' against the 'cultural bolshevists', meaning the left-wing emigrants from Germany,[14] while a Catholic conservative author called for the 'moral national defence' or 'spiritual armament' against National Socialist propaganda.[15] Even at this time there were indications of a sustained struggle for ownership of the term, which probably intensified after 1935. The national unity and self-containedness, which especially prompted the parallel references to 'military', 'economic' and 'spiritual national defence' in the second half of the 1930s, was another instrument of the variable implications of the term and the political strategy. The forces of the left made the 'economic national defence', in the sense of a policy for combating the economic crisis, the precondition for the other dimensions.[16] If the 'spiritual national defence' claimed to safeguard the 'uniqueness' of Switzerland, the question inevitably had to be asked: which Switzerland?

There were both new and old answers to this question in the 1930s. The oldest in relative terms, rooted in the history of the Federation, was the liberal definition of one Carl Hilty: Switzerland as a historically rooted 'voluntary nation' of Christian outlook with an 'ideal mission' of freedom which did not base its national character, as a state, on community of origin, language or 'race'. The key concepts of this tradition were appealed to by the Federal Council in the critical situation at the beginning of the First World War, and are still to be found in fragmentary form in the Federal Council's 'cultural message' of November 1938, which may be seen as the 'Magna Carta' of the 'spiritual national defence': the 'ideal' of Switzerland is the 'cultural community transcending race and language'.[17] This was, as it were, an ideological barrier, amalgamated with the multilingual constitutional reality of federalism, against radical nationalism since the late nineteenth century which had postulated the unity of state, people, culture and 'race'.

In the 1930s, however, a more recent tradition of political thought was more powerful in effect than that liberal inheritance, which had been further weakened by the general crisis of liberalism in the interwar years. The 'cultural message', in particular, under the coordinating authority of the Catholic conservative Federal Councillor Philipp Etter, was dominated by a new conservatism, which had developed in many different ways since the turn of the century and, in its Swiss manifestation, found its consistently most effective and influential propagandist in the man of letters, university professor, political pamphleteer and historian Gonzague de Reynold (1880–1970).[18] This new conservatism was driven by a comprehensive and radical criticism of modernism. The social consequences of industrialisation, class distinction and organisation and the rise of the workers' movement; the cultural change in the form of secularisation and, finally, political democratisation – these essential processes of modernisation since the late nineteenth century were interpreted as the destruction of order and values. In a renewal of old-style counter-revolutionary conservatism, the French Revolution of 1789 was viewed as the source of these processes of destruction. A new 'unity' of society and politics, under the symbol of authority, was seen as the defence against social and political conflict and the cultural pluralism inherent in it. The social foundations of that unity were perceived as being not in the social formations of modernism – urban society, the bourgeoisie and the workers – but in rural society, the peasantry and the old patrician elite. The anti-urban and anti-capitalist 'agrarian ideology', which allowed so many associations and imaginings, was probably the most popular strand in the new conservatism. This current of opinion looked far back into the past for its vision of 'Switzerland', finding the solid foundation of its values in the pre-revolutionary world, and in the supposed 'constants' of Swiss history (de Reynold), and so pulled the ground of historical legitimation from under the feet of the liberal and democratic federal state. At the same time, this vision also looked forward towards a 'different' Switzerland, one that had yet to be created; in this respect it can be seen as part of the enigmatic phenomenon of 'conservative revolution'.[19]

The political thrust of the new conservatism, initially rather vague and enveloped in the general criticism of modern civilisation of the educated classes, became both more selective and more unyielding after 1918. The social confrontation of the general strike also took on a political name with the introduction of the law on proportional representation. The further extension of democracy through this electoral law seemed all the more dangerous in that it was apparently paving the way for socialism – an assumption which the socialists for their part are known to have shared. Anti-socialism became a constituent feature of the 'Swiss' nation in the continuing class polarisation that followed the general strike, renewing itself in clashes over economic and social policy. Because it refers to the great difficulty in overcoming the social divide that split the nation, it is as well to remember that this 'gulf' in social equality was also reinforced by concepts of lifestyle and morals. Labour politics were seen as the expression of 'materialism' encompassing every dangerous form of decadence, and as the 'essence of moral evil'.[20] In view of the perceived association between democracy and socialism, the future course of action was obvious: an anti-liberal and anti-democratic amendment to the constitution, intended to make any such symbiosis structurally impossible.

By various stratagems, a heterogeneous initiative was undertaken with a view to achieving a total revision of the federal constitution. However, it failed emphatically in the referendum of 8 September 1935,[21] but this electoral victory of democracy should not induce us to forget the minorities – varying from region to region and strongest in Catholic and French-speaking cantons – in favour of a total revision (in French-speaking Switzerland, for example, the yes vote was 37.7 per cent as compared with the federal average of 27.6 per cent). Like the similar result of the vote on the banning of freemasonry on 28 November 1937 (prompted by a fascist initiative), this electoral pattern is a reminder of the fragile basis of legitimation for the liberal, citizens' democracy. The fundamental criticism of liberalism and democracy, political parties and parliaments expressed by the new conservatism had a not insignificant level of support within society. That support provided a reference for continuing discussion of an authoritarian constitutional reform and an interpretation of the existing constitution that distinguished the concept of democracy from civil liberalism and endeavoured to give it an authoritarian form.

INFLUENCE OF THE NEW CONSERVATISM

This new conservatism influenced the Federal Council's definition of 'spiritual national defence', the definition of the 'meaning and mission of Switzerland' formulated by Philipp Etter. Taking its cue from the conceptual figure of the 'constants' in the 'spiritual face' of Switzerland, it identified three 'essential' specific features of the state (in this order): its membership of the 'three great spiritual environments of the West' (Italy, France and Germany), the 'federal community' as the 'individuality and essence of democracy', and 'respect for the dignity and freedom of man'. The main focus of democracy, by this definition, had moved away from civil rights and liberal institutions to the institutionally objectivised federal structures of community existence, rooted both symbolically and literally in the Alps. The liberal federal state, by contrast, was sidelined into something resembling 'spiritual conformity' (that is, the Nazi/*Gleichschaltung*), the express intention being to refrain from 'trying to create a watered-down, generically Swiss type'. In complete conformity with the ideas of de Reynold, the 'pillar of state and enemy of democracy' (Roger de Weck), the relationship between citizen and state was to be rooted in authority and obedience. 'The state must once again become the purpose of our sacrifice, not the sacrifice of our purposes!' [22] So it is not surprising, though certainly thought-provoking, that Federal Councillor Etter again presented a programme for authoritarian reform of the constitution in September 1940. [23]

It is one of the major findings of recent research that the objective of a new, authoritarian Switzerland was not a form of 'accommodation' to National Socialism or fascism but a movement of internal origin. On the other hand, there is no overlooking the fact that the new conservatism or 'new Right', dating from the turn of the century, constituted a pan-European phenomenon of self-criticism by bourgeois culture and society. The originators of Swiss political thinking had played their part in this, precisely because of the fact that bourgeois culture (like the labour movement) in Switzerland before the First World War had been strongly linked to, respectively, bourgeois and socialist cultures in neighbouring countries. The new conservatism shared many motivations and concepts with, for example, radical nationalism in the German empire since the turn of the century. Gonzague de Reynold was under the spell of *Action française* and at the same time was giving voice to the convictions of European Catholic conservatism; his speculative and aesthetically inclined habit of thought in interpreting the 'Swiss spirit' was part of the philosophical 'revolution of knowledge' which had abolished the received standards of empirical research and rational argument. [24] In addition, the monumental, heroic style of arts and rhetoric on behalf of the 'spiritual national defence' represented a multinational, epochal phenomenon. It could be said, ironically, that even one of the popular forces in the new Swiss conservatism, the stylisation of the 'danger of domination by foreigners', was an ideological import.

Nevertheless, these pan-European currents in the new conservatism and in the form of 'spiritual national defence' shaped by it had been defeated by the conditions existing in the small state and taken on a specifically Swiss colouration. This process was encouraged by the erosion of common European facets of bourgeois culture under the pressure of imperialistic competition. The idea of domination by foreigners lost something of its actual biological and racial quality in the power gap that divided large and small states, and became a political and social attitude of mind in David's defiance of Goliath.[25] In addition, the fact that Switzerland was multilingual prevented the racial idea from producing any deeper impact or modifying the biological and genetic identification of alleged national unity into geographical determinism. 'A Swiss', it seemed, was made not by 'blood' but by 'soil', Nature and the Alps.[26] The mythologisation of Swiss history in the new conservative thinking, designed to assert an 'objective' unique quality of Switzerland yet sometimes resulting in extravagances which were themselves perceived as 'foreign', thus appears to be an evasion of these obstacles.[27]

Such mutations of similar forms of thinking and ideas not only represented ideological differences associated with tradition but also indicate the political force field within which ideas and values not only come into being but also have to be accepted. It was precisely in this respect that the new conservative form of 'spiritual national defence', as described above, encountered a really decisive obstacle: the National Socialist seizure of power 1933 in Germany. This had the effect of bringing other forms of 'spiritual national defence' into play, which obstructed the attempts at an authoritarian transformation of democracy. The specific, multilayered dynamic of the 'spiritual national defence' in the 1930s evolved under circumstances in which domestic and foreign policy were fundamentally and densely interwoven.

The anti-totalitarian character of the 'spiritual national defence', which as such also turned against the fascist ideology in Italy, did not become strongly marked until after 1933. Despite the irredentist movements in Ticino, fascism was taken less seriously outside the labour movement than National Socialist Germany or treated with understanding and sympathy in the new conservative climate of anti-democratic criticism.[28] The Nazi seizure of power, however, quite swiftly created a 'war of nerves' between Germany and Switzerland, in which the smaller country felt its very existence threatened. The reason this threat was so deeply felt, even before the dramatic events of 1936 onwards, was that it recalled the trauma of the First World War and the inner crisis brought to Switzerland by regional and social conflicts resulting from the effects of the war. However, it was known that the Nazi movement in Germany represented a political force exerting militant pressure for a revision of the Versailles Treaty and the post-war order it had imposed on Europe since 1918–19, on the basis of a radical nationalism directed towards the creation of a greater Germany. One noteworthy liberal diagnosis of the 'German revolution', though it was also shared by the Socialist Party of Switzerland (SPS), identified the 'birth' of National Socialism as having taken place in the 'totalitarian' Germany of the First World War, while its earlier antecedents could be found in the authoritarian German power state of the nineteenth century.[29] The relations between Germany and Switzerland, which had seriously deteriorated since the First World War and suffered from the economic turbulences and problems of the post-war years,[30] lent an additional plausibility to this perception of National Socialism. Representative and influential newspapers of all political parties agreed in their diagnosis of the aggression generated by radical nationalism in Germany. The social democratic press performed a particularly dramatic volte-face in its identification of Switzerland as a nation under threat.[31] In addition, the Swiss labour movement had been very deeply affected by the disaster that had overtaken its German counterpart.[32] Widespread defensive postures and fears of threats soon came to be a feature of diplomatic relations. As early as September 1933 Foreign Minister Giuseppe Motta spoke to the German foreign minister and Goebbels (at a League of Nations conference in Geneva) of the 'deep concern' felt in relation to 'alleged attempts in national socialist circles to annex the German parts of Switzerland'. Shortly afterwards, Federal Councillor Rudolf Minger made it clear to the German ambassador, von Weizsäcker, that although national socialism might be an 'obvious development' for Germany, and one to which he (Minger) was 'sympathetic', it represented a 'danger' to the existence of Switzerland.[33]

The German leadership did not take this seriously, and indeed caused further anxiety to the smaller neutral state by its behaviour. Governmental neutrality was to be converted, by playing on the neutral state of mind of the citizens, into a 'real neutrality'[34] which, in the expected event of war breaking out, was to justify recruiting Switzerland to serve Germany's interests. The formal recognition of governmental neutrality by the top leadership of the Reich, at the instigation of Hitler himself, did not take place until 1937 and was thus rapidly devalued by a variety of events. This reflects the arrogant imperialism of the National Socialist government, which was reluctant to be bound by anything. Prevaricating declarations; arrogant, humiliating sneers at Switzerland; ideological incorporations of German-speaking Switzerland into the 'German sphere'; the political-historical denunciation of 'betrayal of empire'; the propaganda of the Nazi party's foreign organisation in Switzerland; threatened and actual prohibitions on the importation of Swiss newspapers; frontier incidents and attacks such as the 'Jakob case', the kidnapping of an emigrant in Basle in 1935 – after 1933 the totalitarian Nazi state cast its shadow over Switzerland in many ways, even before the annexation of Austria in 1938 first brought Switzerland's fears for its future to fever pitch.[35]

Reaction to this was not confined to the 'spiritual national defence' as an ideologically and politically articulated self-perception of Switzerland in terms of its difference from National Socialist Germany. Because that difference was so wide-ranging, and seemed threatening, the 'spiritual national defence' struck a receptive chord in the public mind which manifested itself in everyday life. As early as the autumn of 1933 private letters from Ernst von Weizsäcker, the new German ambassador in Berne, noted massive anti-German feeling and mocking 'Heil Adolf!' salutes to German motorists, and observed, 'Any non-Nazi just needs to be sent here to turn him into one.'[36] Major sporting events such as football internationals generated a massive explosion of popular feeling in June 1938. Following the Swiss team's sensational victory over 'Greater Germany' in the World Cup in Paris, Basle city centre 'went mad' with a general 'outpouring of hatred against the Third Reich'; 'satisfaction' was triggered by the fact that, following the annexation of Austria, a stop had been put to the 'obsession with the invincibility of the brown-shirted battalions'.[37] This kind of politicisation of non-political events reflects the heightened intensity of the conflict which – as happened later at the zenith of the Cold War – also rubbed off at second hand on dealings between people. In October 1938 the conservative politician Markus Feldmann noted in his diary, 'However unpleasant it may be, you really do have to assume nowadays that every German is an agent and treat him accordingly.'[38] In the view of the German ambassador, 'slander', economic boycott and re-emigration had made the situation of the 'Reich Germans' in Switzerland 'so serious' by the autumn of 1938 that it had become the 'main concern' of the embassy.[39] In the perception of a fundamental threat, anti-Germanism as a political state of mind formed, as it were, a skin that could be clothed in a variety of political ideologies.[40] The losers from this set of political and cultural circumstances, as we know, were – at a very early stage – the 'fronts', those right-wing radical groups which had initially believed themselves to be riding the wave generated by the National Socialist seizure of power.

In these circumstances – an area of conflicting political forces in which a repetition of the Great War threatened – the 'spiritual national defence' took on a multifaceted cultural form and extended into many areas of life. What was 'Swiss', as a political symbol of differentiation and distance from what was 'German', was to shape scientific life, art, music, literature and mass media, together with everyday aesthetics in matters of dress and housing. In German-speaking Switzerland, efforts were made to upgrade the dialect into a written language as a way of demonstrating independence from the enemy's tongue. Technical terms were objected to as German and therefore foreign.[41] All this was regarded by one of the most energetic propagandists of the 'spiritual national defence', the Zurich publisher Adolf Guggenbühl, as 'total democracy', which must permeate every aspect of life.[41] It included the model of the military disciplined citizen, the 'fighting Swiss', which even had an impact on marriage guidance counselling.[43] The male culture of the 'spiritual national defence' may, perhaps, seem to go without saying; its relationship to 'Mother Helvetia', its effects on women and their possible integration into 'Swiss' policy nevertheless deserve more detailed analysis.[44] Finally, one cultural aspect of the 'spiritual national defence', though stronger than the other forces referred to and extending across the political spectrum, was the express emphasis on 'Christian Switzerland'. Here, a Swiss could identify himself with Hilty's tradition or with Catholic conservatism, and distance himself from the National Socialist persecution of the churches; as a rule, this probably did nothing to promote empathy with the plight of the Jewish refugees.[45] Admittedly, the church was unrepresented at Switzerland's great symbolic festival, the National Exhibition of 1939 (the so-called '*Landi*'); just as symptomatic as the complaint itself was one reply to it, that the *Landi* itself was a 'pilgrimage'.[46]

These cultural aspects certainly reflected the effects of a type of conformism, emanating less from the state than from individual social groups, which polarised attitudes and lifestyles as 'Swiss' or 'unSwiss' and thus produced outsiders.[47] This reflects, in a weaker form, the politicisation of culture and the imperative of cultural homogeneity in the totalitarian states as a phenomenon typical of its age. In this context, it should not be forgotten that the Federal Council's 'cultural message' pursued the objectives of 'cultural defence' and 'cultural advertising' at home and abroad as a way of reducing the advantage gained by state-organised cultural propaganda in the other European states.[48] However, the crucial difference is more important than this similarity: in Switzerland there were limits to the pressure to conform, because a basically functional democratic constitution and political activity that took place in public allowed different political positions within the 'spiritual national defence'.

LEFT-WING VARIATIONS

Having already considered the neoconservative form of the 'spiritual national defence', we should compare it with its liberal and left-wing variations. These were to be found in such long-established middle-class newspapers as the *Neue Zürcher Zeitung* or the *Basler Nachrichten*, institutions such as the Zurich Theatre and the labour movement. Its spokesmen were leading journalists and historians, theologians and politicians. Most typical was the newspaper refounded in 1933 under the descriptive title *Die Nation: Independent newspaper for democracy and the national community*, whose adherents came from the labour movement and the democratic peasant opposition, were in alliance with Swiss and German religious socialism, and pursued a policy of co-operation with the liberal, pro-reform circles of the bourgeoisie.[49] In contrast to the neoconservative delegitimisation of the federal state, the liberal version of the 'spiritual national defence' retained the French Revolution and 1848 as a positive inheritance. This however was harmonised in historical thinking with the cooperative-style tradition of the old confederation and the Christian and humanistic tradition to form the spirit of 'democratism' as the foundation of 'Swiss democracy'. The means of 'spiritual national defence' that were also propagated as well, such as the encouragement of Swiss literature, were expressly intended to protect this conception of democracy and its reform (for example, through female suffrage), in order to improve it as a 'dynamic form of state' with the capacity to solve problems that was denied by the critics of democracy.[50] A historical legitimation and communicative structure were thus created to serve as a basis for bridging the traditional political class conflict in the interests of the 'nation'.[51]

It would be precipitate to describe this process of reaching an understanding as being the 'integration' of the labour movement. That movement entered the 'house of Switzerland' – as things stood – under admittedly defensive conditions, in view of the heavy defeats suffered by the labour movements in Italy, Germany and Austria, but with its head held at least half high. The well-known revision of the SPS programme in 1935, its renunciation of the 'class struggle' as a means of changing the system and its commitment to democracy and military national defence; the 'truce' between the metalworkers' union and the employers in 1937 and the gradual (re-)introduction of national symbols such as the Swiss flag at workers' festivals – all these demonstrated allegiance to the nation with no sacrifice of independence.[52] However, the participation of the labour movement in the 'spiritual national defence' was linked to great expectations of social justice from a Swiss 'national community'.[53] This long-established term, which even in Germany was not exclusively National Socialist and had become a fashionable phrase in the 1930s, was now the repository of basic hopes for social security and recognition. Social democrat spokesmen thus repeatedly called upon the 'spiritual national defence' to produce 'deeds' as well as 'words', deeds which would go beyond its current struggle against the economic crisis and unemployment. Ernst Nobs in 1938 identified it as the 'most urgent task of all true Swiss democrats' to break down both the 'all too visible and the invisible class distinctions'. Others expressly campaigned against the 'preservation of the status quo' in the name of the 'spiritual national defence' or referred to a 'defective spiritual national defence' until such time as it took energetic and aggressive action against National Socialism.[54] Despite points in common with the liberal variation, the left-wing form of the 'spiritual national defence' had its own independent form to outside observers, with its explicit expectations of social and economic policy and bitterly critical anti-fascist demonstrations.

The differentiated and multilayered nature of the 'spiritual national defence' after 1933 was more than just a historical and political phenomenon of the ideas underlying political culture. It was also reflected in political practice – in elections and referendums. The Social Democratic Party was able to broaden its base in local elections, and in some cantons, and improved its share of the vote in the 1935 National Council elections.[55] Historically more significant, and perhaps even more important in terms of effect, was the dynamic of the 'crisis initiative' and 'guideline movement' from 1934 onwards.[56] These were cross-party initiatives, focusing on representatives of the liberal and leftist 'spiritual national defence', but they were also a social movement by the 'ordinary people', workers, farmers, salaried employees and small tradesman, against the 'top people', reminiscent even then in many ways of the 'anti-plutocratic' democratic movement of the 1860s. In the 1930s, however, it pursued a modern, Keynesian concept of economic policy and took its stance against the creeping undermining of the parliamentary democracy form of government represented by the Federal Council's emergency resolutions. In both these lines of approach, it stirred up a fundamental debate on the democratic interventionist and welfare state. This, however, only became capable of majority support after the Second World War, as both these initiatives, as we know, just failed. Even so, they did result in a pressure for innovation and a highly symbolic power of veto against the authoritarian transformation of democracy. It must be seen as one of the most notable phenomena of Swiss history in the entire inter-war period that, despite the many symptoms of economic and political crisis, democracy based on referendum was successfully defended.

This of course was a success for evasion, attributable to a probably crucial extent to the way in which the political institutional structure worked and to the culture of political debate that was possible within that structure. The importance of the 'spiritual national defence' as a code phrase and call to arms in the interests of national unity needs to be seen in that context. Because of its multilayered nature, it was in little or no position to achieve that purpose. Admittedly, the 'anti-German' political mentality gave the country stability as viewed from outside; internally, however, only a laborious and minimal political consensus was achieved, to weaken again once the greatest crisis of danger in foreign policy had been passed in 1942.[57] Before 1939, therefore, internal integration on the ground of 'spiritual national defence' should not be overestimated. Mistrust still attached even to this key phrase, and in many middle-class circles social democratic patriotism in the guise of anti-fascism not only lacked credibility but even seemed a threat to neutrality and foreign policy because it was driving Switzerland towards the Western democracies.[58] Apart from the various lines of thrust of domestic and foreign policy within the 'spiritual national defence', there were also unmistakable internal contradictions.

One such contradiction flourished in the field of the debate on federalism. The formula of 'unity in diversity', directed against radical nationalism, was admittedly clearly underlined in 1938 by the recognition of Romansch as the fourth official language. At the same time, however, inconsistencies and political differences of opinion regarding the interpretation of federalism, with all its implications, arose. Although Ernst Laur wanted to legitimise federalism in the spirit of the neoconservative agrarian ideology, he adhered for economic reasons to the federal interventionist state. Conversely, this was rejected in French-speaking Switzerland as being destructive of federalism. These tensions emerged even at that great demonstration of national unity, the National Exhibition of 1939.[59] In addition, little thought had evidently been given within the German-Swiss dialect movement, so typical of the 'spiritual national defence', to its repercussions on the relationship between the linguistic regions. The elevation of German-Swiss literature to become synonymous with 'Swiss literature' necessarily encountered obstructions in the other regions. From the regional perspective, the 'spiritual national defence' seems very much an affair of German-speaking Switzerland, while voices were raised in the West of the country against the 'mystic of unity'.[60]

These internal contradictions also included problems of social acceptance. The class cultures of the bourgeoisie and the workers, rooted in social inequality and earlier conflicts, made it difficult for both sides to reconcile their differences. The substance of the 'truce' in the metalworking industry was meagre, and in other sectors employers continued to refuse to recognise the unions as parties to an agreement. The movement to bring middle-class and socialist sporting associations close together proved equally laborious. Local officials of the unions,

activists and members of the SPS and the workers' cultural organisations expressed reservations and objections to the new course being
steered by the leading groups in the workers' movement. It
undermined subculturally developed self-images and reduced the
division between workers and bourgeois society that was their guarantee of identity.[61] The harmonisation of national and class awareness was
slowed by its opponents even at the 1939 National Exhibition in Zurich.
In labour movement circles there was a sense of disappointment that
they had been almost passed over during the preparations and that no
festival of workers' organisations had been arranged at the festivities
themselves   only 'Labour Days'. At the *Landi*, the memory of which
was a very one-sided one, based on an idyllic rural village, the *Dörfli*
(see p. 213), and – because the timing of the exhibition coincided with
the outbreak of war – the pathos of preparations for defence, the
workers were admittedly able to identify with the wide selection of
'quality work' from industry; but they could do so only as anonymous
workers, who had been denied the right to express their self-awareness.
In an amazing parallel with the figure of the 'unknown soldier', the
subject of national cults of the dead and sacrificed, Federal Councillor
Etter referred to the 'Labour Days' as 'commemorations of the unknown worker'.[62]

These internal regional and social contradictions and problems of
acceptance are a reminder that even the liberal and left-wing variations
of the 'spiritual national defence' were initially very much a matter
confined to informal circles of the functional leadership. It obviously
encouraged (partial) integration of national elites – though admittedly
at the price of excluding the communists – whereas any judgement on
the integration of the masses, despite the mobilising effect of the 'crisis
initiative' and the 'guideline movement', still requires further clarification. The forms and extent of the various social groups responsible
for the 'spiritual national defence' call for a systematic and integrated
examination, since the authorities of the federal state, at any rate, only
became active late in the day, with the development of the cultural
policy and civil defence.[63] In addition to the political and symbolic
manifestations of the 'Swiss' nation, which have often been described,
this analysis should pay more attention to the economic and social
policy aspects of the 'spiritual national defence'. The function of
national integration as social integration operated, after all, against the
background of the world agricultural and industrial economic crisis, in
which National Socialist Germany, soon after 1933, was able to boast of
its economic achievements and successes. What was the reaction to
this?[64] It was probably this context, too, that Karl Barth had in mind in
November 1938 when he called upon Christians against the 'diabolical

church of the anti-Christ' of National Socialism, because the latter, as he put it, was affecting the whole of Europe, and Switzerland too, with the 'intimidating and crippling magnetism of its "spirit", its methods, its tempo, its undeniable vitality or diabolism'. And he followed up these remarks by criticising the 'mildly understanding' distinction between a good thing and its 'outgrowths', and the 'spiritual national defence' too, as 'caricatures of a new Swiss nationalism (with its deep-rooted anti-semitism)', which he claimed was already infected by National Socialism.[65] Barth was no doubt thinking here of the neoconservative variation of the 'spiritual national defence'; but, as an open question, this diagnosis is also aimed retrospectively at the in-depth effect of its other forms. The fact is that, despite all the mental and political defensive postures, the massive power of suggestion of the successes enjoyed by the Nazi regime in the late 1930s must not be forgotten. It seems probable, therefore, that there were also ambivalences in the general view of the 'spiritual national defence'.

EFFECTS OF THE 'SPIRITUAL NATIONAL DEFENCE'

Identifying the multilayered nature of the 'spiritual national defence' and its limitations has made it no easier to form a historical opinion about its effects. The influence it had on attitudes to refugees and emigrants has to be differentiated accordingly. There is a contrast between the anti-Semitically conditioned defensive gesture of the neo-conservative form and the receptiveness and helpfulness of other groups who endorsed the values of the liberal and leftist 'spiritual national defence'. In addition, an overcautious governmental policy of neutrality intervened in the relationship between these variations. This resulted in a very unclear shuttling between rules and exceptions, and in situations which only rarely lead to such blatant public contradictions as they did in the case of Wolfgang Langhoff's book *Die Moorsoldaten*, the first literary report on the violence perpetrated in the early National Socialist concentration camps. It was published by the Adolf Guggenbühl Press in 1935 and caused a sensation, though readings from it were prohibited in Swiss towns.[66] This episode casts some light on the grave phenomenon of the crisis of confidence in the national leadership, which reached a peak in 1940 but – along with other factors – could also trace its origins to the divergent forms of the 'spiritual national defence'. Like the breathtaking silence and ambiguous statements of the Federal Council in the early summer of 1940, the refusal to bring social demo-cratic politicians into the Federal Council at the time of maximum national anxiety suggests how deep the gulf still was between bourgeoisie and workers. The unity of the bourgeois government took precedence over the unity of the nation.[67]

These thoughts on the multilayered profile and various contexts of the 'spiritual national defence' as a phenomenon of political culture in 1930s Switzerland have deliberately been confined to the pre-war period, an attempt being made to identify certain aspects of its objectives, achievements, effects and limitations in that period. This restriction is also based on scepticism about projecting the 'spiritual national defence' as the dominant theme of resistance and defensive and fighting spirit in the Second World War. At the time – typically of many spiritual exaggerations – this was done in the form of the pseudo-religious meaning given to the coincidence in timing between the Zurich National Exhibition and the outbreak of war: the *Landi* was portrayed as 'a national divine service, before our army manned the borders'.[68] André Lasserre interprets the 'spiritual national defence' in a very different way – realistically, giving due weight to the many different contexts, and anthropologically, but along the same lines. He considers that it was critical for the country's self-assertion, as an anti-totalitarian awareness of origin, and thus of identity.[69] It is, however, questionable (and the question is worth asking) whether such a cultural construct is significant in a modern, functionally and socially differentiated, culturally pluralistic and secularised society, if identities are not more restricted and more plural and if images of origin that promise an identity are not more in the nature of imaginings that look to the future and seek answers to the problems of order and meaning of modern society. In this function, however, they themselves remain plural, as the 'Swiss' self-determination embodied in the 'spiritual national defence' demonstrates; especially in its neoconservative and leftist forms, it was in each case striving for a 'different Switzerland' from the status quo.

Since such identity constructs always exist in a given political force field, their significance and effect has in each case to be analysed in these specific and historically variable contexts. The war years, however, were a different environment from the pre- or post-war period. Factors other than mental, ideological and political ones exerted a powerful influence on national integration and self-assertion. In particular, under the extreme life-threatening conditions of the Second World War, the effect of ideas is even more difficult to assess than usual. The deep shock and disorientation felt by Swiss society and the army in the early summer of 1940 shows that the values of the 'spiritual national defence' were no longer sufficient to deal with the totally shocking violence of the modern German style of war. It seems strange how little attention is paid to this deep fear as the obverse side, as it were, of the appeal to steadfastness.[70] It can be inferred from the course of the war, the differences in experience of war and the retrospective treatment of war in the European societies of the twentieth century what complex and tense collective experiences wars represented. The 'post-war societies' had to learn, and were able to learn, that the self-recognition of contradictory histories was more conducive to a libertarian political culture than the legend of an undisputed history.

NOTES

1 Ulrich Hausmann, in review of Robert Gubler, 'Schweizerische Militärradfahrer 1891–1993', Zurich, 1993, *Süddeutsche Zeitung*, 11 June 1993.

2 Werner Möckli, *Schweizergeist – Landigeist? Das schweizerische Selbstverständnis bei Ausbruch des Zweiten Weltkrieges*, Zurich, 1973, pp. 1, 45; Charles Linsmayer, 'Die Krise der Demokratie als Krise ihrer Literatur. Die Literatur der deutschen Schweiz im Zeitalter der geistigen Landesverteidigung', in idem, and Andrea Pfeifer (eds), *Frühling der Gegenwart. Erzählungen III*, Zurich, 1983, pp. 436–93, in this case pp. 463ff.; Ulrich Im Hof, *Mythos Schweiz. Identität – Nation – Geschichte 1291–1991*, Zurich, 1991, pp. 245ff. See on the other hand, the continuation of the 'spiritual national defence' in the post-war period in a climate of anti-communism, conservative neoliberalism and informers to the Swiss state security service: Katharina Bretscher-Spindler, *Vom heissen zum Kalten Krieg. Vorgeschichte und Geschichte der Schweiz im Kalten Krieg 1943–1968*, Zurich, 1997.

3 This refers to the admittedly simplifying terminology or presentation (though it does reflect the political and moral situation and was very influential) of Alice Meyer, *Anpassung oder Widerstand. Die Schweiz zur Zeit des deutschen National-sozialismus*, Frauenfeld, 1965. The view given by Hans Ulrich Jost, 'Bedrohung und Enge (1914–1945)', in Beatrix Mesmer *et al.* (eds), *Geschichte der Schweiz und der Schweizer*, Basle, 1986, pp. 731–819, can be read as a continuing and essentially systematic criticism of the formula of 'accommodation or resistance'.

4 Jost, 'Bedrohung', op. cit., pp. 761, 804ff.

5 Linsmayer op. cit., pp. 463, 467. As Linsmayer and Jost, 'Bedrohung', were first published at the same time (1982–83), they do not refer to each other in their terminology.

6 Linsmayer, op. cit., pp. 466ff.; Edgar Bonjour, *Geschichte der schweizerischen Neutralität*, Vol. 6, Basle, 1970, p. 41.

7 André Lasserre, *Schweiz: Die dunklen Jahre. Öffentliche Meinung 1939–1945*, Zurich, 1992 (French, 1989).

8 Georg Kreis, 'Die Schweiz der Jahre 1918–1948', in *Geschichtsforschung in der Schweiz. Bilanz und Perspektiven – 91*, Basle, 1992, pp. 378–96, esp. pp. 378ff., with important references to the 'as yet unwritten' history of the 'spiritual national defence' (p. 378). Even the wide-ranging NFP 21 (i.e. a research project sponsored by the Swiss National Board of Research) 'Cultural diversity and national identity' included no project specifically focused on the 'spiritual national defence'; see Georg Kreis, *Die Schweiz unterwegs. Schlussbericht des NFP 21 'Kulturelle Vielfalt und nationale Identität'*, Basle, 1993, pp. 62, 65ff., 86, 90 but there are some references to it in sub-projects with other focal points.

9 Aram Mattioli, *Zwischen Demokratie und totalitärer Diktatur. Gonzague de Reynold*

und die Tradition der autoritären Rechten in der Schweiz, Zurich, 1994.

10 Hans Ulrich Jost, *Die reaktionäre Avantgarde. Die Geburt der neuen Rechten in der Schweiz um 1900*, Zurich, 1992; Ruedi Brassel-Moser, *Dissonanzen der Moderne. Aspekte der Entwicklung der politischen Kulturen in der Schweiz der 1920er Jahre*, Zurich 1994; Aram Mattioli (ed.), *Intellektuelle von rechts. Ideologie und Politik in der Schweiz 1918–1939*, Zurich, 1995.

11 Kurt Imhof *et al.* (eds), *Krise und sozialer Wandel*, Vol. 1, 'Zwischen Konflikt und Konkordanz. Analyse von Medienereignissen in der Schweiz in der Vor- und Zwischenkriegszeit', Zurich, 1993; idem, *Krise und sozialer Wandel*, Vol. 2, 'Analyse von Medienereignissen in der Schweiz der Zwischen- und Nachkriegszeit', Zurich, 1996; Andreas Ernst and Erich Wigger (eds), *Die neue Schweiz? Eine Gesellschaft zwischen Integration und Polarisierung (1910–1930)*, Zurich, 1996. Fundamental to these studies are the thoughts on the theory of action and communication of Hansjörg Siegenthaler; see by way of example idem, 'Die Rede von der Kontinuität und Diskontinuität des sozialen Wandels – Das Beispiel der dreissiger Jahre', in Sebastian Brändli *et al.* (eds), *Schweiz im Wandel. Studien zur neueren Gesellschaftsgeschichte, Festschrift für Rudolf Braun zum 60. Geburtstag*, Basle, 1990, pp. 419–34.

12 Pietro Morandi, *Krise und Verständigung. Die Richtlinienbewegung und die Entstehung der Konkordanzdemokratie 1933–1939*, Zurich, 1995.

13 Quoted from Ulrich Niederer, *Geschichte des Schweizerischen Schriftsteller- verbandes. Kulturpolitik und individuelle Förderung: Jakob Bührer als Beispiel*, Tübingen, 1994, p. 119. The remarks that follow cannot replace the missing history of the term.

14 Quoted from Linsmayer, op. cit., p. 441, note 1.

15 Quoted from Martin Dahinden, *Das Schweizerbuch im Zeitalter von National- sozialismus und Geistiger Landesverteidigung*, Berne, 1987, pp. 96ff.

16 See the references in Kurt Imhof, 'Das kurze Leben der geistigen Landes- verteidigung. Von der "Volksgemeinschaft" vor dem Krieg zum Streit über die "Nachkriegsschweiz" im Krieg', in idem *et al.* (eds), *Krise und sozialer Wandel*, Vol. 2, pp. 19–84, in this case pp. 44ff., note 58.

17 As for example in the Federal Council's 'call to arms' of 1 October 1914; quoted from Jacob Ruchti, *Geschichte der Schweiz während des Weltkrieges 1914–1919*, 2 vols, Berne, 1928–30, in this case Vol. 1, p. 140. In the words of Philipp Etter in 1938, this read: 'The concept of the Swiss state is born not of race and not of flesh but of the spirit'; see message from the Federal Council to the Federal Assembly on the organisation and tasks of Swiss cultural defence and cultural propaganda of 9 November 1938, in *Bundesblatt*, 90, 1938, Vol. 2, pp. 985–1033 (hereinafter referred to as the *Kulturbotschaft 1938*), in this case p. 999; see Brassel-Moser, op. cit., pp. 183ff.

18 Mattioli, *Demokratie*, op. cit.

19 Armin Mohler, *Die Konservative Revolution in Deutschland 1918–1932*, 3rd edn, Darmstadt, 1989; Stefan Breuer, *Anatomie der Konservativen Revolution*, Darm- stadt, 1993.

20 According to Fritz Marbach, one of the bridge-builders between the polarised classes, who in 1933 corrected the impression that 'Marxism' had been in power in Switzerland, 'specifically in the hands of those who seem to assume, in an impenetrably mistrustful assessment of human spiritual endeavour, that labour policy has for half a century been the epitomy of everything evil'. Fritz Marbach, *Gewerkschaft – Mittelstand – Fronten. Zur politischen und geistigen Lage der Schweiz*, Berne, undated (1933), p. 70.

21 Peter Stadler, 'Die Diskussion um eine Totalrevision der schweizerischen Bundesverfassung 1933–1935', SZG, 19 (1969), pp. 75–169; for the regional referendum results, Historische Statistik der Schweiz, coordinated by Hansjörg Siegenthaler, edited by Heiner Ritzmann-Blickenstorfer, Zurich, 1996, pp. 1,070ff.

22 All quotations in Kulturbotschaft 1938, pp. 997ff. For the influence of Reynolds on Etter, see Mattioli, Demokratie, op. cit., pp. 243ff.; Roger de Weck, 'Die autoritäre Schweiz und ihr Meisterdenker' (report on Mattioli's biography), in Tagesanzeiger, 31 May 1994.

23 Lasserre, Schweiz, op. cit., pp. 207ff. This same line was also followed by sympathies for Pétain in Western Switzerland; see idem, pp. 124, 127.

24 Ernst Troeltsch, 'Die Revolution in der Wissenschaft', in idem, Gesammelte Schriften, Vol. 4, Tübingen, 1925, pp. 653–77.

25 See the example of the Swiss Society of Authors, which since its foundation in 1912 had been campaigning against the cultural domination by foreigners of German-speaking Switzerland and in the 1930s played an important role in the institutionalisation of the 'spiritual national defence' in cultural policy. At the same time it was also always preoccupied with the economic prospects for Swiss authors. See Niederer, op. cit., especially pp. 61ff.; for the 1930s, see Dahinden, op. cit.

26 Georg Kreis, 'Der "homo alpinus helveticus". Zum schweizerischen Rassen-diskurs der 30er Jahre', in Guy P. Marchal and Aram Mattioli (eds), Erfundene Schweiz. Konstruktionen nationaler Identität, Zurich, 1992, pp. 175–90.

27 Guy P. Marchal, 'Die "Alten Eidgenossen" im Wandel der Zeiten. Das Bild der frühen Eidgenossen im Traditionsbewusstsein und in der Identitätsvorstellung der Schweizer vom 15. bis ins 20. Jahrhundert', in Innerschweiz und frühe Eidgenossenschaft, Vol. 2, Olten, 1990, pp. 309–406, especially pp. 385ff.; idem, 'Mythos im 20. Jahrhundert. Der Wille zum Mythos oder die Versuchung des "neuen Mythos" in einer säkularisierten Welt', in Fritz Graf (ed.), Mythos in mythenloser Gesellschaft, Stuttgart, 1993, pp. 204–29, especially pp. 223ff.

28 See Edgar Bonjour, Geschichte der schweizerischen Neutralität, Vol. 3, Basle, 1970, pp. 143ff.; Katharina Spindler, Die Schweiz und der italienische Faschismus (1922–1930). Der Verlauf der diplomatischen Beziehungen und die Bewertung durch das Bürgertum, Basle, 1976; Theodor Kunz, Die deutschschweizerische Presse und das faschistische Italien 1922–1943, Zurich, 1975.

29 A. Egger, Die deutsche Staatsumwälzung und die schweizerische Demokratie, Berne, 1934, especially p. 14. This brochure, which appeared in the spring of 1934, was immediately recommended by Ernst Nobs. He noted with 'particular satis-faction' that a high-quality body of literature existed as a 'defence against facscist despotism', and particularly singled out in that context publications by such middle-class authors as A. Egger, W. Naef, E. Bovet, A. Oeri and others; Rote Revue, 13, 1933/34, p. 287. On the Swiss reception of the Nazi seizure of power, see Eric Dreifuss, Die Schweiz und das Dritte Reich. Vier deutschschweizerische Zeitungen im Zeitalter des Faschismus 1933–1939, Frauenfeld, 1971, especially pp. 29ff.; however, he does concentrate on domestic policy and disregards foreign policy.

30 Karl H. Pohl, Adolf Müller. Geheimagent und Gesandter in Kaiserreich und Weimarer Republik, Cologne, 1995, pp. 269ff.; Wilfried Feldenkirchen, 'Die Handels-beziehungen zwischen dem Deutschen Reich und der Schweiz, 1914–1945', in VSWG, 74, 1987, pp. 323–50.

31 See the articles in Imhof et al. (eds), Krise und sozialer Wandel, Vols 1 and 2; Manuel

Eisner, '"Wer sind wir?" Wandel der politischen Identität in der Schweiz 1840–1987', in *Schweizerisches Sozialarchiv* (ed.), *Bilder und Leitbilder im sozialen Wandel*, Zurich, 1991, pp. 29–66.

32 Oskar Scheiben, *Krise und Integration. Wandlungen in den politischen Konzeptionen der Sozialdemokratischen Partei der Schweiz 1928–1936*, Zurich, 1987, pp. 143ff.; Hermann Wichers, *Im Kampf gegen Hitler. Deutsche Sozialisten im Schweizer Exil 1933–1940*, Zurich, 1994, pp. 91ff.

33 Note by Neurath dated 26 July 1933, in *Akten zur deutschen auswärtigen Politik 1918–1945 (ADAP)*, Series C, Göttingen, 1971–81, Vol. 1, 2, 453, p. 831; see Motta's report to the National Council dated 27 July 1933, in Swiss Diplomatic Documents, Vol. 10, Berne, 1982, 336, pp. 835ff. Report by Weizsäcker dated 27 October 1933, in *ADAP*, Serie C, Vol. 2, 1, 33, p. 50.

34 This expression is used by von Weizsäcker in his report of 10 May 1937, in *ADAP*, Series C, Vol. 6, 2, 361, p. 784.

35 Bonjour, *Neutralität*, op. cit., Vol. 3, pp. 39ff.; Kurt Humbel, *Nationalsozialistische Propaganda in der Schweiz 1931–1939*, Berne, 1976; Jürg Fink, *Die Schweiz aus der Sicht des Dritten Reiches 1933–1945*, Zurich, 1985; Daniel Bourgeois, *Le Troisième Reich et la Suisse 1933–1941*, Neuchâtel, 1974. For the 'Trial of the Reich', see Christoph Steding, *Das Reich und die Krankheit der europäischen Kultur*, Hamburg, 1938. This unofficial book, pubished by Walter Frank, tried to legitimise radical nationalism and imperialism on the high ground of European history of ideas. It played its part in the scientific and ideological widening of the gap between Germany and Switzerland which found a central point in the debate on Nietzsche and Jacob Burckhardt. See, for example, Edgar Salin, *Jakob Burckhardt und Nietzsche*, Basle, 1938; on Steding, see Helmut Heiber, *Walter Frank und sein Reichsinstitut für Geschichte des neuen Deutschlands*, Stuttgart, 1966, pp. 501ff.

36 Letters dated 4 September 1933 and 16 November 1933, in Leonidas Hill (ed.), *Die Weizsäcker-Papiere 1933–1950*, Frankfurt-am-Main, 1974, p. 76. Weizsäcker was at that time involved in a process of defining an ideological and political position towards National Socialism.

37 According to the Basler social democratic *Arbeiterzeitung*, 10 June 1938. More reticent in language but similar in tone was the *NZZ*. In a departure from journalistic practice, it reported the sporting victory on page 1; *NZZ*, 1034, 10 June 1938; Fred Luchsinger, *Die Neue Zürcher Zeitung im Zeitalter des Zweiten Weltkrieges 1930–1955*, Zurich, 1955, p. 191. A pointer to the almost unknown ambivalence of mass opinion to Nazi Germany is, of course, the fact that at the same time Leni Riefenstahl's film of the Olympic games was being shown with great success in a Zurich cinema; see *NZZ*, 1045, 12 June 1938.

38 Quoted from Werner Rings, *Schweiz im Krieg. 1933–1945*, Zurich, 1974, p. 140.

39 Report by Ambassador Köcher of 18 October 1938, in *ADAP*, Series D, Baden-Baden, 1955, Vol. 5, 529, p. 583. The number of German citizens in Switzerland had more than halved from 134,835 in 1930 to 58,179 in 1941, only a small part of this change presumably being due to naturalisations, which had taken place in relatively large numbers in the 1920s; see *Historische Statistik*, op. cit., p. 146. For more accurate insight, see for example the conditions in Basle, see government report: *Bericht des Regierungsrates über die Abwehr staatsfeindlicher Umtriebe in den Vorkriegs- und Kriegsjahren sowie der Säuberungsaktion nach Kriegsschluss*, Basle, 1946, p. 7.

40 On this metaphorical concept, see Theodor Geiger, *Die soziale Schichtung des deutschen Volkes*, Stuttgart, 1932 (Darmstadt, 1967), pp. 77ff.

41 These areas have still been little explored; see Markus Zürcher, *Unterbrochene*

Tradition. Die Anfänge der Soziologie in der Schweiz, Zurich, 1995, pp. 189ff.; Theo Mäusli, *Jazz und Geistige Landesverteidigung*, Zurich, 1995; Linsmayer, op. cit., pp. 445ff., *passim*; Dahinden, op. cit., pp. 127ff.; Hans Amstutz, *Das Verhältnis zwischen deutscher und französischer Schweiz in den Jahren 1930–1945*, Aarau, 1996, pp. 152ff.

42 Linsmayer, op. cit., pp 441ff.; Möckli, op. cit., pp. 32ff.

43 Linsmayer, op. cit., p. 447.

44 In the context of the meandering debate on federalism, the historian Werner Näf warned in 1938: 'But we also know that this feminine colourfulness of culture [of federalism] contrasts with a masculine will for democracy'; quoted from Amstutz, op. cit., p. 151. It should also be noted that Federal Councillor Etter expressly recommended 'instruction in the history of the fatherland' for 'both boys and girls' (*Kulturbotschaft 1938*, op. cit., p. 1026). In the spring of 1939 a wild controversy flared up in the press regarding unconditional resistance in the event of a German attack, in the form of a 'people's war' in which women would also bear arms. The military described this as 'drug-addicted romanticism' and resolutely rejected the idea of a 'people's war', particular anger being caused not just by the assumption that the army was inadequate but also by the idea of arming women. See G. Wirz, 'Totale Landesverteidigung? Volkskrieg?', *Allgemeine schweizerische Militärzeitung*, 85, 1939, pp. 281–9; Ernst Schürch, 'Volkskrieg', idem, pp. 459–64; Hans G. Wirz, 'Totale Landesverteidigung? Volkskrieg', idem, pp. 466–77. This dispute clearly forms part of the long tradition of controversy over what kind of military constitution is appropriate to Switzerland. In this, the concept of the 'people's defence' or 'people's war' had always been strenuously opposed to the prevalent ideas; for an informative account see Rudolf Jaun, 'Vom Bürger-Militär zum Soldaten-Militär. Die Schweiz im 19. Jahrhundert', in Ute Frevert (ed.), *Militär und Gesellschaft im 19. Jahrhundert*, Stuttgart, 1997, pp. 48–77. The gender-specific policy on population and family, and eugenics also, were deserving of analysis in connection with the 'spiritual national defence'; see the references in Regina Wecker, 'Staatsbürgerschaft, Mutterschaft und Grundrechte', *SZG*, 46, 1996, pp. 383–410.

45 Ernst Staehelin, 'Vom Ringen um die christliche Grundlage der schweizerischen Eidgenossenschaft seit der Geltung der Bundesverfassung von 1874', inaugural address as rector of the University of Basle on 17 November 1939, Basle, 1939; Ursula Käser-Leisibach, *Die begnadeten Sünder. Stimmen aus den Schweizer Kirchen zum Nationalsozialismus 1933–1942*, Winterthur, 1994; Hermann Kocher, *Rationierte Menschlichkeit. Schweizerischer Protestantismus im Spannungsfeld von Flüchtlingsnot und öffentlicher Flüchtlingspolitik der Schweiz 1933–1948*, Zurich, 1996.

46 Möckli, op. cit., p. 41.

47 For the example of the writers, see Linsmayer, op. cit., p. 476. It was the pressure for conformity exerted by the social groups, especially in 1940/41, that Georg Kreis had in mind when he referred in 1979 to 'Swiss totalitarianism' and expressly denied the existence of a 'total state'. However, such a state, and especially a political dictatorship, is one of the fundamental features of 'totalitarianism'. A social pressure to conform or a politically imposed form of social control (in more or less 'narrow' forms) calls for a different term, especially if a profound fear of a deadly threat plays its part in such behaviour, as it did in Switzerland in 1940/41. See Georg Kreis, 'Helvetischer Totalitarismus', *Basler Magazin/Basler Zeitung*, 27 January 1979.

48 *Kulturbotschaft 1938*, op. cit., pp. 994ff.

49 Charles Stirnimann, *Die ersten Jahre des 'Roten Basel' 1935–1938*, Basle, 1988, pp. 170ff.; Mattioli, op. cit., *Demokratie*, pp. 241f.; Morandi, pp. 43ff., *passim*; Ursula Amrein, 'Kulturpolitik und Geistige Landesverteidigung – das Zürcher Schauspielhaus', in Sigrid Weigel and Birgit Erdle (eds), *Fünfzig Jahre danach. Zur Nachgeschichte des Nationalsozialismus*, Zurich, 1996, pp. 281–325. This essay casts an ideologically critical light on the depoliticisation of the theatre since 1938 with its apparently non-political orientation to what was described as timelessly valid classicism, a fusion of neutrality, 'spiritual national defence' and humanitarian values. Similarly critical and highly informative about the hitherto little known early career of Max Frisch is Urs Bircher with the assistance of Kathrin Straub, *Vom langsamen Wachsen eines Zorns. Max Frisch 1911–1955*, Zurich, 1977, pp. 77ff. Both studies identify the 'spiritual national defence' with its neoconservative form and so have no idea of the critical potential of the liberal position. In the case of Max Frisch, this meant the ability, specifically in 1945/46 when self-righteousness was tending to triumph in Switzerland, to move outside the conventional bourgeois–liberal consensus.

50 Egger, op. cit., pp. 25ff., quotations pp. 33, 40. On the conciliatory liberal historical thought, see Möckli, op. cit., pp. 127ff.; Peter Stadler, 'Zwischen Klassenkampf, Ständestaat und Genossenschaft. Politische Ideologien im schweizerischen Geschichtsbild der Zwischenkriegszeit', *HZ*, 219, 1974, pp. 290–358, pp. 311ff.

51 See the articles in Imhof *et al.* (eds), *Krise und sozialer Wandel*, Vols 1 and 2. The reception and discussion of the liberal view of history in the labour movement during the inter-war period merited more accurate analysis; see the reference above, note 29, and the reviews by Ernst Nobs in the *Rote Revue*, for example 18, 1938/39, p. 327 (on A. Jaggi and W. Näf). In this connection, of course, note should be made of the strong 'Grütlian' tradition of social liberalism in the Swiss labour movement of the nineteenth century.

52 Such a surrender is one-sidedly stressed by Scheiben, op. cit., pp. 250ff., with particular reference to the intra-party resistances to the new course. But see Thomas Gerlach, *Ideologie und Organisation. Arbeitgeberverbände und Gewerkschaften in der Schweizer Textilindustrie 1935–1955*, Stuttgart, 1995, pp. 184ff.; Karl Schwaar, *Isolation und Integration. Arbeiterkulturbewegung und Arbeiterbewegungskultur in der Schweiz 1920–1960*, Basle, 1993, pp. 142ff.

53 Imhof, 'Das kurze Leben', op. cit., especially p. 46 ('national community' as a 'core concept'); Oliver Zimmer, 'Die "Volksgemeinschaft". Entstehung und Funktion einer nationalen Einheitssemantik in den 1930er Jahren in der Schweiz', in Imhof *et al.* (eds), *Krise und sozialer Wandel*, Vol. 2, pp. 85–110; Morandi, op. cit., pp. 224ff.

54 Ernst Nobs, 'Besinnung auf die Schweiz', *Rote Revue*, 18, 1938/39, pp. 73–81 (quotation p. 76); K. Killer, 'Geistige Landesverteidigung und Schule', idem, pp. 207–12 (quotation pp. 211ff.); W. Stocker, 'Geistige Landesverteidigung', in idem, pp. 113–17 (quotation p. 116).

55 Stirnimann, op. cit.; Christian Gruber, *Die politischen Parteien der Schweiz im Zweiten Weltkrieg*, Vienna, 1966, pp. 89ff.

56 Morandi, op. cit., *passim*; Möckli, op. cit., pp. 48ff.; Peter Moser, *Der Stand der Bauern. Bäuerliche Politik, Wirtschaft und Kultur gestern und heute*, Frauenfeld, 1994, pp. 116ff.

57 Imhof, 'Das kurze Leben', op. cit., especially pp. 71ff.

58 This attitude was a permanent feature of the *Schweizerische Monatshefte*; by way of example, see Jann von Sprecher, 'Die politische Lage der Schweiz nach dem

Anschluss Österreichs', *Schweizerische Monatshefte*, 18, 1938/39, pp. 1–22. On the SPS's attitude to foreign policy in the years 1938–39, Georg Kreis, *Zensur und Selbstzensur. Die schweizerische Pressepolitik im Zweiten Weltkrieg*, Frauenfeld, 1973, pp. 254ff. In a manifesto of 1 August 1939 the Social Democrats called for 'true' neutrality, 'which maintains correct relations with every state and friendly ones with the democracies'. This was a variation from the Federal Council's formula, also accepted by the SP group in the National Council, of 'maintaining correct and friendly relations with all our neighbours alike'.

59 Werner Baumann, 'Ernst Laur oder "Der Bauernstand muss erhalten werden, koste es, was es wolle"', in Mattioli (ed.), *Intellektuelle*, op. cit., pp. 257–72; Möckli, op. cit., pp. 97ff.; Amstutz, op. cit., pp. 78ff.

60 Amstutz, op. cit., pp. 124ff. (quotation p. 127), 152ff.

61 Gerlach, op. cit., pp. 187ff., 195ff.; Scheiben, op. cit., pp. 250ff.; Schwaar, op. cit., pp. 146ff., 166ff.

62 Schwaar, op. cit., pp. 154ff. (Etter quotation p. 155), p. 267, note 90 (highly informative quotation from an SP newspaper on 'quality work'). Etter's word finds a parallel in the official description of the National Exhibition. A photographic series on the production of a diesel engine, showing the cooperation of director, engineer and both white-collar and blue-collar workers, appears under the heading: 'Das Werk des unbekannten Arbeiters'; *Die Schweiz im Spiegel der Landesausstellung 1939*, 3 vols, Zurich, 1940, here Vol. 1, pp. 233ff. Möckli, *Schweizergeist – Landigeist?* op. cit., is significantly, despite the critical intent, still completely under the spell of the conservative tradition of the *Landi*. This 'modern' side and the relationship between tradition and modernism at the exhibition, its contemporary reception at home and abroad and its after-effects have not yet been appropriately studied; but see the attempts in Kenneth Angst and Alfred Cattani (eds), *Die Landi. Vor fünfzig Jahren in Zürich. Erinnerungen – Dokumente – Betrachtungen*, Stäfa, 1989.

63 This difference becomes significant in Meyer, op. cit., *Anpassung*, pp. 55ff.

64 The question certainly arose, as Arnold Jaggi, *Vom Kampf und Opfer für die Freiheit*, Berne, 1939, reveals. In the armaments boom of the late 1930s German companies (successfully) advertised for skilled workers, which caused a sensation and comparative questions about the living standards of workers in Germany and Switzerland; idem, pp. 36, 75ff., 104ff. (note 18), p. 107 (note 38). On the development of the number of Swiss foreigners in Germany, which increased again after 1936, see *Historische Statistik*, p. 377; Ulrich Herbert, *Fremdarbeiter. Politik und Praxis des 'Ausländer-Einsatzes' in der Kriegswirtschaft des Dritten Reiches*, Berlin, 1985, p. 58. These issues were also a factor for a good many 'deserters'; Linus Reichlin, *Kriegsverbrecher Wipf, Eugen. Schweizer in der Waffen-SS, in deutschen Fabriken und an den Schreibtischen des Dritten Reiches*, Zurich, 1994, pp. 11, 71ff., 146.

65 Karl Barth, 'Die Kirche und die politische Frage von heute', lecture given on 5 December 1938, Zollikon, 1939, quotation pp. 13, 15ff., 29.

66 Werner Mittenzwei, *Exil in der Schweiz*, Leipzig, 1978, pp. 162ff.

67 Bonjour, *Neutralität*, op. cit., Vol. 4, pp. 73ff.; Bernard Degen, *Sozialdemokratie: Gegenmacht? Opposition? Bundesratspartei? Die Geschichte der Regierungsbeteiligung der schweizerischen Sozialdemokraten*, Zurich, 1993, pp. 43ff. On the explicitly sceptical opinion on the effect of the 'spiritual national defence', and especially on the *Landi*, see also Amstutz, op. cit., p. 132, and the down-to-earth assessment of this effect in Hans von Greyerz, 'Der Bundesstaat seit 1848', *Handbuch der Schweizer Geschichte*, Vol. 2, Zurich, 1980, pp. 1,196ff.

68 Quoted from Marchal, 'Die alten Eidgenossen', p. 396.
69 Lasserre, *Schweiz*, op. cit., especially pp. 18ff. and the final conclusions, pp. 427ff.;
    also the chapter by André Lasserre in this volume.
70 See Guisan's breathtaking army orders of 3 June 1940 which bear witness to a
    sense of inferiority by comparison with the German war machine and called
    upon the army to prepare to lay down their lives, using quotations from the
    historical memory of the 'spiritual national defence'. It is particularly note-
    worthy that Guisan identified the sense of disorientation by name, and even
    cited it in detail in his report to the Federal Assembly: 'By contrast, our moral
    preparedness still has to be raised massively. The lack of respect for women,
    alcohol abuse and lack of self-control in all its forms are unworthy of the Swiss
    uniform [!]. The proceedings of the military courts have a sad tale to tell in this
    respect.' Quoted from Henri Guisan, *Bericht an die Bundesversammlung uber den
    Aktivdienst 1939–1945*, printed as manuscript, no place or date, p. 206. See Willi
    Gautschi, *General Henri Guisan. Die schweizerische Armeeführung im Zweiten
    Weltkrieg*, Zurich, 1989, pp. 205ff., 616ff.; Lasserre, *Schweiz*, op. cit., pp. 87ff.; an
    impressive document, Erich Gruner, 'Junge Schweizer erleben den Zweiten
    Weltkrieg', in *Bernische Zeitschrift für Geschichte und Heimatkunde*, 35, 1973, 4, pp.
    129–76.

12

Swiss Memory of the Second World War in the Immediate Post-War Period, 1945–48

LUC VAN DONGEN

THE 'MEMORY' OF WAR IN NON-BELLIGERENT COUNTRIES

Contrary to the situation in other countries[1] and as partially highlighted by the present Jewish assets affair, researchers have previously taken no real interest in the memory of the Second World War in Switzerland. Should this be seen as a historical lacuna, engendered by the spirit of 'spiritual defence'[2] which for so long impregnated the intellectual climate of Switzerland, or evidence that a study of this subject is unnecessary as far as Switzerland is concerned? I will not dwell on the lack of progress by Swiss historians which is apparent in certain areas, one example being the history of the period under discussion. On the other hand, our interpretation of the term 'memory' must be clarified, together with the specific aspects of these problems in connection with Switzerland.

For the French historian Henry Rousso, the history of memory is 'the study of the evolution of the various social practices, their form and their content, whose purpose or effect, explicitly or otherwise, is the representation of the past and the perpetuation of its memory, either within a given group or within society as a whole'.[3] The aim, above all, is to observe the various reversals and usages of the past that are current in public life, and the way in which representations and debates stored away as a result of these 'resurgences' take root in their context. It is, then, this 'public memory'[4] that we must bear in mind when we talk about the 'memory' of the war. What has been commonly called the 'collective memory' is the extension – a risky one, according to psychologists – of an individual phenomenon to a social group, and is only one aspect of public memory in the sense in which we understand it; it will play only an incidental part in this chapter.

Placing memory in its historical perspective inevitably goes hand in hand with reflections on forgetting, because 'even when studied on the scale of a society', as Henry Rousso writes, 'memory can be seen as the organisation of forgetting'.[5] Jacques Picard is saying the same thing when he pleads for a history of oblivion: 'It is always useful, when trying to understand memory, to study the political and social organisation of oblivion.'[6] However, if 'memory' is generally visible – or even blatant – the same is not true of 'forgetting', which is more difficult to grasp. As far as this chapter is concerned, I will place the emphasis more on concealment, which represents, if not deliberate intent, at least easily understood interests. It should be noted that, in the construction of any memory, a part is also played by another important aspect – ignorance. But the charting of oblivion, as of concealment and ignorance, is a function of the state of historical knowledge. Once a previously unknown and highly significant fact has been (re)discovered, that is the time to inquire into the reasons and circumstances for the silence surrounding it.[7]

As for the specific features of the Swiss case, where memory is concerned, I shall first summarise it in broad outline. In his introduction to the *Vichy Syndrome*, Henry Rousso justifies his undertaking mainly through the fact that the years 1939–45 – defeat, the Occupation and especially Vichy – represent a trauma for France, characterised by internal rifts which even brought the country into a state of civil war. Here we have a past built on tragedy, death and slaughter, placing a very heavy burden on memory and complicating the task of the French in coming to terms with their history. Thus, the war can be compared with the French Revolution, the wars in the Vendée, the Paris Commune and, on another level, the Dreyfus case – each of which proved so damaging to national unity and identity.

So what of Switzerland, where national unity and social cohesion have prevailed? The Swiss experience is very far removed from that of France. Switzerland remained neutral, deciding to take no part in the struggle to the death between fascist states and democracies, convinced that this *Sonderfall* (exception or third way) was not only the safest but also the fairest. The territory of Switzerland was safeguarded against military aggression and foreign occupation. The Swiss population, therefore, was not swept up in any 'civil war' between resisters and collaborators. Nor did the country suffer any of the tragedies of war. Admittedly, there were 84 victims of aerial bombing, accidental deaths of serving soldiers, war-related suicides and 17 citizens executed for treason (and covered by a veil of silence from 1945 onward). But there was no grim reality such as to create a tradition of martyrdom or a source of internal discord. To go by the most traditional and most conservative view, it would seem that the people had a steady faith in their rulers, that they had been galvanised by the charismatic figure of their general, and that they had come to terms with themselves after the days of social conflict. As we now know, this vision of Switzerland between 1939 and 1945 is too simplistic by far, the outcome of a teleological judgement which strips history of its ambiguities and virtualities. It disregards, too, the tensions and divisions in the highest circles of government and in the army. Even so, the situation of Switzerland is characterised more by internal unity than by division. So why concern oneself with the memory of an event that has every appearance of being a non-event? First, because, contrary to what many Swiss believe today, the Second World War gave rise to violent arguments after 1945. It is of the greatest interest to follow the course of these flare-ups, debates and silences, too, about the war (and in particular the sensitive topics of the rejection of the Jews, asylum policy in general, economic and financial collaboration with Germany, and so on). Next, there is no escaping the cultural importance of the Second World War, which has become manifest in each 'crisis' of national identity (the Swiss discontent of the 1960s, the debate on the abolition of the army, the crisis of the 1990s) and on every occasion where Switzerland's international destiny is at stake (the debates about Switzerland's accession to the United Nations Organisation and the European Economic Area). The memory of the war, which has become crystallised around certain images and values (neutrality, the redoubt/*réduit*, the army and such like) has become an essential component of the national identity – hence the need to obtain a clearer view of the forces that motivate it.

In undertaking a critical interpretation of the social usages of history throughout the second half of the twentieth century, such a study should surely cast an original light on the history of the 'present day'[8] in Switzerland.

A DOMINANT MEMORY SUBJECTED TO THE POLITICAL CHOICES OF THE TIME

The lines that follow are intended as an initial contribution to the field outlined above. First, I shall endeavour to highlight the main features of the memory of the Second World War in Switzerland from 1945 to 1948, from the standpoint of the relationships between memory and politics.[9] I will stop at 1948 because that date marks both the end of the first phase of 'contact' with the recent past and the involvement of Switzerland in the Cold War – even if the premises for this had already been apparent earlier. Those three decisive years would see the establishment of the mental reflexes and representations specific to the war, which would for many years continue to weigh upon the collective perception of the Swiss. This was the period when the active service generation received its first laurels and where the common memory became fixed. Because of personal experience and the 'conditioning' of minds during the time of conflict, the Swiss population shared a very positive image of the part their country had played during the war. It was, therefore, entirely ready to accept the reassuring image offered to it by its leaders.

A MEMORY SHAPED BY THE INTERNATIONAL SITUATION

The memory that formed in the immediate post-war years was, to a large extent, conditioned by changes in the international context and by the attitude adopted towards Switzerland by certain countries. The main characteristic of Switzerland in 1945 was isolation. We may recall, for example, that on 10 April 1944 the American secretary of state, Cordell Hull, had delivered a sharp criticism of the policy of the neutral countries. Switzerland was accused of prolonging the war by its commercial and financial relations with Germany, its arms shipments and the authorisation it had granted the Axis powers to use the St Gotthard road. In November of that same year, the Allies had given further proof of their hostility towards Switzerland by ordering a total blockade of road and rail traffic. The Soviet Union had even inflicted a serious snub on the Confederation by refusing to restore diplomatic links with Switzerland in November 1944. This crisis cost Federal Councillor Marcel Pilet-Golaz his seat.

Early in 1945, as the noose tightened around the German troops, the Allies stepped up their economic demands and repeated their request for aid for the displaced persons from the concentration camps. Under pressure from the American War Department, the Federal Council's delegate to international assistance works, Edouard de Haller, recommended sending Swiss citizens to provide local protection and food aid to Allied nationals exposed to bombing and the chaos of the situation.

> It is clear that, rightly or wrongly, people were coming to consider that we had not done all we might during the last months of the war …, and that what the victorious nations of tomorrow would feel towards Switzerland would no longer be gratitude but resentment. This is a psychological phenomenon so obvious that there is no need to prove it. Evidence we have gathered from fellow-countrymen recently returning from abroad entirely confirms our conviction that Switzerland will be judged by what it does during the final stage

of the war, not by any meritorious service it may have rendered previously [as the protecting power].[10]

We can conclude from this that the genuine increase in flexibility regarding asylum policy at the end of the war, and the last-minute efforts made to save human life,[11] were not dictated solely by philanthropic considerations. Concern about memory, or, if you like, the future image of the country, also entered into the government's plans. Thus, at the same time as the extremely important negotiations that took place with the allies in 1945/46, Switzerland endeavoured to highlight its humanitarian activities and to be remembered for its virtues. We may remember the 100 million franc subsidy granted by the Federal Council to set up the National Gift (Swiss aid fund) in December 1944.[12] We may also note the plan for an anthology intended to highlight the 'services rendered' by Switzerland during the Second World War. This work, financed by the new head of the Federal Department of Policy, Max Petitpierre, was the successor to another project, the White Paper, and was supposed to include contributions dealing with the ICRC, the Swiss Red Cross, the central agency for prisoners of war, aid to children, hospitalisation and internment, the representation of foreign interests and the National Gift. It was planned, initially, with a view to 'creating a favourable psychological climate for Switzerland's conditional membership of the United Nations'.[13] To carry out the plan, a panel of patriotic writers and faithful servants of their country was conceived: J. Chenevière, C. du Pasquier, M. Zermatten, D. de Rougemont, C. Gorgé, R. de Traz, G. Calgari, F. Ernst, A. Malche, G. Castella, G. de Reynold, L. Savary, R. de Weck, F. Barbey, N. Roger, H. de Ziégler, E. Bauer, Ch. Clerc, J. Freymond, C. Muret, G. Roud and D. Simond.[14] With Switzerland having finally concluded that UN membership was incompatible with its policy of neutrality, the plan was deprived of its raison d'être and, sharing the fate of the White Paper some time earlier, was abandoned in 1947.[15] Even so, the intention spoke volumes. It had been, surely, to erect a sort of 'humanitarian memorial', as this memorandum testifies:

> The enterprise is not without its risks. We must at all costs avoid creating the impression that we are trying to boast, to glory in our attitude which was … only the performance of a sacred duty. Nevertheless, so many acts have been performed during this war, so many acts of devotion have become apparent, that it does seem to me that this would be a – modest – monument to the memory of those six years of conflict.[16]

Between 1945 and 1948, then, Switzerland faced a perilous phase of transition into the post-war world. Changing its diplomatic representatives where necessary, following the principle enunciated by the former Federal Councillor Pilet-Golaz to the effect that policy should be observed but men need not be, the country adjusted to the new international deal. It did not hesitate to pass from the 'faith of the Niebelungen' to 'friendship under stress',[17] a transition reflected in particular by Switzerland's accession to the European Economic Cooperation Organisation (EECO) in April 1948, and the growth of an ardent anti-communist ethos. The public memory of the war, then, grew up little by little within the political and cultural standards of the 'free world'. In 1948, on the occasion of the Prague coup, Switzerland's recent past was no longer a problem internationally. However, the price of assimilation had been a great deal of simplification and silence.

A MEMORY SUBJECT TO NATIONAL IMPERATIVES

Immediately after the German surrender, the Swiss political and military authorities elected to adopt a self-contained and secretive position regarding the war. As the end of hostilities approached, the authorities were torn between fears of Soviet troops arriving on Switzerland's borders and fears of imminent social conflicts echoing those of 1918–19. In March 1945, for example, Lieutenant-Colonel R. Frick, returning from a foreign trip, wrote to warn General Guisan – whom he rightly saw as a wholehearted ally – of the danger of the 'bolshevisation of Europe'.[18] Many other officers, and no doubt many political leaders too, expected a trial of strength comparable to the general strike of 1918. Another fear was that of anti-militarism, a revival of which was expected.[19] Hence, the history of the period then drawing to its end was bound to be carefully supervised by the government.

The attitude adopted by the authorities, and the message they put out, at the end of the war are revealing. With regard to 8 May 1945, the Federal Council adopted an attitude of extreme caution, waiting to see how the Allies would celebrate their victory before deciding on a course of action, which in any case would be significantly influenced by the church.[20] The major concern was to avoid an excess of enthusiasm which might run counter to the policy of neutrality (towards both the Allies and Germany) and cause internal unrest. The decision eventually taken was that a radio address would be given on 8 May and that the bells would be rung throughout the country that same evening. Furthermore, ecumenical religious ceremonies would take place more or less everywhere. In his address the president, Eduard von Steiger of the Agrarian Party, expressed his deep compassion for the sufferings endured by other nations and gave his thanks to the two protective authorities that were to become the cornerstone of the way the war was represented – God and the army. The miraculous fate of Switzerland was described in terms which gave full credit to divine grace and a 'will beyond our understanding'. While notable for its lyricism and humility in its description of the historic events that had just taken place, however, the speech became firmer and more specific in its evaluation of the internal situation. It promised a determined effort to meet the major social challenges of the post-war period: pensions for retired people and surviving dependants, family welfare, the struggle against unemployment, aid to Swiss living abroad, agrarian legislation and such like. Above all it stressed the need for unity, as can be seen from these words, simultaneously unifying and threatening:

> Today, we can say that, in good times and in bad, we were determined to defend our independence, and we did so. We never wavered in that, even when we had no one to rely upon but ourselves ... New tasks now confront us, and we shall tackle them with firmness and resolution, but we shall not allow this country to be disrupted by violence, deceit, cunning and self-importance. The dangers that threatened us from outside our borders have been dispelled. We shall know how to deal with the dangers within.[21]

But in that year, 1945, it was the army more than the civil authority which enjoyed the respect of the people and shaped the beginnings of the public memory. Thus, General Guisan succeeded in imposing upon a reluctant Federal Council the principle of a 'homage to the colours'. This would take place in Berne's Bundesplatz on 19 August 1945 and would be an ideal opportunity to highlight the role of the army in a forward-looking context. In May–August 1945, therefore, the army was called upon to play a key part in the creation of the 'official memory' (or 'dominant memory'), the more so since its leaders were beset by a dual anxiety, about the fate of the army and the international situation. The military command feared that the transition to peace would result in the relaxing of vigilance and the weakening of the armed forces. In a letter dated 3 June 1945 and addressed to von Steiger, Guisan wrote: 'The situation in Europe ... means that we cannot afford anything less than the utmost vigilance. It certainly rules out any break in continuity in the transition from one responsible military authority to another.'[22] Two days earlier, Guisan had received a letter from J. Borel, commanding the 1st Army Corps, along the same lines. Borel wrote: 'Contrary to the widespread opinion among our people ... I believe that there will shortly be further hostilities in Europe, in the form of a conflict between Russia on the one hand and the Allies ... and Switzerland on the other'. It was reasonable to think, in Borel's view, that Russia '[would] take advantage of the chaos of the present situation to try to invade Western Europe and create a Soviet-style new order there'. The USSR could call on 600 divisions and 'a strong fifth column in most of the target countries, including Switzerland', so that the present military team would have to take further precautions before stepping down.[23] Hence, Guisan's position with regard to the Second World War seems dominated by an unusual interest in memory: 'We have gone through an experience that we must not allow to fade from our memories', he declaimed in the Bundesplatz.[24] In his order of the day for 8 May 1945 we find this:

> What is important, then, is that the benefit of this experience, this trial, should not be wasted. If, in the near or more distant future, our army were to be called to arms to defend our independence once again, the generation of 1939 to 1945 will arise again, identify themselves and join the ranks. But those men will only be worthy of their task if they do not reject it in any way, either in their deeds or in their thoughts, and if they pass on to those who follow their courage, their sense of duty and their loyalty.[25]

Guisan returned to this theme again at the time of the Jegenstorf briefing, attended by more than 400 officers:

> Even though, today, public opinion still recognises what you [the officers of the high command, the higher command and the general staff] have done to preserve your country's freedom, there is a danger that their gratitude will soon be forgotten. You will not be able to place much reliance on your 'active service' achievements – however fine and precious to you your memories – our memories – of that period may be. More precisely, you will only be able to rely on those achievements for yourselves and for your comrades … You all represent something else: a great team that was called to serve in the proud school of active service. If that experience did not bring you your baptism of fire, it was still a valuable and splendid influence on your character and intelligence.[26]

A tradition was being 'invented'.[27]

A second form of official intervention also played its part in the creation of memory – the reports. Through them, Switzerland compiled the balance sheet of its activities during the hostilities, but also steered its memory in a particular direction. There are at least four documents of this kind for the years 1945–48 alone:

1. General Guisan's report to the Federal Assembly on the 1939–45 period of active service (to which must be added the reports by the

chief of the general staff, the commanding officer of the air and anti-aircraft forces, the head of training and the head of personnel);
2. The report by the Federal Council to the Federal Assembly on the general's report;
3. The report on anti-democratic activities by Swiss and foreigners in connection with the period of the 1939–45 war (comprising three sections and a supplement);
4. The report by the Federal Council to the Federal Assembly on press arrangements in Switzerland before and during the period of the 1939–45 war.[28]

Guisan's report is a key document for the Swiss memory of the war, since it prompted the first great debate on the years 1939–45. Does that imply an examination of the national conscience? The answer is no, because the document in itself is a purely military balance sheet, and the balance it shows is a panegyric of the army. Drafted by Guisan's right-hand man, Bernard Barbey, it outlines in minute detail how the country's situation evolved from the standpoint of the military command. The main effect of its various chapters, though they un-deniably supplied valuable information to a public avid for further details, was to sanctify Switzerland's act of resistance. As a result, various measures acquired a symbolic value: the second mobilisation of 11 May 1940, the army order of 15 May 1940 ('hold our positions at all costs'), the Alpine redoubt, the two orders of 3 June 1940 ('to the point of supreme sacrifice'), the army order of 2 July 1940 ('the war continues') and the Grütli briefing. Much attention was paid to the 'lessons of history', and the light they were supposed to shed on the organisation of the future army. Guisan wanted to see a newer, younger and more numerous officer class, training and instruction that placed more emphasis on moral and patriotic duty, improved and comprehensive armaments, the preparation of a global strategic theory, the acceptance of the principle of a general in peacetime (a highly controversial issue) and a better distribution of powers between the civil and military authorities. Thus the general stated his personal vision of the national defence, interspersed with many allusions to the social role of the army in maintaining national unity.

As a result of the many heated arguments triggered by this docu-ment, the Federal Council felt obliged to correct certain points. The report by the Federal Council to the Federal Assembly on the general's report must thus be seen as a final summation, relatively technical in nature. The report returns to such contentious issues as the absence of operational plans, the lack of military preparedness, relations between the Federal Council and the general, the question of the inspector-general of the army, the problems within the air force, the case of General Bandi, the night operations by Swiss aircraft, the intelligence service, *Armée et Foyer*, propaganda policy, the recruitment of officers (the famous 'shortcomings of the bourgeoisie'), the violation of secrecy by the general, and so on. Historical trust was not the primary concern of the authorities, as witness this declaration which appears in the early pages of the report:

> The Federal Council knows that the General is in agreement with it regarding the objective of their statements. The issue is not to criticise for the sake of denigration but to strengthen our defensive energy and maintain the strength of our armed forces ... At the present time, preserving confidence in the army and persuading the army that matters are progressing along the right lines are ... much more important than taking sides on particular issues.[29]

Public opinion greeted the Federal Council's report, as a whole, as a necessary reweighing of the facts. The fact remains that, as a military report, an instrument of combat in the service of a new army and a reflection of a particular vision of Switzerland, the Guisan report has three essential consequences. First, it is a 'memorial' to the spirit of resistance in the Swiss people and their army; second, it helps to 'militarise' the memory of the war; and, third, it strengthens the image of a hedgehog Switzerland, owing its fate to its courage alone, since the measures adopted by the general and the general staff merely obeyed, so it would seem, their inherent logic. One may wonder, like Gautschi, whether the controversy surrounding the report was 'an essential filtering stage in a democratic community with a middle-class majority'.[30] It is true that the report represents a break with several years of forced official inhibition. But it is no less undeniable that it bears the stamp of the need for national unity.

The report on so-called 'anti-democratic' activities is another matter.[31] First in terms of its origins, since it owes these to a parliamentary motion signed by more than 80 national councillors. Second, in terms of its scope, since it emanates from the federal public prosecutor's office and is replete with grave ideological implications. It forms part of the story of the official attitude to the 'bad Swiss' and aliens who had become undesirable after 1945. This was the demand voiced by the radical Ernst Boerlin:

> I call upon the Federal Council to give the Federal Assembly and the Swiss people a general and full account, in whatever form it may see fit, of the result of the investigations carried out into the anti-democratic activities of foreign or foreign-sponsored organisations

and individuals in connection with the war period from 1939 to 1945. The account should include those Swiss who were involved in the activities in question.[32]

Boerlin wanted to demonstrate the efficiency of the Swiss police authorities and the extent of the activities that had posed a threat to the state. He also hoped to channel the public's desire for a purge and so help to restore normal relations with Germany and Italy. Finally, he felt that national sentiment would be strengthened by the identification of the 'faux Suisses', an expression much in vogue at that time that referred primarily to communists. Once again, the imperative of national unity makes itself felt. The term 'anti-democratic', as used by the political police, applied to any National Socialist, fascist or communist activity (the political interpretation) and any activity that violated the Swiss regulations intended to guarantee state security and national independence (the police interpretation). The reports thus referred to machinations of this type on Swiss soil from the 1920s onwards. At the end of the third report there is clear evidence of an intent to assimilate Nazism and communism, the extreme right and the extreme left. However, since the prohibition on communist organisations had been lifted, they had become more difficult to prosecute. From that time on, 'the essential thing now is not whether a body is communistic ... but whether it has subversive aims, such as changing our democratic institutions by unlawful means'.[33] The report on anti-democratic activities gave the public memory its moral and ideological tone and also its clear conscience. It established the concept that Switzerland had never deviated from its attachment to democracy and adopted a line of behaviour based on the happy medium. A comment by Pierre Béguin in the *Gazette de Lausanne* clearly illustrates the way in which majority opinion perceived the period 1939–45:

> The Swiss were too clear-headed and too attached to the values upon which they built their national community to allow themselves to be unduly impressed or led astray. With a few exceptions – trouble-makers and delinquents – they did not waver. It would be as well to remember this: even before Hitler had reached the zenith of his power the various 'fronts' had already been devalued, discredited and finally wound up; before he had completed re-arming, everyone in Switzerland was rallying to the principle of national defence and endorsing the principles of democracy without reservation; at a time when he could still do us grievous harm, we were neutralising his agents and friends, heedless of his probable anger. And so this page of our history, which could have been the darkest of all, was in fact one of the brightest. The same thing will happen next time, when

other dangers arise, as long as we remain faithful to ourselves and our national reflexes are still as perfect.[34]

The 'troublemakers' and 'delinquents' are of course to be equated with all those undesirables who were 'purged' in the immediate post-war period. An 'epuration movement' (a term used by the Federal Council to signify a purge of Nazi sympathisers) did in fact take place after the defeat of the totalitarian states. In fact it was directed against two quite separate classes of people: on the one hand compromised aliens (National Socialists and fascists), and on the other the 'bad Swiss' (front members, traitors, spies and so on). Between 1945 and 1948, Switzerland as a whole expelled about 1,600 German and Italian nationals.[35] Meanwhile, the Federal Supreme Court conducted six trials of 102 Swiss citizens between 1946 and 1948, of whom 99 would be given various sentences for political treason, political or military intelligence activities, violation of military secrets, military service abroad, and such like. Notable names among them were P. Benz, G. Oltramare, P. Bonny, R. Fonjallaz, J. Barwirsch, H. Frei, F. Riedweg, T. Stadler, F. Burri and M.-L. Keller.[36] The 'Swiss National Socialists' were found guilty mainly on the basis of Article 266 of the Criminal Code (first paragraph), which makes it a criminal offence for any Swiss to 'commit an act tending to violate the independence of the Confederation or to jeopardise that independence or to cause a foreign power to intervene in the affairs of the Confederation in a manner such as to jeopardise the independence of the Confederation'. Found guilty of having violated the independence of the Confederation, the guilty parties aroused the general anger of the people and of public opinion, in a context totally obscured by Nazi-hunting. Proscribed and excluded from the national consensus, they seemed to fulfil a need for scapegoats and expiatory victims. At the same time, the official ideology declared itself free of any pro-fascist taint, and the public memory of the war was purged, as was clearly apparent in the Oltramare/Bonny/Fonjallaz trial which began on 10 November 1947. Thus we can see that justice, too, plays its part in the creation of memory, by legitimising the common moral attitudes. In the Switzerland of 1945, however, 'doing justice' did not mean meting out justice for genuine crimes but penalising errors which might have had serious consequences.

However, justice was sought only for the 'extremists'. In the case of the signatories of the petition of 15 November 1940 (known as the 'two hundred'), which called for the Swiss press (especially certain leading middle-class titles) to be brought into line, Swiss foreign policy to be adapted to the new order and Swiss withdrawal from the League of Nations, the Federal Council did not in fact see fit to bring any criminal proceedings. On 22 January 1946 it decided to publish the names of the 173 signatories, but at the same time offered an assurance that most of them were good patriots. Although the far-left press regarded it as the death-knell of the middle class, the 'affair of the two hundred' would have no affect on established representations. The conservative press had no problem in demonstrating the misleading nature of a generalisation that condemned the bourgeoisie as a whole, whereas everyone knew that there were strong threats of resistance running through bourgeois circles.[37]

THE COMMUNIST MEMORY

For historical reasons which there is no need to go into here, the aftermath of hostilities saw no confrontation in Switzerland comparable to that which occurred in France, where the 'Gaullist memory' and the 'communist memory' of the war clashed on virtually equal terms.[38] Our interest in far-left attitudes to the recent past can, however, be justified by the fact that despite the almost negligible electoral significance of the Swiss communists (seven seats out of 194 in the 1947 National Council), anti-communism did play a critical part in the political and cultural life of the country. Thus, in conservative public opinion, the communist arguments attracted an attention entirely disproportionate to their genuine strength. Furthermore, it is important to note the extent to which the press of the PST (*Parti suisse du travail*, or Swiss Labour Party), founded in October 1944, was obscured by the Second World War, leading us to refer to the true 'communist memory' as being the only one offered as an alternative to the official memory.

There were four dominant themes of the far left: first, that the Federal Council had pursued a pro-fascist policy; second, that its policy had been subservient to the Axis; third, that the ruling class had been inclined to collaborate with the enemy if attacked; and, fourth, that the communist militants alone could be described as an anti-fascist resistance.[39] The party line, therefore, was identical to that of communists in neighbouring countries, even though Switzerland's wartime situation had been very different. As in France, for example, Léon Nicole and Jean Vincent laid claim to an anti-fascist legitimacy and said nothing of the German–Soviet pact. Claiming collaboration in high places, the PST agitated tirelessly for a complete purge of the leadership. During the early years following the German surrender, feverish efforts were made to re-examine Swiss history from 1917 to 1945 in the light of the most widely shared sentiment of the time – the absolute demonisation of Nazism. In its articles, the far left cited economic collaboration between

Switzerland and Germany,[40] the part played by Marcel Pilet-Golaz, the so-called dependence on Berlin of the Department of Justice and Police, the consideration shown to Nazis resident in Switzerland, Guiseppe Motta's policy towards fascist Italy, the secret mediation by C.-J. Burckhardt between the British and Germans in 1941, the case of the far-right Colonel A. Fonjallaz and the condemnation of the militant socialist Paul Choux in 1936. With regard to General Guisan, the communist press adopted an ambivalent position, fluctuating between sincere respect for his 'resistance' and criticism – sometimes veiled, sometimes open – of a man who was, after all, the incarnation of militarism.[41]

During the years 1945–48, the war served a purpose for the communists which was unparalleled anywhere else. Its exploitation reflects something more than mere political expediency. The frequency of references to the past also reflects a desire to make a statement of identity. The PST was aware of being the only party 'born of the war'. From its point of view, the great conqueror of Hitler was the USSR, whose victory made the foundation of the party possible. The 'new men' of the PST believed they were marching in step with history and dreamed of a world reborn under the aegis of the great fraternal party, as had happened in some other countries. But it must be said that the communist memory would have a negligible impact on the consensus of this age. If the far left failed to understand the special features of the 'Swiss totalitarianism'[42] of 1939–45, any more than it could supply a satisfactory interpretation of the Nazi phenomenon, it often raised pertinent questions and disclosed certain facts that no one would address.[43]

THE DECOY

In the chaos of 1945/46 relating to the war, a great deal of mental confusion abounded. That is the most notable point to arise from an analysis of the various 'affairs' that made the headlines in the immediate post-war period. First came the internment affair, triggered by Radio Moscow on 16 June 1945, and concerning the problem of the Russian internees. Then, still on the subject of internment, came the scandal of the federal officials who had been guilty of fraud, abuse of trust and dishonest management practices. Next came the Hügel affair, much more serious in scope, dealing with the problem of the German–Swiss negotiations of 1940/41 whose purpose had been to smooth over the differences between Switzerland and Germany.[44] This scandal broke at the same time as that of the 'two hundred', and in its turn raised the delicate issue of the relations between a section of the Swiss leadership and certain circles in Germany. Next was the Masson case – brought about by Brigade-Colonel Roger Masson himself – which brought to light certain dubious aspects of the activities of the intelligence service.[45] Finally, although it was a minor matter, the 'affair of the barracks' also revealed the existence of trade in timber with Germany which involved various high-profile Swiss individuals, including the son of General Guisan.

In 1945/46 the Nazi and fascist regimes were regarded everywhere as the 'absolute evil'[46] and were perceived only in terms of moral indignation. In Switzerland, too, the debate reflected this intellectual climate: carried away by their own arguments, certain critics sometimes persuaded themselves that they had really fought against the Nazis. The conflicts revolved around terms like 'resistance', 'assimilation', 'collaboration', 'defeatism' and 'treason', following the example of countries where those phenomena had really occurred. The uncertainty that lies at the heart of Swiss history during the Second World War (what would Switzerland have done if it had been attacked?) lends contemporary controversy something of the appearance of a decoy. The right accused the left of having been slow to recognise the need for national defence, while the left accused the right of appeasement towards the Nazi, fascist and Pétainist regimes. The communists were portrayed as the fifth column of Moscow and the objective allies of the Third Reich from 1939 to 1941. As we have seen, they in their turn described the parties of the right as pro-fascist and pro-Hitler, while condemning the socialists for their participation in government during the war and their anti-democratic attitude to the banning of the communist party. The socialists, for their part, attacked the Catholic right, denouncing its adjustment to the new order and its lurches toward fascism. The latter, in turn, recalled the anti-Soviet positions adopted by the left before 1943.[47] Thus, certain obvious historical facts were denied: the middle-class press, for example, refused to admit the ambiguous attitude it had adopted in 1940. The Catholic conservative movement, for its part, which had indeed been notable for a highly receptive attitude to the language of the authoritarian states (those of Mussolini and Salazar rather than Hitler), nevertheless had no trouble fitting in with the new configuration that had arisen after 1945. Proudly aligning itself with the official myths, it found an easy outlet in fervent patriotism and anti-communism. One René Payot, editor and managing director of the *Journal de Genève*, and well known for the quality of his radio broadcasts from October 1941 onwards, though equally favourable before 1942/43 to 'solidarity for Germanic Europe' and hostile to General de Gaulle, caused no embarrassment whatever to conservative circles when he was awarded the title of 'hero' by the French resistance and the Belgian maquis.[48]

CONCLUSION

In the belligerent countries affected by the Second World War, the immediate post-war years were a period of reconstruction, when wounds were tended and governments endeavoured to rebuild their national communities. The nations were in mourning, sometimes for the effects of internal divisions, and governments found themselves compelled to build a memory based on reconciliation and reparation. The problem was to find a way of absorbing the past. In Switzerland, governing circles did not have to confront the same difficulties, but the memory of the war was nevertheless a not insignificant political issue. The problem was to prevent internal dissensions, to ensure the permanence of the army and to find a way of integrating the country into the new world order. Consequently, the memory that was constructed was subject to imperatives dictated as much by domestic as by foreign policy. In simple terms, the problem was to manufacture a past that met the needs of the present. There is no denying the fundamental role of the army in this process, and the extremely voluntaristic actions of Guisan. As he prepared to step down, he did everything possible – within the limitations imposed by a liberal and democratic state – to make the period of active service nothing less than a garden of remembrance.

In terms of public opinion, the first development of the period 1945–48 was the appearance of a collective need for explanations, following a period in which discussion had been unpatriotic. People were especially interested in the military threats directed against Switzerland, the relations between the Swiss and the Nazis, and the problems of espionage. It should also be noted that some people showed signs of discomfort, or even a guilty conscience. In 1944, for example, the writer Robert de Traz was unhappy at the idea that the Swiss had been left 'marginalised by a human race reborn through tragedy'.[49] A few years later the writer Max Frisch in his turn referred to the sad destiny of Switzerland, 'a void between war and peace, a sense of not being fully involved in events, a period of waiting, a sense of impotence behind a facade of contentment'.[50] Then came the 'affairs' – that 'social theatre', as the historian Pascal Ory called them – which gave rise to such heated controversies and a great deal of political activity. In general terms, the left evinced a desire to know more, while the right clearly felt it was time to 'turn the page'. And yet the socialists, who were relatively critical of the official explanation, were against an extraordinary meeting of the National Council devoted to the attitude of the Confederation in the Second World War. A proposal by the democrat P. Schmid-Ammann, published in *Die Nation* on 9 January 1946, failed to collect the necessary number of signatures.[51] Consequently, borrowing the happy turn of phrase used by Aram Mattioli, we can say that after a brief 'springtime of memory',[52] the 'national reflexes' (Pierre Béguin) regained the upper hand, even on the non-communist left.

At the conclusion of this first phase of memory, and organisation of memory, the image with which one is left is of a Switzerland which unanimously and steadfastly resisted any defeatist temptations, except for a brief period in 1940 when there was a slight moral weakening, fortunately corrected by General Guisan. A slight variation was notable, however, among the military, who were given to stressing the failure of the civil authority in 1940. In the turmoil of ideas that was apparent in the press, the official summary, from the press standpoint, needed to strengthen national unity and be so obvious that it had to be accepted. The result (an unscathed Switzerland) was widely quoted as an over-whelming argument. What answer could there be, in 1946, to those like Olivier Reverdin who declared: 'By their fruits shall ye know them'?[53]

Any tendency towards criticism was restricted both by mental attitudes (Nazi-hunting) and by the status of knowledge. There were subjects that could not be addressed for lack of sufficient information (such as the case of La Charité-sur-Loire) and others that were equally out of court for different reasons: the problem of the turning-back of the Jews does not seem to have been the subject of any particular denunciations in the immediate post-war period – of course, at that time people were unaware of the exact content of the 1938 agreements which introduced the 'J' stamp for the passports of German and Austrian Jews. Another factor, no doubt, is that at that time the full details of the Shoah were still unknown. It was a sign of the times that when the *Voix ouvrière* published an indictment in October 1946 of the former chief of police Heinrich Rothmund it accused him only of having denied entry to Switzerland to 'various categories of refugees'.[54] And the same paper confined itself to praising the production values, screenplay and performances of Leopold Lindtberg's famous film *The Last Chance*, without noting those aspects which nowadays seem to be open to criticism.[55] Nevertheless, the opposition media – the *Voix ouvrière* and *Vorwärts* (communist), *Volksrecht* (socialist), *Die Nation* (progressive) and such like – did challenge the received version of the story and referred to most of the 'grey areas'[56] of the 1930s and 1940s. But, as Switzerland moved forward fully into the climate of the Cold War, even the most moderate dissenting voices were immediately equated with those of the communists, and thus discredited.

In conclusion, we should recall one of the most significant aspects of the war memory in Switzerland during the period under examination – the concealment of the fascistic, reactionary and anti-democratic elements of the conservative ideology that had played a leading part in the spiritual national defence. Switzerland finally achieved its transition to peace as part of a continuing process, and with no serious damage – at least in the short term, though half a century later the hard facts that had been buried in 1945 were to bring about an unprecedented crisis. That continuity had initially been no certainty, but, once established, it would acquire the characteristics of something automatic and help to legitimise the official memory.

NOTES

1 Valuable bibliographical references will be found, for example, in '1945: Consequences and Sequels of the Second World War', proceedings of the international colloquium in Montreal on 2 September 1995, *Bulletin du Comité international d'histoire de la Seconde Guerre mondiale*, special edn, 27/28 May 1995, and in Georges Kantin, Gilles Manceron *et al.*, *Les échos de la mémoire. Tabous et enseignements de la Seconde Guerre mondiale*, Paris, 1981. Reference may also be made to the bibliography published in Henry Rousso and Eric Conan, *Vichy. Un passé qui ne passe pas*, Paris, 1994.
2 Hans Ulrich Jost, 'L'historiographie suisse sous l'emprise de la défense spirituelle', Historical Archive of the Canton of Ticino, 1984, pp. 299–306.
3 Henry Rousso, *Le syndrome de Vichy, de 1944 à nos jours*, Paris, 1990, p. 11.
4 The term was used, in particular, by Nicola Gallerano, 'Histoire et usage public de l'histoire', *Diogène*, 168, October–December 1994, pp. 87–106, and 'La memoria pubblica del fascismo e dell'antifascismo', in *Politiche della memoria*, Rome, 1993, pp. 2–7; Philippe Burrin, 'Vichy', in Pierre Nora (ed.), *Lieux de mémoire*, Vol. 3, 'Les France', Paris, 1992, pp. 321–45.
5 Henry Rousso, op. cit., p. 12.
6 Jacques Picard, 'Eine Politik der Erinnerung. Anmerkungen zu den schweizerischen Erinnerungsfeierlichkeiten zum Ende des Zweiten Weltkrieges in Europa', *Traverse*, 2, 1996, pp. 7–17.
7 Thus, for example, the publication of works on individuals who courageously disobeyed orders to save endangered lives might prompt us, retrospectively, to question the 'forgetting' of such acts since the end of the war (see Alexander Grossmann, *Nur das Gewissen: Carl Lutz und seine Budapester Aktion: Geschichte und Porträt*, Wald, 1986; Stefan Keller, *Délit d'humanité: l'affaire Grüninger*, Geneva, 1994; Theo Tschuy, *Carl Lutz und die Juden von Budapest*, Zurich, 1995). The same applies to the question, recently exhumed by historians, of the subsidiaries of Swiss companies that were active in Germany during the Second World War (see Sophie Pavillon, 'Du potage pour la Wehrmacht', 'Obus sans frontière', 'L'axe de l'aluminium', *Page deux*, June 1996, pp. 58–60, November 1996, pp. 50–3, December 1996, pp. 55–8).

8 Regarding the history of the present era, refer to the excellent work with a preface by Robert Frank, *Ecrire l'histoire du temps présent. En hommage à François Bédarida, Proceedings of the study day of the IHTP* (Institute of Contemporary History) (on 14 May 1992), Paris, 1993. See also Agnès Chauveau and Philippe Tétart (eds), *Questions à l'histoire des temps présents*, Paris, 1992.

9 The essence of what follows has been taken from my licentiateship dissertation given at Geneva University in 1995, 'La Suisse face à la Seconde Guerre mondiale. Emergence et construction d'une mémoire publique 1945–1948', Journal of the Geneva Historical and Archaeological Society, 1997.

10 Edouard de Haller to Max Petitpierre, 16 March 1945, in Swiss Diplomatic Documents, Vol. 15, Berne, 1992, pp. 996–9.

11 See, for example, Alain Dieckhoff, *Rescapés du Génocide. L'action Musy: une opération de sauvetage de Juifs européens en 1944–1945*, Basle, 1994.

12 Regarding the National Gift, Jean-Claude Favez, 'Le Don suisse et la politique étrangère: quelques réflexions', in Barbara Roth-Lochner, Marc Neuenschwander and François Walter (eds), *Des archives à la mémoire: mélanges d'histoire politique, religieuse et sociale offerts à Louis Binz*, Geneva Historical and Archaeological Society, Geneva, 1995.

13 D. Secrétan to C. Gorgé, 21 May 1946, Federal Archive (FA), E 2001 (E) 1/98.

14 FA, E 2001 (E) 1/98.

15 Letter from D. Secrétan to C.-J. Burckhardt, 15 September 1947, and letter from D. Secrétan to A. de Pury, 3 September 1947, FA, E 2001 (E) 1/98.

16 Draft probably compiled by Daniel Secrétan for those approached about participating in the White Paper, undated (late December 1945), unsigned (FA, E 2001 (E) 1/98). For additional information acquired with a view to the publication of the official documents, see Sacha Zala, 'Gebändigte Geschichte. Amtliche Historiographie und ihr Malaise mit der Neutralität, 1945–1961', Swiss Federal Archive files, Vol. 7, Berne, 1998 and his chapter in this volume.

17 Jakob Tanner, 'Or et Granit. La défense nationale et les liens économiques entre la Suisse et le IIIème Reich durant la Seconde Guerre mondiale', *Annuelles*, 1, 1990, p. 45.

18 Report by R. Frick to H. Guisan, 29 September 1945, FA, E 5795/550.

19 Luc van Dongen, 'La Suisse en 1945 et l'enjeu représenté par l'armée, Une Suisse sans armée', *Organe d'échanges et de débats du GSsA*, 26, June 1995, pp. 19–20.

20 Erich Gysling, Mario König and Michael T. Ganz, *1945 – Die Schweiz im Friedensjahr*, Zurich, 1995, 136 pp, and Mario König, '"Front machen gegen einseitigen Siegestaumel". Ein Brief an den Bundesrat, April 1945', *Traverse*, 2, 1995, pp. 122–31.

21 *Gazette de Lausanne*, 9 May 1945.

22 H. Guisan to E. von Steiger, 3 June 1945, FA, E 5795/380.

23 Letter from J. Borel to H. Guisan, 1 June 1945, FA, E 5795/380.

24 *Le Courrier de Genève*, 20 August 1945.

25 Order of the day for 8 May 1945, in H.-R. Kurz, *Cent ans d'armée suisse*, Lugano/Porza, 1981, p. 160.

26 'Rapport de Jegenstorf du 19. 8. 1945', in Henri Guisan, *Rapport du Général Guisan à l'Assemblée fédérale sur le service actif*, Berne, 1946, p. 227.

27 In the sense used by Eric Hobsbawm and T. Ranger, *Invention of Tradition*, Cambridge, 1983.

28 This report was published on 27 December 1946 and debated by the National Council on 11 March 1947, but it seems to have caused no great stir in public opinion at the time of its appearance (because of Christmas?). So I will

deliberately say no more about it in this chapter.

29 'Rapport du Conseil fédéral à l'Assemblée fédérale concernant le rapport du général', Berne, 7 January 1947, p. 5.

30 Willi Gautschi, op. cit., p. 671.

31 *Feuille fédérale*, 1946, I, pp.1ff., II, pp. 165ff., II, p. 203ff., II, p. 1045ff.

32 Bulletin sténographique du conseil national, 5 June 1945, p. 313.

33 Transcript of proceedings of the National Council, 1946, II, p. 262.

34 *Gazette de Lausanne*, 9 January 1946.

35 'Rapport du Conseil fédéral à l'Assemblée fédérale concernant l'activité antidémocratique', supplement to Parts I and II, 25 July 1946, pp. 1,046–55, and 'Rapport du Conseil fédéral sur sa gestion, années 1945–1947'.

36 'Rapport du Conseil fédéral à l'Assemblée fédérale sur les poursuites engagées contre des Suisses nationaux socialistes pour atteinte à l'indépendance de la Confédération, 2. 12. 1948', in *Feuille fédérale*, Vol. III, 1948, pp. 997–1,081. Regarding the case of a Swiss who had been a member of the Waffen-SS, see Linus Reichlin, *Kriegsverbrecher Wipf, Eugen. Schweizer in der Waffen-SS, in deutschen Fabriken und an den Schreibtischen des Dritten Reiches*, Zurich, 1994.

37 Regarding the 'two hundred', see Gerhart Wäger, *Die Sündenböcke der Schweiz. Die Zweihundert im Urteil der geschichtlichen Dokumente 1940–1946*, Olten, 1971.

38 Pierre Nora, 'Gaullistes et communistes', in Pierre Nora (ed.), *Lieux de mémoire*, Vol. III, 'Les France', Paris, 1992, pp. 347–93.

39 I refer the reader to the *Voix ouvrière* for 1945–46, in particular the issues of 22 and 26 January 1946, 9 and 19 February 1946, 28 May 1946 and 27 July 1946.

40 See, for example, the comments in the *Voix ouvrière* regarding the report by the American Senator Kilgore (12 January 1946) or the Washington Accord (May 1946).

41 See, for example, the *Voix ouvrière* of 15 March 1946 and the *Vorwärts*, 3 May 1946.

42 Georg Kreis, 'Die Schweiz und der zweite Weltkrieg. Bilanz und bibliographischer Überblick nach 30 Jahren', in *La seconda guerra mondiale nella prospettiva storica a trent anni dalla epilogo*, Como, 1977, pp. 219–41.

43 It should be noted that the communists were not the only – and certainly not the most lucid – critical voices raised immediately after the war. For example, a more detailed study of the case of the newspaper *Die Nation* and of certain Christian or religious socialist clubs is still needed (L. Ragaz, M. Wolff and so on). Mario König, 'Befangenes Gedenken. Die Schweiz im Rückblick auf den Zweiten Weltkrieg 1945 und 1995', *Bulletin de l'Académie suisse des sciences humaines et sociales*, 1, 1995, pp. 27–32.

44 SS member Klaus Hügel, who styled himself president of the Stuttgart Chamber of Commerce but was in fact working for a dubious organisation, and who from 1942 onwards was an important agent in the German intelligence service, had a number of conversations during 1940 and 1941 with conservative and pro-German officers and representatives of the national press, industry and capital. These, according to Edgar Bonjour, resulted in no specific action. Pilet-Golaz's department had taken no part in the meetings but had been briefed on them and had arranged for visas to be issued to two Germans.

45 Masson, the head of the Swiss intelligence service, had met SS General Walter Schellenberg (his German opposite number from 1942 onwards) on several occasions. In a sensational interview given to a British newspaper, the chief of intelligence asserted that Schellenberg's intervention with Hitler had saved Switzerland from a German attack in March 1943. In fact, this threat was a decoy intended to deceive the Allies. Immediately afterwards, the public learned that

General Guisan had also met Schellenberg in 1943.

46 François Furet, *Le passé d'une illusion. Essai sur l'idée communiste au XXe siècle*, Paris, 1995, p. 410.

47 For the quarrel between socialists and conservative Catholics, see Paul Schmid-Ammann, *Der politische Katholizismus*, Berne, 1945; Martin Rosenberg, *Wer machte in Anpassung?*, Berne, 1945 (collection of articles published in the Lucerne newspaper *Vaterland*) and *'Wir lassen uns nicht manövrieren!' Tatsachen und Feststellungen zum Thema 'Politischer Katholizismus'*, Berne, 1947.

48 On René Payot, see Michel Caillat, *René Payot, un regard ambigu sur la guerre (1939–1942)*, Geneva, 1998.

49 Quoted in Patrice Favre, *La Suisse après la Seconde Guerre mondiale (1944–1946). Politique extérieure et opinion publique*, Fribourg, 1979, p. 44.

50 Quoted in Anne-Françoise Praz, *Du Réduit à l'ouverture. La Suisse de 1940 à 1949*, Prilly, 1995, p. 173.

51 The parliamentary Socialist Party then numbered 54 national councillors. Just 47 signatures would have been enought to call an extraordinary session.

52 Aram Mattioli, *Zwischen Demokratie und totalitärer Diktatur. Gonzague de Reynold und die Tradition der autoritären Rechten in der Schweiz*, Zurich, 1994, p. 291.

53 'People with short memories, to whom we should be grateful that we did not entrust our destiny at the critical moment, are saying that we should have banned all the organisations of the National Socialist Party, expelled suspects on the spot, and recalled the diplomats who were conspiring against us. We could also have declared war on Germany and ordered the Swiss army to force the Rhine crossings! By their fruits shall ye known them. The Federal Council's policy of caution saved our country from invasion' (*Journal de Genève*, 10 January 1946).

54 *Voix ouvrière*, 3 October 1946.

55 *Voix ouvrière*, 13 July 1945.

56 Jakob Tanner has compiled a non-exhaustive list of these 'grey areas': the acceptance of the front members in 1940, Pilet-Golaz's speech of 25 June 1940, the hopes of German victory nourished by some Swiss financial and industrial circles, censorship of the press, the banning of communists, economic relations with Germany, the Nazi gold problem and so on (see Jakob Tanner, *Bundeshaushalt, Währung und Kriegswirtschaft. Eine finanzsoziologische Analyse der Schweiz zwischen 1938 und 1953*, Zurich, 1986, p. 316).

13

The 1946 National Public Survey as a Democratic Challenge[1]

NIKLAUS STETTLER

> What will now, in the transition phase from war to peace, be decided
> on and entered into or perhaps also forgone, will without a doubt
> govern not just the immediate future but also, as we may hope but,
> under certain circumstances may also fear, a very long period to come.
> The key question is: Who will determine the direction, who will be
> active now? We see all too well today that the forces of sedition are at
> work rather than the forces that sustain the state … It is this insight
> that has prompted a small group of students to ask what they can and
> must do for the maintenance of our domestic order.[2]

With these words the 22-year-old law student Andreas Brunner[3]
introduced a hectographed brochure which he sent to a select group of
influential government, business and military leaders, including
Federal Councillor von Steiger and General Guisan. In this brochure,
Brunner outlined the idea of a 'popular survey', a national public
opinion poll in which all recipients of ration stamps would be
encouraged to express their wishes for the country's future. In this
manner, he wanted to help overcome the political apathy he felt he
detected in the general public. At the same time, a number of responsible men would draft a new federal constitution. The results of the
national public opinion survey and the draft constitution would then
guide the 500 men he considered the nation's most important in
conducting a so-called 'elite discussion' to iron out political differences
and prepare a new national consensus. Brunner was convinced that the
public at large would welcome the result of this 'elite discussion', thanks
to the rekindled political interest, and that it could serve as a blueprint
for future action in the post-war era.

Brunner's proposal met with an astonishing response. Most of
the recipients invited the student for a talk and urged him to abandon
the nationwide survey idea. After protracted efforts involving difficult
negotiations, Brunner succeeded in getting the *Neue Helvetische*

Gesellschaft (NHG) to sponsor his project. In February 1946, 2.5 million questionnaires of the *Volksumfrage 1946* were sent out by mail. At the same time, the *Institut Suisse de l'opinion publique* (ISOP, Lausanne) conducted a representative survey. Two years later, the results of both surveys were published in the brochure *Die Schweiz hält durch* (Switzerland perseveres) with a total print run of 70,000 copies.[4]

With the two surveys, a new instrument was introduced into the democratic process. Never before in the history of Switzerland had men and women been questioned in a consultative manner on political issues. Never before had a representative poll been conducted on a Swiss-wide basis. The opinion survey approach elicited opposition in two fundamental respects. First, numerous commentators wondered whether it would not undermine the unity of the people (the *Volksganzen*) by indicating the existence of different groups holding different opinions. Secondly, leading politicians expressed reservations in principle about polling the people. Already in 1942, the liberal expert on public law Zaccaria Giacometti warned that Switzerland had become 'an authoritarian state with totalitarian tendencies'.[5] Even after the disappearance of the external threat, official Switzerland was very reluctant to dismantle the rule-by-decree regime (*Notrechstsregime*), which had mothballed the instruments of direct democracy and reduced the Parliament to a minor role. Once the war was over, it was hardly possible to justify the approach of relying on 'urgent Federal Council decrees' any longer. But for most politicians, a return to democracy appeared problematical. Thus, the popular initiative campaign 'For a Return to Democracy' launched by federalists from the canton of Vaud was opposed by all the major parties and was approved in a nationwide vote in 1949 by the barest of margins. With the appearance of the national public opinion survey, the issue of how much significance should be accorded to public opinion, or what authority should be accorded to the opinions of the 'elite' – which was invariably a self-styled elite – attained a practical dimension. The 'people' appeared to have obtained a voice.

Politicians and journalists thus took the occasion of the opinion survey to express their concept of democracy.[6] Thus, far from being a theoretical exchange, the controversy over the national public opinion survey soon engendered a fundamental discussion of democracy. It is the aim of this chapter to analyse the controversy, drawing on documents from the literary estate of the *Volksumfrage*'s executive director, Andreas Brunner, and pertinent internal ministerial files of some of the federal councillors. In addition, Brunner's collection of newspaper clippings, including letters to the editors, makes it possible to track the public response to this debate.

Despite the obvious importance of the 'democracy issue', historians have accorded it just secondary significance in their treatment of the post-war period. Even the debate accompanying the Vaud initiative has yet to receive appropriate study. To be sure, in some more recent accounts dealing with the vacuum of the immediate post-war era (*le trou de l'immédiat après-guerre* (Herbert Lüthy), the topic of democracy is at least given peripheral treatment, with widely divergent assessments. All the studies emphasise the temporarily broad scope for action in domestic and foreign policy that arose following the first decisive setbacks encountered by the German *Wehrmacht* in 1942/43, a latitude which lasted until 1948–50 but which was hardly exploited by the Federal Council.[7] Whereas the overall social ambience was marked by a sense of new beginnings, official Switzerland sought to calm, to postpone – to survive. As a result, the already meagre pool of ideas for the post-war period gave way to stagnation.[8]

In his study on the political impact on Switzerland of the coming of peace, Mario König concludes that the policies of the Federal Council in the year hostilities ceased were decisively governed by concern that a gap could arise between the authorities and the population. The Federal Council feared its own populace, as the latter might seek to bring suspected collaborators to justice. Calls for resignation were directed in particular at Brunner's favourite discussion partner, Federal Councillor von Steiger.[9]

Like König, Peter Hug also emphasises the authorities' fear of the people. In a study of post-war foreign policy, he points out that incumbent foreign minister Petitpierre would have been able to pursue a more active policy only in concert with reform-minded forces in Switzerland. Militating against such an alliance, however, were both clashes in outlook and the fear of having to accept a pluralist Switzerland.[10] Von Steiger's situation was not much different. If we accept this line of reasoning, then it was primarily the distrust of the people that obstructed a more activist approach to the democracy issue.

Dwelling more on the role of parliament and less on the relationship between the people and the authorities, Georg Kreis comes to other conclusions. Examining primarily the party and programmatic statements relating to the democracy issue, he concludes that the momentum of the anti-parliamentarian campaign had already begun to wane in 1941. From that point on, the ground rules of the parliamentary system were hardly challenged any more.[11] He thus sees the democracy issue as having been resolved in principle even before the end of the war. Thus, the dismantling of the *Notrechtsregime* was little more than a necessary formal correction.

In complete contrast to König and Hug, Kurt Imhof and Heinz

Kleger emphasise the anti-totalitarian tenor of party propaganda rather than the totalitarian tendencies of the political system in post-war Switzerland. In their studies of the press, they demonstrate that the 'spiritual defense of the nation' (*geistige Landesverteidigung*) was based until 1948–50 on an 'anti-totalitarian semantics of community'. Until the start of the Cold War, this was marked by a coalition of the centre. Only in the Catholic People's Party does Imhof see remnants of the anti-democratic positions deriving from the 'Complete Revision Debate' of the 1930s.[12]

These divergent interpretations are, not least, expressions of the authors' different views of what constitutes democracy. Hug's contention, however, that 'official' Switzerland resisted the insight that, in Switzerland, too, a pluralistic society had taken hold, in which divergent positions co-existed, ought to be undisputed.[13] This non-acceptance of the pluralist reality was part and parcel of an understanding of democracy that most people espoused. Following a look at the public opinion surveys and Brunner's Justice Group (*Gerechtigkeitsgruppe*), in which the idea for the national public opinion poll was born, this will be examined at greater length.

THE SURVEYS

In February 1946, more than 2.5 million questionnaires were sent to all households in the name of the NHG to give men and women, young people and adults, the opportunity to participate in the 1946 national public opinion survey (*Volksumfrage 1946*). At the heart of the survey was the so-called 'open question', in which respondents were to answer in 50 words what they 'personally considered the most important issue for the future of the country'. In addition, opinions were requested on the issues of women's suffrage, economic policy, federalism, national defence, neutrality policy (or joining the UN), and the preamble to the Constitution.

Concurrently, the NHG commissioned the ISOP in Lausanne to conduct a representative survey that polled 3,000 selected respondents with a similar set of questions. Here, too, those polled were asked their opinions on women's suffrage, economic policy, federalism, and joining the UN. In addition, the ISOP poll asked questions relating to industrial relations and/or job satisfaction.

The two surveys differed, particularly with respect to methodology. The NHG expected about half-a-million people to return the questionnaires of the national public opinion poll. Thus, the nationwide survey would be able to reflect public opinion only with certain systematic distortions. But this did not bother the NHG, as it was not interested in ascertaining majority relationships. It was looking for 'the best answers'. The ISOP study, by contrast, sought to form a quantitative picture of public opinion.

Because of the inadequate canvassing methods of the national public opinion poll, the results of the two surveys varied markedly. Thus, in the national survey, 30.2 per cent of the responding women sought full suffrage, while only 16.5 per cent did so in the representative sample. Despite this, the NHG gave more emphasis to the results of the popular survey than to the ISOP study. This weighting bias was grounded in an understanding of democracy that was particularly just in the eyes of Brunner. Brunner's concept of a just democracy was essentially informed by the debates conducted in the so-called Justice Group (*Gerechtigkeitsgruppe*) and its predecessors, the Oxford Group Movement and the *Gotthardbund*.

THE JUSTICE GROUP (*GERECHTIGKEITSGRUPPE*)

Andreas Brunner sent his brochure on a national public opinion poll to numerous leading politicians, including a number he knew from the Justice Group. This group had been bringing together various influential Protestant men – scholars, senior civil servants, labour-union leaders, and entrepreneurs – since the summer of 1944, to discuss political issues. For the participants who included, among others, the presidents of the VSM (Swiss Association of Machinery Manufacturers) and the SMUV (Swiss Metalworkers and Watchmakers Union), Schindler and Ilg, and two future federal councillors, Schaffner and Wahlen, the group's linchpin was the book *Gerechtigkeit* (justice, righteousness) by theologian Emil Brunner, Andreas Brunner's father.[14]

A majority of the members of the Justice Group had already become acquainted during the 1930s in the so-called Oxford Group Movement, of which Emil Brunner was the leading Swiss representative.[15] The Missionary Movement, founded in 1921 by the American preacher Frank Buchman, had made it its objective to fight mass atheism in the United States and Western Europe. Young academics in particular were active in it, and, in meditative conversations, learned to commit themselves to the 'leadership of the Holy Spirit'. This 'doctrine of leadership' replaced the exegetic approach to the Bible traditionally practiced in the (established) church. The Oxford Group's adherents were convinced that the 'synagogical understanding of the Bible' in the church ultimately led to the 'total state'.[16]

Numerous Oxford Group members were also politically active. Close to the National Socialist Party (NSDAP), Buchman strove to achieve 'influence through flattery on Hitler' in Germany. Brunner criticised this approach, as he was convinced the 'Christianisation of politics' had to emanate from the individual.[17] In this way, 'the new life would attain clear forms in relations between employer and employee, in the civic life of the city and the country, in relations among the parties, and even among nations'.[18] To make this a reality, a number of Oxford Group members participated in the establishment of the *Gotthardbund* in 1940. This was to become a vehicle to help mould the spiritual defence of the nation (*geistige Landesverteidigung*). However, their conciliatory openness towards, among others, the National Socialists, often led to their rejection by other resistance organisations.[19]

As the tide of the war turned, the *Gotthardbund* lost clout. Now, a number of Oxford Group adherents got together in the Justice Group to ponder the new dangers. They worried that, with the imminent defeat of Germany, workers could become increasingly disoriented and the appeal of the Swiss communists would grow.

They attributed the crisis of orientation to the 'dogma of equality' stemming from the Enlightenment. Since the French Revolution, it was only possible for the individual to discover – 'based on his creaturely equality and inequality' – to what estate he belonged in society in the ranks of the army. But if he failed to achieve this 'recognition', he would be deprived of his sense of identity. Then all would strive to achieve the same and individual differences would be levelled. This 'massification' appeared destined to conjure up (or so was the perception) the threat of social clashes.[20]

To ward off such a scenario, the members of the Justice Group wanted to provide workers with a Christian education in plant settings (*Betriebsgemeinschaften*) which would again provide them with the necessary orientation.[21] At the same time, they sought a 'Christianisation of politics' and, for that, they found the requisite political ethics in Brunner's volume *Gerechtigkeit*, which quickly became the 'scripture' of political Protestantism.

Although the members of the Justice Group were often of divergent opinions on specific political issues, they shared important basic convictions: the condemnation of the Enlightenment, which was seen as the root cause of the destruction of the just order, and the belief in a divine order, in which each person was accorded a preordained position. Convinced that this order was the true desire of all, they wanted to work together to establish this organic society, which was to be based on authority and obedience.[22]

CRITICISM OF THE *NOTRECHTSREGIME* AND THE CONSTITUTION

To bring about this society, the Justice Group sought a new constitution. Their ideas must be seen in the context of a debate on the complete revision of the Federal Constitution, which – following the rejection of an initiative to this effect in 1935 – suddenly became very topical again just before the end of the war.[23]

As Georg Kreis has demonstrated, the constitutional debate had acquired a new twist around 1941. As attacks on parliamentarianism became muted, the demands for better harmonisation of the Constitution with political reality moved to the centre of the debate.[24] With the declaration in 1943 by LDP member Oeri in the Council of States that he sensed 'an increasingly vocal call for more justice and a new constitution', the debate over a complete overhaul of the Constitution became more clearly defined.[25] Against the background of widespread fear of the communists, this now centred on the areas of economic and financial legislation and the desire to establish a binding, uniform constitution. The youth wing of the Liberals, which had spearheaded the drive for such a revision in the 1930s, now adopted demands from the new structural reform programme of the Social Democrats into their forays with the aim of anticipating possible social confrontations. Although the parent party had some sympathy for these demands, the *Freisinn* (Radicals) did not support a total revision for fear the debates would have a polarising effect. Nonetheless, *Der Bund* saw this as evidence of a clear leftward trend, especially in light of the uncertainty which previously prevailed on economic and social policy issues.[26] The Social Democrats of Basle also read the situation this way. In May 1946, they endorsed an initiative by the Young Liberals seeking a cantonal initiative (*Standesinitiative*) for a total revision.[27]

The members of the Justice Group attempted to counter the reform proposals of the Young Liberals by presenting their own, elitist democracy proposals. The group discussed the Constitution issue for the first time in February 1945. Andreas Brunner, who participated in the meeting as secretary, would later report that it was the position taken by Arnold Muggli, section head for rationing in Switzerland's wartime food administration authority, which prompted him to launch the public opinion survey. In the minutes, he recorded Muggli's remarks as follows:

> What it [i.e. Swiss politics] needs in most areas is a uniform doctrine, and the basic policy line ... the absence of which leads to one's losing sight of any and all strategic goals ... We must press the demand for 'tactics in the strategy'. One must ask the question whether the

fulfilment of this demand is not thwarted by a flawed state structure. ... The Federal Council is ... merely the administrator of 'Switzerland Inc.', which has introduced an uncertainty factor into its actions ... As we need a genuine government and a parliament that truly provides leadership, the constitution should be reconstructed in a manner making the government capable of acting and the parliament capable of setting the course.[28]

Brunner expanded the minutes by recording the concerns of his father that the 'people' could 'gradually be infected by alien thinking' if it proved impossible to tap the pool of the unconscious, the 'distinctly Swiss heritage of basic principles'. He cites Werner Kägi, a specialist in public law, as follows: 'Now, at a time when mass politics are being conducted, ... it would be desirable to draw on the capital of sub-conscious principles to counter the dangerous and un-Swiss concept that democracy can be equated with the power of the majority. It must be linked to an acknowledgment of an elite ...'.

For the young Andreas Brunner, these statements contrasted favour-ably with the sombre picture he had conceived of post-war Switzerland. He was convinced that Switzerland was heading for a profound economic and spiritual crisis, one which could only be averted if 'not the egoistic aspirations of the individual, but the needs of the community ... were to be the guiding factors for the actions of the individual in this community'. This, however, would necessitate self-restraint, which could hardly be expected from the common citizen.[29]

He already envisioned 'the people' as entering a state of dissolution. In his eyes, the people were caught in the grip of political apathy due to a profound 'crisis of orientation', which would undermine democ-racy. At the same time, the younger generation yearned for a new vision, one which, at the time, only the communists were offering.[30] The imminent end of press censorship appeared to him only to aggravate the crisis of orientation, and with it the susceptibility to communist visions and the 'massification' of society, because it would be possible to publish anything, whether substantial or irrelevant, while the faculties of judgement would be absent.[31] Finally, he was convinced that the national councillors, with their inability to conduct problem-solving debates, would discredit politics. Thus, with the end of the war, Swiss solidarity was in serious danger, caught between the apathy of the people and party politics. 'What had threatened us from abroad during the war now threatened from within', he concluded.[32] The threats that Brunner identified were standard arguments in the revived debate about a total revision of the Federal Constitution. To a high degree, his assessments were consonant with those of the Catholic–conservative camp, which spoke ominously of the 'decline of Western civilisation'.[33]

From this perspective, the shift in the discussion of the Constitution, described by Kreis, did not represent a departure from authoritarian perceptions of democracy. Werner Kägi, seen by Kreis as an important figure in the new debate, not only called for a return to the Constitution, but was also a vehement opponent of what he called the 'un-Swiss majority-rules principle'. In a similar vein, Muggli's call for effective government, at a time when the Federal Council's willingness to act was no doubt low, but not its ability to act, and at a time when the role of parliament had long been diminished to that of a bystander, can be seen as a resurrection of the old anti-parliamentarianism. Here, the criticism of the *Notrechtsregime* included the existing constitution and could hardly be reconciled with democratic principles.

The following paragraphs examine the extent to which these advocates of a return to the Constitution – especially in their call for democratic procedures – subscribed to authoritarian concepts.

The idea of a council of wise men (*Rat der Weisen*), above all partisan bickering, served as the counterweight to the criticism of the *Notrechts-regime* and of parliamentarianism. Members of the Justice Group conceived of an 'entity of the whole people' (*Einheit des Volksganzen*) which was to find political expression in ideals that were free of conflicts of interest.[34] The 'majority-rules doctrine' (*Majorzdoktrin*), as Brassel labelled this concept, construed 'the people' as a distinct abstract entity with a will of its own, which politicians were supposed to implement. In this way, power struggles and conflicts of interest were to be filtered out. A plurality of opinions would exist for only so long as the right way to implement the will of the people had not yet been found. The scope for differences of opinion was accordingly narrow. Despite its anti-liberal content, this concept had a long tradition in the annals of Swiss radicals.[35]

Building on this tradition, the Justice Group wanted to launch a new Constitution. But it did not confine itself to giving parliament a new role. It foresaw an overhaul of the entire structure of the state. In its eyes, the whole government would have to be 'refounded'; for the Justice Group, the idea that the Constitution should only regulate the relationship of the individual to the state was a mistake. Instead, the individual was to be seen as a part of various communities, and the Constitution ought to define the functions 'man – citizen – family – church – school – vocational group – political party – army – community – Canton – and Confederation'.[36] Such a state – based on communities – should be free of the influence of special interests and incompetent voters. In accordance with a far-reaching principle of 'subsidiarity' (exercise of power at the lowest possible level), large areas of political action would be delegated to non-governmental, depoliticised organisations.[37] Borrowing from corporatist concepts of government in the 1930s, economic policy, for instance, was to be delegated to an economic council composed of representatives of the various professions and trade groups.[38]

The members of the Justice Group publicised their concept of the state widely, but with hardly any response. Only in the *National-Zeitung* did Adolf Gasser warn that Brunner's views were perilously close to the anti-democratic thinking of Gonzaque de Reynolds.[39] But Gasser's sense of democratic outrage remained an isolated outburst. All the same, members of the Justice Group refrained from putting forth specific recommendations for a revision of the Constitution. Even Kägi, the most aggressive among them, toned down his criticism of the Constitution by emphasising that 'it's not a matter of reforming paragraphs. The struggle for the renewal of the basic foundations of our commonweal is first and foremost an educational task.'[40] The Constitution as an orientation aid for 'the people' remained the ultimate objective in the struggle for spiritual unity, one in which relativism had no place alongside inviolable tenets. In his youthful enthusiasm, Andreas Brunner did not confine his efforts to this. He sought ways to bring about the revision and, in the final analysis, chose an instrument which ultimately contradicted his objective.

THE NATIONAL PUBLIC OPINION SURVEY

Brunner wanted to act against the looming menace of 'massification', paralysing fatalism and the politicisation of all domains of life. This appeared imperative to him if the influence of the extreme left was to be curbed. That was why, together with a group of students, he devised his plan to maintain domestic order. The plan foresaw the forging of a new constitution in two phases of 'elite work'. This constitution would reflect the 'basic heritage of Swiss principles' and could represent a kind of 'political catechism'.

In this endeavour, the public opinion survey would serve to shake the populace out of its apathy. To the students, this appeared to be a *sine qua non* for a favourable reception of the draft constitution. They were convinced that a unitary will of the people existed and that, once this will were formulated and recognised as such, the squabbling of the parties could be overcome. Hence they prefaced their campaign with the slogan: 'And who really knows what the people want? Has anyone asked the people? Nobody! That's why we are asking all of you, the whole people, this question: What do the people want?' This was to be explored by means of the instrument known as a public opinion survey, with the maximum possible respondent base in a manner similar to those conducted by the Gallup Institute in the USA.[41] If the respondents subscribed to the proposed solution of 'cooperation – despite different opinions!'[42] they had a chance that their answers would be presented to the group deliberating the Constitution. However, only the best (answers) – at most 3 per cent – would be considered, although the others might be subjected to statistical evaluation.

And, while 'the people' would be pondering what was most important for Switzerland, the framers of the Constitution would be busily working on the political catechism. This small group of creative thinkers (for instance, the Justice Group) would have to remain independent of public office and public pressure. Once they had prepared the catechism, they were to insert a number of replies from the poll into the text.[43]

That would be followed by a second phase of 'elite work' as the draft would be subjected to a 'public comment' process. In the first call for a public opinion survey, this was outlined as follows: 'We all want to, so to say, sit down at a table and write down in this book "What do the people want?"'[44] This 'we all', however, referred only to the 500 (later 300) people identified by the students as the most important individuals in Switzerland, to wit, 'the elite'. In small, politically mixed working groups, they would deliberate the catechism.[45] The overriding objective was unanimity. To achieve this, the select few would have to take part in 'workshops' resembling the military postings during the war. Once the 'Five Hundred' were convinced they had achieved a consensus, they would act to prevent opposition from arising in their own organisations.

Funding for this campaign would come from the sale of the catechism. Already in the autumn of 1945, the SMUV and a number of sizeable companies had made commitments to acquire 50,000 copies. They planned to present the volume to members or employees. Numerous further subscriptions were expected as the survey progressed. The persuasive efforts of the 'elite members' appeared to guarantee acceptance of the catechism. The catechism would also arouse major interest because 'the people' would seek to find their own contributions in it. Having been confronted with a particular major issue during the opinion survey, respondents would now be able to read the right answer. And so the campaign promised to make a serious contribution against 'massification'.

But Brunner's discussions with influential personalities proved sobering. Only the plans for 'elite work' met with a favourable response. The general, for instance, wanted to see the formation of 'an irresistible bloc of all nationally minded forces, if possible with the inclusion of loyal Social Democrats, against the seditious efforts of the Communists, inspired from abroad and directed against our free and democratic order'.[46]

For most of the discussion partners, however, the public deliberations on the Constitution and, with it, the national opinion survey, remained unacceptable. Federal Councillor von Steiger urgently counselled the abandonment of the plan. Pro Helvetia, Brunner's organisational partner of choice, refused to serve as sponsor. And Brunner's attempt to get the survey accredited as an official follow-up activity of the *Sektion Heer und Haus* (unit in charge of troop information) had just as little success.[47]

Ultimately, to obtain the support of the NHG, Brunner had to promise that he would portray the opinion poll solely as an instrument for 'sensitising the people to national objectives and warding off foreign propaganda'. The revision of the Constitution, however, remained the goal of the NHG's commission on the national public opinion survey, in which members of the Justice Group held a majority.[48] Only after the disappointingly low rate of questionnaire return became evident did the group of people, whom I will call the 'initiators', abandon the idea of using the public opinion poll as a vehicle for popularising a new constitution.[49]

At about the same time, the NHG commission redesigned the opinion poll. The commission members were convinced that the question asking about the 'highest priority for the future of the country' would overtax respondents. In order to nevertheless encourage reflection among the respondents, they prefaced this question with six 'simpler' questions dealing with women's suffrage, national defence, federalism, economic policies, the neutrality issue and the preamble to the Federal Constitution.

But, as innocuous as these six 'entry-level' questions were originally intended to be, they became quite important as the project progressed. Seeking to achieve an initial educational impact just by posing the questions, the initiators tried to formulate them so that every man and woman would easily find the right answers. Together with a number of politicians from the centre-right camp who – like themselves – were convinced that they represented political truth bereft of partisan interests, they posed questions such as: 'Do you favour large-scale nationalisation of the economy?' and 'Should the autonomy of the cantons be further curtailed?' These formulations meant that, at the very least, many Social Democrats would be unable to subscribe to these political truths. The suggestive nature of these questions so angered SP Federal Councillor Nobs – he charged that 'the reactionary political and economic intentions' of the campaign 'were so blatantly evident' – that he withdrew his previous support.[50] With that, the Social Democratic involvement, and the purpose of the 'elite work', appeared endangered. Konrad Ilg pointed out that he himself would be unable to make up the loss, as he was isolated within the trade union federation and his party.[51] Despite this, the initiators failed to seek further Social Democratic support and even spurned the offer by SPS president Oprecht to rephrase the questions.[52]

Unexpectedly, the project ran into opposition at the plenary assembly of the NHG. Along with the formulation of the questions, the survey method itself came in for criticism because it did not actually permit the determination of public opinion. This objection struck the initiators as fully extraneous to their intent and they construed it as stubbornly clinging to the Gallup poll technique.[53] From the outset, they had never had the intention of ascertaining public opinion. They had always viewed the public opinion poll merely as a means of spreading the political truth, which would emerge during the course of the 'elite work'. For the critics, by contrast, the idea of a poll elicited an expectation that questions would focus on political attitudes – and that the survey would also reveal majority positions. They therefore could not fail to interpret the deliberate disregard of methodological accuracy as an expression of contempt for the people's will and as a political ploy.

To allay the criticism of NHG delegates, the initiators finally agreed to rephrase the contested questions and to commission the ISOP to conduct a representative survey, running concurrently with the popular survey, designed to yield more conclusive data.[54] But the dispute over methodology revealed different perceptions of the objective of surveys and the role of public opinion in a democracy, differences which could not be fully resolved even by agreeing to the parallel survey. On the one hand stood a liberal perception of the state, which viewed democracy as a means of implementing individual rights and which thus presumed a plurality of interests and opinions. In such a perception, the achievement of compromise required that majorities could be determined. Set against this perception was the concept of democracy held by the initiators, who viewed it as a procedure for determining the 'right positions'. Here, majority views were relevant only insofar as they favoured or impeded the implementation of political truth. For the initiators, the interesting aspect of the poll was not so much what the respondents had to say as the manner in which they expressed it. This by itself was supposed to contribute to the further implementation of the political catechism. Because of these premises, the initiators were unable to accept any methodological modifications of the opinion poll.

ATTITUDES RESEARCH

The controversy at the NHG assembly flared up over the term 'Gallup survey'. Brunner apparently referred to this concept without being more precisely informed about the work of the American institute of public opinion research run by George Gallup, even though he had no intention of conducting a representative survey. At the time, attitudes research was for the most part unknown in Switzerland. Even in the small circle of people familiar with the term 'Gallup poll' – as representative surveys were called – uncertainty prevailed about the methodology.[55] To a wider public, the term connoted primarily something 'American'. As a result, the term was associated with the fascination of America as well as with a widespread rejection of all things American, that is, alien.[56]

Both critics and supporters of public soundings were convinced that the great successes of American public opinion research were only possible because of the advanced state of 'massification'. The statistical tabulation of opinions in the USA was only possible because individual values no longer counted and everyone thought like his neighbour, or so it was argued. Switzerland, by contrast, with its great diversity in a very a small territory, appeared to defy statistical capture. Hence, a survey would be unable to pin down such qualities as cantonal allegiance or cantonal spirit (*Kantönligeist*), 'rivalries between cities' or 'the distinctiveness of every town and every vale'.[57] Opponents of surveys even feared that the collation of opinions into categories would result in negative feedback on society by encouraging group identities and 'massification'.

And it still seemed possible to head off this menace, as the survey proponents were not yet united as to the significance they wanted to accord to public opinion. For the present, they were content to collect information which would help them to orient themselves in the post-war period. In the wide-open situation of the post-war years, many people believed a fresh start was possible. For others, the period was marked by uncertainty. If *Heer und Haus* informants reported the insecurity of the populace, if politicians worried about right-wing populists, and if businesses were unable to assess the sales prospects of their products in the post-war period, one reason was the dearth of reliable information.

It was in this area that marketing and opinion research seemed suited to satisfy the hunger for information. The first institutions which attempted such surveys in Switzerland emerged as early as 1941, in the wake of the fall of France and the Battle of Britain, when hopes arose that the war could be ended. There was huge uncertainty about how a future in a Europe dominated by Germany would be. A number of institutes offered public opinion surveys for guidance. In the ISOP and the *Gesellschaft für Marktforschung* (GfM, Market Research Company), two commercial marketing and opinion research institutes emerged, which – until well into 1945 – concentrated their efforts on acquainting the public with the methods of questioning and emphasising the importance of obtaining additional knowledge.[58] Around that time, a certain W. Jantsch, based in Basle, and the *Gotthardbund* in Zurich, conducted their first polls. The failures of these first polls illustrate just how difficult it was to harmonise such research with the myth of the unity of the people (*Volksganzen*).

Gesellschaft für Marktforschung

At the founding meeting of the GfM, chairman Peter Kaufmann under-scored the importance of opinion research in overcoming the uncertainties concerning the post-war period.[59] His institute arranged regular conferences to illustrate this point. On several occasions, sociologist René König spoke about the dynamics of sales markets, which could be better understood with the help of marketing research.[60] Although the rationing section conducted no scientific opinion research, Arnold Muggli was a welcome speaker with a store of practical experiences. Muggli explained that the job of his unit was not only to determine needs: it also – in the face of tight supplies – had to influence them as well.[61] This summed up the central issue of wartime public opinion polls. The problem was to combine opinion research with opinion shaping. *Heer und Haus* also practised this approach.

Heer und Haus

In 1941, Jantsch, a military chauffeur at the time, approached *Heer und Haus*. Jantsch had already conducted a number of polls in Basle. His ambition was to establish an opinion research institute, which he would then place at the service of the armed forces. Up to that time, *Heer und Haus* had assumed that the determination and moulding of 'popular opinion' went hand-in-hand. And so the officers of *Heer und Haus* were stunned when Jantsch presented the first poll results. His findings suggested a remarkably low level of combat readiness among members of the armed forces. The suspicion immediately arose that Jantsch had provoked the expression of these views. The *Heer und Haus* officer in charge reported at once to the intelligence service (*Nachrichtendienst*): 'Quite apart from the issue proper of establishing a Gallup organisation, it strikes me as interesting to note to whom Jantsch addressed the question about fighting morale ... As for me, I'm of the opinion that such questions should not even be posed.' Still, he did recommend that 'materials relating to the methods be obtained'.[62] Jantsch and his respondents were thereupon investigated. To prevent future dissemination of such sensitive information, the intelligence service also issued a general ban on the publication of opinion poll results. At the same time, it entered into secret negotiations with Jantsch, now under suspicion of espionage, to incorporate the methods fruitfully into their own services.

Heer und Haus, by contrast, preferred to continue relying on confidential monitors who could exercise persuasion as well. Only René Lalive d'Epinay, later to become ISOP director, had the opportunity to conduct smaller polls among course participants. Out of respect for the respondents, he deliberately kept the questions open-ended and dispensed with the profiling of respondents by social groups. This specially developed technique managed to avoid 'the sense, abhorrent to a Swiss man, of an Inquisition'.[63] It permitted 'recognition of the areas in which clarification was required' but provided no insight into group opinions.[64]

Gotthardbund

In the same year, the Zurich section of the *Gotthardbund* began with the establishment of a centre for opinion research. This seemed necessary as 'one couldn't obtain a clear picture of public opinion from the newspapers any longer'.[65] It, too, strove to adapt survey techniques to Switzerland's specific conditions. But a first poll, on the situation of workers with regard to their 'social, economic, political, and religious–ideological outlook', failed for this very reason.

Not much earlier, Elisabeth Noelle, later to establish the (German) *Institut für Demoskopie Allensbach*, had published the first comprehensive, German-language presentation of polling techniques. She wanted 'to keep alive ... the distinction between quantity opinion and quality opinion' and warned against polling 'pettifoggers and gossiping women'.[66] The *Gotthardbund* took a similar view – in total contrast to the father of opinion research, George Gallup – holding that the success of an interview depended less on the trustworthiness of the interviewer than on that of the respondent.[67] For this reason the respondents had to be carefully selected. The survey in question called for polling men and women workers capable of articulating the concerns of workers in a representative way. But, as the students foreseen as interviewers hardly knew any workers, they could not locate the 'ideal workers'. Thus, the survey failed even before it was launched.[68]

Both *Heer und Haus* and the *Gotthardbund* attempted to safeguard 'individual values'. For *Heer und Haus*, this meant dispensing with the identification of a respondent with a group, and thereby avoiding a sociological profile of Switzerland. The *Gotthardbund*, by contrast, tried to avoid giving too much weight to 'the gossip woman' or 'the voice of the doormaid'. Both approaches were useless for canvassing public opinion. With the national public opinion survey, the initiators sought an alternative approach that would not challenge the self-image of Switzerland. But their 'solution', too, encountered difficulties.

IMPERMISSIBLE PLURALISM

In February 1946, all households received a questionnaire, not along with their ration stamps, as had been planned, but by mail, together with a moderately formulated appeal urging participation in the national public opinion poll.[69] The disputed questions were now phrased in a neutral manner: 'Should the influence of the state on the economy (apart from the war economy) be strengthened, dismantled or remain unchanged?'; and: 'Should the dependence of the cantons on the federal government (in principle) be strengthened, reduced or remain unchanged?'[70]

The national public opinion survey received mixed reviews in the press. Initial reactions were for the most part favourable. Unexpectedly, Social Democratic publications praised the educational aspect of the poll. But it did not take long before voices were heard – in centre-right circles as well – which called for a boycott of the survey. The lines of resistance defied the conventional political demarcations.

The initiators were baffled by the harsh criticism from Christian groupings and women's rights organisations, segments they actually wanted to support. Representative for many, Federal Councillor Kobelt sought to have the question about the preamble to the Constitution struck from the survey as it 'doesn't [pose itself] to me and I would therefore not want to pose it'.[71] He feared it could found that, while the preamble enjoyed majority support, it was not endorsed unanimously.

The selected questions also seemed problematical, but even more disturbing for the federal councillor was that a private organisation would place topics on the political agenda without his involvement. This constituted sufficient grounds for him to make a last-ditch attempt to scuttle the entire undertaking. Federal Councillor Petitpierre protested against the fact 'that our people are being asked to express their views [on joining the UN] at a time when the Federal Council has not even issued its recommendation and public opinion has not been sufficiently informed'.[72] The inclusion of the general public in the political process threatened to encroach upon its decision-making prerogatives. Asking the people appeared to the federal councillor to be 'politics from the street', of which he had a fear approaching horror.[73]

The original intent of the initiators had been to support the policies of the Federal Council with their questions. They had assumed the survey would make clear how deeply these policies were anchored in the population. The proposed vetting procedure foresaw that only the best responses would be considered and was coupled with a special appeal to academics to participate in the survey. All this was to guarantee that the quota of responses to be vetted would be filled long before 'the people' were able to make their voice heard. In short, an 'elite survey' was to precede the 'elite work', and public opinion was to be represented by a 'quality elite'.

But the public response to the survey was quite different. In a letter to the editor of the *Neue Zürcher Zeitung* (NZZ), one woman put it this way: 'Our entire neighbourhood was joyfully surprised today by the summons "Questions to the Swiss People". Without having been preceded by a major campaign for the vote, we're being called on to express ourselves on a number of issues in a manner that not even an important constitutional vote could present for decision in such a clear and weighty manner.'[74] She had not realised that there was no intention whatsoever of consulting her and was convinced that, for the first time, her voice would now stand alongside that of other citizens.

This was exactly what politicians and political commentators dreaded. They, who hitherto had been able to present their published opinions as the will of the people, had now, thanks to the poll, been transformed into ordinary citizens whose opinions were only sought if they proved particularly valuable. Without having intended it in this glaring form, the initiators were advocating rule by an educated elite, one which would be determined solely on the basis of the quality of the responses. Editors of smaller papers, in particular, saw this as an attack on their previous role as spokesmen for public opinion.

Even more explosive than the evaluation of the 'open question' was the vetting of the six simple questions. Since no election-style campaign was foreseen for the survey, politicians risked losing their function as brokers of political ideas. In the final analysis, the surveys challenged their role as representatives of 'the people'.

Numerous commentators in regional papers and in Catholic-conservative media sought to remedy the situation by conducting an ex post facto campaign, supplying the answers to the survey in their articles. It was inconceivable to them that the respondents could form an opinion without their intercession. Indeed, they shared this conviction with the initiators. The only point of disagreement was whether the right answers were to be circulated among the people before or after the poll.

By placing the six questions in the survey, an element had been introduced which threatened to undercut the roles of various political factions and the legitimation of the elite. But Brunner acted to soothe worries about the significance of the anticipated results. Thus, he addressed the concerns of women's organisations, which viewed his survey as a variant of the 'trial votes' (*Probeabstimmungen*) which they opposed, and from which they expected bad results, with the argument that 'in a "trial vote", the votes can only be counted. With the national public opinion survey, they will be "weighted" … It will not just be a matter of "majorities". It will be just as important to determine who is of which opinion.'[75] He expressly opposed the majority-rules principle, which he called the principle of *Gleichschaltung* (conformity, or level-ling), and postulated a 'more just' principle of qualitative votes. But he was unable to explain how he would turn this principle into reality. The national opinion survey afforded no means to weight the replies to the six introductory questions, which could only be answered with a 'yes' or a 'no'.

Brunner's pledge to weight the replies appeared to mollify his critics and even in the letter columns of the papers, there were numerous calls to have someone find the correct, Swiss answers. Once again, it appeared possible that the idea of the unitary will of the people, towering above all partisan bickering, could take the day. But the poll incontrovertibly presented the issue of the people's role. Who would now represent this will of the people? How were the replies to be brought into accord with the principle of weighted votes? It was unavoidable that the poll would at least allow for the possibility of a plurality of opinions. But this contradicted the concept of the 'ideal model citizen' (Ruedi Brassel's *ideelle Gesamtbürger*), and with it the prevailing understanding of democracy.

Only after the initiators began to analyse the 52,262 returned questionnaires did it strike them that this was the upshot of their endeavour. Disappointed by the low rate of returns and by the first draft of the catechism, the NHG representatives among the initiators began to have second thoughts about the original plan, which called for the catechism to be drawn up independently of the responses. As one critical voice said of the draft, 'It's pure "Emil Brunner". But the people expect something else, and rightly so.' And NHG president Michaud added that, 'despite everything, we've conducted a popular consulta-tion, and so we ought to frankly recognise it and work with the best responses'.[76] In short, the national opinion survey challenged the prevalent perception of democracy. It did so by bringing up issues for debate independently of the authorities, by postulating a 'quality elite' without equating it with the incumbent opinion makers, by asking the people before they had been 'instructed' and, finally, by implicitly accepting the existence of a plurality of opinions. Beyond that, it violated a fundamental taboo of the *Landigeist* (i.e. *Kantönligeist*). For the first time, it became possible to recognise links between social structure and expressed opinions.

In Switzerland, or so the myth of the classless, solidarity-oriented community would have it, every trait, every preference and opinion was evenly spread throughout the land. In 1942, the director of the GfM had noted that 'public opinion was not a formless shape, but was divided into group opinions, group attitudes, group postures which, in turn, are expressions of clearly definable group livelihoods'.[77] In this abstract form, Kaufmann's utterances hardly aroused any objections. These remarks only encountered opposition once the groups were to be named in functional ways. The application of sociological categories to identify groups, such as size of income, professional standing or political influence, suggested a divisibility of the small units within the federalist system. Politicians and the press responded in anguish when clearly distinguishable groups were detected, for instance, within village communities.[78] Thus, as late as the 1950s, a leading figure in marketing research, Adolf Wirz, could not present his agenda without first prefacing his remarks by asserting that surveys were better suited to societies in which 'a glass wall ... divided the social classes, and in which they ... knew precious little about each other – on either side'.[79]

The national opinion survey had the declared goal of stabilising the unity of Switzerland. This notwithstanding, it laid the foundations for dissecting this Switzerland into groups by calling on the respondents to position themselves in social terms. The quantitative assessment of the questionnaires had to reveal that workers and white-collar employees professed political opinions different from those of company directors or proprietors. In this way, the survey appeared to dissolve entities (such as villages and valleys) in favour of group identities defined according to occupational standing. All of a sudden, it appeared possible to show that, in Switzerland too, there were demonstrable 'social classes' and that a range of different opinions existed side by side. This made it at least possible that the pronouncements of political representatives could be shown not to correspond with the majority views.

The ominous charge that surveys threatened the unity of Switzerland obstructed the work on both polls considerably. While the initiators of the national public opinion survey appeared to have found a way to circumvent the charge by assuring that they would give qualitative assessment a higher priority than quantitative, the ISOP study was unable to sidestep the acceptance of social stratification. It was the prerequisite for the creation of a model that permitted the selection of survey respondents. Still, the institute devoted considerable verbal effort to avoid portraying the necessary social differentiation as an expression of class barriers. All the same, the interview partners had to be selected on the basis of an assessment of their social standing. In short, the elaborate efforts to preserve the image of a unitary popular entity (*Volksganzen*) did not prove very successful.[80] This made it undeniable that, in Switzerland too, different views were espoused by different social groups. The introduction of barriers between the strata did indeed appear to threaten the unity of Switzerland.

LIBERAL IN SPITE OF THEMSELVES

Two years after launching the survey, the results were published in a brochure entitled *Die Schweiz hält durch* (Switzerland perseveres). While it did not contain a draft constitution, it did incorporate Werner Kägi's version of 'Basic Swiss Principles'. The press acknowledged the brochure's publication as an 'honourable and soundly Swiss expression of Swiss thought', and soon put it aside.[81] At most, it served as a catechism for the *Schweizerische Aufklärungsdienst* (a private political initiative), which incorporated it into its own programme.[82]

The reason why *Die Schweiz hält durch*, despite the enormous printing, hardly met with any response was that the book no longer fitted into the political landscape. The dreaded post-war crisis had not materialised. Individual sympathisers of National Socialism were brought to account in 'clean-up' actions without making the collaboration of official Switzerland an issue. In the meantime, food rationing had, for the most part, been lifted and the communist seizure of power in Czechoslovakia was the downfall of the Swiss Communist Party, the PdA (*Partei der Arbeit*, or Workers' Party). The 100th anniversary of the Federal Constitution was marked by jubilee celebrations – political tranquillity had returned. As a result, the project to revamp the Swiss state hardly had any supporters left.

In its contents, too, the brochure contained no surprises. As was to be expected, 95 per cent of the respondents affirmed the national defence policy, the policy of neutrality, and the preamble 'In the Name of God the Almighty'. More than half the respondents favoured the existing federalistic set-up. That just barely a quarter of both women and men favoured full suffrage for women hardly surprised anyone.

For that reason, the few papers which devoted lengthier articles to the surveys focused mainly on differences between the two polls.[83] These were particularly marked – as already mentioned – where women's suffrage and future economic policies were concerned. See the table below.

'Should the influence of the state on the economy (apart from the war economy) be strengthened or dismantled or remain unchanged?' (%)

	be increased	remain unchanged	be reduced	no opinion
Public survey	10.9	32.9	56.2	–
ISOP survey	15.2	30.6	19.6	34.6

ISOP explained this discrepancy by pointing out the low participation of workers in the national opinion survey. But the press viewed it not so much as an expression of divergent groups as an indication of a qualitative difference between the two polls. The national opinion survey simply seemed to be less serious. The commentators still shrank from acknowledging the existence of socially predicated differences of opinion. And with that, the national opinion survey appeared to become an insignificant episode in history. Already, Ernst Bieri, a former member of the student group, had dismissed it in the *NZZ* as an expression of 'unmistakable post-war malaise' which had long since been overcome by the 'bulwark of a conservatively-oriented people'.[84]

This assessment does not do justice to the survey. It was surely correct that Brunner's attempt to preserve the concept of the popular unity had become obsolete now that the ideology of the spiritual defence of the nation had become consolidated in a conservative mentality.[85] But the national opinion survey cannot be reduced to the objective that it strove to achieve. In his youthful enthusiasm, Brunner had, in choosing the survey approach, opted for an instrument which was rooted in a different perception of society. The results of the poll, as published in *Die Schweiz hält durch*, demonstrated that a pluralistic society had taken root in Switzerland. But, as the opinions published were consonant with public opinion, it was nonetheless possible to present the results as an expression of a stable entity. Kägi – and with him most other reviewers – preferred this reading. And so, Brunner's 'elite' appeared to be doing a good job of representing the people. It remained possible to depict democracy as a process of striking a compromise between different 'elite opinions'. Seen from this perspective, it was a violation of the rules that, through the national opinion survey, Swiss women and men were questioned before they were instructed, but there were hardly any repercussions.

Much more significant were the repercussions for the idea of democracy, and the forceful debates which marked the initial phase can be seen as a dispute about this issue. In this debate, too, the formalistic understanding of democracy prevailed. So long as liberty and the relative autonomy of public institutions remained assured and so long as the mode of decision-making was not questioned, democracy appeared to be intact. On the other hand, the independent polling of all men and women also suggested a basic personal right to express opinions. The data-canvassing method allowed for the possibility that different social groups would set divergent political priorities. By admitting the possibility that fissures in the unity of the people (*Volksganzen*) could be construed as evidence of social circumstances, the surveys also provided those who did not feel represented in the conventional political process a 'place' in the political landscape, and, with it, a weight that had to be taken seriously. Thus, the national public opinion survey introduced an instrument in which a pluralistic perception of democracy was inherent.[86] Up to that time, only a few liberals, including Giacometti, had viewed democracy as a system built upon the political rights of the citizen. With the national public opinion survey, this position was put into practice for the first time. The controversy surrounding the two polls made evident that many politicians and commentators had understood and feared the implications, and fought against them.

NOTES

1 I wish to thank Frau E. Brunner-Gyr for her financial assistance, which made this chapter possible. I also wish to thank the Schweizerische Wirtschaftsarchiv (SWA), Basle, which entrusted me with the task of archiving the literary estate of Andreas C. Brunner, and for providing me with the referral for this assignment.

2 Andreas Brunner, 'Vorprojekt zur Volksumfrage', March 1945, SWA Nachlass Andreas C. Brunner, HS 485 E5 (preliminary project for the national public opinion survey).

3 Andreas Brunner became known to a wider public during the 1960s and 1970s. Through his marriage to Elisabeth Gyr, an heiress of Landis & Gyr in Zug, he became a partner in the company, which he led in an innovative fashion. In the political arena, he made his mark as a national councillor for the Freisinnige Party (Liberals, 1968–75) and as the informal father of occupational retirement fund planning. State Councillor Andreas Iten recalled his party colleague: 'Andreas C. Brunner was … a rebel'. He first demonstrated this publicly with the national public opinion survey. See Andreas Iten, *Leichenreden Andreas C. Brunner, 2 May 1923–22 January 1988*.

4 *Die Schweiz hält durch* (Switzerland perseveres), published by the Verein Volksumfrage under the patronage of the Neue Helvetische Gesellschaft, Werner

Kägi (ed.), Zurich, 1948. The print runs included 60,000 copies in German, 9,000 in French and 1,000 in Italian. See also 'Rechenschaftsbericht des Geschäftsführers, 30 March 1949, SWA, HS 485 E11.

5 Zaccaria Giacometti, 'Die gegenwärtige Verfassungslage der Eidgenossenschaft' (The present constitutional situation of the Confederation), lecture held before students of the faculty of law and political sciences of the University of Zurich, in *Schweizerische Hochschulzeitung*, H3, 1942, pp. 139–54.

6 Prominent interest was, to be sure, confined to the launching phase, when it still seemed possible that the survey could yield undesirable results. In 1946 and 1948, Brunner had commissioned the Argus Press Service to collect articles relating to the national public opinion survey. In this manner, two bulky files were filled in 1946. In 1948, there were still about 50 articles. The publication of the results was not noted in important newspapers.

7 I wish to refer here to four publications in particular which bring together a number of studies dealing with the end of the war and with the early post-war years: Erich Gysling, Mario König and Michael T. Ganz, *1945 – Die Schweiz im Friedensjahr*, Zurich, 1995; *Traverse*, Beilage (supplement), 1995/52; Kurt Imhof, Heinz Kleger and Gaetano Romano (eds), *Konkordanz und Kalter Krieg. Analysen von Medienereignissen in der Schweiz der Zwischen- und Nachkriegszeit*, Zurich, 1996; *Itinera*, 18, 'Die Schweiz im internationalen System der Nachkriegszeit 1943–1950', ed. Georg Kreis, Basle, 1996.

8 Emphasising the 'mindlessness': Herbert Lüthy, 'La Suisse des deux aprèsguerres', *Jahrbuch der Neuen Helvetischen Gesellschaft*, 35, 1964, pp. 63–75. Cited in Claus Hässig, 'Intellektuelles Vakuum oder Aufbruchstimmung', *Itinera*, 18, pp. 18–31. Tschäni, by contrast, emphasises the stonewalling against the new: Hans Tschäni, '1945–1995: Die Schweizerfinden', *Traverse*, 2, 1995, pp. 7–10.

9 Mario König, 'Befangenes Denken', *Bulletin der SAGW*, 1, 95, Berne, 1995, pp. 27–32. How strongly the fear of a chasm between people and authorities could seize attention can be seen again in the current discussion about the role of Switzerland during the Second World War. In his address to Parliament of 5 March 1997, Federal Councillor Koller urgently warned against it. See also *Basler Zeitung*, 6 March 1997.

10 Peter Hug, 'Verhinderte oder verpasste Chancen? Die Schweiz und die Vereinten Nationen 1945–1947' (Blocked or Missed Opportunities? Switzerland and the United Nations 1943–1947), *Itinera*, 18, pp. 84–97, p. 92. From the centre-right perspective, a not inconsiderable factor fuelling doubts about the political 'competence' of the people derived from the voting habits of the electorate. Thus, the strong results of the newly established PdA (Communist Party) in the cantons of Basle-Stadt and Vaud in 1944/45 appeared to be evidence enough of the deficient sense of judgement of the 'people'.

11 Georg Kreis, 'Parlamentarismus und Antiparlamentarismus in den Jahren 1933–1945', in *Das Parlament – 'Oberste Gewalt des Bundes'? Festschrift der Bundesversammlung zur 700-Jahr-Feier der Eidgenossenschaft* (Festschrift on the Occasion of the Joint Plenary Session of the Chambers of Parliament Marking the 700th Anniversary of the Swiss Confederation), Berne/Stuttgart, 1991, pp. 301–19, pp. 318ff.

12 Kurt Imhof, 'Die Schweiz im Kalten Krieg oder der "Sonderfall" im Westblock' (Switzerland during the Cold War: or the 'Special Case' in the Western Bloc), *Itinera*, 18, pp. 179–86, pp. 181ff; ibid., 'Das kurze Leben der geistigen Landesverteidigung. Von der "Volksgemeinschaft" vor dem Krieg zum Streit über die "Nachkriegs-schweiz" im Krieg' (The Brief Life of the Spiritual Defence of the

Switzerland and the Second World War

Nation. From the pre-war 'community-nation' to the debate about 'post-war
Switzerland' during the war), in Imhof, Kleger and Romano, op. cit., pp. 19–84,
74, and in Heinz Kleger, 'Die nationale Bürgergesellschaft im Krieg und
Nachkrieg: 1943–1955', ibid., pp. 111–72, 135.

13 Hug, *Itinera*, op. cit., p. 18.
14 Emil Brunner, *Gerechtigkeit*, Zurich, 1943. In the minutes available to me, the
following persons are cited as members during the 1944–46 period: Friedrich
Bernet, secretary of the Confederation of Swiss Employer Organisations (subsequently, management consultant and editor); Karl Brunner, professor of
economics, HSG (St Gallen Graduate School); Emit Brunner, professor of
theology, University of Zurich; Theo Chopard, journalist, FdP, on executive
board of NHG; Charles Ducommun, Price Controls, War Food Administration
and 3GB; Theodor Gut, *Zürichseezeitung*, national councillor, FdP; Konrad Ilg,
SMUV, national councillor, SP; Werner Kägi, lecturer in law, University of
Zurich; Rudolf Meier, farmers' leader, *Bund für Volk und Heimat*; later, *Nationalrat*
BGB and *Regierungsrat* in Zurich; Arnold Muggli, head of Swiss Rations
Management Division; Eberhard Reinhardt, secretary of finance, later, director
of the Swiss Treasury and director-general of Credit Suisse; Hans Schaffner,
head of War Economy Coordination Office, later, federal councillor FdP; Hans
Schindler, Maschinenfabrik Oerlikon, president of VSM (*Verband Schweiz.
Maschinenindustrieller*); Friedrich T. Wahlen, professor, father of the emergency
food resources programme, subsequently, federal councillor for the BGB; H.
Wanner, Aluminium Neuhausen; and Paul Zigerli, civil engineer, national
councillor, EVP. See SWA, HS A1, H. H. Brunner reports that 'interim members'
debaters included: Arthur Steiner, SMUV and SGB; Christian Gasser, Bund der
Subventionslosen, *Gotthardbund*, later, CEO of the Mikron AG; and Gottlieb
Duttweiler, Migros. See Hans Heinrich Brunner, *Mein Vater und sein ültester*,
Zurich, 1986, p. 83.
15 By joining the Oxford Group, Emil Brunner, who had just previously been a
member of the Union of Anti-Militaristic Ministers, did a radical political about-
face. See Ruedi Brassel and Martin Leuenberger, *Willi Kobe, Pazifist, Sozialist und
Pfarrer*, Lucerne, 1994, p. 55.
16 Emil Brunner, *Die Kirchen, die Gruppenbewegung und die Kirche Jesu Christi*, Berlin,
1936, p. 40. Reformed theologians pointed out that this form of searching for
the right way exhibited tendencies that were no less totalitarian. Karl Barth was
one of the most vehement critics of the Oxford Group.
17 Stuart Mews, 'Moralische Aufrüstung', in Horst Balz et al., *Theologisches
Realenzyklopädie*, Vol. 23, Berlin/New York, 1994, pp. 291–94. Brunner's criticism
of Buchman's approach did not go very far. In his apologia for the Oxford Group
– published in 1936 in Berlin – he resorted to anti-Semitic lines of reasoning on
several occasions. See Brunner, *Kirchen*, op. cot.
18 Brunner, *Kirchen*, op. cit., p. 29.
19 The student chapter of the *Gotthardbund* Zurich reported that brochures of the
Oxford Group were used in the army. Archiv für Zeitgeschichte Zurich, Bestand
Gotthardbund. Studentengruppe Zurich, V, 56, 3.5. Regarding criticism of the
Oxfordians see Alice Meyer, *Anpassung oder Widerstand*, Frauenfeld, 1966,
pp. 189ff; Christian Gasser, *Der Gotthardbund*, Berne/Stuttgart, 1984, p. 28.
20 Brunner, *Gerechtigkeit*, op. cit., p. 222.
21 Protokoll Gerechtigkeitsgruppe (Minutes of the Justice Group), 30 September–
1 October, 1944, SWA, HS 485 A 1. Hans Schindler, director of the Maschinenfabrik Oerlikon (MFO), reported corresponding successes at MFO. This

probably accounts for the Oxford Group view of Schindler's MFO as the 'Kingdom of God'. See Brassel and Leuenberger, op. cit., p. 122. For a more detailed account of the 'company congregation' at MFO under the influence of 'moral re-armament' and rationalisation, see Rudolf Jaun, *Management und Arbeiterschaft*, Zurich, 1986, pp. 348–71.

22 Freedom is just 'the second word. The first word, however, is submission', Emil Brunner asserted, in Unser Glaube, Zurich, 1939, p. 77. He sought to proclaim this truth at other centres of orientation. Together with Werner Kägi, he organised a series of discussion evenings for students at the University of Zurich. But these met with little interest. See *Zurcher Student*, 8, January 1945. Andreas Brunner, too, became involved in 'conversion' efforts at the university and at the ETH (the Federal Institute of Technology in Zurich). Together with 'about 40 spiritually live students', he launched a lecture series entitled 'Gespräch zwischen den Fakultäten: "Ich kann nichts dafür", Freiheit, Verantwortung, Determinismus' (An Inter-faculty Dialogue: 'I can't help it': Freedom, Responsibility, and Determinism), which strove to make out basic shared principles in different academic fields of study. SWA, HS 485 C and Universitätsarchiv Zurich, 55.667, Studentisches.

23 On the constitutional debates of the 1930s see Peter Stadler, 'Die Diskussion um eine Totalrevision der Schweiz, Bundesverfassung 1933–1935', *SZG*, 1, 1969, pp. 75–170.

24 Kreis, op. cit., p. 319.

25 Reply of Albert Oeri in the National Council debate on the Oeri proposition (*Postulat*) in favour of the establishment of a constitutional council. In Bulletin of *Nationalrat*, 13/14 December 1943, pp. 307–23.

26 Regarding the constitutional discussions of the Freisinnige Party (liberals), see *Der Bund*, Berne, 26, 28 and 31 July 1946.

27 The Basle parliament (Basler Grosser Rat) linked its initiative (*Standesinitiative*) to calls for the expansion of direct democracy, women's suffrage, the right to introduce legislation, and the elimination of denominational (religious) legal exemptions. See 'Bericht des Bundesrates an die Bundesversammlung über das Initiativbegehren des Kantons Basel-Stadt betr. die Totalrevision der Bundesverfassung vom 27. Nov1959' (Report of the Federal Council to the Plenary Federal Assembly on the initiative proposition of the Canton Basel-City re. the total revision of the Constitution, of 27 November 1959).

28 Protokoll der Gerechtigkeitsgruppe (Minutes of the Justice Group), February 1945, op. cit.

29 Andreas Brunner, 'Studie für das Rationierungsamt über die Möglichkeiten der Aufhebung der Rationierung', 1943, p. 60. SWA, HS 485 B1.

30 On the reports of *Heer und Haus* correspondents on the orientation crisis, see André Lasserre, *Schweiz: Die dunkeln Jahre. Öffentliche Meinung 1939–1945*, Zurich, 1992, pp. 218ff. and 420ff. The theme of the young who seek a new identity was a familiar justification for a revision of the Constitution. See, for example, the National Council debate on the Oeri proposition (*Postulat*) 1943, op. cit.

31 Andreas Brunner, 'Vorbereitungsarbeiten für eine Verfassungsreform', Annex to Brunner, 'Schlussbericht', SWA, HS 485 E10.

32 Andreas Brunner, 'Referat Pro Helvetia', 1945, SWA, HS 485 E4.

33 Kurt Imhof, 'Wiedergeburt der geistigen Landesverteidigung: Kalter Krieg in der Schweiz' (Renaissance of the Spiritual Defence of the Nation: The Cold War and Switzerland), in Imhof, Kleger and Romano, op. cit., pp. 172–248, 184ff.

34 Tributes to personal qualities and interest-free politics were cherished themes in Swiss politics – and a 'wish' often expressed in the national public opinion survey. Thus, the *Gotthardbund* called for a smaller National Council selected on a simple majority basis. See *Gotthardbund, Eidgenossische Ordnung*, Berne, 1941, p. 41. Similar motives prompted Albert Oeri to work for a constitutional council whose members ought to be selected 'solely on the basis of suitability and interest in issues of government', *Basler Nachrichten*, 26 June 1942.

35 Ruedi Brassel, *Dissonanzen der Moderne*, Zurich, 1994, pp. 188ff.

36 Andreas Brunner, 'Expos, – Entwurf über die Verfassungsrevision, 1945', SWA, HS 485 E2.2.

37 Regarding Brunner's concept of 'the plurality of final recourse', see Andreas Brunner, 'Rechtsstaat gegen Totalstaat. Rechtspol. Teil', dissertation Zurich, Wädenswil, 1948. The Justice Group was particularly keen on making sure that old-age retirement benefit schemes would not be made a government task. See Bernhard Degen, *Sozialdemokratie: Gegenmacht? Opposition? Bundesratspartei?*, Zurich, 1993, p. 60; Christian Luchsinger, *Solidarität, Selbständigkeit, Bedürftigkeit*, Zurich, 1995, pp. 38ff. For W. Kägi, as late as 1947, the AHV (social security system) was a symptom of failure (*Symptom für das Versagen*). See also Protokoll der Gerechtigkeitsgruppe, 21 June 1947, op. cit.

38 See also *Gotthardbund, Ordnung*, op. cit., pp. 27ff. The general definition of the term *Berufsgemeinschaft* (vocational associations) included the business and industrial associations, and this included the unions. In the Justice Group, however, a definition of the term ultimately prevailed which was geared more toward the vocational and/or cooperative perspective. Focused on smaller-scale plants, this vocational community embraced rather the communal element of a plant. In larger plants, it could also encompass cooperative-style unions or worker commissions. In the eyes of Ducommun, vocational communities were primarily instruments for overcoming the crisis of orientation of men and women workers. See Ducommun, lecture of 22 January 1941, Archiv für Zeitgeschichte, Studentengruppe, op. cit., V, 56.3.5, 1941–43.

39 Adolf Gasser, 'Federalismus und Demokratie – zwei Gegensätze?' (*NZ*, Basle, 27–28 May 1944.

40 Werner Kägi, 'Expos, zur Verfassungsrevision', 27 October 1945, SWA, HS 485 E6, p. 17 (Expos, on the Revision of the Constitution).

41 Brunner, 'Vorbereitungsarbeiten', op. cit.

42 'Aufrufentwurf zur Volksumfrage', SWA, HS 485 E5.

43 'Plan zuhanden von BR von Steiger', 1945, Annex to Brunner, 'Schlussbericht', op. cit. (Plan for presentation to Federal Councillor von Steiger).

44 'Aufrufentwurf', op. cit.

45 Brunner, 'Vorprojekt', op. cit.

46 'Protokoll einer Besprechung von H.-U. Röbel and A. Brunner – mit General Guisan' (Minutes of a consultation), 8 August 1945. Prepared by A. Brunner, Annex to Brunner, 'Schlussbericht', op. cit.

47 'Aktennotiz über Konferenz vom 6.11.1945, Betr. Weiterführung der Tätigkeit der Sektion "H&H" in der Nachkriegszeit' (Memo of conversation of 6 November 1945 re the continued operation of the section 'H&H' in the post-war period) in FA, E 27, 9315. See also Brunner, 'Referat Pro Helvetia', op. cit. And correspondence with Ernst Laur, August 1945. Annex to Brunner, 'Schlussbericht', op. cit.

48 They were Ilg, Kägi, Muggli and Reinhardt. Also present on several occasions was Ren, Lalive d'Epinay, the erstwhile chief executive of the *Heer und Haus*

division responsible for French-speaking Switzerland, and director of the ISOP. Brunner, 'Schlussbericht', op. cit.

49 Minutes of 24 August 1946, Annex to Brunner, 'Schlussbericht', op. cit. Brunner himself saw the trickle return of the forms as a gain for the constitution drafting. The abandonment became official in February 1947. Letter from Brunner to von Steiger, 11 February 1947, FA, JPD, 4001 (C) 235, 494.

50 Letter from Nobs to Brunner, 28 December 1945, Annex to Brunner, 'Schluss-bericht', op. cit.

51 Letter from Ilg to Brunner, 3 December 1946, SWA, HS 485 E9. See also Oskar Scheiben, 'Konrad Ilgs Weg nach rechts' (Konrad Ilg's road to the right), in *Widerspruch-Sonderband. Arbeitsfrieden – Realität eines Mythos*, Zurich, 1987, pp. 31–6.

52 'Overall, we're surprised by the position taken by NR [National Councillor] Oprecht, but we're convinced that we can't ascribe his positive stance toward the national public opinion survey to his personal views, but alone to the circumstance that we presented the conduct of the national public opinion survey as a self-evident matter and that he had to concede he couldn't gauge the spontaneous reaction of the people. Above all, he can't do anything about the fact that we have 70,000 (sic!) subscriptions in the books.' Letter from Brunner to Kobelt, 29 December 1945, FA, E 27, 9316. Later, Oprecht did not support the opinion survey.

53 Minutes of 16 December 1945, Annex to Brunner, 'Schlussbericht', op. cit.

54 Brunner, 'Schlussbericht', op. cit.

55 August Wohlgensinger, 'Die öffentliche Meinung über Steuern und Finanzpolitik in der Schweiz', dissertation, Fribourg, 1953, p. 13.

56. Mario König, 'Alltag und Politik im Mai 1945 und danach', in Gysling, König and Ganz, op. cit., pp. 86–131, pp. 123ff. (Politics and everyday life in May 1945 and thereafter).

57 *Die Tat*, 13 August 1943. (In a similar vein, E. Weidmann in *Büro und Verkauf*, 5, February 1943, pp. 4ff.)

58 Robert Schnyder von Wartensee, 'Die öffentliche Meinung als Element der staatlichen Willensbildung in der Demokratie', dissertation Berne, Affoltern 1946, p. 132.

59 *NZZ*, Zurich, 27 May 1941.

60 René König, *Zur Sozialpsychologie der modischen Strömungen*, GfM, Zurich, 1944; idem, *Das Problem der Nachahmung – ihre Wirkung im Aufbau des Konsums*, GfM, Zurich, 1945.

61 Arnold Muggli, *Rationierung und Marktforschung*, GfM, Zurich, 1943.

62 Letter from Captain Ernst to Colonel Müller, deputy chief of the Intelligence Department, 14 August 1941, FA, E 27/9057. Certainly, these survey results were not surprising. Ernst von Schenk had reported comparable results in the summer of 1940 in weekly reports about the attitude of the population. These were based on an extremely small respondent base. As the APF feared the reports could damage resistance preparedness, the surveys were soon termi-nated. The reports already prepared were kept locked up: FA, EDI 51/52.

63 Schnyder von Wartensee, op. cit., pp. 125ff. See also Lasserre, op. cit., pp. 58ff.

64 Schnyder von Wartensee, op. cit., p. 137. A similar line of reasoning presumably applied to the decision of Swiss Radio not to conduct a planned listener survey just after the radio directors' conference decided that honouring reasons of state was more important than listener requests. See Ruth Halter-Schmidt, *Schweizer Radio 1939–1945*, Berne/Stuttgart, 1980, pp. 155ff. and p. 187.

65 'Protokoll der ausserordentl. Landsgemeinde der Zürcher Sektion des Gotthard-bundes, 14 March 1941' (Minutes of the special gathering of the Zurich chapter of the Gotthardbund), Archiv für Zeitgeschichte, Zurich, Bestand Gotthard-bund, Landsgemeinden, V. 56.3.3, 1940/1941.

66 Elisabeth Noelle, *Amerikanische Massenbefragung über Politik und Presse*, Berlin, 1940, cited in Gerwin Klinger, 'Das wahre Wesen der Geführten – Zwei demoskopische Projekte des NS-Staates', in *KultuRRevolution*, 29, March 1994, pp. 65–9, p. 66.

67 George Gallup, *A guide to public opinion polls*, Princeton, 1944, pp. 45ff.

68 'Protokolle der Studentengruppe des Gotthardbundes vom 27. Mai und 24. Juni 1941, Archiv für Zeitgeschichte, Studentengruppe', op. cit., V. 56.3.3, 1940/41 (Minutes of the Student Chapter of the Gotthardbund, 27 May and 24 June 1941).

69 To prevent the survey from acquiring the patina of officialdom, Federal Councillor Kobelt barred the distribution of the questionnaire along with the ration stamps. Correspondence Brunner–Kobelt, December 1945–January 1946, FA, E 27, 9316.

70 Umfragebogen zur Volksumfrage 1946 (Questionnaire of the 1946 national pubic opinion survey).

71 Kobelt to Brunner, January 1946, FA, E 27, 9316. On comparable grounds, various newspapers called for a boycott of the poll, for example, the *Rheintalische Volkszeitung of Altstätten* on 16 March 1946.

72 Letter of Petitpierre to Brunner, 19 February 1945, Annex to Brunner, 'Schluss-bericht', op. cit.

73 König, 'Gedenken', op. cit. In March 1946, the *Schweizerische Friedensrat* (Swiss Peace Council) also sought to launch a poll on the topic of joining the UN. But Petitpierre was able to prevent it. See Peter Hug, 'Wer abseits steht, ist immer im Unrecht' (Anyone who stands apart is always in the wrong), in Katharina Rengel (ed.), *Hoffen heisst Handeln. Friedensarbeit in der Schweiz seit 1945*, Zurich, 1995, pp. 39–55.

74 *NZZ*, Zurich, 23 February 1946.

75 Andreas Brunner, *Schweizer Frauenblatt*, Winterthur, 8 March 1946. One call for a boycott can be found in an advertisement of the *Internationale Frauenliga für Friede und Freiheit, Sektion Zürich*, in *Die Frau im Leben und Arbeit*, Aarau, April 1946.

76 Minutes of 24 August 1946, Annex to Brunner, 'Schlussbericht', op. cit.

77 Peter Kaufmann, *Wie das Gallup-Institut die öffentliche Meinung ermittelt*, Thalwil, 1942, p. 38.

78 A case in point about the resistance to knowledge about social stratification is the obstruction of sociology at the University of Zurich during the late 1940s. The internationally acclaimed sociologist and GfM aide, René König, paid the price for crossing this line, with which he proved himself 'little familiar with Swiss conditions'. Fuelled by scepticism concerning this branch of knowledge, he was hounded out of Zurich, and the planned endowment of a sociology chair abandoned. The theological faculty in particular – in which Emil Brunner had a not inconsiderable say – voiced its opposition against social research. See Markus Zürcher, *Unterbrochene Tradition. Die Anfänge der Soziologie in der Schweiz*, Zurich, 1995, pp. 239–85 (Interrupted Tradition: The Beginnings of Sociology in Switzerland).

79 Adolf Wirz, *Durch Marktforschung besser verkaufen*, Zurich, 1953, p. 79.

80 In the concluding report, the ISOP again pointed out the challenges it faced in

designing a model for federalistic Switzerland, 'ISOP-Schlussberlich', in FA, JPD, 1941–1951, 4001 (C) 235, 494. See also Schnyder von Wartensee, op. cit., p. 113.
81 *NZZ*, Zurich, 16 August 1948.
82 Igor Perrig, *Geistige Landesverteidigung im kalten Krieg*, Brig, 1993, pp. 151ff.
83 See, for example, *NZN*, Zurich, 10 July 1948.
84 *NZZ*, Zurich, 16 August 1948.
85 For the redirection of the spiritual defence of the nation (*geistige Landes-verteidigung*), see Imhof, 'Wiedergeburt', op. cit., pp. 180ff. Only recently, the idea was taken up again. With an eye to the jubilee year of 1998, the *Rencontres Suisses*, a citizen-action group established in 1946 with the involvement of several of the advocates of the national public opinion survey, proposed commissioning a larger number of morally and intellectually prominent persons with the task of elaborating a 'Charter' for Switzerland which could serve as the basis for a new national identity and constitution. See *BaZ*, 31 July 1993; *NZZ*, 31 January 1994.
86 This was by no means the end of the debate about the legitimacy of public opinion studies and the concomitant acceptability of pluralism. During the EXPO 1964, the debate reached a renewed climax. A project, in which EXPO visitors were to be polled on various 'explosive' political issues, came under severe fire and, following pressure from the federal government, had to be revised. While the authorities claimed the project was lacking in scientific credentials, various commentators suspected federal censorship. See *NZZ*, 12 and 14 July, 11, 19 and 25 August and 2 September 1964. The results were published in Luc Boltanski, *Le bonheur suisse*, Paris, 1966.

14

Governmental Malaise with History: From the White Paper to the Bonjour Report

SACHA ZALA

For historians, any research into contemporary Swiss history during the 1960s was completely dominated by the monopoly on sources granted to Edgar Bonjour.[1] The continuing research undertaken by the Basle historian was of such political importance that they successfully prevented any work on political history outside government control from 1962 until the mid-1970s: in the early 1960s, other historians were even denied access to documents on the First World War. In 1973 the Federal Archive Regulation of 1966 was revised, reducing the period for which documents were sealed from 50 to 35 years, thus allowing all historians more generous access to sources. Even this liberalisation, however, did not fully open the road to Eldorado as far as the records were concerned, as confirmed by the continuing restrictions on access which, for example, were the subject of Georg Kreis' complaint to the Federal Council in 1975.[2]

My historiographical contribution studies the official attitude to contemporary history in the post-war years and so provides evidence of the construction and dissemination of an artificial view of history which, as a function of a mythic concept of neutrality, formed a constituent element of a basis of community ideology rooted in a continuation of the spiritual defence of Switzerland. It is hardly surprising, therefore, that the stimuli which affected the treatment of Swiss contemporary history in the 1960s came from outside Switzerland. The first of these was the publication, beginning in the 1950s, of the files captured by the (Western) Allies in the *Documents on German Foreign Policy*, which subsequently also appeared in German.[3] Thus the observations which follow can claim a degree of topicality in so far as the Federal Council, in its resolution of 19 December 1996, commissioned the Swiss Independent Expert Commission on the Second World

War to investigate, *inter alia*, 'official historical treatments' and 'reactions to foreign editions of sources'.

There are four aspects of this group of problems that I would like to single out: first, the Swiss White Paper, a publication project worked on by the EPD (*Eidgenössisches Politisches Department*, Federal Political Department) between 1945 and 1948 but eventually unpublished, which has to be seen as a precursor of Bonjour's report;[4] second, the official obstruction of independent research and intrigues against historians intended to prevent any questioning of the official historical record; third, the obstructive attitude towards Allied publication of the *Documents on German Foreign Policy*, with a view to covering up the secret Franco-Swiss military cooperation of 1939–40 (the so-called La Charité-sur-Loire affair) and preventing the dreaded questioning of neutrality; fourth, the instruction to Edgar Bonjour on 6 July 1962 'to prepare for the attention of the Federal Council a comprehensive report on Swiss foreign policy during the last world war', as a direct consequence of articles by journalists and, in particular, the publication of the files on Franco-Swiss military cooperation in the *Documents on German Foreign Policy*.

THE SWISS WHITE PAPER

At the end of the war, even neutral Switzerland confronted the need to settle accounts with the defeated powers. A motion tabled by National Councillor, Ernst Boerlin, on 5 June 1945 called for the exposure of far-right activities, which the Federal Council, in its multi-part report on anti-democratic activities,[5] also exploited as an opportunity to settle accounts with the far left. Subsequently, the then national leadership practised the art of settling scores through reports on several more occasions.[6] Politically, reports were a particularly favourable form of 'controlled management of the past', containing no hidden dangers of explosive revelations. However, repeated questions asked by National Councillors Albert Maag and Urs Dietschi also called for documentary evidence. As a result, consideration was soon given to publishing documents in addition to the reports. Following consultations between Federal Councillor Max Petitpierre and his predecessor Marcel Pilet-Golaz, the historian Werner Näf from Berne was chosen by the Federal Council to review 'the question of a publication' which 'would provide a comprehensive insight into Swiss foreign policy during the war years'. Näf submitted his report in mid-November 1945. He had examined three options: '1. Publication of the Swiss political documents, in other words a "White Paper"; 2. A documented account of Swiss foreign policy during wartime by a

314 Switzerland and the Second World War

historian commissioned by the Federal Council; 3. A future free academic use of the material.'

Näf considered it desirable 'to give the Swiss people an insight into the country's political problems during the war'. However, he added that the enterprise would also encounter 'certain difficulties which must not be overlooked or underestimated', because the interpretation of political decisions and statements would be directly associated with judgements on individuals 'who then held, and in some cases still hold, responsible positions. The danger of misunderstanding or misinterpretation is quite considerable today, at a time when the political mood is a highly emotional one.'

Regarding the first of the three publication options, Näf felt that the 'official publication of a so-called White Paper would be something new in Swiss practice, and indeed this form of documentation, based on the great power model, is not particularly well suited to the essence of Swiss foreign policy', because that policy lacked the 'character of secret diplomacy'. For this reason alone, he thought, 'this form of publication, unsuited to our habits and conditions, should be avoided'. Apart from this reservation, Näf went on to say that any publication of files must 'include *all* important documents' and '*completely* reproduce all items added to the files', because 'any other procedure would not comply with the principles of academic honesty but would create uncertainty and mistrust and hence be extremely counter-productive politically. A review of the files, however, shows me that there are areas whose detailed discussion, although of little material significance, would unnecessarily touch upon sensitive areas which are particularly acute today.' After discussion over various other ideas, Näf concluded that '*publication of documents in the form of a "White Paper" should be avoided*'.

Equally impracticable, he thought, was the option of allowing free academic use of the material in the future, first because 'there could probably be no question of allowing completely free use of these files with immediate effect'[7] and secondly because whether they would be dealt with 'in the true academic sense ... would be a matter of chance and hardly likely in the immediate future', which would not be in line with the intended purpose of an 'early public elucidation of Swiss foreign policy'.

Of the three publication options, then – assuming that publication were to be contemplated at all – only a documented presentation remained as '*the advisable arrangement*'. A descriptive work, added Näf, would have, as compared with publication of documents, 'the definite advantage that the individual activities and events could be placed in context and set against the appropriate *background*'. The presentation would have to be 'documented', so that it would be verifiable, and it might 'in some circumstances' be advisable 'to enclose a formal *documentary appendix* with the description'. The commission should be given to a historian, to be written 'in accordance with academic principles', and 'complete confidence in the person commissioned would be essential'. Näf was convinced that such a publication – 'undertaken in the right way – would have a politically beneficial effect and academic value'.[8]

Subsequently, the project was completely transformed by the EPD. This occurred partly on the basis of information on a similar project in Sweden, but also as a result of a report by Pilet-Golaz and, not least, Näf's own report. All that was now being attempted was a collection of essays on Switzerland's humanitarian activities during the war. This transformation of the White Paper is all the more astonishing in that the original plan for a collection of documents had in no way been conceived as a critical reworking of the past but, rather, as an apologetic presentation of the way neutrality had been handled under Axis pressure. This transformation, then, is clearly illustrative of a policy which Peter Hug has described as compensation for 'Switzerland's failure to participate in the construction of post-war peace by means of nationally exaggerated humanitarian activities'.[9] However, the transformation of the project was not yet a reflection of isolation in foreign policy, since in the spring of 1946 the EPD intended to proceed with the planned publication 'in particular in order to create a psychological climate favourable to conditional Swiss membership of the United Nations'.[10]

It was clear to the Federal Council that the transformation of the publication to a collection of propaganda essays would certainly not meet the need for explanation in domestic policy. So, for a brief period, the EPD pursued a dual approach, also contemplating the option envisaged in the Näf report of a 'documented presentation of Swiss wartime foreign policy by a historian commissioned by the Federal Council',[11] in other words a Bonjour report *ante litteram*. This approach was adopted because the humanitarian pamphlet was useless for the purposes of an apologia in so far as there could be no explanation and no excuse for the evasive policy towards the Axis if the central argument of jeopardy was excluded. Although the form of publication was still undetermined, consideration was being given to the possibility of a report by the Federal Council to the Federal Assembly. Näf was again selected from a shortlist[12] of distinguished historians for this project. However, the trail of this projected publication vanishes after a discussion between Petitpierre and the professor from Berne at the end of February 1946. As is explained below, the aborted project surfaced again in a different form 16 years later with the commission to Edgar Bonjour.

Initially, the further progress of the other humanitarian White Paper proceeded satisfactorily. After careful selection of the authors, some of whom had indicated their willingness for the text to be edited by the authorities, the articles[13] were delivered to the EPD during the latter part of 1946. As soon as the contributions had been received, they were passed on for 'editing'. But the fate of the project then took a different turn. Since by 1947 the original purpose of publication – creating a favourable atmosphere for a Swiss conditional accession to the UN – was no longer on the political agenda, Petitpierre considered whether the work might at least be suitable for use for other propaganda purposes. However, work on the publication became dilatory from the autumn of 1946 and was abandoned altogether in 1947–48, although contact had already been established with publishing houses in Switzerland and elsewhere.[14]

OFFICIAL INTRIGUES AGAINST HISTORIANS

As regards the official obstruction of independent research based on Swiss official files, we can establish that the regulation of 1864, as supplemented by the 1944 regulation on the disclosure and lending of files from the Federal Archive, formally introduced a 50-year period for which the files were sealed, which was not relaxed by the revised regulation of 1957. In Switzerland the sealing of the files from the Second World War period caused no problems, even though the regulations offered no prospect of complete opening of these files until the remote year of 1995. The increased pressure brought to bear on Switzerland from outside for it to 'come to terms with the past' was countered with selective and controlled access to the files on official instructions in the form of official reports.

However, the suppression of foreign documents proved much more difficult. In this case I can demonstrate how the EPD, under the leadership of Federal Councillor Max Petitpierre, did not flinch at intriguing against researchers so that they were refused access by the Allies to the captured German files. Four cases will make this point clear:

First, in a personal and confidential letter of 8 July 1953 to the Swiss ambassador in the United States, Karl Bruggmann, the head of the Department of Political Affairs, Alfred Zehnder, wrote:

> A history student at Berne University, Mr Fritz Steck-Keller, is intending to write a dissertation on 'The spiritual defence of Switzerland in the last world war' ... Experience has shown that he is looking for material designed to compromise individuals. In the

absence of any knowledge to the contrary, it would seem at first glance that he intends to write a sensational book rather than an academically objective study. Having consulted with the office of the Dean of the Phil. I faculty, we have formed the opinion that Mr Steck should be provided, for the purposes of his dissertation, only with the printed reports of the Federal Council and other publications but not with unpublished documents from the Federal Political Department, the Federal Justice and Police Department and the Federal Archive.

This confirms the restrictive way in which the Swiss documents were handled. However, since the foreign office documents in the possession of the Allies also included correspondence from the German embassy in Berne, the EPD was concerned that researchers might gain access to these documents. Zehnder thus continued:

> I now hear that Mr Steck has very close links with American counter-intelligence in Germany, and it is perfectly possible that he may base his sensational publication on the material held by the Americans. We would like to prevent this, specifically because we do not believe it is in Switzerland's interests to allow a campaign to be launched against Switzerland today based on incautious utterances during the war, simply because of a one-sided publication which lays heavy emphasis on personalities. ... Could you not find out who in Washington could give a pointer to the American authorities in Germany and Switzerland to the effect that Mr Steck should not be allowed access to this material on any pretext? I would ask you not to confine yourself to the one specific case, but to try to establish an arrangement which is independent of the Steck case which I mention more by way of illustration. The general idea, then, would be to provoke an instruction from the superior American authorities to the effect that the ... material on Switzerland should not be open for inspection by any private Swiss individual who is unable to produce a recommendation from the Federal Political Department issued for that specific purpose.[15]

Fritz Steck never completed his dissertation and subsequently made a career as a journalist, working in Tokyo as the Far East correspondent of *NZZ* and Radio DRS (and later for the German TV ARD as well). Returning to Switzerland, he became editor of the *Thurgauer Zeitung*. A long-standing employee of the *Echo der Zeit* described him as a serious and highly competent journalist.[16]

Secondly, attempts to prevent independent research were directed not only against students but also against fully qualified historians. In 1954 Rudolf von Albertini took an interest in captured Italian files that had been microfilmed by the Americans. He asked the Swiss embassy in Washington for information. As a result, Legation Counsellor Roy Hunziker examined these microfilms and compiled a list of documents on Switzerland. When the headquarters in Berne learned of this, the matter went straight to the highest echelons of the department. Federal Councillor Petitpierre not only approved a tough personal and confidential letter from Zehnder to Bruggmann but even intended to investigate Hunziker:

> It is extremely annoying to us that the documents to which you refer have fallen into the hands of a private individual.[17] We do not know what Mr Rudolf von Albertini wants with them. He is an outside lecturer in modern history at Zurich University … However, it seems fair to assume that he is looking for topical and possibly sensational material to make his lectures more interesting. If this assumption is correct, Mr von Albertini, and thus Mr Hunziker too, will have done us a severe disservice … A non-selective publication [of the Italian documents] by a Swiss lecturer could have consequences in domestic politics that would not suit us at present. You know from earlier correspondence the skill with which [federal archivist] Prof. [Léon] Kern was able to prevent the publication of certain sensational documents from German archives[18] … As far as Dr von Albertini is concerned, then … we would ask you to tell him that he will be refused any help by the Embassy until such time as further instructions are received from Berne. Such instructions will not be given until we have had the opportunity to talk to Mr von Albertini and find out what sort of chap he is and what he is up to. We are still deeply concerned that a member of your staff so casually offered to help when asked to do so, without thinking that handing over such important documents to a private individual might have very unpleasant consequences for us.[19]

Bruggmann was alarmed by the tone of the letter and immediately cleared up the misunderstanding by telegram: Albertini had not seen any files, but Hunziker had looked through the material and mentioned only 'what he regarded as harmless'. In addition, Bruggmann gave an assurance that, if Albertini had asked for the material, 'we would of course have sent it to you first for censorship'.[20] The department indicated its satisfaction with this explanation, and Zehnder was later able to confirm in a personal and confidential letter to Bruggmann 'that Mr Hunziker has kept within the bounds of what a diplomat must be expected to do in such a difficult situation'.[21] Hunziker subsequently told Albertini that it had proved more complicated to get hold of the microfilm copies because of American censorship regulations: 'At any rate,' Hunziker wrote, 'I couldn't go into the matter any further, because I am being sent to a posting in the Far East and I shall be leaving very shortly.'[22] So the lecturer from Zurich expressed his cordial thanks to the Swiss embassy in Washington and confirmed that he had no alternative 'but to "call the whole thing off"'.[23] The Italian documents which had been kept from Albertini were microfilmed by the Swiss envoys in Washington and passed on for evaluation to the retired federal archivist Léon Kern. In 1959 these copies eventually found their way into the Federal Archive, causing the then archivist Leonhard Haas to assure the minister concerned, Robert Kohli, that they would be stored with all due discretion and shown only to civil servants with the appropriate authorisation.[24] Thus these documents, too, were successfully taken out of circulation.

The third case highlights, ironically, the official obstruction of researchers which even went so far as an attempt to keep the German files from those chosen few who were working on official instructions. Professor Carl Ludwig from Basle, who had been commissioned in July 1954 to write a report[25] for the Federal Assembly on Swiss refugee policy, was refused, at Petitpierre's urging, Swiss diplomatic assistance to obtain access to the German files, even though Federal Councillor Markus Feldmann had acknowledged after 'deep thought' that this 'would probably give a rather peculiar impression'. 'In that case it would be easy to give the impression that the Federal Council intends to draw a veil of secrecy or silence over an essential part of the story of its refugee policy, and any such impression would naturally diminish the importance of the report.'[26] The difference of opinion between the two heads of department ceased to matter when Ludwig announced that he could obtain the document in question 'for himself',[27] as the *Schweizerischer Beobachter* had previously demonstrated when it exposed the Rothmund affair and the 'J' stamp on the basis of the German files.[28]

A fourth example occurred in the autumn of 1958 when the issue of Switzerland's coverage of its own history flared up again. The new revelations were triggered by a series of articles by Johann Wolfgang Brügel. After each volume of the *Documents on German Foreign Policy* had been published, the appropriate files were opened to the public. Drawing on these, over five years Brügel published from London a large number of articles in the *Berner Tagwacht*, the Zurich *Volksrecht* and the Basle *Arbeiter-Zeitung*, which immediately triggered defence reflexes within the EPD. Thus, at the end of November 1958, Armin Daeniker, the Swiss ambassador in the United Kingdom, reported in a confidential letter to Rudolf Bindschedler, head of the EPD legal department, that he had approached the Foreign Office to point out 'the serious consequences that have arisen or may yet arise from Dr Brügel's dispatches to the social democrat newspapers in Switzerland for which he writes. The liberal interpretation of the guidelines has had an effect in terms of political propaganda which is not in line with the intended purpose of those guidelines and must be assessed as obvious abuse.' The British, said Daeniker, had shown 'complete understanding' for his position but would have to reserve the right to examine the question of 'whether and how Dr Brügel could be discreetly refused access to the documents relating to Switzerland'. The problem was that the files had already been released for the purposes of scientific research and – probably because of his academic title – 'Dr Brügel can hardly be denied the status of a scholar'. As a possible solution, Daeniker was considering insisting on the misuse of the documents. Regarding Brügel, the diplomat vouchsafed the information that his journalistic activities, as far as was known, 'were serious in nature' and that personally, too, 'nothing to his disadvantage is known'.[29] The attempt by the EPD to exert influence against Brügel was to be abandoned as early as January 1959, because the British were ultimately unwilling to change the rules for access to the captured German files simply for the sake of Switzerland, since an agreement had already been reached on their return to Germany and the right of public access there. Thus Bindschedler commented resignedly that 'there is no further point in pursuing the Brügel affair'.[30]

OBSTRUCTION AGAINST THE DOCUMENTS ON GERMAN
FOREIGN POLICY

Switzerland's first contact with captured German files came in 1948 in connection with the clarification of the National Socialist activities in Switzerland, when the Federal Prosecutor's Office was looking for evidence in the files of the *Reichssicherheitshauptamt*. The EPD had known since the end of February 1948 that the Swedish foreign ministry had 'now finally obtained the long-sought permission from the British and American authorities'[31] to inspect the files of the German Foreign Office. The EPD thus proposed to extend its researches to these diplomatic documents. The Swiss procedure was nothing unusual – on the contrary, Switzerland had been very late in making its application for access. As far back as September 1945, Sweden had become the first neutral state to sound out the Americans about the possibility of inspecting the diplomatic files.[32] Although the Department of State had refused permission at the time,[33] it subsequently abandoned the position it had adopted and granted access to, for example, Norwegian, Dutch and Danish missions, and later a Swedish mission as well. At the end of January 1952 Switzerland, too, received permission 'for a representative of the Swiss Embassy to be allowed to inspect the

German Foreign Office files'.[34] Shortly afterwards, the Swiss ambassador in the United Kingdom, Henri de Torrenté, was reporting in a secret letter to Petitpierre: the first inspection, he said, had indicated that there were documents 'whose existence you may judge it expedient not to disclose. Indeed, from the Swiss point of view, this seems to me a matter for the greatest caution.'[35] Because of the potentially explosive nature of the issue the EPD considered sending the federal archivist, Professor Léon Kern, to London immediately, and on 22 February 1952 the Federal Council also adopted a resolution to that effect, since 'having regard to the disadvantages that the disclosure of some of these documents might entail for Switzerland, it would be appropriate to obtain advance knowledge of them as soon as possible'.[36] Just a week later, the federal archivist was in London. This visit was followed by others. As a result, Kern was able to inspect the documents relating to Switzerland. They included, in particular, the German documents on Franco-Swiss military cooperation, and the archivist was able to learn that the publishers of the *Documents on German Foreign Policy* had decided to publish these. In a report to Petitpierre he emphasised the problematical aspects of the situation: if the Federal Council should consider publication of certain documents to be inopportune and inconvenient, intervention to that effect with the governments concerned would be a very delicate matter. This was because the editors – in contrast with other editions[37] – had a free hand with the selection of the documents and had been given a promise that their governments would not influence their work. It was improbable, therefore, thought Kern, that the selection already made would be changed.[38] The EPD also learned of the Allied intention to release unpublished documents to the public in due course. The fact that these papers would not – as the Swiss had previously assumed – remain buried in the archives had extensive and unpleasant consequences: 'The precautionary measures we might take will thus have only a temporary effect.'[39]

The matter flared up again on 7 November 1952, when Professor William E. Rappard, director of the Graduate Institute of International Studies in Geneva and an influential adviser to the Federal Council, telephoned Petitpierre and reported that Professor Maurice Baumont, a French lecturer at his institute, knew the content of captured German files which related to discussions between General Guisan and the French army command.[40] Baumont obviously knew what he was talking about, because the Frenchman was one of the senior editors of the Allied edition and jointly responsible, together with his British and American colleagues, for the selection of documents. As a result of Rappard's intervention, Petitpierre indulged in a burst of hectic activity, held numerous discussions, and on 28 November 1952 presented the results of his efforts to the Federal Council. It could be concluded from information that the federal archivist had been able to obtain from Baumont that the British and French were opposed to publication of the documents on Franco-Swiss military cooperation. The position of the Americans was not known, so there was no need to establish contact. The foreign minister concluded from this that it would be premature for the Federal Council to adopt a final position, and the government agreed with this.[41]

In mid-June 1955 Rappard again reported to the foreign minister on indiscretions committed by Baumont, but this time with the latter's agreement, as the editor had come under heavy pressure from the French Foreign Ministry and senior French officers in NATO, who were strenuously opposed to publication of the documents on Franco-Swiss military cooperation. Baumont hoped to obtain political support as a result of his indiscretions, as the American editor, Paul R. Sweet, and his British colleague, Margaret Lambert, had unequivocally decided to publish the documents in question as planned. Although the Frenchman had held out against publication, the other two editors had insisted on publishing everything. On 8 July 1955, Federal President Petitpierre again brought the matter before the Federal Council with the question: 'What to do to avoid publication: approaches to London and Washington? Risk: probable failure – indiscretion: accusations against the Federal Council: it could cause greater interest within the country.'[42] After Petitpierre had informed the Federal Council of the editors' intention to go ahead and publish the compromising documents, he asked the Council members whether the government should undertake any action 'to prevent publication'. Federal Councillor Feldmann considered a political action to be highly dangerous, and advised the Federal Council to avoid any action 'which could cause problems in future regarding public confidence'. 'Are we to accept the risks of [a] demarche in order to protect [the] General? I say no!' was his unambiguous pronouncement. Federal Councillor Philipp Etter, however, tended to favour intervention by the Federal Council 'without commitment', in other words an unofficial attempt to prevent publication, because the matter 'will be a serious blow to our policy of neutrality'. Federal Councillor Hans Streuli went along with Feldmann and advised against any intervention, because 'if it were to come out that [the] Federal Council tried to prevent publication it would create a bad impression!'. After discussion, the government unanimously resolved not to embark on any political initiative. However, it left open the possibility of intervention through the federal archivist.[43]

In February 1956 the Department of State received a letter from the NATO command strongly supporting an initiative by Marshal

Alphonse-Pierre Juin against publication of the documents on Franco-Swiss military cooperation, on the grounds that the matter would be seriously detrimental to NATO policy'.[44] Back in 1952, high-ranking NATO representatives had shown concern regarding the publication of these documents. As a result, Marshal Juin had approached the Quai d'Orsay 'to express the gravest objections regarding the publication of these documents'.[45] Then, in the spring of 1955, Baumont proposed that the agreed selection should be reviewed and the documents complained of by Juin and the Quai d'Orsay omitted. When Sweet and Lambert proved rigidly opposed to this, the Frenchman ceased to exert pressure at editorial level.

However, the publishers in Washington and London were soon to be made aware of the unpleasant consequences of NATO's intervention. Following a similar NATO approach to the Foreign Office, an alarmed Lambert wrote to Sweet on 7 May 1956 that there were further problems: 'The Swiss again, and this time a very high-level approach.'[46] In his reply, Sweet confirmed that the intervention was 'at a very high level', but also pointed out that it had not come directly from the Swiss.[47] Both editors agreed that, if they were to receive a categorical order not to publish the documents, they would resign. As a counter-measure to the NATO intervention the historians in the Department of State presented a carefully worded opinion emphasising that insistence on the omission of the documents could hardly fail to wreck the publication project.[48] It was then agreed that the embassy in Switzerland would be notified and a memorandum drafted for the EPD. Paradoxically, it was not until this defensive step was taken that the whole affair became an official diplomatic matter. On 16 May 1956 the American ambassador in Switzerland, Frances E. Willis, called on Minister Zehnder. On receiving the memorandum, the diplomat reacted swiftly and emphatically: from the Swiss standpoint, he said, publication would be unfortunate and regrettable. They discussed the matter for an hour and a half, the former federal archivist being present for part of the time. Although Kern understood the principles of editorial freedom that governed the Allied edition, he nevertheless asked the ambassador whether the selection of documents made by the three senior editors could be reconsidered. The archivist already knew, of course, that the British and Americans intended to return their captured archives shortly, and that these would then be made accessible to the public in the Federal Republic. Even so, he hoped that a fairly long period would elapse before any researcher turned up the ominous documents in the gigantic mass of files. While Kern was putting the Swiss viewpoint to the ambassador, Zehnder hastened to Petitpierre for instructions. The foreign minister's reaction was even more clearly opposed to publication than that of the secretary-general: 'The principal ground was that publication would render it extremely difficult in the future for the Federal Council to take action in an analogous situation.'[49]

In plain language, Petitpierre indicated to the Americans that in the event of a direct threat the 'armed neutral' might be willing to conclude similar secret agreements on military cooperation – *mutatis mutandis*, in the context of the Cold War, with NATO against the anticipated Soviet aggressor – to those General Guisan had concluded in 1939–40 with the French general staff against the feared German attack. Although the hint was a vague one, It was swiftly picked up in Washington. Petitpierre's argument was not without a certain irony, and could be seen on closer observation to be nothing less than a 'gem of neutrality'. Although the argument was irresistibly clear in terms of the political logic of a bipolar world, and represented a perfect example of the Swiss dialectic between the semblance and substance of neutrality, it was totally paradoxical in terms of the logic of armed neutrality that Switzerland had proclaimed for the purposes of both domestic and foreign policy – *urbi et orbi*: the neutral demands that the evidence of its non-neutrality should be suppressed, because as a neutral it intends to still remain a non-neutral.

Despite the dangerous potential of the affair, the Federal Council was opposed to an official initiative, and Zehnder emphatically made the point to the ambassador that the discussions were highly informal. However, the Swiss desire for suppression of publication was not unknown among diplomatic practices because the Department of State – in perfect compliance with the rules of international courtesy that had been observed since official government documentary publications had first been produced in the nineteenth century[50] – required clearance from Berne before the publication of any Swiss material in the official American series of documents on *Foreign Relations of the United States*.[51] Willis, at any rate, had gathered two essential points from his discussion with Zehnder:

> First, the Swiss Government would be extremely unhappy to see the documents published. Second, if the documents are published, any opportunity of the development of a closer working relationship with the Swiss will be impaired for an indefinite time … We … believe publication of these documents and particularly under our auspices will jeopardise what we believe our long term objectives to be.[52]

Since the French, too, continued to oppose publication, the Department of State discussed the situation with the British embassy in the USA on

24 July 1956. The Americans summarised the matter by referring to the attitudes of the Swiss Federal Council and NATO:

> Since it appeared that publication of these documents by the Allies might affect our relations with the Swiss, our Ambassador in Bern had been asked to take informal soundings. These produced a definite high-level reaction that publication of these documents would be regarded as unfortunate. The Councillor of the Swiss Federal Political Department [Max Petitpierre] made it clear that publicity in this instance would make it extremely difficult for his Government to undertake similar arrangements in case Switzerland should again be under immediate threat of invasion. In addition to these objections from the Swiss, General Gruenther, as a result of conversations with General Juin and other senior officers of NATO, informed the Department that one of the Swiss involved in the 1940 conversations was now the equivalent of a three-star general [Corps Commander Samuel Gonard]. General Gruenther believed that any revelation of this officer's part in these conversations would be personally embarrassing for him and would handicap any negotiations NATO might want to undertake with the Swiss.[53]

The interventions by the American ambassador and the French reached the Department of State along with further protests from the military and the CIA. The Department thus decided to defer publication by means of a ruse until such time as the documents held by the Allies were returned to Germany. On 30 January 1957 the American ambassador was able to inform the Swiss foreign minister that the documents complained of would not be published for the time being.

When the new American administration took office, the publishers of the *Documents on German Foreign Policy* were finally able to bring out their volume – long since prepared for publication – five years late, in the spring of 1961.[54] The news of imminent publication horrified Petitpierre: since his discussion with the American ambassador in 1956 he had, in fact, believed that the matter was 'buried for good'. He still regarded publication as 'absolutely inconceivable'.[55] The foreign minister thus decided to have the American ambassador, Henry Taylor Jr, summoned to see the secretary-general of the EPD. In preparations for the talks Petitpierre asked the minister, Robert Kohli, 'to do your utmost to ensure that this publication does not take place'. The minister was to 'portray any such publication as an "unfriendly act" towards Switzerland, the same terms that the head of the department had also used to Miss Willis, and also to inform Mr Taylor that the American publication would, of course, very significantly influence our future attitude to the American authorities'.[56] So, on 7 February 1961, Kohli explained to the American ambassador that the Swiss had ceased expecting publication and that the intention to publish as now disclosed seemed 'politically imprudent'. The Swiss would, therefore, 'appreciate its abandonment'. In his reply, Taylor pointed out that publication was a matter of agreement between the three Western Allies, and that the Department of State had already succeeded in 1956, at the request of Switzerland, in deferring printing of the documents until a further volume appeared. That volume, however, was now about to be published, and it was hardly possible at this stage to prevent the documents on Franco-Swiss military cooperation being included. The five-year delay achieved in 1956, therefore, could in itself be considered a success. In fact, the volume had already been printed by that time, and was with the binders. 'Any intervention in London or Paris is hardly likely to have any practical value in these circumstances,' observed Kohli in a memorandum to Petitpierre, but 'at any rate the Americans have been left in no doubt that the impending publication is contrary to our wishes.' [57]

When hopes of the continued suppression of the Franco-Swiss cooperation talks finally had to be abandoned, the Federal Council moved into damage limitation mode. Since the publication also included a document on an approach made by Corps Commander Ulrich Wille to the German ambassador in Switzerland, which tainted that senior officer with the suspicion of treason, the Federal Council, at a press conference given on 21 April 1961, shortly before publication of the volume, succeeded in converting the dreaded 'Guisan affair' into a 'Wille affair'. As a last resort, therefore, and in the nick of time, Wille became the sacrifice that would prevent the feared questioning of neutrality as a result of the uproar over another scandal. But the foundations of the neutrality myth were shaken anyway, although the 'affair of the deputy' successfully prevented the full dimensions of this becoming apparent to the Swiss public.

COMMISSIONING OF THE BONJOUR REPORT

On 6 July 1962 the Swiss government resolved to commission the historian Edgar Bonjour 'to prepare *for the Federal Council* a comprehensive report on Switzerland's foreign policy during the last world war'. [58] Following the death of Näf, Bonjour had thus moved forward to first place in the 1946 White Paper shortlist; [59] he had been identified as a suitable and independent figure whose publications had already deserved appreciation from neutral Switzerland. Bonjour had to promise, not 'to say anything to anyone'. Previously, consideration had actually been given to allowing the tried and tested reporting practice to be resumed, former Federal Councillor Philipp Etter being given the delicate task. The incentive to rework the history of Switzerland's neutrality came, of course, from external pressure. The EPD's proposal of 1 May 1962 referred to various publications, some of which cast 'a peculiar light on the mechanics of Swiss neutrality'. In specific terms, the proposal referred to 'two documents in Volume XI of the British publication of documents on German foreign policy', which mentioned 'cooperation between the Swiss and French armies in 1940', and to the book *Spying for Peace* by the British journalist Jon Kimche.[60] In this publication, which created a major sensation in Switzerland, General Guisan was 'disproportionately extolled as the saviour of his country whereas the Federal Council was damned as a complete failure'.[61] This was a blow to the Federal Council, which had been trying for years to prevent publication of details of the Franco-Swiss military cooperation in the *Documents on German Foreign Policy* and so, ultimately, had been screening the general. Not until the secret of the Franco-Swiss military cooperation had come to light, and under pressure from treatments like Kimche's, necessarily speculative because of lack of access to the archives in Switzerland, had the Federal Council allowed itself to be persuaded to open up the privileged one-way street to research by a proven historian into the history of the Second World War.

The 'process of coming to terms', which began with Bonjour's commission, would 'never have begun of its own accord',[62] and but for the publication of the *Documents on German Foreign Policy* 'nothing would ever have been heard of it'.[63] Of course, it would not be until the mid-1970s that investigations into contemporary history became possible in general terms, because the Federal Council's commission to Bonjour was conceived with a view not to publication but, initially, merely for internal explanation. Only pressure from the interested public compelled the Federal Council to approve publication of the Bonjour report. It was to appear in 1970. But there was evidence that the revising of Swiss wartime history was still causing difficulties to the political authorities: first, in the form of the opposition to Bonjour's plans to include an edition of the sources with his report, and, secondly, once Bonjour had been able to carry out his plans anyway by bringing pressure to bear, in the form of the 'censorship of the Federal Political Department', which 'deleted at least one third of the original manuscript, in many cases highly informative documents' from his first documentary supplement, as he himself bitterly stated in his foreword.[64] Once again, the public reacted. The Swiss press raised the cry of scandal, and the historian and National Councillor Walther Hofer tabled a parliamentary question. Bonjour was thus able to incorporate many of the censored documents into the subsequent volumes. But important indications suggest the inescapable conclusion that, in the 1970s, the EPD under the leadership of Federal Councillor Pierre Graber also censored Bonjour's two other documentary supplements.[65] When the last volume of the documents appeared in 1976, the unending story of the 'Swiss White Paper' had finally ended: back in 1945, indeed, Werner Näf had recommended in his report 'that the description be accompanied by a formal *documentary supplement*'.[66] Bonjour himself knew the origins of this long story, and, since he had had to wage open war against government censorship in order to produce his collection of documents, he justified himself in sibylline style with the above quotation from Näf – without mentioning his name, naturally.[67]

CONCLUSION

In the post-war years it is possible clearly to distinguish four phases in the official handling of contemporary history, through which it is possible to trace the initially postulated construction (and gradual crumbling) of an artificial historical construct which was functional to a mythologised concept of neutrality and a constituent part of the basis of 'Swiss special case' in the community ideology:

1. The first short phase lasted until about 1947–48. As Switzerland's foreign policy groped cautiously forward into the post-war community of nations, its objective was to counteract the pressure of foreign criticism and show the humanitarian achievements of neutral Switzerland in their 'right' light by publishing a White Paper.
2. Once the withdrawal of the Federal Council into the new redoubt (réduit) of a mythological special-case construct, favoured by the Cold War, had finally begun, the options for openness were closed, and not only in foreign policy. The official history of Switzerland during the war was constructed and stylised by official reports, in the absence of public access to the files, to constitute an excuse for the political course adopted. This second phase was characterised by a reactive and consistently pursued policy of suppression of independent historical revision. This period lasted until 1961, when the key military secret of neutrality – General Guisan's deals with France – was exposed by the Allied revelations in the *Documents on German Foreign Policy*.
3. Only when the great secret of Franco-Swiss military cooperation had come to light, and under the pressure of the revelations still spouting from the German files, did it become possible and essential to embark upon a revision of Switzerland's own history and exhume the

aborted White Paper project. Thus, in 1962, the Federal Council commissioned Bonjour to write a report. That report subsequently monopolised contemporary Swiss history until the 1970s.

4. It was not until after the Bonjour report had been published and a number of contemporary historians had petitioned the Parliament in 1972 regarding the lifting of the ban on the release of documents of 1945 and before that pressure from the interested public enforced a more liberal attitude to archive access. The revision of the Federal Archive Regulation in 1973 finally created the necessary conditions for the evolution of an independent historiography of Switzerland's role in the Second World War, based on the broader availability of sources.

NOTES

1 This chapter is based on the chapter 'Auswirkungen und Folgen der "Documents on German Foreign Policy" am Beispiel der Schweiz, 1945–1975', of my dissertation: Sacha Zala, *Geschichte unter der Schere politischer Zensur. Amtliche Aktensammlungen im internationalen, Vergleich*, Berne, 1999. A slightly revised version of the chapter appeared as *Gebändigte Geschichte. Amtliche Historiographie und ihr Malaise mit der Geschichte der Neutralität, 1945–1961*, Berne, 1998. For a discussion of censorship of diplomatic documents see my article 'Diplomatic documents', in Derek Jones (ed.), *Censorship: A World Encyclopedia*, Chicago and London, 2000.

2 The Federal Council decision of 22 October 1975, upholding Kreis' complaint, is reprinted in Daniel Stapfer, 'Zeitgeschichtliche Forschung und Recht in der Schweiz. Zur Entwicklung der Akteneinsichtsrechte, 1944–1993', Zurich, 1993 (unpublished licentiateship paper), Annex VI.

3 *Documents on German Foreign Policy, 1918–1945*, Series C, 6 vols, Washington, DC/London, 1957–83; Series D, 13 vols, Washington/London, 1949–64. The German edition later appeared under the series title *Akten zur deutschen auswärtigen Politik*, 1918–1945; Series C, 1933–1937, 6 vols, Göttingen, 1971–81; Series D: 1937–1941, 13 vols, Baden-Baden, 1950–56, 1961, Frankfurt-am-Main, 1962–63, Bonn, 1964, Göttingen, 1969–70.

4 Edgar Bonjour, *Geschichte der Schweizerischen Neutralität*, 9 vols, Basle, 1967–76.

5 *Bericht des Bundesrates an die Bundesversammlung über die antidemokratische Tätigkeit von Schweizern und Ausländern im Zusammenhang mit dem Kriegsgeschehen*, Part 1: 'Nationalsozialismus', Berne, 28 December 1945; Part 2: 'Faschismus', Berne, 17 May 1946; Part 3: 'Kommunismus', Berne, 21 May 1946.

6 General Henri Guisan also practised the art of settling accounts: *Rapport du Général Guisan à l'Assemblée Fédérale sur le service actif, 1939–1945*, 1946 (Annexe I: 'Rapport du Chef de l'Etat-Major Général de l'Armée', Annexe II: 'Rapport du Commandant de l'Aviation et de la D.C.A., Rapport de l'Adjudant Général de l'Armée, Rapport du Chef de l'Instruction de l'Armée, Rapport du Chef du Personnel de l'Armée'). The criticism levelled at the government by Guisan induced the Federal Council to produce a counter-report: *Bericht des Bundesrates an die Bundesversammlung zum Bericht des Generals über den Aktivdienst, 1939–1945,*

1947. The Federal Council also produced reports on press policy (*Bericht des Bundesrates an die Bundesversammlung über die schweizerische Pressepolitik im Zusammenhang mit dem Kriegsgeschehen, 1939–1945*, 1946) and on the war economy (*Die schweizerische Kriegswirtschaft 1939–1948. Bericht des Volkswirtschafts-departementes*, 1950).

7 Even so, Näf was not opposed to a more liberal attitude towards the sealing of the archives. The complete quotation in fact reads: 'Even if, as seems to me to be desirable in itself, the rule requiring relatively long-term sealing of the archives were to be abandoned, even so it would … .'

8 Werner Näf, 'Gutachten betreffend die Frage einer Veröffentlichung über die Beziehungen der Schweiz zum Ausland während der Kriegsjahre 1939–1945', submitted to Federal Councillor Max Petitpierre, Gümligen, 18 November 1945, Swiss Federal Archive (ΓΛ), E 2001 (E), –/1, 98. Emphasis in the original.

9 Peter Hug, 'Verhinderte oder verpasste Chancen? Die Schweiz und die Vereinten Nationen, 1943–1947', *Itinera*, 18, 1996, pp. 84–97, in this case p. 97.

10 Letter from Minister Daniel Secrétan to Minister Camille Gorgé, Berne, 21 May 1946, FA, E 2001 (E), –/1, 98.

11 As note 8.

12 The following professors were listed: Edgar Bonjour (Basle), Werner Kägi (Basle), Richard Feller (Berne), Werner Näf (Berne), Jacques Freymond (Lausanne), Hans Nabholz (Zurich), Jean Rodolphe de Salis (ETH). The preferences were: 1. Näf, 2. Bonjour, 3. de Salis. Memorandum (from Secrétan) to Petitpierre, 4 February 1946, FA, E 2001 (E), –/1, 98.

13 The articles submitted were: Camille Gorgé, 'La représentation des intérêts étrangers'; Jacques Chenevière, 'Le Comité international de la Croix-Rouge. 1 er septembre 1939–30 juin 1946'; Albert Malche, 'L'internement et l'hospitalisation des militaires et des civils'; Guido Calgari, 'Geografia della solidarietà. L'opera del Dono svizzero per le vittime della guerra'; Maurice Zermatten, 'La grande pitié de l'enfance européenne'; Fritz Ernst, 'L'oeuvre de la Croix-Rouge suisse'.

14 The history of the White Paper is also discussed, along with other problems, by Luc van Dongen, *La Suisse face à la Seconde Guerre mondiale, 1945–1948. Emergence et construction d'une mémoire publique*, ed. Geneva Historical and Archaeological Society, Geneva, 1997, and see also his contribution to the present volume.

15 Personal and confidential letter from Zehnder to Bruggmann, Berne, 8 July 1953, FA, E 2001 (E), 1979/28, 4. Reprinted in Zala, *Gebändigte Geschichte* (as note 1).

16 Information provided by Dr Hans Lang to the author, 23 April 1997 and 23 August 1997.

17 This was completely wrong, as Albertini had received only a list.

18 See pp. 320–6.

19 Personal and confidential letter from Zehnder to Bruggmann, Berne, 20 May 1954, FA, E 2001 (E), 1979/28, 2.

20 Telegram from Bruggmann to the FPD, Washington, 29 May 1954, ibid.

21 Personal and confidential letter from Zehnder to Bruggmann, Berne, 22 June 1954, ibid.

22 Letter from Hunziker to Albertini, Washington, 21 July 1954, ibid.

23 Letter from Albertini to Hunziker, Zurich, 31 July 1954, ibid.

24 Letter from Haas to Kohli, Berne, 27 August 1959, ibid.

25 Carl Ludwig, *Die Flüchtlingspolitik der Schweiz in den Jahren 1933 bis 1955. Bericht an den Bundesrat zuhanden der eidgenössischen Räte*, Berne, 1957, subsequently also published as a book (Berne, 1966).

26 Letter from Feldmann to Petitpierre, Berne, 2 November 1954, FA, E 2800 (–),

1967/60, 9.

27 Letter from Petitpierre to Feldmann, Berne, 13 November 1954, ibid.

28 *Der Schweizerische Beobachter*, 28, 31 March 1954, pp. 282–84.

29 Confidential letter from Daeniker to Bindschedler, London, 28 November 1958, FA, E 2001 (E), 1979/28, 4.

30 Confidential letter from Bindschedler to the Swiss embassy in the United Kingdom, Berne, 10 January 1959, ibid.

31 Letter from the Swiss embassy in Sweden to the Department of Political Affairs, Stockholm, 27 February 1948, FA, E 2001 (E), 1967/113, 385.

32 Confidential letter from the US embassy in Sweden to the Secretary of State, Stockholm, 28 September 1945, National Archives Washington (NA), Record Group (RG) 59, Central File (CF) 1945–1949, Box 5674, 840.414/9–2845.

33 The Department of State feared, in fact, that this might have created a precedent for inquiries from other neutral governments. Confidential memorandum from James W. Riddleberger to William P. Cumming, Washington, 11 October 1945, ibid., FW 840.414/9–2845.

34 Confidential memorandum from Torrenté to Zehnder, London, 24 January 1952, FA, E 2001 (E), 1979/28, 4.

35 Secret letter from Torrenté to Petitpierre, London, 5 February 1952, ibid.

36 Extract from the minutes of the Federal Council meeting of 22 February 1952, ibid.

37 See Zala, *Geschichte unter der Schere* (as note 1), pp. 101ff. and *passim*.

38 Report from Kern, Berne, 9 April 1952, FA, E 2001 (E), 1979/28, 4.

39 Confidential letter from Torrenté to Petitpierre, London, 12 March 1952, ibid.

40 Recording by Petitpierre, Berne, 7 November 1952, 11:15, FA, E 2800 (–), 1967/60, 9.

41 Handwritten memorandum from Petitpierre, Berne, 28 November 1952, ibid.

42 Handwritten memorandum from Petitpierre, Berne, 25 June 1955, ibid.

43 Extract from the minutes and handwritten notes on documents from German archives of the Federal Council meetings of 8 July 1955 to 16 March 1956, ibid.

44 Personal and confidential letter from Sweet to Raymond J. Sontag (former senior editor of the *Documents on German Foreign Policy*), Lewes (Delaware), 21 August 1956, Archives of the Hoover Institution on War, Revolution and Peace (AHI), Stanford University, Stanford (CA), Paul R. Sweet Collection. An extract from this document in German translation is reprinted in Paul R. Sweet, 'Der Versuch amtlicher Einflussnahme auf die Edition der "Documents on German Foreign Policy, 1933–1941". Ein Fall aus den fünfziger Jahren', *Vierteljahrshefte für Zeitgeschichte*, 39, 1991, pp. 265–303. Quoted here from the original, p. 2.

45 Letter from Baumont to Sweet (spring 1955). A copy was enclosed with a letter from Rappard to Petitpierre (Geneva, 21 June 1955), FA, E 2800 (–), 1967/60, 9.

46 Letter from Lambert to Sweet, London, 7 May 1956, AHI, Sweet Collection.

47 Personal letter from Sweet to Lambert, Washington, 23 May 1956, ibid.

48 As note 44.

49 Secret letter from Willis to C. Burke Elbrick (Deputy Assistant Secretary for European Affairs), Berne, 16 May 1956, NA, RG 59, CF 1955–1959, Box 4778, 862a.423/5–1656.

50 Zala, *Geschichte unter der Schere* (as note 1), pp. 22–45.

51 For example: telegram from the US embassy in Switzerland to the Secretary of State, Berne, 9 April 1951, NA, RG 59, CF 1950–1954, Box 0096, 023.1/4–951. In addition, Swiss diplomacy was keeping a careful eye on the publications of the American edition of the documents. In March 1955, for example, the Swiss

embassy in the USA sent the FPD the galley proofs of the volume entitled *Foreign Relations of the United States. The Conferences at Malta and Yalta 1945* (Washington, 1955), which related to Switzerland. Interestingly – and this has nothing to do with Switzerland – the history of the publication of this volume, from its suppression to the furore surrounding its pre-publication by the *New York Times*, is a striking example of how the publication of editions of documents is frustrated by political influences. See Zala, *Geschichte unter der Schere* (as note 1), pp. 100–7.

52 As note 49.
53 Confidential memorandum of discussions between John Wesly Jones (Western Europe Division), Marselis C. Parsons Jr (Northern European Affairs) and Lancaster (Western Europe Division) with Frederick John Leishman (First Secretary of the British embassy in the USA), Washington, 24 July 1956, NA, RG 59, CF 1955–1959, Box 4742, 862.423/7–2456.
54 Vol. 11, Series D (as note 3). The documents complained of were Docs 11, 138 and 301.
55 Memorandum from Kohli regarding a discussion with Petitpierre, Berne, 24 January 1961, FA, E 2001 (E), 1979/28, 9.
56 Memorandum from Kohli regarding a discussion with Petitpierre, Berne, 6 February 1961, ibid.
57 Memorandum from Kohli to Petitpierre, Berne, 7 February 1961, ibid.
58 Federal Council resolution of 6 July 1962, No. 1196, FA, E 1004.1. Emphasis mine.
59 See note 12.
60 Jon Kimche, *Spying for Peace*, London 1961. German translation, *General Guisans Zweifrontenkrieg. Die Schweiz zwischen 1939 und 1945*, Frankfurt am Main, 1962.
61 Georg Kreis, 'Die schweizerische Neutralität während des Zweiten Weltkrieges in der historischen Forschung', in Louis-Edouard Roulet (ed.), *Les Etats neutres européens et la Seconde Guerre mondiale*, Neuenburg, 1985, pp. 29–53, in this case p. 31.
62 Georg Kreis, 'Die Schweiz der Jahre 1918–1948', in *Geschichtsforschung in der Schweiz. Bilanz und Perspektiven – 1991*, ed. by the AGGS, Basle, 1992, pp. 378–96, in this case p. 380.
63 *Voix Ouvrière*, 28 April 1961. Emphasis in the original.
64 Bonjour, *Neutralität* (as note 4), Vol. 7, p. 11.
65 Zala, *Geschichte unter der Schere* (as note 1), note 548. I am currently investigating the extent and significance of government censorship of the Bonjour report.
66 As note 8.
67 Bonjour, *Neutralität* (as note 4), Vol. 8, p. 13.

15

Lest We Forget. Switzerland and the Second World War: The Sources

ANDREAS KELLERHALS-MAEDER

Even during the Second World War critical voices were raised against Swiss policies, voices which have never been entirely silenced at any point during the 50 years following the conflict, though for much of that time they represented the dissident views of a small minority.[1] Beginning in the 1970s disputes intensified, and since then the critical voices have multiplied significantly. Since 1995, Switzerland's role in the war has once again been the centre of an intense, often polemical international debate. As a direct consequence of this discussion, in December 1996, the Federal Council (government) and Parliament established an Independent Committee of Experts. This decision arose out of a desire for a serious, critical confrontation of the Swiss past, and of the charges levelled with regard to that past: the justification of such charges is independent of the motives of those voicing them. The establishment of the commission is an important contribution to the 'factualisation' of the debate so urgently called for, and an unequivocal renunciation of political motives, short-term window-dressing, and exploitation of the issues for other ends. The further demand that this process be accelerated makes somewhat less sense. Although research efforts to date have been significant, there remain many grey areas and black holes, which must be alleviated by thorough, source-based and time-intensive scholarship.[2]

A description of the range of sources in the Swiss archive system in general, and in the Swiss Federal Archive in particular, can only serve to underscore the great number and diversity of material awaiting evaluation. But with a view towards what sorts of questions should this corpus be described? And how should a body of archival sources be described in the first place? I address the second question.

Methodological preliminaries: how to describe a body of archival sources

The description of a body of archival sources differs from a bibliography in the same respect in which archives differ from libraries or documentation services. The differences lie not in institutional goals – all serve as information brokers – but rather in the character of the raw material they collect, preserve and transmit as 'memories'.

An archive mediates organically created and transmitted information of common provenance, such as that stemming from a parliament, government, federal or cantonal administration, or from the management, directorate or administration of a legal entity, or from an association, or from a natural person. As an institutional and social memory, an archive performs its amnesia-prevention function by making its raw material available to interested parties, thus ultimately permitting not only access, but also interpretation. Put negatively, an archive does not collect information on specific topics; it offers an open-ended, thematically and temporally unbounded selection of sources sharing a clearly defined provenance.

Archival material includes records generated by administrative procedures, and encompasses both the data content and so-called contextual information. The sources preserved in an archive at one time served, in their original role as official files, as working drafts in administrative decision-making and managerial processes. Such files are collections of bits of text, some of which may have come about almost incidentally, and whose value is not purely informational, but also evidential. Files are archived for the purpose of preserving their evidential value over the long term. The value of the information they contain continues to grow as temporal distance from the originating events increases, transforming them into primary sources for historical research. They both provide information about the past, and serve as a necessary precondition for critical interpretations of this same information. An archive thus contains the raw material used in the construction of very different sorts of recollections and historical representations, a construction whose completion also demands both analysis and reception.

These characteristics give rise to the methodological peculiarities of archival searches. Access to archival materials is mediated not by author or subject indexes, but rather by a combination of diverse information on the creation of official documents and their archival preservation. What we are dealing with is a unique search system, one whose individual search tools are often not clearly distinguishable from the sources themselves. It should also be stressed that the various Swiss archives (Federal Archive, cantonal archives and community and private archives), together with the relevant archives abroad, comprise a cohesive network of mutually complementary but individually unique sources. By contrast, the library system offers nearly identical information at each location.[3]

A description of a body of archival sources can be either general or topical. A general description simply inventories extant sources, while a topical description is oriented towards a specific issue, and towards a set of methodological precepts determined by the mnemonic potential and the relevance of the sources. A description of the disposition of source materials in no way replaces the search tools of an archive. Neither should it in any way prejudice the researcher's decision over which portions of the archival material merit analysis, interpretation, evaluation and discussion.

Under ideal conditions, archives are what makes rational historical treatment possible. Competent archival preservation can make the researcher's job considerably easier. The choice of questions and methods, the systematic search for relevant archival materials, and their critical evaluation are all decisive factors in determining the contents and quality of the final research product.

Whether and how a shared view of the past is agreed upon is ultimately up to the participants in the broader social debate. In this process, a rational treatment of the past is possible only if we are prepared to learn. But we should bear in mind that archives can not guarantee the truth; written materials can be just as deceptive as personal recollections.

Focusing on content: which sources warrant description?

Guidelines for the present source description have been derived from the Federal Decree of 13 December 1996, the corresponding Federal Council Decree of 19 December 1996 and from the research aims of the Independent Committee of Experts: 'Switzerland – Second World War' (July, 1997).

The Federal and Federal Council decrees of December 1996 outline four main areas for research, all targeted at discovering the extent and eventual fate of assets which came to Switzerland as a result of National Socialist and fascist dominion elsewhere. To be investigated are, first, assets belonging to victims which subsequently became classified as dormant; second, looted assets; and third, flight capital (which may also have become classified as dormant). The fourth area comprises the history of previous efforts towards accommodation and amelioration (such as the Washington Agreement and the Registration Decree of 1962), now carried forth by the historical labours of the Independent Commission of Experts. Recent discussion has also raised further moral and political questions.[4]

The research areas mandated by federal decree and the open questions raised and theses advanced in public discussion can not be treated in isolation. The thematic and temporal boundaries of the investigation, and the scope of the sources to be taken into consideration, must be redefined. In the research plan of the Independent Expert Commission, the breadth and complexity of the issues find expression, issuing in a discovery-oriented research strategy.

SEARCHING FOR SOURCES IN THE SWISS FEDERAL ARCHIVE

With regard to the history of Switzerland during the Second World War, the sources and search tools of the Swiss Federal Archive are numerous, broad-based and diverse.[5] The materials in Major Division E, 'The Federal State since 1848' (*Bundesstaat seit 1848*), are surely of central importance. These materials are the most closely tied to the central mission of the Swiss Federal Archive. Also of interest are the sources archived in Major Division J, 'Deposits and Donations (Personal Papers)' (*Depositen und Schenkungen*), whose origins lie primarily in the private sector. Materials in Major Division E are almost all ordered according to the provenance principle. Only the section (*fond*) 'National Defense' (*Landesverteidigung*) subdivision (E 27) is organised by the pertinence principle.[6]

To search the archive is thus to transform a question of content into a provenance-oriented and institutionally informed array of sources, selected and ordered for the purpose of identifying significant collections and individual dossiers. The search space is defined by three parameters: the missions of the originating institutions, their structural organisation and information management in the archive.[7]

The Swiss Federal Archive's *Systematic Overview* provides a useful starting-point for any investigation.[8] For eight distinct topic areas, the *Overview* offers an account of the most important materials in Major Division E, as well as a survey of the private bequests.[9] As far as the research goals of 'Switzerland – Second World War' are concerned, this listing proves rather coarse-grained. Other points of entry thus merit more detailed description.

For collections organised by the pertinence principle – fond E27, 'National Defense' – materials have already been ordered according to thematic principles, making access to desired sources in these records quite easy.

Experience has shown that searching collections organised by the provenance principle is substantially more difficult. For example, a search for sources on the crafting of the Swiss neutrality policy and subsequent discussions of that policy can not begin with a simple keyword search in a subject catalogue. We must rather ask, in what contexts did federal agencies contend with the issues surrounding neutrality? To which agencies were the associated tasks delegated? The very first questions must always ask after the official mandate in the context of which the sought-after files might have come about, and after the institutions charged with pursuing that mandate. A systematic listing of official mandates, and the corresponding listing of agencies responsible for them, are available for the years 1848–1978. Both search tools are also available in electronic form.[10] Insofar as these reference aids are still under development, certain gaps are to be expected, though these may be closed with the benefit of other tools.[11]

Once the right collection has been identified, the next step is to locate the right sources within it. Search tools for this purpose include descriptions of collections, indexes, thematic inventories, accession logs and simple lists.

Fond-level descriptions offer general information on individual record groups, along with accessible documentation on the history of both the archive and the associated agencies.[12] Other search tools are based on the pre-archival structure of agency-specific information management practices (such as agency filing plans) and offer detailed information on the contents of their respective record groups (for example, file numbers, file titles and file dates).

The structure of the agency filing plans provides an ideal reflection of the tasks performed in their respective agencies. They therefore allow us to determine what sort of business we should expect to find documented in the sources corresponding to a given agency (the 'budgeted positions' for archived material).[13] Accession logs document files as they were actually delivered to the archive. In order to gain a general sense of the extent of files in a given collection, we must still go through these logs one by one; their digitalisation will allow us to present them in a cumulative form, increasing ease of use.[14]

Other search tools make fond-spanning research possible. These include specific thematic indexes,[15] and such supplementary tools as catalogues (in particular the Treaty Catalogue),[16] and special indexes for the audiovisual collections, photographs and maps. Theoretically, the combined scope of such instruments covers the entire archive. For pragmatic and economic reasons, however, it is generally preferable to undertake a targeted search for sources of special political weight or evidential value. Official publications or large source compendia are especially suited to such purposes:

- The official stenographic bulletin of the Federal Assembly (Stenographisches Bulletin der Bundesversammlung) began in 1891. Full transcription of Federal Council proceedings began only in 1971. Of primary interest in earlier bulletins are the unpublished minutes of Federal Assembly joint sessions, and of the National Council and Council of States meetings (E 1201 [-], E 1301 [-] and E 1401 [-]). These minutes include topic and speaker indexes. The bulletins are supplemented by the *Übersichten der Verhandlungen der Schweizerischen Bundesversammlung* (Summaries of the Proceedings of the Swiss Federal Assembly, from 1875 on) which list topics of discussion, as well as the transcripts of communiqués in the *Bundesblatt*, and the two-volume compendium on the proceedings of the Federal Assembly 1848–91.[17]
- The chronologically ordered *Protokolle des Bundesrates* (BRB, Protocols of the Federal Council) includes resolutions (but not proceedings) dating back to 1848. See also the corresponding registries (E 1004), along with the *Sammlung der Anträge der Bundeskanzlei und der Departemente* (the Collected Motions of the Federal Chancellery and Departments, E 1001 [-]).
- The 'New Series' of the *Amtliche Sammlung der Bundesgesetze und Verordnungen der Schweizerischen Eidgenossenschaft* (AS, Official Collection of the Federal Laws and Decrees of the Swiss Confederation) begins in 1874. There is also the 1948 *Bereinigte Sammlung* (BS, Abridged Collection) for 1848–1947, which covers all legislation binding in 1948, along with laws passed prior to that year but no longer in effect. The *Systematische Rechtssammlung* (SR, Systematic Legal Collection) begins in 1966.
- The *Schweizerische Bundesblatt* (BB, Swiss federal register) contains communiqués of the Federal Council to the Federal Assembly, reports of the Federal Council, and reports by the Parliament and parliamentary committees dating back to 1849.
- An issue of *Berichte des schweizerischen Bundesrates an die Bundesversammlung über seine Geschäftsführung im Jahre* (Annual Report of the Swiss Federal Council to the Federal Assembly on the Conduct of Business in the Year) is available for each year.
- The *Voranschläge* (Cost Estimates) of the Swiss Confederation and the *Staatsrechnung* (State Budget) have appeared annually.
- Finally, the *Sammlung der Entscheidungen des Bundesgerichts* (BGE,

Collected Decisions of the Federal Court) is available for dates from 1875 onward.

Official publications on parliamentary proceedings, transcripts of resolutions of the Federal Council and so on do more than merely record historical facts. With the help of the bill numbers, file numbers contained in parliamentary questions, and other clues, the records of a given official matter may be traced in files deriving from individual agencies. Archival searching is thus greatly simplified.

Taken together, the search tools listed above constitute a search system. To use this system to locate particular sources is like a police drag-net in which a search is narrowed in an ever-tightening spiral, permitting the increasingly accurate identification of relevant sources and the increasingly confident exclusion of irrelevant material. Once appropriate sources have been found, these in turn point the way to other collections, in which equally important material awaits scrutiny.[18] The full range of contextual information – data on official mandates and the agencies charged with their performance – makes possible the selective, critical organisation of archival material called for by the research task at hand.

OVERVIEW OF MATERIALS IN THE SWISS FEDERAL ARCHIVE

Despite the impressive range of available search tools, not even our archivists aspire to a complete picture of their collections. Whenever new issues appear on the horizon, or when the repertoire of scholarly methods expands, they need time to re-orient themselves. With the current emphasis on unclaimed assets in dormant accounts and the role of financial institutions, scholarly assessments of previous work have changed, and sources once seldom consulted are now the centre of attention.

In response to this change, in the summer of 1996, the Swiss Federal Archive commissioned an analysis of the sources likely to be needed for research in the areas listed in the federal mandate. This analysis was performed by Peter Hug, and presented in September 1996. The broad scope of envisioned research made this analysis extremely difficult. Still, in the Swiss Federal Archive alone, Hug was able to identify roughly 6,000 archival units, or approximately 600 linear metres of sources, of interest to the present investigation.[19] Of course these figures exclude the full range of sources in other public archives, and in numerous (often poorly documented) private sector archives in Switzerland, let alone abroad. Tables 15.1 and 15.2 provide a rough overview.

Table 15.1:
Victim assets/unclaimed assets

Federal Department of Justice and Police:	*Number of archive volumes*	
Justice Division (E 4100)		
– Registration Office (E 4111)	80	
– Estates	260	
– Recommendations	20	
Personal files (Steiger, E 4001 (C); Feldmann, E 400 (D); Rothmund, E 4800 (A))	110	(370)
Federal Political Department		
Dealings with Eastern European Nations (e.g. in E 2001 1967/113)	30	
The 'Heirless assets' policy (E 2001 (E); Agency filing plan locus B.42.13)[20]	15	
Personal files (Petitpierre, E 2800 [-], J.1.3 (-); Stucki, E 2801 (-), J.1.13 [(-))	10	(55)
Department of Economic Affairs		
Swiss Central Clearing Office	20	
Trade Division (E 7110 ff.)	25	(45)
Miscellaneous (e.g. personal files / the Nobs bequest, E 7800 (-), J.1.4 (-))	30	(30)
Total		*500*

Table 15.2:
Looted assets, capital flight, etc.

Federal Department of Justice and Police	*Number of archive documents*	
Justice Division (E 4100)	75	(75)
Federal Political Department (E 2001)		
The 'Looted assets' policy (E 2001 (E), Agency filing plan loci B.51.32, B.52.3)[21]	380	
The protection of Swiss financial interests	660	
Personal files and the Stucki bequest	115	(1,155)
Department of Economic Affairs		
Swiss Compensation Office		
– Corporations, reports, associations	170	
– The liquidation of German assets	1,200	
– Countries division / Old Obligations with Germany	1,470	
– Subdivisions (Finance, Licensing, Shipping)	440	
– Questions of legality	200	
– Trade Division (E 7110 ff.)	150	(3,630)
Federal Banking Commission	400	(400)
Miscellaneous	240	(240)
Total		*5,500*

Do these documents really contain all the relevant sources? Were all pertinent files really preserved? Are all of these sources really germane?

The first question will likely never be answered definitively. Even the most systematic search can only assure us that the probability of having found all of the important files is relatively high.

The second question, whether the transmission and preservation of archival materials has been complete, can be answered with a resounding 'no'. Several factors have had a positive effect on preservation. These include the institutional continuity of the Swiss state since 1848 (continuity which extends to the archive system), the early legal codification of universal record-keeping duties, the early regulation of the administration of paperwork in all public agencies and the existence of often very professionally maintained registries (of which the Federal Department of Foreign Affairs (EPD) provides an outstanding example) and, finally, the pronounced trend towards the creation and maintenance of personal manuscript files (especially in the Federal Department of Justice and Police – witness the Steiger and Rothmund personal files – but also in the EPD and EVD). But, at the same time, other factors have tended to exert a negative influence. Organisational questions were dealt with at several legally distinct levels of the national administrative hierarchy, leading to confusion in the division of administrative labour. Further, both administrative tasks and their assignment to specific agencies were frequently changed. Individual agencies frequently enjoyed relative autonomy, which in some areas, as in the maintenance of the wartime economy, led to the formation of largely independent 'militia-type' hierarchies. In addition, the Swiss Federal Archive lacked the resources necessary to secure their materials. Resistance to the archival mission also arose from within the ranks of archivists, whose education and interests were, for a long time, orientated more towards the Middle Ages than towards contemporary history. And so there are gaps. We need only recall the Federal Police Division's listing of deported refugees (*Rückweisungskartei*), which Carl Ludwig consulted as late as the 1950s, but which never made it to the Federal Archive. And, consider the ongoing practice of deliberately excluding materials deemed unworthy of archival status. The appraisal of materials for possible exclusion remains one of the most controversial chores any archivist must face.[22] On the whole, however, the present state of archival preservation at the federal level is satisfactory, if not without flaws. The federal holdings contain much information now absent from other public and private archives. At the same time, the collections of those other archives allow us, at least in part, to fill in the gaps in federal holdings.

The third question, 'Are the holdings germane to the question at hand?', can be thoroughly addressed only after the sources have been properly scrutinised. The relevance of a given collection depends on various factors (such as research objective and methodology). A deductive, qualitatively oriented research programme would surely have no need for many of the holdings detailed above. For such purposes, many sources will prove useful only as exemplary illustrations. But, as is generally agreed, the most serious gaps in research to date are at the micro-level. It will take 'deep drilling in the ... document massif of the Swiss Archive'[23] to construct an accurate picture of that time, to extract structures and networks from the wealth of systematically preserved detail. From the perspective of the archivist, used to confronting a vast array of sources on a daily basis, an empirical research programme steeped in primary sources is desirable, though to be sure, every research programme must set itself certain limits. We must find a negotiable, responsible middle ground between macro- and micro-analysis. The former seems better suited to discovering the political and economic context, the latter to accomplishing the core research tasks with which we have been charged. For this purpose, a vast wealth of previously neglected material is at our disposal, as the above description should have made amply clear. In particular, we know of large, interesting holdings from the Swiss Compensation Office, the Registration Office for Assets of Disappeared Foreigners, and the Federal Political Department, that have never been systematically exploited.

OVERVIEW OF SOURCES APPROPRIATE TO SPECIFIC RESEARCH TOPICS

Unclaimed assets – refugee policy

The issue of unclaimed assets is tightly connected with that of Swiss refugee policy. The victims of National Socialist persecution sought a safe haven in Switzerland not only for their property, but also for themselves. In recent years, much has been published on these topics, a great deal of it heavily based on work with primary sources. These sources are usually carefully documented.

Research into refugee policy and its counterpart deportation policy, provides an object lesson in the extent to which the archival landscape must be understood as a cohesive Swiss archival system. At the federal level, highly specific gaps in archival preservation emerge. But, with the help of sources which, though they originated in organs of the federal government, are now housed in such institutions as the Geneva State Archive (the files of the Geneva Territorial Military Administration) or, until recently, regional customs districts (customs district files), it is possible to reconstruct the reality of wartime Switzerland, at least in part. Careful research by individual historians has also revealed additional sources in the archives of districts or other administrative units, sources of which the responsible archival administrations were often ignorant. It took the dogged pursuit of many questions by the Israeli Yad Vashem Memorial and the American Holocaust Memorial Museum to bring about our present research in the Swiss Federal Archive and the attendant search for new archival material, an undertaking which, it is worth adding, is not confined to Switzerland.[24]

Thanks to the analysis of new sources it has proved possible to achieve a more accurate representation of Swiss refugee policy, though the precise, authoritative numbers demanded by the present politicised research climate will not be forthcoming.[25]

For inquiries regarding unclaimed assets or official measures taken with regard to those assets in the years since the Second World War, the files of the old Registration Office for the Assets of Disappeared Foreigners (*Meldestelle für die Vermögen verschwundener Ausländer*, E 4111 [A] 1980/13) are of central importance. These files contain numerous references to particular assets and their eventual fate. Many interesting questions can be raised and addressed on the basis of this material.[26] This collection is now used both for scholarly research and in ongoing efforts by banks and the Volcker Commission to resolve the ownership of unclaimed properties. Here the holdings of public archives will help to fill the gaps in bank records.

Looted assets – capital flight

On this constellation of issues, the state of the files is less clear. Though publications have taken up such spectacular examples as the Kurzmeyer case or the story of Baron von der Heydt,[27] no systematic treatment of the whole complex of questions has yet been produced. Nor have professional historians offered any explanation as to why such salient collections as the files of the Swiss Compensation Office remain to this date practically untouched,[28] though they have been accessible for some time.

The Swiss Compensation Office (*Schweizerische Verrechnungsstelle*, hereafter SVSt) was created by a Federal Council resolution of 2 October 1934 as an 'autonomous public institution with corporate organs, separate from and independent of the Federal Government'.[29] The SVSt was originally responsible only for clearing transactions between Switzerland and other countries (it monitored the payment obligations of Swiss debtors, checked the terms under which payments to Swiss creditors could be carried out and developed the technical apparatus required to ensure compliance with individual clearing and payment agreements, and so on). During and following the Second World War, the mission of the SVSt was continually expanded. After having been charged with the enforcement of asset and payment freezes in the early 1940s, it subsequently carried out the Freeze Resolution of 16 February 1945, and in accordance with the Washington Agreement of 25 May 1946, oversaw the liquidation of assets belonging to German nationals residing in Germany. In response to this dramatic increase in responsibilities, the personnel rolls of the SVSt grew steadily until they reached their peak of 819 employees in 1949.

Record-keeping practices in the SVSt were less than satisfactory. No agency filing plans were kept, so today we have only accession logs, supplemented by such SVSt-derived search tools as employment statistics, job descriptions and guidelines for employees, and woefully incomplete descriptions of file locations.[30]

One point of entry into this collection is provided by the charter of the SVSt (E 7160-01 [-] 1976/58, Management). Others include various summaries of SVSt activity (E 7160-04 [-] 1969/107, 1976/60, 1979/37, Planning Office), which incorporate numerous organisational schemata, reports on individual divisions, and data on filing and archiving practices and the destruction of files. Such overviews also list relevant documentation, and, when critical of the SVSt, ground their criticisms in appropriate sources. In addition, the general statistics contained in the sub-collection on the liquidation of German assets (E7160-07 [-] 1968/54) may prove of interest as a preliminary orientation.[31]

Other relevant sources may be found in the files of the Office of the Federal Attorney General. Some of these rulings were generated at the request of the SVSt, others in pursuit of internal initiatives, or in response to queries by other agencies. The filing plan for the EPD also lists broad-based holdings on the topic of looted assets (see B.51.32 and B.52.3). The Federal Court collection also contains important material, in particular the files of the adjudication panel which heard compensation claims regarding assets looted from occupied territories.

The potential benefits of exploring these collections are dramatically illustrated by the example of Eduard von der Heydt. A reconstruction of this case reveals a series of lateral connections to banking concerns and other companies, as well as to several important people. By means of a micro-historical analysis of these connections, we begin to identify networks of personal and institutional influence. These in turn spark follow-up studies, which snowball as new discoveries are made and new opportunities for the formulation of general explanatory theses arise.[32]

With regard to the specific issues surrounding looted gold, the files of the Swiss National Bank (SNB) are of central importance. The SNB has already prepared an appropriate inventory, and released the results of its own investigations to the public. Archival materials on the Federal Court, the Bank for International Settlements, and various private banks should also be taken into account.

Other research topics

The issues of looted assets and capital flight point beyond the bounds of the Second World War, suggesting a seamless thematic transition to more general questions regarding Swiss economic relations. These, in turn, are closely allied to the topic of the wartime economy. From this expanded perspective, many other collections, the enumeration of which would go beyond the scope of this chapter, might prove of interest.[33] Crucial sources will doubtless be found in the EPD and Trade Division collections. Others are lodged in private archives; the Permanent Negotiating Delegation (*Ständige Verhandlungsdelegation*), an important element of federal economic policy, was composed of representatives from both the federal administration and private industry, in particular the *Vorort* or Swiss Federation of Commerce and Industry (*Schweizerischer Handels- und Industrieverein*, SHIV). This wartime economic structure is a typical example of the mixing of state and private interests and responsibilities in militia-style organisations.[34]

For all such issues (looted assets, flight capital, foreign trade relations, the wartime economy and such like), we must ask not only what happened, but why. Research must also address the values of historical actors, the range of actions objectively available to them, and their subjective perceptions of that range. The first reconstructions of the reality of the war years date to the end of the war and to the months immediately following. Here, too, we find the largely defensive, self-justifying attitude of the Swiss government documented in numerous sources, as in Ambassador Stucki's paper, 'The Swiss Position' (*Der Standpunkt der Schweiz*).[35] This presentation of the Swiss case addressed the question of whether Switzerland had profited from the war, and would largely determine the Swiss position in the Washington negotiations. Such legitimising approaches demand critical scrutiny and appropriate analytic attention on the part of the researcher working with these sources. The same is true of all the many accountability reports published after the Second World War.[36]

CONCLUSION

The goal of historical research into the past is knowledge, not judgement or personalisation. Such work is a necessary condition for the rational discussion of an important part of our collective identity, and an important contribution to the development and fortification of our critical self-consciousness. To gain a transparent view of one's past is to strengthen social cohesion and prepare for consciously shaping the future.

Archives are the key to such historical research. Archival materials do not, by themselves, force any particular view of history on us; historiography is the interpretation of sources. For the individual collections in the Swiss archival system to perform their function as the memory of society and state, their contents must be made public to the greatest extent possible. Archival materials should be used in conscious recollection, not consigned to the depths of the social or institutional sub-conscious, let alone destroyed. In this sense – for even the description of a body of archival sources must be guided by certain interests – any description of the archival terrain with its wealth of historical raw material is a plea for source-intensive but pluralistic historical research. The 600 linear metres of sources listed in Peter Hug's analysis are, in the end, no more than a beginning. A culture without history is inconceivable. If the future is to have a history, today's archives must work to ensure conservation by actively disseminating their materials. If, on the other hand, history is to have a future, the activity of historians must go beyond historical construction. The critical analysis of the interactions between Switzerland and miscreant states, the will to confront our own refugee policy, racism and anti-Semitism, both past and present, may pave the way for a political transformation. If our efforts to remember past refugee policies provide an incentive to expand the bounds of possibility as far as possible, then there is hope that history can sensitise us to other contemporary issues, too.

NOTES

1 On the evolution of Swiss historiography, see Georg Kreis, 'Die Schweiz der Jahre 1918–1948', in Boris Schneider and Francis Python (eds), *Geschichtsforschung in der Schweiz. Bilanz und Perspektiven*, Basle, 1992, pp. 378–96.
2 On strategies for saving Switzerland and their rationality or irrationality, see Georg Kohler, 'Die doppelte Schweizer Geschichte oder: wie man souverän wird. Zur Diskussion über die Schweiz und das Dritte Reich', NZZ, 148, 30 June 1996, p. 19.
3 For an introductory survey, see *Informationen Schweiz. Bibliotheken, Archive,*

Dokumentationsstellen, Datenbankanbieter, Aarau, 1994.

4 These charges may be treated as variants of the immorality thesis, the opportunistic enrichment thesis and the war-prolongation thesis, to name just the most provocative. See, for example, Stuart Eizenstat, *US and Allied Efforts to Recover and Restore Gold and Other Assets Stolen or Hidden by Germany during World War II. Preliminary Study,* Washington, 1997, or numerous other publications of the past year. For an introductory survey, see Federal Office of Cultural Affairs (ed.), *Die Rolle der Schweiz im Zweiten Weltkrieg,* Berne, 1997. The long list of studies includes Beat Balzli, *Treuhänder des Reichs. Die Schweiz und die Vermögen der Naziopfer: eine Spurensuche,* Zurich, 1997; Sebastian Speich *et al., Die Schweiz am Pranger. Banken, Bosse und die Nazis,* Vienna and Frankfurt-am-Main, 1997.

5 The ratio of reference aids (search tools) to archival sources is approximately one linear metre of the former to 100–150 linear metres of the latter.

6 The pertinence principle: the organisation of archival resources in accordance with traditional library categories of factual, personal or territorial relevance, without regard to provenance (E<100 signatures). The provenance principle: organization according to the archival tradition of exclusive attention to the conditions of generation, with a view towards preserving the original order (E>999 signatures). In the Swiss Federal Archive, the transition from pertinence to provenance principle may be dated to the 1960s. By and large, with the exception of subdivision E 27, 'National Defense', all files dating from the 1920s and 1930s or later are thus organised by the provenance principle.

7 In what follows, I confine myself to the location of sources by means of archival search tools. It should be clear that there are other means of access, such as references in published literature or published collections of files, such as *Documents diplomatiques suisses 1848–1945;* or ad hoc collections of sources compiled over the last year by Parliamentary Services or the Swiss Federal Archive.

8 *Reihe Inventare,* ed. Swiss Federal Archive; Niklaus Bütikofer *et al., Systematische Beständeübersicht,* 2nd edn, Berne, 1992. The scope of each collection is outlined, along with available reference materials and any special conditions of use which may apply. See http://www.bar.admin.ch/.

9 A cross-institutional overview, indexed by personal names, may be found in *Repertorium der handschriftlichen Nachlässe in den Bibliotheken und Archiven der Schweiz,* compiled by Gaby Knoch-Mund, Basle, 1992.

10 Erich Schärer, 'Die systematische Kompetenzenkartei des Bundesarchivs', in *Studien und Quellen,* 2, 1976, pp. 113–53. The delegation of authority parallels the structure of federal law. There are many sources on administrative history (the history of administrative mandates and organisations). The basic administrative structure of Switzerland is defined in the *Bundesgesetz über die Organisation der Bundesverwaltung* (AS 1914 292, Message of 13 March 1913 in *BBl,* 1913, II, 1) and the *Bundesratsbeschluss betreffend die Zuständigkeit der Departemente und der ihnen unterstellten Amtsstellen zur selbständigen Erledigung von Geschäften* of 17 November 1914 (AS 1914 602). The power of institutional organisation essentially resided in the Parliament, but certain mandates (such as those involving inter-departmental reorganisations) were not subject to referendum or were delegated to the Federal Council (those involving intra-departmental reorganisations). During the First World War, administrative structure was decisively altered, as with the transfer of the Trade Division from the Federal Political Department (*Eidgenössisches Politisches Departement,* hereafter EPD) to the Department of Economic Affairs (*Eidgenössisches Volkswirtschaftsdepartement,* hereafter EVD), albeit only provisionally. After the war, the modifications were

never reversed. Substantive law must be taken into account, as well as organisational law, as the former often (co)determines organisational issues. In addition to the normatively oriented sources on administrative history, the accountability reports of the Federal Council (*Bundesrat*), reports of the trade commissions, budgets, financial reports and so on should all be considered, as they often provide more accurate information on the actual division of responsibilities.

For the period under discussion, we must pay special attention to additional types of administrative fiat which came into play under the national emergency law and the extraordinary executive powers. The conditions of the wartime economy made the practice of delegating new tasks by departmental order especially common. As an illustration, consider the following delegation chain: 1. From the *Bundesgesetz über die Sicherstellung der Landesversorgung mit lebenswichtigen Gütern* of 1 April 1938 (AS 1938 309): 'The Federal Assembly entrusts the Federal Council with the following tasks'. 2. In the *Bundesratsbeschluss Nr. 1 über die Sicherstellung der Landesversorgung* of 19 September 1938 these tasks are delegated to the EVD in accordance with the federal law of April 1938. 3. The *Verfügung des eidgenössischen Volkswirtschaftsdepartements über die Durchführung der Ausfuhrbestimmungen* of 23 September 1938 regulates the performance of this task and delegates it to the Import and Export Section and the Federal Bureau of Price Control.

11 Bärbel Foerster, 'Das Erschliessungskonzept des Schweizerischen Bundesarchivs. Vom Findmittel zum Findsystem', *Studien und Quellen*, 23, 1997, pp. 335–52, offers detailed information on the nature and current state of development of various planned search tools, and further projected customer-oriented innovations. See also Jean-Marc Comment, 'Nouveaux développements de l'informatique aux Archives fédérales', *Studien und Quellen*, 20, 1994, 105–1; Andreas Kellerhals, 'Archivisches Suchen und moderne Informatik', *Studien und Quellen*, 18, 1992, 65–105.

Research on administrative history may be grounded not only in various official publications and the relevant scholarly literature, but to some extent also in internally prepared agency histories and related internal documentation. The latter are listed in the *Dokumentation archivischer Hilfsmittel* (DAH).

12 See, for example, the collection-level description for the Swiss Compensation Office: Swiss Federal Archive, *Analyse des fonds, OSC*, compiled by P. Monn, Berne, 1997. Similar collection-level descriptions are also in preparation for the Trade Division (E 7110) and the War Transportation Office (E 7394).

13 Agency filing plans are listed in the *Dokumentation archivischer Hilfsmittel* (DAH) of the Swiss Federal Archive, and can also be consulted. The basic structure of the inventory for the EPD allows us to determine, for example, that the absence of any files relating to Policy 'D' is not the result of failed transmission; the policy was simply never implemented.

14 To date, only for the EPD collection E 2001 (A)–(E) do we have a comprehensive thematic, accession-independent index, the *Systematische Ordnungskartei* (SOK), which allows us to locate dossiers by cross-referencing agency filing plans with accession data. Otherwise, supplementary reference material is generally confined to personal name indexes. The advent of electronic searching has opened many new opportunities, but problems remain. Some arise, for example, as a result of the multilingual nature of the indexes. A keyword search for 'UNO' would have to be expanded to include keywords 'U.N.O.', 'ONU' and 'O.N.U.'

15 Such special inventories owe their existence to the interests of particular researchers, and accordingly they approach the archive from a variety of

thematic, geographic or other angles. See, for example, the following contributions to the Swiss Federal Archive's series *Reihe Inventare*: Christof Graf, *Zensurakten aus der Zeit des zweiten Weltkrieges. Eine Analyse des Bestandes E 4450. Presse und Funkspruch 1939–1945*, Berne, 1979; Walter Bernecker *et al.*, *Akten zu Lateinamerika. Übersicht über den Bestand E 2001 1896–1965*, Berne, 1991. An analytic inventory on constitutional history is in preparation.

16 This resource is organised by country, and to some extent, depending on the numbers of treaties, by topic and date (as in the heading, 'Germany – Economic Accords 1933–1944'). For economic accords between Switzerland and Germany, the appropriate schematic overview in roughly size A0 located in lot K I 933–946 should also be consulted.

17 This *Repertorium über die Verhandlungen der Bundesversammlung der schweizerischen Eidgenossenschaft* (Fribourg, 1942) was prepared by the Swiss National Archive and commissioned by the *Allgemeine Geschichtsforschende Gesellschaft der Schweiz* (Swiss General Historical Research Society). Needless to say the minutes of Council committees, in particular the Executive Committee of the National Council and Council of States (E 1050.1 [-]), are also of interest, especially with regard to the emergence of the authoritarian concept of the state's role. Compare these materials with later files on the popular initiative, 'Return to Direct Democracy' (Steiger manuscripts 4001 (C) 1: 126 ff.), along with the associated communiqués from the Federal Council to the Federal Assembly regarding the popular desire for a return to direct democracy.

18 When working with archival sources, especially sources stemming from a lengthy administrative procedure, it is often worth looking for comprehensive summaries, which usually turn out to have been prepared for internal use. For example, on the Swiss–Polish correspondence on unclaimed inheritances in Switzerland of 25 June 1949, a 100-page dossier, including a revealing summary, may be found in E 2001 (E), 1987/78, vol. 156 (Registry period 1973–75).

19 Peter Hug, *Analyse der Quellenlage für mögliche Nachforschungen im Zusammenhang mit dem Bundesbeschluss betreffend die historische und rechtliche Untersuchung des Schicksals der infolge der nationalsozialistischen Herrschaft in die Schweiz gelangten Vermögenswerte*, Berne, 1996, p. 7.

20 This entry permits a hierarchical description of the relevant files by topic:
B   Foreign policy
B.4   Foreigners and foreign interests in Switzerland
B.42   Non-resident foreigners
B.42.1   Foreign complaints made in Switzerland.

21 The relevant policies are hierarchically described as follows:
B.5   Neutrality and war
B.51   Neutrality and neutral persons
B.51.3   The legal status of neutral persons and assets in combatant nations
B.51.32 Assets
B.52   Prisoners of war
B.52.3   The treatment of enemy property.

22 Appraisal: 'The analysis of administrative records, performed as part of their assessment, with a view towards determining their meaningfulness and suitability for long-term storage and use. The analysis and estimation of evidential value and information content.' Angelika Menne-Haritz, *Schlüsselbegriffe der Archivterminologie*, Marburg, 1992. There is an extensive scholarly literature on the methodology of appraisal. Though appraisal remains a generally accepted archival practice, one undertaken with extreme care, decisions on what to

archive are always problematic. In the present context, we might cite the partial exclusion of redundant file series from the Swiss Compensation Office as an example of an attempt to stem the flow. A less felicitous decision on the part of the Swiss Federal Archive was the discarding of 45,820 personal dossiers kept by the Central Administration for Refugee Homes and Camps, classified as a redundant duplication of the information in refugee dossiers. Research interests have shifted since 1986, and of course now the value of such files would be assessed otherwise. A detailed description of this liquidation may be found in the Guido Koller inventory cited in note 25.

23 Jakob Tanner, 'Nazifluchtgelder, Operation Safehaven und die Rolle der Schweiz'. In his 'Aspekte der schweizerisch-alliierten Wirtschafts- und Finanzbeziehungen', Linus von Castelmur also draws attention to lacunae at the micro-level. Both may be found in 'Fluchtgelder, Raubgut, und nachrichtenlose Vermögen. Wissensstand und Forschungsperspektiven. Publikation zur Tagung im Schweizerischen Bundesarchiv Bern, 25 Februar 1997', Dossier 6, Berne, Swiss Federal Archive, 1997, pp. 67–72 and 33–6.

24 Similar efforts underway in many different countries were reported at a November 1996 conference at the Centre de Documentation Juive Contemporaine in Paris. A proceedings volume was published in *Revue d'histoire de la Shoa*, 163, May–August 1998.

25 *Studien und Quellen*, 22, 1996, *Die Schweiz und die Flüchtlinge 1933–1945*, contains five papers on this topic, including Guido Koller, 'Entscheidungen über Leben und Tod. Die behördliche Praxis in der schweizerischen Flüchtlingspolitik während des Zweiten Weltkrieges', pp. 17–106. As a follow-up to this work, a comprehensive analytic inventory of sources on Swiss refugee policy has been prepared: Guido Koller and Heinz Roschewski, 'Flüchtlingsakten 1930–1950', *Inventare*, Swiss Federal Archive, Berne, 1999.

26 Consider the many examples in Peter Hug and Marc Perrenoud, see note 23. Open access to these sources is not yet permitted. In accordance with archival regulations, they fall under the normal 30-year embargo. With the permission of the originating agencies, however, certain exceptions may be approved.

27 On this question, see Gian Trepp, 'Die neutrale Schweiz als Marktplatz für Raubgut aus Nazideutschland', in Dossier 6, 39–41, see note 23, or see Beat Balzli (for example, note 4), who offers many interesting examples.

28 Shagra Elam, 'Nazi-Fluchtgelder in der Schweiz', *Widerspruch*, 32, 1996, 137–44.

29 E 7160-01 [-] 1976/58: 223 (the founding documents); E 7160-01 [-] 1979/37: 33 (Presentations and reports on the SVSt. Documentation presented to the finance delegation of the Swiss Parliament).

30 The SVSt files are distributed among the following sub-collections:
   E 7160-01 (-): Management
   E 7160-02 (-): Certification
   E 7160-03 (-): Legal Office
   E 7160-04 (-): Planning Office
   E 7160-05 (-): Personnel Office
   E 7160-06 (-): Liquidation of Old Obligations with Germany
   E 7160-07 (-): Liquidation of German Assets
   E 7160-08 (-): Countries Division – Germany (FRG and GDR)
   E 7160-09 (-): Countries Division (excluding Germany)
   E 7160-10 (-): Financial Transactions Subdivision
   E 7160-11 (-): Licensing Subdivision
   E 7160-12 (-): Shipping Subdivision

E 7160-13 (-): Invisibles Subdivision
E 7160-14 (-): Temporary files of various divisions
J I.117 (-): Files of Erich Mehnert-Frey, Director
J II.104 (-): The SVSt Sport Club
J II.26 (-): The SVSt Employees Association
   The opaque structure of this collection considerably complicates any attempt to work with it, thus explaining, in part, why no one has yet attempted any systematic treatment.
   In a 1957 report to the Administrative Oversight Committee, the Planning Office complains: 'Our operation currently employs roughly thirty file clerks, the majority of whom aren't particularly suited to their tasks. The expansion of our files has led, together with insufficient recognition of their importance, to the assignment of this chore to co-workers who could no longer be used in any other way. In several divisions, individuals who for reasons either of personal health or sheer lack of motivation are incapable of bearing a normal work load now operate as file clerks.' The report goes on to conclude that from now on only female workers should be hired, since they are cheaper! (E 7169-04 [-] 1976/60, vol. 1: *Abklärungen des Rechtsbüros über die Archivierungspflicht und die Archivierungspraxis in verschiedenen öffentlichen Archiven* (Reports of the Legal Office on the Archival Duty and Archival Practice in Various Public Archives, 1951).

31 The appropriate collection description (see note 12) offers more detailed information, supported by a documentary appendix and a source dossier (in preparation). All are available for consultation in the Swiss Federal Archive.

32 For example, research into the von der Heydt case might begin with Federal Attorney's Office dossier C.16.387 (in E 4320 [B] 1990/266:90). These documents contain references to the EPD files (E 2001 [E] 1972/33:173, file number B.22.85.31.1.A, and the W. Stucki manuscripts, E 2801 [-] 1968/84, file number C.M.140.81), to the SVSt files (E 7160-01 [-] 1968/233:171), and to EMD files (E 27 10064, Judge-Advocate (*Oberauditorat*)] E 5330 [-] 1982/1:225f). At the same time, our search would expand thematically, leading us by turns to smuggling by means of diplomatic luggage, information services and military intelligence, to the role of private banks in capital flight and the traffic in looted assets, and finally to the securities market, counterfeiting and the art trade. See Peter Ferdinand Koch, *Geheim-Depot Schweiz. Wie Banken am Holocaust verdienen*, Munich, 1997.

33 See Marc Perrenoud's essay in this volume. On the wartime economy: the decrees of 8 March 1938 delegated the majority of tasks related to the maintenance of the wartime economy to the EVD. Consequently, the following files are of particular interest: those of the General Secretariat of the War Economy Commission (*Kommission für Kriegswirtschaft*), E 7001 (B) and (C), with the personal files of the department head at E 7800 and the Legal Section files at E 7391, the Federal Central Wartime Economy Agency (*Eidgenössische Zentralstelle für Kriegswirtschaft*), E 7004, E 7389 and J.1.138, the bequest of H. Schaffner, agency head from 1942–1948), the War Transport Office (*Kriegstransportamt*), Section for Wartime Risk Abatement (*Sektion für Kriegsrisikoversicherung*, E 7394), and the Trade Division (E 7110), in particular its Import/Export Section (*Sektion für Ein- und Ausfuhr*) and Central Agency for Import and Export Oversight (*Zentralstelle für die Überwachung der Ein- und Ausfuhr*), E 7395. Other important files may be found in the EPD collection (E 2001 [D] and [E], under the filing plan heading C, Economic Policy).

34 The archives of the SHIV leadership are presently lodged in the ETHZ Archive.
35 See E 2001 (E) 5:4, file number F.22.02.1, 'Ist die Schweiz durch den Krieg reicher geworden?' (Did Switzerland Profit from the War? E 6100 [A] 25:2331). Stucki's views were not entirely unopposed. Other opinions may be found, for instance, in the files of the Ad-Hoc Committee of the EPD, founded in 1942. See Antoine Fleury, 'La Suisse et la préparation à l'après-guerre', in Michel Dumoulin (ed.), *Plans des temps de guerre pour l'Europe d'après-guerre, 1940–1947*, Brussels, 1995. Of equal interest in this context are the files of the expert commission established to consider the possible entry of Switzerland into the UN: E 2001 (E)-/5:5, file number F.22.04. Another debate over the relationship between the emerging human rights law on the one hand, and Swiss law together with prior international law on the other, arose in the context of the war crimes trials. Compare Professor E. Hafter's recommendation of 10 January 1944, on the Swiss position with regard to the extradition of alleged war criminals (E 4001 [C]-/1:278, dossier 872).
36 See Luc van Dongen's contribution to this volume, Ch. 12 above.

16

On the Role of the 'Swiss Independent Expert Commission on the Second World War'

JEAN-FRANÇOIS BERGIER

AIMS AND PURPOSES

That the shadow of the past should fall over a nation's present and blur its outlines is not, in itself, anything out of the ordinary. Every nation, every country, tends to preserve – sometimes even to manufacture – the image of its history which suits it best, the image in which it can identify itself and find the outlines of its identity to suit its needs and the circumstances through which it is passing. Every nation and every country feeds on its myths. The function of the historian is not to destroy the myths. The only effect of that is to reproduce the myth in negative form, to create an anti-myth. In any case, the operation generally proves futile. The fact is that myths have their own existence, and though the assaults of historical logic may disturb that existence they cannot destroy it. The historian must recognise the myth for what it is, and distinguish it from the reality which it veils.

The shadow of the past, when identified, generally gives rise to heated intellectual debates; it is often taken up by politicians. It is rare, however, for it to affect or divide an entire nation. Yet that is what happened in Switzerland in 1996. The shadow has become so dense that the Swiss can no longer find their own history within it, and have become disoriented. On this occasion the phenomenon really is exceptional, and it is being reflected in an unprecedented crisis of the Swiss conscience. We must come to terms with the reasons for this obscuring of the past, which extends not just to the period of the Second World War but, in the same way, confuses the memory we have of other controversial episodes in our history. However, this chapter is no place for such an analysis. Its purpose is simply to offer a few comments on the scientific resources committed to dealing with the crisis.

Those resources are unusual. Their deployment cannot fail to raise problems of principle, connected with freedom of research, and problems of application, concerning the field of the inquiries to be carried out. The urgent federal decree of 13 December 1996 initiated the creation of an independent expert commission with instructions to 'study, from a historical and legal standpoint, the fate of assets which found their way to Switzerland after the national socialist regime came to power'. The commission has been vested (Article 5, subclause 2) with the power, within the limits of its mandate, to grant exemption from 'any statutory or contractual duty of secrecy'; on the other hand, its members and assistants are themselves placed under a duty of confidentiality (Article 3), nor do they have the right to disclose to third parties – in particular, to other historians – the information they gather ('the Federal Council shall have exclusive access to all documents and evidence associated with the inquiries' (Article 6)). The question has been posed, and it is a legitimate question, as to whether it is proper to grant a restricted number of designated researchers a privilege which is denied to many others who are equally qualified. Is this not an infringement of freedom of research? I think not, provided that reasonable use is made of this unusual privilege, and that use includes taking account of the general interest; exceptional situations call for exceptional means. The power granted by the legislator to the commission is, no doubt, the only way of circumventing the obstacle of the normal guarantees of secrecy and compelling those who hold confidential information not only to refrain from disposing of it but also to release it for research purposes without thereby breaching their duty of confidentiality.

On the other hand, the 'privilege' enjoyed by the commission does place it under a responsibility to the public, and especially to the community of historians. The commission, obviously, must scrupulously comply with the rules imposed on it (though it played no part whatever in the creation of those rules – it was not appointed until afterwards). However, that is not to say that it has retreated into an ivory tower. Quite the reverse: it intends to make the best possible use of the room for manoeuvre granted to it. Above all, it desires and calls for the closest possible cooperation with all historians who are also concerned with the matters it is covering; it hopes to derive synergistic effects from such cooperation. In any case, the field to be covered is so vast and diverse that the commission could not hope to succeed there alone. It thus sees itself as wide open to communication and dialogue. It will do everything within its power to ensure that the gates which it has the power to open are not slammed shut behind it.

The commission is officially described as 'independent'. Quite clearly, this high-sounding adjective should be interpreted in its relative sense. The commission owes its existence to a federal decree and a mandate. It was established by the federal government, and it is the Confederation which bears the not inconsiderable costs of its activities. The commission has undertaken to report regularly on the progress it has made. It is to submit its conclusions no later (though it is certainly unlikely to be any earlier) than the end of 2001. It is thus subject to a number of constraints which are not easily reconciled with its independence. However, that independence is intended to provide it with three guarantees necessary for the success of its mission: a guarantee of its freedom to organise its own work (within the limits of its budget), its choice of methods and its choice of members; a guarantee that it will not become an instrument intended to provide the government with an immediate response to questions arising from the ramifications of the case and the latest revelations; and, finally, a guarantee that it can resist any pressure brought to bear upon it in order to influence its inquiries and its interpretation of the facts. The experience of the first few months of its activities has clearly shown the commission the high cost of this interpretation of independence, and the absolute necessity to ensure that it is respected, difficult though that may be.

While the federal decree is generous in the powers it grants the commission, it is much less so in defining the terms of reference of the inquiry. It is even ambiguous and – not to put too fine a point on it – clumsy. It was drawn up under pressure resulting from accusations made abroad regarding assets or 'property' deposited in Switzerland and not returned to their rightful owners. Explicitly, the decree refers only to this aspect, leaving the Federal Council (Article 13) free to 'modify the terms of the inquiries'. The latter promptly took advantage of this option in its more detailed instructions to the commission on 19 December 1996, at the same time as it established the commission. Those instructions cite 'the role of Switzerland and its financial position in the context of the Second World War' and cite the following in addition to the famous 'assets in escheat': the trade in gold and foreign currency, Nazi assets, the traffic in cultural goods, arms manufacture, finance for trade operations, the adoption of German enterprises by Swiss companies ('Aryanisation'), the refugee problem and even the way in which historians hitherto have dealt with, or failed to deal with, these issues.

From the outset, and without hesitation, the commission has felt that these instructions impose greater obligations upon it than the decree, as far as the field of its inquiry is concerned. Its investigations thus deal with all the aspects implied by the mandate, and several more besides that are not explicitly mentioned in it but seemed to us (the members of the commission) to be in line with the same general intention:

shedding a full light, where light is needed, on the behaviour of Switzerland and the Swiss before, during and after the war. Not only that, but it intends to propose in its final report a summary of Switzerland's role as a whole and the problems associated with it, incorporating everything that is already known together with any other aspect which the commission may think would add to this summary. The fact is that it is impossible to isolate a problem from its general context, to make it intelligible without seeing it clearly against the overall background of the situation which then confronted our country, within and without. That, incidentally, is why the body that has been formed is not solely a 'commission of historians', which has become the widespread and inaccurate way of referring to it, but a 'commission of experts'. True, only one of its members is not a historian: Professor Joseph Voyame is a lawyer, which makes his function within the group all the more important. Furthermore, the commission is taking the opportunity given to it of instructing experts from disciplines other than history: lawyers, economists, financial analysts, communications specialists and such like.

PLAN OF INQUIRY

During its June 1997 meeting in Zug, the commission evolved a detailed concept and plan of inquiry. It identified no fewer than 26 areas of investigation, or 'boxes', within which information accumulates as it is retrieved from the archives and the oral questioning of witnesses. This inventory of questions is open-ended, and will be added to as the need arises. All these specific aspects of the part played by Switzerland before, during and after the war which are deemed worthy of attention can be classified under six major headings; these have been defined more for the investigators' convenience than on the basis of any internal consistency.

The first section comprises all the general, macrohistorical aspects of Switzerland's foreign relations during the period in question: foreign policy, foreign trade, the country's function as a clearing-house for intelligence and secret service activities, humanitarian activities abroad, and lines of transport from, to and through Switzerland. This section also includes more abstract issues such as the interface or interaction between the various political systems and cultures and their influence on Switzerland, its behaviour and choices, its perceptions of the world at war; and the external influences of events on the dynamism of the Swiss society and economy.

The second section relates to financial structures. It analyses how banks, insurance companies, trusts and other financial institutions behaved before, during and after the war, and how they reacted to the series of political events and the economic stresses arising from them, both in Switzerland itself and in all the countries with which it conducted business relations. How did those institutions, and their executives, assess the opportunities and risks of their operations? What relations did they maintain with the state, to what controls were they subject, or did they attempt to escape any controls?

The third section, directly leading on from the second, tries to study, measure and interpret capital transfer movements. Where appropriate, the commission will identify 'property' that has been improperly retained and will arrange for its return. As we know, this is a particularly complex and difficult aspect, one which has been the prime centre of the criticisms levelled at Switzerland in recent times. The issue is to identify the famous 'property in escheat' (which forms part of the mission of the Volcker Committee), under a private legal agreement between the Swiss Bankers Association and the World Jewish Congress (the Independent Commission of Experts: Switzerland – Second World War and the Volcker Committee are in close contact); but it is also concerned with the escape of Nazi capital and other movements originating in France, Italy and elsewhere. The cultural assets and works of art that have been stolen and resold are another form of looting and transfer, and their disposal on the Swiss market also forms part of this section.

The activities of industrial and commercial undertakings, considered individually (section four), must also be taken into account, although they are not expressly referred to in the commission's mandate; this, incidentally, was used by some undertakings – not many, fortunately – as an excuse to refuse to give Swiss investigators access to their archives. Yet this aspect is essential for a complete understanding of Switzerland's role. The operational policy of the enterprises, and certainly the issue of payments for and the financing of production of imported raw materials and marketing, obviously form part of Swiss investigations.

The last two major sections that have been opened arise from the primarily economic aspect of the previous ones. Section five relates to foreigners and refugees: admission policy, and admission practice which does not necessarily reflect that policy; organisation and financing by the Confederation, the cantons and private, secular or religious aid activities. In this context, we have to examine the issue of racist and anti-Semitic feelings and, more generally, attitudes towards 'other people', foreigners, minorities and marginalised groups (especially gypsies). This forms a substantial file and requires an exceptional effort;

the more so in that the commission had undertaken to present a preliminary (and inevitably incomplete) report on this subject as early as the spring of 1998 originally – which was finally published in November 1999.

The last section deals with the post-war period and the way in which the war years were then perceived. What was the policy of reparations and restitution, and what image of those difficult years did the Swiss retain, or receive? What was the process of the creation of a myth, which in turn has created what I will gladly call 'anti-myths', though these themselves are also a form of alienation from reality?

The list given above is merely a summary. It is neither exhaustive nor definitive, since the essence of research – as we all know – is that it raises additional questions. With this in mind, our provisional inventory can hardly be a preview of the contents table of a final report – a report whose order, form and appearance are as yet unknown.

METHOD

In any case, none of these sections can be partitioned off from the others: interlinking passages have to be provided. Any effective re-working of the history of Switzerland's part in the Second World War must be based on two mutually complementary and interactive approaches. One is analytical: a highly detailed critical summarising of the facts and circumstances revealed by source material, which is the essential basis of our profession. The other is the synthesis approach, identifying the most significant facts and placing them in their chronological and thematic context. It is this aspect that has been insufficiently addressed in Switzerland in the past, and that, no doubt, is what has made us so vulnerable. Producing a synthesis means distancing oneself sufficiently to encompass the full depth of the historical canvas and identify the dominant features of its outline.

Now, in the case of the Second World War, as with any far-reaching historical phenomenon, the depth of the canvas means, first and foremost, time: it is important to see the phenomenon in its long-term context. The war itself, clearly, is the epicentre of an upheaval extending over a much longer period. It was a terrible, apocalyptic event – but, in objective terms, a short-lived one. From September 1939 to May 1945 was only five-and-a-half-years, but the explanation for those years is to be found by placing them in the context of a longer period, extending both backwards and forwards in time. The tribulations we are now experiencing, whose knock-on effect is spreading to one country after another, clearly show that the chapter is far from closed. In a way, viewed from a very long distance, the Second World War was only one critical moment in a story that began before 1914 and seems not to have finished yet.

Looking upstream, as it were, the war forms the continuation of the decades that preceded it. Incidentally, there are some historians (especially economic historians) who see the point and refer more and more often to a 'Thirty Years' War', from 1914 to 1945. That long-term perspective is an important key to pinpointing and assessing the behaviour of Switzerland – and the Swiss – during the war: behaviour that was largely conditioned by everything experienced in the past, in both material and moral terms. Attitudes of mind, reflex actions, a political and administrative culture grew out of the experiences and fears of the First World War, and then of the inter-war period; this memory of what was still a recent past was reflected in reactions to the next war.

Depth of time, thickness of reality: it is just as necessary to emphasise the close correlation and interdependence between all the problems which this war created in Switzerland. Each of them must, imperatively, be interpreted in the context of the whole. Yet in recent or current debates, this correlation has been neglected or even obscured. On the one hand, monographs produced in recent years by qualified researchers have pointed the finger at the critical aspects, as it was their duty to do, though they have also been deliberately underlaid by a degree of revisionist *Schadenfreude*. They have, in general, failed to take sufficient account of the attitudes of mind to which I have just referred, in other words the criteria that could make it possible to form an evaluation of the facts and the behaviour of those involved. Nor have these monographs been sufficiently clear-sighted in considering the context – the interweaving of their subject-matter with the other circumstances of the time. On the other hand, and more importantly, the polemics of recent years, whether launched outside or inside Switzerland, have deliberately isolated the most negative aspects and cited in their support the most accusing testimony, whether reliable or otherwise.

This situation creates the risk of a disjointed view of Switzerland's role in the war. The worst error we could commit would be to reduce this moment in our history to a mere handful of characteristics, considered in isolation: considering trade with Germany without relating it either to trade with other countries or to the precarious domestic situation; considering the question of the gold without taking account of the monetary and social effects that could be expected to arise from it; considering shipments of arms without regard for the needs of national defence. More generally, there is an apparent trend, inspired by the Jewish organisations that are understandably anxious to keep alive the memory of the Holocaust, to regard it as the central event of the war and the only one worthy of commemoration. This is a legitimate attitude from the Jewish standpoint, but a reductionist one from the general standpoint. The Holocaust was a horrifying aberration of the human spirit, but it had little influence on the course of the war as such or, consequently, on the perception which the Swiss have had of the war.

AN OPPORTUNITY FOR HISTORIANS

I have often been asked in recent months whether I think it necessary to 'rewrite the history of Switzerland during the Second World War'. That is the wrong question. All historians know that history – all history – is for ever being 'rewritten'. New sources (or new ways of looking at old sources) constantly supplement or modify our knowledge and force us to tell the story in a different way and revise the interpretations which our predecessors, or even we ourselves, have recently put forward. Above all, every era and every generation asks new and specific questions of history, to which answers have to be found. *Sans cesse sur le métier remettez votre ouvrage* (Untiringly rework the fabric of your verse): Boileau's advice to the poets of his time applies equally well to the historian – and, after all, is not the historian himself something of a poet in his way, shaping the past as he recounts it?

The fact remains that the history of Switzerland during those difficult years calls for a special effort and 'rewriting', partly because of its obvious complexity and partly, too, because of the taboos on the one hand and distortions on the other – distortions in all directions – which have affected the way in which it has been approached over these last 50 or so years. Yet 'rewriting' history does not mean yielding to the temptations of 'revisionism', which comprises substituting one myth for another. 'Rewriting' does not mean suppressing one memory in favour of another: it means bringing them together and reconciling them.

In the present case, this is a difficult undertaking. It calls for patience and subtlety. It can be based only on the most rigorous honesty. It is, or may become, painful too; it demands humility. But the undertaking is a necessary one. Living too long in the chiaroscuro of an idealised or suppressed past becomes unhealthy. The past obscures the present, and confuses the signposts to the future.

So the constraint which is imposed upon us all should be regarded as a benefit. For Switzerland, it at last offers an opportunity to confront its past with equanimity. The clarity we are trying to bring back to that past will never sweep away all the differences of interpretation: they are inherent in that diversity of cultures and sensibilities within Swiss society that give it its richness and originality. The return to clarity will open the way to a genuine constructive debate. It will break the taboos and will make a distinction between experienced reality and imagined reality – myths and anti-myths. It will enable every Swiss, without shame or vanity or second thoughts, to re-examine an accurate and balanced image of a difficult time in his country's history. That history will be released from the threat of manipulation to ideological ends. It will recover its dignity. And, at the same time, let the Swiss acknowledge that this history – all their history, because the Second World War is not the only issue – is not an innocent one. It is a vast heritage that every nation, the Western Judaeo-Christian tradition and humanity as a whole will have to come to terms with afresh. Their future depends upon it.

It is an opportunity, too, for historians. Even though the circumstances surrounding it may be painful, we have been offered a unique opportunity to assert ourselves in the service of society. Never before has such a wide-ranging task been given us; what the public expects of us is unparalleled. Many foreign colleagues have admitted to me that they envy the position we are in, and hope to benefit from it. An opportunity, then, but a heavy responsibility too: to our compatriots and our colleagues. Let us all, together, take the opportunity, take up the responsibility, and carry it through to the end.

Postscript

The following were published after this book was submitted:

Antisemitismus in der Schweiz 1848–1960, ed. Aram Mattioli *et al.*, Zurich, 1998.

Beat Balzli, *Die Schweiz und die Treuhänder des Reiches. Vermögen der Naziopfer: Eine Spurensuche*, Zurich, 1997.

Bilder aus der Schweiz 1939–1945, illustrations Katri Burri; text Thomas Maissen. Zurich, 1997.

Katharina Bretscher-Spindler, *Vom heissen zum Kalten Krieg. Vorgeschichte und Geschichte der Schweiz im Kalten Krieg 1943–1968*, Zurich, 1997.

Thomas Buomberger, *Nazi-Kunstraub. Die Schweiz als Drehscheibe für gestohlene Kulturgüter zur Zeit des Zweiten Weltkriegs*, Zurich, 1998.

Das Geschäft mit der Raubkunst. Fakten, Thesen, Hintergründe, ed. Matthias Frehner. Zurich, 1998.

Der Zweite Weltkrieg und die Schweiz, ed. Kenneth Angst. Mit Beiträgen von H. Bütler, K. Villiger, A. Koller, H. Schaffner, K. Urner, H. Senn, D. Schiendler, W. Hofer and Th. Maissen. Zurich, 1997.

Die Schweiz und die Goldtransaktionen im Zweiten Weltkrieg (Zwischenbericht der Bergier-Kommission UEK), Berne, 1998 (also in French, Italian and English editions and on the Internet).

Michel Fior, *Die Schweiz und das Gold der Reichsbank. Was wusste die schweizerische Nationalbank?* Zurich, 1997 (French original in: *Cahiers de l'Institut d'histoire*, 5, Neuenburg, 1997).

Fluchtgelder, Raubgold und nachrichtenlose Vermögen, Berne, 1997 (Bundesarchiv Dossier 7).

Christine Gehrig-Straube, *Beziehungslose Zeiten. Das schweizerisch-sowjetische Verhältnis zwischen Abbruch und Wiederaufnahme der Beziehungen (1918–1946) auf Grund schweizerischer Akten*, Zurich, 1997.

Stephen P. Halbrook, *Target Switzerland. Swiss Armed Neutrality in World War II*, New York, 1998.

Claudia Hoerschelmann, *Exilland Schweiz. Lebensbedingungen und Schicksale österreichischer Flüchtlinge 1938–1945*, Innsbruck, 1997.

Pascal Ihle, *Die journalistische Landesverteidigung im Zweiten Weltkrieg. Eine kommunikationstheoretische Studie*, Zurich, 1997.

Hans Ulrich Jost, *Politik und Wirtschaft im Krieg. Die Schweiz 1938–1948*, Zurich, 1998.

Franziska Keller, *Oberst Gustav Däniker. Aufstieg und Fall eines Schweizer Berufsoffiziers*, Zurich, 1997.

Krisen und Stabilisierung. Die Schweiz in der Zwischenkriegszeit, ed. Sébastien Guex *et al.*, Zurich, 1998.

Ute Kröger und Peter Exinger, *'In welchen Zeiten leben wir!' Das Schauspielhaus Zürich 1938–1998*, Zurich, 1998.

La Suisse face à l'Empire américain. L'or, le Reich et l'argent des victimes, Genf, 1997.

La Svizzera e la lotta al nazifascismo 1943/1945. A cura di Riccardo Carazzetti e Rodolfo Huber, Locarno, 1998.

Sophie Pavillon, 'Trois filiales d'entreprises suisses en Allemagne du Sud et leur développement durant la période nazi', in (Bundesarchiv), *Studien und Quellen*, 23, 1997, 209–54.

'"Propre. En ordre". La Suisse pendant la Seconde Guerre Mondiale', *Revue d'Histoire de la Shoa*, May/August 1998.

Raubgold, Reduit, Flüchtlinge. Zur Geschichte der Schweiz im Zweiten Weltkrieg, ed. Philipp Sarasin and Regina Wecker, Zurich, 1998.

Rolf Soland, *Zwischen Proletariern und Potentaten. Bundesrat Heinrich Häberlin 1868–1947 und seine Tagebücher*, Zurich, 1997.

Jürg Stadelmann, *Umgang mit Fremden in bedrängter Zeit. Schweizerische Flüchtlingspolitik 1940–1945 und ihre Bedeutung bis heute*, Zurich, 1998.

Paul Stauffer, *'Sechs fruchtbare Jahre ...' Auf den Spuren Carl J. Burckhardts durch den Zweiten Weltkrieg*, Zurich, 1998.

Hans Stutz, *Frontisten und Nationalsozialisten in Luzern 1933–1945*, Lucerne, 1997.

Urs Thaler, *Unerledigte Geschäfte. Zur Geschichte der Schweizerischen Zigarrenfabriken im Dritten Reich*, Zurich, 1998.

Warum wird ein Thema von gesellschaftlicher Bedeutung nicht zum öffentlichen Thema, Schlussbericht der Nationalen Schweizerischen Unesco-Kommission, Berne, 1998.

Was gehen uns unsere Väter an? Jugendliche zu den Spuren des Holocaust in der Schweiz, ed. Hans Saner and H.-Dieter Jendreyko, Basle, 1997.

Hans Wegmüller, *Brot oder Waffen. Der Konflikt zwischen Volkswirtschaft und Armee in der Schweiz 1939–1945*, Zurich, 1998.

Paul Widmer, *Die Schweizer Gesandtschaft in Berlin. Geschichte eines schwierigen diplomatischen Postens*, Zurich, 1997.

Walter Wolf, *Eine namenlose Not bittet um Einlass. Schaffhauser reformierte Kirche im Spannungsfeld 1933–1945*, Schaffhausen, 1997.

Sacha Zala, *Gebändigte Geschichte. Amtliche Historiographie und ihr Malaise mit der Geschichte der Neutralität. 1945–1961*, Berne, 1998 (Bundesarchiv Dossier 7).

Eveline Zeder, *Ein Zuhause für jüdische Flüchtlingskinder. Lilly Volkart und ihr Kinderheim in Ascona 1934–1947*, Zurich, 1998.

Index